LAKE VILLA DISTRICT LIBRARY

Disabilities
SOURCEBOOK

Fourth Edition

Health Reference Series

Fourth Edition

Disabilities
SOURCEBOOK

Basic Consumer Health Information about Disabilities That Affect the Body, Mind, and Senses, Including Birth Defects, Hearing and Vision Loss, Speech Disorders, Learning Disabilities, Psychiatric Disorders, Degenerative Diseases, and Disabilities Caused by Injury and Trauma, Such as Amputation, Spinal Cord Injury, and Traumatic Brain Injury

Along with Facts about Assistive Technology, Physical and Occupational Therapy, Maintaining Health and Wellness, Special Education, Legal, Financial, Education, and Insurance Issues, a Glossary of Related Terms, and Resources for Additional Help and Information

OMNIGRAPHICS

615 Griswold, Ste. 901, Detroit, MI 48226

Bibliographic Note

Because this page cannot legibly accommodate all the copyright notices, the Bibliographic Note portion of the Preface constitutes an extension of the copyright notice.

* * *

OMNIGRAPHICS

Angela L. Williams, *Managing Editor*

***

Copyright © 2018 Omnigraphics

ISBN 978-0-7808-1642-8

E-ISBN 978-0-7808-1643-5

Library of Congress Cataloging-in-Publication Data

Names: Omnigraphics, Inc., issuing body.

Title: Disabilities sourcebook: basic consumer health information about disabilities that affect the body, mind, and senses, including birth defects, hearing and vision loss, speech disorders, learning disabilities, psychiatric disorders, degenerative diseases, and disabilities caused by injury and trauma, such as amputation, spinal cord injury, and traumatic brain injury; along with facts about assistive technology, physical and occupational therapy, maintaining health and wellness, special education, legal, financial, education, and insurance issues, a glossary of related terms, and resources for additional help and information.

Description: Fourth edition. | Detroit, MI: Omnigraphics, [2018] | Series: Health reference series | Includes bibliographical references and index. | Description based on print version record and CIP data provided by publisher; resource not viewed.

Identifiers: LCCN 2018029167 (print) | LCCN 2018030195 (ebook) | ISBN 9780780816435 (eBook) | ISBN 9780780816428 (hardcover: alk. paper)

Subjects: LCSH: People with disabilities--United States--Handbooks, manuals, etc. | People with mental disabilities--United States--Handbooks, manuals, etc.

Classification: LCC HV1553 (ebook) | LCC HV1553.D544 2018 (print) | DDC 362.4--dc23

LC record available at https://lccn.loc.gov/2018029167

Electronic or mechanical reproduction, including photography, recording, or any other information storage and retrieval system for the purpose of resale is strictly prohibited without permission in writing from the publisher.

The information in this publication was compiled from the sources cited and from other sources considered reliable. While every possible effort has been made to ensure reliability, the publisher will not assume liability for damages caused by inaccuracies in the data, and makes no warranty, express or implied, on the accuracy of the information contained herein.

∞

This book is printed on acid-free paper meeting the ANSI Z39.48 Standard. The infinity symbol that appears above indicates that the paper in this book meets that standard.

Printed in the United States

Table of Contents

Preface xiii

Part I: Introduction to Disabilities

Chapter 1 — What Is a Disability? 3

Chapter 2 — Statistics on People with Disabilities
in the United States 11

Chapter 3 — Common Barriers to Participation
Experienced by People with Disabilities 19

Chapter 4 — Myths and Facts about People with
Disabilities 25

Chapter 5 — Women with Disabilities 33

Chapter 6 — Aging and Disabilities 35

Chapter 7 — Communicating with and about People
with Disabilities 47

Chapter 8 — A Guide for Caregivers of People with
Disabilities 55

Chapter 9 — Abuse and People with Disabilities 59

    Section 9.1 — Childhood Bullying 60

    Section 9.2 — Abuse of Children with
    Intellectual Disabilities 63

    Section 9.3 — Violence against Women
    with Disabilities 69

Part II: Types of Disabilities

Chapter 10—Overview of Birth Defects 75
Chapter 11—Cerebral Palsy 83
Chapter 12—Cleft Lip and Palate 95
Chapter 13—Cystic Fibrosis 101
Chapter 14—Inherited Disorders of Metabolism 115
Chapter 15—Muscular Dystrophy 121
Chapter 16—Spina Bifida 133
Chapter 17—Sensory Disabilities 141
    Section 17.1—Hearing Loss 142
    Section 17.2—Hearing Loss in Children 146
    Section 17.3—Vision Loss 150
    Section 17.4—Deaf-Blindness 165
Chapter 18—Speech Disorders 175
    Section 18.1—Aphasia 176
    Section 18.2—Apraxia 180
Chapter 19—Intellectual and Cognitive Disabilities 185
    Section 19.1—Down Syndrome 186
    Section 19.2—Fetal Alcohol Spectrum
                      Disorders 190
    Section 19.3—Shaken Baby Syndrome 194
Chapter 20—Learning Disabilities 197
    Section 20.1—Learning Disabilities:
                      Overview 198
    Section 20.2—Dyscalculia 201
    Section 20.3—Dyslexia 206
    Section 20.4—Dysgraphia 208
    Section 20.5—Dyspraxia 209
Chapter 21—Autism Spectrum Disorders 211
Chapter 22—Attention Deficit Hyperactivity Disorder 217

Chapter 23—Psychiatric Disability and Mental Disorders 221

Chapter 24—Degenerative Diseases That Cause Disability 231
    Section 24.1—Alzheimer Disease 232
    Section 24.2—Amyotrophic Lateral Sclerosis 238
    Section 24.3—Arthritis.................................. 239
    Section 24.4—Multiple Sclerosis 243
    Section 24.5—Parkinson Disease 257

Chapter 25—Disability Caused by Injury and Trauma 275
    Section 25.1—Amputation and Limb Loss 276
    Section 25.2—Back Pain 284
    Section 25.3—Spinal Cord Injury: Understanding Paralysis, Paraplegia, and Quadriplegia 289
    Section 25.4—Traumatic Brain Injury............ 300

Part III: Technologies and Services That Help People with Disabilities and Their Families

Chapter 26—What Is Assistive Technology?.............................. 307

Chapter 27—Rehabilitative and Assistive Technology 311

Chapter 28—Mobility Aids 317
    Section 28.1—Wheelchairs and Other Power-Driven Mobility Devices... 318
    Section 28.2—Tongue-Driven Wheelchairs............................... 320

Chapter 29—Home Use Devices and Modifications.................. 323
    Section 29.1—What Are Home Use Medical Devices?....................... 324

Section 29.2—Adapting Your Living Space to Accommodate Your Disability 327

Chapter 30—Devices for Improving Communication and Hearing 331

Section 30.1—Captions for Deaf and Hard-of-Hearing Viewers 332

Section 30.2—Cochlear Implants 337

Section 30.3—Hearing Aids 340

Section 30.4—Other Hearing Assistive Technology 346

Chapter 31—Therapy and Services to Aid Communication 351

Section 31.1—Child Speech-Language Therapy 352

Section 31.2—Telecommunications Relay Services 355

Chapter 32—Low Vision Devices and Services 357

Section 32.1—Living with Low Vision 358

Section 32.2—Argus Retinal Prosthesis 360

Section 32.3—Implantable Corneal Device to Correct Near Vision 364

Section 32.4—What Is Braille? 366

Section 32.5—Web-Braille 370

Section 32.6—New Technologies for People with Visual Impairment 373

Chapter 33—How Therapists Can Assist People with Disabilities.. 377

Section 33.1—Occupational Therapists 378

Section 33.2—Physiatrists and Physical Therapists 381

Chapter 34—Art and Recreational Therapy 385

Chapter 35—Service Animals and People with Disabilities 391

Chapter 36—Finding Accessible Transportation 395

    Section 36.1—Adapting Motor Vehicles for People with Disabilities............ 396

    Section 36.2—Assistance and Accommodation for Air Travel 405

Chapter 37—Family Support Services 409

    Section 37.1—Understanding Respite and Hospice Care 410

    Section 37.2—Adult Day Care 415

Part IV: Staying Healthy with a Disability

Chapter 38—Nutrition and Weight Management Issues for People with Disabilities....................... 419

    Section 38.1—Nutrition and Disability 420

    Section 38.2—Nutrition for Swallowing Difficulties 422

    Section 38.3—Overweight and Obesity among People with Disabilities 427

Chapter 39—Physical Activity for People with Disabilities 431

    Section 39.1—Exercise Guidelines 432

    Section 39.2—Yoga for People with Disabilities 437

Chapter 40—Personal Hygiene for People with Disabilities 441

    Section 40.1—Dental Care 442

    Section 40.2—How to Bathe Someone with a Disability 447

Chapter 41—Bowel and Bladder Problems Associated with Disability.................................... 451

Chapter 42—Pressure Sores: What They Are and How to Prevent Them.. 461

Chapter 43—Managing Pain... 469

Chapter 44—Coping with Anxiety Disorders and
　　　　　　Depression... 475

Chapter 45—Health Insurance Concerns................................... 485

　　　　Section 45.1—Health Insurance for
　　　　　　　　　　People with Disabilities............ 486

　　　　Section 45.2—Medicaid and Children's
　　　　　　　　　　Health Insurance Program 492

　　　　Section 45.3—Medicaid and Adults with
　　　　　　　　　　Disabilities 496

Chapter 46—Is It a Medical Emergency?..................................... 501

Chapter 47—Rehabilitation: Options for People
　　　　　　with Disabilities... 507

Chapter 48—Choosing a Long-Term Care Setting 519

Part V: Special Education for Children with Disabilities

Chapter 49—Laws about Educating Children
　　　　　　with Disabilities... 529

　　　　Section 49.1—Individuals with
　　　　　　　　　　Disabilities Education Act......... 530

　　　　Section 49.2—Every Student Succeeds Act 532

　　　　Section 49.3—Section 504 of the
　　　　　　　　　　Rehabilitation Act...................... 535

Chapter 50—Evaluating Children for Disability 537

Chapter 51—Early Intervention Services 549

Chapter 52—Individualized Education Programs 559

Chapter 53—Supports, Modifications, and
　　　　　　Accommodations for Students............................. 565

Chapter 54—Students with Disabilities Preparing
　　　　　　for Postsecondary Education............................... 573

Chapter 55—Transitioning Students with
　　　　　　Disabilities to Higher Education and
　　　　　　Adulthood 581

Part VI: Legal, Employment, and Financial Concerns for People with Disabilities

Chapter 56—A Guide to Disability Rights Laws 593

Chapter 57—Questions and Answers about the Americans with Disabilities Act 603

Chapter 58—Housing and Safety Issues for People with Disabilities... 611

    Section 58.1—Centers for Independent Living for Disabled People 612

    Section 58.2—Disability Rights in Housing.... 614

    Section 58.3—Understanding the Fair Housing Amendments Act........ 631

    Section 58.4—Housing Rights for People with Disabilities........................ 637

    Section 58.5—Fire Safety for People with Disabilities and Their Caregivers 640

    Section 58.6—Disaster Preparedness for People with Disabilities and Special Needs..................... 642

Chapter 59—Employees with Disabilities................................. 645

    Section 59.1—Why Work Matters to People with Disabilities............. 646

    Section 59.2—In the Workplace: Reasonable Accommodations for Employees with Disabilities 648

    Section 59.3—Job Accommodation Situations and Solutions 650

    Section 59.4—Accommodating Mental Illness in the Workplace........... 654

Chapter 60—Scholarships and Financial Aid Available to Students with Disabilities............... 659

    Section 60.1—Finding and Applying for Scholarships............................ 660

       Section 60.2—Scholarships for Students with Intellectual Disabilities 662

Chapter 61—Social Security Disability Benefits 667

Chapter 62—Amputation and Social Security Benefits 673

Chapter 63—Tax Benefits and Credits for People with Disabilities 677

Chapter 64—Guardianship for People with Disability............. 687

Chapter 65—Advance Directives and Advance Care Planning for People with Physical and Intellectual Disabilities... 693

Part VII: Additional Help and Information

Chapter 66—Glossary of Terms Related to Disabilities 707

Chapter 67—Directory of Organizations That Help People with Disabilities... 715

Chapter 68—Directory of Organizations for Athletes with Disabilities..................................... 729

Chapter 69—How Can I Get Help Finding and Paying for Assistive Technology?........................ 735

Index.. **741**

Preface

About This Book

Around 12.8 percent of the U.S. population has some type of disability—physical, cognitive, emotional, or sensory disabilities that impair functioning and interfere with daily activities. Although most people with disabilities lead healthy, productive lives, having a disability may increase the risk for illness or injury and interfere with educational goals or employment. In addition, people with more severe disabilities may require help with activities of daily living, such as dressing, bathing, and meal preparation, or even need part- or full-time nursing care.

Disabilities Sourcebook, Fourth Edition offers people with disabilities and their caregivers basic information about birth defects, hearing and vision loss, speech disorders, intellectual and cognitive disabilities, learning disabilities, and other types of impairment caused by chronic illness, injury, and trauma. It discusses assistive technology, home use devices, mobility aids, therapies, and services that foster independence. Information about the importance of nutrition, exercise, personal hygiene, and pain management is also provided. For parents of children with disabilities, the book offers facts about special education, including early intervention services, Individualized Education Programs (IEPs), and other supports. Legal, employment, and financial concerns for people with disabilities are also discussed. The book concludes with a glossary of related terms and directories of resources for additional help and information.

How to Use This Book

This book is divided into parts and chapters. Parts focus on broad areas of interest. Chapters are devoted to single topics within a part.

Part One: Introduction to Disabilities discusses the prevalence of physical, cognitive, emotional, and sensory impairments. It provides statistical data of people with disabilities in the United States. It identifies common barriers that people with disabilities face in mainstream society, such as access to housing, employment, and education, and it offers tips on communicating with and caring for people with disabilities. It explains the effects of aging on disabled people. Abuses sometimes encountered by people with disabilities are also discussed.

Part Two: Types of Disabilities identifies the symptoms, diagnosis, and treatment of the most common forms of disabling conditions, including birth defects, cerebral palsy, cleft lip and palate, inherited disorders of metabolism, muscular dystrophy, spina bifida, and sensory disabilities. The part also discusses speech disorders, intellectual and cognitive disabilities, learning disabilities, autism spectrum disorder, attention deficit hyperactivity disorder, psychiatric disabilities, degenerative diseases, and disabilities caused by injury and trauma.

Part Three: Technologies and Services That Help People with Disabilities and Their Families provides information about devices, therapies, and supports that help people with disabilities attend school, engage in work, and enjoy recreational activities. Facts about mobility aids such as canes and wheelchairs, home use medical devices, communication and hearing aids, and low vision devices are discussed, and information about speech, occupational, physical, and recreational therapies is provided. It also discusses the accessible transportation systems available for the people with disabilities.

Part Four: Staying Healthy with a Disability discusses strategies for maintaining physical health and emotional wellness in people who have disabilities. Patients and caregivers will find information on healthy eating, weight management, personal hygiene, and physical activity, as well as tips on managing bowel and bladder problems, pressure sores, pain, depression, and anxiety. The part concludes with an explanation of health insurance concerns, tips on dealing with hospitalization and rehabilitation, and considerations when choosing a long-term care setting.

Part Five: Special Education for Children with Disabilities identifies laws that support the education of children with disabilities, such as the Individuals with Education Act (IDEA), the Every Student Succeeds Act (ESSA), and Section 504 of the Rehabilitation Act. Facts about evaluating children for disability, early intervention services, individualized education programs (IEPs), and supports, modifications, and accommodations for students are also included.

Part Six: Legal, Employment, and Financial Concerns for People with Disabilities describes disability rights laws that protect people with disabilities from discrimination. It also discusses housing and safety issues for people with disabilities and addresses employment and workplace concerns, Social Security disability benefits, tax benefits, and credits for disabled people. The part concludes explaining the strategy of preparing the people with disability for the future—end-of-life planning.

Part Seven: Additional Help and Information provides a glossary of important terms related to disabilities. A directory of organizations that help people with disabilities and their families is also included, along with a list of organizations for athletes with disabilities, and resources for finding financial help for assistive devices.

Bibliographic Note

This volume contains documents and excerpts from publications issued by the following government agencies: Administration for Community Living (ACL); Agency for Healthcare Research and Quality (AHRQ); Center for Parent Information and Resources (CPIR); Centers for Disease Control and Prevention (CDC); Centers for Medicare and Medicaid Services (CMS); *Eunice Kennedy Shriver* National Institute of Child Health and Human Development (NICHD); Federal Bureau of Prisons (BOP); Federal Communications Commission (FCC); Federal Emergency Management Agency (FEMA); Federal Student Aid; Food and Nutrition Service (FNS); Internal Revenue Service (IRS); Job Corps; National Council on Disability (NCD); National Endowment For the Arts (NEA); National Eye Institute (NEI); National Heart, Lung, and Blood Institute (NHLBI); National Highway Traffic Safety Administration (NHTSA); National Institute of Arthritis and Musculoskeletal and Skin Diseases (NIAMS); National Institute of Biomedical Imaging and Bioengineering (NIBIB); National Institute of Dental and Craniofacial Research (NIDCR); National Institute of Diabetes and Digestive and Kidney Diseases (NIDDK); National Institute of Mental Health (NIMH); National Institute of Neurological Disorders and Stroke (NINDS); National Institute of Standards and Technology

(NIST); National Institute on Aging (NIA); National Institute on Deafness and Other Communication Disorders (NIDCD); National Institutes of Health (NIH); National Science Foundation (NSF); Office of Disease Prevention and Health Promotion (ODPHP); Office on Women's Health (OWH); Substance Abuse and Mental Health Services Administration (SAMHSA); United States Census Bureau; U.S. Agency for International Development (USAID); U.S. Bureau of Labor Statistics (BLS); U.S. Department of Education (ED); U.S. Department of Health and Human Services (HHS); U.S. Department of Homeland Security (DHS); U.S. Department of Housing and Urban Development (HUD); U.S. Department of Justice (DOJ); U.S. Department of Labor (DOL); U.S. Department of Transportation (DOT); U.S. Department of Veterans Affairs (VA); U.S. Equal Employment Opportunity Commission (EEOC); U.S. Fire Administration (FA); U.S. Food and Drug Administration (FDA); U.S. Library of Congress (LOC); U.S. Office of Personnel Management (OPM); and U.S. Social Security Administration (SSA).

It may also contain original material produced by Omnigraphics and reviewed by medical consultants.

About the Health Reference Series

The *Health Reference Series* is designed to provide basic medical information for patients, families, caregivers, and the general public. Each volume takes a particular topic and provides comprehensive coverage. This is especially important for people who may be dealing with a newly diagnosed disease or a chronic disorder in themselves or in a family member. People looking for preventive guidance, information about disease warning signs, medical statistics, and risk factors for health problems will also find answers to their questions in the *Health Reference Series*. The *Series*, however, is not intended to serve as a tool for diagnosing illness, in prescribing treatments, or as a substitute for the physician/patient relationship. All people concerned about medical symptoms or the possibility of disease are encouraged to seek professional care from an appropriate healthcare provider.

A Note about Spelling and Style

Health Reference Series editors use *Stedman's Medical Dictionary* as an authority for questions related to the spelling of medical terms and the *Chicago Manual of Style* for questions related to grammatical structures, punctuation, and other editorial concerns. Consistent adherence is not always possible, however, because the individual volumes within the *Series* include many documents from a wide variety of different producers, and the editor's primary goal is to present material from each source as accurately as is possible. This sometimes means that information in different chapters or sections may follow other guidelines and alternate spelling authorities. For example, occasionally a copyright holder may require that eponymous terms be shown in possessive forms (Crohn's disease vs. Crohn disease) or that British spelling norms be retained (leukaemia vs. leukemia).

Medical Review

Omnigraphics contracts with a team of qualified, senior medical professionals who serve as medical consultants for the *Health Reference Series*. As necessary, medical consultants review reprinted and originally written material for currency and accuracy. Citations including the phrase "Reviewed (month, year)" indicate material reviewed by this team. Medical consultation services are provided to the *Health Reference Series* editors by:

Dr. Vijayalakshmi, MBBS, DGO, MD
Dr. Senthil Selvan, MBBS, DCH, MD
Dr. K. Sivanandham, MBBS, DCH, MS (Research), PhD

Our Advisory Board

We would like to thank the following board members for providing initial guidance on the development of this series:

- Dr. Lynda Baker, Associate Professor of Library and Information Science, Wayne State University, Detroit, MI
- Nancy Bulgarelli, William Beaumont Hospital Library, Royal Oak, MI
- Karen Imarisio, Bloomfield Township Public Library, Bloomfield Township, MI
- Karen Morgan, Mardigian Library, University of Michigan-Dearborn, Dearborn, MI
- Rosemary Orlando, St. Clair Shores Public Library, St. Clair Shores, MI

Health Reference Series *Update Policy*

The inaugural book in the *Health Reference Series* was the first edition of *Cancer Sourcebook* published in 1989. Since then, the *Series* has been enthusiastically received by librarians and in the medical community. In order to maintain the standard of providing high-quality health information for the layperson the editorial staff at Omnigraphics felt it was necessary to implement a policy of updating volumes when warranted.

Medical researchers have been making tremendous strides, and it is the purpose of the *Health Reference Series* to stay current with the most recent advances. Each decision to update a volume is made on an individual basis. Some of the considerations include how much new information is available and the feedback we receive from people who use the books. If there is a topic you would like to see added to the update list, or an area of medical concern you feel has not been adequately addressed, please write to:

Managing Editor
Health Reference Series
Omnigraphics
615 Griswold, Ste. 901
Detroit, MI 48226

Part One

Introduction to Disabilities

Chapter 1

What Is a Disability?

A disability is any condition of the body or mind (impairment) that makes it more difficult for the person with the condition to do certain activities (activity limitation) and interact with the world around them (participation restrictions).

There are many types of disabilities, such as those that affect a person's:

- Vision
- Movement
- Thinking
- Remembering
- Learning
- Communicating
- Hearing
- Mental health
- Social relationships

This chapter contains text excerpted from the following sources: Text in this chapter begins with excerpts from "Disability and Health—Disability Overview," Centers for Disease Control and Prevention (CDC), August 1, 2017; Text beginning with the heading "Healthy Living" is excerpted from "People with Disabilities," Centers for Disease Control and Prevention (CDC), August 3, 2017.

Although "people with disabilities" sometimes refers to a single population, this is actually a diverse group of people with a wide range of needs. Two people with the same type of disability can be affected in very different ways. Some disabilities may be hidden or not easy to see.

According to the World Health Organization (WHO), disability has three dimensions:

1. Impairment in a person's body structure or function, or mental functioning; examples of impairments include loss of a limb, loss of vision, or memory loss.
2. Activity limitation, such as difficulty seeing, hearing, walking, or problem-solving.
3. Participation restrictions in normal daily activities, such as working, engaging in social and recreational activities, and obtaining healthcare and preventive services.

Disability can be:

- Related to conditions that are present at birth and may affect functions later in life, including cognition (memory, learning, and understanding), mobility (moving around in the environment), vision, hearing, behavior, and other areas. These conditions may be:
  - disorders in single genes (for example, Duchenne muscular dystrophy (DMD));
  - disorders of chromosomes (for example, Down syndrome); and
  - the result of the mother's exposure during pregnancy to infections (for example, rubella) or harmful substances, such as alcohol or cigarettes.
- Associated with developmental conditions that become apparent during childhood (for example, autism spectrum disorder (ASD) and attention deficit hyperactivity disorder or ADHD);
- Related to an injury (for example, traumatic brain injury (TBI) or spinal cord injury (SCI));
- Associated with a longstanding condition (for example, diabetes), which can cause a disability such as vision loss, nerve damage, or limb loss;
- Progressive, static (for example, limb loss), or intermittent (for example, some forms of multiple sclerosis (MS)).

What Is a Disability?

What Is Impairment?

Impairment is an absence of or significant difference in a person's body structure or function or mental functioning. For example, problems in the structure of the brain can result in difficulty with mental functions, or problems with the structure of the eyes or ears can result in difficulty with the functions of vision or hearing.

- **Structural impairments** are significant problems with an internal or external component of the body. Examples of these include a type of nerve damage that can result in multiple sclerosis, or a complete loss of a body component, as when a limb has been amputated.
- **Functional impairments** include the complete or partial loss of function of a body part. Examples of these include pain that doesn't go away or joints that no longer move easily.

What Is the Difference between Activity Limitation and Participation Restriction?

The World Health Organization (WHO) published the International Classification of Functioning, Disability and Health (ICF) in 2001. The ICF provides a standard language for classifying body function and structure, activity, participation levels, and conditions in the world around us that influence health. This description helps to assess the health, functioning, activities, and factors in the environment that either help or create barriers for people to fully participate in society.

According to the ICF:

- Activity is the execution of a task or action by an individual.
- Participation is a person's involvement in a life situation.

The ICF acknowledges that the distinction between these two categories is somewhat unclear and combines them, although basically, activities take place at a personal level and participation involves engagement in life roles, such as employment, education, or relationships. Activity limitations and participation restrictions have to do with difficulties an individual experiences in performing tasks and engaging in social roles. Activities and participation can be made easier or more difficult as a result of environmental factors, such as technology, support, and relationships, services, policies, or the beliefs of others.

The ICF includes the following in the categories of activities and participation:

- Learning and applying knowledge
- Managing tasks and demands
- Mobility (moving and maintaining body positions, handling and moving objects, moving around in the environment, moving around using transportation)
- Managing self-care tasks
- Managing domestic life
- Establishing and managing interpersonal relationships and interactions
- Engaging in major life areas (education, employment, managing money, or finances)
- Engaging in community, social, and civic life

It is very important to improve the conditions in communities by providing accommodations that decrease or eliminate activity limitations and participation restrictions for people with disabilities, so they can participate in the roles and activities of everyday life.

Healthy Living

People with disabilities need healthcare and health programs for the same reasons anyone else does—to stay well, active, and a part of the community.

Having a disability does not mean a person is not healthy or that he or she cannot be healthy. Being healthy means the same thing for all of us—getting and staying well so we can lead full, active lives. That means having the tools and information to make healthy choices and knowing how to prevent illness.

Safety

People with disabilities can be at higher risk for injuries and abuse. It is important for parents and other family members to teach their loved one how to stay safe and what to do if they feel threatened or have been hurt in any way.

Assistive Technology

Assistive technologies (AT) are devices or equipment that can be used to help a person with a disability fully engage in life activities. AT's can help enhance functional independence and make daily living tasks easier through the use of aids that help a person travel, communicate with others, learn, work, and participate in social and recreational activities. An example of an assistive technology can be anything from a low-tech device, such as a magnifying glass, to a high tech device, such as a special computer that talks and helps someone communicate. Other examples are wheelchairs, walkers, and scooters, which are mobility aids that can be used by persons with physical disabilities.

School

In order to help a child fully participate in school, plans can be developed around the child's specific needs. These plans, known as 504 plans, are used by general education students not eligible for special education services. By law, children may be eligible to have a 504 plan which lists accommodations related to a child's disability. The 504 plan accommodations may be needed to give the child an opportunity to perform at the same level as their peers. For example, a 504 plan may include your child's assistive technology needs, such as a tape recorder or keyboard for taking notes and a wheelchair accessible environment.

A different plan is needed for children taking special education classes. An Individual Education Plan (IEP) is a legal document that tells the school its duties to your child.

Transitions

For some people with disabilities and their parents, change can be difficult. Planning ahead of time may make transitions easier for everyone.

Transitions occur at many stages of life. For example, the transition from teen years to adulthood can be especially challenging. There are many important decisions to make, such as deciding whether to go to college, a vocational school, or enter the workforce. It is important to begin thinking about this transition in childhood, so that educational transition plans are put in place. Ideally, transition plans from teen years to adulthood are in place by age 14, but no later than age 16. This makes sure the person has the skills he or she needs to begin the next phase of life. This stage in life also involves transitioning one's healthcare services from pediatricians to physicians who primarily treat adults.

Independent Living

Independent living means that a person lives in his or her own apartment or house and needs limited or no help from outside agencies. The person may not need any assistance or might need help with only complex issues such as managing money, rather than day-to-day living skills. Whether an adult with disabilities continues to live at home or moves out into the community depends in large part on his or her ability to manage everyday tasks with little or no help.

For example, can the person clean the house, cook, shop, and pay bills? Is he or she able to use public transportation? Many families prefer to start with some supported living arrangements and move towards increased independence.

Finding Support

For many people with disabilities and those who care for them, daily life may not be easy. Disabilities affect the entire family. Meeting the complex needs of a person with a disability can put families under a great deal of stress—emotional, financial, and sometimes even physical.

However, finding resources, knowing what to expect, and planning for the future can greatly improve overall quality of life. If you have a disability or care for someone who does, it might be helpful to talk with other people who can relate to your experience.

Find a Support Network

By finding support within your community, you can learn more about resources available to meet the needs of families and people with disabilities. This can help increase confidence, enhance quality of life, and assist in meeting the needs of family members.

A national organization that focuses on the disability, such as Spina Bifida Association (SBA), that has a state or local branch, such as Spina Bifida Association in your state, might exist. State or local area Centers for Independent Living (CILs) could also be helpful. United Way offices may be able to point out resources. Look in the phone book or on the web for phone numbers and addresses.

What Is a Disability?

Other ways to connect with other people include camps, organized activities, and sports for people with disabilities. In addition, there are online support groups and networks for people with many different types of disabilities.

Talk with a Mental Health Professional

Psychologists, social workers, and counselors can help you deal with the challenges of living with or caring for someone with a disability. Talk to your primary care physician for a referral.

Chapter 2

Statistics on People with Disabilities in the United States

The *Morbidity and Mortality Weekly Report* (MMWR) has published a report describing the percentage of adults with disabilities in the United States living in communities. This report is based on questions used for the first time in the 2013 Behavioral Risk Factor Surveillance System (BRFSS) that allow respondents to identify specific functional types of disability, such as mobility (serious difficulty walking or climbing stairs), cognitive (serious difficulty concentrating, remembering or making decisions), vision (serious difficulty seeing), self-care (difficulty dressing or bathing) and independent living (difficulty doing errands alone).

According to this report, over 53 million adults living in communities in the United States have a disability. Highest percentages are generally found in southern states and lowest are mostly in mid-western and Rocky Mountain states. Although anyone can have a disability,

---

This chapter contains text excerpted from the following sources: Text in this chapter begins with excerpts from "Key Findings: Prevalence of Disability in the US," Centers for Disease Control and Prevention (CDC), August 20, 2015; Text under the heading "Disability and Functioning" is excerpted from "Disability and Functioning (Noninstitutionalized Adults Aged 18 and Over)," Centers for Disease Control and Prevention (CDC), May 3, 2017.

and a disability can occur at any point in a person's life, disability was more commonly reported by women, older people (65 or more years), and racial and ethnic minority groups. Although progress has been made since the passage of the Americans with Disabilities Act (ADA) 25 years ago giving people with disabilities better opportunities to achieve their potential, studies consistently show that people living with a disability have poorer health than people without a disability, and that many of the health issues related to this poor health are preventable. This MMWR presents important information that public health officials and others can use to help understand and address the needs of people with disabilities in the United States.

Report Limitation

Currently, the BRFSS does not assess deafness or serious difficulty hearing. Therefore, data on the number of people who have hearing difficulties at the state level was not collected. This results in a likely underestimate of the total number of people with disabilities in the United States presented in this report.

Main Findings

- 1 in 5 adults or over 53 million people in the United States have a disability of one form or another, with state-level estimates ranging from 1 in 6 (16.4%; Minnesota) to nearly 1 in 3 (31.5%; Alabama).

Data Table

- The most common functional disability type was mobility disability, reported by about 1 in 8 adults.
- Over a third of adults 65 years or older reported any disability.
- Adults 45–64 years of age were more likely than other age group adults to report a cognitive disability.
- Individuals reporting a higher household income or education level were less likely to report having a disability, compared to individuals in lower income or education levels.
- Women were more likely to report any disability when compared with men (24.4% versus 19.8%). This was also seen for most of the disability types.

Statistics on People with Disabilities in the United States

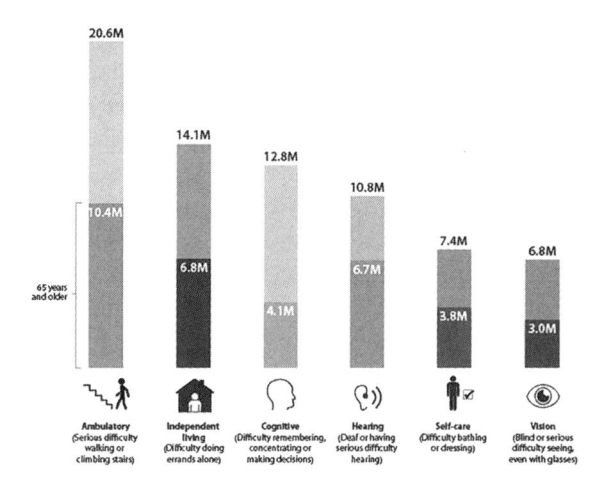

Figure 2.1. *Prevalence of Disabilities for Ages 18+* (Source: "Prevalence of Disabilities for Ages 18+," United States Census Bureau)

- Disability was more frequently reported by non-Hispanic blacks (29.0%) and Hispanic (25.9%) adults than by white non-Hispanic (20.6%) adults.

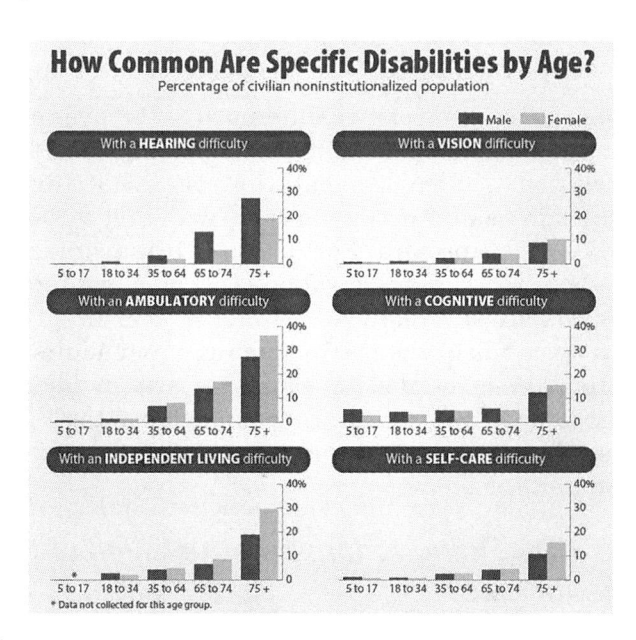

Figure 2.2. *Specific Disabilities by Age* (Source: "Stats for Stories: National Disability Employment Awareness Month," United States Census Bureau)

Implications

- Although disability information has been collected in national surveys for many years, this is the first time functional disability type is included in a state-based health survey. This information can help researchers and public health professionals better understand the makeup of adults with disabilities at a state level, and therefore, better plan programs to address the needs of the different disability populations.

- Variation among states in the percentage of people who reported a disability, with the highest percentage of disability generally found in states in the southern United States, reinforces the importance of assuring that all people with disabilities receive the healthcare and support they need to improve the health and wellbeing of the entire population.

- Because middle-aged adults (45–64 years old) were more likely to report cognitive disabilities than adults in other age groups, further research can be used to help better understand reasons for this, and ways in which their unique needs can be addressed.

- Since the percentage of disability is higher among certain groups such as women, older people, and racial and ethnic minorities, it is important that the programs and resources available for people with disabilities address the needs of these populations.

- The ADA has made a positive difference in the lives of those who have disabilities, providing better access to buildings, transportation, and employment. However, health disparities (differences in health) between people with and without disability are still present. Furthermore, disadvantaged people, namely those with lower education or income and those who are unemployed, are still more likely to report a disability. Working together we can help ensure that children and adults with disabilities receive needed programs, services and healthcare throughout their lives so that they can achieve their full potential, live a quality life, and experience independence in their communities.

What Is CDC Doing to Improve the Lives of People with Disabilities?

Centers for Disease Control and Prevention (CDC) supports 18 state-based disability and health programs and four National Public

Statistics on People with Disabilities in the United States

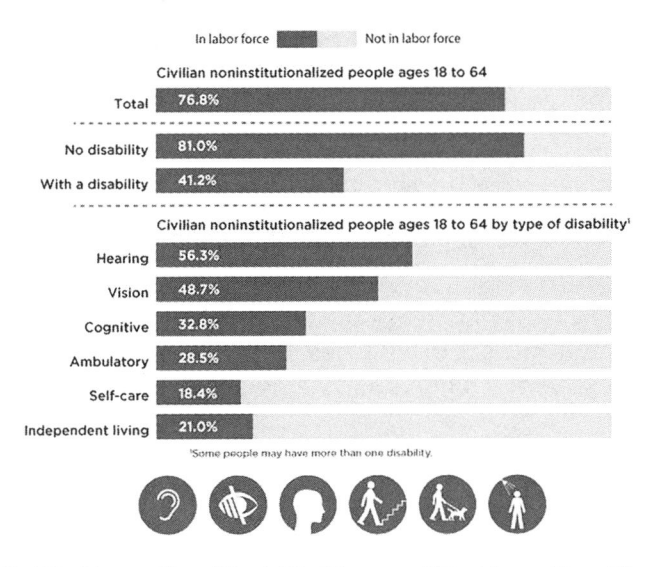

Civilian noninstitutionalized people ages 18 to 64
- Total: 76.8%
- No disability: 81.0%
- With a disability: 41.2%

Civilian noninstitutionalized people ages 18 to 64 by type of disability[1]
- Hearing: 56.3%
- Vision: 48.7%
- Cognitive: 32.8%
- Ambulatory: 28.5%
- Self-care: 18.4%
- Independent living: 21.0%

[1] Some people may have more than one disability.

Figure 2.3. *Working with a Disability* (Source: "Working with a Disability," United States Census Bureau)

Health Practice and Resource Centers which promote healthy lifestyles and work to improve quality of life for people with disabilities. The primary goals of the state programs are to:

- increase health promotion opportunities for people with disabilities;
- improve access to healthcare services for people with disabilities; and
- improve emergency preparedness for people with disabilities.

The CDC's Disability and Health website (www.cdc.gov/ncbddd/disabilityandhealth/index.html) also provides information and resources that public health practitioners, healthcare providers and people interested in the health and wellbeing of people with disabilities can use to increase awareness about disability inclusion. This information and the resources can help ensure that everybody, with and without disabilities, can live, work, learn, and play in their communities.

People are encouraged to visit the updated Disability and Health website (www.cdc.gov/ncbddd/disabilityandhealth) to find helpful information about disability inclusion and learn more about:

- barriers that people with disabilities usually experience in their communities;

- strategies to create inclusive communities; and
- resources to include people with disabilities in public health programs and activities.

CDC also maintains the Disability and Health Data System (DHDS) (www.cdc.gov/ncbddd/disabilityandhealth/dhds/index.html), an online interactive tool that provides instant access to state-level, disability-specific health data. Users can customize the disability and health data they view, making it easy to identify health differences between adults with and without disabilities. In a future update of the system, users will be able to find health data by functional disability type.

Disability and Functioning

Selected Sensory Problems

- Number of adults with hearing trouble: 37.8 million
- Percent of adults with hearing trouble: 15.4 percent
- Number of adults with vision trouble: 25.5 million
- Percent of adults with vision trouble: 10.4 percent

Difficulties in Physical Functioning

- Number of adults unable (or very difficult) to walk a quarter mile: 17.1 million
- Percent of adults unable (or very difficult) to walk a quarter mile: 7.0 percent
- Number of adults with any physical functioning difficulty: 39.5 million
- Percent of adults with any physical functioning difficulty: 16.1 percent

Basic Actions Difficulties or Complex Activity Limitations

- Number of adults aged 18 and over with at least one basic actions difficulty or complex activity limitation: 77.0 million (2015)
- Percent of adults aged 18 and over with at least one basic actions difficulty or complex activity limitation: 33.2 percent (2015)

Statistics on People with Disabilities in the United States

- Number of adults aged 65 and over with at least one basic actions difficulty or complex activity limitation: 26.5 million (2015)
- Percent of adults aged 65 and over with at least one basic actions difficulty or complex activity limitation: 59.8 percent (2015)

Need Help with Personal Care

- Percent of adults aged 65–74 who need help with personal care from other persons: 3.4 percent
- Percent of adults aged 75 and over who need help with personal care from other persons: 10.8 percent

Chapter 3

Common Barriers to Participation Experienced by People with Disabilities

Nearly everyone faces hardships and difficulties at one time or another. But for people with disabilities, barriers can be more frequent and have greater impact. The World Health Organization (WHO) describes barriers as being more than just physical obstacles. Here is the WHO definition of barriers:

Factors in a person's environment that, through their absence or presence, limit functioning and create disability. These include aspects such as:

- A physical environment that is not accessible

- Lack of relevant assistive technology (assistive, adaptive, and rehabilitative devices)

- Negative attitudes of people towards disability

- Services, systems, and policies that are either nonexistent or that hinder the involvement of all people with a health condition in all areas of life

---

This chapter includes text excerpted from "Common Barriers to Participation Experienced by People with Disabilities," Centers for Disease Control and Prevention (CDC), August 1, 2017.

Often there are multiple barriers that can make it extremely difficult or even impossible for people with disabilities to function. Here are the seven most common barriers. Often, more than one barrier occurs at a time.

1. Attitudinal
2. Communication
3. Physical
4. Policy
5. Programmatic
6. Social
7. Transportation

Attitudinal Barriers

Attitudinal barriers are the most basic and contribute to other barriers. For example, some people may not be aware that difficulties in getting to or into a place can limit a person with a disability from participating in everyday life and common daily activities. Examples of attitudinal barriers include:

- **Stereotyping:** People sometimes stereotype those with disabilities, assuming their quality of life is poor or that they are unhealthy because of their impairments.

- **Stigma, prejudice, and discrimination:** Within society, these attitudes may come from people's ideas related to disability— People may see disability as a personal tragedy, as something that needs to be cured or prevented, as a punishment for wrongdoing, or as an indication of the lack of ability to behave as expected in society.

Today, society's understanding of disability is improving as we recognize "disability" as what occurs when a person's functional needs are not addressed in his or her physical and social environment. By not considering disability a personal deficit or shortcoming, and instead thinking of it as a social responsibility in which all people can be supported to live independent and full lives, it becomes easier to recognize and address challenges that all people—including those with disabilities—experience.

Common Barriers Experienced by People with Disabilities

Communication Barriers

Communication barriers are experienced by people who have disabilities that affect hearing, speaking, reading, writing, and or understanding, and who use different ways to communicate than people who do not have these disabilities. Examples of communication barriers include:

- Written health promotion messages with barriers that prevent people with vision impairments from receiving the message. These include:
  - use of small print or no large-print versions of material, and
  - no Braille or versions for people who use screen readers.
- Auditory health messages may be inaccessible to people with hearing impairments, including:
  - videos that do not include captioning, and
  - oral communications without accompanying manual interpretation (such as, American Sign Language).
- The use of technical language, long sentences, and words with many syllables may be significant barriers to understanding for people with cognitive impairments.

Physical Barriers

Physical barriers are structural obstacles in natural or human-made environments that prevent or block mobility (moving around in the environment) or access. Examples of physical barriers include:

- steps and curbs that block a person with mobility impairment from entering a building or using a sidewalk;
- mammography equipment that requires a woman with mobility impairment to stand; and
- absence of a weight scale that accommodates wheelchairs or others who have difficulty stepping up.

Policy Barriers

Policy barriers are frequently related to a lack of awareness or enforcement of existing laws and regulations that require programs and activities be accessible to people with disabilities. Examples of policy barriers include:

- denying qualified individuals with disabilities the opportunity to participate in or benefit from federally funded programs, services, or other benefits;
- denying individuals with disabilities access to programs, services, benefits, or opportunities to participate as a result of physical barriers; and
- denying reasonable accommodations to qualified individuals with disabilities, so they can perform the essential functions of the job for which they have applied or have been hired to perform.

Programmatic Barriers

Programmatic barriers limit the effective delivery of a public health or healthcare program for people with different types of impairments. Examples of programmatic barriers include:

- inconvenient scheduling;
- lack of accessible equipment (such as mammography screening equipment);
- insufficient time set aside for medical examination and procedures;
- little or no communication with patients or participants; and
- provider's attitudes, knowledge, and understanding of people with disabilities.

Social Barriers

Social barriers are related to the conditions in which people are born, grow, live, learn, work and age—or social determinants of health—that can contribute to decreased functioning among people with disabilities. Here are examples of social barriers:

- People with disabilities are far less likely to be employed. The unemployment rate in 2012 for people with disabilities was more than 1 in 10 (13.9%) compared to less than 1 in 10 (6.0%) for those without disabilities.

Common Barriers Experienced by People with Disabilities

- Adults age 25 years and older with disabilities are less likely to have completed high school compared to their peers without disabilities (23.5% compared to 11.1%).
- People with disabilities are more likely to live in poverty compared to people without disabilities (21.6% compared to 12.8%).
- Children with disabilities are almost four times more likely to experience violence than children without disabilities.

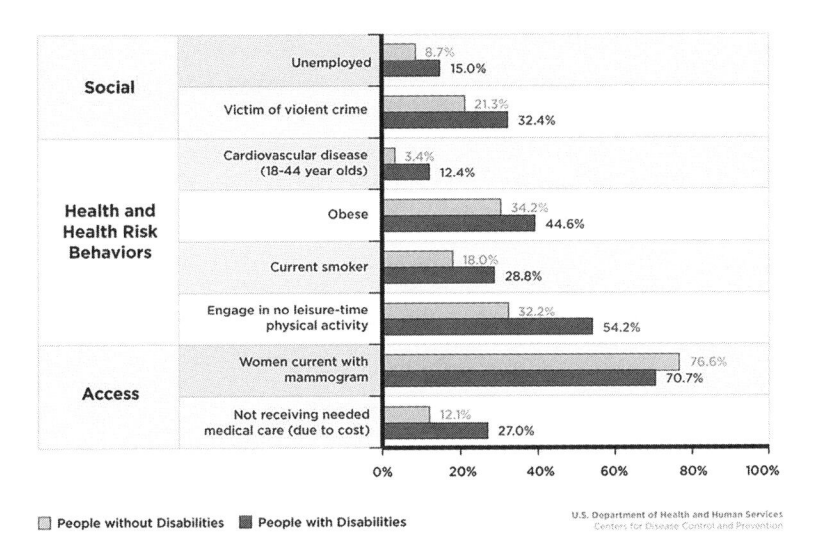

Category	Factor	People without Disabilities	People with Disabilities
Social	Unemployed	8.7%	15.0%
Social	Victim of violent crime	21.3%	32.4%
Health and Health Risk Behaviors	Cardiovascular disease (18-44 year olds)	3.4%	12.4%
Health and Health Risk Behaviors	Obese	34.2%	44.6%
Health and Health Risk Behaviors	Current smoker	18.0%	28.8%
Health and Health Risk Behaviors	Engage in no leisure-time physical activity	32.2%	54.2%
Access	Women current with mammogram	76.6%	70.7%
Access	Not receiving needed medical care (due to cost)	12.1%	27.0%

U.S. Department of Health and Human Services
Centers for Disease Control and Prevention

Figure 3.1. *Factors Affecting the Health of People with Disabilities and without Disabilities*

Transportation Barriers

Transportation barriers are due to a lack of adequate transportation that interferes with a person's ability to be independent and to function in society. Examples of transportation barriers include:

- lack of access to accessible or convenient transportation for people who are not able to drive because of vision or cognitive impairments, and
- public transportation may be unavailable or at inconvenient distances or locations.

Chapter 4

Myths and Facts about People with Disabilities

Understanding Disability Myths and Facts

Despite the passage of key civil rights laws such as the Rehabilitation Act and the Americans with Disabilities Act (ADA), many misunderstandings about people with disabilities persist, particularly in the minds of those who have not experienced disability within their own life or in the lives of people around them. The following highlights several of the most common myths about people with disabilities and the facts that counter these misunderstandings.

Myth: Disability is an unnatural, unusual, and uncommon occurrence.

This chapter contains text excerpted from the following sources: Text under the heading "Understanding Disability Myths and Facts" is excerpted from "A Guide to Interacting with People Who Have Disabilities," U.S. Department of Homeland Security (DHS), September 26, 2013. Reviewed July 2018; Text under the heading "Myths and Misconceptions about Students with Learning Disabilities (LD)" is excerpted from "Supporting Students with Learning Disabilities—Myths and Misconceptions," Job Corps, U.S. Department of Labor (DOL), December 13, 2016; Text under the heading "Common Myths about How Working Will Affect Disability Benefits" is excerpted from "Debunking the Three Biggest Myths about Disability Benefits and Work," U.S. Social Security Administration (SSA), September 10, 2016.

Fact: Disability is a natural part of the human experience. People with disabilities make up a significant portion of the population within all communities, regardless of age, race, ethnicity, or economic status. In 2010, 18.7 percent of the civilian noninstitutionalized population in the United States (about 56.7 million people) had a disability.

Myth: The abilities and needs of people with disabilities can be easily categorized. For example, if a person carries a white cane, they are totally blind; if a person uses a wheelchair, they are unable to stand up.

Fact: People with disabilities do not all have the same abilities and do not all have the same needs for assistance. They are the most knowledgeable about their own needs. For example, many people who carry a white cane have partial vision, and many people who use a wheelchair can stand or walk for short periods.

Myth: An individual's disability is usually observable

Fact: While some individuals' disabilities are observable and identifiable, many are not obvious. For example, the disabilities of individuals who have diabetes, dyslexia, or autism may not be visually apparent.

Myth: With the loss of one of the senses such as sight or hearing, the other senses automatically compensate and become sharper.

Fact: The body's senses do not automatically become sharper, but the individual can learn to become more aware of the information being received through other senses.

Myth: People with disabilities are heroic because they demonstrate bravery and courage by trying to overcome their disability.

Fact: People with disabilities generally do not view themselves as heroes; though some persons with disabilities such as returning military veterans may be considered heroes.

Myth: Most people with disabilities would be better off living in institutions where their needs can be met.

Fact: Federal law supports full inclusion so that people with disabilities have the right to live, learn, work, and participate in the community, utilizing assistive devices and support services if needed.

Myths and Facts about People with Disabilities

Myth: People with mental illness are potentially violent or incapable of participating in the community, and people without disabilities should be protected from them.

Fact: The vast majority of people who are violent do not have mental illness and most people who have mental illness are not violent.

Myth: People with disabilities should be served separately and with special procedures to ensure that they can receive quality services while not affecting the services to others.

Fact: Federal law generally requires that people with disabilities be served in the same setting and circumstances as the rest of the population.

Myth: Simply treating everyone in the same manner will lead to people with disabilities being served appropriately.

Fact: Due to the existence of long-standing physical, communication, and programmatic obstacles, merely treating everyone the same may not ensure equality of opportunity. Federal law requires service providers to remove barriers and take steps to ensure program accessibility for people with disabilities.

Myth: Modifying program procedures and furnishing auxiliary aids such as sign language interpreters or print reading software is too expensive.

Fact: Many modifications and accommodations can be made at low or no cost. In any event, federal law generally requires service providers to furnish auxiliary aids to achieve effective communication with people who have disabilities.

Myths and Misconceptions about Students with Learning Disabilities

The adoption and acceptance of long-standing "myths" and "misconceptions" regarding individuals with learning and attention disabilities continues to fuel prejudicial views, erect attitudinal barriers, and create social stigmas that can have devastating long-term results-emotionally and educationally. Because learning and attention disabilities are not always readily obvious to others, these individuals often get labeled as "stupid," "lazy," "space cadet," "dumb," and other such derogatory terms. These terms only serve to exacerbate the negative self-image that many youth with these disabilities already have about themselves.

Dispelling these myths and misconceptions requires ongoing education and training for the general public as well as service providers, family members, and the student with the disability.

Dispelling the Myths and Misconceptions about Learning Disabilities

Myth: Individuals with learning disabilities (LD) have limited potential.

Fact: Individuals with LD conduct successful and fulfilling lives just as individuals without disabilities do. Greater success is achieved when these individuals are appropriately accommodated or have developed effective compensatory strategies.

Myth: LD is just a polite way to refer to lower overall intelligence and abilities.

Fact: Inherent within the definition of LD is a discrepancy between demonstrated intelligence and specific functioning. It is possible for a student to be both gifted and learning disabled at the same time.

Myth: People with LD are lazy.

Fact: If an individual with a LD has experienced repeated failures, particularly educationally or socially, they often shut down and believe it hurts less to not try than it does to try and fail. The individual may feel he/she has no control over what happens to her/him which is known as learned helplessness. Small doses of success are the best antidote to learned helplessness.

Myth: Given proper instruction, individuals with LD can grow out it.

Fact: Although individuals with LD can and do acquire improved skills, the LD themselves are not cured in the process. Some types of LD can be successfully and permanently remediated but others are thought to be lifelong and may require the acquisition and use of compensatory strategies or accommodations throughout the individual's life span.

Myth: Accommodations provided to students with LD, particularly during testing situations, gives them an unfair advantage over students without disabilities.

Myths and Facts about People with Disabilities

Fact: An accommodation does not tip the scales in the student's favor; it merely levels the playing field. Accommodations provide access to the information thus giving the student with a disability a means to demonstrate his/her knowledge, skills, and abilities. Without modifications, common forms of instruction and examination often inadvertently reflect a student's disability rather than the subject at hand. For example, a student who has a writing disability would be greatly impaired during a written essay exam even though he/she was skilled in the art and mechanics of writing an essay. The use of a word processor allows this student to demonstrate his/her knowledge rather than be judged by the limitations his handwriting difficulties imposed.

Myth: Accommodating the needs of a student with LD means watering down course and program requirements.

Fact: Teaching a student with special learning needs does not mean "less." It may, however, mean "different." The instructional goal should be to find ways to work around the area of deficit and still impart the same body of information and sets of skills.

Myth: Students with LD do not have to work any harder than other students.

Fact: Most students with LD do have to work harder than the average student to achieve success. However, the "silver lining" for those who are willing to put in the extra effort is that being a hard worker is a highly valued characteristic in the work world.

Dispelling the Myths and Misconceptions about Attention Deficit Hyperactivity Disorder (ADHD)

Myth: Attention deficit hyperactivity disorder (ADHD) does not really exist. It is simply an excuse for parents who do not discipline their children.

Fact: Scientific research tells us ADHD is a biologically-based disorder that includes distractibility, impulsiveness, and sometimes hyperactivity. Before a student is diagnosed as ADHD, other possible causes of his/her behavior are ruled out.

Myth: Medication can cure students with ADHD.

Fact: Medicine cannot cure ADHD but can sometimes temporarily moderate its effects. Certain stimulant medications are effective in the majority of the individuals who take it, providing an immediate short-term increase in attention, control, concentration, and goal-directed effort. Medication may also reduce disruptive behaviors, aggression, and hyperactivity.

Myth: Individuals with ADHD will outgrow it.

Fact: ADHD is a lifelong condition although it manifests itself differently dependent upon the age of the individual. Some individuals

- experience a lessening of ADHD symptoms with age,
- develop effective compensatory strategies that make it appear as if the ADHD has gone away, or
- manage the symptoms of the disorder with medication.

Myth: Individuals who can focus their attention in some areas (i.e., video games, etc.) cannot have ADHD.

Fact: ADHD is a neurological difference that makes it very difficult to attend to things that are not interesting to the person involved or that require sustained mental effort. Yet this person can sit for hours and play video games or participate in other activities of interest. This type of focus is known as hyperfocus.

Common Myths about How Working Will Affect Disability Benefits

There are several common myths about how working will affect disability benefits and healthcare coverage. Here are the three most common and why they are wrong.

1. **If I try to go to work, I will automatically lose my Medicare or Medicaid.**

    This is a myth. First, as long as you keep receiving a benefit check of any amount, you will keep your health insurance. If you earn enough that your Social Security Disability Insurance (SSDI) checks stop, Medicare can continue for up to 93 months. If you currently receive Medicaid, you should be eligible to continue to receive Medicaid even after you stop receiving Supplemental Security Income (SSI) benefits due to work. To be eligible you need to meet certain requirements, which include earnings below a threshold amount set by your state. Even if your earnings exceed the state threshold, you

Myths and Facts about People with Disabilities

may still be eligible and should talk to your state Medicaid office.

2. **If I use my Ticket to go to work, Social Security will conduct a medical review of my case, and I will lose my benefits.**

    This is also a myth. Social Security ordinarily reviews your medical condition from time to time to see whether you are still disabled, using a process called the medical Continuing Disability Review, or medical CDR. If you participate in the Ticket program with either an Employment Network or your State Vocational Rehabilitation Agency, and make "timely progress" following your individual work plan, Social Security will not conduct a review of your medical condition. If a medical CDR has already been scheduled for you before you assigned your ticket, Social Security will continue with the medical CDR.

3. **If my checks stop because I go to work and then I have to stop working because of my disability, I will have to reapply for benefits all over again. It took me forever to be approved for benefits and I cannot afford to wait that long again. As a result, I should not try to work.**

    Again, it's a myth. You will not need to reapply if your benefits ended within the past five years due to your earnings and you meet a few other requirements, including that you still have the original medical condition or one related to it that prevents you from working. This is a work incentive called Expedited Reinstatement. You may even be able to receive up to six months of temporary cash benefits in addition to Medicare or Medicaid coverage while U.S. Social Security Administration (SSA) conducts a medical review to determine if your benefits can be reinstated.

Chapter 5

Women with Disabilities

About 27 million women in the United States have disabilities—and the number is growing. More than 50 percent of women older than 65 are living with a disability. The most common cause of disability for women is arthritis or rheumatism.

Women with disabilities may need specialty care to address their individual needs. In addition, they need the same general healthcare as women without disabilities, and they may also need additional care to address their specific needs. However, research has shown that many women with disabilities may not receive regular health screenings within recommended guidelines.

Breast Cancer Screening: The Right to Know

Breast cancer is a major public health concern for all women, including women with disabilities. Women who have disabilities are just as likely as women without disabilities to have ever received a mammogram. However, they are significantly less likely to have been screened within the recommended guidelines. Centers for Disease Control and Prevention (CDC) has developed a family of health promotion materials (e.g., posters, MP3 files, low-tech fliers, print advertisements, and tip sheets) to increase awareness of breast cancer among women with physical disabilities and encourage these women to get screened.

This chapter includes text excerpted from "Women with Disabilities," Centers for Disease Control and Prevention (CDC), August 3, 2017.

Cervical Cancer Screening

Cervical cancer is the easiest female cancer to prevent, with regular screening tests and followup. It also is highly curable when found and treated early. All women are at risk for cervical cancer, including women with disabilities. It occurs most often in women over age 30. It is important to get tested for cervical cancer because 6 out of 10 cervical cancers occur in women who have never received a Pap test (a screening procedure for cervical cancer) or have not been tested in the past five years.

Healthy Living

People with disabilities need healthcare and health programs for the same reasons anyone else does—to stay well, active, and a part of the community.

Having a disability does not mean a person can't be healthy. Being healthy means the same thing for all of us—getting and staying in good physical, mental, and emotional health so we can lead full, active lives. That means having the tools and information to make healthy choices and knowing how to prevent illness.

Intimate Partner Violence (IPV)

Each year, women experience about 4.8 million intimate partner-related physical assaults and rapes. Research has shown that women with a disability are more likely to experience intimate partner violence (IPV) than those without a disability. In fact, researchers found that 37.3 percent of women with a disability were much more likely to report experiencing some form of IPV during their lifetime; this compared with 20.6 percent of women without a disability.

Chapter 6

Aging and Disabilities

Thirty years ago, America was steadily aging. In 1980, approximately 26.1 million people were 65 years of age or older, compared with 3 million in 1900. And Americans were living notably longer than they had in the past—average life expectancy for a child born in 1980 was 73.7 years, up from 47.3 years in 1900. Disability was on the rise among older people. Studies from the 1970s and early 1980s pointed to modest increases in the prevalence of disability. For example, in 1976, 4.8 million older people reported limitations in the number or kinds of major activities they could undertake.

It was widely believed that aging invariably brought with it frailty and loss of independence. One study, for example, predicted that technology would save people's lives, but still leave them disabled and an increasing burden on society. However, groundbreaking research from projects such as the Baltimore Longitudinal Study of Aging (www.grc.nia.nih.gov/branches/blsa/blsanew.htm), initiated in 1958, began to suggest that disease and disability were not inevitable consequences of aging.

The growth in the aging population, the increase in life expectancy, and concerns about disability led to the founding in 1974 of the

---

This chapter contains text excerpted from the following sources: Text in this chapter begins with excerpts from "Disability in Older Adults," National Institutes of Health (NIH), June 30, 2018; Text under the heading "Reducing Chronic Disease and Disability" is excerpted from "Reducing Chronic Disease in Older Age," National Institute on Aging (NIA), National Institutes of Health (NIH), July 25, 2018.

National Institute on Aging (NIA) within the National Institutes of Health (NIH). The Institute was charged with "the conduct and support of biomedical, social, and behavioral research, training, health information dissemination, and other programs with respect to the aging process and diseases and other special problems and needs of the aged."

People continue to live longer and the U.S. population is increasingly older. The leading edge of the Baby Boom turns 65 in 2011, part of a rapid growth in population aging in the United States—and worldwide. 39 million people in the United States are age 65 or older, and life expectancy at birth has reached 78.3 years. Most notable is the growth in the population of individuals age 85 and older who are at highest risk for disease and disability.

Research demonstrates that disease and disability are not an inevitable part of aging. Disability rates can be reduced, as evidenced by data from the National Long Term Care Survey (NLTCS) (www.nltcs.aas.duke.edu), which found that between 1982 and 1999, the prevalence of physical disability in older Americans decreased from 26 percent to 20 percent. Additionally, there is evidence from the Health and Retirement Study (HRS) (hrsonline.isr.umich.edu) that the probability of being cognitively impaired at a given age has been decreasing (from the mid-1990s up until at least 2004), although the rapidly increasing population of older adults means that the absolute number of cognitive impaired individuals is still increasing.

However, it remains unclear whether the decline in rates of disability s continued since 1999, and researchers are analyzing multiple data sources to ascertain the trend. There is some evidence suggesting that while the decline in disability may have continued among the oldest old (those age 85+), the decline in disability ended or was reversed in the new cohorts recently entering old age.

Factors thought to have contributed to this decline in disability rates include improved medical treatment (particularly treatments such as beta-blockers and angiotensin-converting enzyme (ACE) inhibitors for cardiovascular disease (CVD)), positive behavioral changes, more widespread use of assistive technologies, rising education levels, and improvements in socioeconomic status. The NIH supports research to understand the underlying causes of this decline in order to develop behavioral and multi-level interventions to maintain and accelerate this trend.

Scientists are identifying factors that contribute to healthier aging and longer life expectancy. Epidemiologic studies suggest that lifespan and health are determined by both genetic and environmental

Aging and Disabilities

influences, with genetics accounting for about 35 percent of lifespan and modifiable environmental factors contributing most to this complex interaction.

Interventions are being developed to improve how older people function. Researchers at the NIH-supported Claude D. Pepper Older Americans Independence Centers (OAIC) (www.peppercenter.org/public/home.cfm), for example, have developed effective ways to prevent falls, improve muscle function (size, strength, and power), and reduce delirium related to hospital stays. One NIH study dramatically demonstrated that even 90-year-olds can improve muscle strength and mobility with simple weight training exercises.

However, downward trends in disability may be threatened by recent increases in obesity levels. According to the National Health Interview Survey (NHIS) (www.cdc.gov/nchs/nhis.htm), the disability rate among people ages 18–59 rose significantly from the 1980s through the 1990s, with the growing prevalence of obesity factoring into the trend. Obesity and overweight put people at increased risk for potentially disabling chronic diseases such as heart disease, type 2 diabetes, high blood pressure, stroke, osteoarthritis, respiratory problems, and some forms of cancer.

Researchers may find ways to identify those most at risk for specific types of disability. NIH investigators have identified several markers, including grip strength, gait (walking) speed, circulating levels of the protein IL-6, and measures of lung function, that can be used to predict the onset of limitations in mobility. Researchers are currently conducting a genome-wide association study to identify genes and genomic regions associated with trajectories of change in each of these markers.

The National Health and Aging Trends Study (NHATS) (web.jhu.edu/popaging/nhats.html), a new nationwide NIH-funded study of 12,000 people age 65 and older, will provide data to disentangle the physical, social, technological and environmental factors in disability prevalence, onset, and recovery. The study will also help us understand the social and economic consequences of late-life disability for individuals, families, and society.

The HRS (hrsonline.isr.umich.edu), a nationwide NIH-funded survey of more than 22,000 people age 50 and older, is allowing researchers to examine the interactions among physical and mental health, insurance coverage, financial well-being, family support, work status, retirement planning and the impact of these variables on disability. Improved ability to forecast disability trends will help give policymakers more accurate projections of national expenditures for the

Social Security and Medicare programs. Researchers will also assess disability risks in understudied populations within the United States, minorities, and the medically underserved.

Research may bring new treatments to prevent or minimize disability from stroke, diabetes, and other acute and chronic health problems. For example, NIH-supported researchers are developing interventions to improve quadriceps muscle function after total knee replacement and muscle conditioning (muscle size, strength, and power) in community-dwelling individuals at high risk for falls and mobility disability. Other studies are evaluating the ability of an exercise and health promotion intervention to facilitate maintenance of physical and cognitive function in older adults with mild cognitive impairment (often a precursor condition to Alzheimer disease (AD)). In addition, researchers are conducting a clinical trial of testosterone in men with impaired physical functioning.

Interventions are being developed to prevent disability in older people. For example, the ongoing Lifestyle Interventions and Independence for Elders (LIFE) Study (www.thelifestudy.org/public/index.cfm) will assess the effect of an exercise intervention to prevent mobility disability in older adults. NIA also funds a randomized trial of a social engagement intervention, the Experience Corps (www.experiencecorps.org/index.cfm), which places older volunteers, mostly inner-city residents, in elementary schools in cognitively demanding and socially productive roles. Preliminary data have shown improvements in both mental and physical health for seniors, as well as benefits for the schools.

Reducing Chronic Disease in Older Age

Chronic disease and disability can compromise the quality of life for older people. Some 79 percent of people age 70 and older have at least one of seven potentially disabling chronic conditions (arthritis, hypertension, heart disease, diabetes, respiratory diseases, stroke, and cancer). The burden of such chronic conditions and disability poses a challenge not only to individuals, but to families, employers, and to the healthcare system as well. Research to improve understanding of the risk and protective factors for chronic disease and disability can offer effective prevention strategies.

Benefits of Exercise

Regular exercise is essential to maintain health and function at any age. In older adults, it has been shown that exercise in four key areas—endurance, strength, balance, and flexibility—can improve function and reduce disease. Endurance activity is important for function of the heart, lungs, and circulatory system and may help prevent such diseases as diabetes, colon cancer, heart disease, and stroke. Even in very old adults, strength exercises build muscles, increase metabolism, and help to keep weight and blood sugar in check. Strength exercises have been shown to help prevent osteoporosis. Balance and flexibility exercises help prevent falls and other injuries. As research continues to measure such benefits, investigators also are delving deeper into how exercise does what it does. Better understanding in this area, for instance, in how exercise affects metabolic processes within the older body, may lead to new and innovative interventions.

Fitness Affects Mortality Risk Regardless of Body Fat

Both obesity and being unfit increase risk for chronic disease and death. However, the interrelationship between fitness, body fat, and mortality has not been clear. Recent research suggests that it is fitness, not fat, that may count most. In one study, investigators followed men 30–83 years of age for an average of eight years, classifying participants according to body fat as well as relative fitness based on exercise testing. Not surprisingly, the study showed that the higher the level of fat, the lower the level of fitness. But what intrigued researchers most were data showing that, within each category of body fat, "fit" men were at lower risk of death. Most strikingly, among those more fit, obesity was not significantly related to risk of death. In another study, low fitness increased mortality risk in men approximately fivefold for cardiovascular disease (CVD), and threefold for all-cause mortality. These findings suggest that, beyond interventions focusing on weight-loss to prevent and treat obesity-associated conditions, there may also be important benefits for the obese from improved fitness.

Stress Testing May Not Be Needed for Starting an Exercise Program

The role of exercise stress testing and safety monitoring for older people who want to start an exercise program is unclear. Current guidelines for routine exercise stress testing may deter older people from beginning an exercise program, either because of the cost of testing or because it may lead people to believe that exercise poses higher risks than it actually does. The latest research suggests that, in the absence of cardiovascular contraindications, the benefits of exercise for the elderly, balanced against a somewhat minor increase in risk, may be sufficient for starting an exercise program without prior exercise stress testing.

Identifying Gene Variants That Influence the Interaction between Exercise and Cholesterol Levels

The increase in body fat and loss of muscle mass that occur with age raise risk for disease, including diabetes and CVD. Proper diet and/or exercise can be effective in helping to prevent or improve these conditions. However, there can be large variation in response to these interventions, in part because of genetic influences. Detection of specific genes affecting obesity, muscle mass, and blood cholesterol levels may provide a way to identify individuals likely to respond favorably to a particular intervention. In overweight, postmenopausal women, one genetic variation of an enzyme, lipoprotein lipase (LPL), was found to be associated with lower levels of both total cholesterol and low-density lipoprotein (LDL-cholesterol), risk factors for heart disease. The same LPL gene variant was found in older men with greater exercise-induced increases in high-density lipoprotein (HDL-cholesterol), a protective factor against heart disease. In another study, variants of the gene for *apolipoprotein E (APOE)*, previously shown to influence blood cholesterol levels, were related to exercise-induced increases in HDL-cholesterol in middle-aged and older, overweight men. One form (APOE2) was associated with greater exercise-induced increases in HDL, compared with other variants of the *APOE* gene. Knowledge of how such specific gene variants interact with each other and with exercise and diet will lead to the development of more targeted and individualized prevention and treatment strategies.

Treatment and Prevention of Disease

Treatment of disease in older people can be complicated by the presence of other diseases and disorders and by the use of multiple medications to treat various conditions. Potential interactions of multiple medications, including those of prescribed drugs with over-the-counter (OTC) drugs and dietary supplements, represent additional concerns. Moreover, compliance with treatment regimens can be difficult, as older patients often must maintain a complex schedule for taking several different medications. Research is ongoing to determine the best treatment approaches for older patients, particularly those with multiple comorbidities, and to identify strategies for improving compliance and minimizing potentially harmful effects of multiple medications.

Inadequate Treatment of Hypertension and Atrial Fibrillation (AF) in the Elderly

According to national surveys, 60–70 percent of older Americans aged 60 years and older have high blood pressure. Despite the considerable amount of scientific evidence that hypertension is an important risk factor for CVD in all age groups, survey data suggest that in hypertensives over age 70, only 25 percent of African Americans and only 18 percent of white Americans have achieved the blood pressure goals (140/90 mmHg) recommended by the Joint National Committee (JNC) on the Prevention, Detection, Evaluation, and Treatment of High Blood Pressure. Uncontrolled or inadequately controlled high blood pressure can lead to heart attack, stroke, heart failure, kidney disease, dementia or blindness. Another common cardiovascular problem is AF, a heart rhythm abnormality that can lead to circulating blood clots. Warfarin, a drug used to inhibit blood clotting, dramatically reduces the risk of stroke in patients with AF. Two recent studies suggest that older patients may be under-treated for both hypertension and AF. One found that developing new strategies to improve blood pressure control in older hypertensive patients might prevent an estimated 15 percent of heart attacks in this population. The other found that many patients with AF and at least one additional stroke risk factor, especially high blood pressure, did not receive appropriate warfarin therapy when such treatment may have been appropriate. These findings suggest the need for new strategies to enhance the appropriate use of currently available warfarin and antihypertensive treatments in standard clinical care.

Commonly Prescribed Diuretic Protects against Osteoporosis

The lifetime risk of osteoporotic fracture in the United States is 40 percent in women and 13 percent in men. Because age-related bone loss increases susceptibility to fracture, strategies aimed at preserving bone mass are important. Large observational studies have consistently shown that the use of thiazide diuretics, usually prescribed to treat high blood pressure, is associated with higher bone density and about a 30 percent lower risk of hip fracture. Investigators recently completed a clinical trial to directly test the effect of taking thiazides on bone density in older men and women with normal blood pressure. Among healthy older adults, low-dose hydrochlorothiazide did preserve bone density at the hip and spine. The modest effects observed over three years, if accumulated over 10–20 years, may explain the 30 percent reduction in hip fracture risk associated with thiazides in the earlier observational studies. The results of this trial suggest that low-dose thiazide therapy may have a role in strategies to prevent osteoporosis.

Molecular Understanding of Disease Processes: Diabetes, Atherosclerosis

Diabetes is one of the leading causes of death and disability in the United States. Type 2 diabetes, the most common form, usually develops in adults over 40 and is most common in adults 55 and older. Diabetes accelerates the narrowing of blood vessels by atherosclerosis and is a major risk factor for peripheral arterial disease. Atherosclerosis, which impairs blood circulation by narrowing arteries, is the most common form of occlusive vascular disease, a factor in both heart attacks and strokes. Most individuals with peripheral arterial disease have atherosclerosis, and symptoms can include painful cramping in leg muscles during physical activity. Studies reported here include: a new molecular approach for treating type 2 diabetes; gene therapy advances in possible treatment for peripheral artery disease; and advances in understanding and preventing the atherosclerotic process and how to reverse it.

Exendin-4 as a Treatment for Type 2 Diabetes

Type 2 diabetes mellitus (DM) is caused by an inability of the beta cells of the pancreas to compensate for increasing insulin demands; consequently, blood glucose levels rise. Scientists are searching for compounds that act on the pancreatic beta cells to prevent this progressive rise in blood glucose. Glucagon-like peptide 1 (GLP-1), a gut peptide, can stimulate beta cells to produce more insulin even in type 2 DM; however, its biologic half-life is short and its effects quickly wear off. Exendin-4, a newly studied peptide analog of GLP-1, is long-lived and more potent than GLP-1, and has been shown to reduce blood glucose levels in rodents. A recent study with small numbers of diabetic and nondiabetic humans demonstrated Exendin-4's efficacy in inducing insulin and normalizing blood sugar, even in diabetics. In the near future, an exendin-like drug possibly may become an effective treatment for type 2 DM.

Gene Transfer in Animal Model Stimulates Growth of New Vessels for Treatment of Peripheral Muscle Ischemia

Patients with blocked arteries in limbs are at risk of disabling symptoms in the part of the limb to which blood flow has been interrupted (ischemia). Restoring blood flow involves treatment with factors that promote artery regrowth (angiogenic factors). Until now, these angiogenic factors have been successfully tested only in animals whose blood supply is permanently blocked, and clinical trials in humans with similar permanent blockages are underway. Whether angiogenic treatment could also be used to treat people with intermittent ischemia, a condition in which the symptoms associated with blockage can recur periodically, is not known. Research is suggesting that intervention may be possible. In one recent study, scientists delivered an angiogenic factor by gene transfer into normal rat leg muscle several weeks before inducing ischemia by interrupting blood flow to the same leg. In that study, the angiogenic factor markedly increased formation of new blood vessels to the normal muscle, and these new blood vessels played a role in restoring blood flow and normal metabolism more quickly to the limb following ischemia. Successful development of this technique in humans might permit early intervention in patients with intermittent ischemia.

Regulation of TGF-β Type II Receptor and Atherosclerosis

Atherosclerosis or narrowing of the arteries is the major risk factor for both heart disease and stroke and is a major complication after arteries have been surgically enlarged by balloon angioplasty. Throughout life, artery wall cells successfully repair injuries related to smoking, high blood pressure or cholesterol, making new cells to replace damaged ones. But constant exposure to such stresses eventually causes the artery wall cells to lose control of their replication. The growing mass of cells forms plaque, which eventually clogs the vessels and causes reduced blood flow. New research is helping to identify the complex series of cellular events causing cells to lose control of their division. In normal circumstances, a protein called TGF-ß1 prevents excessive cell division. It acts on the cells through binding to a protein receptor on the cell surface, the TGF-ß1 receptor, causing intracellular changes that stop cells dividing. In atherosclerotic lesions, it has been shown, unrestricted growth in some cells is caused by mutations in this receptor, inactivating it. Another way of preventing normal receptor function is to make too little TGF-ß1 receptor to be effective. One protein that inhibits the production of TGF-ß1 receptor is called Egr-1. This protein is found at very high levels in plaques, perhaps being induced by artery injury. Finding drugs to repress the activity of Egr-1 may be one way of keeping the key TGF-ß1 receptor functioning effectively to stop excessive cell division and prevent atherosclerosis.

Selected Future Research Directions to Reduce Disease and Disability

Cardiovascular Disease: Its Impact on Aging and Role in Dementia

Diseases of the heart and blood vessels are the leading cause of hospitalization and death in older Americans. The National Institute on Aging (NIA) is pursuing a broad program of basic and clinical cardiovascular research, often in collaboration with the National Heart, Lung, and Blood Institute (NHLBI). Characterization of age-associated changes in both the structure and function of the heart and blood vessels is vital to the development of newer, more effective prevention and treatment of CVD. Research priorities include identifying genetic and environmental risk factors for hypertension, heart disease, and stroke as well as development of subclinical measures to predict development of CVD. Studies are ongoing to determine the causes of age-associated increases in vascular stiffness, a potential risk factor for CVD. Other research will focus on age-related changes in the structure and function of the heart's conduction system that can increase the risk of cardiac arrhythmias, especially atrial fibrillation that if uncorrected can lead to strokes. Additional priorities include determining the reasons for gender and racial differences in the aging cardiovascular system, delineating the relationship of cardiac enlargement to aging and disease development, reducing the progression of early atherosclerotic disease, and identification and testing of new therapeutic targets for congestive heart failure. Further, the interrelationships among CVD, cerebrovascular disease, and age-related cognitive declines, including dementia, need to be explored. Such research will help to better understand the range of factors that may contribute to mild cognitive deficits in elders and to develop improved methods for early identification of people at risk for dementia. Additional efforts in this area will look at new approaches for treatment and prevention, such as examining combined use of treatments targeted at CVD, cerebrovascular disease, hypertension, and AD pathology. New technological developments in cardiac, vascular, and brain imaging and monitoring will be exploited to advance understanding of these disorders and their comorbidities, in animal models, including nonhuman primates, and in humans.

Treating and Reducing the Risk of Cancer

The second leading cause of death among the elderly is cancer. People age 65 and over account for 70 percent of cancer mortality in the United States. In collaboration with the National Cancer Institute (NCI), the NIA supports a research initiative to expand participation of older cancer patients in clinical trials and is expanding basic and clinical research on breast, prostate, and colon cancers. This research focuses on age-related changes that contribute to increased cancer incidence and mortality in older people, aggressive tumor behavior in the aged patient, the contributions of environmental versus hereditary factors to the risk of cancer, and the impact of previous or concurrent conditions and disabilities on the cancer experience of older patients. Specific research topics include: dose adjustment for antitumor agents and radiation therapy, diagnostic cancer imaging, the effect of coexisting diseases on cancer treatment and survival outcome, survival advantages or disadvantages of minority or ethnic populations, and underlying biological or environmental basis for cancers, such as prostate cancer, that disproportionately affect particular groups.

Type 2 Diabetes: An Age-Related Pathology

Unlike insulin-dependent diabetes, in which the pancreas makes no insulin, people with noninsulin-dependent diabetes (NIDDM) produce some insulin. However, not enough insulin is produced or the individual's cells are resistant to the insulin's action. NIDDM patients can often control their condition by weight loss through diet and exercise. Complications of diabetes are pervasive, including damage to the eyes, blood vessels, nervous system, and kidneys. A number of research lines within the NIA portfolio address issues relevant to diabetes. Work described earlier on a potential future drug treatment for type 2 diabetes, Exendin-4, is continuing. Increasing levels of physical activity and participation in exercise are often recommended for the prevention and treatment of common metabolic conditions such as obesity and insulin resistance/diabetes. NIA-funded scientists are investigating whether the metabolic benefits of exercise are mediated through body composition changes and/or occur independently of changes in body fat or leanness.

Potential Role of Caloric Restriction (CR) in Prevention of Multiple Diseases

In animal models, chronic CR has been shown to extend lifespan and delay the onset of age-related pathologies. A recent Request for Applications (RFA), has invited proposals for exploratory human studies on the effects of caloric restriction interventions on physiology, body composition, and risk factors for age-related pathologies, and encourages the use of such outcome measures as insulin sensitivity and glucose metabolism. Another current RFA is soliciting research proposals on the molecular and neural mechanisms underlying the beneficial effects of caloric restriction, and includes as a major objective investigation of the role played by reduction of blood glucose levels in the lifespan extension effects.

Enhancing Musculoskeletal Function

Osteoporosis, osteoarthritis, and age-related loss of muscle mass (or sarcopenia) contribute to frailty and injury among older people. The NIA supports several research initiatives to define the underlying mechanisms of aging in bone, muscle, and joints, and to design and evaluate effective prevention and intervention strategies for age-related musculoskeletal decline. In one area, scientists are exploring factors that may act to predispose older people to fractures. The role of exercise continues to be closely scrutinized. The physiological effects of exercise on muscle and bone are being examined, and the development of interventions to encourage older people to begin and maintain an exercise regimen is particularly important. Also, NIA participates in the National Institutes of Health (NIH) Federal Working Group on Bone Diseases (FWGBD), convened quarterly to provide opportunities for sharing information, identifying collaborative projects and carrying out specific joint activities such as conferences and research initiatives. In collaboration with the National Institute of Arthritis and Musculoskeletal and Skin Diseases (NIAMS), NIA will continue to evaluate future opportunities, currently encouraging researchers studying Paget's disease and osteogenesis imperfecta to focus on the effects of aging in patients with these conditions.

Chapter 7

Communicating with and about People with Disabilities

About 50 million Americans report having a disability. Most Americans will experience a disability sometime during the course of their lives. Disabilities can affect people in different ways, even when one person has the same type of disability as another person. Some disabilities may be hidden or not easy to see.

People-First Language

People-first language is used to speak appropriately and respectfully about an individual with a disability. People-first language emphasizes the person first not the disability. For example, when referring to a

---

This chapter contains text excerpted from the following sources: Text in this chapter begins with excerpts from "Communicating with and about People with Disabilities," Centers for Disease Control and Prevention (CDC), July 23, 2010. Reviewed July 2018; Text under the heading "Communicating with and about People with Disabilities in General" is excerpted from "Communicating with and about People with Disabilities," U.S. Department of Labor (DOL), October 1, 2002. Reviewed July 2018; Text beginning with the heading "Communicating with and about People with Disabilities in the Workplace" is excerpted from "Effective Interaction: Communicating with and about People with Disabilities in the Workplace," U.S. Department of Labor (DOL), March 20, 2007. Reviewed July 2018.

person with a disability, refer to the person first by using phrases such as: "a person who...," "a person with..." or, "person who has..."

Here are suggestions on how to communicate with and about people with disabilities.

Table 7.1. How to Communicate with and about People with Disabilities

People-First Language	Language to Avoid
Person with a disability	The disabled, handicapped
Person without a disability	Normal person, healthy person
Person with an intellectual, cognitive, developmental disability	Retarded, slow, simple, moronic, defective or retarded, afflicted, special person
Person with an emotional or behavioral disability, person with a mental health or a psychiatric disability	Insane, crazy, psycho, maniac, nuts
Person who is hard of hearing	Hearing impaired, suffers a hearing loss
Person who is deaf	Deaf and dumb, mute
Person who is blind/visually impaired	The blind
Person who has a communication disorder, is unable to speak, or uses a device to speak	Mute, dumb
Person who uses a wheelchair	Confined or restricted to a wheelchair, wheelchair bound
Person with a physical disability	Crippled, lame, deformed, invalid, spastic
Person with epilepsy or seizure disorder	Epileptic
Person with multiple sclerosis	Afflicted by MS
Person with cerebral palsy	CP victim
Accessible parking or bathrooms	Handicapped parking or bathroom
Person of short stature	Midget
Person with Down syndrome	Mongoloid
Person who is successful, productive	Has overcome his/her disability, is courageous

Communicating with and about People with Disabilities in General

The Americans with Disabilities Act (ADA), other laws and the efforts of many disability organizations have made strides in improving

Communicating with and about People with Disabilities

accessibility in buildings, increasing access to education, opening employment opportunities and developing realistic portrayals of persons with disabilities in television programming and motion pictures. Where progress is still needed is in communication and interaction with people with disabilities. Individuals are sometimes concerned that they will say the wrong thing, so they say nothing at all—thus further segregating people with disabilities. Listed here are some suggestions on how to relate to and communicate with and about people with disabilities.

Words

Positive language empowers. When writing or speaking about people with disabilities, it is important to put the person first. Group designations such as "the blind," "the retarded," or "the disabled" are inappropriate because they do not reflect the individuality, equality or dignity of people with disabilities. Further, words like "normal person" imply that the person with a disability isn't normal, whereas "person without a disability" is descriptive but not negative. The accompanying chart shows examples of positive and negative phrases.

Table 7.2. Examples of Positive and Negative Phrases

Positive Phrases	Negative Phrases
Person with an intellectual, cognitive, developmental disability	Retarded; mentally defective
Person who is blind, person who is visually impaired	The blind
Person with a disability	The disabled; handicapped
Person who is deaf	The deaf; deaf and dumb
Person who is hard of hearing	Suffers a hearing loss
Person who has multiple sclerosis	Afflicted by MS
Person with cerebral palsy	CP victim
Person with epilepsy, person with seizure disorder	Epileptic
Person who uses a wheelchair	Confined or restricted to a wheelchair
Person who has muscular dystrophy	Stricken by MD
Person with a physical disability, physically disabled	Crippled; lame; deformed
Unable to speak, uses synthetic speech	Dumb; mute

Table 7.2. Continued

Positive Phrases	Negative Phrases
Person with psychiatric disability	Crazy; nuts
Person who is successful, productive	Has overcome his/her disability; is courageous (when it implies the person has courage because of having a disability)

Actions

Etiquette considered appropriate when interacting with people with disabilities is based primarily on respect and courtesy. Outlined below are tips to help you in communicating with persons with disabilities.

General Tips for Communicating with People with Disabilities

- When introduced to a person with a disability, it is appropriate to offer to shake hands. People with limited hand use or who wear an artificial limb can usually shake hands. (Shaking hands with the left hand is an acceptable greeting.)

- If you offer assistance, wait until the offer is accepted. Then listen to or ask for instructions.

- Treat adults as adults. Address people who have disabilities by their first names only when extending the same familiarity to all others.

- Relax. Don't be embarrassed if you happen to use common expressions such as "See you later" or "Did you hear about that?" that seem to relate to a person's disability.

- Don't be afraid to ask questions when you're unsure of what to do.

Tips for Communicating with Individuals Who Are Blind or Visually Impaired

- Speak to the individual when you approach him or her.

- State clearly who you are; speak in a normal tone of voice.

- When conversing in a group, remember to identify yourself and the person to whom you are speaking.

- Never touch or distract a service dog without first asking the owner.

Communicating with and about People with Disabilities

- Tell the individual when you are leaving.
- Do not attempt to lead the individual without first asking; allow the person to hold your arm and control her or his own movements.
- Be descriptive when giving directions; verbally give the person information that is visually obvious to individuals who can see. For example, if you are approaching steps, mention how many steps.
- If you are offering a seat, gently place the individual's hand on the back or arm of the chair so that the person can locate the seat.

Tips for Communicating with Individuals Who Are Deaf or Hard of Hearing

- Gain the person's attention before starting a conversation (i.e., tap the person gently on the shoulder or arm).
- Look directly at the individual, face the light, speak clearly, in a normal tone of voice, and keep your hands away from your face. Use short, simple sentences. Avoid smoking or chewing gum.
- If the individual uses a sign language interpreter, speak directly to the person, not the interpreter.
- If you telephone an individual who is hard of hearing, let the phone ring longer than usual. Speak clearly and be prepared to repeat the reason for the call and who you are.
- If you do not have a Text Telephone (TTY), dial 711 to reach the national telecommunications relay service, which facilitates the call between you and an individual who uses a TTY.

Tips for Communicating with Individuals with Mobility Impairments

- If possible, put yourself at the wheelchair user's eye level.
- Do not lean on a wheelchair or any other assistive device.
- Never patronize people who use wheelchairs by patting them on the head or shoulder.
- Do not assume the individual wants to be pushed—ask first.
- Offer assistance if the individual appears to be having difficulty opening a door.

- If you telephone the individual, allow the phone to ring longer than usual to allow extra time for the person to reach the telephone.

Tips for Communicating with Individuals with Speech Impairments

- If you do not understand something the individual says, do not pretend that you do. Ask the individual to repeat what he or she said and then repeat it back.
- Be patient. Take as much time as necessary.
- Try to ask questions which require only short answers or a nod of the head.
- Concentrate on what the individual is saying.
- Do not speak for the individual or attempt to finish her or his sentences.
- If you are having difficulty understanding the individual, consider writing as an alternative means of communicating, but first, ask the individual if this is acceptable.

Tips for Communicating with Individuals with Cognitive Disabilities

- If you are in a public area with many distractions, consider moving to a quiet or private location.
- Be prepared to repeat what you say, orally or in writing.
- Offer assistance completing forms or understanding written instructions and provide extra time for decision making. Wait for the individual to accept the offer of assistance; do not "overassist" or be patronizing.
- Be patient, flexible and supportive. Take time to understand the individual and make sure the individual understands you.

Communicating with and about People with Disabilities in the Workplace

As children, we are curious—pointing to anything unfamiliar and asking questions. We have few, if any, inhibitions. As adults, we learn to censor our queries, feeling uncomfortable with anything unfamiliar.

Communicating with and about People with Disabilities

This is true when we are faced with new technologies. It is true when we are faced with tackling new projects for which we may not feel prepared. It is often true when we meet people who speak a different language or come from a different culture.

It is human nature and not unusual, therefore, to be concerned about interactions with people who use wheelchairs, who are blind, who are deaf, or whom we find difficult to understand. We may be concerned that we will say the wrong thing, ask an inappropriate question, or unintentionally offend. We do not want to appear uninformed or insensitive.

A key to any effective communication is to focus on the communication itself—what information needs to be transmitted and how best to transmit it. Positive language empowers. When writing or speaking about people with disabilities, it is important to put the person first—to focus on the person, not the disability. Group designations, such as "the blind," "the deaf" or "the disabled" are not empowering. It is important to use words that reflect individuality, equality or dignity—the person who is blind, the child who is deaf, the individual with a disability, for example.

General Tips for Interacting with People with Disabilities

Appropriate etiquette when interacting with people with disabilities is based primarily on respect and courtesy. Below are a few tips to help you communicate effectively.

- When speaking with a person with a disability, talk directly to the person, not his or her companion. This applies whether the person has a mobility impairment, a speech impairment, a cognitive impairment, is blind or deaf and uses an interpreter.

- Extend common courtesies to people with disabilities. Extend your hand to shake hands or hand over business cards. If the individual cannot shake your hand or grasp the card, he or she will tell you, and direct where you may place the card.

- If the person has a speech impairment and you are having difficulty understanding what he or she is saying, ask the individual to repeat, rather than pretending to understand. Listen carefully, and repeat back what you think you heard to ensure effective communication.

- If you believe that an individual with a disability needs assistance, go ahead and offer the assistance—but wait for your offer to be accepted before you try to help.
- If you are interviewing a job candidate with a disability, listen to what the individual has to offer. Do not make assumptions about what that person can or cannot do.
- If you are speaking to a person who is blind, be sure to identify yourself at the beginning of the conversation and announce when you are leaving. Don't be afraid to use common expressions that refer to sight, such as, "See you later."
- If you wish to get the attention of a person who is deaf, tap the person gently on the shoulder or arm. Look directly at the person, and speak clearly in a normal tone of voice. Keep your hands away from your face, and use short, simple sentences. If the person uses a sign language interpreter, speak directly to the person, not to the interpreter.
- If you encounter an individual with a service animal, such as a dog, please do not touch or distract the animal. Service animals are working, and it breaks their training to interact with others when they are on duty. When the animal is not working, some owners may allow interaction.
- If you are having a conversation with a person who uses a wheelchair, if at all possible put yourself at the person's eye level. Never lean on or touch a person's wheelchair or any other assistive device. A person's assistive device is part of the person's personal space, and it is jarring or disturbing for anyone to have his or personal space invaded.
- If you are speaking with an individual with a cognitive disability, you may need to repeat or rephrase what you say. If you are giving instructions on how to perform a task, you may also need to give the instructions in writing.

Chapter 8

A Guide for Caregivers of People with Disabilities

Caregivers provide care to people who need some degree of ongoing assistance with everyday tasks on a regular or daily basis. The recipients of care can live either in residential or institutional settings, range from children to older adults, and have chronic illnesses or disabling conditions.

Approximately, 25 percent of U.S. adults 18 years of age and older reported providing care or assistance to a person with a long-term illness or disability in the past 30 days, according to 2009 data from Centers for Disease Control and Prevention's (CDC) state-based Behavioral Risk Factor Surveillance System (BRFSS). This is termed "informal or unpaid care" because it is provided by family or friends rather than by paid caregivers. The one year value of this unpaid caregiver activity was estimated as $450 million dollars in 2009.

This chapter includes text excerpted from the following sources: Text in this chapter begins with excerpts from "Caregiving Index—Alzheimer's Disease and Healthy Aging," Centers for Disease Control and Prevention (CDC), March 28, 2018; Text under the heading "Caregiving Tips for Families of People with Disabilities" is excerpted from "Family Caregivers," Centers for Disease Control and Prevention (CDC), August 3, 2017.

Caregiving Tips for Families of People with Disabilities

These general caregiving tips provide families with information on how to stay healthy and positive. Keep in mind that these tips can be used to address many family issues. Information, support, advocacy, empowerment, care, and balance can be the foundation for a healthy family and are appropriate no matter what the challenge.

Be Informed

- Gather information about your family member's condition, and discuss issues with others involved in the care of your family member. Being informed will help you make more knowledgeable health decisions and improve your understanding about any challenges your family might face.
- Notice how others care for the person with special needs. Be aware of signs of mental or physical abuse.

Get Support

- Family members and friends can provide support in a variety of ways and oftentimes want to help. Determine if there are big or small things they can do to assist you and your family.
- Join a local or online support group. A support group can give you the chance to share information and connect with people who are going through similar experiences. A support group may help combat the isolation and fear you may experience as a caregiver.
- Don't limit your involvement to support groups and associations that focus on a particular need or disability. There are also local and national groups that provide services, recreation, and information for people with disabilities.
- Friends, family, healthcare providers, support groups, community services, and counselors are just a few of the people available to help you and your family.

Be an Advocate

- Be an advocate for your family member with a disability. Caregivers who are effective advocates may be more successful at getting better service.

A Guide for Caregivers of People with Disabilities

- Ask questions. For example, if your family member with a disability uses a wheelchair and you want to plan a beach vacation, find out if the beaches are accessible via a car, ramp, portable walkway mat, or other equipment.

- Inform other caregivers of any special conditions or circumstances. For example, if your family member with a disability has a latex allergy, remind dental or medical staff each time you visit them.

- Document the medical history of your family member with a disability, and keep this information current.

- Make sure your employer understands your circumstances and limitations. Discuss your ability to travel or to work weekends or evenings. Arrange for flexible scheduling when needed.

- Become familiar with the Americans with Disabilities Act (ADA), the Family Medical Leave Act (FMLA), and other state and national provisions. Know how and when to apply them to your situation.

Be Empowering

- Focus on what you and your family member with a disability can do.

- Find appropriate milestones and celebrate them.

- If someone asks you questions about the family member with a disability, let him or her answer when possible. Doing so may help empower the individual to engage with others.

- When appropriate, teach your family member with a disability to be as independent and self-assured as possible. Always keep health and safety issues in mind.

Take Care of Yourself

- Take care of yourself. Caring for a family member with a disability can wear out even the strongest caregiver. Stay healthy for yourself and those you care for.

- Work hard to maintain your personal interests, hobbies, and friendships. Don't let caregiving consume your entire life. This is not healthy for you or those you care for. Balance is key.

- Allow yourself not to be the perfect caregiver. Set reasonable expectations to lower stress and make you a more effective caregiver.
- Delegate some caregiving tasks to other reliable people.
- Take a break. Short breaks, like an evening walk or relaxing bath, are essential. Long breaks are nurturing. Arrange a retreat with friends or get away with a significant other when appropriate.
- Don't ignore signs of illness: if you get sick, see a healthcare provider. Pay attention to your mental and emotional health as well. Remember, taking good care of yourself can help the person you care for as well. Exercising and eating healthy also are important.

Keep Balance in the Family

- Family members with a disability may require extra care and attention. Take time for all family members, taking into account the needs of each individual. For example, it's important for parents of a child with a disability to also spend time with each other and with any other children they might have.
- Consider respite care. "Respite" refers to short-term, temporary care provided to people with disabilities so that their families can take a break from the daily routine of caregiving.

Chapter 9

Abuse and People with Disabilities

Chapter Contents

Section 9.1—Childhood Bullying 60
Section 9.2—Abuse of Children with Intellectual
 Disabilities... 63
Section 9.3—Violence against Women with
 Disabilities... 69

Section 9.1

Childhood Bullying

This section includes text excerpted from "Bullying and Children and Youth with Disabilities and Special Health Needs," StopBullying.gov, U.S. Department of Health and Human Services (HHS), October 1, 2017.

What Is Bullying?

Childhood bullying is unwanted, aggressive behavior among school-aged children. It involves a real or perceived power imbalance and the behavior is repeated, or has the potential to be repeated, over time. Both kids who are bullied and kids who bully others may have serious, lasting problems.

Who Gets Bullied?

Children with physical, developmental, intellectual, emotional, and sensory disabilities are more likely to be bullied than their peers. Any number of factors—physical vulnerability, social skill challenges, or intolerant environments—may increase their risk. Research suggests that some children with disabilities may bully others as well.

Kids with special health needs, such as epilepsy or food allergies, may also be at higher risk of being bullied. For kids with special health needs, bullying can include making fun of kids because of their allergies or exposing them to the things they are allergic to. In these cases, bullying is not just serious; it can mean life or death.

A small but growing amount of research shows that:

- Children with attention deficit hyperactivity disorder (ADHD) are more likely than other children to be bullied. They also are somewhat more likely than others to bully their peers.

- Children with autism spectrum disorder (ASD) are at increased risk of being bullied and left out by peers. In a study of 8- to 17-year-olds, researchers found that children with ASD were more than three times as likely to be bullied as their peers.

- Children with epilepsy are more likely to be bullied by peers, as are children with medical conditions that affect their appearance, such as cerebral palsy, muscular dystrophy, and spina bifida. These children frequently report being called names related to their disability.

Abuse and People with Disabilities

- Children with hemiplegia (paralysis of one side of their body) are more likely than other children their age to be bullied and have fewer friends.
- Children who have diabetes and are dependent on insulin may be especially vulnerable to peer bullying.
- Children who stutter may be more likely to be bullied. In one study, 83 percent of adults who stammered as children said that they were teased or bullied; 71 percent of those who had been bullied said it happened at least once a week.
- Children with learning disabilities (LD) are at a greater risk of being bullied. At least one study also has found that children with LD may also be more likely than other children to bullying their peers.

Effects of Bullying

Kids who are bullied are more likely to have:

- Depression and anxiety. Signs of these include increased feelings of sadness and loneliness, changes in sleep and eating patterns, and loss of interest in activities they used to enjoy. These issues may persist into adulthood.
- Health complaints
- Decreased academic achievement—grade point average (GPA) and standardized test scores—and school participation. They are more likely to miss, skip, or drop out of school.

Bullying, Disability Harassment, and the Law

Bullying behavior can become "disability harassment," which is prohibited under Section 504 of the *Rehabilitation Act of 1973* and *Title II of the Americans with Disabilities Act of 1990*. According to the U.S. Department of Education (ED), disability harassment is "intimidation or abusive behavior toward a student based on disability that creates a hostile environment by interfering with or denying a student's participation in or receipt of benefits, services, or opportunities in the institution's program."

Disability harassment can take different forms including verbal harassment, physical threats, or threatening written statements. When a school learns that disability harassment may have occurred, the school must investigate the incident(s) promptly and respond appropriately. Disability harassment can occur in any location that is connected with school—classrooms, the cafeteria, hallways, the playground, athletic fields, or school buses. It also can occur during school-sponsored events.

What Parents Can Do

If you believe a child with special needs is being bullied:

- Be supportive of the child and encourage him or her to describe who was involved and how and where the bullying happened. Be sure to tell the child that it is not his or her fault and that nobody deserves to be bullied or harassed. Do not encourage the child to fight back. This may make the problem worse.

- Ask the child specific questions about his or her friendships. Be aware of signs of bullying, even if the child doesn't call it that. Children with disabilities do not always realize they are being bullied. They may, for example, believe that they have a new friend although this "friend" is making fun of them.

- Talk with the child's teacher immediately to see whether he or she can help to resolve the problem.

- Put your concerns in writing and contact the principal if the bullying or harassment is severe or the teacher doesn't fix the problem. Explain what happened in detail and ask for a prompt response. Keep a written record of all conversations and communications with the school.

- Ask the school district to convene a meeting of the Individualized Education Program (IEP) or the Section 504 teams. These groups ensure that the school district is meeting the needs of its students with disabilities. This meeting will allow parents to explain what has been happening and will let the team review the child's IEP or 504 plans and make sure that the school is taking steps to stop the harassment. Parents, if your child needs counseling or other supportive services because of the harassment, discuss this with the team. Work with the school to help establish a system-wide bullying prevention program that includes support systems for bullied children. As the U.S. Department of Education (ED) (2000) recognizes, "creating a supportive school climate is the most important step in preventing harassment."

Abuse and People with Disabilities

- Explore whether the child may also be bullying other younger, weaker students at school. If so, his or her IEP may need to be modified to include help to change the aggressive behavior.

- Be persistent. Talk regularly with the child and with school staff to see whether the behavior has stopped.

Section 9.2

Abuse of Children with Intellectual Disabilities

This section contains text excerpted from the following sources: Text beginning with the heading "Children with Developmental Disabilities" is excerpted from "Aggressive Behavior and Violence," Centers for Disease Control and Prevention (CDC), July 18, 2017; Text beginning with the heading "Keeping Children with Disabilities Safe" is excerpted from "Keeping Children with Disabilities Safe," Centers for Disease Control and Prevention (CDC), June 22, 2018.

Children with Developmental Disabilities

Most children with developmental disabilities are not any more violent or aggressive than other children. However, some children may feel a lot of frustration related to their developmental disability. This frustration is sometimes shown through aggression or even self-harming behaviors, such as banging their head or cutting their skin.

Other children have conditions that are more directly connected to aggressive behavior. For example, children with oppositional defiant disorder are often annoyed and angry, and they argue with adults in order to gain control.

There are many reasons children with developmental disabilities may have aggression problems. It is important to remember that everyone has times when they get frustrated or angry, and children should be taught that frustration is normal. It is best to try to understand the reasons behind the aggression and violence. Knowing this will help parents and health professionals work toward reducing the problems;

teaching the child ways to cope with frustration should be part of this plan.

Aggressive Behavior

Aggressive behavior is common among youth, especially young children. However, families and health professionals can take steps to help reduce violence and aggression. Some examples: Stay calm, praise positive behavior, and work with the child's health professional.

Examples of physical aggression:

- Biting
- Hitting
- Kicking

Examples of verbal aggression:

- Saying "no" to parents' or teachers' rules
- Screaming or shouting
- Using foul language

The anger or frustration of toddlers is usually reactive or impulsive in response to something that has happened to them, such as having a toy taken away. As children grow and develop more advanced language, social skills, and planning ability, proactive or planned aggressive behavior may become more common.

Aggressive behaviors that cause damage to objects or harm people or animals are considered violent behaviors. Not all violence comes from physical aggression; verbal aggression can also cause harm.

What Can We Do?

Parents

There is no single way to reduce aggression and violence in all children. Some things to consider are the child's age, their disability, and goals for the family. Here are some ways parents can try to create an environment in which violence and aggression are less common.

- Walk the talk! Do not use aggression or violence yourself.
- Do your best to keep your home life calm, supportive, and respectful.

- If your child is acting aggressively, reinforce alternative or competing behaviors. For example, have a drawing pad handy, or play a game that requires your child's calm attention, such as "eye spy."

- Be sure to praise good behavior immediately and often.

- Help your child articulate his or her feelings. Talking through their emotions helps children of all ages.

- Work with your child to develop strategies to calm him or her when he or she feels scared, angry, or frustrated.

- For some children, it is best to explain consequences for misbehavior ahead of time. It is important that the child understands the consequences before they are enforced.

- Once you have set up consequences, enforce them! If bad behavior is not addressed regularly, it may continue or even get worse.

- Notice when and where your child is most aggressive or violent, and try to avoid those places.

- Tell your child's healthcare providers as many details about your child's behavior as possible. He or she will be able to offer tips and work with you to develop a plan.

Health Professionals

Health professionals help reduce or prevent aggression and violent behaviors. Depending on the child, here are some of the more common ways:

- Direct therapy at symptoms that are causing the most impairment or the most impairing diagnosis (e.g., attention deficit hyperactivity disorder, aggression, or compulsions).

- Offer alternative training and other programs that help caregivers reduce aggression in their daily routine.

Keeping Children with Disabilities Safe

We all want to keep our children safe and secure and help them to be happy and healthy. Preventing injuries and harm is not very different for children with disabilities compared to children without disabilities. However, finding the right information and learning about the kinds of risks children might face at different ages is often not easy for parents of children with disabilities. Each child is different—and the general recommendations that are available to keep children safe should be tailored to fit your child's skills and abilities.

There are steps that parents and caregivers can take to keep children with disabilities safe.

To keep all children safe, parents and caregivers need to:

- Know and learn about what things are unique concerns or a danger for their child.

- Plan ways to protect their child and share the plan with others.

- Remember that their child's needs for protection will change over time.

What Parents and Caregivers Can Do

Parents or caregivers can talk to their child's doctor or healthcare professional about how to keep him or her safe. Your child's teacher or child care provider might also have some good ideas. Once you have ideas about keeping your child safe, make a safety plan and share it with your child and other adults who might be able to help if needed.

Here are some things to think about when making a safety plan for your child:

Moving around and Handling Things

Does your child have challenges with moving around and handling things around them? Sometimes children are faced with unsafe situations, especially in new places. Children who have limited ability to move, see, hear, or make decisions, and children who do not feel or understand pain might not realize that something is unsafe, or might have trouble getting away.

Take a look around the place where your child will be to make sure every area your child can reach is safe for your child. Check your child's clothing and toys—are they suitable for his or her abilities, not just age and size? For example, clothing and toys that are meant for older children might have strings that are not safe for a child who cannot easily untangle themselves, or toys might have small parts that are not safe for children who are still mouthing toys.

Safety Equipment

Do you have the right kind of safety equipment? Safety equipment is often developed for age and size, and less for ability.

For example, a major cause of child death is motor vehicle crashes. Keeping your child safe in the car is important. When choosing the right car seat, you might need to consider whether your child has difficulties sitting up or sitting still in the seat, in addition to your child's age, height, and weight. If you have a child with disabilities, talk to your healthcare professional about the best type of car seat or booster seat and the proper seat position for your child. You can also ask a certified child passenger safety technician who is trained in special needs.

Other examples of special safety equipment:

- Life jackets may need to be specially fitted for your child.
- Smoke alarms that signal with a light and vibration may be better in a home where there is a child who cannot hear.
- Handrails and safety bars can be put into homes to help a child who has difficulty moving around or a child who is at risk for falling.

Speak to your healthcare professional about the right equipment for your child and have this equipment ready and available before you may need it.

Talking and Understanding

Does your child have problems with talking or understanding? Children who have problems communicating might have limited ability to learn about safety and danger.

For example, children who cannot hear might miss spoken instructions. Children who have trouble understanding or remembering might not learn about safety as easily as other children. Children who have a hard time communicating might not be able to ask questions about safety. Adults might think that children with disabilities are aware of dangers when they actually are not.

Parents and caregivers may need to find different ways to teach their children about safety, such as:

- Showing them what to do
- Using pretend play to rehearse
- Practicing on a regular basis

Parents and caregivers may need to find different ways to let their children communicate that they are in danger. For example, you might teach your child to use a whistle, bell, or alarm can alert others to danger. Tell adults who take care of your child about the ways to communicate with your child if there is any danger.

It's also useful to contact your local fire department and explain any special circumstances you have, so that they don't have to rely on the child or others to explain their special needs in case of an emergency.

Making Decisions

Does your child have problems with making decisions? Children might have limited ability to make decisions either because of developmental delays or limits in their thinking skills, or in their ability to stop themselves from doing things that they want, but should not do.

For example, children with attention deficit hyperactivity disorder (ADHD) or fetal alcohol spectrum disorders (FASDs) might be very impulsive and fail to think about the results of their actions. People often put more dangerous things higher up, so that little children cannot reach them. Your older child might be able to reach something that he or she is not ready to handle safely. Check your child's environment, particularly new places.

Some children might also have problems distinguishing when situations and people are safe or dangerous. They might not know what to do. Parents and caregivers can give children specific instructions on how to behave in certain situations that might become dangerous.

Moving and Exploring

Does your child have enough chances to move and explore? Children with disabilities often need some extra protection. But just like all children, they also need to move and explore so that they can develop healthy bodies and minds.

Some parents of children with special needs worry about their children needing extra protection. It is not possible to protect children from every bump and bruise. Exploring can help children learn what's safe and what might be difficult or dangerous. Being fit and healthy can help children stay safe, and an active lifestyle is important for long-term health.

Children with disabilities might find it hard to take part in sports and active play—for example, equipment may need to be adjusted, coaches may need extra information and support to help a child with a disability, or a communication problem may make it more difficult for some children to play as part of a team.

Talk to your child's teachers, potential coaches, care providers, or health professional about ways to find the right balance between being safe and being active.

Other Concerns

Do you have other concerns? Every child is different. This is not a complete list of questions and concerns, these are just examples. Your questions and concerns may be different. Speak with your healthcare provider, teacher, or child care provider to learn more about keeping your child safe.

Section 9.3

Violence against Women with Disabilities

This section includes text excerpted from the following sources: Text in this section begins with excerpts from "Advancing Women and Girls with Disabilities," U.S. Agency for International Development (USAID), August 24, 2015; Text beginning with the heading "Women with Disabilities and Violence" is excerpted from "Violence against Women with Disabilities," Office on Women's Health (OWH), U.S. Department of Health and Human Services (HHS), March 2, 2018.

Persons with disabilities are the world's largest minority, representing 15 percent of the global population. 80 percent of this population live in developing countries.

Women and girls with disabilities are subjected to multiple layers of discrimination. Based on their gender and disability status they often face "double discrimination." This inequality is exacerbated for women and girls with disabilities who are members of marginalized ethnic or racial groups or part of the lesbian, gay, bisexual, transgender and intersex community.

Unemployment rates are highest among women with disabilities. The United Nations estimates that 75 percent of women with disabilities are unemployed and women with disabilities who are employed often earn less than their male counterparts and women without disabilities. Gender disparities also exist in education. While the overall literacy rate for persons with disabilities is 3 percent, United Nations Educational, Scientific and Cultural Organization (UNESCO) estimates that it is just 1 percent for women and girls with disabilities.

Women and girls with disabilities often face disproportionately high rates of gender-based violence, sexual abuse, neglect, maltreatment, and exploitation. Studies show that women and girls with disabilities are twice as likely to experience gender-based violence compared to women and girls without disabilities. Women with disabilities are often denied reproductive healthcare and at times are even subjected to forced sterilization. When healthcare services are available, they may not be physically accessible for women with varying types of disabilities, or healthcare providers don't know how to accommodate them.

The exclusion and violence against women and girls with disabilities in any country carries heavy financial and social consequences. Discrimination against persons with disabilities hinders economic development, limits democracy, and erodes societies. Perhaps because of the challenges they face, women and girls with disabilities are poised to be leaders within their communities and can greatly contribute to the economic development of their countries.

Disability inclusion is U.S. Agency for International Development (USAID) policy. The agency supports disability-specific programs to address targeted needs, and seeks to integrate disability into all the programs. The USAID Disability Policy requires the inclusion of persons with disabilities in the programs, stating that:

- Issues related to disability are integral to international development

- Consultation with members of the disability community is critical

- Investing in and strengthening disabled people's organizations is vital in promoting the human rights of persons with disabilities

USAID is committed to empowering and including women and girls with disabilities. Here are just a couple examples of the programs that USAID support:

- Mobility International USA's Women's Institute on Leadership and Disability (WILD), supported by the USAID Leadership, Management and Governance Project, brings together emerging women leaders with disabilities from Africa, Asia, Eurasia,

Abuse and People with Disabilities

Latin America, and the Middle East to strengthen leadership skills, create new visions, and build international networks of support for inclusive international development programming. Christiana Yaghr of Ghana, who works with the Ghana National Association for the Deaf, participated in the WILD program.

- In Vietnam, women with disabilities are gaining employment in the Information and Technology (IT) field. Since 2007, USAID and Catholic Relief Services (CRS) have collaborated with the Hanoi College of Information Technology and Van Lang University in Ho Chi Minh City to provide training in advanced computer skills, such as graphic design, 3D modeling, and web development, for youth with disabilities from all over Vietnam. To date, the program has trained more than 700 students with disabilities in Hanoi and Ho Chi Minh City, and over 80 percent of graduates have since found jobs.

Women with Disabilities and Violence

Research suggests that women with disabilities are more likely to experience domestic violence, emotional abuse, and sexual assault than women without disabilities. Women with disabilities may also feel more isolated and feel they are unable to report the abuse, or they may be dependent on the abuser for their care. Like many women who are abused, women with disabilities are usually abused by someone they know, such as a partner or family member.

How Can I Recognize Signs of Abuse in a Loved One with a Disability?

Relatives must be strong advocates for their loved ones with disabilities. If you have a relative with a disability, learn the signs of abuse, especially if your relative has trouble communicating.

Report abuse to adult protective services if you notice any of the following with a loved one who has a disability:

- Suddenly being unable to meet essential day-to-day living needs that affect health, safety, or well-being
- Lack of contact with friends or family
- Visible handprints or bruising on the face, neck, arms, or wrists
- Burns, cuts, or puncture wounds

- Unexplained sprains, fractures, or dislocations
- Signs of injuries to internal organs, such as vomiting
- Wearing torn, stained, soiled, or bloody clothing
- Appearing hungry, malnourished, disoriented, or confused

Each state has an adult protective services agency.

How Common Is Violence or Abuse against Women with Disabilities?

Women with a disability are more likely to experience violence or abuse compared to women without a disability. Some studies show that women with a disability may be more likely to experience violence or abuse by a current or former partner compared to women without disabilities.

Who Commits Violence or Abuse against Women with Disabilities?

Most often, violence or abuse against women with disabilities is by their spouses or partners. But women with disabilities can also face abuse from caregivers or personal assistants. Women with disabilities who need help with daily activities like bathing, dressing, or eating may be more at risk of abuse because they are physically or mentally more vulnerable and can have many different caregivers in their life.

What Should I Do If I Suspect Abuse against a Woman with a Disability?

Report any suspected abuse to adult protective services. Each state has an adult protective services agency.

Part Two

Types of Disabilities

Chapter 10

Overview of Birth Defects

Birth Defects Are Common[1]

Birth defects are common, costly, and critical conditions that affect 1 in every 33 babies born in the United States each year. Every 4½ minutes, a baby is born with a birth defect in the United States. That means nearly 120,000 babies are affected by birth defects each year.

Birth defects are structural changes present at birth that can affect almost any part or parts of the body (e.g., heart, brain, foot). They may affect how the body looks, works, or both. Birth defects can vary from mild to severe. The well-being of each child affected with a birth defect depends mostly on which organ or body part is involved and how much it is affected. Depending on the severity of the defect and what body part is affected, the expected lifespan of a person with a birth defect may or may not be affected.

What Are the Types of Birth Defects?[2]

There are two main categories of birth defects.

This chapter includes text excerpted from documents published by two public domain sources. Text under the headings marked 1 are excerpted from "Facts about Birth Defects," Centers for Disease Control and Prevention (CDC), June 19, 2018; Text under the headings marked 2 are excerpted from "Birth Defects," *Eunice Kennedy Shriver* National Institute of Child Health and Human Development (NICHD), September 1, 2017.

Structural Birth Defects

Structural birth defects are related to a problem with the structure of body parts. These can include:

- Cleft lip or cleft palate
- Heart defects, such as missing or misshaped valves
- Abnormal limbs, such as a clubfoot
- Neural tube defects, such as spina bifida, and problems related to the growth and development of the brain and spinal cord

Functional or Developmental Birth Defects

Functional or developmental birth defects are related to a problem with how a body part or body system works or functions. These problems can include:

- **Nervous system or brain problems.** These include intellectual and developmental disabilities, behavioral disorders, speech or language difficulties, seizures, and movement trouble. Some examples of birth defects that affect the nervous system include Down syndrome, Prader-Willi syndrome (PWS), and Fragile X syndrome.

- **Sensory problems.** Examples include hearing loss and visual problems, such as blindness or deafness.

- **Metabolic disorders.** These involve problems with certain chemical reactions in the body, such as conditions that limit the body's ability to rid itself of waste materials or harmful chemicals. Two common metabolic disorders are phenylketonuria and hypothyroidism.

- **Degenerative disorders.** These are conditions that might not be obvious at birth but cause one or more aspects of health to steadily get worse. Examples of degenerative disorders are muscular dystrophy and X-linked adrenoleukodystrophy (X-ALD), which leads to problems of the nervous system and the adrenal glands and was the subject of the movie "Lorenzo's Oil."

Some birth defects affect many parts or processes in the body, leading to both structural and functional problems.

Causes of Birth Defects[1]

Birth defects can occur during any stage of pregnancy. Most birth defects occur in the first three months of pregnancy, when the organs of the baby are forming. This is a very important stage of development. However, some birth defects occur later in pregnancy. During the last six months of pregnancy, the tissues and organs continue to grow and develop.

For some birth defects, like fetal alcohol syndrome (FAS), we know the cause. But for most birth defects, we don't know what causes them. For most birth defects, we think they are caused by a complex mix of factors. These factors include our genes (information inherited from our parents), our behaviors, and things in the environment. But, we don't fully understand how these factors might work together to cause birth defects.

While we still have more work to do, we have learned a lot about birth defects through past research. For example, some things might increase the chances of having a baby with a birth defect, such as:

- Smoking, drinking alcohol, or taking certain "street" drugs during pregnancy.
- Having certain medical conditions, such as being obese or having uncontrolled diabetes before and during pregnancy.
- Taking certain medications, such as isotretinoin (a drug used to treat severe acne).
- Having someone in your family with a birth defect. To learn more about your risk of having a baby with a birth defect, you can talk with a clinical geneticist or a genetic counselor.
- Being an older mother, typically over the age of 34 years.

Having one or more of these risks doesn't mean you'll have a pregnancy affected by a birth defect. Also, women can have a baby born with a birth defect even when they don't have any of these risks. It is important to talk to your doctor about what you can do to lower your risk.

Identifying Birth Defects[1]

A birth defect can be found before birth, at birth, or any time after birth. Most birth defects are found within the first year of life.

Some birth defects (such as cleft lip) are easy to see, but others (such as heart defects or hearing loss) are found using special tests, such as echocardiograms (an ultrasound picture of the heart), X-rays, or hearing tests.

How Do Healthcare Providers Diagnose Birth Defects?[2]

Diagnosis of birth defects depends on the specific problem and parts or systems of the body that are affected.

Many structural problems, such as clubfoot or cleft palate, are detected and diagnosed after a physical examination of the baby immediately after birth. For other conditions, newborn screening or prenatal testing is the only way to detect and diagnose problems.

This information focuses on structural birth defects, their causes, their prevention, and their treatments. Functional/developmental birth defects are addressed more completely in the intellectual and developmental disabilities content and in condition-specific topics.

Newborn Screening

Newborn screening, a process that tests infants' blood for different health conditions, including many birth defects, provides one method of detecting problems. Newborn screening does not diagnose any specific conditions but detects that a problem may exist. By detecting problems immediately after birth, conditions can be diagnosed and treated before they have lifelong effects.

In addition, newborn screening routinely includes test for hearing problems, as well as pulse oximetry (test of baby's pulse rate and blood oxygen levels) to detect critical congenital heart defects.

Infants who are at high risk for certain conditions—for example, because of their family history—can undergo additional testing at birth to detect these conditions and treat them if needed. This type of screening has been effective in detecting some cases of Menkes disease, allowing for treatment to begin before health problems occur.

Prenatal Screening

During pregnancy, women have routine tests, such as blood and urine tests, to check for diabetes, signs of infection, or disorders of pregnancy such as preeclampsia. Blood tests also measure the levels of certain substances in a woman's blood that determine the risk of the fetus for certain chromosomal disorders and neural tube defects. Ultrasound screenings, creating a picture using sound, allow providers to view the developing fetus in the womb. Some birth defects, such as spina bifida, are detectable on ultrasounds.

Healthcare providers recommend that certain pregnant women, including those who are older than 35 years of age and those with a family history of certain conditions, get additional prenatal tests to screen for birth defects. Prenatal detection allows doctors to start treatment as early as possible for some birth defects.

Noninvasive Prenatal Testing

Noninvasive prenatal testing (NIPT) is not a routine prenatal test but is used when a routine test suggests that the fetus may have a chromosomal disorder, such as having an extra or missing chromosome in each cell, which occurs in disorders such as Down syndrome, Patau syndrome, and Edwards syndrome.

NIPT analyzes the placental deoxyribonucleic acid (DNA) present in the mother's blood; it does not require cell samples from inside the womb.

Experts recommend NIPT only for high-risk pregnancies. This method does not detect open neural tube defects, nor does it predict late pregnancy complications.

Amniocentesis

Amniocentesis is a test that is usually performed to determine whether a fetus has a genetic disorder. In this test, a doctor takes a small amount of fluid from the womb using a long needle. The fluid, called amniotic fluid, contains cells that have genetic material that is the same as the fetus's genetic material. A laboratory grows the cells and then examines their genetic material for any problems. Some birth defects that can be detected with amniocentesis are Down syndrome and certain types of muscular dystrophy.

There is a slight risk of pregnancy loss with amniocentesis, so women should discuss the procedure with their healthcare provider before making a decision about the test.

Chorionic Villus Sampling (CVS)

This test extracts cells from inside the womb to determine whether the fetus has a genetic disorder. Using a long needle, the doctor takes cells from the chorionic villi, which are tissues in the placenta, the organ in the womb that nourishes the fetus. The genetic material in the chorionic villus cells is identical to that of the fetal cells.

Like amniocentesis, chorionic villus sampling (CVS) can be used to test for chromosomal disorders and other genetic problems. CVS can be done earlier in pregnancy than amniocentesis, but it is also associated with a slightly higher risk of miscarriage than amniocentesis. Women who are considering CVS should discuss the test and the risks with her healthcare provider.

What Are the Treatments for Birth Defects?[2]

Because the symptoms and problems caused by birth defects vary, treatments for birth defects also vary. Treatments range from medications and therapies to surgeries and assistive devices.

This information focuses on structural birth defects, their causes, their prevention, and their treatments. Functional/developmental birth defects are addressed more completely in the intellectual and developmental disabilities content and in the condition-specific topics.

For example:

- Steroid medications, such as prednisone, can help people with muscular dystrophy increase muscle strength, ability, and respiratory function and slow the progression of weakness. Physical therapy is also useful for building strength and reducing weakness.

- Infants with cerebral palsy may receive sensory-motor therapy using Velcro-covered "sticky mittens" to help them "snag" and explore objects they are unable to grasp in the hand.

- Assistive devices include orthopedic braces to help patients with limb defects to walk and cochlear implants for hearing impairment.

- In the Management of Myelomeningocele Study (MOMS), conducted through *Eunice Kennedy Shriver* National Institute of Child Health and Human Development's (NICHD) Maternal-Fetal Surgery Network, researchers tested a surgical procedure to correct a severe form of spina bifida while the fetus was still in the womb. Although the surgery itself carried risks, it greatly reduced health complications for the infants who received it, including greater likelihood of being able to walk without assistance.

- Gene therapy approaches, in which a gene that is mutated or missing is replaced by a normal version of the gene, are being tested for a variety of genetic disorders. Some examples of disorders that are being treated successfully with gene therapy include genetic disorders of the immune system, the muscles, and the eyes. NICHD-supported research on Duchenne muscular dystrophy (DMD) used genome editing techniques to improve leg grip strength in a mouse model by "turning on" a gene for a specific protein used in muscles.

Preventing Birth Defects[1]

Not all birth defects can be prevented. But, there are things that a woman can do before and during pregnancy to increase her chance of having a healthy baby:

- Be sure to see your healthcare provider regularly and start prenatal care as soon as you think you might be pregnant.
- Get 400 micrograms (mcg) of folic acid every day, starting at least one month before getting pregnant.
- Don't drink alcohol, smoke, or use "street" drugs.
- Talk to a healthcare provider about any medications you are taking or thinking about taking. This includes prescription and over-the-counter (OTC) medications and dietary or herbal supplements. Don't stop or start taking any type of medication without first talking with a doctor.
- Learn how to prevent infections during pregnancy.
- If possible, be sure any medical conditions are under control, before becoming pregnant. Some conditions that increase the risk for birth defects include diabetes and obesity.

Living with a Birth Defect[1]

Babies who have birth defects often need special care and interventions to survive and to thrive developmentally. State birth defects tracking programs provide one way to identify and refer children as early as possible for services they need. Early intervention is vital to improving outcomes for these babies. If your child has a birth defect, you should ask his or her doctor about local resources and treatment. Geneticists, genetic counselors, and other specialists are another resource.

Chapter 11

Cerebral Palsy

What Is Cerebral Palsy?

Cerebral palsy (CP) refers to a group of neurological disorders that appear in infancy or early childhood and permanently affect body movement and muscle coordination cerebral palsy is caused by damage to or abnormalities inside the developing brain that disrupt the brain's ability to control movement and maintain posture and balance. The term cerebral refers to the brain; palsy refers to the loss or impairment of motor function.

CP affects the motor area of the brain's outer layer (called the cerebral cortex), the part of the brain that directs muscle movement.

In some cases, the cerebral motor cortex hasn't developed normally during fetal growth. In others, the damage is a result of injury to the brain either before, during, or after birth. In either case, the damage is not repairable and the disabilities that result are permanent.

Children with CP exhibit a wide variety of symptoms, including:

- Lack of muscle coordination when performing voluntary movements (ataxia)

- Stiff or tight muscles and exaggerated reflexes (spasticity)

- Weakness in one or more arm or leg

This chapter includes text excerpted from "Cerebral Palsy: Hope through Research," National Institute of Neurological Disorders and Stroke (NINDS), July 24, 2018.

- Walking on the toes, a crouched gait, or a "scissored" gait
- Variations in muscle tone, either too stiff or too floppy
- Excessive drooling or difficulties swallowing or speaking
- Shaking (tremor) or random involuntary movements
- Delays in reaching motor skill milestones
- Difficulty with precise movements such as writing or buttoning a shirt

The symptoms of CP differ in type and severity from one person to the next, and may even change in an individual over time. Symptoms may vary greatly among individuals, depending on which parts of the brain have been injured. All people with cerebral palsy have problems with movement and posture, and some also have some level of intellectual disability, seizures, and abnormal physical sensations or perceptions, as well as other medical disorders. People with CP also may have impaired vision or hearing, and language, and speech problems.

CP is the leading cause of childhood disabilities, but it doesn't always cause profound disabilities. While one child with severe CP might be unable to walk and need extensive, lifelong care, another child with mild CP might be only slightly awkward and require no special assistance. The disorder isn't progressive, meaning it doesn't get worse over time. However, as the child gets older, certain symptoms may become more or less evident.

A study by the Centers for Disease Control and Prevention (CDC) shows the average prevalence of CP is 3.3 children per 1,000 live births.

There is no cure for cerebral palsy, but supportive treatments, medications, and surgery can help many individuals improve their motor skills and ability to communicate with the world.

What Are the Early Signs of Cerebral Palsy?

The signs of cerebral palsy usually appear in the early months of life, although specific diagnosis may be delayed until age two years or later. Infants with CP frequently have developmental delay, in which they are slow to reach developmental milestones such as learning to roll over, sit, crawl, or walk. Some infants with CP have abnormal muscle tone. Decreased muscle tone (hypotonia) can make them appear relaxed, even floppy. Increased muscle tone (hypertonia) can make them seem stiff or rigid. In some cases, an early period of hypotonia

Cerebral Palsy

will progress to hypertonia after the first 2–3 months of life. Children with CP may also have unusual posture or favor one side of the body when they reach, crawl, or move. It is important to note that some children without CP also might have some of these signs.

Some early warning signs:

In a baby younger than 6 months of age:

- The baby's head lags when picked up or lying on its back
- The baby feels stiff
- The baby feels floppy
- When picked up, the baby's legs get stiff and cross or scissor

In a baby older than 6 months of age:

- The baby doesn't roll over in either direction
- The baby cannot bring its hands together
- The baby has difficulty bringing its hands to its mouth
- The baby reaches out with only one hand while keeping the other fisted

In a baby older than 10 months of age:

- The baby crawls in a lopsided manner, pushing off with one hand and leg while dragging the opposite hand and leg
- The baby cannot stand holding onto support

What Causes Cerebral Palsy

Cerebral palsy is caused by abnormal development of part of the brain or by damage to parts of the brain that control movement. This damage can occur before, during, or shortly after birth. The majority of children have congenital CP (that is, they were born with it), although it may not be detected until months or years later. A small number of children have acquired cerebral palsy, which means the disorder begins after birth. Some causes of acquired CP include brain damage in the first few months or years of life, brain infections such as bacterial meningitis or viral encephalitis, problems with blood flow to the brain, or head injury from a motor vehicle accident, a fall, or child abuse.

In many cases, the cause of cerebral palsy is unknown. Possible causes include genetic abnormalities, congenital brain malformations, maternal infections or fevers, or fetal injury, for example. The following types of brain damage may cause its characteristic symptoms:

- **Damage to the white matter of the brain (periventricular leukomalacia, or PVL).** The white matter of the brain is responsible for transmitting signals inside the brain and to the rest of the body. Damage from PVL looks like tiny holes in the white matter of an infant's brain. These gaps in brain tissue interfere with the normal transmission of signals. Researchers have identified a period of selective vulnerability in the developing fetal brain, a period of time between 26 and 34 weeks of gestation, in which periventricular white matter is particularly sensitive to insults and injury.

- **Abnormal development of the brain (cerebral dysgenesis).** Any interruption of the normal process of brain growth during fetal development can cause brain malformations that interfere with the transmission of brain signals. Mutations in the genes that control brain development during this early period can keep the brain from developing normally. Infections, fevers, trauma, or other conditions that cause unhealthy conditions in the womb also put an unborn baby's nervous system at risk.

- **Bleeding in the brain (intracranial hemorrhage).** Bleeding inside the brain from blocked or broken blood vessels is commonly caused by fetal stroke. Some babies suffer a stroke while still in the womb because of blood clots in the placenta that block blood flow in the brain. Other types of fetal stroke are caused by malformed or weak blood vessels in the brain or by blood-clotting abnormalities. Maternal high blood pressure (hypertension) is a common medical disorder during pregnancy and is more common in babies with fetal stroke. Maternal infection, especially pelvic inflammatory disease, has also been shown to increase the risk of fetal stroke.

- **Severe lack of oxygen in the brain.** Asphyxia, a lack of oxygen in the brain caused by an interruption in breathing or poor oxygen supply, is common for a brief period of time in babies due to the stress of labor and delivery. If the supply of oxygen is cut off or reduced for lengthy periods, an infant can develop a type of brain damage called hypoxic-ischemic encephalopathy (HIE), which destroys tissue in the cerebral motor cortex and other areas of the brain. This kind of damage can also be caused by severe maternal low blood pressure, rupture of the uterus, detachment of the placenta, or problems involving the umbilical cord, or severe trauma to the head during labor and delivery.

What Are the Risk Factors of Cerebral Palsy?

There are some medical conditions or events that can happen during pregnancy and delivery that may increase a baby's risk of being born with CP. These risks include:

- **Low birthweight and premature birth.** Premature babies (born less than 37 weeks into pregnancy) and babies weighing less than 5½ pounds at birth have a much higher risk of developing cerebral palsy than full-term, heavier weight babies. Tiny babies born at very early gestational ages are especially at risk.

- **Multiple births.** Twins, triplets, and other multiple births—even those born at term—are linked to an increased risk of cerebral palsy. The death of a baby's twin or triplet further increases the risk.

- **Infections during pregnancy.** Infections such as toxoplasmosis, rubella (German measles), cytomegalovirus, and herpes, can infect the womb and placenta. Inflammation triggered by infection may then go on to damage the developing nervous system in an unborn baby. Maternal fever during pregnancy or delivery can also set off this kind of inflammatory response.

- **Blood type incompatibility between mother and child.** Rh incompatibility is a condition that develops when a mother's Rh blood type (either positive or negative) is different from the blood type of her baby. The mother's system doesn't tolerate the baby's different blood type and her body will begin to make antibodies that will attack and kill her baby's blood cells, which can cause brain damage.

- **Exposure to toxic substances.** Mothers who have been exposed to toxic substances during pregnancy, such as methylmercury, are at a heightened risk of having a baby with cerebral palsy.

- **Mothers with thyroid abnormalities, intellectual disability, excess protein in the urine, or seizures.** Mothers with any of these conditions are slightly more likely to have a child with CP.

There are also medical conditions during labor and delivery, and immediately after delivery that act as warning signs for an increased risk of CP. However, most of these children will not develop CP. Warning signs include:

- **Breech presentation.** Babies with cerebral palsy are more likely to be in a breech position (feet first) instead of head first at the beginning of labor. Babies who are unusually floppy as fetuses are more likely to be born in the breech position.

- **Complicated labor and delivery.** A baby who has vascular or respiratory problems during labor and delivery may already have suffered brain damage or abnormalities.

- **Small for gestational age.** Babies born smaller than normal for their gestational age are at risk for cerebral palsy because of factors that kept them from growing naturally in the womb.

- **Low Apgar score.** The Apgar score is a numbered rating that reflects a newborn's physical health. Doctors periodically score a baby's heart rate, breathing, muscle tone, reflexes, and skin color during the first minutes after birth. A low score at 10–20 minutes after delivery is often considered an important sign of potential problems such as CP.

- **Jaundice.** More than 50 percent of newborns develop jaundice (a yellowing of the skin or whites of the eyes) after birth when bilirubin, a substance normally found in bile, builds up faster than their livers can break it down and pass it from the body. Severe, untreated jaundice can kill brain cells and can cause deafness and CP.

- **Seizures.** An infant who has seizures faces a higher risk of being diagnosed later in childhood with CP.

Can Cerebral Palsy Be Prevented?

Cerebral palsy related to genetic abnormalities cannot be prevented, but a few of the risk factors for congenital cerebral palsy can be managed or avoided. For example, rubella, or German measles, is preventable if women are vaccinated against the disease before becoming pregnant. Rh incompatibilities can also be managed early in pregnancy. Acquired cerebral palsy, often due to head injury, is often

Cerebral Palsy

preventable using common safety tactics, such as using car seats for infants and toddlers.

How Is Cerebral Palsy Diagnosed?

Most children with cerebral palsy are diagnosed during the first two years of life. But if a child's symptoms are mild, it can be difficult for a doctor to make a reliable diagnosis before the age of four or five.

Doctors will order a series of tests to evaluate the child's motor skills. During regular visits, the doctor will monitor the child's development, growth, muscle tone, age-appropriate motor control, hearing and vision, posture, and coordination, in order to rule out other disorders that could cause similar symptoms. Although symptoms may change over time, CP is not progressive. If a child is continuously losing motor skills, the problem more likely is a condition other than CP—such as a genetic or muscle disease, metabolism disorder, or tumors in the nervous system.

Lab tests can identify other conditions that may cause symptoms similar to those associated with CP.

Neuroimaging techniques that allow doctors to look into the brain (such as magnetic resonance imaging (MRI) scan can detect abnormalities that indicate a potentially treatable movement disorder. Neuroimaging methods include:

- **Cranial ultrasound** uses high-frequency sound waves to produce pictures of the brains of young babies. It is used for high-risk premature infants because it is the least intrusive of the imaging techniques, although it is not as successful as computed tomography or magnetic resonance imaging at capturing subtle changes in white matter—the type of brain tissue that is damaged in CP.

- **Computed tomography (CT)** uses X-rays to create images that show the structure of the brain and the areas of damage.

- **Magnetic resonance imaging (MRI)** uses a computer, a magnetic field, and radio waves to create an anatomical picture of the brain's tissues and structures. MRI can show the location and type of damage and offers finer levels of details than CT.

Another test, an electroencephalogram, uses a series of electrodes that are either taped or temporarily pasted to the scalp to detect electrical activity in the brain. Changes in the normal electrical pattern may help to identify epilepsy.

Some metabolic disorders can masquerade as CP. Most of the childhood metabolic disorders have characteristic brain abnormalities or malformations that will show up on an MRI.

Other types of disorders can also be mistaken for CP or can cause specific types of CP. For example, coagulation disorders (which prevent blood from clotting or lead to excessive clotting) can cause prenatal or perinatal strokes that damage the brain and produce symptoms characteristic of CP, most commonly hemiparetic CP. Referrals to specialists such as a child neurologist, developmental pediatrician, ophthalmologist, or otologist aid in a more accurate diagnosis and help doctors develop a specific treatment plan.

How Is Cerebral Palsy Treated?

Cerebral palsy can't be cured, but treatment will often improve a child's capabilities. Many children go on to enjoy near-normal adult lives if their disabilities are properly managed. In general, the earlier treatment begins, the better chance children have of overcoming developmental disabilities or learning new ways to accomplish the tasks that challenge them.

There is no standard therapy that works for every individual with cerebral palsy. Once the diagnosis is made, and the type of CP is determined, a team of healthcare professionals will work with a child and his or her parents to identify specific impairments and needs, and then develop an appropriate plan to tackle the core disabilities that affect the child's quality of life.

Physical therapy, usually begun in the first few years of life or soon after the diagnosis is made, is a cornerstone of CP treatment. Specific sets of exercises (such as resistive, or strength training programs) and activities can maintain or improve muscle strength, balance, and motor skills, and prevent contractures. Special braces (called orthotic devices) may be used to improve mobility and stretch spastic muscles.

Occupational therapy focuses on optimizing upper body function, improving posture, and making the most of a child's mobility. Occupational therapists help individuals address new ways to meet everyday activities such as dressing, going to school, and participating in day-to-day activities.

Recreation therapy encourages participation in art and cultural programs, sports, and other events that help an individual expand physical and cognitive skills and abilities. Parents of children who participate in recreational therapies usually notice an improvement in their child's speech, self-esteem, and emotional well-being.

Speech and language therapy can improve a child's ability to speak, more clearly, help with swallowing disorders, and learn new ways to communicate—using sign language and/or special communication devices such as a computer with a voice synthesizer, or a special board covered with symbols of everyday objects and activities to which a child can point to indicate his or her wishes.

Treatments for problems with eating and drooling are often necessary when children with CP have difficulty eating and drinking because they have little control over the muscles that move their mouth, jaw, and tongue. They are also at risk for breathing food or fluid into the lungs, as well as for malnutrition, recurrent lung infections, and progressive lung disease.

Drug Treatments

Oral medications such as diazepam, baclofen, dantrolene sodium, and tizanidine are usually used as the first line of treatment to relax stiff, contracted, or overactive muscles. Some drugs have some risk side effects such as drowsiness, changes in blood pressure, and risk of liver damage that require continuous monitoring. Oral medications are most appropriate for children who need only mild reduction in muscle tone or who have widespread spasticity.

- **Botulinum toxin (BT-A)**, injected locally, has become a standard treatment for overactive muscles in children with spastic movement disorders such as CP. BT-A relaxes contracted muscles by keeping nerve cells from overactivating muscle. The relaxing effect of a BT-A injection lasts approximately 3 months. Undesirable side effects are mild and short-lived, consisting of pain upon injection and occasionally mild flu-like symptoms. BT-A injections are most effective when followed by a stretching program including physical therapy and splinting. BT-A injections work best for children who have some control over their motor movements and have a limited number of muscles to treat, none of which is fixed or rigid.

- **Intrathecal baclofen** therapy uses an implantable pump to deliver baclofen, a muscle relaxant, into the fluid surrounding the spinal cord. Baclofen decreases the excitability of nerve cells in the spinal cord, which then reduces muscle spasticity throughout the body. The pump can be adjusted if muscle tone is worse at certain times of the day or night. The baclofen pump is most appropriate for individuals with chronic, severe stiffness or uncontrolled muscle movement throughout the body.

Surgery

Orthopedic surgery is often recommended when spasticity and stiffness are severe enough to make walking and moving about difficult or painful. For many people with CP, improving the appearance of how they walk—their gait—is also important. Surgeons can lengthen muscles and tendons that are proportionately too short, which can improve mobility and lessen pain. Tendon surgery may help the symptoms for some children with CP but could also have negative long-term consequences. Orthopedic surgeries may be staggered at times appropriate to a child's age and level of motor development. Surgery can also correct or greatly improve spinal deformities in people with CP. Surgery may not be indicated for all gait abnormalities and the surgeon may request a quantitative gait analysis before surgery.

Surgery to cut nerves. Selective dorsal rhizotomy (SDR) is a surgical procedure recommended for cases of severe spasticity when all of the more conservative treatments—physical therapy, oral medications, and intrathecal baclofen—have failed to reduce spasticity or chronic pain. A surgeon locates and selectively severs overactivated nerves at the base of the spinal column. SDR is most commonly used to relax muscles and decrease chronic pain in one or both of the lower or upper limbs. It is also sometimes used to correct an overactive bladder. Potential side effects include sensory loss, numbness, or uncomfortable sensations in limb areas once supplied by the severed nerve.

Assistive Devices

Assistive devices such as computers, computer software, voice synthesizers, and picture books can greatly help some individuals with CP improve communications skills. Other devices around the home or workplace make it easier for people with CP to adapt to activities of daily living.

Orthotic devices help to compensate for muscle imbalance and increase independent mobility. Braces and splints use external force to correct muscle abnormalities and improve function such as sitting or walking. Other orthotics help stretch muscles or the positioning of a joint. Braces, wedges, special chairs, and other devices can help people

Cerebral Palsy

sit more comfortably and make it easier to perform daily functions. Wheelchairs, rolling walkers, and powered scooters can help individuals who are not independently mobile. Vision aids include glasses, magnifiers, and large-print books and computer typeface. Some individuals with CP may need surgery to correct vision problems. Hearing aids and telephone amplifiers may help people hear more clearly.

Complementary and Alternative Therapies

Many children and adolescents with CP use some form of complementary or alternative medicine. Controlled clinical trials involving some of the therapies have been inconclusive or showed no benefit and the therapies have not been accepted in mainstream clinical practice. Although there are anecdotal of some benefit in some children with CP, these therapies have not been approved by the U.S. Food and Drug Administration (FDA) for the treatment of CP. Such therapies include hyperbaric oxygen therapy, special clothing worn during resistance exercise training, certain forms of electrical stimulation, assisting children in completing certain motions several times a day, and specialized learning strategies. Also, dietary supplements, including herbal products, may interact with other products or medications a child with CP may be taking or have unwanted side effects on their own. Families of children with CP should discuss all therapies with their doctor.

Stem cell therapy is being investigated as a treatment for cerebral palsy, but research is in early stages and large-scale clinical trials are needed to learn if stem cell therapy is safe and effective in humans. Stem cells are capable of becoming other cell types in the body. Scientists are hopeful that stem cells may be able to repair damaged nerves and brain tissues. Studies in the United States are examining the safety and tolerability of umbilical cord blood stem cell infusion in children with CP.

Chapter 12

Cleft Lip and Palate

Cleft lip and cleft palate are birth defects that occur when a baby's lip or mouth do not form properly during pregnancy. Together, these birth defects commonly are called "orofacial clefts."

What Is Cleft Lip?

The lip forms between the fourth and seventh weeks of pregnancy. As a baby develops during pregnancy, body tissue and special cells from each side of the head grow toward the center of the face and join together

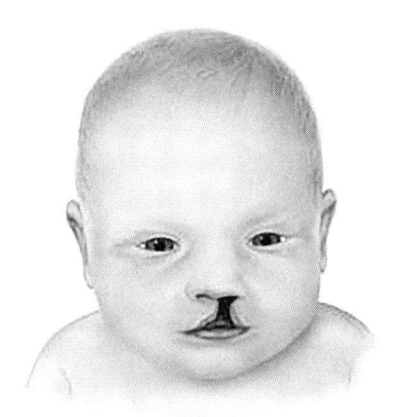

Figure 12.1. *Baby with Cleft Lip*

This chapter includes text excerpted from "Facts about Cleft Lip and Cleft Palate," Centers for Disease Control and Prevention (CDC), November 21, 2017.

to make the face. This joining of tissue forms the facial features, like the lips and mouth. A cleft lip happens if the tissue that makes up the lip does not join completely before birth. This results in an opening in the upper lip. The opening in the lip can be a small slit or it can be a large opening that goes through the lip into the nose. A cleft lip can be on one or both sides of the lip or in the middle of the lip, which occurs very rarely. Children with a cleft lip also can have a cleft palate.

What Is Cleft Palate?

The roof of the mouth (palate) is formed between the sixth and ninth weeks of pregnancy. A cleft palate happens if the tissue that makes up the roof of the mouth does not join together completely during pregnancy. For some babies, both the front and back parts of the palate are open. For other babies, only part of the palate is open.

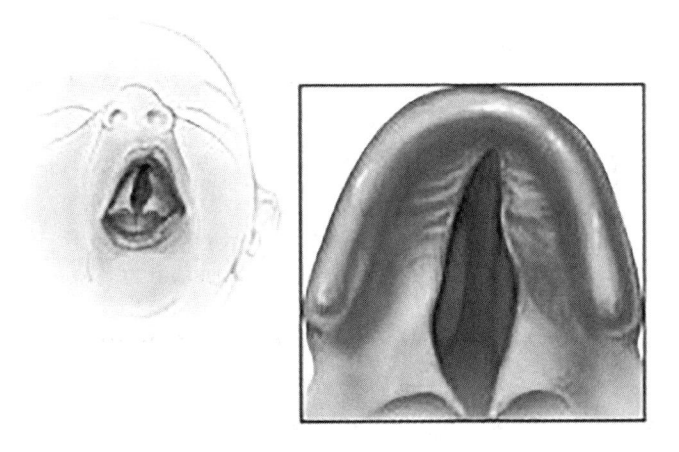

Figure 12.2. *Baby with Cleft Palate*

Other Problems

Children with a cleft lip with or without a cleft palate or a cleft palate alone often have problems with feeding and speaking clearly and can have ear infections. They also might have hearing problems and problems with their teeth.

Occurrence

Centers for Disease Control and Prevention (CDC) estimated that, each year in the United States, about 2,650 babies are born with a

Cleft Lip and Palate

cleft palate and 4,440 babies are born with a cleft lip with or without a cleft palate. Isolated orofacial clefts, or clefts that occur with no other major birth defects, are one of the most common types of birth defects in the United States. Depending on the cleft type, the rate of isolated orofacial clefts can vary from 50–80 percent of all clefts.

Causes and Risk Factors

The causes of orofacial clefts among most infants are unknown. Some children have a cleft lip or cleft palate because of changes in their genes. Cleft lip and cleft palate are thought to be caused by a combination of genes and other factors, such as things the mother comes in contact with in her environment, or what the mother eats or drinks, or certain medications she uses during pregnancy.

Like the many families of children with birth defects, CDC wants to find out what causes them. Understanding the factors that are more common among babies with a birth defect will help us learn more about the causes. CDC funds the Centers for Birth Defects Research and Prevention (CBDRP), which collaborate on large studies such as the National Birth Defects Prevention Study (NBDPS; births 1997–2011) and the Birth Defects Study To Evaluate Pregnancy exposureS (BD-STEPS; began with births in 2014), to understand the causes of and risks for birth defects, including orofacial clefts.

CDC reported on important findings from research studies about some factors that increase the chance of having a baby with an orofacial cleft:

- **Smoking**—Women who smoke during pregnancy are more likely to have a baby with an orofacial cleft than women who do not smoke.

- **Diabetes**—Women with diabetes diagnosed before pregnancy have an increased risk of having a child with a cleft lip with or without cleft palate, compared to women who did not have diabetes.

- **Use of certain medicines**—Women who used certain medicines to treat epilepsy, such as topiramate or valproic acid, during the first trimester (the first 3 months) of pregnancy have an increased risk of having a baby with cleft lip with or without cleft palate, compared to women who didn't take these medicines.

CDC continues to study birth defects, such as cleft lip and cleft palate, and how to prevent them. If you are pregnant or thinking about becoming pregnant, talk with your doctor about ways to increase your chances of having a healthy baby.

Diagnosis

Orofacial clefts, especially cleft lip with or without cleft palate, can be diagnosed during pregnancy by a routine ultrasound. They can also be diagnosed after the baby is born, especially cleft palate. However, sometimes certain types of cleft palate (for example, submucous cleft palate and bifid uvula) might not be diagnosed until later in life.

Management and Treatment

Services and treatment for children with orofacial clefts can vary depending on the severity of the cleft; the child's age and needs; and the presence of associated syndromes or other birth defects, or both.

Surgery to repair a cleft lip usually occurs in the first few months of life and is recommended within the first 12 months of life. Surgery to repair a cleft palate is recommended within the first 18 months of life or earlier if possible. Many children will need additional surgical procedures as they get older. Surgical repair can improve the look and appearance of a child's face and might also improve breathing, hearing, and speech and language development. Children born with orofacial clefts might need other types of treatments and services, such as special dental or orthodontic care or speech therapy.

Because children with orofacial clefts often require a variety of services that need to be provided in a coordinated manner throughout childhood and into adolescence and sometimes adulthood, the American Cleft Palate-Craniofacial Association (ACPA) recommends services and treatment by cleft and craniofacial teams. Cleft and craniofacial teams provide a coordinated approach to care for children with orofacial clefts. These teams usually consist of experienced and qualified physicians and healthcare providers from different specialties. Cleft and craniofacial teams and centers are located throughout the United States and other countries. Resources are available to help in choosing a cleft and craniofacial team.

With treatment, most children with orofacial clefts do well and lead a healthy life. Some children with orofacial clefts may have issues with self-esteem if they are concerned with visible differences between themselves and other children. Parent-to-parent support groups can prove to be useful for families of babies with birth defects of the head and face, such as orofacial clefts.

Chapter 13

Cystic Fibrosis

Cystic fibrosis, or CF, is an inherited disease of the secretory glands. Secretory glands include glands that make mucus and sweat. "Inherited" means the disease is passed from parents to children through genes. People who have CF inherit two faulty genes for the disease—one from each parent. The parents likely don't have the disease themselves. CF mainly affects the lungs, pancreas, liver, intestines, sinuses, and sex organs.

Causes of Cystic Fibrosis

A defect in the *CFTR* gene causes CF. This gene makes a protein that controls the movement of salt and water in and out of your body's cells. In people who have CF, the gene makes a protein that doesn't work well. This causes thick, sticky mucus and very salty sweat.

Research suggests that the *CFTR* protein also affects the body in other ways. This may help explain other symptoms and complications of CF. More than a thousand known defects can affect the *CFTR* gene. The type of defect you or your child has may affect the severity of CF. Other genes also may play a role in the severity of the disease.

How Is Cystic Fibrosis Inherited?

Every person inherits two *CFTR* genes—one from each parent. Children who inherit a faulty *CFTR* gene from each parent will have

---

This chapter includes text excerpted from "Cystic Fibrosis," National Heart, Lung, and Blood Institute (NHLBI), May 22, 2018.

CF. Children who inherit one faulty *CFTR* gene and one normal *CFTR* gene are "CF carriers." CF carriers usually have no symptoms of CF and live normal lives. However, they can pass the faulty *CFTR* gene to their children.

The image below shows how two parents who are both CF carriers can pass the faulty *CFTR* gene to their children.

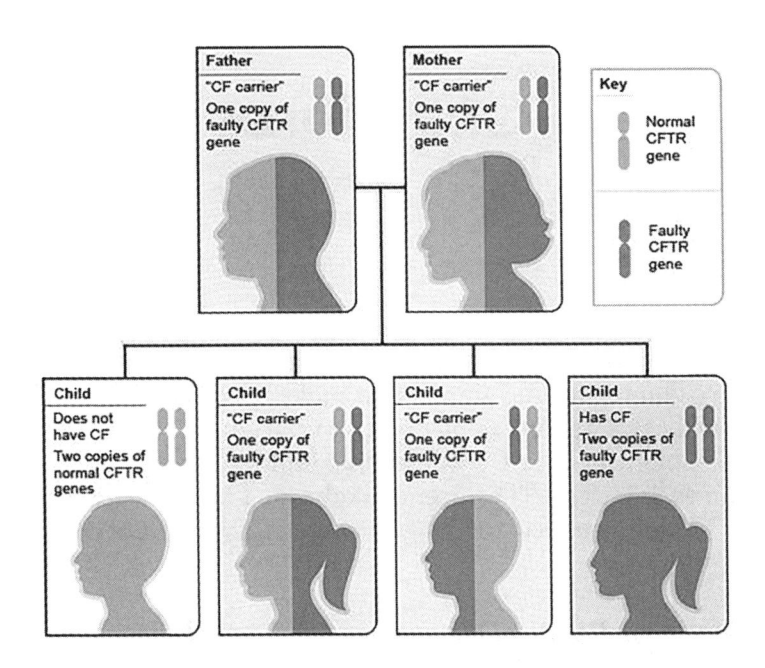

Figure 13.1. *Inheritance Pattern for Cystic Fibrosis*

The image shows how CFTR genes are inherited. A person inherits two copies of the CFTR gene—one from each parent. If each parent has a normal CFTR gene and a faulty CFTR gene, each child has a 25 percent chance of inheriting two normal genes; a 50 percent chance of inheriting one normal gene and one faulty gene; and a 25 percent chance of inheriting two faulty genes.

Risk Factors of Cystic Fibrosis

CF affects both males and females and people from all racial and ethnic groups. However, the disease is most common among Caucasians of Northern European descent. CF also is common among Latinos and American Indians, especially the Pueblo and Zuni. The disease is less common among African Americans and Asian Americans. More than 10 million Americans are carriers of a faulty CF gene. Many of them don't know that they're CF carriers.

Cystic Fibrosis

Signs, Symptoms, and Complications of Cystic Fibrosis

The signs and symptoms of CF vary from person to person and over time. Sometimes you'll have few symptoms. Other times, your symptoms may become more severe. One of the first signs of CF that parents may notice is that their baby's skin tastes salty when kissed, or the baby doesn't pass stool when first born. Most of the other signs and symptoms of CF happen later. They're related to how CF affects the respiratory, digestive, or reproductive systems of the body.

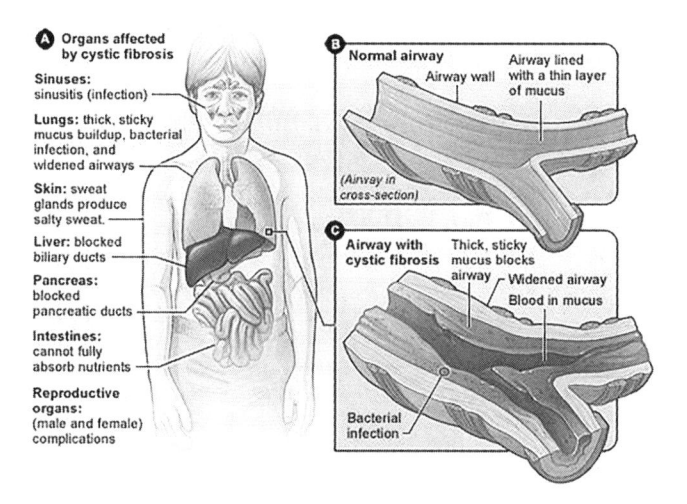

Figure 13.2. *Cystic Fibrosis*

Figure A shows the organs that CF can affect. Figure B shows a cross-section of a normal airway. Figure C shows an airway with CF. The widened airway is blocked by thick, sticky mucus that contains blood and bacteria.

Respiratory System Signs and Symptoms

People who have CF have thick, sticky mucus that builds up in their airways. This buildup of mucus makes it easier for bacteria to grow and cause infections. Infections can block the airways and cause frequent coughing that brings up thick sputum (spit) or mucus that's sometimes bloody.

People who have CF tend to have lung infections caused by unusual germs that don't respond to standard antibiotics. For example, lung infections caused by bacteria called mucoid Pseudomonas are much more common in people who have CF than in those who don't. An infection caused by these bacteria may be a sign of CF.

People who have CF have frequent bouts of sinusitis, an infection of the sinuses. The sinuses are hollow air spaces around the eyes, nose, and forehead. Frequent bouts of bronchitis and pneumonia also can occur. These infections can cause long-term lung damage.

As CF gets worse, you may have more serious problems, such as pneumothorax or bronchiectasis. Some people who have CF also develop nasal polyps (growths in the nose) that may require surgery.

Digestive System Signs and Symptoms

In CF, mucus can block tubes, or ducts, in your pancreas (an organ in your abdomen). These blockages prevent enzymes from reaching your intestines.

As a result, your intestines can't fully absorb fats and proteins. This can cause ongoing diarrhea or bulky, foul-smelling, greasy stools. Intestinal blockages also may occur, especially in newborns. Too much gas or severe constipation in the intestines may cause stomach pain and discomfort.

A hallmark of CF in children is poor weight gain and growth. These children are unable to get enough nutrients from their food because of the lack of enzymes to help absorb fats and proteins.

As CF gets worse, other problems may occur, such as:

- Pancreatitis. This is a condition in which the pancreas becomes inflamed, which causes pain.
- Rectal prolapse. Frequent coughing or problems passing stools may cause rectal tissue from inside you to move out of your rectum.
- Liver disease due to inflamed or blocked bile ducts.
- Diabetes
- Gallstones

Reproductive System Signs and Symptoms

Men who have CF are infertile because they're born without a vas deferens. The vas deferens is a tube that delivers sperm from the testes to the penis. Women who have CF may have a hard time getting pregnant because of mucus blocking the cervix or other CF complications.

Cystic Fibrosis

Other Signs, Symptoms, and Complications

Other signs and symptoms of CF are related to an upset of the balance of minerals in your blood. CF causes your sweat to become very salty. As a result, your body loses large amounts of salt when you sweat. This can cause dehydration (a lack of fluid in your body), increased heart rate, fatigue (tiredness), weakness, decreased blood pressure, heat stroke, and, rarely, death. CF also can cause clubbing and low bone density. Clubbing is the widening and rounding of the tips of your fingers and toes. This sign develops late in CF because your lungs aren't moving enough oxygen into your bloodstream. Low bone density also tends to occur late in CF. It can lead to bone-thinning disorders called osteoporosis and osteopenia.

Diagnosis of Cystic Fibrosis

Doctors diagnose CF based on the results from various tests.

Newborn Screening

All states screen newborns for CF using a genetic test or a blood test. The genetic test shows whether a newborn has faulty *CFTR* genes. The blood test shows whether a newborn's pancreas is working properly.

Sweat Test

If a genetic test or blood test suggests CF, a doctor will confirm the diagnosis using a sweat test. This test is the most useful test for diagnosing CF. A sweat test measures the amount of salt in sweat.

For this test, the doctor triggers sweating on a small patch of skin on an arm or leg. He or she rubs the skin with a sweat-producing chemical and then uses an electrode to provide a mild electrical current. This may cause a tingling or warm feeling.

Sweat is collected on a pad or paper and then analyzed. The sweat test usually is done twice. High salt levels confirm a diagnosis of CF.

Other Tests

If you or your child has CF, your doctor may recommend other tests, such as:

- Genetic tests to find out what type of *CFTR* defect is causing your CF

- A chest X-ray. This test creates pictures of the structures in your chest, such as your heart, lungs, and blood vessels. A chest X-ray can show whether your lungs are inflamed or scarred, or whether they trap air.

- A sinus X-ray. This test may show signs of sinusitis, a complication of CF.

- Lung function tests. These tests measure how much air you can breathe in and out, how fast you can breathe air out, and how well your lungs deliver oxygen to your blood.

- A sputum culture. For this test, your doctor will take a sample of your sputum (spit) to see whether bacteria are growing in it. If you have bacteria called mucoid Pseudomonas, you may have more advanced CF that needs aggressive treatment.

Prenatal Screening

If you're pregnant, prenatal genetic tests can show whether your fetus has CF. These tests include amniocentesis and chorionic villus sampling (CVS).

In amniocentesis, your doctor inserts a hollow needle through your abdominal wall into your uterus. He or she removes a small amount of fluid from the sac around the baby. The fluid is tested to see whether both of the baby's *CFTR* genes are normal.

In CVS, your doctor threads a thin tube through the vagina and cervix to the placenta. The doctor removes a tissue sample from the placenta using gentle suction. The sample is tested to see whether the baby has CF.

Cystic Fibrosis Carrier Testing

People who have one normal *CFTR* gene and one faulty *CFTR* gene are CF carriers. CF carriers usually have no symptoms of CF and live normal lives. However, carriers can pass faulty *CFTR* genes on to their children.

If you have a family history of CF or a partner who has CF (or a family history of it) and you're planning a pregnancy, you may want to find out whether you're a CF carrier.

A genetics counselor can test a blood or saliva sample to find out whether you have a faulty CF gene. This type of testing can detect faulty CF genes in 9 out of 10 cases.

Treatment for Cystic Fibrosis

CF has no cure. However, treatments have greatly improved in recent years. The goals of CF treatment include:

- Preventing and controlling lung infections
- Loosening and removing thick, sticky mucus from the lungs
- Preventing or treating blockages in the intestines
- Providing enough nutrition
- Preventing dehydration (a lack of fluid in the body)
- Depending on the severity of CF, you or your child may be treated in a hospital

Specialists Involved

If you or your child has CF, you may be treated by a CF specialist. This is a doctor who is familiar with the complex nature of CF. Often, a CF specialist works with a medical team of nurses, physical therapists, dietitians, and social workers. CF specialists often are located at major medical centers.

The United States also has more than 100 CF Care Centers. These centers have teams of doctors, nurses, dietitians, respiratory therapists, physical therapists, and social workers who have special training related to CF care. Most CF Care Centers have pediatric and adult programs or clinics.

Treatment for Lung Problems

The main treatments for lung problems in people who have CF are chest physical therapy (CPT), exercise, and medicines. Your doctor also may recommend a pulmonary rehabilitation (PR) program.

Chest Physical Therapy (CPT)

CPT also is called chest clapping or percussion. It involves pounding your chest and back over and over with your hands or a device to loosen the mucus from your lungs so that you can cough it up.

You might sit down or lie on your stomach with your head down while you do CPT. Gravity and force help drain the mucus from your lungs.

Some people find CPT hard or uncomfortable to do. Several devices have been developed that may help with CPT, such as:

- An electric chest clapper, known as a mechanical percussor.
- An inflatable therapy vest that uses high-frequency airwaves to force the mucus that's deep in your lungs toward your upper airways so you can cough it up.
- A small, handheld device that you exhale through. The device causes vibrations that dislodge the mucus.
- A mask that creates vibrations that help break the mucus loose from your airway walls.

Breathing techniques also may help dislodge mucus so you can cough it up. These techniques include forcing out a couple of short breaths or deeper breaths and then doing relaxed breathing. This may help loosen the mucus in your lungs and open your airways.

Exercise

Aerobic exercise that makes you breathe harder can help loosen the mucus in your airways so you can cough it up. Exercise also helps improve your overall physical condition.

However, CF causes your sweat to become very salty. As a result, your body loses large amounts of salt when you sweat. Thus, your doctor may recommend a high-salt diet or salt supplements to maintain the balance of minerals in your blood.

If you exercise regularly, you may be able to cut back on your CPT. However, you should check with your doctor first.

Medicines

If you have CF, your doctor may prescribe antibiotics, anti-inflammatory medicines, bronchodilators, or medicines to help clear the mucus. These medicines help treat or prevent lung infections, reduce swelling and open up the airways, and thin mucus. If you have mutations in a gene called G551D, which occurs in about 5 percent of people who have CF, your doctor may prescribe the oral medicine ivacaftor (approved for people with CF who are 6 years of age and older).

Antibiotics are the main treatment to prevent or treat lung infections. Your doctor may prescribe oral, inhaled, or intravenous (IV) antibiotics.

Cystic Fibrosis

Oral antibiotics often are used to treat mild lung infections. Inhaled antibiotics may be used to prevent or control infections caused by the bacteria mucoid *Pseudomonas*. For severe or hard-to-treat infections, you may be given antibiotics through an IV tube (a tube inserted into a vein). This type of treatment may require you to stay in a hospital.

Anti-inflammatory medicines can help reduce swelling in your airways due to ongoing infections. These medicines may be inhaled or oral.

Bronchodilators help open the airways by relaxing the muscles around them. These medicines are inhaled. They're often taken just before CPT to help clear mucus out of your airways. You also may take bronchodilators before inhaling other medicines into your lungs.

Your doctor may prescribe medicines to reduce the stickiness of your mucus and loosen it up. These medicines can help clear out mucus, improve lung function, and prevent worsening lung symptoms.

Treatments for Advanced Lung Disease

If you have advanced lung disease, you may need oxygen therapy. Oxygen usually is given through nasal prongs or a mask.

If other treatments haven't worked, a lung transplant may be an option if you have severe lung disease. A lung transplant is a surgery to remove a person's diseased lung and replace it with a healthy lung from a deceased donor.

Pulmonary Rehabilitation (PR)

Your doctor may recommend PR as part of your treatment plan. PR is a broad program that helps improve the well-being of people who have chronic (ongoing) breathing problems.

PR doesn't replace medical therapy. Instead, it's used with medical therapy and may include:

- Exercise training
- Nutritional counseling
- Education on your lung disease or condition and how to manage it
- Energy-conserving techniques
- Breathing strategies
- Psychological counseling and/or group support

PR has many benefits. It can improve your ability to function and your quality of life. The program also may help relieve your breathing problems. Even if you have advanced lung disease, you can still benefit from PR.

Treatment for Digestive Problems

CF can cause many digestive problems, such as bulky stools, intestinal gas, a swollen belly, severe constipation, and pain or discomfort. Digestive problems also can lead to poor growth and development in children.

Nutritional therapy can improve your strength and ability to stay active. It also can improve growth and development in children. Nutritional therapy also may make you strong enough to resist some lung infections. A nutritionist can help you create a nutritional plan that meets your needs.

In addition to having a well-balanced diet that's rich in calories, fat, and protein, your nutritional therapy may include:

- Oral pancreatic enzymes to help you digest fats and proteins and absorb more vitamins

- Supplements of vitamins A, D, E, and K to replace the fat-soluble vitamins that your intestines can't absorb

- High-calorie shakes to provide you with extra nutrients

- A high-salt diet or salt supplements that you take before exercising

- A feeding tube to give you more calories at night while you're sleeping. The tube may be threaded through your nose and throat and into your stomach. Or, the tube may be placed directly into your stomach through a surgically made hole. Before you go to bed each night, you'll attach a bag with a nutritional solution to the entrance of the tube. It will feed you while you sleep.

Other treatments for digestive problems may include enemas and mucus-thinning medicines to treat intestinal blockages. Sometimes surgery is needed to remove an intestinal blockage.

Your doctor also may prescribe medicines to reduce your stomach acid and help oral pancreatic enzymes work better.

Treatments for Cystic Fibrosis Complications

A common complication of CF is diabetes. The type of diabetes associated with CF often requires different treatment than other types of diabetes.

Another common CF complication is the bone-thinning disorder osteoporosis. Your doctor may prescribe medicines that prevent your bones from losing their density.

Living with Cystic Fibrosis

If you or your child has CF, you should learn as much as you can about the disease. Work closely with your doctors to learn how to manage CF.

Ongoing Care

Having ongoing medical care by a team of doctors, nurses, and respiratory therapists who specialize in CF is important. These specialists often are located at major medical centers or CF Care Centers.

The United States has more than 100 CF Care Centers. Most of these centers have pediatric and adult programs or clinics.

It's standard to have CF checkups every 3 months. Talk with your doctor about whether you should get an annual flu shot and other vaccines. Take all of your medicines as your doctor prescribes. In between checkups, be sure to contact your doctor if you have:

- Blood in your mucus, increased amounts of mucus, or a change in the color or consistency of your mucus
- Decreased energy or appetite
- Severe constipation or diarrhea, severe abdominal pain, or vomit that's dark green
- A fever, which is a sign of infection (however, you may still have a serious infection that needs treatment even if you don't have a fever)

Transition of Care

Better treatments for CF allow people who have the disease to live longer now than in the past. Thus, the move from pediatric care to adult care is an important step in treatment.

If your child has CF, encourage him or her to learn about the disease and take an active role in treatment. This will help prepare your child for the transition to adult care.

CF Care Centers can help provide age-appropriate treatment throughout the transition period and into adulthood. They also will support the transition to adult care by balancing medical needs with other developmental factors, such as increased independence, relationships, and employment.

Talk with your child's healthcare team for more information about how to help your child move from pediatric care to adult care.

Lifestyle Changes

In between medical checkups, you can practice good self-care and follow a healthy lifestyle.

For example, follow a healthy diet. A healthy diet includes a variety of fruits, vegetables, and whole grains. Talk with your doctor about what types and amounts of foods you should include in your diet.

Other lifestyle changes include:

- Not smoking and avoiding tobacco smoke
- Washing your hands often to lower your risk of infection
- Exercising regularly and drinking lots of fluids
- Doing chest physical therapy (as your doctor recommends)

Other Concerns

Although CF requires daily care, most people who have the disease are able to attend school and work. Adults who have CF can expect to have normal sex lives. Most men who have the disease are infertile (unable to have children). However, modern fertility treatments may help them.

Women who have CF may find it hard to get pregnant, but they usually can have children. If you have CF, you should talk with your doctor if you're planning a pregnancy. Although CF can cause fertility problems, men and women who have the disease should still have protected sex to avoid sexually transmitted diseases (STDs).

Emotional Issues

Living with CF may cause fear, anxiety, depression, and stress. Talk about how you feel with your healthcare team. Talking to a professional counselor also can help. If you're very depressed, your doctor may recommend medicines or other treatments that can improve your quality of life.

Cystic Fibrosis

Joining a patient support group may help you adjust to living with CF. You can see how other people who have the same symptoms have coped with them. Talk with your doctor about local support groups or check with an area medical center.

Support from family and friends also can help relieve stress and anxiety. Let your loved ones know how you feel and what they can do to help you.

Chapter 14

Inherited Disorders of Metabolism

Metabolism is the process of chemical transformation that occurs within the cells of organisms and is required to drive life-sustaining cellular processes.

The primary objectives of metabolism are to

- absorb food and transform it into building blocks for cells and tissues;
- break down food in order to provide energy for cellular processes; and
- eliminate waste that is left over from these metabolic processes.

Metabolic chemical transformations usually occur in sequences called "metabolic pathways" and are catalyzed by enzymes. Enzymes manage metabolic pathways by regulating various interdependent biochemical reactions in response to changes in the cell environment—an essential function for cell function and survival. Molecular substances called "cofactors" help these enzymes during chemical transformations.

A metabolic disorder is an abnormal biochemical reaction that disrupts the normal metabolic process. A metabolic disorder can be congenital or acquired. A congenital disorder is characterized by a

---

"Inherited Disorders of Metabolism," © 2018 Omnigraphics. Reviewed July 2018.

defective gene that leads to specific enzyme deficiencies. An acquired metabolic disorder is usually caused by either a deficiency in a certain metabolic substrate or an enzyme deficiency induced by some agent or organism outside of the body. Such deficiencies disrupt normal metabolic pathways and prevent the body from synthesizing important substrates such as amino acids, fatty acids, organic acids, and other macromolecules.

Incidence of Inborn Errors of Metabolism

Mutations in human genes are estimated to number some 30,000, and can cause an astounding number of disorders. Thousands of inherited metabolic disorders (IEMs) arise from gene mutation, and new ones continue to emerge. These mutations challenge clinicians and patients alike. While some inherited metabolic disorders (such as Gaucher disease) are rare, others (such as diabetes or gout) are widespread. Collectively, Inborn errors of metabolism (IEM) represents a significant burden on the population in terms of morbidity, mortality, and healthcare costs.

Etiology of Inborn Errors of Metabolism

The code or blueprint for human enzyme production is usually carried on a pair of genes. Most people with IEM inherit two defective copies of the gene—one from each parent. Parents may be "carriers" who have one defective and one normal copy of the gene in question and, therefore, have no symptoms of the IEM. The offspring of two carriers of the same defective gene copies, however, cannot synthesize enough effective enzymes and, therefore, develop the genetic metabolic disorder. This form of genetic transmission from parents to offspring is called "autosomal recessive inheritance." The defective gene is caused by a mutation in the gene, which renders the gene dysfunctional or ineffective. The defective gene is preserved through generations, leading to IEM in subsequent generations.

IEM may also be caused by X-linked recessive inheritance. In this type of inheritance, the defective maternal gene is passed on to the offspring via the X chromosome (sex chromosome).

The third type of genetic defect involves mitochondrial inheritance. Mitochondria are cell organelles that generate chemical energy to power the cell's metabolic activities. These contain copies of their own DNA, all of which are inherited from the mother. The mitochondrial DNA code for enzymes necessary for normal mitochondrial function, and mutations in them lead to dysfunction of the mitochondria and inadequate production of energy.

Classification of Inborn Errors of Metabolism

Disorders Involving Complex Molecules

Disorders involving synthesis of cholesterol, a type of lipid with multiple biochemical functions in the body, are the most common type of metabolic diseases belonging to this class. Hypercholesterolemia, characterized by elevated levels of blood cholesterol, often leads to lipid deposition on arterial walls (atherosclerosis), a major risk factor for cardiovascular diseases. IEM could also lead to impaired storage in lysosomes (the cell organelles that contain enzymes involved in several aspects of energy metabolism).

Lysosomes contain the enzymes responsible for breaking down proteins and lipids. Impaired activity of lysosomal enzymes results in the buildup of complex molecules such as glycolipids and glycoproteins. This buildup could lead to organ damage and severe neurological complications. The most common lipid storage disorder is Gaucher disease, which is characterized by a deficiency of the enzyme glucocerebrosidase. Symptoms include enlarged spleen, liver malfunction, painful bone lesions, swollen lymph nodes, and neurologic complications.

Disorders That Give Rise to Toxic Substances

This metabolic disorder results in toxic substances accumulating in the body as the result of a defective enzyme in metabolic pathways that involve amino acid and organic acid metabolism or sugar intolerances. These disorders typically present as a symptom-free period followed by a period of acute "intoxication." Symptoms such as vomiting, lethargy, coma, and liver failure are common and may be complicated by other organ failure and developmental delay. Phenylketonuria, resulting from the insufficiency of phenylalanine hydroxylase, leads to the buildup of phenylalanine in the blood. Buildup of toxic metabolites can also arise from organic acidemias or urea-cycle defects.

Organic acidemias result from abnormally elevated levels of organic acids in body fluids and tissues. A common disorder of this type is the maple syrup urine disease (MSUD)—so called because of the characteristic odor of maple syrup that results from the accumulation of amino acids in the blood and the urine.

Disorders Involving Energy Metabolism

Metabolic disorders of this type are due to a malfunction in energy production, or utilization, at the cellular level. Glycogen storage diseases are a common subtype of disorders involving energy metabolism. Glucose and glycogen stored in the liver and muscles provides a ready source of fuel for many types of body tissues. But defects in enzymes involved in glycogen breakdown can lead to a number of metabolic diseases, depending on the specific enzyme and metabolic pathway involved. For example, von Gierke disease is a metabolic disease involving the enzyme, glucose-6-phosphatase, and has an incidence with American population of approximately 1 in 50,000 to 100,000 births.

Oxidation of fatty acids in the liver mitochondria is also a source of energy and any dysfunction of the enzymes involved in the catabolism of fatty acids can lead to metabolic disorders. Metabolic diseases arising from impaired energy metabolism can also result from disorders of the mitochondria; the presentation of disease depending largely on the organ affected by the defective mitochondria. While minor defects do not have any significant clinical consequence and may simply manifest as "exercise intolerance," other defects involving mitochondria of brain and muscles may have multi-organ impact and serious clinical implications. Some of the disorders in this class include mitochondrial encephalomyopathy, lactic acidosis, and Leigh syndrome, characterized by progressive loss of mental and movement abilities, resulting in death within two to three years, usually due to respiratory failure.

Symptoms of Inborn Errors of Metabolism

IEM may be rare or widespread and usually encompass a wide spectrum of diseases that vary considerably in their etiology, onset, symptoms, and progression. IEM may present as multisystemic diseases, and the severity of symptoms usually depends on the importance of the defective enzyme or cofactor in the metabolic pathway. The adverse effects of metabolic dysfunction can fall into one or more of the following categories:

- Inability of the body to synthesize essential substances, such as amino acids (building blocks of protein) that perform specific functions
- Buildup of metabolites to toxic levels
- Interference with other metabolic pathways

The metabolic dysfunction arising from IEM can have clinically significant consequences. While in some cases, IEM can be fatal in

Inherited Disorders of Metabolism

infancy or childhood in other cases, people reach adulthood before any major symptoms manifest.

Common symptoms of IEM may include:

- elevated blood levels of metabolites (such as sugar and ammonia)
- abnormal liver function tests
- blood cell abnormalities
- growth failure
- developmental delays (delayed milestones)

When metabolic diseases associated with IEM manifest early in life, they can lead to permanent neurological damage. This is because the central nervous system continues to develop until adolescence and is particularly susceptible to the deprivation of vital metabolic components and accumulation of toxic metabolites arising from enzymatic defects. Consequently, patients with metabolic dysfunction may experience seizures, pain, sleep problems, and bowel or bladder problems. They may also suffer from cognitive and sensory impairment and other long-term effects that affect major organ systems in the body.

Screening of Inborn Errors of Metabolism

Newborn screening for inherited metabolic disorders makes it possible to provide timely and effective intervention and prevent permanent disabilities, neurologic complications, and other adverse outcomes. A clinical suspicion of an IEM is generally followed up with biochemical genetic laboratory studies. These studies involve highly specialized procedures for assessing levels of various metabolites in blood, cerebrospinal fluid, urine, muscle, or other tissues. Recent advances in gas chromatography-mass spectrometry (GC-MS) have transformed the way the whole population can be screened for IEM. Prenatal screening using GC-MS offers rapid, more specific, and sensitive evaluation for IEM as compared to traditional assays and also makes it possible to screen for a number of previously unscreened IEM. If screening laboratory tests point toward a specific metabolic disease, further confirmatory tests are required before a diagnosis can be established.

Managing Inborn Errors of Metabolism

Treatment modalities largely depend on the type and severity of metabolic dysfunctions arising from IEM. Treatment begins soon after a diagnosis is established and is usually individualized. While conservative treatment is based on dietary restrictions, dietary supplementation, enzyme replacement therapies, or toxin removal, newer treatment options based on organ/bone marrow transplantation or gene transfer therapies are also being increasingly considered. For rare disorders of impaired metabolism that do not have an approved treatment protocol, supportive measures are provided to patients without actually treating the underlying cause of the disease.

References

1. "Inborn Error of Metabolism," ScienceDirect, n.d.
2. "The NIH MINI Study: Metabolism, Infection, and Immunity in Inborn Errors of Metabolism," National Human Genome Research Institute (NHGRI), February 22, 2013.

Chapter 15

Muscular Dystrophy

What Is Muscular Dystrophy?

Muscular dystrophy (MD) refers to a group of more than 30 genetic diseases that cause progressive weakness and degeneration of skeletal muscles used during voluntary movement. The word dystrophy is derived from the Greek dys, which means "difficult" or "faulty," and troph, or "nourish." These disorders vary in age of onset, severity, and pattern of affected muscles. All forms of MD grow worse as muscles progressively degenerate and weaken. Many individuals eventually lose the ability to walk.

Some types of MD also affect the heart, gastrointestinal system, endocrine glands, spine, eyes, brain, and other organs. Respiratory and cardiac diseases may occur, and some people may develop a swallowing disorder. MD is not contagious and cannot be brought on by injury or activity.

What Causes Muscular Dystrophy

All of the muscular dystrophies are inherited and involve a mutation in one of the thousands of genes that program proteins critical to muscle integrity. The body's cells don't work properly when a protein is altered or produced in insufficient quantity (or sometimes missing

---

This chapter includes text excerpted from "Muscular Dystrophy: Hope through Research," National Institute of Neurological Disorders and Stroke (NINDS), July 6, 2018.

completely). Many cases of MD occur from spontaneous mutations that are not found in the genes of either parent, and this defect can be passed to the next generation.

Genes are like blueprints: they contain coded messages that determine a person's characteristics or traits. They are arranged along 23 rod-like pairs of chromosomes, with one half of each pair being inherited from each parent. Each half of a chromosome pair is similar to the other, except for one pair, which determines the sex of the individual. Muscular dystrophies can be inherited in three ways:

- Autosomal dominant inheritance occurs when a child receives a normal gene from one parent and a defective gene from the other parent. Autosomal means the genetic mutation can occur on any of the 22 nonsex chromosomes in each of the body's cells. Dominant means only one parent needs to pass along the abnormal gene in order to produce the disorder. In families where one parent carries a defective gene, each child has a 50 percent chance of inheriting the gene and, therefore, the disorder. Males and females are equally at risk and the severity of the disorder can differ from person to person.

- Autosomal recessive inheritance means that both parents must carry and pass on the faulty gene. The parents each have one defective gene but are not affected by the disorder. Children in these families have a 25 percent chance of inheriting both copies of the defective gene and a 50 percent chance of inheriting one gene, and therefore, becoming a carrier, able to pass along the defect to their children. Children of either sex can be affected by this pattern of inheritance.

- X-linked (or sex-linked) recessive inheritance occurs when a mother carries the affected gene on one of her two X chromosomes and passes it to her son (males always inherit an X chromosome from their mother and a Y chromosome from their father, while daughters inherit an X chromosome from each parent). Sons of carrier mothers have a 50 percent chance of inheriting the disorder. Daughters also have a 50 percent chance of inheriting the defective gene but usually are not affected, since the healthy X chromosome they receive from their father can offset the faulty one received from their mother. Affected fathers cannot pass an X-linked disorder to their sons but their daughters will be carriers of that disorder. Carrier females occasionally can exhibit milder symptoms of MD.

How Many People Have Muscular Dystrophy?

MD occurs worldwide, affecting all races. Its incidence varies, as some forms are more common than others. Its most common form in children, Duchenne muscular dystrophy, affects approximately 1 in every 3,500–6,000 male births each year in the United States.* Some types of MD are more prevalent in certain countries and regions of the world. Many muscular dystrophies are familial, meaning there is some family history of the disease. Duchenne cases often have no prior family history. This is likely due to the large size of the dystrophin gene that is implicated in the disorder, making it a target for spontaneous mutations.

* *Centers for Disease Control and Prevention (CDC), National Center on Birth Defects and Developmental Disabilities (NCBDDD), July 17, 2013.*

How Does Muscular Dystrophy Affect Muscles?

Muscles are made up of thousands of muscle fibers. Each fiber is actually a number of individual cells that have joined together during development and are encased by an outer membrane. Muscle fibers that make up individual muscles are bound together by connective tissue.

Muscles are activated when an impulse, or signal, is sent from the brain through the spinal cord and peripheral nerves (nerves that connect the central nervous system to sensory organs and muscles) to the neuromuscular junction (the space between the nerve fiber and the muscle it activates). There, a release of the chemical acetylcholine triggers a series of events that cause the muscle to contract.

The muscle fiber membrane contains a group of proteins—called the dystrophin-glycoprotein complex (DGC)—which prevents damage as muscle fibers contract and relax. When this protective membrane is damaged, muscle fibers begin to leak the protein creatine kinase (needed for the chemical reactions that produce energy for muscle contractions) and take on excess calcium, which causes further harm. Affected muscle fibers eventually die from this damage, leading to progressive muscle degeneration.

Although MD can affect several body tissues and organs, it most prominently affects the integrity of muscle fibers. The disease causes muscle degeneration, progressive weakness, fiber death, fiber branching and splitting, phagocytosis (in which muscle fiber material is broken down and destroyed by scavenger cells), and, in some cases, chronic or permanent shortening of tendons and muscles. Also, overall muscle strength and tendon reflexes are usually lessened or lost due to the replacement of muscle by connective tissue and fat.

Are There Other Muscular Dystrophy-Like Conditions?

There are many other heritable diseases that affect the muscles, the nerves, or the neuromuscular junction. Such diseases as inflammatory myopathy, progressive muscle weakness, and cardiomyopathy (heart muscle weakness that interferes with pumping ability) may produce symptoms that are very similar to those found in some forms of MD), but they are caused by different genetic defects. The differential diagnosis for people with similar symptoms includes congenital myopathy, spinal muscular atrophy, and congenital myasthenic syndromes. The sharing of symptoms among multiple neuromuscular diseases, and the prevalence of sporadic cases in families not previously affected by MD, often makes it difficult for people with MD to obtain a quick diagnosis. Gene testing can provide a definitive diagnosis for many types of MD, but not all genes have been discovered that are responsible for some types of MD. Some individuals may have signs of MD, but carry none of the currently recognized genetic mutations. Studies of other related muscle diseases may, however, contribute to what we know about MD.

How Do the Muscular Dystrophies Differ?

There are nine major groups of the muscular dystrophies. The disorders are classified by the extent and distribution of muscle weakness, age of onset, rate of progression, severity of symptoms, and family history (including any pattern of inheritance). Although some forms of MD become apparent in infancy or childhood, others may not appear until middle age or later. Overall, incidence rates and severity vary, but each of the dystrophies causes progressive skeletal muscle deterioration, and some types affect cardiac muscle.

How Are the Muscular Dystrophies Diagnosed?

Both the individual's medical history and a complete family history should be thoroughly reviewed to determine if the muscle disease is secondary to a disease affecting other tissues or organs or is an inherited condition. It is also important to rule out any muscle weakness resulting from prior surgery, exposure to toxins, or current

Muscular Dystrophy

medications that may affect the person's functional status or rule out many acquired muscle diseases. Thorough clinical and neurological exams can rule out disorders of the central and/or peripheral nervous systems, identify any patterns of muscle weakness and atrophy, test reflex responses and coordination, and look for contractions.

Various laboratory tests may be used to confirm the diagnosis of MD.

Blood and urine tests can detect defective genes and help identify specific neuromuscular disorders. For example:

- Creatine kinase is an enzyme that leaks out of damaged muscle. Elevated creatine kinase levels may indicate muscle damage, including some forms of MD, before physical symptoms become apparent. Levels are significantly increased in the early stages of Duchenne and Becker MD. Testing can also determine if a young woman is a carrier of the disorder.

- The level of serum aldolase, an enzyme involved in the breakdown of glucose, is measured to confirm a diagnosis of skeletal muscle disease. High levels of the enzyme, which is present in most body tissues, are noted in people with MD and some forms of myopathy.

- Myoglobin is measured when injury or disease in skeletal muscle is suspected. Myoglobin is an oxygen-binding protein found in cardiac and skeletal muscle cells. High blood levels of myoglobin are found in people with MD.

- Polymerase chain reaction (PCR) can detect some mutations in the dystrophin gene. Also known as molecular diagnosis or genetic testing, PCR is a method for generating and analyzing multiple copies of a fragment of deoxyribonucleic acid (DNA).

- Serum electrophoresis is a test to determine quantities of various proteins in a person's DNA. A blood sample is placed on specially treated paper and exposed to an electric current. The charge forces the different proteins to form bands that indicate the relative proportion of each protein fragment.

Exercise tests can detect elevated rates of certain chemicals following exercise and are used to determine the nature of the MD or other muscle disorder. Some exercise tests can be performed bedside while others are done at clinics or other sites using sophisticated equipment. These tests also assess muscle strength. They are performed when the person is relaxed and in the proper position to allow technicians to measure muscle function against gravity and detect even slight muscle weakness. If weakness in respiratory muscles is suspected, respiratory capacity may be measured by having the person take a deep breath and count slowly while exhaling.

Genetic testing looks for genes known to either cause or be associated with inherited muscle disease. DNA analysis and enzyme assays can confirm the diagnosis of certain neuromuscular diseases, including MD. Genetic linkage studies can identify whether a specific genetic marker on a chromosome and a disease are inherited together. They are particularly useful in studying families with members in different generations who are affected. An exact molecular diagnosis is necessary for some of the treatment strategies that are currently being developed. Advances in genetic testing include whole exome and whole genome sequencing, which will enable people to have all of their genes screened at once for disease-causing mutations, rather than have just one gene or several genes tested at a time. Exome sequencing looks at the part of the individual's genetic material, or genome, that "code for" (or translate) into proteins.

Genetic counseling can help parents who have a family history of MD determine if they are carrying one of the mutated genes that cause the disorder. Two tests can be used to help expectant parents find out if their child is affected.

- Amniocentesis, done usually at 14–16 weeks of pregnancy, tests a sample of the amniotic fluid in the womb for genetic defects (the fluid and the fetus have the same DNA). Under local anesthesia, a thin needle is inserted through the woman's abdomen and into the womb. About 20 milliliters of fluid (roughly 4 teaspoons) is withdrawn and sent to a lab for evaluation. Test results often take 1–2 weeks.

- Chorionic villus sampling, or CVS, involves the removal and testing of a very small sample of the placenta during early pregnancy. The sample, which contains the same DNA as the fetus, is removed by catheter or a fine needle inserted through the cervix or by a fine needle inserted through the abdomen. The tissue is tested for genetic changes identified in an affected family member. Results are usually available within 2 weeks.

Diagnostic imaging can help determine the specific nature of a disease or condition. One such type of imaging, called magnetic resonance imaging (MRI), is used to examine muscle quality, any atrophy or abnormalities in size, and fatty replacement of muscle tissue, as well as to monitor disease progression. MRI scanning equipment creates a strong magnetic field around the body. Radio waves are then passed through the body to trigger a resonance signal that can be detected at different angles within the body. A computer processes this resonance into either a three-dimensional picture or a two-dimensional "slice" of the tissue being scanned. MRI is a noninvasive, painless procedure. Other forms of diagnostic imaging for MD include phosphorus magnetic resonance spectroscopy, which measures cellular response to exercise and the amount of energy available to muscle fiber, and ultrasound imaging (also known as sonography), which uses high-frequency sound waves to obtain images inside the body. The sound wave echoes are recorded and displayed on a computer screen as a real-time visual image. Ultrasound may be used to measure muscle bulk. MRI scans of the brain may be useful in diagnosing certain forms of congenital muscular dystrophy where structural brain abnormalities are typically present.

Muscle biopsies are used for diagnostic purposes, and in research settings, to monitor the course of disease and treatment effectiveness. Using local or general anesthesia, a physician or surgeon can remove a small sample of muscle for analysis. The sample may be gathered either surgically, through a slit made in the skin, or by needle biopsy, in which a thin hollow needle is inserted through the skin and into the muscle. A small piece of muscle remains in the hollow needle when it is removed from the body. The muscle specimen is stained and examined to determine whether the person has muscle disease, nerve disease (neuropathy), inflammation, or another myopathy. Muscle biopsies can sometimes also assist in carrier testing. With the advent of accurate molecular techniques, muscle biopsy is less frequently needed to diagnose muscular dystrophies. Muscle biopsy is still necessary to make the diagnosis in most of the acquired muscle diseases.

Immunofluorescence testing can detect specific proteins such as dystrophin within muscle fibers. Following biopsy, fluorescent markers are used to stain the sample that has the protein of interest.

Electron microscopy can identify changes in subcellular components of muscle fibers. Electron microscopy can also identify changes that characterize cell death, mutations in muscle cell mitochondria, and an increase in connective tissue seen in muscle diseases such as

MD. Changes in muscle fibers that are evident in a rare form of distal MD can be seen using an electron microscope.

Neurophysiology studies can identify physical and/or chemical changes in the nervous system.

- Nerve conduction velocity studies measure the speed and strength with which an electrical signal travels along a nerve. A small surface electrode stimulates a nerve, and a recording electrode detects the resulting electrical signal either elsewhere on the same nerve or on a muscle controlled by that nerve. The response can be assessed to determine whether nerve damage is present.

- Repetitive stimulation studies involve electrically stimulating a motor nerve several times in a row to assess the function of the neuromuscular junction. The recording electrode is placed on a muscle controlled by the stimulated nerve, as is done for a routine motor nerve conduction study.

- Electromyography (EMG) can record muscle fiber and motor unit activity. A tiny needle containing an electrode is inserted through the skin into the muscle. The electrical activity detected in the muscle can be displayed on a monitor, and can also be heard when played through a speaker. Results may reveal electrical activity characteristic of MD or other neuromuscular disorders.

How Are the Muscular Dystrophies Treated?

There is no specific treatment that can stop or reverse the progression of any form of MD. All forms of MD are genetic and cannot be prevented at this time, aside from the use of prenatal screening interventions. However, available treatments are aimed at keeping the person independent for as long as possible and prevent complications that result from weakness, reduced mobility, and cardiac and respiratory difficulties. Treatment may involve a combination of approaches, including physical therapy, drug therapy, and surgery. The available treatments are sometimes quite effective and can have a significant impact on life expectancy and quality of life.

Assisted ventilation is often needed to treat respiratory muscle weakness that accompanies many forms of MD, especially in the later stages. Air that includes supplemental oxygen is fed through a flexible mask (or, in some cases, a tube inserted through the esophagus

Muscular Dystrophy

and into the lungs) to help the lungs inflate fully. Since respiratory difficulty may be most extreme at night, some individuals may need overnight ventilation. Many people prefer noninvasive ventilation, in which a mask worn over the face is connected by a tube to a machine that generates intermittent bursts of forced air that may include supplemental oxygen. Some people with Duchenne MD, especially those who are overweight, may develop obstructive sleep apnea and require nighttime ventilation. Individuals on a ventilator may also require the use of a gastric feeding tube.

Drug therapy may be prescribed to delay muscle degeneration. Corticosteroids such as prednisone can slow the rate of muscle deterioration in Duchenne MD and help children retain strength and prolong independent walking by as much as several years. However, these medicines have side effects such as weight gain, facial changes, loss of linear (height) growth, and bone fragility that can be especially troubling in children. Immunosuppressive drugs such as cyclosporine and azathioprine can delay some damage to dying muscle cells. Drugs that may provide short-term relief from myotonia (muscle spasms and weakness) include mexiletine; phenytoin; baclofen, which blocks signals sent from the spinal cord to contract the muscles; dantrolene, which interferes with the process of muscle contraction; and quinine. The U.D. Food and Drug Administration (FDA) has granted accelerated approval of the drug Exondys 51 to treat individuals who have a confirmed mutation of the dystrophin gene amenable to exon 15 skipping. The accelerated approval means the drug can be administered to selected individuals who meet the rare disease criteria while the company works on additional trials to learn more about the effectiveness of the drug. (Drugs for myotonia may not be effective in myotonic MD but work well for myotonia congenita, a genetic neuromuscular disorder characterized by the slow relaxation of the muscles.) Respiratory infections may be treated with antibiotics.

Physical therapy can help prevent deformities, improve movement, and keep muscles as flexible and strong as possible. Options include passive stretching, postural correction, and exercise. A program is developed to meet the individual's needs. Therapy should begin as soon as possible following diagnosis, before there is joint or muscle tightness.

- Passive stretching can increase joint flexibility and prevent contractures that restrict movement and cause loss of function. When done correctly, passive stretching is not painful. The therapist or other trained health professional slowly moves the joint as far as possible and maintains the position for about 30 seconds. The movement is repeated several times during the session. Passive stretching on children may be easier following a warm bath or shower.

- Regular, moderate exercise can help people with MD maintain range of motion and muscle strength, prevent muscle atrophy, and delay the development of contractures. Individuals with a weakened diaphragm can learn coughing and deep breathing exercises that are designed to keep the lungs fully expanded.

- Postural correction is used to counter the muscle weakness, contractures, and spinal irregularities that force individuals with MD into uncomfortable positions. When possible, individuals should sit upright, with feet at a 90-degree angle to the floor. Pillows and foam wedges can help keep the person upright, distribute weight evenly, and cause the legs to straighten. Armrests should be at the proper height to provide support and prevent leaning.

- Support aids such as wheelchairs, splints and braces, other orthopedic appliances, and overhead bed bars (trapezes) can help maintain mobility. Braces are used to help stretch muscles and provide support while keeping the person ambulatory. Spinal supports can help delay scoliosis. Night splints, when used in conjunction with passive stretching, can delay contractures. Orthotic devices such as standing frames and swivel walkers help people remain standing or walking for as long as possible, which promotes better circulation and improves calcium retention in bones.

- Repeated low-frequency bursts of electrical stimulation to the thigh muscles may produce a slight increase in strength in some boys with Duchenne MD, though this therapy has not been proven to be effective.

Occupational therapy may help some people deal with progressive weakness and loss of mobility. Some individuals may need to learn new job skills or new ways to perform tasks while other persons may need to change jobs. Assistive technology may include modifications to home and workplace settings and the use of motorized wheelchairs, wheelchair accessories, and adaptive utensils.

Muscular Dystrophy

Speech therapy may help individuals whose facial and throat muscles have weakened. Individuals can learn to use special communication devices, such as a computer with voice synthesizer

Dietary changes have not been shown to slow the progression of MD. Proper nutrition is essential, however, for overall health. Limited mobility or inactivity resulting from muscle weakness can contribute to obesity, dehydration, and constipation. A high-fiber, high-protein, low-calorie diet combined with recommended fluid intake may help. Feeding techniques can help people with MD who have a swallowing disorder and find it difficult to pass from or liquid from the mouth to the stomach.

Corrective surgery is often performed to ease complications from MD.

- Tendon or muscle-release surgery is recommended when a contracture becomes severe enough to lock a joint or greatly impair movement. The procedure, which involves lengthening a tendon or muscle to free movement, is usually performed under general anesthesia. Rehabilitation includes the use of braces and physical therapy to strengthen muscles and maintain the restored range of motion. A period of immobility is often needed after these orthopedic procedures, thus the benefits of the procedure should be weighed against the risk of this period of immobility, as the latter may lead to a setback.

- Individuals with either Emery-Dreifuss or MD may require a pacemaker at some point to treat cardiac problems.

- Surgery to reduce the pain and postural imbalance caused by scoliosis may help some individuals. Scoliosis occurs when the muscles that support the spine begin to weaken and can no longer keep the spine straight. The spinal curve, if too great, can interfere with breathing and posture, causing pain. One or more metal rods may need to be attached to the spine to increase strength and improve posture. Another option is spinal fusion, in which bone is inserted between the vertebrae in the spine and allowed to grow, fusing the vertebrae together to increase spinal stability.

- People with myotonic dystrophy often develop cataracts, a clouding of the lens of the eye that blocks light. Cataract surgery involves removing the cloudy lens to improve the person's ability to see.

What Is the Prognosis for Muscular Dystrophy?

The prognosis varies according to the type of MD and the speed of progression. Some types are mild and progress very slowly, allowing normal life expectancy, while others are more severe and result in functional disability and loss of ambulation. Life expectancy often depends on the degree of muscle weakness, as well as the presence and severity of respiratory and/or cardiac complications.

Chapter 16

Spina Bifida

The human nervous system develops from a small, specialized plate of cells along the back of an embryo (called the neural plate). Early in development, the edges of this plate begin to curl up toward each other, creating the neural tube—a narrow sheath that closes to form the brain and spinal cord of the embryo. As development progresses, the top of the tube becomes the brain and the remainder becomes the spinal cord. This process is usually complete by the 28th day of pregnancy. But if problems occur during this process, the result can be brain disorders called neural tube defects, including spina bifida.

What Is Spina Bifida?

Spina bifida, which literally means "cleft spine," is characterized by the incomplete development of the brain, spinal cord, and/or meninges (the protective covering around the brain and spinal cord). It is the most common neural tube defect in the United States—affecting 1,500–2,000 of the more than 4 million babies born in the country each year. An estimated 166,000 individuals with spina bifida live in the United States.

This chapter includes text excerpted from "Spina Bifida Fact Sheet," National Institute of Neurological Disorders and Stroke (NINDS), July 6, 2018.

What Are the Different Types of Spina Bifida?

There are four types of spina bifida:

1. Occulta
2. Closed neural tube defects
3. Meningocele
4. Myelomeningocele

Occulta is the mildest and most common form in which one or more vertebrae are malformed. The name "occulta," which means "hidden," indicates that a layer of skin covers the malformation or opening in the vertebrae. This form of spina bifida, present in 10–20 percent of the general population, rarely causes disability or symptoms.

Closed neural tube defects make up the second type of spina bifida. This form consists of a diverse group of defects in which the spinal cord is marked by malformations of fat, bone, or meninges. In most instances there are few or no symptoms; in others, the malformation causes incomplete paralysis with urinary and bowel dysfunction.

In the third type, meningocele, spinal fluid, and meninges protrude through an abnormal vertebral opening; the malformation contains no neural elements and may or may not be covered by a layer of skin. Some individuals with meningocele may have few or no symptoms while others may experience such symptoms as complete paralysis with bladder and bowel dysfunction.

Myelomeningocele, the fourth form, is the most severe and occurs when the spinal cord/neural elements are exposed through the opening in the spine, resulting in partial or complete paralysis of the parts of the body below the spinal opening. The impairment may be so severe that the affected individual is unable to walk and may have bladder and bowel dysfunction.

What Causes Spina Bifida

The exact cause of spina bifida remains a mystery. No one knows what disrupts complete closure of the neural tube, causing this malformation to develop. Scientists suspect the factors that cause spina bifida are multiple: genetic, nutritional, and environmental factors all play a role. Research studies indicate that insufficient intake of folic acid—a common B vitamin—in the mother's diet is a key factor in causing spina bifida and other neural tube defects. Prenatal vitamins typically contain folic acid as well as other vitamins.

What Are the Signs and Symptoms of Spina Bifida?

The symptoms of spina bifida vary from person to person, depending on the type and level of involvement. Closed neural tube defects are often recognized early in life due to an abnormal tuft or clump of hair or a small dimple or birthmark on the skin at the site of the spinal malformation.

Meningocele and myelomeningocele generally involve a fluid-filled sac—visible on the back—protruding from the spinal canal. In meningocele, the sac may be covered by a thin layer of skin. In most cases of myelomeningocele, there is no layer of skin covering the sac and an area of abnormally developed spinal cord tissue is usually exposed.

What Are the Complications of Spina Bifida?

Complications of spina bifida can range from minor physical problems with little functional impairment to severe physical and mental disabilities. It is important to note, however, that most people with spina bifida are of normal intelligence. Spina bifida's impact is determined by the size and location of the malformation, whether it covered, and which spinal nerves are involved. All nerves located below the malformation are affected to some degree. Therefore, the higher the malformation occurs on the back, the greater the amount of nerve damage and loss of muscle function and sensation.

In addition to abnormal sensation and paralysis, another neurological complication associated with spina bifida is Chiari II malformation—a condition common in children with myelomeningocele—in which the brain stem and the cerebellum (hindbrain) protrude downward into the spinal canal or neck area. This condition can lead to compression of the spinal cord and cause a variety of symptoms including difficulties with feeding, swallowing, and breathing control; choking; and changes in upper arm function (stiffness, weakness).

Chiari II malformation may also result in a blockage of cerebrospinal fluid, causing a condition called hydrocephalus, which is an abnormal buildup of cerebrospinal fluid in and around the brain. Cerebrospinal fluid is a clear liquid that surrounds the brain and spinal cord. The buildup of fluid puts damaging pressure on these structures. Hydrocephalus is commonly treated by surgically implanting a shunt—a hollow tube—in the brain to drain the excess fluid into the abdomen.

Some newborns with myelomeningocele may develop meningitis, an infection in the meninges. Meningitis may cause brain injury and can be life threatening.

Children with both myelomeningocele and hydrocephalus may have learning disabilities, including difficulty paying attention, problems with language and reading comprehension, and trouble learning math.

Additional problems such as latex allergies, skin problems, gastrointestinal conditions, and depression may occur as children with spina bifida get older.

How Is Spina Bifida Diagnosed?

In most cases, spina bifida is diagnosed prenatally, or before birth. However, some mild cases may go unnoticed until after birth (postnatal). Very mild forms (spinal bifida occulta), in which there are no symptoms, may never be detected.

Prenatal Diagnosis

The most common screening methods used to look for spina bifida during pregnancy are second trimester (16–18 weeks of gestation) maternal serum alpha-fetoprotein (MSAFP) screening and fetal ultrasound. The MSAFP screen measures the level of a protein called alpha-fetoprotein (AFP), which is made naturally by the fetus and placenta. During pregnancy, a small amount of AFP normally crosses the placenta and enters the mother's bloodstream. If abnormally high levels of this protein appear in the mother's bloodstream, it may indicate that the fetus has an "open" (not skin-covered) neural tube defect. The MSAFP test, however, is not specific for spina bifida and requires correct gestational dates to be most accurate; it cannot definitively determine that there is a problem with the fetus. If a high level of AFP is detected, the doctor may request additional testing, such as an ultrasound or amniocentesis to help determine the cause.

The second trimester MSAFP screen described above may be performed alone or as part of a larger, multiple-marker screen. Multiple-marker screens look not only for neural tube defects, but also for other birth defects, including Down syndrome and other chromosomal abnormalities. First trimester screens for chromosomal abnormalities also exist but signs of spina bifida are not evident until the second trimester when the MSAFP screening is performed.

Amniocentesis—an exam in which the doctor removes samples of fluid from the amniotic sac that surrounds the fetus—may also be used to diagnose spina bifida. Although amniocentesis cannot reveal the severity of spina bifida, finding high levels of AFP and other proteins may indicate that the disorder is present.

Postnatal Diagnosis

Mild cases of spina bifida (occulta, closed) not diagnosed during prenatal testing may be detected postnatally by plain film X-ray examination. Individuals with the more severe forms of spina bifida often have muscle weakness in their feet, hips, and legs that result in deformities that may be present at birth. Doctors may use magnetic resonance imaging (MRI) or a computed tomography (CT) scan to get a clearer view of the spinal cord and vertebrae. If hydrocephalus is suspected, the doctor may request a CT scan and/or X-ray of the skull to look for extra cerebrospinal fluid inside the brain.

How Is Spina Bifida Treated?

There is no cure for spina bifida. The nerve tissue that is damaged cannot be repaired nor can function be restored to the damaged nerves. Treatment depends on the type and severity of the disorder. Generally, children with the mildest form need no treatment, although some may require surgery as they grow.

The key early priorities for treating myelomeningocele are to prevent infection from developing in the exposed nerves and tissue through the spinal defect, and to protect the exposed nerves and structures from additional trauma. Typically, a child born with spina bifida will have surgery to close the defect and minimize the risk of infection or further trauma within the first few days of life.

Selected medical centers continue to perform fetal surgery for treatment of myelomeningocele through a National Institutes of Health (NIH) experimental protocol (Management of Myelomeningocele Study, or MOMS). Fetal surgery is performed in utero (within the uterus) and involves opening the mother's abdomen and uterus and sewing shut the abnormal opening over the developing baby's spinal cord. Some doctors believe the earlier the defect is corrected, the better the baby's outcome. Although the procedure cannot restore lost neurological function, it may prevent additional loss from occurring.

The surgery is considered experimental and there are risks to the fetus as well as to the mother. The major risks to the fetus are those that might occur if the surgery stimulates premature delivery, such as organ immaturity, brain hemorrhage, and death. Risks to the mother include infection, blood loss leading to the need for transfusion, gestational diabetes, and weight gain due to bed rest.

Still, the benefits of fetal surgery are promising, and include less exposure of the vulnerable spinal nerve tissue and bone to the intrauterine environment, in particular, the amniotic fluid, which is considered toxic. As an added benefit, doctors have discovered that the procedure may affect the way the fetal hindbrain develops in utero, decreasing the severity of certain complications—such as Chiari II and hydrocephalus—and in some cases, eliminating the need for surgery to implant a shunt.

Twenty to fifty percent of children with myelomeningocele develop a condition called progressive tethering, or tethered cord syndrome; their spinal cord becomes fastened to an immovable structure—such as overlying membranes and vertebrae—causing the spinal cord to become abnormally stretched with the child's growth. This condition can cause loss of muscle function to the legs, as well as changes in bowel and bladder function. Early surgery on a tethered spinal cord may allow the child to return to their baseline level of functioning and prevent further neurological deterioration.

Some children will need subsequent surgeries to manage problems with the feet, hips, or spine. Individuals with hydrocephalus generally will require additional surgeries to replace the shunt, which can be outgrown or become clogged or infected.

Some individuals with spina bifida require assistive devices such as braces, crutches, or wheelchairs. The location of the malformation on the spine often indicates the type of assistive devices needed. Children with a defect high on the spine will have more extensive paralysis and will often require a wheelchair, while those with a defect lower on the spine may be able to use crutches, leg braces, or walkers. Beginning special exercises for the legs and feet at an early age may help prepare the child for walking with those braces or crutches when he or she is older.

Treatment for bladder and bowel problems typically begins soon after birth, and may include bladder catheterizations and bowel management regimens.

Can Spina Bifida Be Prevented?

Folic acid, also called folate, is an important vitamin in the development of a healthy fetus. Although taking this vitamin cannot guarantee having a healthy baby, it can help. Some studies have shown that by adding folic acid to their diets, women of childbearing age significantly reduce the risk of having a child with a neural tube defect, such as spina bifida. Therefore, it is recommended that all women of childbearing age consume 400 micrograms of folic acid daily. Foods high in folic acid include dark green vegetables, egg yolks, and some fruits. Many foods—such as some breakfast cereals, enriched breads, flours, pastas, rice, and other grain products—are now fortified with folic acid. Many multivitamins contain the recommended dosage of folic acid as well.

Women who already have a child with spina bifida, who have spina bifida themselves, or who have already had a pregnancy affected by any neural tube defect are at greater risk of having another child with spina bifida or another neural tube defect; 5–10 times the risk to the general population. These women may benefit from taking a higher daily dose of folic acid before they consider becoming pregnant.

What Is the Prognosis for Spina Bifida?

Children with spina bifida can lead active lives. Prognosis, activity, and participation depend on the number and severity of abnormalities and associated personal and environmental factors. Most children with the disorder have normal intelligence and can walk, often with assistive devices. If learning problems develop, appropriate educational interventions are helpful.

Chapter 17

Sensory Disabilities

Chapter Contents

Section 17.1—Hearing Loss... 142
Section 17.2—Hearing Loss in Children 146
Section 17.3—Vision Loss... 150
Section 17.4—Deaf-Blindness 165

Section 17.1

Hearing Loss

> This section includes text excerpted from "Hearing Loss and Older Adults," National Institute on Deafness and Other Communication Disorders (NIDCD), March 2016.

What Is Hearing Loss?

Hearing loss is a sudden or gradual decrease in how well you can hear. It is one of the most common conditions affecting older and elderly adults. Approximately one in three people between the ages of 65 and 74 have hearing loss and nearly half of those older than 75 have difficulty hearing. Having trouble hearing can make it hard to understand and follow a doctor's advice, to respond to warnings, and to hear doorbells and alarms. It can also make it hard to enjoy talking with friends and family. All of this can be frustrating, embarrassing, and even dangerous.

What Should I Do If I Have Trouble Hearing?

Hearing problems can be serious. The most important thing you can do if you think you have a hearing problem is to seek professional advice. There are several ways to do this. You can start with your primary care physician, an otolaryngologist, an audiologist, or a hearing aid specialist. Each has a different type of training and expertise. Each can be an important part of your hearing healthcare.

An otolaryngologist, is a doctor who specializes in diagnosing and treating diseases of the ear, nose, and throat. An otolaryngologist will try to find out why you're having trouble hearing and offer treatment options. He or she may also refer you to another hearing professional, an audiologist. An audiologist has specialized training in identifying and measuring the type and degree of hearing loss and recommending treatment options. Audiologists also may be licensed to fit hearing aids. Another source of hearing aids is a hearing aid specialist, who is licensed by a state to conduct and evaluate basic hearing tests, offer counseling, and fit and test hearing aids.

Why Am I Losing My Hearing?

Hearing loss happens for different reasons. Many people lose their hearing slowly as they age. This condition is known as presbycusis.

Doctors do not know why presbycusis affects some people more than others, but it seems to run in families. Another reason for hearing loss with aging may be years of exposure to loud noise. This condition is known as noise-induced hearing loss. Many construction workers, farmers, musicians, airport workers, yard and tree care workers, and people in the armed forces have hearing problems even in their younger and middle years because of too much exposure to loud noise.

Hearing loss can also be caused by viral or bacterial infections, heart conditions or stroke, head injuries, tumors, and certain medicines.

What Treatments and Devices Can Help Hearing Loss?

Your treatment will depend on your hearing loss, so some treatments will work better for you than others. There are a number of devices and aids that can improve hearing loss. Here are the most common ones:

- Hearing aids are electronic instruments you wear in or behind your ear. They make sounds louder. Things sound different when you wear a hearing aid, but an audiologist or hearing aid specialist can help you get used to it. To find the hearing aid that works best for you, you may have to try more than one. Ask your audiologist or hearing specialist whether you can have a trial period with a few different hearing aids. Both of you can work together until you are comfortable.

- Cochlear implants are small electronic devices surgically implanted in the inner ear that help provide a sense of sound to people who are profoundly deaf or hard-of-hearing. If your hearing loss is severe, your doctor may recommend a cochlear implant in one ear or both.

- Assistive listening devices include telephone and cell phone amplifying devices, smartphone or tablet "apps," and closed circuit systems (induction coil loops) in places of worship, theaters, and auditoriums.

- Lip reading or speech reading is another option that helps people with hearing problems follow conversational speech. People who use this method pay close attention to others when they talk, by watching how the speaker's mouth and body move.

Can My Friends and Family Help Me with My Hearing Loss?

Yes. You and your family can work together to make hearing easier. Here are some things you can do:

- Tell your friends and family about your hearing loss. They need to know that hearing is hard for you. The more you tell the people you spend time with, the more they can help you.
- Ask your friends and family to face you when they talk so that you can see their faces. If you watch their faces move and see their expressions, it may help you to understand them better.
- Ask people to speak louder, but not shout. Tell them they do not have to talk slowly, just more clearly.
- Turn off the TV or the radio if you aren't actively listening to it.
- Be aware of noise around you that can make hearing more difficult. When you go to a restaurant, do not sit near the kitchen or near a band playing music. Background noise makes it hard to hear people talk.

Working together to hear better may be tough on everyone for a while. It will take time for you to get used to watching people as they talk and for people to get used to speaking louder and more clearly. Be patient and continue to work together. Hearing better is worth the effort.

Are There Different Styles of Hearing Aids?

There are three basic styles of hearing aids. The styles differ by size, their placement on or inside the ear, and the degree to which they amplify sound.

Behind-the-ear (BTE) hearing aids consist of a hard plastic case worn behind the ear and connected to a plastic earmold that fits inside the outer ear. The electronic parts are held in the case behind the ear. Sound travels from the hearing aid through the earmold and into the ear. BTE aids are used by people of all ages for mild to profound hearing loss. A new kind of BTE aid is an open-fit hearing aid. Small, open-fit aids fit behind the ear completely, with only a narrow tube inserted into the ear canal, enabling the canal to remain open. For this reason, open-fit hearing aids may be a good choice for people who experience a buildup of earwax, since this type of aid is less likely to

Sensory Disabilities

be damaged by such substances. In addition, some people may prefer the open-fit hearing aid because their perception of their voice does not sound "plugged up."

In-the-ear (ITE) hearing aids fit completely inside the outer ear and are used for mild to severe hearing loss. The case holding the electronic components is made of hard plastic. Some ITE aids may have certain added features installed, such as a telecoil. A telecoil is a small magnetic coil that allows users to receive sound through the circuitry of the hearing aid, rather than through its microphone. This makes it easier to hear conversations over the telephone. A telecoil also helps people hear in public facilities that have installed special sound systems, called induction loop systems. Induction loop systems can be found in many churches, schools, airports, and auditoriums. ITE aids usually are not worn by young children because the casings need to be replaced often as the ear grows.

Canal aids fit into the ear canal and are available in two styles. The in-the-canal (ITC) hearing aid is made to fit the size and shape of a person's ear canal. A completely-in-canal (CIC) hearing aid is nearly hidden in the ear canal. Both types are used for mild to moderately severe hearing loss.

Because they are small, canal aids may be difficult for a person to adjust and remove. In addition, canal aids have less space available for batteries and additional devices, such as a telecoil. They usually are not recommended for young children or for people with severe to profound hearing loss because their reduced size limits their power and volume.

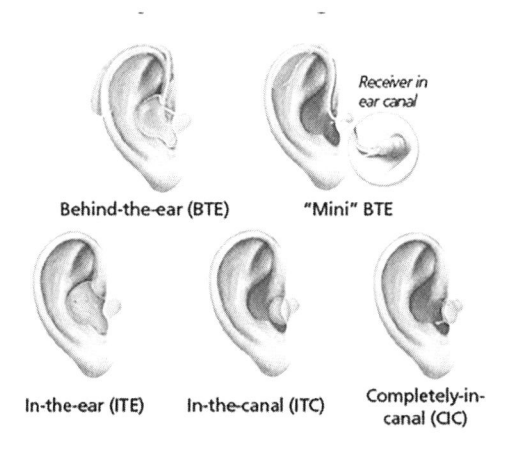

Figure 17.1. *Styles of Hearing Aids*

Are New Types of Hearing Aids Available?

Although they work differently than the hearing aids described above, implantable hearing aids are designed to help increase the transmission of sound vibrations entering the inner ear. A middle ear implant (MEI) is a small device attached to one of the bones of the middle ear. Rather than amplifying the sound traveling to the eardrum, an MEI moves these bones directly. Both techniques have the net result of strengthening sound vibrations entering the inner ear so that they can be detected by individuals with sensorineural hearing loss. A bone-anchored hearing aid (BAHA) is a small device that attaches to the bone behind the ear. The device transmits sound vibrations directly to the inner ear through the skull, bypassing the middle ear. BAHAs are generally used by individuals with middle ear problems or deafness in one ear. Because surgery is required to implant either of these devices, many hearing specialists feel that the benefits may not outweigh the risks.

Section 17.2

Hearing Loss in Children

This section includes text excerpted from "Basics about Hearing Loss in Children," Centers for Disease Control and Prevention (CDC), April 11, 2018.

Hearing loss can affect a child's ability to develop speech, language, and social skills. The earlier children with hearing loss start getting services, the more likely they are to reach their full potential. If you think that a child might have hearing loss, ask the child's doctor for a hearing screening as soon as possible. Don't wait!

Signs and Symptoms

The signs and symptoms of hearing loss are different for each child. If you think that your child might have hearing loss, ask the child's doctor for a hearing screening as soon as possible. Don't wait!

Sensory Disabilities

Even if a child has passed a hearing screening before, it is important to look out for the following signs.

Signs in Babies

- Does not startle at loud noises
- Does not turn to the source of a sound after six months of age
- Does not say single words, such as "dada" or "mama" by one year of age
- Turns head when he or she sees you but not if you only call out his or her name. This sometimes is mistaken for not paying attention or just ignoring, but could be the result of a partial or complete hearing loss.
- Seems to hear some sounds but not others

Signs in Children

- Speech is delayed
- Speech is not clear
- Does not follow directions. This sometimes is mistaken for not paying attention or just ignoring, but could be the result of a partial or complete hearing loss.
- Often says, "Huh?"
- Turns the TV volume up too high

Babies and children should reach milestones in how they play, learn, communicate and act. A delay in any of these milestones could be a sign of hearing loss or other developmental problem.

Screening and Diagnosis

Hearing screening can tell if a child might have hearing loss. Hearing screening is easy and is not painful. In fact, babies are often asleep while being screened. It takes a very short time—usually only a few minutes.

Babies

All babies should have a hearing screening no later than one month of age. Most babies have their hearing screened while still in the hospital. If a baby does not pass a hearing screening, it's very important to get a full hearing test as soon as possible, but no later than three months of age.

Children

Children should have their hearing tested before they enter school or any time there is a concern about the child's hearing. Children who do not pass the hearing screening need to get a full hearing test as soon as possible.

Treatments and Intervention Services

No single treatment or intervention is the answer for every person or family. Good treatment plans will include close monitoring, follow-ups, and any changes needed along the way. There are many different types of communication options for children with hearing loss and for their families. Some of these options include:

- Learning other ways to communicate, such as sign language
- Technology to help with communication, such as hearing aids and cochlear implants
- Medicine and surgery to correct some types of hearing loss
- Family support services

Causes and Risk Factors

Hearing loss can happen any time during life—from before birth to adulthood.

Following are some of the things that can increase the chance that a child will have hearing loss:

- A genetic cause: About one out of two cases of hearing loss in babies is due to genetic causes. Some babies with a genetic cause for their hearing loss might have family members who also have a hearing loss. About one out of two babies with genetic hearing loss have a "syndrome." This means they have other conditions in addition to the hearing loss, such as Down syndrome or Usher syndrome.
- One out of four cases of hearing loss in babies is due to maternal infections during pregnancy, complications after birth, and head trauma. For example, the child:
  - Was exposed to infection, such as, before birth

Sensory Disabilities

- Spent five days or more in a hospital neonatal intensive care unit (NICU) or had complications while in the NICU
- Needed a special procedure like a blood transfusion to treat bad jaundice
- Has head, face or ears shaped or formed in a different way than usual
- Has a condition like a neurological disorder that may be associated with hearing loss
- Had an infection around the brain and spinal cord called meningitis
- Received a bad injury to the head that required a hospital stay
- For about one out of four babies born with hearing loss, the cause is unknown.

Prevention

Following are tips for parents to help prevent hearing loss in their children:

- Have a healthy pregnancy
- Learn how to during pregnancy
- Make sure your child gets all the regular childhood vaccines
- Keep your child away from high noise levels, such as from very loud toys

Get Help

- If you think that your child might have hearing loss, ask the child's doctor for a hearing screening as soon as possible. Don't wait!
- If your child does not pass a hearing screening, ask the child's doctor for a full hearing test as soon as possible.
- If your child has hearing loss, talk to the child's doctor about treatment and intervention services.

Hearing loss can affect a child's ability to develop speech, language, and social skills. The earlier children with hearing loss start getting services, the more likely they are to reach their full potential. If you are a parent and you suspect your child has hearing loss, trust your instincts and speak with your child's doctor.

Section 17.3

Vision Loss

> The section includes text excerpted from the following sources: Text in this section begins with excerpts from "The Burden of Vision Loss," Centers for Disease Control and Prevention (CDC), October 30, 2017; Text under the heading "Age-Related Macular Degeneration" is excerpted from "Facts about Age-Related Macular Degeneration," National Eye Institute (NEI), September 2015; Text under the heading "Glaucoma" is excerpted from "Facts about Glaucoma," National Eye Institute (NEI), September 2015; Text under the heading "Cataract" is excerpted from "Facts about Cataract," National Eye Institute (NEI), September 2015; Text under the heading "Diabetic Retinopathy" is excerpted from "Facts about Diabetic Eye Disease," National Eye Institute (NEI), September 2015.

In 2015, a total of 1.02 million people were blind, and approximately 3.22 million people in the United States had vision impairment (VI), as defined by the best-corrected visual acuity in the better-seeing eye. In addition, 8.2 million people had VI due to uncorrected refractive error. By 2050, the numbers of these conditions are projected to double to approximately 2.01 million people who are blind, or having VI of 20/200 or worse, 6.95 million people with VI, and 16.4 million with VI due to uncorrected refractive error.

Through 2050, the number of people with VI are projected to continue to increase and remain higher among non-Hispanic white individuals compared with other racial/ethnic groups for both men and women. In 2050, the second highest number of VI cases is projected to shift from African American to Hispanic adults.

Vision Loss among Top Ten Disabilities

An analysis of the 1999 Survey of Income and Program Participation (SIPP) revealed blindness or vision problems to be among the top

10 disabilities among adults aged 18 years and older. Vision loss has serious consequences for the individual as well as those who care for and about people who have compromised vision because it impedes the ability to read, drive, prepare meals, watch television, and attend to personal affairs. Reduced vision among mature adults has been shown to result in social isolation, family stress, and ultimately a greater tendency to experience other health conditions or die prematurely.

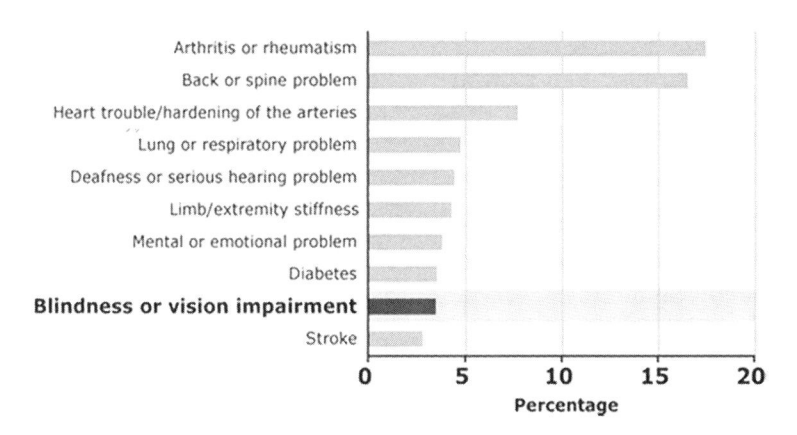

Figure 17.2. *Prevalence of Disabilities and Associated Health Conditions among Adults in United States*

Estimated Growth in Population

During the next three decades, the population of adults with vision impairment and age-related eye diseases is estimated to double because of the rapidly aging U.S. population. In addition, the epidemic of diabetes, as well as other chronic diseases, will contribute to an increasing population of people who experience vision loss.

Age-Related Macular Degeneration

Age-related macular degeneration (AMD) is a common eye condition and a leading cause of vision loss among people age 50 and older. It causes damage to the macula, a small spot near the center of the retina and the part of the eye needed for sharp, central vision, which lets us see objects that are straight ahead.

In some people, AMD advances so slowly that vision loss does not occur for a long time. In others, the disease progresses faster and may lead to a loss of vision in one or both eyes. As AMD progresses, a blurred area near the center of vision is a common symptom. Over time, the blurred area may grow larger or you may develop blank spots in your central vision. Objects also may not appear to be as bright as they used to be.

AMD by itself does not lead to complete blindness, with no ability to see. However, the loss of central vision in AMD can interfere with simple everyday activities, such as the ability to see faces, drive, read, write, or do close work, such as cooking or fixing things around the house.

The Macula

The macula is made up of millions of light-sensing cells that provide sharp, central vision. It is the most sensitive part of the retina, which is located at the back of the eye. The retina turns light into electrical signals and then sends these electrical signals through the optic nerve to the brain, where they are translated into the images we see. When the macula is damaged, the center of your field of view may appear blurry, distorted, or dark.

Who Is at Risk?

Age is a major risk factor for AMD. The disease is most likely to occur after age 60, but it can occur earlier. Other risk factors for AMD include:

- **Smoking.** Research shows that smoking doubles the risk of AMD.
- **Race.** AMD is more common among Caucasians than among African-Americans or Hispanics/Latinos.
- **Family history and genetics.** People with a family history of AMD are at higher risk. At last count, researchers had identified nearly 20 genes that can affect the risk of developing AMD. Many more genetic risk factors are suspected. You may see offers for genetic testing for AMD. Because AMD is influenced by so many genes plus environmental factors such as smoking and nutrition, there are currently no genetic tests that can diagnose AMD, or predict with certainty who will develop it. The American Academy of Ophthalmology (AAO) currently recommends against routine genetic testing for AMD, and insurance generally does not cover such testing.

Sensory Disabilities

How Is Age-Related Macular Degeneration Detected?

The early and intermediate stages of AMD usually start without symptoms. Only a comprehensive dilated eye exam can detect AMD. The eye exam may include the following:

- **Visual acuity test.** This eye chart measures how well you see at distances.

- **Dilated eye exam.** Your eye care professional places drops in your eyes to widen or dilate the pupils. This provides a better view of the back of your eye. Using a special magnifying lens, he or she then looks at your retina and optic nerve for signs of AMD and other eye problems.

- **Amsler grid.** Your eye care professional also may ask you to look at an Amsler grid. Changes in your central vision may cause the lines in the grid to disappear or appear wavy, a sign of AMD.

- **Fluorescein angiogram (FA).** In this test, which is performed by an ophthalmologist, a fluorescent dye is injected into your arm. Pictures are taken as the dye passes through the blood vessels in your eye. This makes it possible to see leaking blood vessels, which occur in a severe, rapidly progressive type of AMD (see below). In rare cases, complications to the injection can arise, from nausea to more severe allergic reactions.

- **Optical coherence tomography (OCT).** You have probably heard of ultrasound, which uses sound waves to capture images of living tissues. OCT is similar except that it uses light waves, and can achieve very high-resolution images of any tissues that can be penetrated by light—such as the eyes. After your eyes are dilated, you'll be asked to place your head on a chin rest and hold still for several seconds while the images are obtained. The light beam is painless.

During the exam, your eye care professional will look for drusen, which are yellow deposits beneath the retina. Most people develop some very small drusen as a normal part of aging. The presence of medium-to-large drusen may indicate that you have AMD.

Another sign of AMD is the appearance of pigmentary changes under the retina. In addition to the pigmented cells in the iris (the colored part of the eye), there are pigmented cells beneath the retina. As these cells break down and release their pigment, your eye care professional may see dark clumps of released pigment and later, areas that are less pigmented. These changes will not affect your eye color.

How Is Age-Related Macular Degeneration Treated?

Neovascular AMD typically results in severe vision loss. However, eye care professionals can try different therapies to stop further vision loss. You should remember that the therapies described below are not a cure. The condition may progress even with treatment.

- **Injections.** One option to slow the progression of neovascular AMD is to inject drugs into the eye. With neovascular AMD, abnormally high levels of vascular endothelial growth factor (VEGF) are secreted in your eyes. VEGF is a protein that promotes the growth of new abnormal blood vessels. Anti-VEGF injection therapy blocks this growth. If you get this treatment, you may need multiple monthly injections. Before each injection, your eye will be numbed and cleaned with antiseptics. To further reduce the risk of infection, you may be prescribed antibiotic drops. A few different anti-VEGF drugs are available. They vary in cost and in how often they need to be injected, so you may wish to discuss these issues with your eye care professional.

- **Photodynamic therapy (PDT).** This technique involves laser treatment of select areas of the retina. First, a drug called verteporfin will be injected into a vein in your arm. The drug travels through the blood vessels in your body, and is absorbed by new, growing blood vessels. Your eye care professional then shines a laser beam into your eye to activate the drug in the new abnormal blood vessels, while sparing normal ones. Once activated, the drug closes off the new blood vessels, slows their growth, and slows the rate of vision loss. This procedure is less common than anti-VEGF injections, and is often used in combination with them for specific types of neovascular AMD.

- **Laser surgery.** Eye care professionals treat certain cases of neovascular AMD with laser surgery, though this is less common than other treatments. It involves aiming an intense "hot" laser at the abnormal blood vessels in your eyes to destroy them. This laser is not the same one used in photodynamic therapy which may be referred to as a "cold" laser. This treatment is more likely to be used when blood vessel growth is limited to a compact area in your eye, away from the center of the macula, that can be easily targeted with the laser. Even so, laser treatment also may destroy some surrounding healthy tissue. This often results in a small blind spot where the laser has scarred the retina. In some cases, vision immediately after the surgery may be worse than it was before. But the surgery may also help prevent more severe vision loss from occurring years later.

Glaucoma

Glaucoma is a group of diseases that damage the eye's optic nerve and can result in vision loss and blindness. However, with early detection and treatment, you can often protect your eyes against serious vision loss.

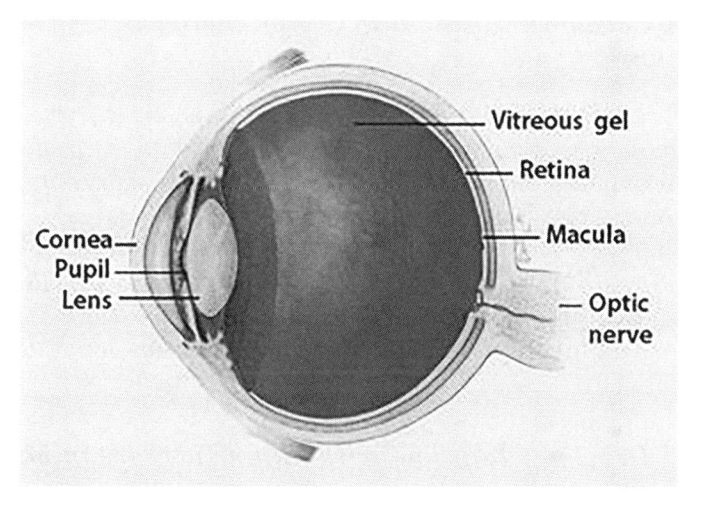

Figure 17.3. *Optic Nerve*

The optic nerve is a bundle of more than 1 million nerve fibers. It connects the retina to the brain. The retina is the light-sensitive tissue at the back of the eye. A healthy optic nerve is necessary for good vision.

How Does the Optic Nerve Get Damaged by Open-Angle Glaucoma?

Several large studies have shown that eye pressure is a major risk factor for optic nerve damage. In the front of the eye is a space called the anterior chamber. A clear fluid flows continuously in and out of the chamber and nourishes nearby tissues. The fluid leaves the chamber at the open angle where the cornea and iris meet. (See diagram below.) When the fluid reaches the angle, it flows through a spongy meshwork, like a drain, and leaves the eye.

In open-angle glaucoma, even though the drainage angle is "open," the fluid passes too slowly through the meshwork drain. Since the fluid builds up, the pressure inside the eye rises to a level that may damage the optic nerve. When the optic nerve is damaged from increased pressure, open-angle glaucoma and vision loss—may result. That's why controlling pressure inside the eye is important.

Another risk factor for optic nerve damage relates to blood pressure. Thus, it is important to also make sure that your blood pressure is at a proper level for your body by working with your medical doctor.

Can I Develop Glaucoma If I Have Increased Eye Pressure?

Not necessarily. Not every person with increased eye pressure will develop glaucoma. Some people can tolerate higher levels of eye pressure better than others. Also, a certain level of eye pressure may be high for one person but normal for another.

Whether you develop glaucoma depends on the level of pressure your optic nerve can tolerate without being damaged. This level is different for each person. That's why a comprehensive dilated eye exam is very important. It can help your eye care professional determine what level of eye pressure is normal for you.

Can I Develop Glaucoma without an Increase in My Eye Pressure?

Yes. Glaucoma can develop without increased eye pressure. This form of glaucoma is called low-tension or normal-tension glaucoma. It is a type of open-angle glaucoma.

Who Is at Risk for Open-Angle Glaucoma?

Anyone can develop glaucoma. Some people, listed below, are at higher risk than others:

- African Americans over age 40
- Everyone over age 60, especially Mexican Americans
- People with a family history of glaucoma

Sensory Disabilities

A comprehensive dilated eye exam can reveal more risk factors, such as high eye pressure, thinness of the cornea, and abnormal optic nerve anatomy. In some people with certain combinations of these high-risk factors, medicines in the form of eyedrops reduce the risk of developing glaucoma by about half.

Glaucoma Symptoms

At first, open-angle glaucoma has no symptoms. It causes no pain. Vision stays normal. Glaucoma can develop in one or both eyes.

Without treatment, people with glaucoma will slowly lose their peripheral (side) vision. As glaucoma remains untreated, people may miss objects to the side and out of the corner of their eye. They seem to be looking through a tunnel. Over time, straight-ahead (central) vision may decrease until no vision remains.

How Is Glaucoma Detected?

Glaucoma is detected through a comprehensive dilated eye exam that includes the following:

- **Visual acuity test.** This eye chart test measures how well you see at various distances.

- **Visual field test.** This test measures your peripheral (side vision). It helps your eye care professional tell if you have lost peripheral vision, a sign of glaucoma.

- **Dilated eye exam.** In this exam, drops are placed in your eyes to widen, or dilate, the pupils. Your eye care professional uses a special magnifying lens to examine your retina and optic nerve for signs of damage and other eye problems. After the exam, your close-up vision may remain blurred for several hours.

- **Tonometry** is the measurement of pressure inside the eye by using an instrument called a tonometer. Numbing drops may be applied to your eye for this test. A tonometer measures pressure inside the eye to detect glaucoma.

- **Pachymetry** is the measurement of the thickness of your cornea. Your eye care professional applies a numbing drop to your eye and uses an ultrasonic wave instrument to measure the thickness of your cornea.

Can Glaucoma Be Cured?

No. There is no cure for glaucoma. Vision lost from the disease cannot be restored.

Glaucoma Treatments

Immediate treatment for early-stage, open-angle glaucoma can delay progression of the disease. That's why early diagnosis is very important.

Glaucoma treatments include medicines, laser trabeculoplasty, conventional surgery, or a combination of any of these. While these treatments may save remaining vision, they do not improve sight already lost from glaucoma.

Cataract

A cataract is a clouding of the lens in the eye that affects vision. Most cataracts are related to aging. Cataracts are very common in older people. By age 80, more than half of all Americans either have a cataract or have had cataract surgery.

A cataract can occur in either or both eyes. It cannot spread from one eye to the other.

What Is the Lens?

The lens is a clear part of the eye that helps to focus light, or an image, on the retina. The retina is the light-sensitive tissue at the back of the eye.

In a normal eye, light passes through the transparent lens to the retina. Once it reaches the retina, light is changed into nerve signals that are sent to the brain.

The lens must be clear for the retina to receive a sharp image. If the lens is cloudy from a cataract, the image you see will be blurred.

What Causes Cataracts?

The lens lies behind the iris and the pupil. It works much like a camera lens. It focuses light onto the retina at the back of the eye, where an image is recorded. The lens also adjusts the eye's focus, letting us see things clearly both up close and far away. The lens is made of mostly water and protein. The protein is arranged in a precise way that keeps the lens clear and lets light pass through it.

But as we age, some of the protein may clump together and start to cloud a small area of the lens. This is a cataract. Over time, the cataract may grow larger and cloud more of the lens, making it harder to see.

Researchers suspect that there are several causes of cataract, such as smoking and diabetes. Or, it may be that the protein in the lens just changes from the wear and tear it takes over the years.

How Do Cataracts Affect Vision?

Age-related cataracts can affect your vision in two ways:

Clumps of protein reduce the sharpness of the image reaching the retina. The lens consists mostly of water and protein. When the protein clumps up, it clouds the lens and reduces the light that reaches the retina. The clouding may become severe enough to cause blurred vision. Most age-related cataracts develop from protein clumpings. When a cataract is small, the cloudiness affects only a small part of the lens. You may not notice any changes in your vision. Cataracts tend to "grow" slowly, so vision gets worse gradually. Over time, the cloudy area in the lens may get larger, and the cataract may increase in size. Seeing may become more difficult. Your vision may get duller or blurrier.

The clear lens slowly changes to a yellowish/brownish color, adding a brownish tint to vision. As the clear lens slowly colors with age, your vision gradually may acquire a brownish shade. At first, the amount of tinting may be small and may not cause a vision problem. Over time, increased tinting may make it more difficult to read and perform other routine activities. This gradual change in the amount of tinting does not affect the sharpness of the image transmitted to the retina. If you have advanced lens discoloration, you may not be able to identify blues and purples. You may be wearing what you believe to be a pair of black socks, only to find out from friends that you are wearing purple socks.

When Are You Most Likely to Have a Cataract?

The term "age-related" is a little misleading. You don't have to be a senior citizen to get this type of cataract. In fact, people can have an age-related cataract in their 40s and 50s. But during middle age, most cataracts are small and do not affect vision. It is after age 60 that most cataracts cause problems with a person's vision.

Who Is at Risk for Cataract?

The risk of cataract increases as you get older. Other risk factors for cataract include:

- Certain diseases (for example, diabetes)
- Personal behavior (smoking, alcohol use)
- The environment (prolonged exposure to ultraviolet sunlight)

What Are the Symptoms of a Cataract?

The most common symptoms of a cataract are:

- Cloudy or blurry vision
- Colors seem faded
- Glare. Headlights, lamps, or sunlight may appear too bright. A halo may appear around lights.
- Poor night vision
- Double vision or multiple images in one eye. (This symptom may clear as the cataract gets larger.)
- Frequent prescription changes in your eyeglasses or contact lenses

These symptoms also can be a sign of other eye problems. If you have any of these symptoms, check with your eye care professional.

Are There Different Types of Cataract?

Yes. Although most cataracts are related to aging, there are other types of cataract:

1. **Secondary cataract.** Cataracts can form after surgery for other eye problems, such as glaucoma. Cataracts also can develop in people who have other health problems, such as diabetes. Cataracts are sometimes linked to steroid use.

2. **Traumatic cataract.** Cataracts can develop after an eye injury, sometimes years later.

3. **Congenital cataract.** Some babies are born with cataracts or develop them in childhood, often in both eyes. These cataracts may be so small that they do not affect vision. If they do, the lenses may need to be removed.

Sensory Disabilities

4. **Radiation cataract.** Cataracts can develop after exposure to some types of radiation.

How Is a Cataract Detected?

Cataract is detected through a comprehensive eye exam that includes:

1. **Visual acuity test.** This eye chart test measures how well you see at various distances.
2. **Dilated eye exam.** Drops are placed in your eyes to widen, or dilate, the pupils. Your eye care professional uses a special magnifying lens to examine your retina and optic nerve for signs of damage and other eye problems. After the exam, your close-up vision may remain blurred for several hours.
3. **Tonometry.** An instrument measures the pressure inside the eye. Numbing drops may be applied to your eye for this test.

Your eye care professional also may do other tests to learn more about the structure and health of your eye.

How Is a Cataract Treated?

The symptoms of early cataract may be improved with new eyeglasses, brighter lighting, anti-glare sunglasses, or magnifying lenses. If these measures do not help, surgery is the only effective treatment. Surgery involves removing the cloudy lens and replacing it with an artificial lens.

A cataract needs to be removed only when vision loss interferes with your everyday activities, such as driving, reading, or watching TV. You and your eye care professional can make this decision together. Once you understand the benefits and risks of surgery, you can make an informed decision about whether cataract surgery is right for you. In most cases, delaying cataract surgery will not cause long-term damage to your eye or make the surgery more difficult. You do not have to rush into surgery.

Sometimes a cataract should be removed even if it does not cause problems with your vision. For example, a cataract should be removed if it prevents examination or treatment of another eye problem, such as age-related macular degeneration or diabetic retinopathy.

If you choose surgery, your eye care professional may refer you to a specialist to remove the cataract.

If you have cataracts in both eyes that require surgery, the surgery will be performed on each eye at separate times, usually four weeks apart.

Diabetic Retinopathy

Diabetic retinopathy affects blood vessels in the light-sensitive tissue called the retina that lines the back of the eye. It is the most common cause of vision loss among people with diabetes and the leading cause of vision impairment and blindness among working-age adults.

What Causes Diabetic Retinopathy?

Chronically high blood sugar from diabetes is associated with damage to the tiny blood vessels in the retina, leading to diabetic retinopathy. The retina detects light and converts it to signals sent through the optic nerve to the brain. Diabetic retinopathy can cause blood vessels in the retina to leak fluid or hemorrhage (bleed), distorting vision. In its most advanced stage, new abnormal blood vessels proliferate (increase in number) on the surface of the retina, which can lead to scarring and cell loss in the retina.

Diabetic retinopathy may progress through four stages:

1. **Mild nonproliferative retinopathy.** Small areas of balloon-like swelling in the retina's tiny blood vessels, called microaneurysms, occur at this earliest stage of the disease. These microaneurysms may leak fluid into the retina.

2. **Moderate nonproliferative retinopathy.** As the disease progresses, blood vessels that nourish the retina may swell and distort. They may also lose their ability to transport blood. Both conditions cause characteristic changes to the appearance of the retina and may contribute to diabetic macular edema (DME).

3. **Severe nonproliferative retinopathy.** Many more blood vessels are blocked, depriving blood supply to areas of the retina. These areas secrete growth factors that signal the retina to grow new blood vessels.

4. **Proliferative diabetic retinopathy (PDR).** At this advanced stage, growth factors secreted by the retina trigger the proliferation of new blood vessels, which grow along the inside surface of the retina and into the vitreous gel, the fluid

that fills the eye. The new blood vessels are fragile, which makes them more likely to leak and bleed. Accompanying scar tissue can contract and cause retinal detachment—the pulling away of the retina from the underlying tissue, like wallpaper peeling away from a wall. Retinal detachment can lead to permanent vision loss.

Who Is at Risk for Diabetic Retinopathy?

People with all types of diabetes (type 1, type 2, and gestational) are at risk for diabetic retinopathy. Risk increases the longer a person has diabetes. Between 40 and 45 percent of Americans diagnosed with diabetes have some stage of diabetic retinopathy, although only about half are aware of it. Women who develop or have diabetes during pregnancy may have rapid onset or worsening of diabetic retinopathy.

What Is the Symptoms of Diabetic Retinopathy?

The early stages of diabetic retinopathy usually have no symptoms. The disease often progresses unnoticed until it affects vision. Bleeding from abnormal retinal blood vessels can cause the appearance of "floating" spots. These spots sometimes clear on their own. But without prompt treatment, bleeding often recurs, increasing the risk of permanent vision loss. If DME occurs, it can cause blurred vision.

How Is Diabetic Retinopathy Detected?

Diabetic retinopathy is detected during a comprehensive dilated eye exam that includes:

1. **Visual acuity testing.** This eye chart test measures a person's ability to see at various distances.

2. **Tonometry.** This test measures pressure inside the eye.

3. **Pupil dilation.** Drops placed on the eye's surface dilate (widen) the pupil, allowing a physician to examine the retina and optic nerve.

4. **Optical coherence tomography (OCT).** This technique is similar to ultrasound but uses light waves instead of sound waves to capture images of tissues inside the body. OCT provides detailed images of tissues that can be penetrated by light, such as the eye.

A comprehensive dilated eye exam allows the doctor to check the retina for:

1. Changes to blood vessels
2. Leaking blood vessels or warning signs of leaky blood vessels, such as fatty deposits
3. Swelling of the macula (DME)
4. Changes in the lens
5. Damage to nerve tissue

If severe diabetic retinopathy is suspected, a fluorescein angiogram may be used to look for damaged or leaky blood vessels. In this test, a fluorescent dye is injected into the bloodstream, often into an arm vein. Pictures of the retinal blood vessels are taken as the dye reaches the eye.

How Can People with Diabetes Protect Their Vision?

Vision lost to diabetic retinopathy is sometimes irreversible. However, early detection and treatment can reduce the risk of blindness by 95 percent. Because diabetic retinopathy often lacks early symptoms, people with diabetes should get a comprehensive dilated eye exam at least once a year. People with diabetic retinopathy may need eye exams more frequently. Women with diabetes who become pregnant should have a comprehensive dilated eye exam as soon as possible. Additional exams during pregnancy may be needed.

Studies such as the Diabetes Control and Complications Trial (DCCT) have shown that controlling diabetes slows the onset and worsening of diabetic retinopathy. DCCT study participants who kept their blood glucose level as close to normal as possible were significantly less likely than those without optimal glucose control to develop diabetic retinopathy, as well as kidney and nerve diseases. Other trials have shown that controlling elevated blood pressure and cholesterol can reduce the risk of vision loss among people with diabetes.

Treatment for diabetic retinopathy is often delayed until it starts to progress to PDR, or when DME occurs. Comprehensive dilated eye exams are needed more frequently as diabetic retinopathy becomes more severe. People with severe nonproliferative diabetic retinopathy have a high risk of developing PDR and may need a comprehensive dilated eye exam as often as every 2–4 months.

Sensory Disabilities

How Is Proliferative Diabetic Retinopathy (PDR) Treated?

For decades, PDR has been treated with scatter laser surgery, sometimes called panretinal laser surgery or panretinal photocoagulation. Treatment involves making 1,000 to 2,000 tiny laser burns in areas of the retina away from the macula. These laser burns are intended to cause abnormal blood vessels to shrink. Although treatment can be completed in one session, two or more sessions are sometimes required. While it can preserve central vision, scatter laser surgery may cause some loss of side (peripheral), color, and night vision. Scatter laser surgery works best before new, fragile blood vessels have started to bleed. Recent studies have shown that anti-VEGF treatment not only is effective for treating DME, but is also effective for slowing progression of diabetic retinopathy, including PDR, so anti-VEGF is increasingly used as a first-line treatment for PDR.

Section 17.4

Deaf-Blindness

> The section includes text excerpted from the following sources: Text beginning with the heading "What Is Deaf-Blindness?" is excerpted from "Overview on Deaf-Blindness," Education Resources Information Center (ERIC), U.S. Department of Education (ED), October 2008. Reviewed July 2018; Text under the heading "Interveners and Children Who Are Deaf-Blind" is excerpted from "Interveners and Children Who Are Deaf-Blind," U.S. Department of Education (ED), December 14, 2015.

What Is Deaf-Blindness?

It may seem that deaf-blindness refers to a total inability to see or hear. However, in reality deaf-blindness is a condition in which the combination of hearing and visual losses in children cause "such severe communication and other developmental and educational needs that they cannot be accommodated in special education programs solely for children with deafness or children with blindness" or multiple disabilities. Children who are called deaf-blind are singled out educationally because impairments of sight and hearing require thoughtful and unique educational approaches in order to ensure that children with this disability have the opportunity to reach their full potential.

A person who is deaf-blind has a unique experience of the world. For people who can see and hear, the world extends outward as far as his or her eyes and ears can reach. For the young child who is deaf-blind, the world is initially much narrower. If the child is profoundly deaf and totally blind, his or her experience of the world extends only as far as the fingertips can reach. Such children are effectively alone if no one is touching them. Their concepts of the world depend upon what or whom they have had the opportunity to physical contact.

If a child who is deaf-blind has some usable vision and/or hearing, as many do, her or his world will be enlarged. Many children called deaf-blind have enough vision to be able to move about in their environments, recognize familiar people, see sign language at close distances, and perhaps read large print. Others have sufficient hearing to recognize familiar sounds, understand some speech, or develop speech themselves. The range of sensory impairments included in the term "deaf-blindness" is great.

Who Is Deaf-Blind, and What Are the Causes of Deaf-Blindness?

As far as it has been possible to count them, there are over 10,000 children (ages birth to 22 years) in the United States who have been classified as deaf-blind. It has been estimated that the adult deaf-blind population numbers 35,000–40,000. The causes of deaf-blindness are many. Below is a list of many of the possible etiologies of deaf-blindness.

Major Causes of Deaf-Blindness

- Syndromes
  - Down
  - Usher
  - Trisomy 13
- Multiple congenital anomalies
  - CHARGE association
  - Hydrocephaly

- Microcephaly
- Fetal alcohol syndrome (FAS)
- Maternal drug abuse
- Congenital prenatal dysfunction
  - Acquired immunodeficiency syndrome (AIDS)
  - Herpes
  - Rubella
  - Syphilis
  - Toxoplasmosis
- Postnatal causes
  - Asphyxia
  - Encephalitis
  - Head injury/trauma
  - Meningitis
  - Stroke

Some people are deaf-blind from birth. Others may be born deaf or hard-of-hearing and become blind or visually impaired later in life; or the reverse may be the case. Still others may be adventitiously deaf-blind—that is, they are born with both sight and hearing but lose some or all of these senses as a result of accident or illness. Deaf-blindness is often accompanied by additional disabilities. Causes such as maternal rubella can also affect the heart and the brain. Some genetic syndromes or brain injuries that cause deaf-blindness may also cause cognitive disabilities and/or physical disabilities.

What Are the Challenges Facing a Person Who Is Deaf-Blind?

A person who is deaf-blind must somehow make sense of the world using the limited information available to him or her. If the person's sensory disabilities are great, and if people in the environment have not made an effort to order the world for him or her in a way that makes it easier to understand, this challenge may be overwhelming. Behavioral and emotional difficulties often accompany deaf-blindness and are the natural outcomes of the child's or adult's inability to understand and communicate.

People who can see and hear often take for granted the information that those senses provide. Events such as the approach of another person, an upcoming meal, the decision to go out, a change in routine are all signaled by sights and sounds that allow a person to prepare for them. The child or adult who misses these cues because of limited sight and/or hearing may come to experience the world as an unpredictable, and possibly threatening, place. To a great extent, persons who are deaf-blind must depend upon the goodwill and sensitivity of those around them to make their world safe and understandable.

The challenge of learning to communicate is perhaps the greatest one that children who are deaf-blind face. It is also the greatest opportunity, since communication and language hold the power to make their thoughts, needs, and desires known. The ability to use words can also open up worlds beyond the reach of their fingertips through the use of interpreters, books, and an ever-increasing array of electronic communication devices. In order to learn language, children who are deaf-blind must depend upon others to make language accessible to them. Given that accessibility, children who are deaf-blind face the challenges of engaging in interactions to the best of their abilities and of availing themselves of the language opportunities provided for them.

A person who is deaf-blind also faces, further, the challenge of learning to move about in the world as freely and independently as possible. Adult individuals also must eventually find adult living and work situations that allow them to use their talents and abilities in the best way possible. Many adults who are deaf-blind lead independent or semi-independent lives and have productive work and enjoyable social lives. The achievement of such success depends in large part upon the education they have received since childhood, and particularly upon the communication with others that they have been able to develop.

What Are the Particular Challenges Facing the Family, Teachers, and Caregivers of a Person Who Is Deaf-Blind?

Communication

The disability of deaf-blindness presents unique challenges to families, teachers, and caregivers, who must make sure that the person

Sensory Disabilities

who is deaf-blind has access to the world beyond the limited reach of his or her eyes, ears, and fingertips. The people in the environment of children or adults who are deaf-blind must seek to include them—moment-by-moment—in the flow of life and in the physical environments that surround them. If they do not, the child will be isolated and will not have the opportunity to grow and to learn. If they do, the child will be afforded the opportunity to develop to his or her fullest potential.

The most important challenge for parents, caregivers, and teachers is to communicate meaningfully with the child who is deaf-blind. Continual good communication will help foster his or her healthy development. Communication involves much more than mere language. Good communication can best be thought of as conversation. Conversations employ body language and gestures, as well as both signed and spoken words. A conversation with a child who is deaf-blind can begin with a partner who simply notices what the child is paying attention to at the moment and finds a way to let the child know that his or her interest is shared.

This shared interest, once established, can become a topic around which a conversation can be built. Mutual conversational topics are typically established between a parent and a sighted or hearing child by making eye contact and by gestures such as pointing or nodding, or by exchanges of sounds and facial expressions. Lacking significant amounts of sight and hearing, children who are deaf-blind will often need touch in order for them to be sure that their partner shares their focus of attention. The parent or teacher may, for example, touch an interesting object along with the child in a nondirective way. Or, the mother may imitate a child's movements, allowing the child tactual access to that imitation, if necessary. (This is the tactual equivalent of the actions of a mother who instinctively imitates her child's babbling sounds.) Establishing a mutual interest like this will open up the possibility for conversational interaction.

Teachers, parents, siblings, and peers can continue conversations with children who are deaf-blind by learning to pause after each turn in the interaction to allow time for response. These children frequently have very slow response times. Respecting the child's own timing is crucial to establishing successful interactions. Pausing long enough to allow the child to take another turn in the interaction, then responding to that turn, pausing again, and so on—this back-and-forth exchange becomes a conversation. Such conversations, repeated consistently, build relationships and become the eventual basis for language learning.

As the child who is deaf-blind becomes comfortable interacting nonverbally with others, she or he becomes ready to receive some form of symbolic communication as part of those interactions. Often it is helpful to accompany the introduction of words (spoken or signed) with the use of simple gestures and/or objects which serve as symbols or representations for activities. Doing so may help a child develop the understanding that one thing can stand for another, and will also enable him or her to anticipate events.

Think of the many thousands of words and sentences that most children hear before they speak their own first words. A child who is deaf-blind needs comparable language stimulation, adjusted to his or her ability to receive and make sense of it. Parents, caregivers, and teachers face the challenge of providing an environment rich in language that is meaningful and accessible to the child who is deaf-blind. Only with such a rich language environment will the child have the opportunity to acquire language herself or himself. Those around the child can create a rich language environment by continually commenting on the child's own experience using sign language, speech, or whatever symbol system is accessible to the child. These comments are best made during conversational interactions. A teacher or a parent may, for example, use gesture or sign language to name the object that he or she and the child are both touching, or name the movement that they share. This naming of objects and actions, done many, many times, may begin to give the child who is deaf-blind a similar opportunity afforded to the hearing child—that of making meaningful connections between words and the things for which they stand.

Principal communication systems for persons who are deaf-blind are these:

- Touch cues
- Gestures
- Object symbols
- Picture symbols
- Sign language
- Fingerspelling
- Signed English
- Pidgin Signed English
- Braille writing and reading
- Tadoma method of speech reading

Sensory Disabilities

- American Sign Language
- Large print writing and reading
- Lip-reading speech

Along with nonverbal and verbal conversations, a child who is deaf-blind needs a reliable routine of meaningful activities, and some way or ways that this routine can be communicated to her or him. Touch cues, gestures, and use of object symbols are some typical ways in which to let a child who is deaf-blind know what is about to happen to her or him. Each time before the child is picked up, for example, the caregiver may gently lift his or her arms a bit, and then pause, giving the child time to ready herself or himself for being handled. Such consistency will help the child to feel secure and to begin to make the world predictable, thus allowing the child to develop expectations. Children and adults who are deaf-blind and are able to use symbolic communication may also be more reliant on predictable routine than people who are sighted and hearing. Predictable routine may help to ease the anxiety which is often caused by the lack of sensory information.

Orientation and Mobility

In addition, the child who is deaf-blind will need help learning to move about in the world. Without vision, or with reduced vision, he or she will not only have difficulty navigating, but may also lack the motivation to move outward in the first place. Helping a young child who is deaf-blind learn to move may begin with thoughtful attention to the physical space around him or her (crib or other space) so that whatever movements the child instinctively makes are rewarded with interesting stimulation that motivates further movement. Orientation and mobility specialists can help parents and teachers to construct safe and motivating spaces for the young child who is deaf-blind. In many instances, children who are deaf-blind may also have additional physical and health problems that limit their ability to move about. Parents and teachers may need to include physical and occupational therapists, vision teachers, health professionals, and orientation and mobility specialists on the team to plan accessible and motivating spaces for these children. Older children or adults who have lost vision can also use help from trained specialists in order to achieve as much confidence and independence as possible in moving about in their world.

Individualized Education

Education for a child or youth with deaf-blindness needs to be highly individualized; the limited channels available for learning necessitate organizing a program for each child that will address the child's unique ways of learning and his or her own interests. Assessment is crucial at every step of the way. Sensory deficits can easily be misled even experienced educators into underestimating (or occasionally overestimating) intelligence and constructing in appropriate programs.

Helen Keller said, "Blindness separates a person from things, but deafness separates him from people." This potential isolation is one important reason why it is necessary to engage the services of persons familiar with the combination of both blindness and deafness when planning an educational program for a child who is deaf-blind. Doing so will help a child or youth with these disabilities receive an education which maximizes her or his potential for learning and for meaningful contact with her or his environment. The earlier these services can be obtained, the better for the child.

Transition

When a person who is deaf-blind nears the end of his or her school-based education, transition and rehabilitation help will be required to assist in planning so that as an adult the individual can find suitable work and living situations. Because of the diversity of needs, such services for a person who is deaf-blind can rarely be provided by a single person or agency; careful and respectful teamwork is required among specialists and agencies concerned with such things as housing, vocational and rehabilitation needs, deafness, blindness, orientation and mobility, medical needs, and mental health.

The adult who is deaf-blind must be central to the transition planning. The individual's own goals, directions, interests, and abilities must guide the planning at every step of the way. Skilled interpreters, family members, and friends who know the person well can help the adult who is deaf-blind have the most important voice in planning his or her own future.

Inclusion in Family

Clearly, the challenges for parents, teachers, and caregivers of children who are deaf-blind are many. Not least among them is the challenge of including the child in the flow of family and community life. Since such a child does not necessarily respond to care in the ways we might expect, parents will be particularly challenged in their efforts to include her or him. The mother or father of an infant who can see is usually rewarded with smiles and lively eye contact from the child. The parent of a child who is deaf-blind must look for more subtle yards: small hand or body movements, for instance, may be the child's way of expressing pleasure or connection. Parents may also need to change their perceptions regarding typical developmental milestones. They can learn, as many have, to rejoice as fully in the ability of their child who is deaf-blind to sign a new word, or to feed herself, or to return a greeting as they do over another child's college scholarship or success in basketball or election to class office.

Parents, then, may need to shift expectations and perceptions in significant ways. They also need to do the natural grieving that accompanies the birth of a child who is disabled. Teachers and caregivers must also make these perceptual shifts. Parents' groups and resources for teachers can provide much-needed support for those who live and work with children and adults who are deaf-blind. Such supports will help foster the mutually rewarding inclusion of children who are deaf-blind into their families and communities.

Interveners and Children Who Are Deaf-Blind

Technology, supports, and services for children who are deaf-blind have come a long way since Helen Keller first responded to Anne Sullivan's efforts to help her learn.

The importance of intervener services for many children who are deaf-blind children cannot be overstated. The National Center on Deaf-Blindness (NCDB) defines this service as providing access to information and communication and facilitating the development of social and emotional well-being for children who are deaf-blind.

In educational environments, intervener services are provided by an individual, typically a paraeducator, who has received specialized training in deaf-blindness and the process of intervention. An intervener provides consistent one-to-one support to a student who is deaf-blind (age three through 21) throughout the instructional day.

The NCDB is funded by Office of Special Education and Rehabilitative Services (OSERS) Office of Special Education Programs (OSEP) as a national technical assistance center to improve the quality of life and educational opportunities for the roughly 10,000 children who are deaf-blind. Deaf-blindness is a low incidence disability and within this population of children there is great variability. Ninety percent of children who are identified as deaf-blind have additional physical, medical and/or cognitive disabilities. Without support, these children are cut off from most, if not all, communication and activities in their environments. Thus, it is clear that many of these children can, and do, benefit from services offered by trained interveners.

Chapter 18

Speech Disorders

Chapter Contents

Section 18.1—Aphasia 176
Section 18.2—Apraxia 180

Section 18.1

Aphasia

This section contains text excerpted from the following sources: Text beginning with the heading "What Is Aphasia?" is excerpted from "Aphasia," National Institute on Deafness and Other Communication Disorders (NIDCD), March 6, 2017; Text under the heading "Preventing Aphasia" is excerpted from "What Is Aphasia," MedlinePlus, National Institutes of Health (NIH), May 31, 2017.

What Is Aphasia?

Aphasia is a disorder that results from damage to portions of the brain that are responsible for language. For most people, these areas are on the left side of the brain. Aphasia usually occurs suddenly, often following a stroke or head injury, but it may also develop slowly, as the result of a brain tumor or a progressive neurological disease. The disorder impairs the expression and understanding of language as well as reading and writing. Aphasia may co-occur with speech disorders, such as dysarthria or apraxia of speech, which also result from brain damage.

Who Can Acquire Aphasia?

Most people who have aphasia are middle-aged or older, but anyone can acquire it, including young children. About 1 million people in the United States currently have aphasia, and nearly 180,000 Americans acquire it each year, according to the National Aphasia Association (NAA).

What Causes Aphasia

Aphasia is caused by damage to one or more of the language areas of the brain. Most often, the cause of the brain injury is a stroke. A stroke occurs when a blood clot or a leaking or burst vessel cuts off blood flow to part of the brain. Brain cells die when they do not receive their normal supply of blood, which carries oxygen and important nutrients. Other causes of brain injury are severe blows to the head, brain tumors, gunshot wounds, brain infections, and progressive neurological disorders, such as Alzheimer disease.

What Types of Aphasia Are There?

There are two broad categories of aphasia: fluent and nonfluent, and there are several types within these groups.

Speech Disorders

Damage to the temporal lobe of the brain may result in Wernicke aphasia, the most common type of fluent aphasia. People with Wernicke aphasia may speak in long, complete sentences that have no meaning, adding unnecessary words and even creating made-up words.

For example, someone with Wernicke aphasia may say, "You know that smoodle pinkered and that I want to get him round and take care of him like you want before."

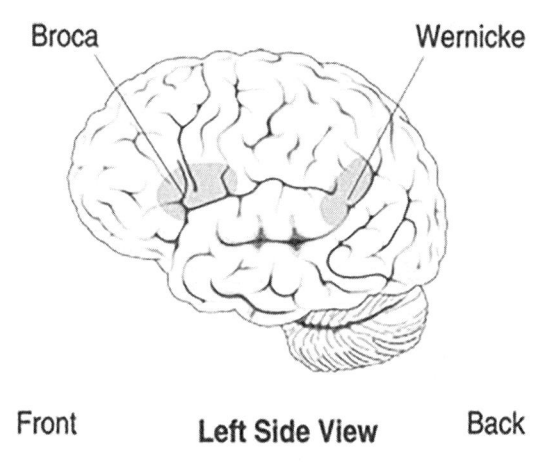

Figure 18.1. *Areas of the Brain Affected by Broca and Wernicke Aphasia*

As a result, it is often difficult to follow what the person is trying to say. People with Wernicke aphasia are often unaware of their spoken mistakes. Another hallmark of this type of aphasia is difficulty understanding speech.

The most common type of nonfluent aphasia is Broca aphasia. People with Broca aphasia have damage that primarily affects the frontal lobe of the brain. They often have right-sided weakness or paralysis of the arm and leg because the frontal lobe is also important for motor movements. People with Broca aphasia may understand speech and know what they want to say, but they frequently speak in short phrases that are produced with great effort. They often omit small words, such as "is," "and" and "the."

For example, a person with Broca aphasia may say, "Walk dog," meaning, "I will take the dog for a walk," or "book book two table," for "There are two books on the table." People with Broca aphasia typically understand the speech of others fairly well. Because of this, they are often aware of their difficulties and can become easily frustrated.

Another type of aphasia, global aphasia, results from damage to extensive portions of the language areas of the brain. Individuals with global aphasia have severe communication difficulties and may be extremely limited in their ability to speak or comprehend language. They may be unable to say even a few words or may repeat the same words or phrases over and over again. They may have trouble understanding even simple words and sentences.

There are other types of aphasia, each of which results from damage to different language areas in the brain. Some people may have difficulty repeating words and sentences even though they understand them and can speak fluently (conduction aphasia). Others may have difficulty naming objects even though they know what the object is and what it may be used for (anomic aphasia).

Sometimes, blood flow to the brain is temporarily interrupted and quickly restored. When this type of injury occurs, which is called a transient ischemic attack (TIA), language abilities may return in a few hours or days.

How Is Aphasia Diagnosed?

Aphasia is usually first recognized by the physician who treats the person for his or her brain injury. Most individuals will undergo a magnetic resonance imaging (MRI) or computed tomography (CT) scan to confirm the presence of a brain injury and to identify its precise location. The physician also typically tests the person's ability to understand and produce language, such as following commands, answering questions, naming objects, and carrying on a conversation.

If the physician suspects aphasia, the patient is usually referred to a speech-language pathologist, who performs a comprehensive examination of the person's communication abilities. The person's ability to speak, express ideas, converse socially, understand language, and read and write are all assessed in detail.

How Is Aphasia Treated?

Following a brain injury, tremendous changes occur in the brain, which helps it to recover. As a result, people with aphasia often see dramatic improvements in their language and communication abilities in the first few months, even without treatment. But in many cases, some aphasia remains following this initial recovery period. In these instances, speech-language therapy is used to help patients regain their ability to communicate.

Research has shown that language and communication abilities can continue to improve for many years and are sometimes accompanied by new activity in brain tissue near the damaged area. Some of the factors that may influence the amount of improvement include the cause of the brain injury, the area of the brain that was damaged and its extent, and the age and health of the individual.

Aphasia therapy aims to improve a person's ability to communicate by helping him or her to use remaining language abilities, restore language abilities as much as possible, and learn other ways of communicating, such as gestures, pictures, or use of electronic devices. Individual therapy focuses on the specific needs of the person, while group therapy offers the opportunity to use new communication skills in a small-group setting.

Technologies have provided new tools for people with aphasia. "Virtual" speech pathologists provide patients with the flexibility and convenience of getting therapy in their homes through a computer. The use of speech-generating applications on mobile devices like tablets can also provide an alternative way to communicate for people who have difficulty using spoken language.

Increasingly, patients with aphasia participate in activities, such as book clubs, technology groups, and art and drama clubs. Such experiences help patients regain their confidence and social self-esteem, in addition to improving their communication skills. Stroke clubs, regional support groups formed by people who have had a stroke, are available in most major cities. These clubs can help a person and his or her family adjust to the life changes that accompany stroke and aphasia.

Family involvement is often a crucial component of aphasia treatment because it enables family members to learn the best way to communicate with their loved one.

Family members are encouraged to:

- Participate in therapy sessions, if possible

- Simplify language by using short, uncomplicated sentences

- Repeat the content words or write down key words to clarify meaning as needed

- Maintain a natural conversational manner appropriate for an adult

- Minimize distractions, such as a loud radio or TV, whenever possible

- Include the person with aphasia in conversations
- Ask for and value the opinion of the person with aphasia, especially regarding family matters
- Encourage any type of communication, whether it is speech, gesture, pointing, or drawing
- Avoid correcting the person's speech
- Allow the person plenty of time to talk
- Help the person become involved outside the home. Seek out support groups, such as stroke clubs

Preventing Aphasia

One way to prevent aphasia is to lower your chance of a stroke by improving your cardiovascular health. Another is to protect your head from injury, such as by wearing a helmet when you ride a bike.

Section 18.2

Apraxia

This section includes text excerpted from "Apraxia of Speech," National Institute on Deafness and Other Communication Disorders (NIDCD), October 31, 2017.

What Is Apraxia of Speech?

Apraxia of speech (AOS)—also known as acquired apraxia of speech, verbal apraxia, or childhood apraxia of speech (CAS) when diagnosed in children—is a speech sound disorder. Someone with AOS has trouble saying what he or she wants to say correctly and consistently. AOS is a neurological disorder that affects the brain pathways involved in planning the sequence of movements involved in producing speech. The brain knows what it wants to say, but cannot properly plan and sequence the required speech sound movements.

AOS is not caused by weakness or paralysis of the speech muscles (the muscles of the jaw, tongue, or lips). Weakness or paralysis of the speech muscles results in a separate speech disorder, known as dysarthria. Some people have both dysarthria and AOS, which can make diagnosis of the two conditions more difficult.

The severity of AOS varies from person to person. It can be so mild that it causes trouble with only a few speech sounds or with pronunciation of words that have many syllables. In the most severe cases, someone with AOS might not be able to communicate effectively by speaking, and may need the help of alternative communication methods.

What Are the Types and Causes of Apraxia of Speech?

There are two main types of AOS:

1. **Acquired AOS** can affect someone at any age, although it most typically occurs in adults. Acquired AOS is caused by damage to the parts of the brain that are involved in speaking and involves the loss or impairment of existing speech abilities. It may result from a stroke, head injury, tumor, or other illness affecting the brain. Acquired AOS may occur together with other conditions that are caused by damage to the nervous system. One of these is dysarthria, as mentioned earlier. Another is aphasia, which is a language disorder.

2. **Childhood AOS** is present from birth. This condition is also known as developmental apraxia of speech, developmental verbal apraxia, or articulatory apraxia. Childhood AOS is not the same as developmental delays in speech, in which a child follows the typical path of speech development but does so more slowly than is typical. The causes of childhood AOS are not well understood. Imaging and other studies have not been able to find evidence of brain damage or differences in the brain structure of children with AOS. Children with AOS often have family members who have a history of a communication disorder or a learning disability. This observation and research findings suggest that genetic factors may play a role in the disorder. Childhood AOS appears to affect more boys than girls.

What Are the Symptoms of Apraxia of Speech?

People with either form of AOS may have a number of different speech characteristics, or symptoms:

- Distorting sounds. People with AOS may have difficulty pronouncing words correctly. Sounds, especially vowels, are often distorted. Because the speaker may not place the speech structures (e.g., tongue, jaw) quite in the right place, the sound comes out wrong. Longer or more complex words are usually harder to say than shorter or simpler words. Sound substitutions might also occur when AOS is accompanied by aphasia.

- Making inconsistent errors in speech. For example, someone with AOS may say a difficult word correctly but then have trouble repeating it, or may be able to say a particular sound one day and have trouble with the same sound the next day.

- Groping for sounds. People with AOS often appear to be groping for the right sound or word, and may try saying a word several times before they say it correctly.

- Making errors in tone, stress, or rhythm. Another common characteristic of AOS is the incorrect use of prosody. Prosody is the rhythm and inflection of speech that we use to help express meaning. Someone who has trouble with prosody might use equal stress, segment syllables in a word, omit syllables in words and phrases, or pause inappropriately while speaking.

Children with AOS generally understand language much better than they are able to use it. Some children with the disorder may also have other speech problems, expressive language problems, or motor-skill problems.

How Is Apraxia of Speech Diagnosed?

Professionals known as speech-language pathologists play a key role in diagnosing and treating AOS. Because there is no single symptom or test that can be used to diagnose AOS, the person making the diagnosis generally looks for the presence of several of a group of symptoms, including those described earlier. Ruling out other conditions, such as muscle weakness or language production problems (e.g., aphasia), can help with the diagnostic process.

Informal testing for both acquired and childhood AOS, a speech-language pathologist may ask the patient to perform speech tasks such as repeating a particular word several times or repeating a list of words of increasing length (for example, love, loving, lovingly). For acquired AOS, a speech-language pathologist may also examine the patient's ability to converse, read, write, and perform nonspeech movements. To diagnose childhood AOS, parents and professionals may need to observe a child's speech over a period of time.

How Is Apraxia of Speech Treated?

In some cases, people with acquired AOS recover some or all of their speech abilities on their own. This is called spontaneous recovery.

Children with AOS will not outgrow the problem on their own. They also do not acquire the basics of speech just by being around other children, such as in a classroom. Therefore, speech-language therapy is necessary for children with AOS as well as for people with acquired AOS who do not spontaneously recover all of their speech abilities.

Speech-language pathologists use different approaches to treat AOS, and no single approach has been proven to be the most effective. Therapy is tailored to the individual and is designed to treat other speech or language problems that may occur together with AOS. Frequent, intensive, one-on-one speech-language therapy sessions are needed for both children and adults with AOS. (The repetitive exercises and personal attention needed to improve AOS are difficult to deliver in group therapy.) Children with severe AOS may need intensive speech-language therapy for years, in parallel with normal schooling, to obtain adequate speech abilities.

In severe cases, adults and children with AOS may need to find other ways to express themselves. These might include formal or informal sign language; a notebook with pictures or written words that can be pointed to and shown to other people; or an electronic communication device—such as a smartphone, tablet, or laptop computer—that can be used to write or produce speech. Such assistive communication methods can also help children with AOS learn to read and better understand spoken language by stimulating areas of the brain involved in language and literacy.

Some adults and children will make more progress during treatment than others. Support and encouragement from family members and friends and extra practice in the home environment are important.

Chapter 19

Intellectual and Cognitive Disabilities

Chapter Contents

Section 19.1—Down Syndrome 186
Section 19.2—Fetal Alcohol Spectrum Disorders 190
Section 19.3—Shaken Baby Syndrome....................................... 194

Section 19.1

Down Syndrome

The section includes text excerpted from "Facts about Down Syndrome," Centers for Disease Control and Prevention (CDC), February 15, 2018.

What Is Down Syndrome?

Down syndrome is a condition in which a person has an extra chromosome. Chromosomes are small "packages" of genes in the body. They determine how a baby's body forms during pregnancy and how the baby's body functions as it grows in the womb and after birth. Typically, a baby is born with 46 chromosomes. Babies with Down syndrome have an extra copy of one of these chromosomes, chromosome 21. A medical term for having an extra copy of a chromosome is 'trisomy.' Down syndrome is also referred to as Trisomy 21. This extra copy changes how the baby's body and brain develop, which can cause both mental and physical challenges for the baby.

Even though people with Down syndrome might act and look similar, each person has different abilities. People with Down syndrome usually have an IQ (a measure of intelligence) in the mildly-to-moderately low range and are slower to speak than other children.

Some common physical features of Down syndrome include:

- A flattened face, especially the bridge of the nose
- Almond-shaped eyes that slant up
- A short neck
- Small ears
- A tongue that tends to stick out of the mouth
- Tiny white spots on the iris (colored part) of the eye
- Small hands and feet
- A single line across the palm of the hand (palmar crease)
- Small pinky fingers that sometimes curve toward the thumb
- Poor muscle tone or loose joints
- Shorter in height as children and adults

Intellectual and Cognitive Disabilities

Occurrence

Down syndrome remains the most common chromosomal condition diagnosed in the United States. Each year, about 6,000 babies born in the United States have Down syndrome. This means that Down syndrome occurs in about 1 out of every 700 babies.

Types of Down Syndrome

There are three types of Down syndrome. People often can't tell the difference between each type without looking at the chromosomes because the physical features and behaviors are similar.

- **Trisomy 21:** About 95 percent of people with Down syndrome have Trisomy 21. With this type of Down syndrome, each cell in the body has 3 separate copies of chromosome 21 instead of the usual 2 copies.

- **Translocation Down syndrome:** This type accounts for a small percentage of people with Down syndrome (about 3%). This occurs when an extra part or a whole extra chromosome 21 is present, but it is attached or "trans-located" to a different chromosome rather than being a separate chromosome 21.

- **Mosaic Down syndrome:** This type affects about 2 percent of the people with Down syndrome. Mosaic means mixture or combination. For children with mosaic Down syndrome, some of their cells have 3 copies of chromosome 21, but other cells have the typical two copies of chromosome 21. Children with mosaic Down syndrome may have the same features as other children with Down syndrome. However, they may have fewer features of the condition due to the presence of some (or many) cells with atypical number of chromosomes.

Causes and Risk Factors of Down Syndrome

- The extra chromosome 21 leads to the physical features and developmental challenges that can occur among people with Down syndrome. Researchers know that Down syndrome is caused by an extra chromosome, but no one knows for sure why Down syndrome occurs or how many different factors play a role.

- One factor that increases the risk of having a baby with Down syndrome is the mother's age. Women who are 35 years or older when they become pregnant are more likely to have a pregnancy affected by Down syndrome than women who become pregnant at a younger age. However, the majority of babies with Down syndrome are born to mothers less than 35 years old, because there are many more births among younger women.

Diagnosis of Down Syndrome

There are two basic types of tests available to detect Down syndrome during pregnancy: screening tests and diagnostic tests. A screening test can tell a woman and her healthcare provider whether her pregnancy has a lower or higher chance of having Down syndrome. Screening tests do not provide an absolute diagnosis, but they are safer for the mother and the developing baby. Diagnostic tests can typically detect whether or not a baby will have Down syndrome, but they can be more riskier for the mother and developing baby. Neither screening nor diagnostic tests can predict the full impact of Down syndrome on a baby; no one can predict this.

Screening Tests for Down Syndrome

Screening tests often include a combination of a blood test, which measures the amount of various substances in the mother's blood (e.g., maternal serum alpha-fetoprotein screening (MSAFP), Triple Screen, Quad-screen), and an ultrasound, which creates a picture of the baby. During an ultrasound, one of the things the technician looks at is the fluid behind the baby's neck. Extra fluid in this region could indicate a genetic problem. These screening tests can help determine the baby's risk of Down syndrome. Rarely, screening tests can give an abnormal result even when there is nothing wrong with the baby. Sometimes, the test results are normal and yet they miss a problem that does exist.

Diagnostic Tests for Down Syndrome

Diagnostic tests are usually performed after a positive screening test in order to confirm a Down syndrome diagnosis. Types of diagnostic tests include:

- **Chorionic villus sampling (CVS)**—examines material from the placenta
- **Amniocentesis**—examines the amniotic fluid (the fluid from the sac surrounding the baby)

Intellectual and Cognitive Disabilities

- **Percutaneous umbilical blood sampling (PUBS)** — examines blood from the umbilical cord

These tests look for changes in the chromosomes that would indicate a Down syndrome diagnosis.

Other Health Problems Associated with Down Syndrome

Many people with Down syndrome have the common facial features and no other major birth defects. However, some people with Down syndrome might have one or more major birth defects or other medical problems. Some of the more common health problems among children with Down syndrome are listed below.

- Hearing loss
- Obstructive sleep apnea, which is a condition where the person's breathing temporarily stops while asleep
- Ear infections
- Eye diseases
- Heart defects present at birth

Healthcare providers routinely monitor children with Down syndrome for these conditions.

Treatments for Down Syndrome

Down syndrome is a lifelong condition. Services early in life will often help babies and children with Down syndrome to improve their physical and intellectual abilities. Most of these services focus on helping children with Down syndrome develop to their full potential. These services include speech, occupational, and physical therapy, and they are typically offered through early intervention programs in each state. Children with Down syndrome may also need extra help or attention in school, although many children are included in regular classes.

Section 19.2

Fetal Alcohol Spectrum Disorders

This section includes text excerpted from "Basics about FASDs," Centers for Disease Control and Prevention (CDC), May 10, 2018.

Fetal alcohol spectrum disorders (FASDs) are a group of conditions that can occur in a person whose mother drank alcohol during pregnancy. These effects can include physical problems and problems with behavior and learning. Often, a person with an FASD has a mix of these problems.

Cause and Prevention of Fetal Alcohol Spectrum Disorders

FASDs are caused by a woman drinking alcohol during pregnancy. Alcohol in the mother's blood passes to the baby through the umbilical cord. When a woman drinks alcohol, so does her baby.

There is no known safe amount of alcohol during pregnancy or when trying to get pregnant. There is also no safe time to drink during pregnancy. Alcohol can cause problems for a developing baby throughout pregnancy, including before a woman knows she's pregnant. All types of alcohol are equally harmful, including all wines and beer.

To prevent FASDs, a woman should not drink alcohol while she is pregnant, or when she might get pregnant. This is because a woman could get pregnant and not know for up to 4–6 weeks. In the United States, nearly half of pregnancies are unplanned.

If a woman is drinking alcohol during pregnancy, it is never too late to stop drinking. Because brain growth takes place throughout pregnancy, the sooner a woman stops drinking the safer it will be for her and her baby. Resources are available here.

FASDs are completely preventable if a woman does not drink alcohol during pregnancy—so why take the risk?

Signs and Symptoms of Fetal Alcohol Spectrum Disorders

FASDs refer to the whole range of effects that can happen to a person whose mother drank alcohol during pregnancy. These conditions can affect each person in different ways, and can range from mild to severe.

Intellectual and Cognitive Disabilities

A person with an FASD might have

- abnormal facial features, such as a smooth ridge between the nose and upper lip (this ridge is called the philtrum)
- small head size
- shorter-than-average height
- low body weight
- poor coordination
- hyperactive behavior
- difficulty with attention
- poor memory
- difficulty in school (especially with math)
- learning disabilities
- speech and language delays
- intellectual disability or low IQ
- poor reasoning and judgment skills
- sleep and sucking problems as a baby
- vision or hearing problems
- problems with the heart, kidneys, or bones

Types of Fetal Alcohol Spectrum Disorders

Different terms are used to describe FASDs, depending on the type of symptoms.

- **Fetal alcohol syndrome (FAS):** FAS represents the most involved end of the FASD spectrum. Fetal death is the most extreme outcome from drinking alcohol during pregnancy. People with FAS might have abnormal facial features, growth problems, and central nervous system (CNS) problems. People with FAS can have problems with learning, memory, attention span, communication, vision, or hearing. They might have a mix of these problems. People with FAS often have a hard time in school and trouble getting along with others.
- **Alcohol-related neurodevelopmental disorder (ARND):** People with ARND might have intellectual disabilities and

problems with behavior and learning. They might do poorly in school and have difficulties with math, memory, attention, judgment, and poor impulse control.

- **Alcohol-related birth defects (ARBD):** People with ARBD might have problems with the heart, kidneys, or bones or with hearing. They might have a mix of these.

- **Neurobehavioral disorder associated with prenatal alcohol exposure (ND-PAE):** ND-PAE was first included as a recognized condition in the *Diagnostic and Statistical Manual 5 (DSM 5)* of the American Psychiatric Association (APA) in 2013. A child or youth with ND-PAE will have problems in three areas:

  1. Thinking and memory, where the child may have trouble planning or may forget material he or she has already learned,

  2. Behavior problems, such as severe tantrums, mood issues (for example, irritability), and difficulty shifting attention from one task to another, and

  3. Trouble with day-to-day living, which can include problems with bathing, dressing for the weather, and playing with other children. In addition, to be diagnosed with ND-PAE, the mother of the child must have consumed more than minimal levels of alcohol before the child's birth, which APA defines as more than 13 alcoholic drinks per month of pregnancy (that is, any 30-day period of pregnancy) or more than 2 alcoholic drinks in one sitting.

Diagnosis of Fetal Alcohol Spectrum Disorders

The term FASDs is not meant for use as a clinical diagnosis. Centers for Disease Control and Prevention (CDC) worked with a group of experts and organizations to review the research and develop guidelines for diagnosing FAS. The guidelines were developed for FAS only. CDC and its partners are working to put together diagnostic criteria for other FASDs, such as ARND.

Diagnosing FAS can be hard because there is no medical test, like a blood test, for it. And other disorders, such as ADHD (attention deficit hyperactivity disorder) and Williams syndrome, have some symptoms like FAS.

Intellectual and Cognitive Disabilities

To diagnose FAS, doctors look for

- abnormal facial features (e.g., smooth ridge between nose and upper lip)
- lower-than-average height, weight, or both
- central nervous system problems (e.g., small head size, problems with attention and hyperactivity, poor coordination)
- prenatal alcohol exposure; although confirmation is not required to make a diagnosis

Treatment of Fetal Alcohol Spectrum Disorders

FASDs last a lifetime. There is no cure for FASDs, but research shows that early intervention treatment services can improve a child's development.

There are many types of treatment options, including medication to help with some symptoms, behavior and education therapy, parent training, and other alternative approaches. No one treatment is right for every child. Good treatment plans will include close monitoring, followups, and changes as needed along the way.

Also, "protective factors" can help reduce the effects of FASDs and help people with these conditions reach their full potential.

Protective factors include:

- Diagnosis before 6 years of age
- Loving, nurturing, and stable home environment during the school years
- Absence of violence
- Involvement in special education and social services

Get Help

If you or the doctor thinks there could be a problem, ask the doctor for a referral to a specialist (someone who knows about FASDs), such as a developmental pediatrician, child psychologist, or clinical geneticist. In some cities, there are clinics whose staffs have special training in diagnosing and treating children with FASDs. To find doctors and clinics in your area visit the National and State Resource Directory from the National Organization on Fetal Alcohol Syndrome (NOFAS).

At the same time as you ask the doctor for a referral to a specialist, call your state or territory's early intervention program to request a free evaluation to find out if your child can get services to help. This is sometimes called a Child Find evaluation. You do not need to wait for a doctor's referral or a medical diagnosis to make this call.

Where to call for a free evaluation from the state depends on your child's age:

- If your child is younger than 3 years old, Call your state or territory's early intervention program (www.cdc.gov/ncbddd/actearly/parents/states.html) and say: "I have concerns about my child's development and I would like to have my child evaluated to find out if he/she is eligible for early intervention services."

- If your child is 3 years old or older, contact your local public school system.

Even if your child is not old enough for kindergarten or enrolled in a public school, call your local elementary school or board of education and ask to speak with someone who can help you have your child evaluated.

Section 19.3

Shaken Baby Syndrome

This section contains text excerpted from the following sources: Text beginning with the heading "What's the Problem?" is excerpted from "Shaken Baby Syndrome," Centers for Disease Control and Prevention (CDC), September 15, 2017; Text beginning with the heading "Treatment" is excerpted from "Shaken Baby Syndrome Information Page," National Institute of Neurological Disorders and Stroke (NINDS), July 2, 2018.

What Is Shaken Baby Syndrome?

Shaken baby syndrome (SBS) is a severe form of physical child abuse. SBS may be caused from vigorously shaking an infant by the shoulders, arms, or legs. The "whiplash" effect can cause intracranial

Intellectual and Cognitive Disabilities

(within the brain) or intraocular (within the eyes) bleeding. Often there is no obvious external head trauma. Still, children with SBS may display some outward signs:

- Change in sleeping pattern or inability to be awakened
- Confused, restless, or agitated state
- Convulsions or seizures
- Loss of energy or motivation
- Slurred speech
- Uncontrollable crying
- Inability to be consoled
- Inability to nurse or eat

SBS can result in death, mental retardation or developmental delays, paralysis, severe motor dysfunction, spasticity, blindness, and seizures.

Who's at Risk for Shaken Baby Syndrome?

Small children are especially vulnerable to this type of abuse. Their heads are large in comparison to their bodies, and their neck muscles are weak. Children under one year of age are at highest risk, but SBS has been reported in children up to five years of age. Shaking often occurs in response to a baby crying or having a toilet-training accident. The perpetrator tends to be male and is primarily the biological father or the mother's boyfriend or partner. Caregivers are responsible for about 9–21 percent of cases. The explanation typically provided by the caregiver—"I was playing with the baby"—does not begin to account for the severity of trauma. Many times there is also a history of child abuse.

Can Shaken Baby Syndrome Be Prevented?

SBS is completely preventable. However, it is not known whether educational efforts will effectively prevent this type of abuse. Home visitation programs are shown to prevent child abuse in general. Because the child's father or the mother's partner often causes SBS, they should be included in home visitation programs. Home visits bring community resources to families in their homes. Health professionals provide information, healthcare, psychological support, and other services that can help people to be more effective parents and caregivers.

The Bottom Line on Shaken Baby Syndrome

- Shaking a baby can cause death or permanent brain damage. It can result in lifelong disability.

- Healthy strategies for dealing with a crying baby include: finding the reason for the crying; checking for signs of illness or discomfort, such as diaper rash, teething, tight clothing; feeding or burping; soothing the baby by rubbing its back; gently rocking; offering a pacifier; singing or talking; taking a walk using a stroller or a drive in a properly-secured car seat; or calling the doctor if sickness is suspected.

- All babies cry. Caregivers often feel overwhelmed by a crying baby. Calling a friend, relative, or neighbor for support or assistance let's the caregiver take a break from the situation. If immediate support is not available, the caregiver could place the baby in a crib (making sure the baby is safe), close the door, and check on the baby every five minutes.

Treatment of Shaken Baby Syndrome

Emergency treatment for a baby who has been shaken usually includes life-sustaining measures such as respiratory support and surgery to stop internal bleeding and bleeding in the brain. Doctors may use brain scans, such as magnetic resonance imaging (MRI) and computed tomography (CT), to make a more definite diagnosis.

Prognosis of Shaken Baby Syndrome

In comparison with accidental traumatic brain injury (TBI) in infants, shaken baby injuries have a much worse prognosis. Damage to the retina of the eye can cause blindness. The majority of infants who survive severe shaking will have some form of neurological or mental disability, such as cerebral palsy (CP) or cognitive impairment, which may not be fully apparent before 6 years of age. Children with shaken baby syndrome (SBS) may require lifelong medical care.

Chapter 20

Learning Disabilities

Chapter Contents

Section 20.1—Learning Disabilities: Overview.......................... 198
Section 20.2—Dyscalculia... 201
Section 20.3—Dyslexia 206
Section 20.4—Dysgraphia 208
Section 20.5—Dyspraxia.. 209

Section 20.1

Learning Disabilities: Overview

This section includes text excerpted from "What Are the Indicators of Learning Disabilities?" *Eunice Kennedy Shriver* National Institute of Child Health and Human Development (NICHD), January 12, 2016.

Many children have difficulty with reading, writing, or other learning-related tasks at some point, but this does not mean they have learning disabilities. A child with a learning disability often has several related signs, and these persist over time. The signs of learning disabilities vary from person to person. Common signs that a person may have learning disabilities include the following:

- Difficulty with reading and/or writing
- Problems with math skills
- Difficulty remembering
- Problems paying attention
- Trouble following directions
- Poor coordination
- Difficulty with concepts related to time
- Problems staying organized

A child with a learning disability also may exhibit one or more of the following:

- Impetuous behavior
- Inappropriate responses in school or social situations
- Difficulty staying on task (easily distracted)
- Difficulty finding the right way to say something
- Inconsistent school performance
- Immature way of speaking
- Difficulty listening well
- Problems dealing with new things in life
- Problems understanding words or concepts

Learning Disabilities

These signs alone are not enough to determine that a person has a learning disability. A professional assessment is necessary to diagnose a learning disability.

Each learning disability has its own signs. Also, not every person with a particular disability will have all of the signs of that disability.

Children being taught in a second language that they are learning sometimes act in ways that are similar to the behaviors of someone with a learning disability. For this reason, learning disability assessment must take into account whether a student is bilingual or a second language learner.

Below are some common learning disabilities and the signs associated with them:

Dyslexia

People with dyslexia usually have trouble making the connections between letters and sounds and with spelling and recognizing words.

People with dyslexia often show other signs of the condition. These may include:

- Failure to fully understand what others are saying
- Difficulty organizing written and spoken language
- Delayed ability to speak
- Poor self-expression (for example, saying "thing" or "stuff" for words not recalled)
- Difficulty learning new vocabulary, either through reading or hearing
- Trouble learning foreign languages
- Slowness in learning songs and rhymes
- Slow reading as well as giving up on longer reading tasks
- Difficulty understanding questions and following directions
- Poor spelling
- Difficulty recalling numbers in sequence (for example, telephone numbers and addresses)
- Trouble distinguishing left from right

Dysgraphia

Dysgraphia is characterized by problems with writing. This disorder may cause a child to be tense and awkward when holding a pen or pencil, even to the extent of contorting his or her body. A child with very poor handwriting that he or she does not outgrow may have dysgraphia.

Other signs of this condition may include:

- A strong dislike of writing and/or drawing
- Problems with grammar
- Trouble writing down ideas
- A quick loss of energy and interest while writing
- Trouble writing down thoughts in a logical sequence
- Saying words out loud while writing
- Leaving words unfinished or omitting them when writing sentences

Dyscalculia

Signs of this disability include problems understanding basic arithmetic concepts, such as fractions, number lines, and positive and negative numbers.

Other symptoms may include:

- Difficulty with math-related word problems
- Trouble making change in cash transactions
- Messiness in putting math problems on paper
- Trouble recognizing logical information sequences (for example, steps in math problems)
- Trouble with understanding the time sequence of events
- Difficulty with verbally describing math processes

Dyspraxia

A person with dyspraxia has problems with motor tasks, such as hand-eye coordination, that can interfere with learning. Some other symptoms of this condition include:

Learning Disabilities

- Problems organizing oneself and one's things
- Breaking things
- Trouble with tasks that require hand-eye coordination, such as coloring within the lines, assembling puzzles, and cutting precisely
- Poor balance
- Sensitivity to loud and/or repetitive noises, such as the ticking of a clock
- Sensitivity to touch, including irritation over bothersome-feeling clothing

Section 20.2

Dyscalculia

This section contains text excerpted from the following sources: Text beginning with the heading "What Is Dyscalculia?" is excerpted from "Infographic: Does Your Child Struggle with Math?" *Eunice Kennedy Shriver* National Institute of Child Health and Human Development (NICHD), December 30, 2017; Text beginning with the heading "Symptoms" is © 2017 Omnigraphics. Reviewed July 2018.

What Is Dyscalculia?

Dyscalculia is not as well known as dyslexia, but both are learning disabilities.

Dyscalculia = Math
Causes trouble with

- Understanding arithmetic (numbers) concepts and solving arithmetic problems
- Estimating time, measuring, and budgeting

Also called a Math Learning Disability.

How Many People Have Dyscalculia?

Boys are slightly more likely to have dyscalculia than girls.

What Are the Risk Factors for Dyscalculia?

By Age 4

Has trouble

- Listing numbers in correct order
- Matching number words or written digits to number of objects
- Counting objects

Age 6–12

Has regular and lasting trouble

- Performing addition, subtraction, multiplication, or division appropriate to grade level
- Recognizing math errors

Age 12+

Has trouble

- Estimating (informed guessing)
- Making exact calculations
- Understanding graphs and charts
- Understanding fractions and decimals

How Can Adults Reduce the Risk of Dyscalculia in Young Children?

Show the child that numbers are a normal part of everyday life.

- Mention numbers to your child while doing everyday activities— like grocery shopping or setting the table.
- Count out loud and show the child both the written number word ("three") and digit ("3").
- Count actual objects the child can see.
- Compare objects in everyday conversation using words that describe size or amount.

Symptoms of Dyscalculia

In early childhood, dyscalculia is typified by general difficulty with numbers, recognizing patterns, and sorting objects by shape or size. As children enter school and math learning progresses, the characteristics may include trouble with simple addition, subtraction, multiplication, and division, as well as difficulty retaining numerical concepts and applying math to common situations.

Teens with dyscalculia continue to have problems as math becomes increasingly complex and more is expected of them. Symptoms for this age group, as well as adults, can include:

- Lack of understanding of time, often late or miscalculating how long tasks will take
- Difficulty applying math principles to everyday life, such as calculating the area of a room or the amount of a tip
- Poor sense of direction, easily gets lost or worries about getting lost
- Trouble judging distances between objects
- May do well in classes that require reading and writing skills, such as English and history, but struggles in those that rely on numbers, like algebra and science
- Trouble with measurements, as in recipes or woodworking, especially when conversions are necessary (pints to ounces, for example)
- Difficulty understanding information in chart or graph form
- Good recall of spoken or printed words, but has trouble remembering numbers and patterns

Diagnosis of Dyscalculia

Most often, various types of learning disabilities are identified when children are quite young, and this is usually the case with dyscalculia. But often younger students do so well in other areas, and the level of math being taught is simple enough, that they are able to mask the symptoms. As a result, in some cases dyscalculia may not be diagnosed until the teen years, when work with numbers becomes considerably more complex and students start to fall behind.

There is no single cause for dyscalculia, but because some of the underlying problems can be neurological or genetic, the first step in diagnosis should be a physical examination by a doctor who is aware that the teen has been exhibiting some of the above symptoms. If no physical cause can be determined, then the student should be evaluated by a specialist in learning disabilities, who will review past performance, administer a variety of tests, and ask questions to determine the individual's skills and understanding of various concepts. Some of the evaluation process will likely include:

- Questions about areas in which the teen feels he or she has had difficulty
- Questions about times when the student has felt hopeless or frustrated about math
- Probing for other learning disabilities that may be contributing factors
- An evaluation of basic math skills (counting, addition, subtraction, etc.)
- Determining whether the teen can discern patterns and organize objects logically
- Testing for the ability to estimate quantity
- Gauging the individual's facility with money (making change, estimating costs, etc.)
- Evaluating the ability to tell time and determine how long tasks will take
- Assessing the student's ability to find alternate ways to solve problems

An important part of diagnosis is to evaluate how well the teen is able to understand math concepts and apply them to common situations, rather than just having him or her perform a series of calculations. For math learning to move forward, it's critical that the student develop a solid grasp of underlying principles, and this won't happen without an accurate assessment of the teen's history and current status.

Treatment of Dyscalculia

Dyscalculia cannot be cured, and it won't improve on its own. But with treatment by a trained professional, along with dedication on the part of the student and support from teachers, parents, and

Learning Disabilities

peers, math skills can be improved considerably. Some strategies include:

- Helping students be aware of their strengths and weaknesses so they can understand and make use of their own unique learning style
- Devising real-life examples that link math skills to everyday situations
- Breaking complex problems into smaller, more easily managed parts
- Using visual aids, such as drawings or physical objects, to help solve math problems
- Talking through the problem-solving process verbally
- Using graph paper to help organize ideas
- Working on a calculator when this is appropriate
- Circling computation signs before trying to solve a problem
- Covering up most of a math exercise or test with a piece of paper to make it easier to concentrate on one problem at a time
- Playing math-related video games
- Reading math problems aloud and continuing to talk while working on a solution
- Reviewing new skills, discussing, and asking questions before moving on to the next task
- Engaging a tutor to help with review, practice, and any particular areas of difficulty
- Working with a classmate or other peer on homework assignments or to review the day's lessons

References

1. "Dyscalculia," National Center for Learning Disabilities (NCLD), 2007.
2. "Dyscalculia: Indications, Treatment and Strategies," NoBullying.com, September 4, 2016.
3. Morin, Amanda. "Treatment Options for Dyscalculia," Understood.org., n.d.

4. Morin, Amanda. "Understanding Dyscalculia," Understood.org, n.d.

5. "What Is Dyscalculia?" Dyslexia SPELD Foundation (DSF), 2014.

Section 20.3

Dyslexia

This section contains text excerpted from the following sources: Text in this section begins with excerpts from "Dyslexia Information Page," National Institute of Neurological Disorders and Stroke (NINDS), June 12, 2018; Text beginning with the heading "What is Dyslexia?" is excerpted from "What is Dyslexia?" MedlinePlus, National Institutes of Health (NIH), December 30, 2015.

Dyslexia is a brain-based type of learning disability that specifically impairs a person's ability to read. These individuals typically read at levels significantly lower than expected despite having normal intelligence. Although the disorder varies from person to person, common characteristics among people with dyslexia are difficulty with phonological processing (the manipulation of sounds), spelling, and/or rapid visual-verbal responding. In individuals with adult onset of dyslexia, it usually occurs as a result of brain injury or in the context of dementia; this contrasts with individuals with dyslexia who simply were never identified as children or adolescents. Dyslexia can be inherited in some families, and studies have identified a number of genes that may predispose an individual to developing dyslexia.

Dyslexia Impairs a Person's Ability to Read

Individuals typically read at significantly lower levels than expected despite having normal intelligence. Although it varies from person to person, people with dyslexia have difficulty with sound processing, spelling, and/or rapid visual-verbal responding. Adult onset of dyslexia usually results from brain injury or dementia; this contrasts with those with dyslexia who simply were never identified as children or adolescents. Dyslexia can be inherited in some families. Few studies have identified a number of genes that may predispose an individual to developing dyslexia.

Dyslexia Symptoms

People with dyslexia often show:

- Difficulty and slowness in reading words
- Difficulty understanding text that is read (poor comprehension)
- Problems with spelling
- Delayed speech (learning to talk later than most other children)
- Difficulty with rhyming

Treating Dyslexia

The main focus of treatment should be on a person's specific learning problems, typically by modifying the teaching environment and methods.

- **Special teaching techniques.** The use of explicit, systematic instruction to teach and directly support children's efforts to learn to read and recognize words. This occurs over time.
- **Classroom modifications.** For example, teachers can give students with dyslexia extra time to finish tasks and provide taped tests that allow the child to hear the questions instead of reading them.
- **Use of technology.** Children with dyslexia may benefit from listening to books on tape or using word-processing programs with spell-check features.

What Is the Prognosis for Dyslexia?

For those with dyslexia, the prognosis is mixed. The disability affects such a wide range of people and produces such different symptoms and varying severity that predictions are hard to make. Prognosis is generally good, however, for individuals whose dyslexia is identified early, who have supportive family and friends and a strong self-image, and who are involved in proper remediation.

Section 20.4

Dysgraphia

This section includes text excerpted from "Dysgraphia Information Page," National Institute of Neurological Disorders and Stroke (NINDS), June 21, 2018.

Dysgraphia is a neurological disorder characterized by writing disabilities. Specifically, the disorder causes a person's writing to be distorted or incorrect. In children, the disorder generally emerges when they are first introduced to writing. They make inappropriately sized and spaced letters, or write wrong or misspelled words, despite thorough instruction. Children with the disorder may have other learning disabilities; however, they usually have no social or other academic problems. Cases of dysgraphia in adults generally occur after some trauma. In addition to poor handwriting, dysgraphia is characterized by wrong or odd spelling, and production of words that are not correct (i.e., using "boy" for "child").

Cause of Dysgraphia

The cause of the disorder is unknown, but in adults, it is usually associated with damage to the parietal lobe of the brain.

Treatment of Dysgraphia

Treatment for dysgraphia varies and may include treatment for motor disorders to help control writing movements. Other treatments may address impaired memory or other neurological problems. Some physicians recommend that individuals with dysgraphia use computers to avoid the problems of handwriting.

Prognosis of Dysgraphia

Some individuals with dysgraphia improve their writing ability, but for others, the disorder persists.

Section 20.5

Dyspraxia

This section includes text excerpted from "Developmental Dyspraxia Information Page," National Institute of Neurological Disorders and Stroke (NINDS), June 15, 2018.

Developmental dyspraxia is a disorder characterized by an impairment in the ability to plan and carry out sensory and motor tasks. Generally, individuals with the disorder appear "out of sync" with their environment.

Symptoms of Dyspraxia

Symptoms vary and may include poor balance and coordination, clumsiness, vision problems, perception difficulties, emotional and behavioral problems, difficulty with reading, writing, and speaking, poor social skills, poor posture, and poor short-term memory. Although individuals with the disorder may be of average or above average intelligence, they may behave immaturely.

Treatment of Dyspraxia

Treatment is symptomatic and supportive and may include occupational and speech therapy, and "cueing" or other forms of communication such as using pictures and hand gestures. Many children with the disorder require special education.

Prognosis of Dyspraxia

Developmental dyspraxia is a lifelong disorder. Many individuals are able to compensate for their disabilities through occupational and speech therapy.

Chapter 21

Autism Spectrum Disorders

What Is Autism Spectrum Disorder?

Autism spectrum disorder (ASD) refers to a group of complex neurodevelopment disorders characterized by repetitive and characteristic patterns of behavior and difficulties with social communication and interaction. The symptoms are present from early childhood and affect daily functioning. The term "spectrum" refers to the wide range of symptoms, skills, and levels of disability in functioning that can occur in people with ASD. Some children and adults with ASD are fully able to perform all activities of daily living while others require substantial support to perform basic activities. The *Diagnostic and Statistical Manual of Mental Disorders (DSM-5)* includes Asperger syndrome, childhood disintegrative disorder, and pervasive developmental disorders not otherwise specified (PDD-NOS) as part of ASD rather than as separate disorders. A diagnosis of ASD includes an assessment of intellectual disability and language impairment. ASD occurs in every racial and ethnic group, and across all socioeconomic levels. However, boys are significantly more likely to develop ASD than girls. The analysis from the Centers for Disease Control and Prevention (CDC) estimates that 1 in 68 children has ASD.

This chapter includes text excerpted from "Autism Spectrum Disorder Fact Sheet," National Institute of Neurological Disorders and Stroke (NINDS), September 2015.

What Are Some Common Signs of Autism Spectrum Disorder?

Even as infants, children with ASD may seem different, especially when compared to other children their own age. They may become overly focused on certain objects, rarely make eye contact, and fail to engage in typical babbling with their parents. In other cases, children may develop normally until the second or even third year of life, but then start to withdraw and become indifferent to social engagement. The severity of ASD can vary greatly and is based on the degree to which social communication, insistence of sameness of activities and surroundings, and repetitive patterns of behavior affect the daily functioning of the individual.

Social Impairment and Communication Difficulties

Many people with ASD find social interactions difficult. The mutual give-and-take nature of typical communication and interaction is often particularly challenging. Children with ASD may fail to respond to their names, avoid eye contact with other people, and only interact with others to achieve specific goals. Often children with ASD do not understand how to play or engage with other children and may prefer to be alone. People with ASD may find it difficult to understand other people's feelings or talk about their own feelings.

People with ASD may have very different verbal abilities ranging from no speech at all to speech that is fluent, but awkward and inappropriate. Some children with ASD may have delayed speech and language skills, may repeat phrases, and give unrelated answers to questions. In addition, people with ASD can have a hard time using and understanding nonverbal cues such as gestures, body language, or tone of voice. For example, young children with ASD might not understand what it means to wave goodbye. People with ASD may also speak in flat, robot-like or a sing-song voice about a narrow range of favorite topics, with little regard for the interests of the person to whom they are speaking.

Repetitive and Characteristic Behaviors

Many children with ASD engage in repetitive movements or unusual behaviors such as flapping their arms, rocking from side to side, or twirling. They may become preoccupied with parts of objects like the wheels on a toy truck. Children may also become obsessively interested in a particular topic such as airplanes or memorizing train schedules. Many people with ASD seem to thrive so much on routine that changes to the daily patterns of life—like an unexpected stop on the way home from school—can be very challenging. Some children may even get angry or have emotional outbursts, especially when placed in a new or overly stimulating environment.

What Disorders Are Related to Autism Spectrum Disorder?

Certain known genetic disorders are associated with an increased risk for autism, including Fragile X syndrome (which causes intellectual disability) and tuberous sclerosis (which causes benign tumors to grow in the brain and other vital organs)—each of which results from a mutation in a single, but different, gene. Researchers have discovered other genetic mutations in children diagnosed with autism, including some that have not yet been designated as named syndromes. While each of these disorders is rare, in aggregate, they may account for 20 percent or more of all autism cases.

People with ASD also have a higher than average risk of having epilepsy. Children whose language skills regress early in life—before age 3—appear to have a risk of developing epilepsy or seizure-like brain activity. About 20–30 percent of children with ASD develop epilepsy by the time they reach adulthood. Additionally, people with both ASD and intellectual disability have the greatest risk of developing a seizure disorder.

How Is Autism Spectrum Disorder Diagnosed?

ASD symptoms can vary greatly from person to person depending on the severity of the disorder. Symptoms may even go unrecognized for young children who have mild ASD or less debilitating handicaps.

Autism spectrum disorder is diagnosed by clinicians based on symptoms, signs, and testing according to the *Diagnostic and Statistical Manual of Mental Disorders-V,* a guide created by the American Psychiatric Association (APA) used to diagnose mental disorders. Children should be screened for developmental delays during periodic checkups and specifically for autism at 18- and 24-month well-child visits.

Very early indicators that require evaluation by an expert include:

- No babbling or pointing by age 1
- No single words by age 16 months or two-word phrases by age 2

- No response to name
- Loss of language or social skills previously acquired
- Poor eye contact
- Excessive lining up of toys or objects
- No smiling or social responsiveness

Later indicators include:
- Impaired ability to make friends with peers
- Impaired ability to initiate or sustain a conversation with others
- Absence or impairment of imaginative and social play
- Repetitive or unusual use of language
- Abnormally intense or focused interest
- Preoccupation with certain objects or subjects
- Inflexible adherence to specific routines or rituals

If screening instruments indicate the possibility of ASD, a more comprehensive evaluation is usually indicated. A comprehensive evaluation requires a multidisciplinary team, including a psychologist, neurologist, psychiatrist, speech therapist, and other professionals who diagnose and treat children with ASD. The team members will conduct a thorough neurological assessment and in-depth cognitive and language testing. Because hearing problems can cause behaviors that could be mistaken for ASD, children with delayed speech development should also have their hearing tested.

What Causes Autism Spectrum Disorder

Scientists believe that both genetics and environment likely play a role in ASD. There is great concern that rates of autism have been increasing in recent decades without full explanation as to why. Researchers have identified a number of genes associated with the disorder. Imaging studies of people with ASD have found differences in the development of several regions of the brain. Studies suggest that ASD could be a result of disruptions in normal brain growth very early in development. These disruptions may be the result of defects in genes that control brain development and regulate how brain cells communicate with each other. Autism is more common in children born prematurely. Environmental factors may also play a role in gene function and development, but no specific environmental causes have yet been identified. The theory that parental practices are responsible for ASD has long been disproved. Multiple studies have shown that vaccination to prevent childhood infectious diseases does not increase the risk of autism in the population.

What Role Do Genes Play in Autism?

Twin and family studies strongly suggest that some people have a genetic predisposition to autism. Identical twin studies show that if one twin is affected, then the other will be affected between 36–95 percent of the time. There are a number of studies in progress to determine the specific genetic factors associated with the development of ASD. In families with one child with ASD, the risk of having a second child with the disorder also increases. Many of the genes found to be associated with autism are involved in the function of the chemical connections between brain neurons (synapses). Researchers are looking for clues about which genes contribute to increased susceptibility. In some cases, parents and other relatives of a child with ASD show mild impairments in social communication skills or engage in repetitive behaviors. Evidence also suggests that emotional disorders such as bipolar disorder and schizophrenia occur more frequently than average in the families of people with ASD.

In addition to genetic variations that are inherited and are present in nearly all of a person's cells, research has also shown that *de novo*, or spontaneous, gene mutations can influence the risk of developing autism spectrum disorder. *De novo* mutations are changes in sequences of deoxyribonucleic acid or DNA, the hereditary material in humans, which can occur spontaneously in a parent's sperm or egg cell or during fertilization. The mutation then occurs in each cell as the fertilized egg divides. These mutations may affect single genes or they may be changes called copy number variations, in which stretches of DNA containing multiple genes are deleted or duplicated. Studies have shown that people with ASD tend to have more copy number *de novo* gene mutations than those without the disorder, suggesting that for some the risk of developing ASD is not the result of mutations in individual genes but rather spontaneous coding mutations across many genes. *De novo* mutations may explain genetic disorders in which an affected child has the mutation in each cell but the parents do not and there is no family pattern to the disorder. Autism risk also increases in children born to older parents. There is still much research to be done to determine the potential role of environmental factors on spontaneous mutations and how that influences ASD risk.

Do Symptoms of Autism Change over Time?

For many children, symptoms improve with age and behavioral treatment. During adolescence, some children with ASD may become depressed or experience behavioral problems, and their treatment may need some modification as they transition to adulthood. People with ASD usually continue to need services and supports as they get older, but depending on severity of the disorder, people with ASD may be able to work successfully and live independently or within a supportive environment.

How Is Autism Treated?

There is no cure for ASD. Therapies and behavioral interventions are designed to remedy specific symptoms and can substantially improve those symptoms. The ideal treatment plan coordinates therapies and interventions that meet the specific needs of the individual. Most healthcare professionals agree that the earlier the intervention, the better.

Educational/behavioral interventions: Early behavioral/educational interventions have been very successful in many children with ASD. In these interventions, therapists use highly structured and intensive skill-oriented training sessions to help children develop social and language skills, such as applied behavioral analysis, which encourages positive behaviors and discourages negative ones. In addition, family counseling for the parents and siblings of children with ASD often helps families cope with the particular challenges of living with a child with ASD.

Medications: While medication can't cure ASD or even treat its main symptoms, there are some that can help with related symptoms such as anxiety, depression, and obsessive-compulsive disorder. Antipsychotic medications are used to treat severe behavioral problems. Seizures can be treated with one or more anticonvulsant drugs. Medication used to treat people with attention deficit disorder can be used effectively to help decrease impulsivity and hyperactivity in people with ASD. Parents, caregivers, and people with autism should use caution before adopting any unproven treatments.

Chapter 22

Attention Deficit Hyperactivity Disorder

Attention deficit hyperactivity disorder (ADHD) is one of the most common neurodevelopmental disorders of childhood. It is usually first diagnosed in childhood and often lasts into adulthood. Children with ADHD may have trouble paying attention, controlling impulsive behaviors (may act without thinking about what the result will be), or be overly active.

Signs and Symptoms of Attention Deficit Hyperactivity Disorder

It is normal for children to have trouble focusing and behaving at one time or another. However, children with ADHD do not just grow out of these behaviors. The symptoms continue and can cause difficulty at school, at home, or with friends.

A child with ADHD might

- daydream a lot;
- forget or lose things a lot;
- squirm or fidget;

This chapter includes text excerpted from "Attention-Deficit/Hyperactivity Disorder (ADHD)—Basic Information," Centers for Disease Control and Prevention (CDC), May 31, 2017.

- talk too much;
- make careless mistakes or take unnecessary risks;
- have a hard time resisting temptation;
- have trouble taking turns; or
- have difficulty getting along with others

Types of Attention Deficit Hyperactivity Disorder

There are three different types of ADHD, depending on which types of symptoms are strongest in the individual:

- **Predominantly inattentive presentation:** It is hard for the individual to organize or finish a task, to pay attention to details, or to follow instructions or conversations. The person is easily distracted or forgets details of daily routines.

- **Predominantly hyperactive-impulsive presentation:** The person fidgets and talks a lot. It is hard to sit still for long (e.g., for a meal or while doing homework). Smaller children may run, jump or climb constantly. The individual feels restless and has trouble with impulsivity. Someone who is impulsive may interrupt others a lot, grab things from people, or speak at inappropriate times. It is hard for the person to wait their turn or listen to directions. A person with impulsiveness may have more accidents and injuries than others.

- **Combined presentation:** Symptoms of the above two types are equally present in the person.

Because symptoms can change over time, the presentation may change over time as well.

Causes of Attention Deficit Hyperactivity Disorder

Scientists are studying cause(s) and risk factors in an effort to find better ways to manage and reduce the chances of a person having ADHD. The cause(s) and risk factors for ADHD are unknown, but current research shows that genetics plays an important role. Studies of twins link genes with ADHD.

In addition to genetics, scientists are studying other possible causes and risk factors including:

- Brain injury

Attention Deficit Hyperactivity Disorder

- Exposure to environmental (e.g., lead) during pregnancy or at a young age
- Alcohol and tobacco use during pregnancy
- Premature delivery
- Low birth weight

Research does not support the popularly held views that ADHD is caused by eating too much sugar, watching too much television, parenting, or social and environmental factors such as poverty or family chaos. Of course, many things, including these, might make symptoms worse, especially in certain people. But the evidence is not strong enough to conclude that they are the main causes of ADHD.

Diagnosis of Attention Deficit Hyperactivity Disorder

Deciding if a child has ADHD is a several step process. There is no single test to diagnose ADHD, and many other problems, like anxiety, depression, sleep problems, and certain types of learning disabilities, can have similar symptoms. One step of the process involves having a medical exam, including hearing and vision tests, to rule out other problems with symptoms like ADHD. Another part of the process may include a checklist for rating ADHD symptoms and taking a history of the child from parents, teachers, and sometimes, the child.

Treatments of Attention Deficit Hyperactivity Disorder

In most cases, ADHD is best treated with a combination of behavior therapy and medication. For preschool-aged children (4–5 years of age) with ADHD, behavior therapy, particularly training for parents, is recommended as the first line of treatment. No single treatment is the answer for every child and good treatment plans will include close monitoring, followups and any changes needed along the way.

Managing Symptoms of Attention Deficit Hyperactivity Disorder: Staying Healthy

Being healthy is important for all children and can be especially important for children with ADHD. In addition to behavioral therapy and medication, having a healthy lifestyle can make it easier for your child to deal with ADHD symptoms. Here are some healthy behaviors that may help:

- Eating a healthful diet centered on fruits, vegetables, whole grains, legumes (for example, beans, peas, and lentils), lean protein sources, and nuts and seeds
- Participating in physical activity for at least 60 minutes each day
- Limiting the amount of daily screen time from TVs, computers, phones, etc.
- Getting the recommended amount of sleep each night based on age

Get Help

If you or your doctor has concerns about ADHD, you can take your child to a specialist such as a child psychologist or developmental pediatrician, or you can contact your local early intervention agency (for children under 3) or public school (for children 3 and older). You can fill out a symptoms checklist and take it to the child's doctor.

The Centers for Disease Control and Prevention (CDC) sponsors the National Resource Center (NRC) on ADHD (www.help4adhd.org/NRC.aspx), a program of CHADD—Children and Adults with attention deficit hyperactivity disorder. Their website has links to information for people with ADHD and their families. The National Resource Center (NRC) operates a call center with trained staff to answer questions about ADHD. The number is 800-233-4050.

Chapter 23

Psychiatric Disability and Mental Disorders

Anxiety Disorders

Anxiety disorders are characterized by excessive fear or anxiety that is difficult to control and negatively and substantially impacts daily functioning. Fear refers to the emotional response to a real or perceived threat while anxiety is the anticipation of a future threat. These disorders can range from specific fears (called phobias), such as the fear of flying or public speaking, to more generalized feelings of worry and tension. Anxiety disorders typically develop in childhood and persist to adulthood. Specific anxiety disorders include generalized anxiety disorder (GAD), panic disorder, separation anxiety disorder (SAD), and social anxiety disorder (social phobia).

National prevalence data indicate that nearly 40 million people in the United States (18%) experience an anxiety disorder in any given year. According to Substance Abuse and Mental Health Services Administration's (SAMHSA) report, lifetime phobias and generalized anxiety disorders are the most prevalent among adolescents between the ages of 13 and 18 and have the earliest median age of first onset, around age 6. Phobias and generalized anxiety usually first appear around age 11, and they are the most prevalent anxiety disorders in adults.

This chapter includes text excerpted from "Mental Disorders," Substance Abuse and Mental Health Services Administration (SAMHSA), October 27, 2015.

Evidence suggests that many anxiety disorders may be caused by a combination of genetics, biology, and environmental factors. Adverse childhood experiences may also contribute to risk for developing anxiety disorders.

Attention Deficit Hyperactivity Disorder (ADHD)

Attention deficit hyperactivity disorder (ADHD) is defined by a persistent pattern of inattention (for example, difficulty keeping focus) and/or hyperactivity-impulsivity (for example, difficulty controlling behavior, excessive and inappropriate motor activity). Children with ADHD have difficulty performing well in school, interacting with other children, and following through on tasks. Adults with ADHD are often extremely distractible and have significant difficulties with organization. There are three subtypes of the disorder:

- Predominantly hyperactive/impulsive
- Predominantly inattentive
- Combined hyperactive/inattentive

ADHD is one of the more common mental disorders diagnosed among children. Data from the National Health Interview Survey (NHIS) indicate that parents of 8.4 percent of children aged 3–17 years had been informed that their child had ADHD. For youth ages 13–18, the prevalence rate is 9 percent. The disorder occurs four times as often among boys than girls. It is estimated that the prevalence of ADHD among adults is 2.5 percent.

Research suggests that ADHD has a high degree of heritability, however, the exact gene or constellation of genes that give rise to the disorder are not known. Environmental risk factors may include low birth weight, smoking and alcohol use during pregnancy, exposure to lead, and history of child maltreatment.

The three overarching features of ADHD include inattention, hyperactivity, and impulsivity. Inattentive children may have trouble paying close attention to details, make careless mistakes in schoolwork, are easily distracted, have difficulty following through on tasks, such as homework assignments, or quickly become bored with a task. Hyperactivity may be defined by fidgeting or squirming, excessive talking, running about, or difficulty sitting still. Finally, impulsive children may be impatient, may blurt out answers to questions prematurely, have trouble waiting their turn, may frequently interrupt conversations, or intrude on others' activities.

Psychiatric Disability and Mental Disorders

Bipolar and Related Disorders

People with bipolar and related disorders experience atypical, dramatic swings in mood, and activity levels that go from periods of feeling intensely happy, irritable, and impulsive to periods of intense sadness and feelings of hopelessness. Individuals with this disorder experience discrete mood episodes, characterized as either a:

- Manic episode—abnormally elevated, expansive, or irritable mood accompanied by increased energy or activity that substantially impairs functioning

- Hypomanic episode—similar to a manic episode, however, not severe enough to cause serious social or occupational problems

- Major depressive episode (MDE)—persistent depressed mood or loss of interest or pleasure

- Mixed state—includes symptoms of both a manic episode and a major depressive episode

People exhibiting these symptoms are most frequently identified as having one of two types of bipolar disorders: bipolar I disorder or bipolar II disorder. The bipolar I diagnosis is used when there has been at least one manic episode in a person's life. The bipolar II diagnosis is used when there has been a more regular occurrence of depressive episodes along with a hypomanic episode, but not a full-blown manic episode. Cyclothymic disorder, or cyclothymia, is a diagnosis used for a mild form of bipolar disorder.

The combined prevalence of bipolar I disorder, bipolar II disorder and cyclothymia is estimated at 2.6 percent of the U.S. adult population and 11.2 percent for 13–18 year olds.

A family history of bipolar disorder is the strongest risk factor for the condition, and the level of risk increases with the degree of kinship.

As mentioned previously, bipolar disorders are characterized by manic and depressive episodes. In children, manic episodes may present as an excessively silly or joyful mood that is unusual for the child or an uncharacteristically irritable temperament and are accompanied by unusual behavioral changes, such as decreased need for sleep, risk-seeking behavior, and distractibility. Depressive episodes may present as a persistent, sad mood, feelings of worthlessness or guilt, and loss of interest in previously enjoyable activities. Behavioral changes associated with depressive episodes may include fatigue or loss of energy, gaining or losing a significant amount of weight, complaining about pain, or suicidal thoughts or plans.

Depressive Disorders (Including Major Depressive Disorder)

Depressive disorders are among the most common mental health disorders in the United States. They are characterized by a sad, hopeless, empty, or irritable mood, and somatic and cognitive changes that significantly interfere with daily life. Major depressive disorder (MDD) is defined as having a depressed mood for most of the day and a marked loss of interest or pleasure, among other symptoms, present nearly every day for at least a two-week period. In children and adolescents, MDD may manifest as an irritable rather than a sad disposition. Suicidal thoughts or plans can occur during an episode of major depression, which can require immediate attention (to be connected to a skilled, trained counselor at a local crisis center, people can call 800-272-TALK (800-272-8255) anytime 24/7).

Based on the National Survey on Drug Use and Health (NSDUH) data, 6.6 percent of adults aged 18 or older had a major depressive episode (MDE), which was defined by the 4th edition of the *Diagnostic and Statistical Manual of Mental Disorders (DSM-IV)*. The NSDUH data also show that the prevalence of MDE among adolescents aged 12–17 was 11.4 percent, while female youths were about three times as likely as male youths to experience an MDE.

MDD is thought to have many possible causes, including genetic, biological, and environmental factors. Adverse childhood experiences and stressful life experiences are known to contribute to risk for MDD. In addition, those with closely related family members (for example, parents or siblings) who are diagnosed with the disorder are at increased risk.

A diagnosis for MDD at a minimum requires that symptoms of depressed mood (for example, feelings of sadness, emptiness, hopelessness) and loss of interest or pleasure in activities are present. Additional symptoms may include significant weight loss or gain, insomnia or hypersomnia, feelings of restlessness, lethargy, feelings of worthlessness or excessive guilt, distractibility, and recurrent thoughts of death, including suicidal ideation. Symptoms must be present for at least two-weeks and cause significant impairment or dysfunction in daily life.

Disruptive, Impulse Control, and Conduct Disorders

This class of disorders is characterized by problems with self-control of emotions or behaviors that violate the rights of others and/or

Psychiatric Disability and Mental Disorders

bring a person into conflict with societal norms or authority figures. Oppositional defiant disorder (ODD) and conduct disorder are the most prominent of this class of disorders in children.

Oppositional Defiant Disorder

Children with oppositional defiant disorder display a frequent and persistent pattern of angry or irritable mood, argumentative/defiant behavior, or vindictiveness. Symptoms are typically first seen in the preschool years, and often precede the development of conduct disorder.

The average prevalence of ODD is estimated at 3.3 percent and occurs more often in boys than girls.

Children who experienced harsh, inconsistent, or neglectful child-rearing practices are at increased risk for developing ODD.

Symptoms of ODD include angry/irritable mood, argumentative/defiant behavior, or vindictiveness. A child with an angry/irritable mood may often lose their temper, be frequently resentful, or easily annoyed. Argumentative or defiant children are frequently combative with authority figures or adults and often refuse to comply with rules. They may also deliberately annoy others or blame others for their mistakes or misbehavior. These symptoms must be evident for at least six months and observed when interacting with at least one individual who is not a sibling.

Conduct Disorder

Occurring in children and teens, conduct disorder is a persistent pattern of disruptive and violent behaviors that violate the basic rights of others or age-appropriate social norms or rules, and causes significant impairment in the child or family's daily life.

An estimated 8.5 percent of children and youth meet criteria for conduct disorder at some point in their life. Prevalence increases from childhood to adolescence and is more common among males than females.

Conduct disorder may be preceded by temperamental risk factors, such as behavioral difficulties in infancy and below-average intelligence. Similar to ODD, environmental risk factors may include harsh or inconsistent child-rearing practices and/or child maltreatment. Parental criminality, frequent changes of caregivers, large family size, familial psychopathology, and early institutional living may also contribute to risk for developing the disorder. Community-level risk factors may include neighborhood exposure to violence, peer rejection, and association with a delinquent peer group. Children with a parent or sibling with conduct disorder or other behavioral health disorders (for example, ADHD, schizophrenia, severe alcohol use disorder) are more likely to develop the condition. Children with conduct disorder often present with other disorders as well, including ADHD, learning disorders, and depression.

The primary symptoms of conduct disorder include aggression to people and animals (for example, bullying or causing physical harm), destruction of property (for example, fire-setting), deceitfulness or theft (for example, breaking and entering), and serious violations of rules (for example, truancy, elopement). Symptoms must be present for 12 months and fall into one of three subtypes depending on the age at onset (childhood, adolescent, or unspecified).

Obsessive-Compulsive and Related Disorders

Obsessive-compulsive disorder (OCD) is defined by the presence of persistent thoughts, urges, or images that are intrusive and unwanted (obsessions), or repetitive and ritualistic behaviors that a person feels are necessary in order to control obsessions (compulsions). OCD tends to begin in childhood or adolescence, with most individuals being diagnosed by the age of 19.

In the United States, the 12-month prevalence rate of OCD is estimated at 1.2 percent or nearly 2.2 million American adults.

The causes of OCD are largely unknown, however, there is some evidence that it runs in families and is associated with environmental risk factors, such as child maltreatment or traumatic childhood events.

Prerequisites for OCD include the presence of obsessions, compulsions, or both. Obsessions may include persistent thoughts (for example, of contamination), images (for example, of horrific scenes), or urges (for example, to jump from a window) and are perceived as unpleasant and involuntary. Compulsions include repetitive behaviors that the person is compelled to carry out ritualistically in response to an obsession or according to a rigid set of rules. Compulsions are carried out in an effort to prevent or reduce anxiety or distress, and yet are clearly excessive or unrealistic. A common example of an OCD symptom is a person who is obsessed with germs and feels compelled to wash their hands excessively. OCD symptoms are time-consuming and cause significant dysfunction in daily life.

Schizophrenia Spectrum and Other Psychotic Disorders

The defining characteristic of schizophrenia and other psychotic disorders is abnormalities in one or more of five domains: delusions, hallucinations, disorganized thinking, grossly disorganized or abnormal motor behavior, and negative symptoms, which include diminished emotional expression and a decrease in the ability to engage in self-initiated activities. Disorders in this category include schizotypal disorder, schizoaffective disorder, and schizophreniform disorder. The most common diagnosis in this category is schizophrenia.

Schizophrenia

Schizophrenia is a brain disorder that impacts the way a person thinks (often described as a "thought disorder"), and is characterized by a range of cognitive, behavioral, and emotional experiences that can include: delusions, hallucinations, disorganized thinking, and grossly disorganized or abnormal motor behavior. These symptoms are chronic and severe, significantly impairing occupational and social functioning.

The lifetime prevalence of schizophrenia is estimated to be about 1 percent of the population. Childhood-onset schizophrenia (defined as onset before age 13) is much rarer, affecting approximately 0.01 percent of children. Symptoms of schizophrenia typically manifest between the ages of 16 and 30.

While family history of psychosis is often not predictive of schizophrenia, genetic predisposition correlates to risk for developing the disease. Physiological factors, such as certain pregnancy and birth complications and environmental factors, such as season of birth (late winter/early spring) and growing up in an urban environment may be associated with increased risk for schizophrenia.

People with schizophrenia can experience what are termed positive or negative symptoms. Positive symptoms are psychotic behaviors including:

- Delusions of false and persistent beliefs that are not part of the individual's culture. For example, people with schizophrenia may believe that their thoughts are being broadcast on the radio.

- Hallucinations that include hearing, seeing, smelling, or feeling things that others cannot. Most commonly, people with the disorder hear voices that talk to them or order them to do things.

- Disorganized speech that involves difficulty organizing thoughts, thought-blocking, and making up nonsensical words.
- Grossly disorganized or catatonic behavior.

Negative symptoms may include flat affect, disillusionment with daily life, isolating behavior, lack of motivation, and infrequent speaking, even when forced to interact. As with other forms of serious mental illness, schizophrenia is related to homelessness, involvement with the criminal justice system, and other negative outcomes.

Trauma- and Stressor-Related Disorders

The defining characteristic of trauma- and stressor-related disorders is previous exposure to a traumatic or stressful event. The most common disorder in this category is posttraumatic stress disorder (PTSD).

Posttraumatic Stress Disorder

Posttraumatic stress disorder (PTSD) is characterized as the development of debilitating symptoms following exposure to a traumatic or dangerous event. These can include re-experiencing symptoms from an event, such as flashbacks or nightmares, avoidance symptoms, changing a personal routine to escape having to be reminded of an event, or being hyper-aroused (easily startled or tense) that makes daily tasks nearly impossible to complete. PTSD was first identified as a result of symptoms experienced by soldiers and those in war; however, other traumatic events, such as rape, child abuse, car accidents, and natural disasters have also been shown to give rise to PTSD.

It is estimated that more than 7.7 million people in the United States could be diagnosed as having a PTSD with women being more likely to have the disorder when compared to men.

Risk for PTSD is separated into three categories, including pretraumatic, peritraumatic, and posttraumatic factors.

- Pretraumatic factors include childhood emotional problems by age 6, lower socioeconomic status, lower education, prior exposure to trauma, childhood adversity, lower intelligence, minority racial/ethnic status, and a family psychiatric history. Female gender and younger age at exposure may also contribute to pretraumatic risk.

Psychiatric Disability and Mental Disorders

- Peritraumatic factors include the severity of the trauma, perceived life threat, personal injury, interpersonal violence, and dissociation during the trauma that persists afterward.

- Posttraumatic risk factors include negative appraisals, ineffective coping strategies, subsequent exposure to distressing reminders, subsequent adverse life events, and other trauma-related losses.

Diagnosis of PTSD must be preceded by exposure to actual or threatened death, serious injury, or violence. This may entail directly experiencing or witnessing the traumatic event, learning that the traumatic event occurred to a close family member or friend, or repeated exposure to distressing details of the traumatic event. Individuals diagnosed with PTSD experience intrusive symptoms (for example, recurrent upsetting dreams, flashbacks, distressing memories, intense psychological distress), avoidance of stimuli associated with the traumatic event, and negative changes in cognition and mood corresponding with the traumatic event (for example, dissociative amnesia, negative beliefs about oneself, persistent negative affect, feelings of detachment or estrangement). They also experience significant changes in arousal and reactivity associated with the traumatic events, such as hypervigilance, distractibility, exaggerated startle response, and irritable or self-destructive behavior.

Chapter 24

Degenerative Diseases That Cause Disability

Chapter Contents

Section 24.1—Alzheimer Disease 232
Section 24.2—Amyotrophic Lateral Sclerosis 238
Section 24.3—Arthritis 239
Section 24.4—Multiple Sclerosis 243
Section 24.5—Parkinson Disease 257

Section 24.1

Alzheimer Disease

This section includes text excerpted from "Alzheimer's Disease Fact Sheet," National Institute on Aging (NIA), National Institutes of Health (NIH), August 17, 2016.

Alzheimer disease (AD) is an irreversible, progressive brain disorder that slowly destroys memory and thinking skills, and eventually the ability to carry out the simplest tasks. In most people with Alzheimer, symptoms first appear in their mid-60s. Estimates vary, but experts suggest that more than 5 million Americans may have Alzheimer.

AD is ranked as the sixth leading cause of death in the United States, but estimates indicate that the disorder may rank third, just behind heart disease and cancer, as a cause of death for older people.

Changes in the Brain

Scientists continue to unravel the complex brain changes involved in the onset and progression of AD. It seems likely that damage to the brain starts a decade or more before memory and other cognitive problems appear. During this preclinical stage of AD, people seem to be symptom-free, but toxic changes are taking place in the brain. Abnormal deposits of proteins form amyloid plaques and tau tangles throughout the brain, and once healthy neurons stop functioning, lose connections with other neurons, and die.

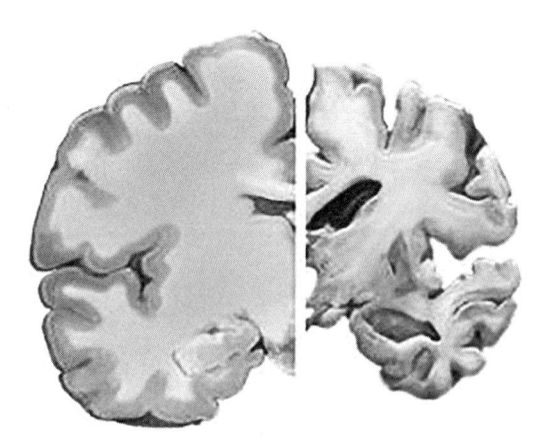

Figure 24.1. *Healthy Brain versus Severe Alzheimer*

Degenerative Diseases That Cause Disability

The damage initially appears to take place in the hippocampus, the part of the brain essential in forming memories. As more neurons die, additional parts of the brain are affected, and they begin to shrink. By the final stage of Alzheimer, damage is widespread, and brain tissue has shrunk significantly.

Signs and Symptoms of Alzheimer Disease

Memory problems are typically one of the first signs of cognitive impairment related to AD. Some people with memory problems have a condition called mild cognitive impairment (MCI). In MCI, people have more memory problems than normal for their age, but their symptoms do not interfere with their everyday lives. Movement difficulties and problems with the sense of smell have also been linked to MCI. Older people with MCI are at greater risk for developing Alzheimer, but not all of them do. Some may even go back to normal cognition.

The first symptoms of Alzheimer vary from person to person. For many, decline in nonmemory aspects of cognition, such as word-finding, vision/spatial issues, and impaired reasoning or judgment, may signal the very early stages of AD. Researchers are studying biomarkers (biological signs of disease found in brain images, cerebrospinal fluid, and blood) to see if they can detect early changes in the brains of people with MCI and in cognitively normal people who may be at greater risk for Alzheimer. Studies indicate that such early detection may be possible, but more research is needed before these techniques can be relied upon to diagnose Alzheimer disease in everyday medical practice.

Mild Alzheimer Disease

As AD progresses, people experience greater memory loss and other cognitive difficulties. Problems can include wandering and getting lost, trouble handling money and paying bills, repeating questions, taking longer to complete normal daily tasks, and personality and behavior changes. People are often diagnosed in this stage.

Moderate Alzheimer Disease

In this stage, damage occurs in areas of the brain that control language, reasoning, sensory processing, and conscious thought. Memory loss and confusion grow worse, and people begin to have problems recognizing family and friends. They may be unable to learn new things, carry out multistep tasks such as getting dressed, or cope with new situations. In addition, people at this stage may have hallucinations, delusions, and paranoia and may behave impulsively.

Severe Alzheimer Disease

Ultimately, plaques and tangles spread throughout the brain, and brain tissue shrinks significantly. People with severe Alzheimer cannot communicate and are completely dependent on others for their care. Near the end, the person may be in bed most or all of the time as the body shuts down.

What Causes Alzheimer Disease

Scientists don't yet fully understand what causes AD in most people. There is a genetic component to some cases of early-onset Alzheimer disease. Late-onset Alzheimer arises from a complex series of brain changes that occur over decades. The causes probably include a combination of genetic, environmental, and lifestyle factors. The importance of any one of these factors in increasing or decreasing the risk of developing Alzheimer may differ from person to person.

The Basics of Alzheimer

Scientists are conducting studies to learn more about plaques, tangles, and other biological features of AD. Advances in brain imaging techniques allow researchers to see the development and spread of abnormal amyloid and tau proteins in the living brain, as well as changes in brain structure and function. Scientists are also exploring the very earliest steps in the disease process by studying changes in the brain and body fluids that can be detected years before Alzheimer symptoms appear. Findings from these studies will help in understanding the causes of Alzheimer and make diagnosis easier.

One of the great mysteries of AD is why it largely strikes older adults. Research on normal brain aging is shedding light on this question. For example, scientists are learning how age-related changes in the brain may harm neurons and contribute to Alzheimer damage. These age-related changes include atrophy (shrinking) of certain parts of the brain, inflammation, production of unstable molecules called free radicals, and mitochondrial dysfunction (a breakdown of energy production within a cell).

Genetics

Most people with Alzheimer have the late-onset form of the disease, in which symptoms become apparent in their mid-60s. The *apolipoprotein E (APOE)* gene is involved in late-onset Alzheimer. This gene has several forms. One of them, *APOE ε4*, increases a person's risk of developing the disease and is also associated with an earlier age of disease onset. However, carrying the *APOE ε4* form of the gene does not mean that a person will definitely develop AD, and some people with no *APOE ε4* may also develop the disease.

Also, scientists have identified a number of regions of interest in the genome (an organism's complete set of deoxyribonucleic acid (DNA)) that may increase a person's risk for late-onset Alzheimer to varying degrees.

Early-onset Alzheimer disease (EOFAD) occurs between a person's 30s to mid-60s and represents less than 10 percent of all people with Alzheimer. Some cases are caused by an inherited change in one of three genes, resulting in a type known as early-onset familial AD, or FAD. For other cases of early-onset Alzheimer, research suggests there may be a genetic component related to factors other than these three genes.

Most people with Down syndrome develop Alzheimer. This may be because people with Down syndrome have an extra copy of chromosome 21, which contains the gene that generates harmful amyloid.

Health, Environmental, and Lifestyle Factors

Research suggests that a host of factors beyond genetics may play a role in the development and course of AD. There is a great deal of interest, for example, in the relationship between cognitive decline and vascular conditions such as heart disease, stroke, and high blood pressure, as well as metabolic conditions such as diabetes and obesity. Ongoing research will help us understand whether and how reducing risk factors for these conditions may also reduce the risk of Alzheimer.

A nutritious diet, physical activity, social engagement, and mentally stimulating pursuits have all been associated with helping people stay healthy as they age. These factors might also help reduce the risk of cognitive decline and AD. Clinical trials are testing some of these possibilities.

Diagnosis of Alzheimer Disease

Doctors use several methods and tools to help determine whether a person who is having memory problems has "possible Alzheimer dementia" (dementia may be due to another cause) or "probable Alzheimer dementia" (no other cause for dementia can be found).

To diagnose Alzheimer, doctors may:

- Ask the person and a family member or friend questions about overall health, past medical problems, ability to carry out daily activities, and changes in behavior and personality

- Conduct tests of memory, problem solving, attention, counting, and language

- Carry out standard medical tests, such as blood and urine tests, to identify other possible causes of the problem

- Perform brain scans, such as computed tomography (CT), magnetic resonance imaging (MRI), or positron emission tomography (PET), to rule out other possible causes for symptoms

These tests may be repeated to give doctors information about how the person's memory and other cognitive functions are changing over time.

AD can be definitely diagnosed only after death, by linking clinical measures with an examination of brain tissue in an autopsy.

People with memory and thinking concerns should talk to their doctor to find out whether their symptoms are due to Alzheimer or another cause, such as stroke, tumor, Parkinson disease, sleep disturbances, side effects of medication, an infection, or a non-Alzheimer dementia. Some of these conditions may be treatable and possibly reversible.

If the diagnosis is Alzheimer, beginning treatment early in the disease process may help preserve daily functioning for some time, even though the underlying disease process cannot be stopped or reversed. An early diagnosis also helps families plan for the future. They can take care of financial and legal matters, address potential safety issues, learn about living arrangements, and develop support networks.

In addition, an early diagnosis gives people greater opportunities to participate in clinical trials that are testing possible new treatments for AD or other research studies.

Treatment of Alzheimer Disease

AD is complex, and it is unlikely that any one drug or other intervention can successfully treat it. Current approaches focus on helping people maintain mental function, manage behavioral symptoms, and

Degenerative Diseases That Cause Disability

slow down certain problems, such as memory loss. Researchers hope to develop therapies targeting specific genetic, molecular, and cellular mechanisms so that the actual underlying cause of the disease can be stopped or prevented.

Maintaining Mental Function

Several medications are approved by the U.S. Food and Drug Administration (FDA) to treat symptoms of Alzheimer. Donepezil (Aricept®), rivastigmine (Exelon®), and galantamine (Razadyne®) are used to treat mild to moderate Alzheimer (donepezil can be used for severe Alzheimer as well). Memantine (Namenda®) is used to treat moderate to severe Alzheimer. These drugs work by regulating neurotransmitters, the chemicals that transmit messages between neurons. They may help reduce symptoms and help with certain behavioral problems. However, these drugs don't change the underlying disease process. They are effective for some but not all people, and may help only for a limited time. The FDA has also approved Aricept® and Namzaric®, a combination of Namenda® and Aricept®, for the treatment of moderate to severe AD.

Managing Behavior

Common behavioral symptoms of Alzheimer include sleeplessness, wandering, agitation, anxiety, and aggression. Scientists are learning why these symptoms occur and are studying new treatments—drug and nondrug—to manage them. Research has shown that treating behavioral symptoms can make people with Alzheimer more comfortable and makes things easier for caregivers.

Section 24.2

Amyotrophic Lateral Sclerosis

This section includes text excerpted from "Amyotrophic Lateral Sclerosis (ALS) Information Page," National Institute of Neurological Disorders and Stroke (NINDS), June 15, 2018.

Amyotrophic lateral sclerosis (ALS) is a rapidly progressive, fatal disease that affects the nerve cells (neurons) in that brain and spinal cord that control voluntary muscle movement. Our voluntary muscles produce movements like walking, breathing, chewing, and talking. Nerve cells called motor neurons—that connect from the brain and spinal cord to the rest of the body—begin to degenerate and die, and stop sending messages to muscles. The muscles gradually weaken, waste away, and twitch, and the brain can't start and control voluntary movement.

Symptoms of Amyotrophic Lateral Sclerosis

Symptoms are usually first noticed in the arms and hands, legs, or swallowing muscles. People with ALS lose their strength and become unable to move their arms and legs, and to hold the body upright. Some individuals eventually can't breathe on their own. Although ALS doesn't usually impair a person's mind or personality, several studies suggest that some people with ALS may develop cognitive problems involving word fluency, decision making, and memory.

Causes of Amyotrophic Lateral Sclerosis

Most cases of ALS happen with no known cause, while a small percentage of cases are inherited.

Treatment of Amyotrophic Lateral Sclerosis

No cure has yet been found for ALS. However, the drugs riluzole and edaravone have approved by the U.S. Food and Drug Administration (FDA) to treat ALS. Riluzole prolongs life by 2–3 months but does not relieve symptoms. Edaravone can slow the clinical decline in daily functioning of people with ALS. The FDA has also approved the NeuRx Diaphragm Pacing System (DPS)™, which uses implanted electrodes and a battery pack to cause the diaphragm (breathing muscle) to contract, to help certain individuals who have ALS before the onset of severe respiratory failure. Other treatments are designed to relieve symptoms and improve the quality of life for people with ALS. Drugs are available to help individuals with spasticity, pain, panic attacks, and depression. Physical therapy, occupational therapy, and rehabilitation may help to prevent joint immobility and slow muscle weakness and atrophy. Individuals with ALS may eventually consider forms of mechanical ventilation (respirators).

Prognosis of Amyotrophic Lateral Sclerosis

Regardless of the part of the body first affected by the disease, muscle weakness and atrophy spread to other parts of the body as the disease progresses. Individuals have increasing problems with moving, swallowing, and speaking or forming words. Eventually, people with ALS will not be able to stand or walk, get in or out of bed on their own, or use their hands and arms. In later stages of the disease, individuals have difficulty breathing as the muscles of the respiratory system weaken. Although ventilation support can ease problems with breathing and prolong survival, it does not affect the progression of ALS. Most people with ALS die from respiratory failure, usually within 3–5 years from the onset of symptoms. However, about 10 percent of those individuals with ALS survive for 10 or more years.

Section 24.3

Arthritis

This section includes text excerpted from "Arthritis," National Institute of Arthritis and Musculoskeletal and Skin Diseases (NIAMS), April 30, 2017.

"Arthritis" literally means joint inflammation. Although joint inflammation is a symptom or sign rather than a specific diagnosis, the term arthritis is often used to refer to any disorder that affects the joints. Joints are places where two bones meet, such as your elbow or knee.

There are different types of arthritis. In some diseases in which arthritis occurs, other organs, such as your eyes, heart, or skin, can also be affected.

Fortunately, current treatments allow most people with arthritis to lead active and productive lives.

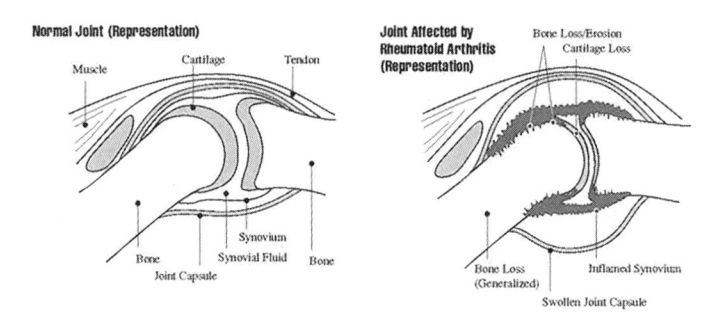

Figure 24.2. *Normal Joint and Joint Affected by Rheumatoid Arthritis*

What Are the Types of Arthritis?

There are several types of arthritis. Common ones include:

- **Ankylosing spondylitis (AS)** is arthritis that affects the spine. It often involves redness, heat, swelling, and pain in the spine or in the joint where the bottom of the spine joins the pelvic bone.

- **Gout** is caused by crystals that build up in the joints. It usually affects the big toe, but many other joints may be affected.

- **Juvenile arthritis (JA)** is the term used to describe arthritis in children. Arthritis is caused by inflammation of the joints.

- **Osteoarthritis (OA)** usually comes with age and most often affects the fingers, knees, and hips. Sometimes osteoarthritis follows a joint injury. For example, you might have badly injured your knee when young and develop arthritis in your knee joint years later.

- **Psoriatic arthritis** can occur in people who have psoriasis (scaly red and white skin patches). It affects the skin, joints, and areas where tissues attach to bone.

- **Reactive arthritis** is pain or swelling in a joint that is caused by an infection in your body. You may also have red, swollen eyes and a swollen urinary tract.

Degenerative Diseases That Cause Disability

- **Rheumatoid arthritis (RA)** happens when the body's own defense system doesn't work properly. It affects joints and bones (often of the hands and feet), and may also affect internal organs and systems. You may feel sick or tired, and you may have a fever.

Arthritis is seen with other conditions. These include:

- Lupus happens when the body's defense system harms the joints, heart, skin, kidneys, and other organs.
- Infection that gets into a joint and destroys the cushion between the bones.

What Are the Symptoms of Arthritis?

Symptoms of arthritis can include:

- Pain, redness, heat, and swelling in your joints
- Trouble moving around
- Fever
- Weight loss
- Breathing problems
- Rash or itch

These symptoms may also be signs of other illnesses.

What Causes Arthritis

There are probably many genes that make people more likely to have arthritis. Research has found some of these genes. If you have the gene linked with arthritis, something in your environment—such as a virus or injury—may trigger the condition.

Is There an Arthritis Test?

To diagnosis you with arthritis or another rheumatic disease, your doctor may:

- Ask you about your medical history
- Give you a physical exam
- Take samples for a laboratory test
- Take X-rays

How Is Arthritis Treated?

There are many treatments that can help relieve pain and help you live with arthritis. You should talk to your doctor about the best treatments for you, which can include:

- Medications to relieve pain, slow the condition, and prevent further damage.
- Surgery to repair joint damage or relieve pain.

Who Treats Arthritis

Doctors who diagnose and treat arthritis and other rheumatic disease include:

- A general practitioner, such as your family doctor
- A rheumatologist, who treats arthritis and other diseases of the bones, joints, and muscles

Living with Arthritis

There are many things you can do to help you live with arthritis and other rheumatic diseases, including:

- Take your medications when and how you're supposed to.
- Exercise to reduce joint pain and stiffness. It also helps with losing weight, which reduces stress on the joints. You should speak to your doctor about a safe, well-rounded exercise program.
- Use heat and cold therapies to reduce joint pain and swelling.
- Try relaxation therapy to help reduce pain by learning ways to relax your muscles.
- Use splints and braces to support weakened joints or allow them to rest. You should see your doctor to make sure your splint or brace fits well.
- Use assistive devices, such as a cane or shoe insert, to ease the pain when walking. Other devices can help you open a jar, close zippers, or hold pencils.

Section 24.4

Multiple Sclerosis

This section includes text excerpted from "Multiple Sclerosis: Hope Through Research," National Institute of Neurological Disorders and Stroke (NINDS), July 6, 2018.

Multiple sclerosis (MS) is the most common disabling neurological disease of young adults. It most often appears when people are between 20–40 years old. However, it can also affect children and older people.

What Is Multiple Sclerosis?

Multiple sclerosis (MS) is a neuroinflammatory disease that affects myelin, a substance that makes up the membrane (called the myelin sheath) that wraps around nerve fibers (axons). Myelinated axons are commonly called white matter. Researchers have learned that MS also damages the nerve cell bodies, which are found in the brain's gray matter, as well as the axons themselves in the brain, spinal cord, and optic nerve (the nerve that transmits visual information from the eye to the brain). As the disease progresses, the brain's cortex shrinks (cortical atrophy).

The term MS refers to the distinctive areas of scar tissue (sclerosis or plaques) that are visible in the white matter of people who have MS. Plaques can be as small as a pinhead or as large as the size of a golf ball. Doctors can see these areas by examining the brain and spinal cord using a type of brain scan called magnetic resonance imaging (MRI).

While MS sometimes causes severe disability, it is only rarely fatal and most people with MS have a normal life expectancy.

What Are Plaques Made of and Why Do They Develop?

Plaques, or lesions, are the result of an inflammatory process in the brain that causes immune system cells to attack myelin. The myelin sheath helps to speed nerve impulses traveling within the nervous system. Axons are also damaged in MS, although not as extensively, or as early in the disease, as myelin.

Under normal circumstances, cells of the immune system travel in and out of the brain patrolling for infectious agents (viruses, for example) or unhealthy cells. This is called the "surveillance" function of the immune system.

Surveillance cells usually won't spring into action unless they recognize an infectious agent or unhealthy cells. When they do, they produce substances to stop the infectious agent. If they encounter unhealthy cells, they either kill them directly or clean out the dying area and produce substances that promote healing and repair among the cells that are left.

Researchers have observed that immune cells behave differently in the brains of people with MS. They become active and attack what appears to be healthy myelin. It is unclear what triggers this attack. MS is one of many autoimmune disorders, such as rheumatoid arthritis and lupus, in which the immune system mistakenly attacks a person's healthy tissue as opposed to performing its normal role of attacking foreign invaders like viruses and bacteria. Whatever the reason, during these periods of immune system activity, most of the myelin within the affected area is damaged or destroyed. The axons also may be damaged. The symptoms of MS depend on the severity of the immune reaction as well as the location and extent of the plaques, which primarily appear in the brain stem, cerebellum, spinal cord, optic nerves, and the white matter of the brain around the brain ventricles (fluid-filled spaces inside of the brain).

What Are the Signs and Symptoms of Multiple Sclerosis?

The symptoms of MS usually begin over one to several days, but in some forms, they may develop more slowly. They may be mild or severe and may go away quickly or last for months. Sometimes the initial symptoms of MS are overlooked because they disappear in a day or so and normal function returns. Because symptoms come and go in the majority of people with MS, the presence of symptoms is called an attack, or in medical terms, an exacerbation. Recovery from symptoms is referred to as remission, while a return of symptoms is called a relapse. This form of MS is, therefore, called relapsing-remitting MS (RRMS), in contrast to a more slowly developing form called primary progressive MS. Progressive MS can also be a second stage of the illness that follows years of relapsing-remitting symptoms.

A diagnosis of MS is often delayed because MS shares symptoms with other neurological conditions and diseases.

The first symptoms of MS often include:

- Vision problems such as blurred or double vision or optic neuritis, which causes pain in the eye and a rapid loss of vision

Degenerative Diseases That Cause Disability

- Weak, stiff muscles, often with painful muscle spasms
- Tingling or numbness in the arms, legs, trunk of the body, or face
- Clumsiness, particularly difficulty staying balanced when walking
- Bladder control problems, either inability to control the bladder or urgency
- Dizziness that doesn't go away

MS may also cause later symptoms such as:

- Mental or physical fatigue which accompanies the above symptoms during an attack
- Mood changes such as depression or euphoria
- Changes in the ability to concentrate or to multitask effectively
- Difficulty making decisions, planning, or prioritizing at work or in private life

Some people with MS develop transverse myelitis (TM), a condition caused by inflammation in the spinal cord. Transverse myelitis causes loss of spinal cord function over a period of time lasting from several hours to several weeks. It usually begins as a sudden onset of lower back pain, muscle weakness, or abnormal sensations in the toes and feet, and can rapidly progress to more severe symptoms, including paralysis. In most cases of transverse myelitis, people recover at least some function within the first 12 weeks after an attack begins. Transverse myelitis can also result from viral infections, arteriovenous malformations, or neuroinflammatory problems unrelated to MS. In such instances, there are no plaques in the brain that suggest previous MS attacks.

Neuromyelitis optica is a disorder associated with transverse myelitis as well as optic nerve inflammation. Patients with this disorder usually have antibodies against a particular protein in their spinal cord, called the aquaporin channel. These patients respond differently to treatment than most people with MS.

Most individuals with MS have muscle weakness, often in their hands and legs. Muscle stiffness and spasms can also be a problem. These symptoms may be severe enough to affect walking or standing. In some cases, MS leads to partial or complete paralysis. Many people with MS find that weakness and fatigue are worse when they have a fever or when they are exposed to heat. MS exacerbations may occur following common infections.

Tingling and burning sensations are common, as well as the opposite, numbness and loss of sensation. Moving the neck from side to side or flexing it back and forth may cause "Lhermitte sign," a characteristic sensation of MS that feels like a sharp spike of electricity coursing down the spine.

While it is rare for pain to be the first sign of MS, pain often occurs with optic neuritis and trigeminal neuralgia (TN), a neurological disorder that affects one of the nerves that runs across the jaw, cheek, and face. Painful spasms of the limbs and sharp pain shooting down the legs or around the abdomen can also be symptoms of MS.

Most individuals with MS experience difficulties with coordination and balance at some time during the course of the disease. Some may have a continuous trembling of the head, limbs, and body, especially during movement, although such trembling is more common with other disorders such as Parkinson disease.

Fatigue is common, especially during exacerbations of MS. A person with MS may be tired all the time or may be easily fatigued from mental or physical exertion.

Urinary symptoms, including loss of bladder control and sudden attacks of urgency, are common as MS progresses. People with MS sometimes also develop constipation or sexual problems.

Depression is a common feature of MS. A small number of individuals with MS may develop more severe psychiatric disorders such as bipolar disorder and paranoia, or experience inappropriate episodes of high spirits, known as euphoria.

People with MS, especially those who have had the disease for a long time, can experience difficulty with thinking, learning, memory, and judgment. The first signs of what doctors call cognitive dysfunction may be subtle. The person may have problems finding the right word to say, or trouble remembering how to do routine tasks on the job or at home. Day-to-day decisions that once came easily may now be made more slowly and show poor judgment. Changes may be so small or happen so slowly that it takes a family member or friend to point them out.

How Many People Have Multiple Sclerosis?

No one knows exactly how many people have MS. Experts think there are currently 250,000–350,000 people in the United States diagnosed with MS. This estimate suggests that approximately 200 new cases are diagnosed every week. Studies of the prevalence (the proportion of individuals in a population having a particular disease) of MS indicate that the rate of the disease has increased steadily during the twentieth century.

As with most autoimmune disorders, twice as many women are affected by MS as men. MS is more common in colder climates. People of Northern European descent appear to be at the highest risk for the disease, regardless of where they live. Native Americans of North and South America, as well as Asian American populations, have relatively low rates of MS.

What Causes Multiple Sclerosis

The ultimate cause of MS is damage to myelin, nerve fibers, and neurons in the brain and spinal cord, which together make up the central nervous system (CNS). But how that happens, and why, are questions that challenge researchers. Evidence appears to show that MS is a disease caused by genetic vulnerabilities combined with environmental factors.

Although there is little doubt that the immune system contributes to the brain and spinal cord tissue destruction of MS, the exact target of the immune system attacks and which immune system cells cause the destruction isn't fully understood.

Researchers have several possible explanations for what might be going on. The immune system could be:

- Fighting some kind of infectious agent (for example, a virus) that has components which mimic components of the brain (molecular mimicry)
- Destroying brain cells because they are unhealthy
- Mistakenly identifying normal brain cells as foreign

The last possibility has been the favored explanation for many years. Research now suggests that the first two activities might also play a role in the development of MS. There is a special barrier, called the blood–brain barrier (BBB), which separates the brain and spinal cord from the immune system. If there is a break in the barrier, it exposes the brain to the immune system for the first time. When this happens, the immune system may misinterpret the brain as "foreign."

Genetic Susceptibility

Susceptibility to MS may be inherited. Studies of families indicate that relatives of an individual with MS have an increased risk for developing the disease. Experts estimate that about 15 percent of individuals with MS have one or more family members or relatives who also have MS. But even identical twins, whose deoxyribonucleic acid (DNA) is exactly the same, have only a 1 in 3 chance of both having the disease. This suggests that MS is not entirely controlled by genes. Other factors must come into play.

Research suggests that dozens of genes and possibly hundreds of variations in the genetic code (called gene variants) combine to create vulnerability to MS. Some of these genes have been identified. Most of the genes identified so far are associated with functions of the immune system. Additionally, many of the known genes are similar to those that have been identified in people with other autoimmune diseases as type 1 diabetes, rheumatoid arthritis or lupus. Researchers continue to look for additional genes and to study how they interact with each other to make an individual vulnerable to developing MS.

Sunlight and Vitamin D

A number of studies have suggested that people who spend more time in the sun and those with relatively high levels of vitamin D are less likely to develop MS. Bright sunlight helps human skin produce vitamin D. Researchers believe that vitamin D may help regulate the immune system in ways that reduce the risk of MS. People from regions near the equator, where there is a great deal of bright sunlight, generally have a much lower risk of MS than people from temperate areas such as the United States and Canada. Other studies suggest that people with higher levels of vitamin D generally have less severe MS and fewer relapses.

Smoking

A number of studies have found that people who smoke are more likely to develop MS. People who smoke also tend to have more brain lesions and brain shrinkage than nonsmokers. The reasons for this are currently unclear.

Infectious Factors and Viruses

A number of viruses have been found in people with MS, but the virus most consistently linked to the development of MS is Epstein Barr virus (EBV), the virus that causes mononucleosis.

Degenerative Diseases That Cause Disability

Only about 5 percent of the population has not been infected by EBV. These individuals are at a lower risk for developing MS than those who have been infected. People who were infected with EBV in adolescence or adulthood and who, therefore, develop an exaggerated immune response to EBV are at a significantly higher risk for developing MS than those who were infected in early childhood. This suggests that it may be the type of immune response to EBV that predisposes to MS, rather than EBV infection itself. However, there is still no proof that EBV causes MS.

Autoimmune and Inflammatory Processes

Tissue inflammation and antibodies in the blood that fight normal components of the body and tissue in people with MS are similar to those found in other autoimmune diseases. Along with overlapping evidence from genetic studies, these findings suggest that MS results from some kind of disturbed regulation of the immune system.

How Is Multiple Sclerosis Diagnosed?

There is no single test used to diagnose MS. Doctors use a number of tests to rule out or confirm the diagnosis. There are many other disorders that can mimic MS. Some of these other disorders can be cured, while others require different treatments than those used for MS. Therefore, it is very important to perform a thorough investigation before making a diagnosis.

In addition to a complete medical history, physical examination, and a detailed neurological examination, a doctor will order an MRI scan of the head and spine to look for the characteristic lesions of MS. MRI is used to generate images of the brain and/or spinal cord. Then a special dye or contrast agent is injected into a vein and the MRI is repeated. In regions with active inflammation in MS, there is disruption of the blood–brain barrier and the dye will leak into the active MS lesion.

Doctors may also order evoked potential tests, which use electrodes on the skin and painless electric signals to measure how quickly and accurately the nervous system responds to stimulation. In addition, they may request a lumbar puncture (sometimes called a "spinal tap") to obtain a sample of cerebrospinal fluid. This allows them to look for proteins and inflammatory cells associated with the disease and to rule out other diseases that may look similar to MS, including some infections and other illnesses. MS is confirmed when positive signs of the disease are found in different parts of the nervous system at more than one-time interval and there is no alternative diagnosis.

Are There Treatments Available for Multiple Sclerosis?

There is still no cure for MS, but there are treatments for initial attacks, medications and therapies to improve symptoms, and developed drugs to slow the worsening of the disease. These new drugs have been shown to reduce the number and severity of relapses and to delay the long-term progression of MS.

Treatments for Attacks

The usual treatment for an initial MS attack is to inject high doses of a steroid drug, such as methylprednisolone, intravenously (into a vein) over the course of 3–5 days. It may sometimes be followed by a tapered dose of oral steroids. Intravenous steroids quickly and potently suppress the immune system, and reduce inflammation. Clinical trials have shown that these drugs hasten recovery.

The American Academy of Neurology (AAN) recommends using plasma exchange as a secondary treatment for severe flare-ups in relapsing forms of MS when the patient does not have a good response to methylprednisolone. Plasma exchange, also known as plasmapheresis, involves taking blood out of the body and removing components in the blood's plasma that are thought to be harmful. The rest of the blood, plus replacement plasma, is then transfused back into the body. This treatment has not been shown to be effective for secondary progressive or chronic progressive forms of MS.

Treatments to Help Reduce Disease Activity and Progression

During the past 20 years, researchers have made major breakthroughs in MS treatment due to new knowledge about the immune system and the ability to use MRI to monitor MS in patients. As a result, a number of medical therapies have been found to reduce relapses in persons with relapsing-remitting MS. These drugs are called disease-modulating drugs.

There is debate among doctors about whether to start disease-modulating drugs at the first signs of MS or to wait until the course of the disease is better defined before beginning treatment. On one hand, U.S.

Food and Drug Administration (FDA)-approved medications to treat MS work best early in the course of the disease and work poorly, if at all, later in the progressive phase of the illness. Clinical trials have shown convincingly that delaying treatment, even for the 1–2 years that it may take for patients with MS to develop a second clinical attack, may lead to an irreversible increase in disability. In addition, people who begin treatment after their first attack have fewer brain lesions and fewer relapses over time.

On the other hand, initiating treatment in patients with a single attack and no signs of previous MS lesions, before MS is diagnosed, poses risks because all FDA-approved medications to treat MS are associated with some side effects. Therefore, the best strategy is to have a thorough diagnostic work-up at the time of first attack of MS. The work-up should exclude all other diseases that can mimic MS so that the diagnosis can be determined with a high probability. The diagnostic tests may include an evaluation of the cerebrospinal fluid and repeated MRI examinations. If such a thorough work-up cannot confirm the diagnosis of MS with certainty, it may be prudent to wait before starting treatment. However, each patient should have a scheduled follow-up evaluation by his or her neurologist 6–12 months after the initial diagnostic evaluation, even in the absence of any new attacks of the disease. Ideally, this evaluation should include an MRI examination to see if any new MS lesions have developed without causing symptoms.

It appeared that a minority of people with MS had very mild disease or "benign MS" and would never get worse or become disabled. This group makes up 10–20 percent of those with MS. Doctors were concerned about exposing such benign MS patients to the side effects of MS drugs. However, data from the long-term followup of these patients indicate that after 10–20 years, some of these patients become disabled. Therefore, evidence supports discussing the start of therapy early with all people who have MS, as long as the MS diagnosis has been thoroughly investigated and confirmed. There is an additional small group of individuals (approximately 1%) whose course will progress so rapidly that they will require aggressive and perhaps even experimental treatment.

The FDA-approved therapies for MS are designed to modulate or suppress the inflammatory reactions of the disease. They are most effective for relapsing-remitting MS at early stages of the disease. These treatments include injectable beta interferon drugs. Interferons are signaling molecules that regulate immune cells. Potential side effects of beta interferon drugs include flu-like symptoms, such as fever, chills, muscle aches, and fatigue, which usually fade with continued therapy. A few individuals will notice a decrease in the effectiveness of the drugs after 18–24 months of treatment due to the development of antibodies that neutralize the drugs' effectiveness. If the person has flare-ups or worsening symptoms, doctors may switch treatment to alternative drugs.

Glatiramer acetate is another injectable immune-modulating drug used for MS. Exactly how it works is not entirely clear, but research has shown that it changes the balance of immune cells in the body. Side effects with glatiramer acetate are usually mild, but it can cause skin reactions and allergic reactions. It is approved only for relapsing forms of MS.

The drug mitoxantrone, which is administered intravenously four times a year, has been approved for especially severe forms of relapsing-remitting and secondary progressive MS. This drug has been associated with development of certain types of blood cancers in up to one percent of patients, as well as with heart damage. Therefore, this drug should be used as a last resort to treat patients with a form of MS that leads to rapid loss of function and for whom other treatments did not stop the disease.

Natalizumab works by preventing cells of the immune system from entering the brain and spinal cord. It is administered intravenously once a month. It is a very effective drug for many people, but it is associated with an increased risk of a potentially fatal viral infection of the brain called progressive multifocal encephalopathy (PML). People who take natalizumab must be carefully monitored for symptoms of PML, which include changes in vision, speech, and balance that do not remit like an MS attack. Therefore, natalizumab is generally recommended only for individuals who have not responded well to the other approved MS therapies or who are unable to tolerate them. Other side effects of natalizumab treatment include allergic and hypersensitivity reactions.

The FDA approved fingolimod, the first MS drug that can be taken orally as a pill, to treat relapsing forms of MS. The drug prevents white blood cells called lymphocytes from leaving the lymph nodes and entering the blood and the brain and spinal cord. The decreased number of lymphocytes in the blood can make people taking fingolimod more susceptible to infections. The drug may also cause problems with eyes and with blood pressure and heart rate. Because of this, the drug must be administered in a doctor's office for the first time and the treating physician must evaluate the patient's vision and blood pressure during an early follow-up examination. The exact frequency of rare side effects (such as severe infections) of fingolimod is unknown.

The FDA approved ocrelizumab (brand name Ocrevus) to treat adults with relapsing forms of MS and primary progressive multiple sclerosis.

Other FDA-approved drugs to treat relapsing forms of MS in adults include dimethyl fumarate and teriflunomide, both taken orally.

Table 24.1. Disease Modifying Drugs

Trade Name	Generic Name
Avonex	interferon beta-1a
Betaseron	interferon beta-1b
Rebif	interferon beta-1a
Copaxone	glatiramer acetate
Tysabri	natalizumab
Novantrone	mitoxantrone
Gilenya	fingolimod

How Do Doctors Treat the Symptoms of Multiple Sclerosis?

MS causes a variety of symptoms that can interfere with daily activities but which can usually be treated or managed to reduce their impact. Many of these issues are best treated by neurologists who have advanced training in the treatment of MS and who can prescribe specific medications to treat the problems.

Vision Problems

Eye and vision problems are common in people with MS but rarely result in permanent blindness. Inflammation of the optic nerve or damage to the myelin that covers the optic nerve and other nerve fibers can cause a number of symptoms, including blurring or graying of vision, blindness in one eye, loss of normal color vision, depth perception, or a dark spot in the center of the visual field (scotoma).

Uncontrolled horizontal or vertical eye movements (nystagmus) and "jumping vision" (opsoclonus) are common to MS, and can be either mild or severe enough to impair vision.

Double vision (diplopia) occurs when the two eyes are not perfectly aligned. This occurs commonly in MS when a pair of muscles that control a specific eye movement aren't coordinated due to weakness in one or both muscles. Double vision may increase with fatigue or as the result of spending too much time reading or on the computer. Periodically resting the eyes may be helpful.

Weak Muscles, Stiff Muscles, Painful Muscle Spasms, and Weak Reflexes

Muscle weakness is common in MS, along with muscle spasticity. Spasticity refers to muscles that are stiff or that go into spasms without any warning. Spasticity in MS can be as mild as a feeling of tightness in the muscles or so severe that it causes painful, uncontrolled spasms. It can also cause pain or tightness in and around the joints. It also frequently affects walking, reducing the normal flexibility or "bounce" involved in taking steps.

Tremor

People with MS sometimes develop tremor, or uncontrollable shaking, often triggered by movement. Tremor can be very disabling. Assistive devices and weights attached to limbs are sometimes helpful for people with tremor. Deep brain stimulation and drugs such as clonazepam also may be useful.

Problems with Walking and Balance

Many people with MS experience difficulty walking. In fact, studies indicate that half of those with relapsing-remitting MS will need some kind of help walking within 15 years of their diagnosis if they remain untreated. The most common walking problem in people with MS experience is ataxia—unsteady, uncoordinated movements—due to damage with the areas of the brain that coordinate movement of muscles. People with severe ataxia generally benefit from the use of a cane, walker, or other assistive device. Physical therapy can also reduce walking problems in many cases.

The FDA approved the drug dalfampridine to improve walking in patients with MS. It is the first drug approved for this use. Clinical trials showed that patients treated with dalfampridine had faster walking speeds than those treated with a placebo pill.

Fatigue

Fatigue is a common symptom of MS and may be both physical (for example, tiredness in the legs) and psychological (due to depression). Probably the most important measures people with MS can take to

Degenerative Diseases That Cause Disability

counter physical fatigue are to avoid excessive activity and to stay out of the heat, which often aggravates MS symptoms. On the other hand, daily physical activity programs of mild to moderate intensity can significantly reduce fatigue. An antidepressant such as fluoxetine may be prescribed if the fatigue is caused by depression. Other drugs that may reduce fatigue in some individuals include amantadine and modafinil.

Fatigue may be reduced if the person receives occupational therapy to simplify tasks and/or physical therapy to learn how to walk in a way that saves physical energy or that takes advantage of an assistive device. Some people benefit from stress management programs, relaxation training, membership in an MS support group, or individual psychotherapy. Treating sleep problems and MS symptoms that interfere with sleep (such as spastic muscles) may also help.

Pain

People with MS may experience several types of pain during the course of the disease.

Trigeminal neuralgia is a sharp, stabbing, facial pain caused by MS affecting the trigeminal nerve as it exits the brainstem on its way to the jaw and cheek. It can be treated with anticonvulsant or antispasmodic drugs, alcohol injections, or surgery.

People with MS occasionally develop central pain, a syndrome caused by damage to the brain and/or spinal cord. Drugs such as gabapentin and nortriptyline sometimes help to reduce central pain.

Burning, tingling, and prickling (commonly called "pins and needles") are sensations that happen in the absence of any stimulation. The medical term for them is dysesthesias" They are often chronic and hard to treat.

Chronic back or other musculoskeletal pain may be caused by walking problems or by using assistive aids incorrectly. Treatments may include heat, massage, ultrasound treatments, and physical therapy to correct faulty posture and strengthen and stretch muscles.

Problems with Bladder Control and Constipation

The most common bladder control problems encountered by people with MS are urinary frequency, urgency, or the loss of bladder control. The same spasticity that causes spasms in legs can also affect the bladder. A small number of individuals will have the opposite problem—retaining large amounts of urine. Urologists can help with treatment of bladder-related problems. A number of medical treatments are available. Constipation is also common and can be treated with a high-fiber diet, laxatives, and other measures.

Sexual Issues

People with MS sometimes experience sexual problems. Sexual arousal begins in the central nervous system, as the brain sends messages to the sex organs along nerves running through the spinal cord. If MS damages these nerve pathways, sexual response—including arousal and orgasm—can be directly affected. Sexual problems may also stem from MS symptoms such as fatigue, cramped or spastic muscles, and psychological factors related to lowered self-esteem or depression. Some of these problems can be corrected with medications. Psychological counseling also may be helpful.

Depression

Studies indicate that clinical depression is more frequent among people with MS than it is in the general population or in persons with many other chronic, disabling conditions. MS may cause depression as part of the disease process, since it damages myelin and nerve fibers inside the brain. If the plaques are in parts of the brain that are involved in emotional expression and control, a variety of behavioral changes can result, including depression. Depression can intensify symptoms of fatigue, pain, and sexual dysfunction. It is most often treated with selective serotonin reuptake inhibitor (SSRI) antidepressant medications, which are less likely than other antidepressant medications to cause fatigue.

Inappropriate Laughing or Crying

MS is sometimes associated with a condition called pseudobulbar affect that causes inappropriate and involuntary expressions of laughter, crying, or anger. These expressions are often unrelated to mood; for example, the person may cry when they are actually very happy, or laugh when they are not especially happy. The FDA approved the first treatment specifically for pseudobulbar affect, a combination of the drugs dextromethorphan and quinidine. The condition can also be treated with other drugs such as amitriptyline or citalopram.

Cognitive Changes

Half-to three-quarters of people with MS experience cognitive impairment, which is a phrase doctors use to describe a decline in the ability to think quickly and clearly and to remember easily. These cognitive changes may appear at the same time as the physical symptoms or they may develop gradually over time. Some individuals with MS may feel as if they are thinking more slowly, are easily distracted, have trouble remembering, or are losing their way with words. The right word may often seem to be on the tip of their tongue.

Some experts believe that it is more likely to be a cognitive decline, rather than physical impairment, that causes people with MS to eventually withdraw from the workforce. A number of neuropsychological tests have been developed to evaluate the cognitive status of individuals with MS. Based on the outcomes of these tests, a neuropsychologist can determine the extent of strengths and weaknesses in different cognitive areas. Drugs such as donepezil, which is usually used for Alzheimer disease, may be helpful in some cases.

Section 24.5

Parkinson Disease

This section includes text excerpted from "Parkinson's Disease: Hope Through Research," National Institute of Neurological Disorders and Stroke (NINDS), July 6, 2018.

What Is Parkinson Disease?

Parkinson disease (PD) is a degenerative disorder of the central nervous system that belongs to a group of conditions called movement disorders. It is both chronic, meaning it persists over a long period of time, and progressive, meaning its symptoms grow worse over time. As nerve cells (neurons) in parts of the brain become impaired or die, people may begin to notice problems with movement, tremor, stiffness in the limbs or the trunk of the body, or impaired balance. As these symptoms become more pronounced, people may have difficulty walking, talking, or completing other simple tasks. Not everyone with one or more of these symptoms has PD, as the symptoms appear in other diseases as well.

The precise cause of PD is unknown, although some cases of PD are hereditary and can be traced to specific genetic mutations. Most cases are sporadic—that is, the disease does not typically run in families. It is thought that PD likely results from a combination of genetic susceptibility and exposure to one or more unknown environmental factors that trigger the disease.

PD is the most common form of parkinsonism, in which disorders of other causes produce features and symptoms that closely resemble PD. While most forms of parkinsonism have no known cause, there are cases in which the cause is known or suspected or where the symptoms result from another disorder.

No cure for PD exists today, but research is ongoing and medications or surgery can often provide substantial improvement with motor symptoms.

What Causes Parkinson Disease

PD occurs when nerve cells, or neurons, in the brain die or become impaired. Although many brain areas are affected, the most common symptoms result from the loss of neurons in an area near the base of the brain called the substantia nigra. Normally, the neurons in this area produce an important brain chemical known as dopamine. Dopamine is a chemical messenger responsible for transmitting signals between the substantia nigra and the next "relay station" of the brain, the corpus striatum, to produce smooth, purposeful movement. Loss of dopamine results in abnormal nerve firing patterns within the brain that cause impaired movement. Studies have shown that most people with Parkinson have lost 60–80 percent or more of the dopamine-producing cells in the substantia nigra by the time symptoms appear, and that people with PD also have loss of the nerve endings that produce the neurotransmitter norepinephrine. Norepinephrine, which is closely related to dopamine, is the main chemical messenger of the sympathetic nervous system, the part of the nervous system that controls many autonomic functions of the body, such as pulse and blood pressure. The loss of norepinephrine might explain several of the nonmotor features seen in PD, including fatigue and abnormalities of blood pressure regulation.

The affected brain cells of people with PD contain Lewy bodies— deposits of the protein alpha-synuclein. Researchers do not yet know why Lewy bodies form or what role they play in the disease. Some research suggests that the cell's protein disposal system may fail in people with PD, causing proteins to build up to harmful levels and trigger cell death. Additional studies have found evidence that clumps of protein that develop inside brain cells of people with PD may contribute to the death of neurons. Some researchers speculate that the protein buildup in Lewy bodies is part of an unsuccessful attempt to protect the cell from the toxicity of smaller aggregates, or collections, of synuclein.

Genetics. Scientists have identified several genetic mutations associated with PD, including the alpha-synuclein gene, and many more genes have been tentatively linked to the disorder. Studying the genes responsible for inherited cases of PD can help researchers understand both inherited and sporadic cases. The same genes and proteins that are altered in inherited cases may also be altered in sporadic cases by environmental toxins or other factors. Researchers also hope that discovering genes will help identify new ways of treating PD.

Environment. Exposure to certain toxins has caused parkinsonian symptoms in rare circumstances (such as exposure to 1-methyl-4-phenyl-1,2,3,6-tetrahydropyridine (MPTP), an illicit drug, or in miners exposed to the metal manganese). Other still-unidentified environmental factors may also cause PD in genetically susceptible individuals.

Mitochondria. Several lines of research suggest that mitochondria may play a role in the development of PD. Mitochondria are the energy-producing components of the cell and abnormalities in the mitochondria are major sources of free radicals—molecules that damage membranes, proteins, DNA, and other parts of the cell. This damage is often referred to as oxidative stress. Oxidative stress-related changes, including free radical damage to DNA, proteins, and fats, have been detected in the brains of individuals with PD. Some mutations that affect mitochondrial function have been identified as causes of PD.

While mitochondrial dysfunction, oxidative stress, inflammation, toxins, and many other cellular processes may contribute to PD, the actual cause of the cell loss death in PD is still undetermined.

What Genes Are Linked to Parkinson Disease?

Several genes have been definitively linked to PD. The first to be identified was alpha-synuclein. In the 1990s, researchers at National Institutes of Health (NIH) and other institutions studied the genetic profiles of a large Italian family and three Greek families with familial PD and found that their disease was related to a mutation in this gene. They found a second alpha-synuclein mutation in a German family with PD. These findings prompted studies of the role of alpha-synuclein in PD, which led to the discovery that Lewy bodies seen in all cases of PD contain alpha-synuclein protein. This discovery revealed the link between hereditary and sporadic forms of the disease.

In 2003, researchers studying inherited PD discovered that the disease in one large family was caused by a triplication of the normal alpha-synuclein gene on one copy of chromosome 4 (a chromosome is a threadlike structure of a protein and the genetic material DNA). This triplication caused people in the affected family to produce too much of the normal alpha-synuclein. This study showed that an excess of the normal form of synuclein could result in PD, just as the abnormal form does.

Other genes linked to PD include parkin, DJ-1, PINK1, and LRRK2. DJ-1 and PINK1 cause rare, early-onset forms of PD. The parkin gene is translated into a protein that normally helps cells break down and recycle proteins. DJ-1 normally helps regulate gene activity and protect cells from oxidative stress. PINK1 codes for a protein active in mitochondria. Mutations in this gene appear to increase susceptibility to cellular stress.

Mutations in LRRK2 were originally identified in several English and Basque families as a cause of a late-onset PD. Subsequent studies have identified mutations of this gene in other families with PD as well as in a small percentage of people with apparently sporadic PD. LRRK2 mutations are a major cause of PD in North Africa and the Middle East.

Another interesting association is with the GBA gene, which makes the enzyme glucocerebrosidase. Mutations in both GBA genes cause Gaucher disease (in which fatty acids, oils, waxes, and steroids accumulate in the brain), but different changes in this gene are associated with an increased risk for Parkinson disease as well. Investigators seek to understand what this association can tell us about PD risk factors and potential treatments.

Who Gets Parkinson Disease?

Estimates suggest that about 50,000 Americans are diagnosed with PD each year, although some estimates are much higher. Getting an accurate count of the number of cases is difficult because many people in the early stages of the disease may assume their symptoms are the result of normal aging and do not seek medical attention. Diagnosis is sometimes complicated by the fact that other conditions may produce symptoms of PD and there is no definitive test for the disease. People with PD may sometimes be told by their doctors that they have other disorders, and people with PD-like diseases may be incorrectly diagnosed as having PD.

PD affects about 50 percent more men than women, and the reasons for this discrepancy are unclear. While PD occurs in people throughout the world, a number of studies have found a higher incidence in developed countries. Other studies have found an increased risk in people who live in rural areas with increased pesticide use. However, those apparent risks are not fully characterized.

One clear risk factor for PD is age. The average age of onset is 60 years, and the incidence rises significantly with advancing age. However, about 5–10 percent of people with PD have "early-onset" disease that begins before the age of 50. Some early-onset cases are linked to specific gene mutations such as parkin. People with one or more close relatives who have PD have an increased risk of developing the disease themselves, but the total risk is still about 2–5 percent unless the family has a known gene mutation for the disease. An estimated 15–25 percent of people with PD have a known relative with the disease.

In very rare cases, parkinsonian symptoms may appear in people before the age of 20. This condition is called juvenile parkinsonism. It often begins with dystonia and bradykinesia, and the symptoms often improve with levodopa medication.

What Are the Symptoms of Parkinson Disease?

The four primary symptoms of PD are:

Tremor. The tremor associated with PD has a characteristic appearance. Typically, the tremor takes the form of a rhythmic back-and-forth motion at a rate of 4-6 beats per second. It may involve the thumb and forefinger and appear as a "pill rolling" tremor. Tremor often begins in a hand, although sometimes a foot or the jaw is affected first. It is most obvious when the hand is at rest or when a person is under stress. Tremor usually disappears during sleep or improves with intentional movement. It is usually the first symptom that causes people to seek medical attention.

Rigidity. Rigidity, or a resistance to movement, affects most people with PD. The muscles remain constantly tense and contracted so that the person aches or feels stiff. The rigidity becomes obvious when another person tries to move the individual's arm, which will move only in ratchet-like or short, jerky movements known as "cogwheel" rigidity.

Bradykinesia. This slowing down of spontaneous and automatic movement is particularly frustrating because it may make simple tasks difficult. The person cannot rapidly perform routine movements. Activities once performed quickly and easily—such as washing or dressing—may take much longer. There is often a decrease in facial expressions.

Postural instability. Postural instability, or impaired balance, causes affected individuals to fall easily.

PD does not affect everyone the same way, and the rate of progression and the particular symptoms differ among individuals.

PD symptoms typically begin on one side of the body. However, the disease eventually affects both sides. Even after the disease involves both sides of the body, the symptoms are often less severe on one side than on the other.

Friends or family members may be the first to notice changes in someone with early PD. They may see that the person's face lacks expression and animation (known as "masked face") or that the person moves more slowly.

Early symptoms of PD may be subtle and occur gradually. Affected people may feel mild tremors or have difficulty getting out of a chair. Activities may take longer to complete than in the past and individuals may note some stiffness in addition to slowness. They may notice that they speak too softly or that their handwriting is slow and looks cramped or small. This very early period may last a long time before the more classical and obvious motor (movement) symptoms appear.

As the disease progresses, the symptoms of Parkinson disease may begin to interfere with daily activities. Affected individuals may not be able to hold utensils steady or they may find that the shaking makes reading a newspaper difficult. People with PD often develop a so-called parkinsonian gait that includes a tendency to lean forward, taking small quick steps as if hurrying (called festination), and reduced swinging in one or both arms. They may have trouble initiating movement (start hesitation), and they may stop suddenly as they walk (freezing).

A number of other symptoms may accompany PD, and some can be treated with medication or physical therapy.

- **Depression.** This common disorder may appear early in the course of the disease, even before other symptoms are noticed. Some people lose their motivation and become dependent on family members. Fortunately, depression typically can be treated successfully with antidepressant medications such as amitriptyline or fluoxetine.

Degenerative Diseases That Cause Disability

- **Emotional changes.** Some people with PD become fearful and insecure, while others may become irritable or uncharacteristically pessimistic.

- **Difficulty with swallowing and chewing.** Muscles used in swallowing may work less efficiently in later stages of the disease. Food and saliva may collect in the mouth and back of the throat, which can result in choking or drooling. These problems may also make it difficult to get adequate nutrition. Speech-language therapists, occupational therapists (who help people learn new ways to perform activities of daily living), and dieticians can often help with these problems.

- **Speech changes.** About half of all individuals with PD have speech difficulties that may be characterized as speaking too softly or in a monotone. Some may hesitate before speaking, slur, or speak too fast. A speech therapist may be able to help these individuals reduce some of these problems.

- **Urinary problems or constipation.** In some people with PD, bladder and bowel problems can occur due to the improper functioning of the autonomic nervous system, which is responsible for regulating smooth muscle activity. Medications can effectively treat some of these symptoms.

- **Skin problems.** In PD, the skin on the face may become oily, particularly on the forehead and at the sides of the nose. The scalp may become oily too, resulting in dandruff. In other cases, the skin can become very dry. Standard treatments for skin problems can help.

- **Sleep problems.** Sleep problems are common in PD and include difficulty staying asleep at night, restless sleep, nightmares and emotional dreams, and drowsiness or sudden sleep onset during the day. Another common problem is "REM behavior disorder," in which people act out their dreams, potentially resulting in injury to themselves or their bed partners. The medications used to treat PD may contribute to some of these sleep issues. Many of these problems respond to specific therapies.

- **Dementia or other cognitive problems.** Some people with PD may develop memory problems and slow thinking. Cognitive problems become more severe in late stages of PD, and a diagnosis of Parkinson disease dementia (PDD) may be given. Memory, social judgment, language, reasoning, or other mental skills may be affected. There is currently no way to halt PD dementia, but drugs such as rivastigmine, donepezil, or memantine may help. The medications used to treat the motor symptoms of PD may cause confusion and hallucinations.

- **Orthostatic hypotension.** Orthostatic hypotension is a sudden drop in blood pressure when a person stands up from a lying down or seated position. This may cause dizziness, lightheadedness, and, in extreme cases, loss of balance or fainting. Studies have suggested that, in PD, this problem results from a loss of nerve endings in the sympathetic nervous system that controls heart rate, blood pressure, and other automatic functions in the body. The medications used to treat PD may also contribute to this symptom. Orthostatic hypotension may improve by increasing salt intake. Physicians treating the disorder may also reduce antihypertensive drug dosage or by prescribing medications such as fludrocortisone.

- **Muscle cramps and dystonia.** The rigidity and lack of normal movement associated with PD often causes muscle cramps, especially in the legs and toes. Massage, stretching, and applying heat may help with these cramps. PD can also be associated with dystonia—sustained muscle contractions that cause forced or twisted positions. Dystonia in PD is often caused by fluctuations in the body's level of dopamine. Management strategies may involve adjusting medications.

- **Pain.** Many people with PD develop aching muscles and joints because of the rigidity and abnormal postures often associated with the disease. Treatment with levodopa and other dopaminergic drugs often alleviates these pains to some extent. Certain exercises may help.

- **Fatigue and loss of energy.** Many people with PD often have fatigue, especially late in the day. Fatigue may be associated with depression or sleep disorders, but it may also result from muscle stress or from overdoing activity when the person feels well. Fatigue may also result from akinesia—trouble initiating or carrying out movement. Exercise, good sleep habits, staying mentally active, and not forcing too many activities in a short time may help to alleviate fatigue.

- **Sexual dysfunction.** Because of its effects on nerve signals from the brain, PD may cause sexual dysfunction. PD-related

Degenerative Diseases That Cause Disability

depression or use of certain medications may also cause decreased sex drive and other problems. People should discuss these issues with their physician as they may be treatable.

Hallucinations, delusions, and other psychotic symptoms can be caused by the drugs prescribed for PD. Reducing PD medications dosages or changing medications may be necessary if hallucinations occur. If such measures are not effective, doctors sometimes prescribe drugs called atypical antipsychotics, which include clozapine and quetiapine. The typical antipsychotic drugs, which include haloperidol, worsen the motor symptoms of PD and should not be used.

Parkinsonism Resulting from Neurological Disorders

- **Arteriosclerotic parkinsonism.** Sometimes known as pseudoparkinsonism, vascular parkinsonism, or atherosclerotic parkinsonism, arteriosclerotic parkinsonism involves damage to the brain due to multiple strokes. Tremor is rare in this type of parkinsonism, while dementia and difficulties with gait are common. Antiparkinsonian drugs are of little help to people with this form of parkinsonism.

- **Posttraumatic parkinsonism.** Also known as posttraumatic encephalopathy or "punch-drunk syndrome," parkinsonian symptoms can develop after a severe head injury or frequent head trauma associated with boxing or other activities. This type of trauma can also cause a form of dementia called chronic traumatic encephalopathy.

- **Essential tremor.** Sometimes called benign essential tremor or familial tremor, this common condition tends to run in families and progresses slowly over time. The tremor is usually equal in both hands and increases when the hands are moving. It may involve the head but usually spares the legs. Essential tremor is not the same as Parkinson disease and does not usually lead to it, although in some cases the two conditions may overlap in one person. People with essential tremor have no other parkinsonian features. Essential tremor does not respond to levodopa or to most other PD drugs, but there are medications to treat it.

- **Normal pressure hydrocephalus (NPH).** It is an abnormal increase of cerebrospinal fluid (CSF) in the brain's ventricles, or cavities. This causes the ventricles to enlarge, putting pressure on the brain. Symptoms include problems with walking, impaired bladder control leading to increased urinary frequency or incontinence, and progressive mental impairment and dementia. The person may also have a general slowing of movements or may complain that his or her feet feel "stuck." These symptoms may sometimes be mistaken for PD. They do not respond to Parkinson medications. Brain scans, intracranial pressure monitoring, and other tests can help to diagnose NPH. NPH can sometimes be treated by surgically implanting a CSF shunt that drains excess cerebrospinal fluid into the abdomen, where it is absorbed.

- **Parkinsonism accompanying other conditions.** Parkinsonian symptoms appear in individuals with other, clearly distinct neurological disorders such as Wilson disease, Huntington disease, Alzheimer disease, spinocerebellar ataxias (SCA), and Creutzfeldt-Jakob disease (CJD). Each of these disorders has specific features that help to distinguish it from PD.

Environmental Causes for Parkinson Disease

- **Postencephalitic parkinsonism.** Just after the first World War, the viral disease encephalitis lethargica (EL) affected almost 5 million people throughout the world, and then suddenly disappeared in the 1920s. Known as sleeping sickness in the United States, this disease killed one-third of its victims and led to postencephalitic parkinsonism in many others. This resulted in a movement disorder that appeared sometimes years after the initial illness. (In 1973, neurologist Oliver Sacks published Awakenings, an account of his work in the late 1960s with surviving postencephalitic patients in a New York hospital. Using the then-experimental drug levodopa, Dr. Sacks was able to temporarily "awaken" these individuals from their statue-like state). In rare cases, other viral infections, including western equine encephalomyelitis (WEE), eastern equine encephalomyelitis (EEE), and Japanese B encephalitis (JE), have caused parkinsonian symptoms.

- **Drug-induced parkinsonism.** A reversible form of parkinsonism sometimes results from use of certain drugs, such as chlorpromazine and haloperidol, which are typically prescribed for patients with psychiatric disorders. Some drugs used for stomach disorders (metoclopramide), high blood pressure

Degenerative Diseases That Cause Disability

(reserpine), and others such as valproate can cause tremor and bradykinesia. Stopping the medication or lowering the dosage of these medications usually causes the symptoms to go away.

- **Toxin-induced parkinsonism.** Some toxins can cause parkinsonism by various mechanisms. The chemical MPTP also causes a permanent form of parkinsonism that closely resembles PD. Investigators discovered this reaction in the 1980s when heroin addicts in California who had taken an illicit street drug contaminated with MPTP began to develop severe parkinsonism. This discovery, which showed that a toxic substance could damage the brain and produce parkinsonian symptoms, led to a dramatic breakthrough in Parkinson research.
- **Parkinsonism-dementia complex of Guam.** This disease occurs among the Chamorro populations of Guam and the Mariana Islands and may be accompanied by a motor neuron disease resembling amyotrophic lateral sclerosis (Lou Gehrig disease). The course of the disease is rapid, with death typically occurring within 5 years.

How Is Parkinson Disease Diagnosed?

There are currently no blood or laboratory tests that diagnose sporadic PD. Therefore, the diagnosis is based on medical history and a neurological examination. In some cases PD can be difficult to diagnose accurately early on in the course of the disease. Early signs and symptoms of PD may sometimes be dismissed as the effects of normal aging. Doctors may sometimes request brain scans or laboratory tests in order to rule out other disorders. However, computed tomography (CT) and magnetic resonance imaging (MRI) brain scans of people with PD usually appear normal. Since many other diseases have similar features but require different treatments, making a precise diagnosis is important so that people can receive the proper treatment.

How Is Parkinson Disease Treated?

At present, there is no cure for PD, but medications or surgery can often provide improvement in the motor symptoms.

Drug Therapy

Medications for PD fall into three categories. The first category includes drugs that increase the level of dopamine in the brain. The most common drugs for PD are dopamine precursors—substances such as levodopa that cross the blood–brain barrier (BBB) and are then changed into dopamine. Other drugs mimic dopamine or prevent or slow its breakdown.

The second category of PD drugs affects other neurotransmitters in the body in order to ease some of the symptoms of the disease. For example, anticholinergic drugs interfere with production or uptake of the neurotransmitter acetylcholine. These can be effective in reducing tremors.

The third category of drugs prescribed for PD includes medications that help control the nonmotor symptoms of the disease, that is, the symptoms that don't affect movement. For example, people with PD-related depression may be prescribed antidepressants.

- **Levodopa/Carbidopa.** The cornerstone of therapy for PD is the drug levodopa (also called L-dopa). Nerve cells can use levodopa to make dopamine and replenish the brain's reduced supply. People cannot simply take dopamine pills because dopamine does not easily pass through the blood–brain barrier. (The blood–brain barrier is a protective lining of cells inside blood vessels that regulate the transport of oxygen, glucose, and other substances in the brain.) Usually, people are given levodopa combined with another substance called carbidopa. When added to levodopa, carbidopa prevents the conversion of levodopa into dopamine except for in the brain; this stops or diminishes the side effects due to dopamine in the bloodstream. Levodopa/carbidopa is often very successful at reducing or eliminating the tremors and other motor symptoms of PD during the early stages of the disease. It allows the majority of people with PD to extend the period of time in which they can lead active, productive lives.

    Although levodopa/carbidopa helps most people with PD, not all symptoms respond equally to the drug. Levodopa usually helps most with bradykinesia and rigidity. Problems with balance may not respond.

    People often see noticeable improvement in their symptoms after starting levodopa/carbidopa therapy. However, they may need to increase the dose gradually for maximum benefit. Levodopa is often so effective that some people may not show symptoms during the early stages of the disease as long as they take the medicine. But levodopa is not a cure. Although it can

Degenerative Diseases That Cause Disability

reduce the symptoms of PD, it does not replace lost nerve cells and it does not stop the progression of the disease.

- Levodopa/carbidopa can have a variety of side effects. The most common initial side effects include nausea, low blood pressure, and restlessness. The nausea and vomiting caused by levodopa are greatly reduced by the right combination of levodopa and carbidopa. The drug also can cause drowsiness or sudden sleep onset, which can make driving and other activities dangerous. Long-term use of levodopa sometimes causes hallucinations and psychosis. In March 2017, the FDA approved safinamide tablets as an add-on treatment for individuals with PD how are currently taking levodopa/carbidopa and experiencing "off" episodes (when the person's medications are not working well, causing an increase in PD symptoms).

- Dyskinesias, or involuntary movements such twisting and writhing, commonly develop in people who take levodopa over an extended period. These movements may be either mild or severe. Some doctors start younger individuals with PD on drugs that act directly like dopamine itself and add levodopa later in the course of the disease. The dosage of levodopa is sometimes reduced in order to lessen these drug-induced movements. The drug amantadine may help control dyskinesias but if dyskinesias are severe, surgical treatment such as deep brain stimulation may be considered.

Other difficulties may be encountered later in the disease course. People with PD may begin to notice more pronounced symptoms before their first dose of medication in the morning and between doses as the period of effectiveness after each dose begins to shorten, called the wearing-off effect. People experience sudden, unpredictable "off periods," where the medications do not seem to be working. One approach to alleviating these side effects is to take levodopa more often and in smaller amounts. People with PD should never stop taking levodopa without their physician's input, because rapidly withdrawing the drug can have potentially serious side effects.

In addition to levodopa/carbidopa, there are other available treatments:

- **Dopamine agonists.** These drugs, which include apomorphine, pramipexole, ropinirole, and rotigotine, mimic the role of dopamine in the brain. They can be given alone or with levodopa. They are somewhat less effective than levodopa in treating PD symptoms, but work for longer periods of time. Many of the potential side effects are similar to those associated with the use of levodopa, including drowsiness, sudden sleep onset, hallucinations, confusion, dyskinesias, edema (swelling due to excess fluid in body tissues), nightmares, and vomiting. In rare cases, they can cause an uncontrollable desire to gamble, hypersexuality, or compulsive shopping.

- **Monoamine Oxidase B (MAO-B) inhibitors.** These drugs inhibit the enzyme monoamine oxidase B, or MAO-B, which breaks down dopamine in the brain. MAO-B inhibitors cause dopamine to accumulate in surviving nerve cells and reduce the symptoms of PD. Studies supported by the National Institute of Neurological Disorders and Stroke (NINDS) have shown that selegiline (also called deprenyl) can delay the need for levodopa therapy by up to a year or more. When selegiline is given with levodopa, it appears to enhance and prolong the response to levodopa and thus may reduce wearing-off. Selegiline is usually well-tolerated, although side effects may include nausea, orthostatic hypotension, or insomnia. It should not be taken with the antidepressant fluoxetine or the sedative meperidine, because combining selegiline with these drugs can be harmful. The drug rasagiline is used in treating the motor symptoms of PD with or without levodopa. Whether rasagiline slows progression of PD is still controversial.

- **Catechol-O-methyltransferase (COMT) inhibitors.** COMT stands for catechol-O-methyltransferase, another enzyme that breaks down dopamine. The drug entacapone and tolcapone prolong the effects of levodopa by preventing the breakdown of dopamine. COMT inhibitors can decrease the duration of "off periods" of one's dose of levodopa. The most common side effect is diarrhea. The drugs cause nausea, sleep disturbances, dizziness, urine discoloration, abdominal pain, low blood pressure, or hallucinations. In a few rare cases, tolcapone has caused severe liver disease, and people taking tolcapone need regular monitoring of their liver function.

- **Amantadine.** This antiviral drug can help reduce symptoms of PD and levodopa-induced dyskinesia. It is often used alone in the early stages of the disease. It may also be used with an anticholinergic drug or levodopa. After several months,

Degenerative Diseases That Cause Disability

amantadine effectiveness wears off in up to half of the people taking it. Amantadine side effects may include insomnia, mottled skin, edema, agitation, or hallucinations. Researchers are not certain how amantadine works in PD, but it may increase the effects of dopamine.

- **Anticholinergics.** These drugs, which include trihexyphenidyl, benztropine, and ethopropazine, decrease the activity of the neurotransmitter acetylcholine and can be particularly effective for tremor. Side effects may include dry mouth, constipation, urinary retention, hallucinations, memory loss, blurred vision, and confusion.

When recommending a course of treatment, a doctor will assess how much the symptoms disrupt the person's life and then tailor therapy to the person's particular condition. Since no two people will react the same way to a given drug, it may take time and patience to get the dose just right. Even then, symptoms may not be completely alleviated.

Table 24.2. Medications to Treat the Motor Symptoms of Parkinson Disease

Category	Generic	Brand Name
Drugs that increase brain levels of dopamine	Levodopa/carbidopa	Parcopa, Sinemet
Drugs that mimic dopamine (dopamine agonists)	Apomorphine Pramipexole Ropinirole Rotigotine	Apokyn Mirapex Requip Neupro
Drugs that inhibit dopamine breakdown (MAO-B inhibitors)	Rasagiline Selegiline (deprenyl)	Azilect Eldepryl, Zelapar
Drugs that inhibit dopamine breakdown (COMT inhibitors)	Entacapone Tolcapone	Comtan Tasmar
Drugs that decrease the action of acetylcholine (anticholinergics)	Benztropine Ethopropazine Trihexyphenidyl	Cogentin Parsidol Artane
Drugs with an unknown mechanism of action for PD	Amantadine	Symmetrel

Surgery

Before the discovery of levodopa, surgery was an option for treating PD. Studies in the past few decades have led to great improvements in surgical techniques, and surgery is again considered for people with PD for whom drug therapy is no longer sufficient.

Pallidotomy and Thalamotomy. The earliest types of surgery for PD involved selectively destroying specific parts of the brain that contribute to PD symptoms. Surgical techniques have been refined and can be very effective for the motor symptoms of PD. The most common lesion surgery is called pallidotomy. In this procedure, a surgeon selectively destroys a portion of the brain called the globus pallidus. Pallidotomy can improve symptoms of tremor, rigidity, and bradykinesia, possibly by interrupting the connections between the globus pallidus and the striatum or thalamus. Some studies have also found that pallidotomy can improve gait and balance and reduce the amount of levodopa people require, thus reducing drug-induced dyskinesias. Another procedure, called thalamotomy, involves surgically destroying part of the thalamus; this approach is useful primarily to reduce tremor.

Because these procedures cause permanent destruction of small amounts of brain tissue, they have largely been replaced by deep brain stimulation for treatment of PD. However, a new method using focused ultrasound from outside the head is being tested because it creates lesions without the need for surgery.

Deep Brain Stimulation or DBS, uses an electrode surgically implanted into part of the brain, typically the subthalamic nucleus or the globus pallidus. Similar to a cardiac pacemaker, a pulse generator (battery pack) that is implanted in the chest area under the collarbone sends finely controlled electrical signals to the electrode(s) via a wire placed under the skin. When turned on using an external wand, the pulse generator and electrodes painlessly stimulate the brain in a way that helps to block signals that cause many of the motor symptoms of PD. DBS is approved by the U.S. Food and Drug Administration (FDA) and is widely used as a treatment for PD.

DBS can be used on one or both sides of the brain. If it is used on just one side, it will affect symptoms on the opposite side of the body. DBS is primarily used to stimulate one of three brain regions: the subthalamic nucleus, the globus pallidus interna, or the thalamus. Stimulation of either the globus pallidus or the subthalamic nucleus can reduce tremor, bradykinesia, and rigidity. Stimulation of the thalamus is useful primarily for reducing tremor.

People who initially responded well to treatment with levodopa tend to respond well to DBS. While the motor function benefits of DBS can be substantial, it usually does not help with speech problems, "freezing," posture, balance, anxiety, depression, or dementia.

One advantage of DBS compared to pallidotomy and thalamotomy is that the electrical current can be turned off using a handheld device. The pulse generator also can be externally programmed.

Individuals must return to the medical center frequently for several months after DBS surgery in order to have the stimulation adjusted very carefully to give the best results. After a few months, the number of medical visits usually decreases significantly, though individuals may occasionally need to return to the center to have their stimulator checked. The battery for the pulse generator must be surgically replaced every three to five years. DBS does not stop PD from progressing, and some problems may gradually return. DBS is not a good option for everyone. It is generally appropriate for people with levodopa-responsive PD who have developed dyskinesias or other disabling "off" symptoms despite drug therapy. It is not generally an option for people with memory problems, hallucinations, severe depression, poor health, or a poor response to levodopa. DBS has not been demonstrated to be of benefit for "atypical" parkinsonian syndromes such as multiple system atrophy, progressive supranuclear palsy, or posttraumatic parkinsonism, which also do not improve with Parkinson medications.

As with any brain surgery, DBS has potential complications, including stroke or brain hemorrhage. These complications are rare, however. There is also a risk of infection, which may require antibiotics or even replacement of parts of the DBS system.

Complementary and Supportive Therapies

A wide variety of complementary and supportive therapies may be used for PD. Among these therapies are standard physical, occupational, and speech therapy techniques, which can help with such problems as gait and voice disorders, tremors and rigidity, and cognitive decline. Other types of supportive therapies include:

Diet. At this time there are no specific vitamins, minerals, or other nutrients that have any proven therapeutic value in PD. An NINDS clinical study of the dietary supplement coenzyme Q10 was stopped in 2011 when results from an interim analysis showed active treatment with the supplement was unlikely to demonstrate a statistically significant difference than from a placebo. The NINDS and other components of the National Institutes of Health are funding research to determine if caffeine, antioxidants, and other dietary factors may be beneficial for preventing or treating PD. While there is currently no proof that any specific dietary factor is beneficial, a normal, healthy diet can promote overall well-being for people with PD just as it would for anyone else. Eating a fiber-rich diet and drinking plenty of fluids also can help alleviate constipation. A high protein diet, however, may limit levodopa's absorption, highlighting the importance of the timing of medications.

Exercise. Exercise can help people with PD improve their mobility and flexibility. Some doctors prescribe physical therapy or muscle-strengthening exercises to tone muscles and to put underused and rigid muscles through a full range of motion. The effects of exercise on disease progression are not known, but it may improve body strength so that the person is less disabled. Exercises also improve balance, helping people minimize gait problems, and can strengthen certain muscles so that people can speak and swallow better. Exercise can improve emotional well-being and general physical activity, such as walking, gardening, swimming, calisthenics, and using exercise machines, can have other benefits. An NINDS-funded clinical trial demonstrated the benefit of tai chi exercise compared to resistance or stretching exercises. People with PD should always check with their doctors before beginning a new exercise program.

Other complementary and supportive therapies that are used by some individuals with PD include massage therapy, yoga, hypnosis, acupuncture, and the Alexander technique, which optimizes posture and muscle activity.

Another important therapeutic approach involves speech and swallowing evaluation and therapy. Certain techniques can help with the low voice volume that individuals with Parkinson often experience.

Chapter 25

Disability Caused by Injury and Trauma

Chapter Contents

Section 25.1—Amputation and Limb Loss 276
Section 25.2—Back Pain.. 284
Section 25.3—Spinal Cord Injury: Understanding
 Paralysis, Paraplegia, and Quadriplegia 289
Section 25.4—Traumatic Brain Injury 300

Section 25.1

Amputation and Limb Loss

This section contains text excerpted from the following sources: Text in this section begins with excerpts from "Limb Prosthetics Services and Devices," National Institute of Standards and Technology (NIST), April 28, 2017; Text under the heading "National Limb Loss Resource Center" is excerpted from "National Limb Loss Resource Center," Administration for Community Living (ACL), September 20, 2017.

There are an estimated 1.9 million amputees in the United States and approximately 185,000 amputations surgeries performed each year. Of those amputations performed, 82 percent are due to peripheral vascular disease and diabetes. However, there are other causes of amputation. Approximately 8,900 children receive amputations each year due to lawn mower accidents. Birth defects result in a life-long need for prosthetic devices. About 6,000 of these are upper extremity amputees in a given year. Walter Reed Army Medical Center (WRAMC) is treating about 1,000 military amputees. The U.S. Department of Veterans Affairs (VA) has 40,000 amputees currently receiving services in the VA healthcare system.

The overall annual numbers of amputees in the United States, as well in the Veterans Administration healthcare system are accelerating because of diabetes-related limb amputations. The growth rate of the over-65 age group is nearly triple that of the under-65 age group. More than 65 percent of amputations are performed on people age 50 and older. There is a direct correlation between age and the onset of diabetes and vascular disease, which are the leading causes of amputations. Limb loss does not affect just the aged. Every day in the United States, children are born with missing limbs, and teenagers suffer amputations as a result of accidents or cancer.

Types of Amputation

Amputations are generally classified according to the level at which they are performed. Some amputation levels are referred to by the name of the surgeon credited with developing the amputation technique used.

Disability Caused by Injury and Trauma

Lower-Extremity Amputations

Syme Amputation

Developed about 1842 by James Syme, a leading Scottish surgeon, the Syme amputation leaves the long bones of the shank (the tibia and fibula) virtually intact, only a small portion at the very end being removed. The tissues of the heel, which are ideally suited to withstand high pressures, are preserved, and this, in combination with the long bones, usually permits the patient to bear the full weight of his body on the end of the stump. Because the amputation stump is nearly as long as the unaffected limb, a person with Syme amputation can usually get about the house without a prosthesis even though normal foot and ankle action has been lost. Atrophy of the severed muscles that were formerly attached to bones in the foot to provide ankle action results in a stump with a bulbous end which, though not of the most pleasing appearance, is quite an advantage in holding the prosthesis in place. Since its introduction, Syme operation has been looked upon with both favor and disfavor among surgeons. It seems to be the consensus now that "the Syme" should be performed in preference to amputation at a higher level if possible. In the case of most women, though, "the Syme" is undesirable because of the difficulty of providing a prosthesis that matches the shape of the other leg.

Below-Knee Amputations (BKAs)

Any amputation above the Syme level and below the knee joint is known as a below-knee amputation (BKA). Because circulatory troubles have often developed in long below-knee stumps, and because the muscles that activate the shank are attached at a level close to the knee joint, the below-knee amputation is usually performed at the junction of the upper and middle third sections. Thus nearly full use of the knee is retained-an important factor in obtaining a gait of nearly normal appearance. However, it is rare for a below-knee amputee to bear a significant amount of weight on the end of the stump; thus the design of prostheses must provide for weight-bearing through other areas. Several types of surgical procedures have been employed to obtain weight-bearing through the end of the below-knee stump, but none has found widespread use.

Knee-Bearing Amputations

Complete removal of the lower leg, or shank, is known as a knee disarticulation. When the operation is performed properly, the result is an efficient, though bulbous, stump capable of carrying the weight-bearing forces through the end. Unfortunately, the length causes some problems in providing an efficient prosthesis because the space used normally to house the mechanism needed to control the artificial shank properly is occupied by the end of the stump. Nevertheless, prostheses have been highly beneficial in knee-disarticulation cases. Development of adequate devices for obtaining control of the shank is currently underway, and such devices should be generally available in the near future.

Several amputation techniques have been devised in an attempt to overcome the problems posed by the length and shape of the true knee-disarticulation stump. The Gritti-Stokes procedure entails placing the kneecap, or patella, directly over the end of the femur after it has been cut off about two inches above the end. When the operation is performed properly, excellent results are obtained, but extreme skill and expert postsurgical care are required. Variations of the Gritti-Stokes amputation have been introduced from time to time but have never been used widely.

Above-Knee Amputations

Amputations through the thigh are among the most common. Total body weight cannot be taken through the end of the stump but can be accommodated through the ischium, that part of the pelvis upon which a person normally sits.

Hip Disarticulation and Hemipelvectomy

A true hip disarticulation involves removal of the entire femur, but whenever feasible the surgeon leaves as much of the upper portion of the femur as possible in order to provide additional stabilization between the prosthesis and the wearer, even though no additional function can be expected over the true hip disarticulation. Both types of stump are provided with the same type of prosthesis. With slight modification the same type of prosthesis can be used by the hemipelvectomy patient, that is, when half of the pelvis has been removed. It is surprising how well hip-disarticulation and hemipelvectomy patients have been able to function when fitted with the newer type of prosthesis.

Upper-Extremity Amputations

Partial-Hand Amputations

If sensation is present the surgeon will save any functional part of the hand in lieu of disarticulation at the wrist. Any method of obtaining some form of grasp, or prehension, is preferable to the best prosthesis. If the result is unsightly, the stump can be covered with a plastic glove, lifelike in appearance, for those occasions when the wearer is willing to sacrifice function for appearance. Many prosthetists have developed special appliances for partial-hand amputations that permit more function than any of the artificial hands and hooks yet devised and, at the same time, permit the patient to make full use of the sensation remaining in the stump. Such devices are usually individually designed and fitted.

Wrist Disarticulation

Removal of the hand at the wrist joint was once condemned because it was thought to be too difficult to fit so as to yield more function than a shorter forearm stump. However, with plastic sockets based on anatomical and physiological principles, the wrist disarticulation case can now be fitted so that most of the pronation-supination of the forearm-an important function of the upper extremity-can be used. In the case of the wrist disarticulation, nearly all the normal forearm pronation-supination is present. Range of pronation-supination decreases rapidly as length of stump decreases; when 60 percent of the forearm is lost, no pronation-supination is possible.

Amputations through the Forearm

Amputations through the forearm are commonly referred to as below-elbow amputations and are classified as long, short, and very short, depending upon the length of stump. Stumps longer than 55 percent of total forearm length are considered long, between 35 and 55 percent as short, and less than 35 percent as very short. Long stumps retain the rotation function in proportion to length; long and short stumps without complications possess full range of elbow motion and full power about the elbow, but often very short stumps are limited in both power and motion about the elbow. Devices and techniques have been developed to make full use of all functions remaining in the stump.

Disarticulation at the Elbow

Disarticulation at the elbow consists of removal of the forearm, resulting in a slightly bulbous stump but usually one with good end-weight-bearing characteristics. The long bulbous end, while presenting some fitting problems, permits good stability between socket and stump, and thus allows use of nearly all the rotation normally present in the upper arm-a function much appreciated by the amputee.

Above-Elbow Amputation

Any amputation through the upper arm is generally referred to as an above-elbow amputation. In practice, stumps in which less than 30 percent of the humerus remains are treated as shoulder disarticulation cases; those with more than 90 percent of the humerus remaining are fitted as elbow disarticulation cases.

Shoulder Disarticulation and Forequarter Amputation

Removal of the entire arm is known as shoulder disarticulation but, whenever feasible, the surgeon will leave intact as much of the humerus as possible to provide stability between the stump and the socket. When it becomes necessary to remove the clavicle and scapula, the operation is known as a forequarter, or interscapulothoracic, amputation. The very short above-elbow, the shoulder disarticulation, and the forequarter cases are all provided with essentially the same type of prosthesis.

The Postsurgical Period

The period between the time of surgery and time of fitting the prosthesis is an important one if a good functional stump, and thus the most efficient use of a prosthesis, is to be obtained. The surgeon and others on his hospital staff will do everything possible to ensure the best results, but ideal results require the wholehearted cooperation of the patient.

It is not unnatural for the patient to feel extremely depressed during the first few days after surgery, but after he becomes aware of the possibilities of recovery, the outlook becomes brighter, and he generally enters cooperatively into the rehabilitation phase.

As soon as the stump has healed sufficiently, exercise of the stump is started in order to keep the muscles healthy and reduce the possibility of muscle contractures. Contracture scan be prevented easily, but it is most difficult and sometimes impossible to correct them. At first, exercises are administered by a therapist or nurse; later the patient is instructed concerning the type and amount of exercise that should be undertaken. The patient is also instructed in methods and amount of massage that should be given the stump to aid in the reduction of the stump size. Further, to aid shrinkage, cotton-elastic bandages are wrapped around the stump and worn continuously until a prosthesis is fitted. The bandage is removed and reapplied at regular intervals—four times during the day, and at bedtime. It is most important that a clean bandage is available for use each day.

The amputee is taught to apply the bandage unless it is physically impossible for him to do so, in which case some member of his family must be taught the proper method for use at home. To reduce the possibility of contractures, the lower-extremity stump must not be propped up on pillows. Wheelchairs should be used as little as possible; crutch walking is preferred, but the above-knee stump must not be allowed to rest on the crutch handle.

Prostheses for Various Types of Amputation

Much time and attention have been devoted to the development of mechanical components, such as knee and ankle units, for artificial limbs, yet by far the most important factors affecting the successful use of a prosthesis are the fit of the socket to the stump and the alignment of the various parts of the limb in relation to the stump and other parts of the body.

Thus, though many parts of a prosthesis may be mass-produced, it is necessary for each limb to be assembled in correct alignment and fitted to the stump to meet the individual requirements of the intended user. To make and fit artificial limbs properly requires a complete understanding of anatomical and physiological principles and of mechanics; craftsmanship and artistic ability are also required.

In general, an artificial limb should be as light as possible and still withstand the loads imposed upon it. In the U.S. willow and woods of similar characteristics have formed the basis of construction for more limbs than any other material, though aluminum, leather-and-steel combinations, and fiber have been used widely. Wood construction is still the type most used in the United States for above-knee prostheses, but plastic laminates similar to those so popular in small-boat construction are the materials of choice for virtually all other types of prostheses. Plastic laminates are light in weight, easy to keep clean, and do not absorb perspiration. They may be molded easily and rapidly over contours such as those found on a plaster model of a stump. Plastic laminates can be made extremely rigid or with any degree of flexibility required in artificial-limb construction. In some instances, especially in upper-extremity sockets, the fact that most plastic laminates do not permit water vapor to pass to the atmosphere has caused discomfort, but a porous type has been developed by the Army Medical Biomechanical Research Laboratory (AMBRL) (formerly the Army Prosthetics Research Laboratory). Except experimentally, its use thus far has been restricted to artificial arms. Of course, most of the mechanical parts are made of steel or aluminum, depending upon their function.

As in the case of the tailor making a suit, the first step in fabrication of a prosthesis is to take the necessary measurements for a good fit. If the socket is to be fabricated of a plastic laminate, an impression of the stump is made. Most often this is accomplished by wrapping the stump with a wet plaster-of-Paris bandage and allowing it to dry, as a physician does in applying a cast when a bone is broken.

The cast, or wrap, is removed from the stump and filled with a plaster-of-Paris solution to form an exact model of the stump which-after being modified to provide relief for any tender spots, to ensure that weight will be taken in the proper places, and to take full advantage of the remaining musculature can be used for molding a plastic-laminate socket. Often a "check" socket of cloth impregnated with beeswax is made over the model and tried on the stump to determine the correctness of the modifications.

For upper-extremity cases the socket is attached to the rest of the prosthesis and a harness is fabricated and installed for operation of the various parts of the artificial arm. For the lower-extremity case the socket is fastened temporarily to an adjustable, or temporary, leg for walking trials. With this device, the prosthetist can easily adjust the alignment until both he and the amputee are satisfied that the optimum arrangement has been reached. A prosthesis can now be made incorporating the same alignment achieved with the adjustable leg.

There are many kinds of artificial limbs available for each type of amputation, and much has been written concerning the necessity for prescribing limbs to meet the needs of each individual. This, of course, is true particularly in the case of persons in special or arduous occupations, or with certain medical problems, but actually, limbs for a given type of amputation vary to only a small degree.

National Limb Loss Resource Center

The mission of the National Limb Loss Resource Center (operated by the Amputee Coalition) is to reach out to and empower people affected by limb loss to achieve their full potential through education, support, advocacy, and the promotion of limb loss prevention. The National Limb Loss Resource Center programs use both traditional and innovative approaches to educate and inform people with limb loss, their family members, healthcare providers, policy makers, community members, and the general public about limb loss and limb difference. Resources include information and referral by phone and email, support groups and peer support, educational events, and a national website.

Goals of the Mission of the National Limb Loss Resource Center

- Operate and maintain an information and referral center to provide persons with limb loss, their family members, and caregivers with information and resources to increase the independence and well-being of people with limb loss (PWLL) and respond to inquiries about limb loss from the media and general public.

- Collect, develop, and disseminate patient education materials that provide PWLL, their family members, and caregivers with information and resources to increase their independence and well-being.

- Develop and disseminate programs and services that increase the independence and well-being of PWLL and their family members and help PWLL fully participate in social life.

- Develop and conduct consumer educational events for PWLL, their family members, and caregivers to increase the independence and well-being of PWLL and to help them age well with limb loss.

- Conduct national outreach for the development and dissemination of patient education materials, programs and services, provide technical support and assistance to local limb loss support groups, and raise awareness about the limb loss community.

- Develop and maintain partnerships and collaborations that create innovative solutions to address the needs of PWLL, their family members, and caregivers.

- Collaborate with federal agencies and other national organizations that have a vested interest in the amputee community.

- Monitor and evaluate the performance of National Limb Loss Resource Center objectives and activities.

Section 25.2

Back Pain

This section includes text excerpted from "Low Back Pain Fact Sheet," National Institute of Neurological Disorders and Stroke (NINDS), July 6, 2018.

If you have lower back pain, you are not alone. About 80 percent of adults experience low back pain at some point in their lifetimes. It is the most common cause of job-related disability and a leading contributor to missed work days. In a large survey, more than a quarter of adults reported experiencing low back pain during the past 3 months.

Men and women are equally affected by low back pain, which can range in intensity from a dull, constant ache to a sudden, sharp sensation that leaves the person incapacitated. Pain can begin abruptly as a result of an accident or by lifting something heavy, or it can develop over time due to age-related changes of the spine. Sedentary lifestyles also can set the stage for low back pain, especially when a weekday routine of getting too little exercise is punctuated by strenuous weekend workout.

Most low back pain is acute, or short term, and lasts a few days to a few weeks. It tends to resolve on its own with self-care and there is no residual loss of function. The majority of acute low back pain is mechanical in nature, meaning that there is a disruption in the way the components of the back (the spine, muscle, intervertebral discs, and nerves) fit together and move.

Subacute low back pain is defined as pain that lasts between 4 and 12 weeks.

Chronic back pain is defined as pain that persists for 12 weeks or longer, even after an initial injury or underlying cause of acute low back pain has been treated. About 20 percent of people affected by acute low back pain develop chronic low back pain with persistent symptoms at one year. In some cases, treatment successfully relieves chronic low back pain, but in other cases pain persists despite medical and surgical treatment.

What Causes Lower Back Pain

The vast majority of low back pain is mechanical in nature. In many cases, low back pain is associated with spondylosis, a term that refers to the general degeneration of the spine associated with normal

Disability Caused by Injury and Trauma

wear and tear that occurs in the joints, discs, and bones of the spine as people get older. Some examples of mechanical causes of low back pain include:

- **Sprains and strains** account for most acute back pain. Sprains are caused by overstretching or tearing ligaments, and strains are tears in tendon or muscle. Both can occur from twisting or lifting something improperly, lifting something too heavy, or overstretching. Such movements may also trigger spasms in back muscles, which can also be painful.

- **Intervertebral disc degeneration** is one of the most common mechanical causes of low back pain, and it occurs when the usually rubbery discs lose integrity as a normal process of aging. In a healthy back, intervertebral discs provide height and allow bending, flexion, and torsion of the lower back. As the discs deteriorate, they lose their cushioning ability.

- **Herniated or ruptured discs** can occur when the intervertebral discs become compressed and bulge outward (herniation) or rupture, causing low back pain.

- **Radiculopathy** is a condition caused by compression, inflammation and/or injury to a spinal nerve root. Pressure on the nerve root results in pain, numbness, or a tingling sensation that travels or radiates to other areas of the body that are served by that nerve. Radiculopathy may occur when spinal stenosis or a herniated or ruptured disc compresses the nerve root.

- **Sciatica** is a form of radiculopathy caused by compression of the sciatic nerve, the large nerve that travels through the buttocks and extends down the back of the leg. This compression causes shock-like or burning low back pain combined with pain through the buttocks and down one leg, occasionally reaching the foot. In the most extreme cases, when the nerve is pinched between the disc and the adjacent bone, the symptoms may involve not only pain, but numbness and muscle weakness in the leg because of interrupted nerve signaling. The condition may also be caused by a tumor or cyst that presses on the sciatic nerve or its roots.

- **Spondylolisthesis** is a condition in which a vertebra of the lower spine slips out of place, pinching the nerves exiting the spinal column.

- **A traumatic injury,** such as from playing sports, car accidents, or a fall can injure tendons, ligaments or muscle resulting in low back pain. Traumatic injury may also cause the spine to become overly compressed, which in turn can cause an intervertebral disc to rupture or herniate, exerting pressure on any of the nerves rooted to the spinal cord. When spinal nerves become compressed and irritated, back pain and sciatica may result.

- **Spinal stenosis** is a narrowing of the spinal column that puts pressure on the spinal cord and nerves that can cause pain or numbness with walking and over time leads to leg weakness and sensory loss.

- **Skeletal irregularities** include scoliosis, a curvature of the spine that does not usually cause pain until middle age; lordosis, an abnormally accentuated arch in the lower back; and other congenital anomalies of the spine.

Low back pain is rarely related to serious underlying conditions, but when these conditions do occur, they require immediate medical attention. Serious underlying conditions include:

- **Infections** are not a common cause of back pain. However, infections can cause pain when they involve the vertebrae, a condition called osteomyelitis; the intervertebral discs, called discitis; or the sacroiliac joints connecting the lower spine to the pelvis, called sacroiliitis.

- **Tumors** are a relatively rare cause of back pain. Occasionally, tumors begin in the back, but more often they appear in the back as a result of cancer that has spread from elsewhere in the body.

- **Cauda equina syndrome (CES)** is a serious but rare complication of a ruptured disc. It occurs when disc material is pushed into the spinal canal and compresses the bundle of lumbar and sacral nerve roots, causing loss of bladder and bowel control. Permanent neurological damage may result if this syndrome is left untreated.

- **Abdominal aortic aneurysms (AAA)** occur when the large blood vessel that supplies blood to the abdomen, pelvis, and legs becomes abnormally enlarged. Back pain can be a sign that the aneurysm is becoming larger and that the risk of rupture should be assessed.

- **Kidney stones** can cause sharp pain in the lower back, usually on one side.

Other underlying conditions that predispose people to low back pain include:

- **Inflammatory diseases of the joints** such as arthritis, including osteoarthritis and rheumatoid arthritis as well as spondylitis, an inflammation of the vertebrae, can also cause low back pain. Spondylitis is also called spondyloarthritis or spondyloarthropathy.
- **Osteoporosis** is a metabolic bone disease marked by a progressive decrease in bone density and strength, which can lead to painful fractures of the vertebrae.
- **Endometriosis** is the buildup of uterine tissue in places outside the uterus.
- **Fibromyalgia**, a chronic pain syndrome involving widespread muscle pain and fatigue.

Can Back Pain Be Prevented?

Recurring back pain resulting from improper body mechanics is often preventable by avoiding movements that jolt or strain the back, maintaining correct posture, and lifting objects properly. Many work-related injuries are caused or aggravated by stressors such as heavy lifting, contact stress (repeated or constant contact between soft body tissue and a hard or sharp object), vibration, repetitive motion, and awkward posture. Using ergonomically designed furniture and equipment to protect the body from injury at home and in the workplace may reduce the risk of back injury.

The use of lumbar supports in the form of wide elastic bands that can be tightened to provide support to the lower back and abdominal muscles to prevent low back pain remains controversial. Such supports are widely used despite a lack of evidence showing that they actually prevent pain. Multiple studies have determined that the use of lumbar supports provides no benefit in terms of the prevention and treatment of back pain. Although there have been anecdotal case reports of injury reduction among workers using lumbar support belts, many companies that have back belt programs also have training and ergonomic awareness programs. The reported injury reduction may be related to a combination of these or other factors. Furthermore, some caution is advised given that wearing supportive belts may actually lead to or aggravate back pain by causing back muscles to weaken from lack of use.

Recommendations for Keeping One's Back Healthy

Following any period of prolonged inactivity, a regimen of low-impact exercises is advised. Speed walking, swimming, or stationary bike riding 30 minutes daily can increase muscle strength and flexibility. Yoga also can help stretch and strengthen muscles and improve posture. Consult a physician for a list of low-impact, age-appropriate exercises that are specifically targeted to strengthening lower back and abdominal muscles.

- Always stretch before exercise or other strenuous physical activity.
- Don't slouch when standing or sitting. The lower back can support a person's weight most easily when the curvature is reduced. When standing, keep your weight balanced on your feet.
- At home or work, make sure work surfaces are at a comfortable height.
- Sit in a chair with good lumbar support and proper position and height for the task. Keep shoulders back. Switch sitting positions often and periodically walk around the office or gently stretch muscles to relieve tension. A pillow or rolled-up towel placed behind the small of the back can provide some lumbar support. During prolonged periods of sitting, elevate feet on a low stool or a stack of books.
- Wear comfortable, low-heeled shoes.
- Sleeping on one's side with the knees drawn up in a fetal position can help open up the joints in the spine and relieve pressure by reducing the curvature of the spine. Always sleep on a firm surface.
- Don't try to lift objects that are too heavy. Lift from the knees, pull the stomach muscles in, and keep the head down and in line with a straight back. When lifting, keep objects close to the body. Do not twist when lifting.
- Maintain proper nutrition and diet to reduce and prevent excessive weight gain, especially weight around the waistline

- Quit smoking. Smoking reduces blood flow to the lower spine, which can contribute to spinal disc degeneration. Smoking also increases the risk of osteoporosis and impedes healing. Coughing due to heavy smoking also may cause back pain.

Section 25.3

Spinal Cord Injury: Understanding Paraplegia, and Quadriplegia

This section includes text excerpted from "Spinal Cord Injury: Hope through Research," National Institute of Neurological Disorders and Stroke (NINDS), July 6, 2018.

The spinal cord is a tight bundle of neural cells (neurons and glia) and nerve pathways (axons) that extend from the base of the brain to the lower back. It is the primary information highway that receives sensory information from the skin, joints, internal organs, and muscles of the trunk, arms, and legs, which is then relayed upward to the brain. It also carries messages downward from the brain to other body systems. Millions of nerve cells situated in the spinal cord itself also coordinate complex patterns of movements such as rhythmic breathing and walking. Together, the spinal cord and brain make up the central nervous system (CNS), which controls most functions of the body.

The spinal cord is made up of neurons, glia, and blood vessels. The neurons and their dendrites (branching projections that receive input from axons of other neurons) reside in an H-shaped or butterfly-shaped region called gray matter. The gray matter of the cord contains lower motor neurons, which branch out from the cord to muscles, internal organs, and tissue in other parts of the body and transmit information commands to start and stop muscle movement that is under voluntary control. Upper motor neurons are located in the brain and send their long processes (axons) to the spinal cord neurons. Other types of nerve cells found in dense clumps of cells that sit just outside the spinal cord (called sensory ganglia) relay information such as temperature, touch, pain, vibration, and joint position back to the brain.

What Is a Spinal Cord Injury?

The vertebrae normally protect the soft tissues of the spinal cord, but they can be broken or dislocated in a variety of ways that puts harmful pressure on the spinal cord. Injuries can occur at any level of the spinal cord. The segment of the cord that is injured, and the severity of the damage to the nervous tissue, will determine which body functions are compromised or lost. An injury to a part of the spinal cord causes physiological consequences to parts of the body controlled by nerves at and below the level of the injury.

Motor vehicle accidents and catastrophic falls are the most common causes of physical trauma that breaks, crushes, or presses on the vertebrae and can cause irreversible damage at the corresponding level of the spinal cord and below. Severe trauma to the cervical cord results in paralysis of most of the body, including the arms and legs, and is called tetraplegia (though the older term, quadriplegia, is still in common use). Trauma to the thoracic nerves in the upper, middle, or lower back results in paralysis of the trunk and lower extremities, called paraplegia.

Penetrating injuries, such as gunshot or knife wounds, damage the spinal cord; however, most traumatic injuries do not completely sever the spinal cord. Instead, an injury is more likely to cause fractures and compression of the vertebrae, which then crush and destroy the axons that carry signals up and down the spinal cord. A spinal cord injury can damage a few, many, or almost all of the axons that cross the site of injury. A variety of cells located in and around the injury site may also die. Some injuries in which there is little or no nerve cell death but only pressure-induced blockage of nerve signaling or only demyelination without axonal damage will allow almost complete recovery. Others in which there is complete cell death across even a thin horizontal level of the spinal cord will result in complete paralysis.

Facts and Figures about Spinal Cord Injury

- There are an estimated 12,000 spinal cord injuries every year in the United States alone.

- More than a quarter of a million Americans are currently living with spinal cord injuries.

- The cost of managing the care of spinal cord injury patients is $3 billion each year.
- The largest proportion of spinal cord injuries (36.5%) occurs during car accidents; more than a quarter are the result of falls; and the rest are due to acts of violence (primarily gunshot wounds), sporting accidents, and other less common causes.
- The average age at injury has risen and is now 42.6 years.
- 80 percent of spinal cord injury patients are men.

What Happens When the Spinal Cord Is Injured?

Traumatic spinal cord injury usually begins with a sudden, mechanical blow or rupture to the spine that fractures or dislocates vertebrae. The damage begins at the moment of primary injury, when the cord is stretched or displaced by bone fragments or disc material. Nerve signaling stops immediately but may not return rapidly even if there is no structural damage to the cord. In severe injury, axons are cut or damaged beyond repair, and neural cell membranes are broken. Blood vessels may rupture and cause bleeding into the spinal cord's central tissue, or bleeding can occur outside the cord, causing pressure by the blood clot on the cord.

Within minutes, the spinal cord near the site of severe injury swells within the spinal canal. This may increase pressure on the cord and cut blood flow to spinal cord tissue. Blood pressure can drop, sometimes dramatically, as the body loses its ability to self-regulate. All these changes can cause a condition known as spinal shock that can last from several hours to several days.

There is some controversy among neurologists about the extent and impact of spinal shock, and even its definition in terms of physiological characteristics. It appears to occur in approximately half of the cases of spinal cord injury and is usually directly related to the size and severity of the injury. During spinal shock, the entire spinal cord below the lesion becomes temporarily disabled, causing complete paralysis, loss of all reflexes, and loss of sensation below the affected cord level.

The primary injury initiates processes that continue for days or weeks. It sets off a cascade of biochemical and cellular events that kills neurons, strips axons of their protective myelin covering, and triggers an inflammatory immune system response. This is the beginning of the secondary injury process. Days, or sometimes even weeks later, after this second wave of damage has passed, the area of destruction has increased—sometimes to several segments above and below the original injury.

- **Changes in blood flow cause ongoing damage.** The major reduction in blood flow to the site following the initial injury can last for as long as 24 hours and become progressively worse if there is continued compression of the cord due to swelling or bleeding. Because of the greater blood flow needs of gray matter, the impact is greater on the central cord than on the outlying white matter. Blood vessels in the gray matter also become leaky, sometimes as early as 5 minutes after injury, which initiates spinal cord swelling. Cells that line the still-intact blood vessels in the spinal cord also begin to swell, and this further reduces blood flow to the injured area. The combination of leaking, swelling, and sluggish blood flow prevents the normal delivery of oxygen and nutrients to neurons, causing many of them to die.

- **Excessive release of neurotransmitters kills nerve cells.** After the injury, an excessive release of neurotransmitters (chemicals that allow neurons to signal each other) can cause additional damage by overstimulating nerve cells. The neurotransmitter glutamate is commonly used by axons in the spinal cord to stimulate activity in other neurons. But when spinal cells are injured, their axons flood the area with glutamate and trigger additional nerve cell damage. This process kills neurons near the injury site and the myelin-forming oligodendrocytes at and beyond the injured area.

- **An invasion of immune system cells creates inflammation.** Under normal conditions, the blood–brain barrier (BBB) keeps potentially destructive immune system cells from entering the brain or spinal cord. This barrier is a naturally-occurring result of closely spaced cells along the blood vessels that prevent many substances from leaving the blood and entering brain tissues. But when the blood–brain barrier breaks down, immune system cells—primarily white blood cells (WBC)—can invade the spinal cord tissue and trigger an inflammatory response. This inflammatory response can cause additional damage to some neurons and may kill others.

- **Free radicals attack nerve cells.** Another consequence of inflammation is the increased production of highly reactive forms of oxygen molecules called free radicals—chemicals that modify the chemical structure of other molecules in damaging ways, for example, damaging cell membranes. Free radicals are produced naturally as a by-product of normal oxygen metabolism in small enough amounts that they cause no harm. But injury to the spinal cord causes cells to overproduce free radicals, which destroy critical molecules of the cell.

- **Nerve cells self-destruct.** For reasons that are still unclear, spinal cord injury sets off apoptosis—a normal process of cell death that helps the body get rid of old and unhealthy cells. Apoptosis kills oligodendrocytes in damaged areas of the spinal cord days to weeks after the injury. Apoptosis can strip myelin from intact axons in adjacent ascending and descending pathways, causing the axons to become dysfunctional and disrupting the spinal cord's ability to communicate with the brain.

- **Scarring occurs.** Following a spinal cord injury, astrocytes (star-shaped glial cells that support the brain and spinal cord) wall off the injury site by forming a scar, which creates a physical and chemical barrier to any axons which could potentially regenerate and reconnect. Even if some intact myelinated axons remain, there may not be enough to convey any meaningful information to or from the brain.

Researchers are especially interested in studying the mechanisms of this wave of secondary damage because finding ways to stop it could save spinal cord tissue and thereby enable greater functional recovery.

What Immediate Treatments Are Available for Spinal Cord Injuries?

Injury to the spine isn't always obvious. Any injury that involves the head and neck, pelvic fractures, penetrating injuries in the area of the spine, or injuries that result from falling from heights should raise concerns regarding an unstable spinal column. Until imaging of the spine is done at an emergency or trauma center, people who might have spine injury should be cared for as if any significant movement of the neck or back could cause further damage.

At the accident scene, emergency personnel will immobilize the head and neck to prevent movement, put a rigid collar around the neck, and carefully place the person on a rigid backboard to prevent further damage to the spinal cord. Sedation may be given to relax the person and prevent movement. A breathing tube may be inserted if the injury is to the high cervical cord and the individual is at risk of respiratory arrest.

At the hospital or trauma center, realigning the spine using a rigid brace or axial traction (using a mechanical force to stretch the spine and relieve pressure on the spinal cord) is usually done as soon as possible to stabilize the spine and prevent additional damage. Fractured vertebrae, bone fragments, herniated discs, or other objects compressing the spinal column may need to be surgically removed. Spinal decompression surgery to relieve pressure within the spinal column also may be necessary in the days after injury. Results of a neurosurgical study show that, in some cases, earlier surgery is associated with better functional recovery.

How Are Spinal Cord Injuries Diagnosed?

The emergency room physician will test the individual to see if there is any movement or sensation at or below the level of injury. Methods to assess autonomic function also have been established (American Spinal Injury Association, or ASIA, Autonomic Standards Classification). Emergency medical tests for a spinal cord injury include:

- Magnetic resonance imaging (MRI), which uses computer-generated radio waves and a powerful magnetic field to produce detailed three-dimensional images of body structures, including tissues, organs, bones, and nerves. It can document brain and spinal trauma from injury, as well as aid in diagnosing brain and spinal cord tumors, herniated disks, vascular (blood vessel) irregularities, bleeding and inflammation that might compress the spine and spinal cord, and injury to the ligaments that support the cervical spine.

- Computerized tomography (CT) provides rapid, clear two-dimensional X-ray images of organs, bones, and tissues. Neurological CT scans are used to view the brain and spine. CT is excellent in detecting bone fractures, bleeding, and spinal stenosis (narrowing of the spinal canal), but CT has less ability to image the spinal cord or identify ligament injury associated with an unstable spine than MRI.

- Plane X-rays (which demonstrate the planes of bone on bone) of the person's chest and skull are often taken as part of a neurological workup. X-rays can be used to view most parts of the body, such as a joint or major organ system. In a conventional X-ray, a concentrated burst of low-dose ionized radiation is passed through the body and onto a photographic plate. Since calcium in bones absorbs X-rays more easily than soft tissue or muscle, the bony structure appears white on the film. Vertebral misalignment or fracture can be seen within minutes. X-rays taken in different neck positions (i.e., flexion and extension views) detect instability of the cervical spine. Tissue masses such as injured ligaments or a bulging disc are not visible on conventional X-rays.

How Does a Spinal Cord Injury Affect the Rest of the Body and How Is It Treated?

People who survive a spinal cord injury often have medical complications resulting in bladder, bowel, and sexual dysfunction. They may also develop chronic pain, autonomic dysfunction, and spasticity (increased tone in and contractions of muscles of the arms and legs), but this is highly variable and poorly understood. Higher levels of injury may have an increased susceptibility to respiratory and heart problems.

- **Breathing.** A spinal cord injury high in the neck can affect the nerves and muscles in the neck and chest that are involved with breathing. Respiratory complications are often an indication of the severity of spinal cord injury. About one-third of those with injury to the neck area will need help with breathing and require respiratory support via intubation, which involves inserting a tube connected to a machine that pushes oxygen into the lungs and removes carbon dioxide) through the nose or throat and into the airway. This may be temporary or permanent depending upon the severity and location of injury. Any injury to the spinal cord between the C1-C4 segments, which supply the phrenic nerves leading to the diaphragm, can stop breathing. (The phrenic nerves cause the diaphragm to move and the lungs to expand.) People with these injuries need immediate ventilatory support. People with high cervical cord injury may have trouble coughing and clearing secretions from their lungs. Special training regarding breathing and swallowing may be needed.

- **Pneumonia.** Respiratory complications are the leading cause of death in people with spinal cord injury, commonly as a result of pneumonia. Intubation increases the risk of developing ventilator-associated pneumonia; individuals with spinal cord injury who are intubated have to be carefully monitored and treated with antibiotics if symptoms of pneumonia appear. Attention to clearing secretions and preventing aspiration of mouth contents into the lungs can prevent pneumonia.

- **Circulatory problems.** Spinal cord injuries can cause a variety of changes in circulation, including blood pressure instability, abnormal heart rhythms (arrhythmias) that may appear days after the injury, and blood clots. Because the brain's control of the cardiac nerves is cut off, the heart can beat at a dangerously slow pace, or it can pound rapidly and irregularly. Arrhythmias are more common and severe in the most serious injuries. Low blood pressure also often occurs due to changes in nervous system control of blood vessels, which then widen, causing blood to pool in the small arteries far away from the heart. Blood pressure needs to be closely monitored to keep blood and oxygen flowing through the spinal cord tissue, with the understanding that baseline blood pressure can be significantly lower than usual in people living with spinal cord injuries. Since muscle movement contributes to moving blood back to the heart, people with spinal cord injuries are at triple the usual risk for blood clots due to stagnation of blood flow in the large veins in the legs. Treatment includes anticoagulant drugs and compression stockings to increase blood flow in the lower legs and feet.

- **Spasticity and muscle tone.** When the spinal cord is damaged, information from the brain can no longer regulate reflex activity. Reflexes may become exaggerated over time, causing muscle spasticity. Muscles may waste away or diminish due to underuse. If spasms become severe enough, they may require medical treatment. For some, spasms can be as much of a help as they are a hindrance, since spasms can tone muscles that would otherwise waste away. Some people can even learn to use the increased tone in their legs to help them turn over in bed, propel them into and out of a wheelchair, or stand.

- **Autonomic dysreflexia.** The autonomic nervous system controls involuntary actions such as blood pressure, heartbeat, and bladder and bowel function. Autonomic dysreflexia is a life-threatening reflex action that primarily affects those with injuries to the neck or upper back. It happens when there is

Disability Caused by Injury and Trauma

an irritation, pain, or stimulus to the nervous system below the level of injury. The irritated area tries to send a sensory signal to the brain, but the signal may be misdirected, causing a runaway reflex action in the spinal cord that has been disconnected from the brain's regulation. Unlike spasms that affect muscles, autonomic dysreflexia affects blood vessels and organ systems controlled by the sympathetic nervous system. Anything that causes pain or irritation can set off autonomic dysreflexia, including a full bladder, constipation, cuts, burns, bruises, sunburn, pressure of any kind on the body, or tight clothing. Symptoms of its onset may include flushing or sweating, a pounding headache, anxiety, sudden increase in blood pressure, vision changes, or goosebumps on the arms and legs. Emptying the bladder or bowels and removing or loosening tight clothing are just a few of the possibilities that should be tried to relieve whatever is causing the irritation. If possible, the person should be kept in a sitting position, rather than lying flat, to keep blood flowing to the lower extremities and help reduce blood pressure.

- **Pressure sores (or pressure ulcers).** Pressure sores are areas of skin tissue that have broken down because of continuous pressure on the skin and reduced blood flow to the area. People with paraplegia and tetraplegia are susceptible to pressure sores because they may lose all or part of skin sensations and cannot shift their weight. As a result, individuals must be shifted periodically by a caregiver if they cannot shift positions themselves. Good nutrition and hygiene can also help prevent pressure sores by encouraging healthy skin. Special motorized rotating beds may be used to prevent and treat sores.

- **Pain.** Some people who have spinal cord nerve are paralyzed often develop neurogenic pain—pain or an intense burning or stinging sensation may be unremitting due to hypersensitivity in some parts of the body. It can either be spontaneous or triggered by a variety of factors and can occur even in parts of the body that have lost normal sensation. Almost all people with spinal cord injury are prone to normal musculoskeletal pain as well, such as shoulder pain due to overuse of the shoulder joint from using a wheelchair. Treatments for chronic pain include medications, acupuncture, spinal or brain electrical stimulation, and surgery. However, none of these treatments are completely effective at relieving neurogenic pain.

- **Bladder and bowel problems.** Most spinal cord injuries affect bladder and bowel functions because the nerves that control the involved organs originate in the segments near the lower end of the spinal cord and lose normal brain input. Although the kidneys continue to produce urine, bladder control may be lost and the risk of bladder and urinary tract infections increases. Some people may need to use a catheter to empty their bladders. The digestive system may be unaffected, but people recovering from a spinal cord injury may need to learn ways to empty their bowels. A change in diet may be needed to help with control.

- **Sexual function.** Depending on the level of injury and recovery from the trauma, sexual function and fertility may be affected. A urologist and other specialists can suggest different options for sexual functioning and health.

- **Depression.** Many people living with a spinal cord injury may develop depression as a result of lifestyle changes. Therapy and medicines may help treat depression.

Once someone has survived the injury and begins to cope psychologically and emotionally, the next concern is how to live with disabilities. Doctors are now able to predict with reasonable accuracy the likely long-term outcome of spinal cord injuries. This helps people experiencing spinal cord injury (SCI) set achievable goals for themselves, and gives families and loved ones a realistic set of expectations for the future.

How Does Rehabilitation Help People Recover from Spinal Cord Injuries?

No two people will experience the same emotions after surviving a spinal cord injury, but almost everyone will feel frightened, anxious, or confused about what has happened. It's common for people to have very mixed feelings: relief that they are still alive, but disbelief at the nature of their disabilities.

Rehabilitation programs combine physical therapies with skill-building activities and counseling to provide social and emotional support. The education and active involvement of the newly injured person and his or her family and friends is crucial.

A rehabilitation team is usually led by a doctor specializing in physical medicine and rehabilitation (called a physiatrist), and often includes social workers, physical and occupational therapists, recreational therapists, rehabilitation nurses, rehabilitation psychologists, vocational counselors, nutritionists, a case worker, and other specialists.

In the initial phase of rehabilitation, therapists emphasize regaining communication skills and leg and arm strength. For some individuals, mobility will only be possible with the assistance of devices such as a walker, leg braces, or a wheelchair. Communication skills such as writing, typing, and using the telephone may also require adaptive devices for some people with tetraplegia.

Physical therapy includes exercise programs geared toward muscle strengthening. Occupational therapy helps redevelop fine motor skills, particularly those needed to perform activities of daily living such as getting in and out of a bed, self-grooming, and eating. Bladder and bowel management programs teach basic toileting routines. People acquire coping strategies for recurring episodes of spasticity, autonomic dysreflexia, and neurogenic pain.

Vocational rehabilitation includes identifying the person's basic work skills and physical and cognitive capabilities to determine the likelihood for employment; identifying potential workplaces and any assistive equipment that will be needed, and; arranging for a user-friendly workplace. If necessary, educational training is provided to develop skills for a new line of work that may be less dependent upon physical abilities and more dependent upon computer or communication skills. Individuals with disabilities that prevent them from returning to the workforce are encouraged to maintain productivity by participating in activities that provide a sense of satisfaction and self-esteem, such as educational classes, hobbies, memberships in special interest groups, and participation in family and community events.

Recreation therapy encourages people with SCI to participate in recreational sports or activities at their level of mobility, as well as achieve a more balanced and normal lifestyle that provides opportunities for socialization and self-expression.

Adaptive devices also may help people with spinal cord injury to regain independence and improve mobility and quality of life. Such devices may include a wheelchair, electronic stimulators, assisted gait training, neural prostheses, computer adaptations, and other computer-assisted technology.

Section 25.4

Traumatic Brain Injury

> This section contains text excerpted from the following sources: Text in this section begins with excerpts from "TBI: Get the Facts," Centers for Disease Control and Prevention (CDC), April 27, 2017; Text beginning with the heading "Treatment" is excerpted from "Traumatic Brain Injury Information Page," National Institute of Neurological Disorders and Stroke (NINDS), June 18, 2018.

Traumatic brain injury (TBI) is a major cause of death and disability in the United States. TBIs contribute to about 30 percent of all injury deaths. Every day, 153 people in the United States die from injuries that include TBI. Those who survive a TBI can face effects that last a few days, or the rest of their lives. Effects of TBI can include impaired thinking or memory, movement, sensation (e.g., vision or hearing), or emotional functioning (e.g., personality changes, depression). These issues not only affect individuals but can have lasting effects on families and communities.

What Is a Traumatic Brain Injury?

A TBI is caused by a bump, blow, or jolt to the head that disrupts the normal function of the brain. Not all blows or jolts to the head result in a TBI. The severity of a TBI may range from "mild" (i.e., a brief change in mental status or consciousness) to "severe" (i.e., an extended period of unconsciousness or memory loss after the injury). Most TBIs that occur each year are mild, commonly called concussions.

How Big Is the Problem?

- In 2013, about 2.8 million TBI-related emergency department (ED) visits, hospitalizations, and deaths occurred in the United States.
  - TBI contributed to the deaths of nearly 50,000 people.
  - TBI was a diagnosis in more than 282,000 hospitalizations and 2.5 million ED visits. These consisted of TBI alone or TBI in combination with other injuries.
- Over the span of six years (2007–2013), while rates of TBI-related ED visits increased by 47 percent, hospitalization rates decreased by 2.5 percent and death rates decreased by 5 percent.

Disability Caused by Injury and Trauma

- In 2012, an estimated 329,290 children (age 19 or younger) were treated in United States EDs for sports and recreation-related injuries that included a diagnosis of concussion or TBI.
  - From 2001–2012, the rate of ED visits for sports and recreation-related injuries with a diagnosis of concussion or TBI, alone or in combination with other injuries, more than doubled among children (age 19 or younger).

What Are the Leading Causes of Traumatic Brain Injury?

- In 2013, falls were the leading cause of TBI. Falls accounted for 47 percent of all TBI-related ED visits, hospitalizations, and deaths in the United States. Falls disproportionately affect the youngest and oldest age groups:
  - More than half (54%) of TBI-related ED visits hospitalizations, and deaths among children 0–14 years were caused by falls.
  - Nearly 4 in 5 (79%) TBI-related ED visits, hospitalizations, and deaths in adults aged 65 and older were caused by falls.
- Being struck by or against an object was the second leading cause of TBI, accounting for about 15 percent of TBI-related ED visits, hospitalizations, and deaths in the United States in 2013.
  - Over 1 in 5 (22%) TBI-related ED visits, hospitalizations, and deaths in children less than 15 years of age were caused by being struck by or against an object.
- Among all age groups, motor vehicle crashes were the third overall leading cause of TBI-related ED visits, hospitalizations, and deaths (14%). When looking at just TBI-related deaths, motor vehicle crashes were the third leading cause (19%) in 2013.
- Intentional self-harm was the second leading cause of TBI-related deaths (33%) in 2013.

Risk Factors for Traumatic Brain Injury

Among TBI-related deaths in 2013:

- Rates were highest for persons 75 years of age and older.

- The leading cause of TBI-related death varied by age.
  - Falls were the leading cause of death for persons 65 years of age or older.
  - Intentional self-harm was the leading cause of death for persons 25–64 years of age.
  - Motor vehicle crashes were the leading cause of death for persons 5–24 years of age.
  - Assaults were the leading cause of death for children ages 0–4 years.

Among nonfatal TBI-related injuries in 2013:

- Hospitalization rates were highest among persons 75 years of age and older.
- Rates of ED visits were highest for persons 75 years of age and older and children 0–4 years of age.
- Falls were the leading cause of TBI-related ED visits for all but one age group.
  - Being struck by or against an object was the leading cause of TBI-related ED visits for persons 15–24 years of age.
- The leading cause of TBI-related hospitalizations varied by age:
  - Falls were the leading cause among children 0–14 years of age and adults 45 years of age and older.
  - Motor vehicle crashes were the leading cause of hospitalizations for adolescents and persons 15–44 years of age.

Treatment of Traumatic Brain Injury

Anyone with signs of moderate or severe TBI should receive medical attention as soon as possible. Because little can be done to reverse the initial brain damage caused by trauma, medical personnel try to stabilize an individual with TBI and focus on preventing further injury. Primary concerns include ensuring proper oxygen supply to the brain and the rest of the body, maintaining adequate blood flow, and controlling blood pressure. Imaging tests help in determining the diagnosis and prognosis of a TBI patient. A blood test to evaluate mild traumatic brain injury in adults was approved by the U.S.

Food and Drug Administration (FDA). People with mild to moderate injuries may receive skull and neck X-rays to check for bone fractures or spinal instability. For moderate to severe cases, the imaging test is a computed tomography (CT) scan. Moderately to severely injured patients receive rehabilitation that involves individually tailored treatment programs in the areas of physical therapy, occupational therapy, speech/language therapy, physiatry (physical medicine), psychology/psychiatry, and social support.

Prognosis of Traumatic Brain Injury

Approximately half of severely head-injured patients will need surgery to remove or repair hematomas (ruptured blood vessels) or contusions (bruised brain tissue). Disabilities resulting from a TBI depend upon the severity of the injury, the location of the injury, and the age and general health of the individual. Some common disabilities include problems with cognition (thinking, memory, and reasoning), sensory processing (sight, hearing, touch, taste, and smell), communication (expression and understanding), and behavior or mental health (depression, anxiety, personality changes, aggression, acting out, and social inappropriateness). More serious head injuries may result in stupor, an unresponsive state, but one in which an individual can be aroused briefly by a strong stimulus, such as sharp pain; coma, a state in which an individual is totally unconscious, unresponsive, unaware, and unarousable; vegetative state, in which an individual is unconscious and unaware of his or her surroundings, but continues to have a sleep-wake cycle and periods of alertness; and a persistent vegetative state (PVS), in which an individual stays in a vegetative state for more than a month.

Part Three

Technologies and Services That Help People with Disabilities and Their Families

Chapter 26

What Is Assistive Technology?

Assistive technology (AT) is any service or tool that helps older adults or persons with disabilities perform activities that might otherwise be difficult or impossible. For older adults, such technology may be a walker to improve mobility or an amplification device to make sounds easier to hear. It could also include a magnifying glass for someone who has poor vision or a scooter that makes it possible for someone to travel over distances that are too far to walk. In short, AT is anything that aids continued participation in daily activities. AT allows many people to live independently without long-term nursing or home healthcare. For some, it is critical to the ability to perform simple activities of daily living, such as bathing.

Choosing Assistive Technology

Older adults should carefully evaluate their needs before purchasing AT. Using AT may change the mix of services that they require

---

This chapter contains text excerpted from the following sources: Text in this chapter begins with excerpts from "Assistive Technology," Eldercare Locator, U.S. Administration on Aging (AOA), October 20, 2015; Text under the heading "Some Examples of Assistive Technologies" is excerpted from "What Are Some Types of Assistive Devices and How Are They Used?" *Eunice Kennedy Shriver* National Institute of Child Health and Human Development (NICHD), December 1, 2016.

or affect the way that those services are provided. Needs assessment and planning are very important.

Usually, a needs assessment is most effective when done by a team working with the older adult in a place where the AT will be used. For example, someone who has trouble communicating or hearing might consult his or her doctor, an audiology specialist, a speech-language therapist, and family and friends. Together, they can identify precise challenges and help select the most effective devices available at the lowest cost. A professional member of the team, such as the audiology specialist, can also arrange for any training needed to use the equipment.

When considering AT, it is useful to consider high-tech and low-tech solutions. Older adults should also think about how their needs might change over time. High-tech devices tend to be more expensive but may address many different needs. Low-tech equipment is usually less expensive but also less adaptable.

Paying for Assistive Technology

Medicare

Right now, no single private insurance plan or public program will pay for all types of AT under any circumstances. However, Medicare Part B will cover up to 80 percent of the cost, if the items are durable medical equipment—devices that are "primarily and customarily used to serve a medical purpose, and generally are not useful to a person in the absence of illness or injury." Contact Medicare to determine whether a particular type of AT is covered.

Medicaid

Depending on where you live, the state-run Medicaid program may pay for some AT. Keep in mind that when Medicaid covers part of the cost, the benefits do not usually provide the total amount needed to buy an expensive piece of equipment, such as a power wheelchair.

Older adults who are eligible for veteran benefits may be eligible for assistance from the U.S. Department of Veterans Affairs (VA), which has a model structure in place to pay for the large volume of equipment that it buys. The VA also invests in training people to use assistive devices.

U.S. Department of Veterans Affairs Health Benefits Service Center

Subsidy programs provide some types of AT at a reduced cost or for free. Many businesses and nonprofit groups offer discounts, grants, or

What Is Assistive Technology?

rebates to get consumers to try a specific product. Older adults should be cautious about participating in subsidy programs run by businesses with commercial interests in the product or service because of the potential for fraud.

Local Resources for Assistive Technology

Most states have at least one agency that deals specifically with AT issues. The Assistive Technology Act (Tech Act) provides funds for the development of statewide consumer information and training programs. Find your state programs by visiting www.at3center.net/home.

Some Area Agencies on Aging (AAA) have programs or link to services that assist older people to obtain low-cost assistive technology. To locate your AAA, call the Eldercare Locator at 800-677-1116 or visit www.eldercare.acl.gov.

Local civic, faith-based, and veterans' organizations, as well as senior centers, may also be able to refer you to AT resources.

Some Examples of Assistive Technologies

- Mobility aids, such as wheelchairs, scooters, walkers, canes, crutches, prosthetic devices, and orthotic devices
- Hearing aids
- Cognitive assistance, including computer or electrical assistive devices
- Computer software and hardware, such as voice recognition programs, screen readers, and screen enlargement applications
- Automatic page-turners, book holders, and adapted pencil grips
- Closed captioning in movies and television programs
- Building modifications include ramps, automatic door openers, grab bars, and wider doorways
- Specially designed wheelchairs for organized sports, such as basketball, tennis, and racing
- Adaptive switches for toys and games
- Kitchen implements
- Medication dispensers

Chapter 27

Rehabilitative and Assistive Technology

What Is Rehabilitative and Assistive Technology?

Rehabilitative and assistive technology refers to tools, equipment, or products that can help a person with a disability to function successfully at school, home, work, and in the community. Assistive technology can be as simple as a magnifying glass or as complex as a computerized communication system. An assistive device can be as large as an automated wheelchair lift for a van or as small as a handheld hook to assist with buttoning a shirt. The term "rehabilitative technology" is sometimes used to refer to aids used to help people recover their functioning after injury or illness. But the term often is used interchangeably with the term "assistive technology."

The *Eunice Kennedy Shriver* National Institute of Child Health and Human Development (NICHD) supports research for developing technologies, devices, computerized and robotic devices, and other aids aimed at helping people with disabilities achieve their full potential. Rehabilitative engineering involves the application of engineering and scientific principles to study how people with disabilities function in society. It includes studying barriers to optimal function and designing

---

This chapter includes text excerpted from "Rehabilitative and Assistive Technology: Condition Information," *Eunice Kennedy Shriver* National Institute of Child Health and Human Development (NICHD), December 1, 2016.

solutions so that people with disabilities can interact successfully in their environments.

What Are Some Types of Assistive Devices and How Are They Used?

Some examples of assistive technologies are as follows:

- People with physical disabilities that affect movement can use mobility aids, such as wheelchairs, scooters, walkers, canes, crutches, prosthetic devices, and orthotic devices, to enhance their mobility

- Hearing aids can improve hearing ability in persons with hearing problems

- Cognitive assistance, including computer or electrical assistive devices, can help people function following brain injury

- Computer software and hardware, such as voice recognition programs, screen readers, and screen enlargement applications, help people with mobility and sensory impairments use computer technology

- In the classroom and elsewhere, assistive devices, such as automatic page-turners, book holders, and adapted pencil grips, allow learners with disabilities to participate in educational activities

- Closed captioning allows people with hearing impairments to enjoy movies and television programs

- Barriers in community buildings, businesses, and workplaces can be removed or modified to improve accessibility. Such modifications include ramps, automatic door openers, grab bars, and wider doorways.

- Lightweight, high-performance wheelchairs have been designed for organized sports, such as basketball, tennis, and racing

- Adaptive switches make it possible for a child with limited motor skills to play with toys and games

- Many types of devices help people with disabilities perform such tasks as cooking, dressing, and grooming. Kitchen implements are available with large, cushioned grips to help people with weakness or arthritis in their hands. Medication dispensers with alarms can help people remember to take their medicine on time. People who use wheelchairs for mobility can use extendable reaching devices to reach items on shelves.

What Are Some Types of Rehabilitative Technologies?

Rehabilitative technologies are any technologies that help people recover function after injury or illness. Just a few examples include the following:

- **Robotics.** Specialized robots help people regain function in arms or legs after a stroke.
- **Virtual reality (VR).** People who are recovering from injury can retrain themselves to perform motions within a virtual environment.
- **Musculoskeletal modeling and simulations.** These computer simulations of the human body can pinpoint the underlying mechanical problems in a person with a movement-related disability. This can help design better assistive aids or physical therapies.
- **Transcranial magnetic stimulation (TMS).** TMS sends magnetic impulses through the skull to stimulate the brain. This system can help people who have had a stroke recover movement and brain function.
- **Transcranial direct current stimulation (tDCS).** In tDCS, a mild electrical current travels through the skull and stimulates the brain of patients recovering from stroke. This can help recover movement.
- **Motion analysis.** Motion analysis captures video of human motion with specialized computer software that analyzes the motion in detail. The technology gives healthcare providers a detailed picture of a person's specific movement challenges to be used as a guide for proper therapy.

For What Conditions Are Assistive Devices Used?

Some disabilities are quite visible, and others are "hidden." Most disabilities can be grouped into four major categories:

1. **Cognitive disability:** Intellectual and learning disabilities/disorder, distractibility, reading disorders, inability to remember or focus on large amounts of information.

2. **Hearing disability:** Hearing loss or impaired hearing.

3. **Physical disability:** Paralysis, difficulties with walking or other movement, inability to use a computer mouse, slow response time, limited fine or gross motor control.

4. **Visual disability:** Blindness, low vision, color blindness.

Mental illness, including anxiety disorders, mood disorders, eating disorders, and psychosis, for example, is also a disability. Hidden disabilities can include some people with visual impairments and those with dexterity difficulties, such as repetitive strain injury. People who are hard of hearing or have mental health difficulties also may be included in this category.

Some people have disabling medical conditions that may be regarded as hidden disabilities—for example, epilepsy; diabetes; sickle cell conditions; Human immunodeficiency virus (HIV)/acquired immunodeficiency syndrome (AIDS); cystic fibrosis (CF); cancer; and heart, liver or kidney problems. The conditions may be short term or long term, stable or progressive, constant or unpredictable and fluctuating, controlled by medication or another treatment, or untreatable. Many people with hidden disabilities can benefit from assistive technologies for certain activities or during certain stages of their diseases or conditions.

People who have spinal cord injuries (SPIs), traumatic brain injury (TBI), cerebral palsy (CP), muscular dystrophy (MD), spina bifida, osteogenesis imperfecta (OI), multiple sclerosis (MS), demyelinating diseases, myelopathy, progressive muscular atrophy (PMA), amputations, or paralysis often benefit from complex rehabilitative technology. This means that the assistive devices these people use are individually configured to help each person with his or her own unique disability.

How Does Rehabilitative and Assistive Technology Benefit People with Disabilities?

Deciding which type of rehabilitative or assistive technology would be most helpful for a person with a disability is usually made by the disabled person and his or her family and caregivers, along with a team of professionals and consultants. The team is trained to match particular assistive technologies to specific needs to help the person function more independently. The team may include family doctors, regular and special education teachers, speech-language pathologists, rehabilitation engineers, occupational therapists, and other specialists,

Rehabilitative and Assistive Technology

including representatives from companies that manufacture assistive technology.

Assistive technology enables students with disabilities to compensate for the impairments they experience. This specialized technology promotes independence and decreases the need for other educational support.

Appropriate assistive technology helps people with disabilities overcome or compensate, at least in part, for their limitations. Rehabilitative technology can help restore function in people who have developed a disability due to disease, injury, or aging. Rehabilitative and assistive technology can enable individuals to:

- Care for themselves and their families
- Work
- Learn in schools and other educational institutions
- Access information through computers and reading
- Enjoy music, sports, travel, and the arts
- Participate fully in community life

Assistive technology also benefits employers, teachers, family members, and everyone who interacts with users of the technology. Increasing opportunities for participation benefits everyone.

As assistive technologies are becoming more commonplace, people without disabilities are benefiting from them. For example, people who are poor readers or for whom English is a second language are taking advantage of screen readers. The aging population is making use of screen enlargers and magnifiers.

Chapter 28

Mobility Aids

Chapter Contents

Section 28.1—Wheelchairs and Other Power-
　　　　　　　Driven Mobility Devices 318
Section 28.2—Tongue-Driven Wheelchairs 320

Section 28.1

Wheelchairs and Other Power-Driven Mobility Devices

This section includes text excerpted from "Wheelchairs, Mobility Aids, and Other Power-Driven Mobility Devices," ADA.gov, U.S. Department of Justice (DOJ), January 31, 2014. Reviewed July 2018.

People with mobility, circulatory, respiratory, or neurological disabilities use many kinds of devices for mobility. Some use walkers, canes, crutches, or braces. Some use manual or power wheelchairs or electric scooters. In addition, advances in technology have given rise to new devices, such as Segways®, that some people with disabilities use as mobility devices, including many veterans injured while serving in the military. And more advanced devices will inevitably be invented, providing more mobility options for people with disabilities.

This section is designed to help Title II entities (state and local governments) and Title III entities (businesses and nonprofit organizations that serve the public) (together, "covered entities") understand how the new rules for mobility devices apply to them. These rules went into effect on March 15, 2011.

- Covered entities must allow people with disabilities who use manual or power wheelchairs or scooters, and manually-powered mobility aids such as walkers, crutches, and canes, into all areas where members of the public are allowed to go.

- Covered entities must also allow people with disabilities who use other types of power-driven mobility devices into their facilities, unless a particular type of device cannot be accommodated because of legitimate safety requirements. Where legitimate safety requirements bar accommodation for a particular type of device, the covered entity must provide the service it offers in alternate ways if possible.

- The rules set out five specific factors to consider in deciding whether or not a particular type of device can be accommodated.

Wheelchairs

Most people are familiar with the manual and power wheelchairs and electric scooters used by people with mobility disabilities. The term "wheelchair" is defined in the new rules as "a manually-operated or power-driven device designed primarily for use by an individual with a mobility disability for the main purpose of indoor or of both indoor and outdoor locomotion."

Other Power-Driven Mobility Devices

In recent years, some people with mobility disabilities have begun using less traditional mobility devices such as golf cars or Segways®. These devices are called "other power-driven mobility device" (OPDMD) in the rule. OPDMD is defined in the new rules as "any mobility device powered by batteries, fuel, or other engines that is used by individuals with mobility disabilities for the purpose of locomotion, including golf cars, electronic personal assistance mobility devices such as the Segway® PT, or any mobility device designed to operate in areas without defined pedestrian routes, but that is not a wheelchair." When an OPDMD is being used by a person with a mobility disability, different rules apply under the Americans with Disabilities Act (ADA) than when it is being used by a person without a disability.

Choice of Device

People with disabilities have the right to choose whatever mobility device best suits their needs. For example, some people may choose to use a manual wheelchair rather than a power wheelchair because it enables them to maintain their upper body strength. Similarly, someone who is able to stand may choose to use a Segway® rather than a manual wheelchair because of the health benefits gained by standing. A facility may be required to allow a type of device that is generally prohibited when being used by someone without a disability when it is being used by a person who needs it because of a mobility disability. For example, if golf cars are generally prohibited in a park, the park may be required to allow a golf car when it is being used because of a person's mobility disability, unless there is a legitimate safety reason that it cannot be accommodated.

Section 28.2

Tongue-Driven Wheelchairs

This section includes text excerpted from "Tongue-Driven Wheelchair Out-Maneuvers the Competition," National Institute of Biomedical Imaging and Bioengineering (NIBIB), January 2, 2014. Reviewed July 2018.

Researchers funded by the National Institute of Biomedical Imaging and Bioengineering (NIBIB) have demonstrated that their novel Tongue Drive System (TDS) is superior to other assistive devices used by individuals with tetraplegia.

In a small clinical trial, the researchers showed for the first time that individuals with tetraplegia can maneuver a wheelchair three times faster using the TDS and with the same accuracy as the currently used sip-and-puff system. The speed and accuracy of the TDS was even more impressive given that the study participants had years of daily experience using the sip-and-puff technology, which requires inhaling and exhaling through a straw attached to a pneumatic switch that maneuvers the wheelchair.

The new technology offers a significant measure of increased independence for those reliant on assistive technologies to perform daily life tasks. The work was performed by a team led by Maysam Ghovanloo, Ph.D., Georgia Institute of Technology, and was published in the November 27 issue of Science Translational Medicine.

The TDS takes advantage of the fact that virtually all paralyzed individuals remain able to move their tongue. The researchers have seized upon this phenomenon to turn the tongue of individuals with tetraplegia into a highly sensitive and accurate joystick. The system employs a magnetic tongue stud worn by the user to wirelessly relay the position of the tongue to the computerized wheelchair. The complete system allows an individual to use his tongue to steer the wheelchair much like a radio-controlled toy car is guided using a joystick.

Participants also tested the use of the Tongue Drive to operate a computer. Able-bodied individuals and individuals with tetraplegia tested moving a computer cursor to click on random targets on the screen, as well as navigating a maze with the cursor. Eleven individuals with tetraplegia compared the TDS to the sip-and-puff system and 23 able-bodied individuals compared the Tongue Drive to the computer mouse and keypad. Both groups adapted to use of the Tongue Drive with just 30 minutes of training and improved rapidly with additional experience.

At the end of the trials the participants reported that, compared to their current assistive technology, they preferred the TDS, which allows a more seamless, less cumbersome interaction with their environment. Unlike other assistive technologies that are mounted on the wheelchair or on a computer, they also liked the fact that the TDS is worn on the body and remains usable even when they are transferred to bed or another wheelchair.

Grace Peng, Ph.D. Program Director at NIBIB adds "We have been thrilled to support and watch this revolutionary rehabilitation work of Dr. Ghovanloo's team unfold. It is particularly rewarding that this work was supported by an American Recovery and Reinvestment Act (ARRA) National Institutes of Health (NIH) Challenge Grant. ARRA grants were special two-year grants to design innovative solutions to our most challenging biomedical research problems. This work is a significant step towards vastly improving the independence and quality of life of individuals with tetraplegia, and is a true ARRA Challenge Grant success story."

Currently, testing of the TDS has been confined to the lab or hospital. The research team is planning tests outside of the laboratory to see how patients function with the TDS in their homes, workplaces, and a variety of other environments.

Chapter 29

Home Use Devices and Modifications

Chapter Contents

Section 29.1—What Are Home Use Medical Devices?.............. 324
Section 29.2—Adapting Your Living Space to
　　　　　　　Accommodate Your Disability 327

Section 29.1

What Are Home Use Medical Devices?

This section contains text excerpted from the following sources: Text under the heading "Home Use Devices" is excerpted from "Home Use Devices," U.S. Food and Drug Administration (FDA), March 26, 2018; Text beginning with the heading "What Devices Does FDA Recommend for Home Use?" is excerpted from "Frequently Asked Questions about Home Use Devices," U.S. Food and Drug Administration (FDA), February 4, 2018.

Home Use Devices

A home use medical device is a medical device intended for users in any environment outside of a professional healthcare facility. This includes devices intended for use in both professional healthcare facilities and homes.

- A user is a patient (care recipient), caregiver, or family member that directly uses the device or provides assistance in using the device.

- A qualified healthcare professional is a licensed or nonlicensed healthcare professional with proficient skill and experience with the use of the device so that they can aid or train care recipients and caregivers to use and maintain the device.

What Devices Does the FDA Recommend for Home Use?

The U.S. Food and Drug Administration (FDA) is responsible for regulating companies that manufacture, repackage, relabel, and import medical devices sold in the United States. This is accomplished through scientific review of premarket data submitted by a medical device manufacturer to establish a device's safety and efficacy and then once on the market, monitoring medical device adverse event reports to detect and correct device-related problems in a timely manner.

It is important to note because the FDA's scope of work is to regulate the medical device industry, the FDA cannot and does not recommend specific medical devices for use in any setting. Review the instructions for use for a device you plan to use in the home before deciding on the one best for a particular patient population.

Home Use Devices and Modifications

Where Can I Buy Home Use Devices?

Home use devices are often sold to patients who have a prescription for that given device at hospitals or at pharmacies. Medical devices are also cleared or approved for sale directly to the consumer and these are called over-the-counter (OTC) products. Medical devices are also available at many online retailers. If you buy a home use device online, make sure you are buying from a reliable source. Also, check the store's return policy and customer support statement before you place an order.

Who Do I Contact If My Device Breaks or Doesn't Work Properly?

Make sure you have phone numbers for your homecare agency, doctor, or the device manufacturer to call if your device is not working properly. You should also report the problem to your doctor, to the manufacturer of your medical device and to FDA through the MedWatch Reporting Program.

Who Can Write a Prescription for a Medical Device?

Each state has laws and regulations that determine who can write a prescription for a medical device in that state. FDA defers to the states on determining who can write a valid prescription.

Do I Need a Prescription for My Device?

Not all medical devices require a prescription; however, many medical devices do require a prescription (for example, contact lenses).

How Can I Find Out If My Medical Device Has Been Recalled?

You can search FDA's online public recall database.

I Can't Find the Instructions for Use. Where Can I Find the Information?

If you do not have the instructions, contact your healthcare provider.

Where Do I Report a Serious Injury, Death, or Medical Device Malfunction?

You may report a problem by phone, fax, online or mail:

- Toll-Free: 800-332-1088
- Toll-Free Fax: 800-FDA-0178 (800-332-0178)
- MedWatch Online
- **Regular Mail:** Use postage-paid FDA Form 3500
- **Mail to:** MedWatch 5600 Fishers Ln., Rockville, MD 20852-9787

How Do I Clean My Device?

Follow the manufacturer's instructions. If you do not have the instructions, contact your healthcare provider.

Where Do I Dispose of Hazardous Waste, Such as Needles or Tubing?

Dispose of your hazardous waste according to the manufacturer's instructions. You may also wish to contact your pharmacist, nearest hospital, solid waste company, or state or local government for additional information about proper disposal.

Is My Home Wiring Compatible with the Medical Device?

The FDA has developed a checklist with important questions to ask when considering home use medical devices. Discuss these issues with your healthcare provider.

Section 29.2

Adapting Your Living Space to Accommodate Your Disability

This section includes text excerpted from "Home Modifications," Administration for Community Living (ACL), April 1, 2017.

Home modifications are changes made to adapt living spaces to meet the needs of people with physical limitations so that they can continue to live independently and safely. These modifications may include adding assistive technology or making structural changes to a home. Modifications can range from something as simple as replacing cabinet door knobs with pull handles to full-scale construction projects that require installing wheelchair ramps and widening doorways. The main benefit of making home modifications is that they promote independence and prevent accidents. According to a 2000 AARP housing survey, "89 percent of older Americans want to stay in their current homes for as long as possible," but other studies show that most homes are not designed to accommodate the needs of people over age 65. A house that was perfectly suitable for a senior at age 55, for example, may have too many stairs or slippery surfaces for a person who is 70 or 80.

How Can I Tell What Home Modifications Are Right for Me?

The best way to begin planning for home modifications is by defining the basic terms used and asking some simple questions. According to the Rehabilitation Engineering and Assistive Technology Society of North America (RESNA), home modifications should improve the following features of a home:

- **Accessibility.** Improving accessibility means making doorways wider, clearing spaces to make sure a wheelchair can pass through, lowering countertop heights for sinks and kitchen cabinets, installing grab bars, and placing light switches and electrical outlets at heights that can be reached easily.

- **Adaptability.** Adaptability features are changes that can be made quickly to accommodate the needs of seniors or individuals with disabilities without having to completely redesign the home or use different materials for essential fixtures. Examples include installing grab bars in bathroom walls and movable cabinets under the sink so that someone in a wheelchair can use the space.

- **Universal design.** Universal design features are usually built into a home when the first blueprints or architectural plans are drawn. These features include appliances, fixtures, and floor plans that are easy for all people to use, flexible enough so that they can be adapted for special needs, sturdy and reliable, and functional with a minimum of effort and understanding of the mechanisms involved.

Where Do I Begin?

Before you make home modifications, you should evaluate your current and future needs by going through your home room by room and answering a series of questions to highlight where changes might be made. Several checklists are available to help you conduct this review. The National Resource Center on Supportive Housing and Home Modifications (NRCSHHM) is a good place to start.

You can begin your survey by examining areas of your home. Here are some questions to ask:

Appliances, Kitchen, Bathroom

- Are cabinet door knobs easy to use?
- Are stove controls easy to use and clearly marked?
- Are faucets easy to use?
- Are there grab bars where needed?

Doors, Windows

- Are your doors and windows easy to open and close?
- Are your door locks sturdy and easy to operate?
- Are your doors wide enough to accommodate a walker or wheelchair?
- Do your doors have peepholes or viewing?

Electrical Outlets, Switches, Safety Devices

- Are light or power switches easy to turn on and off?

Home Use Devices and Modifications

- Are electrical outlets easy to reach?
- Are the electrical outlets properly grounded to prevent shocks?
- Are your extension cords in good condition?
- Can you hear the doorbell in every part of the house?
- Do you have smoke detectors throughout your home?
- Do you have an alarm system?
- Is the telephone readily available for emergencies?
- Would you benefit from having an assistive device to make it easier to hear and talk on the telephone?

Floors

- Are all of the floors in your home on the same level?
- Are steps up and down marked in some way?
- Are all floor surfaces safe and covered with nonslip or nonskid materials?
- Do you have scatter rugs or doormats that could be hazardous?

Hallways, Steps, Stairways

- Are hallways and stairs in good condition?
- Do all of your hallways and stairs have smooth, safe surfaces?
- Do your stairs have steps that are big enough for your whole foot?
- Do you have handrails on both sides of the stairway?
- Are your stair rails wide enough for you to grasp them securely?
- Would you benefit from building a ramp to replace the stairs or steps inside or outside of your home?

Lighting, Ventilation

- Do you have night lights where they are needed?
- Is the lighting in each room sufficient for the use of the room?
- Is the lighting bright enough to ensure safety?
- Is each room well-ventilated with good air circulation?

Once you have explored all the areas of your home that could benefit from remodeling, you might make a list of potential problems and possible solutions.

- Are all appliances and utensils conveniently and safely located?
- Can the oven and refrigerator be opened easily?
- Can you sit down while working?
- Can you get into and out of the bathtub or shower easily?
- Is the kitchen counter height and depth comfortable for you?
- Is the water temperature regulated to prevent scalding or burning?
- Would you benefit from having convenience items, such as a handheld showerhead, a garbage disposal, or a trash compactor?

Where Can I Learn More about Home Modifications?

The National Resource Center on Supportive Housing and Home Modifications is one of the best sources for more information about home modifications. The center is a major clearinghouse for news on government-assisted housing, assisted living policies, home modifications for older people, training and education courses.

Some area Agencies on Aging (AAA) have programs or link to services that assist older people to obtain home modifications. You can call the Eldercare Locator at 800-677-1116 or visit the website (www.eldercare.gov).

Chapter 30

Devices for Improving Communication and Hearing

Chapter Contents

Section 30.1—Captions for Deaf and Hard-of-Hearing Viewers 332
Section 30.2—Cochlear Implants 337
Section 30.3—Hearing Aids 340
Section 30.4—Other Hearing Assistive Technology 346

Section 30.1

Captions for Deaf and Hard-of-Hearing Viewers

This section contains text excerpted from the following sources: Text beginning with the heading "What Are Captions?" is excerpted from "Captions for Deaf and Hard-of-Hearing Viewers," National Institute on Deafness and Other Communication Disorders (NIDCD), July 5, 2017; Text beginning with the heading "Closed Captioning on Television" is excerpted from "Closed Captioning on Television," Federal Communications Commission (FCC), April 11, 2018.

What Are Captions?

Captions are words displayed on a television, computer, mobile device, or movie screen that describe the audio or sound portion of a program or video. Captions allow viewers who are deaf or hard-of-hearing to follow the dialogue and the action of a program simultaneously. For people with hearing loss who are not deaf, captions can even make the spoken words easier to hear—because hearing, like vision, is influenced by our expectations (When you have an idea of what someone might be about to say, his or her speech may seem more clear). Captions can also provide information about who is speaking or about sound effects that may be important to understand a news story, a political event, or the plot of a program.

Captions are created from the program's transcript. A captioner separates the dialogue into captions and makes sure the words appear in sync with the audio they describe. Computer software encodes the captioning information and combines it with the audio and video to create a new master tape or digital file of the program. Ideally, the captions should appear near the bottom of the screen—not in the middle, where misplaced captions can cover the newscaster's face or the basketball hoop or quarterback.

Open and Closed Captions

Captions may be "open" or "closed." Open captions are always in view and cannot be turned off, whereas closed captions can be turned on and off by the viewer (using the menu settings on any television).

Closed captioning is available on digital television sets, including high-definition television sets, manufactured after July 1, 2002. Some digital captioning menus allow the viewer to control the caption display, including font style, text size and color, and background color.

Real-Time Captioning

Real-time captions, or communication access real-time translation, are created as an event takes place. A captioner (often trained as a court reporter or stenographer) uses a stenotype machine with a phonetic keyboard and special software. A computer translates the phonetic symbols into English captions almost instantaneously. The slight delay is based on the captioner's need to hear and code the word, and on computer processing time. Real-time captioning can be used for programs that have no script; live events, including congressional proceedings; news programs; and nonbroadcast meetings, such as the national meetings of professional associations.

Although most real-time captioning is more than 98 percent accurate, the audience will see occasional errors. The captioner may mishear a word, hear an unfamiliar word, or have an error in the software dictionary.

Electronic Newsroom Captions

Electronic newsroom captions (ENR) are created from a news script computer or teleprompter and are commonly used for live newscasts. Only material that is scripted can be captioned using this technique. Therefore, spontaneous commentary, live field reports, breaking news, and sports and weather updates may not be captioned using ENR, and real-time captioning is needed.

Edited and Verbatim Captions

Captions can be produced as either edited or verbatim captions. Edited captions summarize ideas and shorten phrases. Verbatim captions include all of what is said. Although there are situations in which edited captions are preferred for ease in reading (such as for children's programs), most people who are deaf or hard-of-hearing prefer the full access provided by verbatim texts.

Rear-Window Captioning

Some movie theaters across the country offer this type of captioning system. An adjustable Lucite panel attaches to the viewer's seat and reflects the captions from a light-emitting diode (LED) panel at the back of the theater.

Captioned Telephone

A captioned telephone has a built-in screen to display in text (captions) whatever the other person on the call is saying. When an outgoing call is placed on a captioned telephone, the call is connected to a captioned telephone service (CTS). A specially trained CTS operator hears the person you want to talk to and repeats what that person says. Speech recognition technology automatically transcribes the CTS operator's voice into text that is displayed on the captioned telephone screen.

The Law

The Americans with Disabilities Act (ADA) of 1990 requires businesses and public accommodations to ensure that individuals with disabilities are not excluded from or denied services because of the absence of auxiliary aids. Captions are considered one type of auxiliary aid. Since the passage of the ADA, the use of captioning has expanded. Entertainment, educational, informational, and training materials are captioned for deaf and hard-of-hearing audiences at the time they are produced and distributed.

The Television Decoder Circuitry Act of 1990 requires that all televisions larger than 13 inches sold in the United States after July 1993 have a special built-in decoder that enables viewers to watch closed-captioned programming. The Telecommunications Act of 1996 directs the Federal Communications Commission (FCC) to adopt rules requiring closed captioning of most television programming.

Captions and the Federal Communications Commission

The FCC's rules on closed captioning became effective January 1, 1998. They require people or companies that distribute television programs directly to home viewers to caption those programs. The rules required all nonexempt programs to be closed captioned by January 1, 2006; after that date, captioning was also required for all new nonexempt programs. As of January 1, 2010, all new nonexempt Spanish language video programming must also be provided with captions.

Who Is Required to Provide Closed Captions?

Congress requires video program distributors (cable operators, broadcasters, satellite distributors, and other multichannel video

Devices for Improving Communication and Hearing

programming distributors) to close caption their TV programs. The FCC rules ensure that viewers have full access to programming, address captioning quality, and provide guidance to video programming distributors and programmers. The rules require that captions be accurate, synchronous, complete, and properly placed. In addition, the rules distinguish between prerecorded, live, and near-live programming, and explain how the standards apply to each type of programming, recognizing the greater challenges involved with captioning live or near-live programming.

What Programs Are Exempt?

Some advertisements, public service announcements, non-English-language programs (with the exception of Spanish programs), locally produced and distributed nonnews programming, textual programs, early-morning programs, and nonvocal musical programs are exempt from captioning.

To find out more about the FCC rules and captions, including information on the complaint process, call:

Toll-Free Voice: 888-CALL-FCC (888-225-5322)
Toll-Free TTY: 888-TELL-FCC (888-835-5322)

Closed Captioning on Television

Closed captioning displays the audio portion of a television program as text on the TV screen, providing a critical link to news, entertainment, and information for individuals who are deaf or hard-of-hearing. Congress requires video programming distributors (VPDs)—cable operators, broadcasters, satellite distributors, and other multichannel video programming distributors—to close caption their TV programs.

Federal Communications Commission Closed Captioning Rules

The FCC rules for TV closed captioning ensure that viewers who are deaf and hard of hearing have full access to programming, address captioning quality and provide guidance to video programming distributors and programmers. The rules apply to all television programming with captions, requiring that captions be:

- **Accurate:** Captions must match the spoken words in the dialogue and convey background noises and other sounds to the fullest extent possible.

- **Synchronous:** Captions must coincide with their corresponding spoken words and sounds to the greatest extent possible and must be displayed on the screen at a speed that can be read by viewers.

- **Complete:** Captions must run from the beginning to the end of the program to the fullest extent possible.

- **Properly placed:** Captions should not block other important visual content on the screen, overlap one another or run off the edge of the video screen.

The rules distinguish between prerecorded, live, and near-live programming and explain how the standards apply to each type of programming, recognizing the greater hurdles involved with captioning live and near-live programming.

Exempt Programming

There are two categories of exemptions from the closed captioning rules, self-implementing, and economically burdensome:

- Self-implementing exemptions include public service announcements shorter than 10 minutes and not paid for with federal dollars, programming shown from 2 a.m. to 6 a.m., and programming that is primarily textual. There is also an exemption for locally produced nonnews programming with no repeat value.

- The FCC has established procedures for petitioning for an exemption from the closed captioning rules when compliance would be economically burdensome. Find out about the economically burdensome exemption.

- Even if a program or a provider is exempt under the commission's rules, it may still have obligations under other federal laws to make its video programming accessible to individuals with disabilities.

What If You Experience Closed Captioning Problems?

You may contact your Vital Product Data (VPD) to report the problem at the time that the problem occurs to see if you can get the problem fixed. You can find your VPD's contact information on your bill, or, if you have broadcast-only TV, the contact information for the TV

Devices for Improving Communication and Hearing

station should be in the phone directory. Also, you can search the FCC's VPD Registry. VPDs must provide the FCC with contact information for the receipt and handling of immediate closed captioning concerns by consumers, and contact information for written closed captioning complaints.

For captioning problems during nonemergency programming, you may file a written complaint with either the FCC or your VPD. If you file your complaint with the FCC, the FCC will forward the complaint to your VPD. FCC rules require that your written complaint must be filed within 60 days of the captioning problem. After receiving a complaint, either directly from you or from the FCC, the VPD has 30 days to respond to the complaint. If you filed your complaint with your VPD and they do not respond within 30 days, or if a dispute remains, you can send your complaint to the FCC.

Section 30.2

Cochlear Implants

This section includes text excerpted from "Cochlear Implants," National Institute on Deafness and Other Communication Disorders (NIDCD), March 6, 2017.

What Is a Cochlear Implant?

A cochlear implant is a small, complex electronic device that can help to provide a sense of sound to a person who is profoundly deaf or severely hard-of-hearing. The implant consists of an external portion that sits behind the ear and a second portion that is surgically placed under the skin. An implant has the following parts:

- A microphone, which picks up sound from the environment

- A speech processor, which selects and arranges sounds picked up by the microphone

- A transmitter and receiver/stimulator, which receive signals from the speech processor and convert them into electric impulses

- An electrode array, which is a group of electrodes that collects the impulses from the stimulator and sends them to different regions of the auditory nerve

An implant does not restore normal hearing. Instead, it can give a deaf person a useful representation of sounds in the environment and help him or her to understand speech.

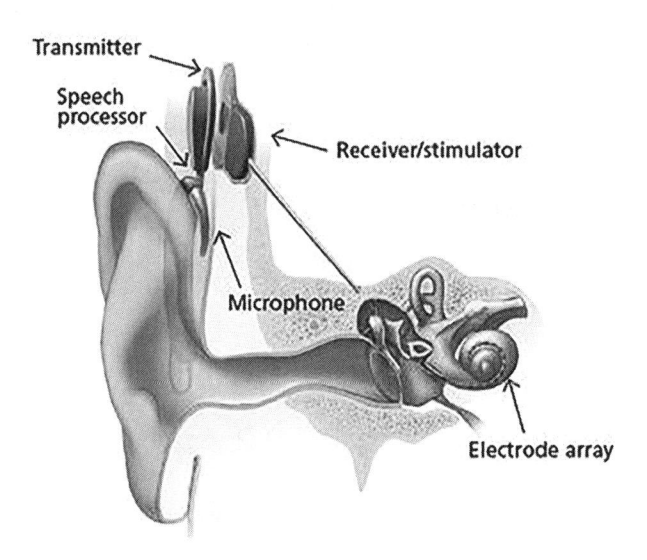

Figure 30.1. *Ear with Cochlear Implant*

How Does a Cochlear Implant Work?

A cochlear implant is very different from a hearing aid. Hearing aids amplify sounds so they may be detected by damaged ears. Cochlear implants bypass damaged portions of the ear and directly stimulate the auditory nerve. Signals generated by the implant are sent by way of the auditory nerve to the brain, which recognizes the signals as sound. Hearing through a cochlear implant is different from normal hearing and takes time to learn or relearn. However, it allows many people to recognize warning signals, understand other sounds in the environment, and understand speech in person or over the telephone.

Who Gets Cochlear Implants?

Children and adults who are deaf or severely hard-of-hearing can be fitted for cochlear implants. As of December 2012, approximately

Devices for Improving Communication and Hearing

324,200 registered devices have been implanted worldwide. In the United States, roughly 58,000 devices have been implanted in adults and 38,000 in children. (Estimates provided by the U.S. Food and Drug Administration (FDA), as reported by cochlear implant manufacturers.)

The FDA first approved cochlear implants in the mid-1980s to treat hearing loss in adults. Since 2000, cochlear implants have been FDA-approved for use in eligible children beginning at 12 months of age. For young children who are deaf or severely hard-of-hearing, using a cochlear implant while they are young exposes them to sounds during an optimal period to develop speech and language skills. Research has shown that when these children receive a cochlear implant followed by intensive therapy before they are 18 months old, they are better able to hear, comprehend sound and music, and speak than their peers who receive implants when they are older. Studies have also shown that eligible children who receive a cochlear implant before 18 months of age develop language skills at a rate comparable to children with normal hearing, and many succeed in mainstream classrooms.

Some adults who have lost all or most of their hearing later in life can also benefit from cochlear implants. They learn to associate the signals from the implant with sounds they remember, including speech, without requiring any visual cues such as those provided by lipreading or sign language.

How Does Someone Receive a Cochlear Implant?

Use of a cochlear implant requires both a surgical procedure and significant therapy to learn or relearn the sense of hearing. Not everyone performs at the same level with this device. The decision to receive an implant should involve discussions with medical specialists, including an experienced cochlear-implant surgeon. The process can be expensive. For example, a person's health insurance may cover the expense, but not always. Some individuals may choose not to have a cochlear implant for a variety of personal reasons. Surgical implantations are almost always safe, although complications are a risk factor, just as with any kind of surgery. An additional consideration is learning to interpret the sounds created by an implant. This process takes time and practice. Speech-language pathologists and audiologists are frequently involved in this learning process. Prior to implantation, all of these factors need to be considered.

What Does the Future Hold for Cochlear Implants?

The National Institute on Deafness and Other Communication Disorders (NIDCD) supports research to enhance the benefits of cochlear implants. Scientists are exploring whether using a shortened electrode array, inserted into a portion of the cochlea, for example, can help individuals whose hearing loss is limited to the higher frequencies while preserving their hearing of lower frequencies. Researchers also are looking at the potential benefits of pairing a cochlear implant in one ear with either another cochlear implant or a hearing aid in the other ear.

Section 30.3

Hearing Aids

This section includes text excerpted from "Hearing Aids," National Institute on Deafness and Other Communication Disorders (NIDCD), July 2015.

What Is a Hearing Aid?

A hearing aid is a small electronic device that you wear in or behind your ear. It makes some sounds louder so that a person with hearing loss can listen, communicate, and participate more fully in daily activities. A hearing aid can help people hear more in both quiet and noisy situations. However, only about one out of five people who would benefit from a hearing aid actually uses one.

A hearing aid has three basic parts: a microphone, amplifier, and speaker. The hearing aid receives sound through a microphone, which converts the sound waves to electrical signals and sends them to an amplifier. The amplifier increases the power of the signals and then sends them to the ear through a speaker.

How Can Hearing Aids Help?

Hearing aids are primarily useful in improving the hearing and speech comprehension of people who have hearing loss that results

Devices for Improving Communication and Hearing

from damage to the small sensory cells in the inner ear, called hair cells. This type of hearing loss is called sensorineural hearing loss. The damage can occur as a result of disease, aging, or injury from noise or certain medicines. A hearing aid magnifies sound vibrations entering the ear. Surviving hair cells detect the larger vibrations and convert them into neural signals that are passed along to the brain. The greater the damage to a person's hair cells, the more severe the hearing loss, and the greater the hearing aid amplification needed to make up the difference. However, there are practical limits to the amount of amplification a hearing aid can provide. In addition, if the inner ear is too damaged, even large vibrations will not be converted into neural signals. In this situation, a hearing aid would be ineffective.

How Can I Find out If I Need a Hearing Aid?

If you think you might have hearing loss and could benefit from a hearing aid, visit your physician, who may refer you to an otolaryngologist or audiologist. An otolaryngologist is a physician who specializes in ear, nose, and throat disorders and will investigate the cause of the hearing loss. An audiologist is a hearing health professional who identifies and measures hearing loss and will perform a hearing test to assess the type and degree of loss.

Are There Different Styles of Hearing Aids?

There are three basic styles of hearing aids. The styles differ by size, their placement on or inside the ear, and the degree to which they amplify sound.

- **Behind-the-ear (BTE)** hearing aids consist of a hard plastic case worn behind the ear and connected to a plastic earmold that fits inside the outer ear. The electronic parts are held in the case behind the ear. Sound travels from the hearing aid through the earmold and into the ear. BTE aids are used by people of all ages for mild to profound hearing loss. A kind of BTE aid is an open-fit hearing aid. Small, open-fit aids fit behind the ear completely, with only a narrow tube inserted into the ear canal, enabling the canal to remain open. For this reason, open-fit hearing aids may be a good choice for people who experience a buildup of earwax, since this type of aid is less likely to be damaged by such substances. In addition, some people may prefer the open-fit hearing aid because their perception of their voice does not sound "plugged up."

- **In-the-ear (ITE)** hearing aids fit completely inside the outer ear and are used for mild to severe hearing loss. The case holding the electronic components is made of hard plastic. Some ITE aids may have certain added features installed, such as a telecoil. A telecoil is a small magnetic coil that allows users to receive sound through the circuitry of the hearing aid, rather than through its microphone. This makes it easier to hear conversations over the telephone. A telecoil also helps people hear in public facilities that have installed special sound systems, called induction loop systems. Induction loop systems can be found in many churches, schools, airports, and auditoriums. ITE aids usually are not worn by young children because the casings need to be replaced often as the ear grows.

- **Canal** aids fit into the ear canal and are available in two styles. The in-the-canal (ITC) hearing aid is made to fit the size and shape of a person's ear canal. A completely-in-canal (CIC) hearing aid is nearly hidden in the ear canal. Both types are used for mild to moderately severe hearing loss. Because they

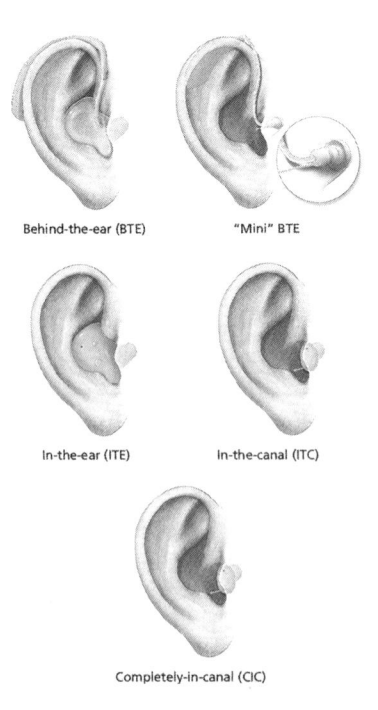

Figure 30.2. *Styles of Hearing Aids*

are small, canal aids may be difficult for a person to adjust and remove. In addition, canal aids have less space available for batteries and additional devices, such as a telecoil. They usually are not recommended for young children or for people with severe to profound hearing loss because their reduced size limits their power and volume.

Do All Hearing Aids Work the Same Way?

Hearing aids work differently depending on the electronics used. The two main types of electronics are analog and digital.

1. Analog aids convert sound waves into electrical signals, which are amplified. Analog/adjustable hearing aids are custom built to meet the needs of each user. The aid is programmed by the manufacturer according to the specifications recommended by your audiologist. Analog/programmable hearing aids have more than one program or setting. An audiologist can program the aid using a computer, and you can change the program for different listening environments—from a small, quiet room to a crowded restaurant to large, open areas, such as a theater or stadium. Analog/programmable circuitry can be used in all types of hearing aids. Analog aids usually are less expensive than digital aids.

2. Digital aids convert sound waves into numerical codes, similar to the binary code of a computer, before amplifying them. Because the code also includes information about a sound's pitch or loudness, the aid can be specially programmed to amplify some frequencies more than others. Digital circuitry gives an audiologist more flexibility in adjusting the aid to a user's needs and to certain listening environments. These aids also can be programmed to focus on sounds coming from a specific direction. Digital circuitry can be used in all types of hearing aids.

Which Hearing Aid Will Work Best for Me?

The hearing aid that will work best for you depends on the kind and severity of your hearing loss. If you have a hearing loss in both of your ears, two hearing aids are generally recommended because two aids provide a more natural signal to the brain. Hearing in both ears also will help you understand speech and locate from where the sound is coming. You and your audiologist should select a hearing aid that best suits your needs and lifestyle. Price is also a key consideration because hearing aids range from hundreds to several thousand dollars. Similar to other equipment purchases, style and features affect cost. However, don't use price alone to determine the best hearing aid for you. Just because one hearing aid is more expensive than another does not necessarily mean that it will better suit your needs.

A hearing aid will not restore your normal hearing. With practice, however, a hearing aid will increase your awareness of sounds and their sources. You will want to wear your hearing aid regularly, so select one that is convenient and easy for you to use. Other features to consider include parts or services covered by the warranty, estimated schedule and costs for maintenance and repair, options and upgrade opportunities, and the hearing aid company's reputation for quality and customer service.

What Questions Should I Ask before Buying a Hearing Aid?

Before you buy a hearing aid, ask your audiologist these important questions:

- What features would be most useful to me?
- What is the total cost of the hearing aid? Do the benefits of newer technologies outweigh the higher costs?
- Is there a trial period to test the hearing aids? (Most manufacturers allow a 30- to 60-day trial period during which aids can be returned for a refund.) What fees are nonrefundable if the aids are returned after the trial period?
- How long is the warranty? Can it be extended? Does the warranty cover future maintenance and repairs?
- Can the audiologist make adjustments and provide servicing and minor repairs? Will loaner aids be provided when repairs are needed?
- What instruction does the audiologist provide?

How Can I Adjust to My Hearing Aid?

Hearing aids take time and patience to use successfully. Wearing your aids regularly will help you adjust to them. Become familiar with

Devices for Improving Communication and Hearing

your hearing aid's features. With your audiologist present, practice putting in and taking out the aid, cleaning it, identifying right and left aids, and replacing the batteries. Ask how to test it in listening environments where you have problems with hearing.

Learn to adjust the aid's volume and to program it for sounds that are too loud or too soft. Work with your audiologist until you are comfortable and satisfied. You may experience some of the following problems as you adjust to wearing your new aid.

- **My hearing aid feels uncomfortable.** Some individuals may find a hearing aid to be slightly uncomfortable at first. Ask your audiologist how long you should wear your hearing aid while you are adjusting to it.

- **My voice sounds too loud.** The "plugged-up" sensation that causes a hearing aid user's voice to sound louder inside the head is called the occlusion effect, and it is very common for new hearing aid users. Check with your audiologist to see if a correction is possible. Most individuals get used to this effect over time.

- **I get feedback from my hearing aid.** A whistling sound can be caused by a hearing aid that does not fit or work well or is clogged by earwax or fluid. See your audiologist for adjustments.

- **I hear background noise.** A hearing aid does not completely separate the sounds you want to hear from the ones you do not want to hear. Sometimes, however, the hearing aid may need to be adjusted. Talk with your audiologist.

- **I hear a buzzing sound when I use my cell phone.** Some people who wear hearing aids or have implanted hearing devices experience problems with the radio frequency interference caused by digital cell phones. Both hearing aids and cell phones are improving, however, so these problems are occurring less often. When you are being fitted for a new hearing aid, take your cell phone with you to see if it will work well with the aid.

Section 30.4

Other Hearing Assistive Technology

This section includes text excerpted from "Assistive Devices for People with Hearing, Voice, Speech, or Language Disorders," National Institute on Deafness and Other Communication Disorders (NIDCD), March 6, 2017.

What Are Assistive Devices?

The terms assistive device or assistive technology can refer to any device that helps a person with hearing loss or a voice, speech, or language disorder to communicate. These terms often refer to devices that help a person to hear and understand what is being said more clearly or to express thoughts more easily. With the development of digital and wireless technologies, more and more devices are becoming available to help people with hearing, voice, speech, and language disorders communicate more meaningfully and participate more fully in their daily lives.

What Types of Assistive Devices Are Available?

Health professionals use a variety of names to describe assistive devices:

- Assistive listening devices (ALDs) help amplify the sounds you want to hear, especially where there's a lot of background noise. ALDs can be used with a hearing aid or cochlear implant to help a wearer hear certain sounds better.

- Augmentative and alternative communication (AAC) devices help people with communication disorders to express themselves. These devices can range from a simple picture board to a computer program that synthesizes speech from text.

- Alerting devices connect to a doorbell, telephone, or alarm that emits a loud sound or blinking light to let someone with hearing loss know that an event is taking place.

What Types of Assistive Listening Devices Are Available?

Several types of ALDs are available to improve sound transmission for people with hearing loss. Some are designed for large facilities

Devices for Improving Communication and Hearing

such as classrooms, theaters, places of worship, and airports. Other types are intended for personal use in small settings and for one-on-one conversations. All can be used with or without hearing aids or a cochlear implant. ALD systems for large facilities include hearing loop systems, frequency-modulated (FM) systems, and infrared systems.

Hearing loop (or induction loop) systems use electromagnetic energy to transmit sound. A hearing loop system involves four parts:

- A sound source, such as a public address system, microphone, or home TV or telephone

- An amplifier

- A thin loop of wire that encircles a room or branches out beneath carpeting

- A receiver worn in the ears or as a headset

Amplified sound travels through the loop and creates an electromagnetic field that is picked up directly by a hearing loop receiver or a telecoil, a miniature wireless receiver that is built into many hearing aids and cochlear implants. To pick up the signal, a listener must be wearing the receiver and be within or near the loop. Because the sound is picked up directly by the receiver, the sound is much clearer, without as much of the competing background noise associated with many listening environments. Some loop systems are portable, making it possible for people with hearing loss to improve their listening environments, as needed, as they proceed with their daily activities. A hearing loop can be connected to a public address system, a television, or any other audio source. For those who don't have hearing aids with embedded telecoils, portable loop receivers are also available.

FM systems use radio signals to transmit amplified sounds. They are often used in classrooms, where the instructor wears a small microphone connected to a transmitter and the student wears the receiver, which is tuned to a specific frequency, or channel. People who have a telecoil inside their hearing aid or cochlear implant may also wear a wire around the neck (called a neckloop) or behind their aid or implant (called a silhouette inductor) to convert the signal into magnetic signals that can be picked up directly by the telecoil. FM systems can transmit signals up to 300 feet and are able to be used in many public places. However, because radio signals are able to penetrate walls, listeners in one room may need to listen to a different channel than those in another room to avoid receiving mixed signals. Personal FM systems operate in the same way as larger scale systems and can be used to help people with hearing loss to follow one-on-one conversations.

Infrared systems use infrared light to transmit sound. A transmitter converts sound into a light signal and beams it to a receiver that is worn by a listener. The receiver decodes the infrared signal back to sound. As with FM systems, people whose hearing aids or cochlear implants have a telecoil may also wear a neckloop or silhouette inductor to convert the infrared signal into a magnetic signal, which can be picked up through their telecoil. Unlike induction loop or FM systems, the infrared signal cannot pass through walls, making it particularly useful in courtrooms, where confidential information is often discussed, and in buildings where competing signals can be a problem, such as classrooms or movie theaters. However, infrared systems cannot be used in environments with too many competing light sources, such as outdoors or in strongly lit rooms.

Personal amplifiers are useful in places in which the above systems are unavailable or when watching TV, being outdoors, or traveling in a car. About the size of a cell phone, these devices increase sound levels and reduce background noise for a listener. Some have directional microphones that can be angled toward a speaker or other source of sound. As with other ALDs, the amplified sound can be picked up by a receiver that the listener is wearing, either as a headset or as earbuds.

What Types of Augmentative and Alternative Communication Devices Are Available for Communicating Face-to-Face?

The simplest AAC device is a picture board or touch screen that uses pictures or symbols of typical items and activities that make up a person's daily life. For example, a person might touch the image of a glass to ask for a drink. Many picture boards can be customized and expanded based on a person's age, education, occupation, and interests.

Keyboards, touch screens, and sometimes a person's limited speech may be used to communicate desired words. Some devices employ a text display. The display panel typically faces outward so that two people can exchange information while facing each other. Spelling and word prediction software can make it faster and easier to enter information.

Devices for Improving Communication and Hearing

Speech-generating devices go one step further by translating words or pictures into speech. Some models allow users to choose from several different voices, such as male or female, child or adult, and even some regional accents. Some devices employ a vocabulary of prerecorded words while others have an unlimited vocabulary, synthesizing speech as words are typed in. Software programs that convert personal computers into speaking devices are also available.

What Augmentative and Alternative Communication Devices Are Available for Communicating by Telephone?

For many years, people with hearing loss have used text telephone or telecommunications devices, called teletypewriter (TTY) or telecommunications device for the deaf (TDD) machines, to communicate by phone. This same technology also benefits people with speech difficulties. A TTY machine consists of a typewriter keyboard that displays typed conversations onto a readout panel or printed on paper. Callers will either type messages to each other over the system or, if a call recipient does not have a TTY machine, use the national toll-free telecommunications relay service at 711 to communicate. Through the relay service, a communications assistant serves as a bridge between two callers, reading typed messages aloud to the person with hearing while transcribing what's spoken into type for the person with hearing loss.

With today's electronic communication devices, however, TTY machines have almost become a thing of the past. People can place phone calls through the telecommunications relay service using almost any device with a keypad, including a laptop, personal digital assistant, and cell phone. Text messaging has also become a popular method of communication, skipping the relay service altogether.

Another system uses voice recognition software and an extensive library of video clips depicting American Sign Language (ASL) to translate a signer's words into text or computer-generated speech in real time. It is also able to translate spoken words back into sign language or text.

Finally, for people with mild to moderate hearing loss, captioned telephones allow you to carry on a spoken conversation, while providing a transcript of the other person's words on a readout panel or computer screen as backup.

What Types of Alerting Devices Are Available?

Alerting or alarm devices use sound, light, vibrations, or a combination of these techniques to let someone know when a particular event is occurring. Clocks and wake-up alarm systems allow a person to choose to wake up to flashing lights, horns, or a gentle shaking.

Visual alert signalers monitor a variety of household devices and other sounds, such as doorbells and telephones. When the phone rings, the visual alert signaler will be activated and will vibrate or flash a light to let people know. In addition, remote receivers placed around the house can alert a person from any room. Portable vibrating pagers can let parents and caretakers know when a baby is crying. Some baby monitoring devices analyze a baby's cry and light up a picture to indicate if the baby sounds hungry, bored, or sleepy.

Chapter 31

Therapy and Services to Aid Communication

Chapter Contents

Section 31.1—Child Speech-Language Therapy 352

Section 31.2—Telecommunications Relay Services 355

Section 31.1

Child Speech-Language Therapy

This section contains text excerpted from the following sources: Text in this section begins with excerpts from "Language and Speech Disorders," Centers for Disease Control and Prevention (CDC), May 23, 2018; Text under the heading "Who Are Speech-Language Pathologists?" is excerpted from "Speech-Language Pathologists," U.S. Bureau of Labor Statistics (BLS), U.S. Department of Labor (DOL), July 2, 2018; Text beginning with the heading "Questions You May Want to Ask Your Child's Speech-Language Pathologist" is excerpted from "Questions You May Want to Ask Your Child's Speech-Language Pathologist," Centers for Disease Control and Prevention (CDC), November 2012. Reviewed July 2018.

If a child has a problem with language or speech development, talk to a healthcare provider about an evaluation. An important first step is to find out if the child may have a hearing loss. Hearing loss may be difficult to notice particularly if a child has hearing loss only in one ear or has partial hearing loss, which means they can hear some sounds but not others.

A language development specialist like a speech-language pathologist will conduct a careful assessment to determine what type of problem with language or speech the child may have.

Overall, learning more than one language does not cause language disorders, but children may not follow exactly the same developmental milestones as those who learn only one language. Developing the ability to understand and speak in two languages depends on how much practice the child has using both languages, and the kind of practice. If a child who is learning more than one language has difficulty with language development, careful assessment by a specialist who understands the development of skills in more than one language may be needed.

Treatment for Language or Speech Disorders and Delays

Children with language problems often need extra help and special instruction. Speech-language pathologists can work directly with children and their parents, caregivers, and teachers. Having a language or speech delay or disorder can qualify a child for early intervention (for children up to 3 years of age) and special education services (for children aged 3 years and older). Schools can do their own testing for language or speech disorders to see if a child needs intervention. An evaluation by a healthcare professional is needed if there are other concerns about the child's hearing, behavior, or emotions. Parents, healthcare providers, and the school can work together to find the right referrals and treatment.

Who Are Speech-Language Pathologists?

Speech-language pathologists (SLPs) (sometimes called speech therapists) assess, diagnose, treat, and help to prevent communication and swallowing disorders in children and adults. Speech, language, and swallowing disorders result from a variety of causes, such as a stroke, brain injury, hearing loss, developmental delay, Parkinson disease, a cleft palate, or autism.

SLPs typically do the following:

- Evaluate levels of speech, language, or swallowing difficulty
- Identify treatment options
- Create and carry out an individualized treatment plan that addresses specific functional needs
- Teach children and adults how to make sounds and improve their voices and maintain fluency
- Help individuals improve vocabulary and sentence structure used in oral and written language
- Work with children and adults to develop and strengthen the muscles used to swallow
- Counsel individuals and families on how to cope with communication and swallowing disorders

SLPs work with children and adults who have problems with speech and language, including related cognitive or social communication problems. They may be unable to speak at all, or they may speak with difficulty or have rhythm and fluency problems, such as stuttering. SLPs may work with people who are unable to understand the language or with those who have voice disorders, such as inappropriate pitch or a harsh voice.

SLPs also must complete administrative tasks, including keeping accurate records and documenting billing information. They record their initial evaluations and diagnoses, track treatment progress, and note any changes in an individual's condition or treatment plan.

Some SLPs specialize in working with specific age groups, such as children or the elderly. Others focus on treatment programs for specific communication or swallowing problems, such as those resulting from strokes, trauma, or a cleft palate.

In medical facilities, SLPs work with physicians and surgeons, social workers, psychologists, occupational therapists, physical therapists, and other healthcare workers. In schools, they evaluate students for speech and language disorders and work with teachers, other school personnel, and parents to develop and carry out individual or group programs, provide counseling, and support classroom activities.

Questions You May Want to Ask Your Child's Speech-Language Pathologist

1. What kind of training and experience do you have working with children who are deaf or hard of hearing? What age group have you worked with?
2. What communication option(s) do you use in therapy (for example: Signing Exact English (SEE), American Sign Language (ASL), Cued Speech, Auditory-Verbal, etc.)?
3. What is your experience and comfort level using these communication options?
4. How do you test my child's speech and language development? How often will you check my child's progress?
5. How do you decide the amount of time my child will spend on speech production, language (spoken or signed), and auditory (hearing) training?
6. What are my costs for the different types of therapies? Where do I go to get help with these costs?
7. Can I observe a speech therapy session with another child who has hearing loss?

Questions to Help the Child at Home

1. Can you tell me where I can learn more about the different types of communication options?
2. What tips can I use or activities can I do to support my child's communication at home?
3. Can you suggest any other resources in the community for our family?

Therapy and Services to Aid Communication

Section 31.2

Telecommunications Relay Services

This section includes text excerpted from "Telecommunications Relay Services," National Institute on Deafness and Other Communication Disorders (NIDCD), March 6, 2017.

What Are Telecommunication Relay Services?

A telecommunications relay service (TRS) provides a communications assistant (CA) that allows people who are deaf, hard of hearing, or speech impaired to communicate with people who use a standard telephone.

A TRS offers two options:

1. Voice carry-over (VCO)

2. Hearing carry-over (HCO)

VCO allows a person with a hearing impairment to speak directly to the other party and then read the response typed by a CA. HCO allows a person with a speech impairment to hear the other party and relay the typed response back to the telephone user through the CA. This service allows individuals with communication disorders to communicate with all telephone users.

Title IV of the Americans with Disabilities Act (ADA) of 1990 (which took full effect on July 26, 1993) requires all U.S. telephone companies to provide telecommunications relay services.

How Can I Use a Telecommunication Relay Service?

To reach a TRS, dial 711 and the assistant can place the 10-digit call on behalf of the text telephone device (TTY or TDD) user.

You can dial 711 to access all telecommunications relay services anywhere in the United States. The relay service is free. In the event of an emergency, TDD or TTY users can call 911 directly and do not need to make a TRS call via 711.

Communications assistants are trained to be unobtrusive. An assistant's responsibility is to relay the conversation exactly as it is received. All relay calls are confidential.

Regardless of which long-distance company or organization is providing a state's relay service, callers can continue to use the long-distance company of their choice.

Where Can I Find Additional Information about Telecommunication Relay Services?

For more information on TRS, please visit the Federal Communications Commission (FCC).

The National Institute on Deafness and Other Communication Disorders (NIDCD) maintains a directory of organizations that provide information on the normal and disordered processes of hearing, balance, taste, smell, voice, speech, and language.

Use the following keywords to help you find organizations that can answer questions and provide information on telecommunications relay services:

- Advice on the ADA
- Assistive technology
- Telecommunications

Chapter 32

Low Vision Devices and Services

Chapter Contents

Section 32.1—Living with Low Vision 358
Section 32.2—Argus Retinal Prosthesis 360
Section 32.3—Implantable Corneal Device to
 Correct Near Vision 364
Section 32.4—What Is Braille? 366
Section 32.5—Web-Braille 370
Section 32.6—New Technologies for People with
 Visual Impairment 373

Section 32.1

Living with Low Vision

This section includes text excerpted from "What You Should Know," National Eye Institute (NEI), January 24, 2013. Reviewed July 2018.

What Is Low Vision?

When you have low vision, eyeglasses, contact lenses, medicine, or surgery may not help. Activities like reading, shopping, cooking, writing, and watching TV may be hard to do.

In fact, millions of Americans lose some of their sight every year. While vision loss can affect anyone at any age, low vision is most common for those over age 65.

Low vision is usually caused by eye diseases or health conditions. Some of these include age-related macular degeneration (AMD), cataract, diabetes, and glaucoma. Eye injuries and birth defects are some other causes. Whatever the cause, lost vision cannot be restored. It can, however, be managed with proper treatment and vision rehabilitation.

You should visit an eye care professional if you experience any changes to your eyesight.

What Causes Low Vision

Low vision can result from a variety of diseases, disorders, and injuries that affect the eye. Many people with low vision have age-related macular degeneration, cataract, glaucoma, or diabetic retinopathy. Age-related macular degeneration accounts for almost 45 percent of all cases of low vision.

How Many People Have Low Vision?

Millions of Americans have low vision. About 135 million people around the world have low vision.

How Do I Know If I Have Low Vision?

Below are some signs of low vision. Even when wearing your glasses or contact lenses, do you still have difficulty with:

- Recognizing the faces of family and friends?

Low Vision Devices and Services

- Reading, cooking, sewing, or fixing things around the house?
- Selecting and matching the color of your clothes?
- Seeing clearly with the lights on or feeling like they are dimmer than normal?
- Reading traffic signs or the names of stores?

These could all be early warning signs of vision loss or eye disease. The sooner vision loss or eye disease is detected by an eye care professional, the greater your chances of keeping your remaining vision.

What Should a Person Do If He or She Has Low Vision?

First, note the kinds of vision problems that are occurring. Some warning signs include the following:

- Trouble reading, cooking, or sewing
- Trouble seeing because the lights don't seem as bright as usual
- Trouble recognizing the faces of friends and relatives
- Trouble crossing the street or reading signs

A person who is having these vision difficulties should immediately make an appointment with an eye care professional for an eye examination. If the person's vision cannot be treated by conventional methods, such as glasses, contact lenses, medication, or surgery, then he or she should ask the eye care professional for information about vision rehabilitation. These services may include eye examinations, a low vision evaluation, training on how to use visual and adaptive devices, support groups, and training on how to perform everyday activities in new ways.

What Should a Person Do If He or She Knows Someone with Low Vision?

Urge that person to make an appointment with an eye care professional for an eye examination. Then help the person find out about low vision and vision rehabilitation services and encourage him or her to take advantage of all available resources.

How Much Does a Low Vision Evaluation Cost?

While costs vary by region, typically a low vision evaluation costs between $100 and $200.

Is a Low Vision Examination Covered by Health Insurance, Medicaid, or Medicare?

Policies vary by state, but generally, Medicare will cover low vision examinations performed by eye care professionals. Private health insurance usually does not cover low vision examinations, but should check with the insurance carrier to be sure.

Section 32.2

Argus Retinal Prosthesis

This section includes text excerpted from "Artificial Retina Receives FDA Approval," National Science Foundation (NSF), February 14, 2013. Reviewed July 2018.

The U.S. Food and Drug Administration (FDA) granted market approval to an artificial retina technology, the first bionic eye to be approved for patients in the United States. The prosthetic technology was developed in part with support from the National Science Foundation (NSF).

The device, called the Argus® II Retinal Prosthesis System, transmits images from a small, eyeglass-mounted camera wirelessly to a microelectrode array implanted on a patient's damaged retina. The array sends electrical signals via the optic nerve, and the brain interprets a visual image.

The FDA approval currently applies to individuals who have lost sight as a result of severe to profound retinitis pigmentosa (RP), an ailment that affects one in every 4,000 Americans. The implant allows some individuals with RP, who are completely blind, to locate objects, detect movement, improve orientation and mobility skills and discern shapes such as large letters.

The Argus II is manufactured by, and will be distributed by, Second Sight Medical Products of Sylmar, California, which is part of the team of scientists and engineers from the university, federal and private sectors who spent nearly two decades developing the system with public and private investment.

"Seeing my grandmother go blind motivated me to pursue ophthalmology and biomedical engineering to develop a treatment for patients for whom there was no foreseeable cure," says the technology's codeveloper, Mark Humayun, associate director of research at the Doheny Eye Institute (DEI) at the University of Southern California (USC) and director of the NSF Engineering Research Center for Biomimetic MicroElectronic Systems (BMES). "It was an interdisciplinary approach grounded in biomedical engineering that has allowed us to develop the Argus II, making it the first commercially approved retinal implant in the world to restore sight to some blind patients," Humayun adds.

The effort by Humayun and his colleagues has received early and continuing support from NSF, the National Institutes of Health (NIH) and the U.S. Department of Energy (DOE), with grants totaling more than $100 million. The private sector's support nearly matched that of the federal government.

"The retinal implant exemplifies how NSF grants for high-risk, fundamental research can directly result in ground-breaking technologies decades later," said Acting NSF Assistant Director for Engineering Kesh Narayanan. "In collaboration with the Second Sight team and the courageous patients who volunteered to have experimental surgery to implant the first-generation devices, the researchers of NSF's Biomimetic MicroElectronic Systems Engineering Research (BMES ERC) Center are developing technologies that may ultimately have as profound an impact on blindness as the cochlear implant has had for hearing loss."

Although some treatments to slow the progression of degenerative diseases of the retina are available, no treatment has existed that could replace the function of lost photoreceptors in the eye.

The researchers began their retinal prosthesis research in the late 1980s to address that need, and in 1994 Humayun received his first NSF grant, an NSF Young Investigator Award, which built upon additional support from the Whittaker Foundation. Humayun used the funding to develop the first conceptualization of the Argus II's underlying artificial retina technology.

Since that time, he and his collaborators—including Wentai Liu of the University of California, Los Angeles and fellow USC researchers

Jim Weiland and Eugene de Juan, Jr.—received six additional NSF grants, totaling $40 million, some of which was part of NSF's funding for BMES, launched in 2003. BMES drives research into a range of sophisticated prosthetic technologies to treat blindness, paralysis and other conditions.

"We were encouraged by the team's exploratory work in the 1980s and 1990s, supported by NSF and others, which revealed that healthy neural pathways can carry information to the brain, even though other parts of the eye are damaged," adds Narayanan. "The retinal prosthesis they developed from that work simulates the most complex part of the eye. Based on the promise of that implant, we decided in 2003 to entrust the research team with an NSF Engineering Research Center," says Narayanan. "The center was to scale up technology development and increase device sensitivity and biocompatibility, while simultaneously preparing students for the workforce and building partnerships to speed the technology to the marketplace, where it could make a difference in people's lives. The center has succeeded with all of those goals."

The researchers' efforts have bridged cellular biology—necessary for understanding how to stimulate the retinal ganglion cells without permanent damage—with microelectronics, which led to the miniaturized, low-power integrated chip for performing signal conversion, conditioning and stimulation functions. The hardware was paired with software processing and tuning algorithms that convert visual imagery to stimulation signals, and the entire system had to be incorporated within hermetically sealed packaging that allowed the electronics to operate in the vitreous fluid of the eye indefinitely. Finally, the research team had to develop new surgical techniques in order to integrate the device with the body, ensuring accurate placement of the stimulation electrodes on the retina.

"The artificial retina is a great engineering challenge under the interdisciplinary constraint of biology, enabling technology, regulatory compliance, as well as sophisticated design science," adds Liu. "The artificial retina provides an interface between biotic and abiotic systems. Its unique design characteristics rely on system-level optimization, rather than the more common practice of component optimization, to achieve miniaturization and integration. Using the most advanced semiconductor technology, the engine for the artificial retina is a 'system on a chip' of mixed voltages and mixed analog-digital design, which provides self-contained power and data management and other functionality. This design for the artificial retina facilitates both surgical procedures and regulatory compliance."

The Argus II design consists of an external video camera system matched to the implanted retinal stimulator, which contains a microelectrode array that spans 20 degrees of visual field. The NSF BMES ERC has developed a prototype system with an array of more than 15 times as many electrodes and an ultra-miniature video camera that can be implanted in the eye. However, this prototype is many years away from being available for patient use.

"The external camera system-built into a pair of glasses-streams video to a belt-worn computer, which converts the video into stimulus commands for the implant," says Weiland. "The belt-worn computer encodes the commands into a wireless signal that is transmitted to the implant, which has the necessary electronics to receive and decode both wireless power and data. Based on those data, the implant stimulates the retina with small electrical pulses. The electronics are hermetically packaged and the electrical stimulus is delivered to the retina via a microelectrode array."

In 1998, Robert Greenberg founded Second Sight to develop the technology for the marketplace. While under development, the Argus I and Argus II systems have won wide recognition, including a 2010 Popular Mechanics Breakthrough Award and a 2009 R&D 100 Award, but it is only with FDA approval that the technology can now be made available to patients.

"An artificial retina can offer hope to those with retinitis pigmentosa, as it may help them achieve a level of visual perception that enhances their quality of life, enabling them to perform functions of daily living more easily and the chance to enjoy simple pleasures we may take for granted," says Narayanan. "Such success is the result of fundamental studies in several fields, technology improvements based on those results and feedback from clinical trials—all enabled by sustained public and private investment from entities like NSF."

Section 32.3

Implantable Corneal Device to Correct Near Vision

This section includes text excerpted from "FDA Approves Implantable Device That Changes the Shape of the Cornea to Correct near Vision," U.S. Food and Drug Administration (FDA), June 29, 2016.

The U.S. Food and Drug Administration (FDA) approved the Raindrop Near Vision Inlay, a device implanted in the cornea (the clear, front surface) of one eye to improve near vision in certain patients with presbyopia. It is the second FDA-approved implantable corneal device for correction of near vision in patients who have not had cataract surgery and the first implantable device that changes the shape of the cornea to achieve improved vision.

Presbyopia is the loss of the ability to change the focusing power of the eye, resulting in diminished near vision. The focusing power of the eye decreases in nearly all adults over the course of their lifetime. It usually occurs in the fourth or fifth decade of life due to normal aging. Some people may develop symptoms of presbyopia sooner than others, but nearly everyone will eventually develop symptoms and may require some method of near vision correction. Bifocals and reading glasses are a common correction method. Corneal inlay surgery is an elective option for those who may not want to wear glasses.

"Given the prevalence of presbyopia and the aging of the baby boomer population, the need for near vision correction will likely rise in the coming years," said William Maisel, M.D., M.P.H., deputy director for science and chief scientist in the FDA's Center for Devices and Radiological Health (CDRH). "The Raindrop Near Vision Inlay provides a new option for surgical, outpatient treatment of presbyopia."

The Raindrop Near Vision Inlay is a clear device made of a hydrogel material and resembles a tiny contact lens smaller than the eye of a needle. It is indicated for use in patients 41–65 years old who, in addition to not having had cataract surgery, are unable to focus clearly on near objects or small print and need reading glasses with +1.50 to +2.50 diopters of power—but do not need glasses or contacts for clear distance vision.

To insert the device, an eye surgeon uses a laser to create a flap in the cornea of the patient's nondominant eye, implants the device into the opening, and puts the flap back in place. The inlay provides a steeper surface that can help the eye focus on near objects or print. The natural lens of the eye typically performs this function by changing shape, but in patients with presbyopia, the lens becomes hardened and ineffective at focusing on close-up objects, which causes poor near vision. By reshaping the curvature of the cornea, the inlay corrects the refractive error that results in near vision problems.

The safety and effectiveness of the Raindrop Near Vision Inlay were studied in a clinical trial of 373 subjects implanted with the device. Two years after implantation, 92 percent of patients included in the analysis (336 out of 364) were able to see with 20/40 vision or better at near distances with the inlay-implanted eye.

The Raindrop Near Vision Inlay implantation may cause or worsen problems with glare, halos, foreign body sensation, and pain. There is a risk of developing infection, inflammation, a new dry eye condition or exacerbation of an existing dry eye condition, retinal detachment, or a decrease in distance vision. The device may cause complications of the cornea, such as corneal scarring, swelling, inflammation, thinning, clouding or melting. The device may cause certain tissue in the eye to grow into the cornea (epithelial ingrowth), causing clouding. Some patients may require a second surgery to remove or replace the inlay.

The Raindrop Near Vision Inlay is not recommended for patients who: have severe dry eye or an active eye infection or inflammation; exhibit signs of corneal disease characterized by general thinning and cone-shaped protrusion in the center of the cornea (keratoconus); have abnormal features of the outer part of the eye (cornea) to be implanted; have certain autoimmune or connective tissue diseases; do not have enough corneal thickness to withstand the procedure; have a recent herpes eye infection or problems resulting from a previous infection or have uncontrolled glaucoma or uncontrolled diabetes.

The Raindrop Near Vision Inlay is manufactured by Revision Optics, Inc. of Lake Forest, California. The FDA, an agency within the U.S. Department of Health and Human Services (HHS), protects the public health by assuring the safety, effectiveness, and security of human and veterinary drugs, vaccines and other biological products for human use, and medical devices. The agency also is responsible for the safety and security of our nation's food supply, cosmetics, dietary supplements, products that give off electronic radiation, and for regulating tobacco products.

Section 32.4

What Is Braille?

This section includes text excerpted from "NLS Factsheet: About Braille," U.S. Library of Congress (LOC), October 23, 2010. Reviewed July 2018.

Braille is a system of touch reading and writing in which raised dots represent the letters of the alphabet and numbers, as well as music notes and symbols. Braille contains symbols for punctuation marks and provides a system of contractions and short-form words to save space, making it an efficient method of tactile reading.

Braille is read by moving one or more fingers along each line. Both hands are usually involved in the reading process, and reading is generally done with the index fingers. Usually, one hand reads the majority of one line while the other hand locates the beginning of the next. Average reading speed is approximately 125 words per minute, but greater speeds of up to 200 words per minute are possible.

By using braille, blind people can review and study the written word. They may become aware of conventions such as spelling, punctuation, paragraphing, and footnotes. Most important, braille provides blind individuals access to a wide range of reading materials—educational and recreational reading as well as informational manuals. Blind people also are able to pursue hobbies and cultural enrichment with such braille materials as music scores, hymnals, playing cards, and board games.

The History of Braille

The system of embossed writing invented by Louis Braille in 1821 gradually came to be accepted throughout the world as the fundamental form of written communication for blind individuals.

Various methods—many of them raised versions of print letters—had been attempted over the years to enable blind people to read. The braille system has succeeded because it is based on a rational sequence of signs devised for the fingertips, rather than imitating signs devised for the eyes. In addition, braille can be written by blind people and used for any notation that follows an accepted sequence, such as numerals, musical notes, or chemical tables.

Braille has undergone many modifications, particularly the addition of contractions representing groups of letters or whole words that appear frequently in a language. The use of contractions permits faster reading and helps reduce the size of braille books, making them less cumbersome.

Several groups have been established over the past century to modify and standardize the braille code. The major goal is to develop easily understood contractions without making the code too complex.

The official braille code, English Braille, American Edition, was first published in 1932 by what is now the Braille Authority of North America (BANA). This organization represents many agencies and consumer groups and has been responsible for updating and interpreting the basic literary braille code and the specialized codes for music, mathematics, computer braille, and other uses in the United States and Canada. Other countries have similar authorities.

Louis Braille: A Remarkable Inventor

In 1821 a blind twelve-year-old boy took a secret code devised for the military and recognized in it the basis for written communication for blind individuals. Louis Braille, enrolled at the National Institute of the Blind in Paris, spent many years developing and refining the system of raised dots that has come to be known by his name.

The original military code was called night writing and was used by soldiers to communicate after dark. It was based on a twelve-dot cell, two-dots wide by six-dots high. Each dot or combination of dots within the cell stood for a phonetic sound. The problem with the military code was that a single fingertip could not feel all the dots with one touch.

Braille created a reading method based on a cell of six dots. This crucial improvement meant that a fingertip could encompass the entire cell unit with one impression and move rapidly from one cell to the next.

Braille himself was blind from the age of three. He was born in the village of Coupvray near Paris on January 4, 1809. One day he was playing with a sharp tool belonging to his father, a harness maker. The child accidentally injured one eye with the tool and developed an infection that later caused total blindness.

Until 1819, Braille attended the local village school, where his superior mental abilities put him at the head of his class. He received a scholarship to the National Institute of the Blind, where he was the youngest student. Soon afterward, he began the development of the embossed code. In 1829 he published the code in Procédé pour Ecrire les Paroles, la Musique et le Plain-Chant au Moyen de Points, which also contained a braille music code based on the same six-dot cell.

Disabilities Sourcebook, Fourth Edition

After he developed his system for reading and writing, Braille remained at the institute as an instructor. Eventually, an incessant cough made it impossible for him to lecture. He died at the age of forty-three, and was buried in the family plot in the village cemetery in Coupvray. In 1952, on the centennial of his death, his body was ceremoniously transferred to the Pantheon in Paris. A monument to Louis Braille stands in the main square of Coupvray.

The Braille Alphabet

The braille cell, an arrangement of six dots, is the basic unit for reading and writing braille. Sixty-three different patterns are possible from these six dots. For purposes of identification and description, these dots are numbered downward 1-2-3 on the left and 4-5-6 on the right:

$$1 \bullet \ \bullet \ 4$$
$$2 \bullet \ \bullet \ 5$$
$$3 \bullet \ \bullet \ 6$$

Figure 32.1. *Braille Dots*

(Note: As shown here, the "•" symbol represents a raised braille dot in the six-dot configuration. The "o" symbol represents a position in the cell where no braille dot occurs.)

The first ten letters of the alphabet (a–j) use only the dots in the upper two rows of the cell.

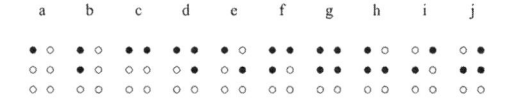

Figure 32.2. *Braille Alphabets (A-J)*

The next ten letters of the alphabet (k–t) are formed by adding dot 3 to each of the first ten letters.

Figure 32.3. *Braille Alphabets (K–T)*

Low Vision Devices and Services

The remaining letters, except for w, are formed by adding dots 3 and 6 to each of the first five letters.

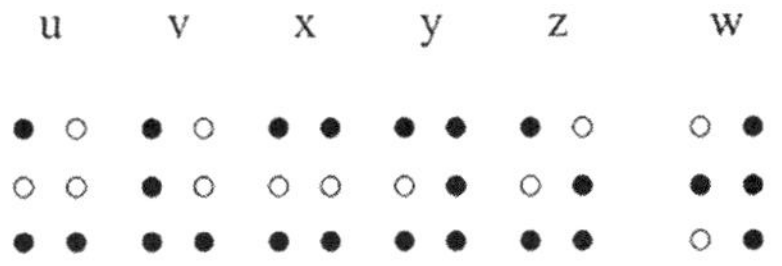

Figure 32.4. *Braille Alphabets (U-Z) and W*

The letter "w" is an exception because the French alphabet did not contain a "w" when the code was created; the symbol for "w" was added later.

Braille and Advances in Technology

Access to information in braille has evolved considerably in recent years. Braille can now be translated and formatted with a computer. Braille characters can be entered directly into a computer with six keys on the computer's keyboard. In addition, text that is entered into a computer via scanning or typing can be put into braille by using special software programs. Braille embossers can take the output from a computer and produce single- or double-sided braille materials in a fraction of the time it took to create braille by hand. While this process represents a major advance in braille production, computer-assisted braille translation is not perfect and materials must always be checked by a qualified braille proofreader.

Blind individuals use devices with refreshable braille displays to take notes, read braille materials, prepare school assignments, and perform many other tasks in braille that were not possible even twenty years ago. These advances in braille technology have had a profound impact on educational and professional opportunities available to blind braille readers.

Braille Transcribers and Proofreaders

Throughout the United States, dedicated braille transcribers and proofreaders work, often on a volunteer basis, to produce braille materials. These materials supplement the books and magazines produced in quantity by National Library Service (NLS) and other organizations. Sighted and blind individuals may become certified after completing a lengthy, detailed course of braille transcribing, culminating in the award by the Library of Congress (LOC) of a certificate of proficiency in the appropriate braille code.

Their activities include transcribing print material into braille, duplicating/embossing copies, binding braille books, preparing materials for use with electronic refreshable braille displays, and proofreading.

Many braille transcribers and proofreaders work as volunteers for NLS and its national network of cooperating libraries that distributes books and magazines to blind and physically handicapped readers, state departments of special education, and local school systems.

Many individuals work as volunteers to gain the experience necessary to be hired by braille production agencies and school systems. The National Braille Association (NBA), a professional organization for transcribers, provides transcribers with guidance and professional development opportunities.

Brailling is a skill that requires training, intellectual curiosity, patience, meticulousness, and the abilities to work under pressure and to understand and follow directions. Braille transcribers report a great sense of accomplishment in learning a completely new system of reading and writing, and in empowering blind people to independently access the reading materials they need for education, work, and other life activities.

Section 32.5

Web-Braille

"Web-Braille," © 2018 Omnigraphics.
Reviewed July 2018.

Braille is a system of raised dots that enables blind and visually impaired readers to read with their fingers on letters embossed onto paper. Braille system, which remains virtually unchanged to this day, was invented in the early 1800s by a French educator Louis Braille.

What Is Web-Braille?

The Library of Congress (LOC) offers an electronic platform for braille readers called "Web-Braille," and the National Library Service for the Blind and Physically Handicapped (NLS) offers eligible Braille readers access to Web-Braille digital book files. There are currently more than 2,700 electronic braille books available on the Internet, and about 40 new titles are added in braille each month and made accessible to users immediately.

Web-Braille provides braille books and magazines in an electronic format for braille readers. The text is produced by the NLS. Braille readers can access the Web-Braille website using a user ID and password that they receive when they register and subscribe to the service.

Web-Braille files are in grade 2 braille electronic form format and require braille display, braille-aware notetaker, or braille embosser equipment in order to read. To a sighted person, the braille text file looks like gibberish when viewed by a word processor, but the file is legible when viewed using the right equipment. All Web-Braille books and magazines have a book BR number, a volume number—which is the name of the book or magazine—and a ".brf" file extension.

What Does Web-Braille Contain?

The NLS produces thousands of books and magazines at a rate of about 40 new braille titles each month that are made accessible to users immediately. Web-Braille books include books published by NLS since 1992 and a few hundred older titles. Magazines dating from May 2001 are available on Web-Braille and are available no more than one day after the hard-copy magazine is shipped to the readers.

Who Can Use Web-Braille?

Access to Web-Braille is limited and permission for use is given only to certain institutions and NLS patrons in accordance with copyright laws. Some institutions that are eligible to use Web-Braille include public and private schools that teach braille to blind and visually impaired students, schools for the blind, and nonprofit organizations that help to produce braille books. Agencies can also use Web-Braille files to produce braille-only copies, but are not allowed to produce unencrypted e-text versions of the content or to make large-print versions without prior permission from the copyright holder.

How Does a User Register for Web-Braille Services?

Eligible users approach a cooperating network library and express interest in gaining access to Web-Braille services. An account can then be created with an e-mail address and a six- to eight-character password. Once the user is registered and the subscription is activated, the new user will receive access instructions in an e-mail.

How Does a User Locate Specific Books for Web-Braille Services?

There are two ways to locate specific Web-Braille books:

Online Catalog. The NLS online catalog has links to Web-Braille books. In order to retrieve specific Web-Braille titles, key in the words "web braille" without a hyphen in the "annotation, notes, contents" fields. A list containing a link to each volume of Web-Braille titles appears. To access a particular volume, a user ID and password is necessary.

Braille Book Review. The main Web-Braille page allows access to online versions of Braille Book Review. The web version contains all new braille books published since July–August 1999.

References

1. "Web Braille," John R. Ashcroft, Missouri Secretary of State, n.d.

2. "Web-Braille—New Internet Service for Visually Impaired," Library of Congress, November 1999.

3. "Web-Braille," National Library Service for the Blind and Physically Handicapped, Library of Congress, July 2001.

4. "Web-Braille," Montana.gov, n.d.

Low Vision Devices and Services

Section 32.6

New Technologies for People with Visual Impairment

This section includes text excerpted from "Five Innovations Harness New Technologies for People with Visual Impairment, Blindness," National Eye Institute (NEI), February 3, 2017.

February is low vision awareness month. During 2017 low vision awareness month (www.nei.nih.gov/nehep/lvam), the National Eye Institute (NEI), part of the National Institutes of Health (NIH), highlighted new technologies and tools in the works to help the 4.1 million Americans living with low vision or blindness. The innovations aim to help people with vision loss more easily accomplish daily tasks, from navigating office buildings to crossing a street. Many of the innovations take advantage of computer vision, a technology that enables computers to recognize and interpret the complex assortment of images, objects, and behaviors in the surrounding environment.

Low vision means that even with glasses, contact lenses, medicine, or surgery, people find everyday tasks difficult to do. It can affect many aspects of life, from walking in crowded places to reading or preparing a meal, explained Cheri Wiggs, Ph.D., program director for low vision and blindness rehabilitation at the NEI. The tools needed to stay engaged in everyday activities vary based on the degree and type of vision loss. For example, glaucoma causes loss of peripheral vision, which can make walking or driving difficult. By contrast, age-related macular degeneration (AMD) affects central vision, creating difficulty with tasks such as reading, she said.

Here's a look at a few NEI-funded technologies under development that aim to lessen the impact of low vision and blindness.

Co-Robotic Cane

Navigating indoors can be especially challenging for people with low vision or blindness. While existing global positioning system (GPS)-based assistive devices can guide someone to a general location such as a building, GPS isn't much help in finding specific rooms, said Cang Ye, Ph.D., of the University of Arkansas at Little Rock. Ye has developed a co-robotic cane that provides feedback on a user's surrounding environment.

Ye's prototype cane has a computerized 3D camera to "see" on behalf of the user. It also has a motorized roller tip that can propel the cane toward a desired location, allowing the user to follow the cane's direction. Along the way, the user can speak into a microphone and a speech recognition system interprets verbal commands and guides the user via a wireless earpiece. The cane's credit card-sized computer stores preloaded floor plans. However, Ye envisions being able to download floor plans via wireless fidelity (Wi-Fi) upon entering a building. The computer analyzes three-dimensional 3D information in real time and alerts the user of hallways and stairs. The cane gauges a person's location in the building by measuring the camera's movement using a computer vision method. That method extracts details from a current image captured by the camera and matches them with those from the previous image, thus determining the user's location by comparing the progressively changing views, all relative to a starting point. In addition to receiving NEI support, Ye was awarded a grant from the NIH's Coulter College Commercializing Innovation (C3i) Program to explore commercialization of the robotic cane.

Robotic Glove Finds Door Handles, Small Objects

In the process of developing the co-robotic cane, Ye realized that closed doorways pose yet another challenge for people with low vision and blindness. "Finding the door knob or handle and getting the door open slows you way down," he said. To help someone with low vision locate and grasp small objects more quickly, he designed a fingerless glove device.

On the back surface is a camera and a speech recognition system, enabling the user to give the glove voice commands such as "door handle," "mug," "bowl," or "bottle of water." The glove guides the user's hand via tactile prompts to the desired object. "Guiding the person's hand left or right is easy," Ye said. "An actuator on the thumb's surface takes care of that in a very intuitive and natural way." Prompting a user to move his or her hand forward and backward, and getting a feel for how to grasp an object, is more challenging.

Ye's colleague Yantao Shen, Ph.D., University of Nevada, Reno, developed a novel hybrid tactile system that comprises an array of cylindrical pins that send either a mechanical or electrical stimulus. The electric stimulus provides an electrotactile sensation, meaning that it excites the nerves on the skin of the hand to simulate a sense of touch. Picture four cylindrical pins in alignment down the length of your index finger. One by one, starting with the pin closest to your fingertip, the pins pulse in a pattern indicating that the hand should move backward.

The reverse pattern indicates the need for forward motion. Meanwhile, a larger electrotactile system on the palm uses a series of cylindrical pins to create a 3D representation of the object's shape. For example, if your hand is approaching the handle of a mug, you would sense the handle's shape in your palm so that you could adjust the position of your hand accordingly. As your hand moves toward the mug handle, any slight shifts in angle are noted by the camera and the tactile sensation on your palm reflects such changes.

Smartphone Crosswalk App

Street crossings can be especially dangerous for people with low vision. James Coughlan, Ph.D., and his colleagues at the Smith-Kettlewell Eye Research Institute (SKERI) have developed a smartphone app that gives auditory prompts to help users identify the safest crossing location and stay within the crosswalk.

The app harnesses three technologies and triangulates them. A global positioning system (GPS) is used to pinpoint the intersection where a user is standing. Computer vision is then used to scan the area for crosswalks and walk lights. That information is integrated with a geographic information system (GIS) database containing a crowdsourced, detailed inventory about an intersection's quirks, such as the presence of road construction or uneven pavement. The three technologies compensate for each other's weaknesses. For example, while computer vision may lack the depth perception needed to detect a median in the center of the road, such local knowledge would be included in the GIS template. And while GPS can adequately localize the user to an intersection, it cannot identify on which corner a user is standing. Computer vision determines the corner, as well as where the user is in relation to the crosswalk, the status of the walk lights and traffic lights, and the presence of vehicles.

CamIO System Helps Explore Objects in a Natural Way

Imagine a system that enables visually impaired biology students to explore a 3D anatomical model of a heart by touching an area and hearing "aortic arch" in response. The same system could also be used to get an auditory readout of the display on a device such as a glucose monitor. The prototype system, designed with a low-cost camera connected to a laptop computer, can make physical objects—from 2D maps to digital displays on microwaves—fully accessible to users with low vision or blindness.

The CamIO (short for camera input-output), also under development by Coughlan, provides real-time audio feedback as the user explores an object in a natural way, turning it around and touching it. Holding a finger stationary on 3D or 2D objects, signals the system to provide an audible label of the location in question or an enhanced image on a laptop screen. CamIO was conceived by Joshua Miele, Ph.D., a blind scientist at Smith-Kettlewell who develops and evaluates novel sound/touch interfaces to help people with vision loss. Coughlan plans to develop a smartphone app version of CamIO. In the meantime, software for the laptop version will be available for free download.

High-Powered Prisms, Periscopes for Severe Tunnel Vision

People with retinitis pigmentosa (RP) and glaucoma can lose most of their peripheral vision, making it challenging to walk in crowded places like airports or malls. People with severe peripheral field vision loss can have a residual central island of vision that's as little as 1–2 percent of their full visual field. Eli Peli, O.D., of Schepens Eye Research Institute, Boston, has developed lenses constructed of many adjacent one-millimeter wide prisms that expand the visual field while preserving central vision. Peli designed a high-powered prism, called a multiplexing prism that expands one's field of view by about 30 degrees. "That's an improvement, but it's not good enough," explained Peli.

In a study, he and his colleagues mathematically modeled people walking in crowded places and found that the risk of collision is highest when other pedestrians are approaching from a 45-degree angle. To reach that degree of peripheral vision, he and his colleagues are employing a periscope-like concept. Periscopes, such as those used to see the ocean surface from a submarine, rely on a pair of parallel mirrors that shift an image, providing a view that would otherwise be out of sight. Applying a similar concept, but with nonparallel mirrors, Peli and colleagues have developed a prototype that achieves a 45-degree visual field. Their next step is to work with optical labs to manufacture a cosmetically acceptable prototype that can be mounted into a pair of glasses. "It would be ideal if we could design magnetic clip-ons spectacles that could be easily mounted and removed," he said.

Chapter 33

How Therapists Can Assist People with Disabilities

Chapter Contents

Section 33.1—Occupational Therapists 378
Section 33.2—Physiatrists and Physical Therapists 381

Section 33.1

Occupational Therapists

This section contains text excerpted from the following sources: Text in this section begins with excerpts from "Occupational Therapy—VA Palo Alto Healthcare System," U.S. Department of Veterans Affairs (VA), June 8, 2018; Text under the heading "What Do Occupational Therapists Do?" is excerpted from "Occupational Therapy—VA Boston Healthcare System," U.S. Department of Veterans Affairs (VA), June 9, 2015; Text under the heading "Role of an Occupational Therapist in Evaluation and Treatment" is excerpted from "Occupational Therapists," U.S. Bureau of Labor Statistics (BLS), U.S. Department of Labor (DOL), April 13, 2018.

In simplest terms, occupational therapy is a healthcare profession that works with people with physical, mental, or developmental conditions to develop, recover, or maintain their daily living skills.

Occupational therapy is a client-centered practice in which the client has an integral part in the therapeutic process. The occupational therapy process includes an individualized evaluation during which the client/family and occupational therapist determine the individual's goals; a customized intervention to improve the person's ability to perform daily activities and reach his/her goals; and an outcomes evaluation to monitor progression towards meeting the client's goals.

Occupational therapy interventions focus on adapting the environment, modifying the task, teaching the skill, and educating the client/family in order to increase participation in, and performance of, daily activities.

What Do Occupational Therapists Do?

Occupational therapists (OTs) help people across the lifespan participate in the things they want and need to do through the therapeutic use of everyday activities.

Common areas of treatment are as follows:

- Activities of daily living (bathing, dressing, feeding, and grooming)
- Bathroom safety
- Kitchen safety and cooking
- Community reintegration

How Therapists Can Assist People with Disabilities

- Fine motor skills (difficulty using hands)
- Decreased strength or range of motion in arms
- Visual problems (legal blindness or one side neglect)
- Memory and problem solving
- Energy conservation (breathing techniques and pacing strategies)
- Joint protection for arthritic hands (how to grasp things correctly)
- Positioning (in bed, chair or wheelchair)
- Stress and/or anxiety management (relaxation techniques)
- Adaptive devices
- Assistive technology
- Wheelchair and seating
- Driver training

Role of an Occupational Therapist in Evaluation and Treatment

OTs typically do the following:

- Review patients' medical history, ask the patients questions, and observe them doing tasks
- Evaluate a patient's condition and needs
- Develop a treatment plan for patients, identifying specific goals and the types of activities that will be used to help the patient work toward those goals
- Help people with various disabilities perform different tasks, such as teaching a stroke victim how to get dressed
- Demonstrate exercises—for example, stretching the joints for arthritis relief—that can help relieve pain in people with chronic conditions
- Evaluate a patient's home or workplace and, on the basis of the patient's health needs, identify potential improvements, such as labeling kitchen cabinets for an older person with poor memory

- Educate a patient's family and employer about how to accommodate and care for the patient
- Recommend special equipment, such as wheelchairs and eating aids, and instruct patients on how to use that equipment
- Assess and record patients' activities and progress for patient evaluations, for billing, and for reporting to physicians and other healthcare providers

Patients with permanent disabilities, such as cerebral palsy, often need help performing daily tasks. Therapists show patients how to use appropriate adaptive equipment, such as leg braces, wheelchairs, and eating aids. These devices help patients perform a number of daily tasks, allowing them to function more independently.

Some occupational therapists work with children in educational settings. They evaluate disabled children's abilities, modify classroom equipment to accommodate children with disabilities, and help children participate in school activities. Therapists also may provide early intervention therapy to infants and toddlers who have, or are at risk of having, developmental delays.

Therapists who work with the elderly help their patients lead more independent and active lives. They assess patients' abilities and environment and make recommendations to improve the patients' everyday lives. For example, therapists may identify potential fall hazards in a patient's home and recommend their removal.

In some cases, occupational therapists help patients create functional work environments. They evaluate the workspace, recommend modifications, and meet with the patient's employer to collaborate on changes to the patient's work environment or schedule.

OTs also may work in mental health settings, where they help patients who suffer from developmental disabilities, mental illness, or emotional problems. Therapists teach these patients skills such as managing time, budgeting, using public transportation, and doing household chores in order to help them cope with, and engage in, daily life activities. In addition, therapists may work with individuals who have problems with drug abuse, alcoholism, depression, or other disorders. They may also work with people who have been through a traumatic event, such as a car accident.

Some OTs, such as those employed in hospitals, work as part of a healthcare team along with doctors, registered nurses, and other types of therapists. They may work with patients who have chronic conditions, such as diabetes, or help rehabilitate a patient recovering from hip replacement surgery. OTs also oversee the work of occupational therapy assistants and aides.

If your ability to move and function has been compromised by injury or disease, physical therapy may help you return to health and normal functioning. OTs rely on evidence-based therapy to treat patients after surgery, sports injuries, heart and lung problems, weakness or pain, and a wide range of complex conditions that affect muscles, bones, ligaments, and tendons.

Section 33.2

Physiatrists and Physical Therapists

This section contains text excerpted from the following sources: Text under the heading "What Is Physical Medicine and Rehabilitation?" is excerpted from "Physical Medicine and Rehabilitation—PM&R," U.S. Department of Veterans Affairs (VA), June 9, 2015; Text under the heading "Duties of a Physical Therapist" is excerpted from "Physical Therapists," U.S. Bureau of Labor Statistics (BLS), U.S. Department of Labor (DOL), April 13, 2018; Text under the heading "Computer Models Could Help Design Physical Therapy Regimens" is excerpted from "Computer Models Could Help Design Physical Therapy Regimens," National Institute of Biomedical Imaging and Bioengineering (NIBIB), January 9, 2017.

What Is Physical Medicine and Rehabilitation?

Physical Medicine and Rehabilitation (PM&R) physicians or physiatrists are nerve, muscle, and bone experts who treat injuries or illnesses that affect how you move. Rehabilitation physicians are medical doctors who have completed training in the medical specialty of physical medicine and rehabilitation.

Specifically, rehabilitation physicians:

- diagnose and treat pain;

- restore maximum function lost through injury, illness or disabling conditions;

- treat the whole person, not just the problem area;

- provide nonsurgical treatments; and

- explain your medical problems and treatment/prevention plan.

The job of a rehabilitation physician is to treat any disability resulting from disease or injury, from sore shoulders to amputations. The focus is on the development of a comprehensive integrated program for putting the pieces of a person's life back together after injury or disease—without surgery.

Rehabilitation physicians take the time needed to accurately pinpoint the source of an ailment. They then design a treatment plan that can be carried out by the patients themselves or with the help of the rehabilitation physician's medical team. This medical team might include other physicians and health professionals, such as neurologists, orthopedic surgeons, and physical therapists. By providing an appropriate treatment plan, rehabilitation physicians help patients stay as active as possible at any age. Their broad medical expertise allows them to treat disabling conditions throughout a person's lifetime. Both inpatient and outpatient physiatry consultation services are available.

Duties of a Physical Therapist

Physical therapists, sometimes called PTs, help injured or ill people improve their movement and manage their pain. These therapists are often an important part of rehabilitation, treatment, and prevention of patients with chronic conditions, illnesses, or injuries.

Physical therapists typically do the following:

- Review patients' medical history and any referrals or notes from doctors, surgeons, or other healthcare workers

- Diagnose patients' functions and movements by observing them stand or walk and by listening to their concerns, among other methods

- Develop individualized plans of care for patients, outlining the patients' goals and the expected outcomes of the plans

- Use exercises, stretching maneuvers, hands-on therapy, and equipment to ease patients' pain, help them increase their mobility, prevent further pain or injury, and facilitate health and wellness

- Evaluate and record a patient's progress, modifying a plan of care and trying new treatments as needed

How Therapists Can Assist People with Disabilities

- Educate patients and their families about what to expect from the recovery process and how best to cope with challenges throughout the process

Physical therapists provide care to people of all ages who have functional problems resulting from back and neck injuries; sprains, strains, and fractures; arthritis; amputations; neurological disorders, such as stroke or cerebral palsy (CP); injuries related to work and sports; and other conditions.

Physical therapists are educated to use a variety of different techniques to care for their patients. These techniques include exercises; training in functional movement, which may include the use of equipment such as canes, crutches, wheelchairs, and walkers; and special movements of joints, muscles, and other soft tissue to improve movement and decrease pain.

The work of physical therapists varies by type of patient. For example, a patient working to recover mobility lost after a stroke needs different care from a patient who is recovering from a sports injury. Some physical therapists specialize in one type of care, such as orthopedics or geriatrics. Many physical therapists also help patients to maintain or improve mobility by developing fitness and wellness programs that encourage healthier and more active lifestyles.

Physical therapists work as part of a healthcare team, overseeing the work of physical therapist assistants and aides and consulting with physicians and surgeons and other specialists.

Computer Models Could Help Design Physical Therapy Regimens

After a stroke, patients typically have trouble walking and few are able to regain the gait they had before suffering a stroke. Researchers funded by the National Institute of Biomedical Imaging and Bioengineering (NIBIB) have developed a computational walking model that could help guide patients to their best possible recovery after a stroke. Computational modeling uses computers to simulate and study the behavior of complex systems using mathematics, physics, and computer science. In this case, researchers are developing a computational modeling program that can construct a model of the patient from the patient's walking data collected on a treadmill and then predict how the patient will walk after different planned rehabilitation treatments. They hope that one day the model will be able to predict the best gait a patient can achieve after completing rehabilitation, as well as recommend the best rehabilitation approach to help the patient achieve an optimal recovery.

Currently, there is no way for a clinician to determine the most effective rehabilitation treatment prescription for a patient. Clinicians cannot always know which treatment approach to use, or how the approach should be implemented to maximize walking recovery. B.J. Fregly, Ph.D. and his team at the University of Florida developed a computational modeling approach to help answer these questions. They tested the approach on a patient who had suffered a stroke.

The team first measured how the patient walked at his preferred speed on a treadmill. Using those measurements, they then constructed a neuromusculoskeletal computer model of the patient that was personalized to the patient's skeletal anatomy, foot contact pattern, muscle force-generating ability, and neural control limitations. Fregly and his team found that the personalized model was able to predict accurately the patient's gait at a faster walking speed, even though no measurements at that speed were used for constructing the model.

Chapter 34

Art and Recreational Therapy

Art therapy is based on the idea that the creative process of art making is healing and life enhancing, and is a form of nonverbal communication of thoughts and feelings. Art therapy encourages personal growth, increases self-understanding and assists in emotional reparation. Participation in this treatment modality does not require any artistic training. The therapists involved in providing this treatment are all trained registered / licensed art therapists.

Art therapy helps individuals to

- create meaning;
- achieve insight;

This chapter contains text excerpted from the following sources: Text in this chapter begins with excerpts from "What Is Art Therapy?" U.S. Department of Veterans Affairs (VA), April 11, 2017; Text under the heading "Historical Context of Research into the Arts and Health" is excerpted from "The National Endowment for the Arts Guide to Community-Engaged Research in the Arts and Health," National Endowment For the Arts (NEA), December 3, 2016; Text under the heading "Creative Art Therapy and the Integrated Healthcare Model" is excerpted from "Creative Arts Therapy a Useful Tool for Military Patients," National Endowment For the Arts (NEA), November 12, 2015; Text under the heading "Creative Art Therapists" is excerpted from "Creative Arts Therapies Fact Sheet," U.S. Department of Veterans Affairs (VA), March 2018; Text under the heading "Therapeutic Recreation" is excerpted from "Recreation Therapy Service Fact Sheet," U.S. Department of Veterans Affairs (VA), March 2018; Text under the heading "Recreational Therapy: Restoring Function, Recreating Lives" is excerpted from "Recreational Therapy: Restoring Function, Recreating Lives," U.S. Department of Veterans Affairs (VA), April 17, 2015.

- find relief from overwhelming emotions or trauma and posttraumatic stress disorder (PTSD);
- resolve conflicts and problems, enrich daily life; and
- achieve an increased sense of well-being.

Historical Context of Research into the Arts and Health

Therapeutic uses of the arts have been documented since antiquity. For centuries, artists, philosophers, physicians, and others have proposed specific benefits of the arts for health and well-being. For instance, early examples about the therapeutic value of music date back at least to the 18th century, when references to music appeared in medical texts and references to medicine in music treatises.

An interest in using the arts to influence health developed substantially in the 20th century when arts professionals formalized distinct arts therapies by founding professional organizations and creating educational training programs. Among these interventions are music therapy, visual art therapy, dance/movement therapy, drama therapy, and several other genre-based forms of creative arts therapy.

Creative Art Therapy and the Integrated Healthcare Model

Creative arts therapy is a noninvasive and cost-effective medical treatment in which certified creative arts therapists work closely with other health professionals to create individual treatment plans with measurable outcomes. Patients may receive therapies such as painting, ceramics, music therapy, and therapeutic writing to improve health conditions for a wide range of medical, physical, neurological, and psychological health issues, such as depression, anxiety, cognitive function, memory, and impaired motor skills. Patients have described how art therapy activities have improved their cognitive skills and ability to process trauma and confront issues relating to frustrations, transitions, and grief.

Creative Art Therapists

Creative arts therapists are human service professionals who use arts modalities and creative processes to promote wellness, recovery, rehabilitation through unique personal interactions. Each creative arts therapy discipline has its own set of professional standards and requisite qualifications. Creative arts therapists are highly skilled, credentialed professionals having completed extensive coursework and clinical training.

Qualified creative arts therapists develop treatment goals, provide clinical interventions, monitor and document progress, and serve on interdisciplinary teams. Therapists plan and carry out treatment interventions to facilitate sensory integration, ambulation, community reentry, and reality orientation; to diminish emotional stress, muscular dysfunction; and to treat psychosocial dysfunction; while providing a sense of achievement and progress and channeling energies into acceptable forms of behavior.

Care Standards

Creative arts therapists adhere to standards of care that promote optimal outcomes for patients. Creative arts therapists utilize a wide range of techniques in clinical interventions that emphasize the healing potential and influence of the arts for rehabilitation, recovery, and improved quality of life.

Populations Served

Creative arts therapists create nonthreatening group and individual artistic experiences for individuals of all ages who confront life challenges related to physical and mental health conditions, on a daily basis. Creative arts therapists provide and promote creative self-expression that is personally driven and individually focused.

Research

Research supports the effectiveness of creative arts therapies interventions in many areas, including overall physical rehabilitation and facilitating movement. Creative arts therapies further help patients to increase motivation to become engaged in treatment, provide emotional support for patients and their families, and create an outlet to safely express feelings. Research findings and clinical observations attest to the positive outcomes that can result from creative arts therapies, and especially for those who may be resistive to other treatment approaches.

Therapeutic Recreation

Veterans Health Administration (VHA) is the first national healthcare system to establish Recreation as a section under the

Rehabilitation Medicine Service Office and included the creative arts. The complexity and interdependence of each patient's physiological, psychological, social, emotional, and social needs were recognized and therapeutic recreation developed into a specialized professional field. Each of the creative arts disciplines also developed, researched, and defined the distinctions between creative arts for personal use and the therapeutic applications of those arts. Later the Recreation "Section" was expanded to become a separate service within the U.S. Department of Veterans Affairs (VA) and the old image of diversionary "fun and games" changed to one of therapy.

Recreational Therapy: Restoring Function, Recreating Lives

Thousands of veterans receive "recreational therapy" from VA. For America's veterans, therapeutic recreation promotes health and wellness along with reducing or eliminating activity limitations and restrictions caused by an illness or disabling condition. The role of a recreation therapist in the VHA is to work in conjunction with interdisciplinary team members, Veterans, families, and friends to assist in a continuum of care from admission to discharge.

The benefits of recreation therapy for Veterans include improving physical well being such as weight management and controlling diabetes and hypertension. The therapy can also improve social functioning and help Veterans develop new leisure skills. It can enhance creative expression and break down barriers for cultural expression.

A final transition to home and to the community is a goal for many Veterans and recreation therapy helps create the catalyst for successful community re-entry.

Larry Long, Director, Veterans Health Administration Recreation Therapy Program, describes the role of the recreation therapy: "Recreation therapists provide treatment services and recreation activities to Veterans with disabilities, illnesses or other disabling conditions. They treat and maintain the physical, mental and emotional well-being of the patient using a variety of techniques, including arts and crafts, sports, games, dance, music and community integration activities.

"Recreation therapists assist in maintaining the health of Veterans receiving care at VA facilities for a variety of conditions, including those who are geriatric, chemically dependent, spinal cord injured, visually impaired and others. They also assist Veterans with disabilities to integrate into the community by helping them use community resources and recreational activities."

Art and Recreational Therapy

Therapeutic recreation is based upon a holistic framework that focuses on all aspects of improving an individual's health and functioning. By providing structured and unstructured therapy-driven services, providers use therapeutic recreation for improving physical abilities, building confidence and promoting greater self-reliance.

Chapter 35

Service Animals and People with Disabilities

This chapter provides guidance on the term "service animal" and the service animal provisions in the department's revised regulations.

- Beginning on March 15, 2011, only dogs are recognized as service animals under titles II and III of the Americans with Disabilities Act (ADA).

- A service animal is a dog that is individually trained to do work or perform tasks for a person with a disability.

- Generally, title II and title III entities must permit service animals to accompany people with disabilities in all areas where members of the public are allowed to go.

How "Service Animal" Is Defined

Service animals are defined as dogs that are individually trained to do work or perform tasks for people with disabilities. Examples of such work or tasks include guiding people who are blind, alerting people who are deaf, pulling a wheelchair, alerting and protecting a person who is having a seizure, reminding a person with mental illness to take prescribed medications, calming a person with posttraumatic

---

This chapter includes text excerpted from "Service Animals," ADA.gov, U.S. Department of Justice (DOJ), July 2011. Reviewed July 2018.

stress disorder (PTSD) during an anxiety attack, or performing other duties. Service animals are working animals, not pets. The work or task a dog has been trained to provide must be directly related to the person's disability. Dogs whose sole function is to provide comfort or emotional support do not qualify as service animals under the ADA.

This definition does not affect or limit the broader definition of "assistance animal" under the Fair Housing Act or the broader definition of "service animal" under the Air Carrier Access Act (ACAA). Some state and local laws also define service animal more broadly than the ADA does. Information about such laws can be obtained from that State's attorney general's office.

Where Service Animals Are Allowed

Under the ADA, State and local governments, businesses, and non-profit organizations that serve the public generally must allow service animals to accompany people with disabilities in all areas of the facility where the public is normally allowed to go. For example, in a hospital, it would be inappropriate to exclude a service animal from areas such as patient rooms, clinics, cafeterias, or examination rooms. However, it may be appropriate to exclude a service animal from operating rooms or burn units where the animal's presence may compromise a sterile environment.

Service Animals Must Be under Control

Under the ADA, service animals must be harnessed, leashed, or tethered, unless these devices interfere with the service animal's work or the individual's disability prevents using these devices. In that case, the individual must maintain control of the animal through voice, signal, or other effective controls.

Inquiries, Exclusions, Charges, and Other Specific Rules Related to Service Animals

- When it is not obvious what service an animal provides, only limited inquiries are allowed. Staff may ask two questions:

    1. Is the dog a service animal required because of a disability?

    2. What work or task has the dog been trained to perform?

    Staff cannot ask about the person's disability, require medical documentation, require a special identification card or training

Service Animals and People with Disabilities

documentation for the dog, or ask that the dog demonstrate its ability to perform the work or task.

- Allergies and fear of dogs are not valid reasons for denying access or refusing service to people using service animals. When a person who is allergic to dog dander and a person who uses a service animal must spend time in the same room or facility, for example, in a school classroom or at a homeless shelter, they both should be accommodated by assigning them, if possible, to different locations within the room or different rooms in the facility.

- A person with a disability cannot be asked to remove his service animal from the premises unless

  1. the dog is out of control and the handler does not take effective action to control it or

  2. the dog is not housebroken. When there is a legitimate reason to ask that a service animal be removed, staff must offer the person with the disability the opportunity to obtain goods or services without the animal's presence.

- Establishments that sell or prepare food must allow service animals in public areas even if state or local health codes prohibit animals on the premises.

- People with disabilities who use service animals cannot be isolated from other patrons, treated less favorably than other patrons, or charged fees that are not charged to other patrons without animals. In addition, if a business requires a deposit or fee to be paid by patrons with pets, it must waive the charge for service animals.

- If a business such as a hotel normally charges guests for damage that they cause, a customer with a disability may also be charged for damage caused by himself or his service animal.

- Staffs are not required to provide care or food for a service animal.

Miniature Horses

In addition to the provisions about service dogs, the department's revised ADA regulations have a new, separate provision about miniature horses that have been individually trained to do work or perform tasks for people with disabilities. (Miniature horses generally range in height from 24–34 inches measured to the shoulders and generally weigh between 70 and 100 pounds.) Entities covered by the ADA must modify their policies to permit miniature horses where reasonable. The regulations set out four assessment factors to assist entities in determining whether miniature horses can be accommodated in their facility. The assessment factors are:

1. whether the miniature horse is housebroken;
2. whether the miniature horse is under the owner's control;
3. whether the facility can accommodate the miniature horse's type, size, and weight; and
4. whether the miniature horse's presence will not compromise legitimate safety requirements necessary for safe operation of the facility.

Chapter 36

Finding Accessible Transportation

Chapter Contents

Section 36.1—Adapting Motor Vehicles for People
with Disabilities 396

Section 36.2—Assistance and Accommodation for
Air Travel.. 405

Section 36.1

Adapting Motor Vehicles for People with Disabilities

This section includes text excerpted from "Adapting Motor Vehicles for People with Disabilities," National Highway Traffic Safety Administration (NHTSA), June 2015.

New and existing adaptive technologies continue to broaden opportunities for people with disabilities to drive both comfortably and safely. Some of these adaptive technologies are as simple as swivel seats for more convenient access. Others, such as hand controls, may be necessary for a driver to safely operate a vehicle. Whatever your requirements, chances are good that adaptive equipment is available to support your special driving needs and allow you to maintain the freedom offered by the open road.

The information in this section is based on the experience of driver rehabilitation specialists and other professionals who work with people who require adaptive devices for their motor vehicles. The steps outlined here represent a proven process—evaluating your needs, making sure the vehicle "fits" you properly, choosing appropriate features, installing and knowing how to use adaptive devices, practicing good vehicle maintenance—that can help you avoid costly mistakes when modifying or purchasing a vehicle to accommodate your driving requirements.

Also included is general information on cost savings, licensing requirements, and organizations to contact for additional assistance. Although the section focuses on drivers of modified vehicles, it also contains important information for people who drive passengers with disabilities.

Investigate Cost-Saving Opportunities and Licensing Requirements

Cost-Saving Opportunities

With such a wide range of adaptive equipment solutions available, associated costs for modifying a vehicle can vary greatly depending on an individual's needs. Some adaptive equipment, such as a special seat back cushion, can provide a better view of the road for as little as $50. More complex equipment, such as hand controls, can be purchased for

Finding Accessible Transportation

under $1,000. However, a new vehicle modified with adaptive equipment will cost anywhere from $20,000–$80,000. Whether you are modifying a vehicle you now own or purchasing a new vehicle with adaptive equipment, it pays to do your homework first. By consulting with a driver rehabilitation specialist before you buy, you can learn what adaptive equipment you need now or may need in the future, avoid paying for equipment you don't need, and learn about opportunities for public and private financial assistance.

There are programs that may help pay part or all of the cost of vehicle modification. For information, contact your state's Department of Vocational Rehabilitation (VR) or another agency that provides vocational services, and, if appropriate, the U.S. Department of Veterans Affairs (VA). You can find phone numbers for these state and federal agencies online or in your local phone book.

Also be aware of the following:

- Some nonprofits that advocate for individuals with disabilities offer programs that may help pay for adaptive devices. Generally, these groups and programs represent local resources. To learn about any available programs in your area, contact your state government office that handles services for persons with disabilities.

- Automotive insurance may cover all or part of the cost of adaptive equipment if your need for such equipment is a result of a motor vehicle crash.

- Workers' compensation typically covers the cost of adaptive equipment if your need for such equipment is a result of a job-related injury.

- Most major vehicle manufacturers offer rebates on adaptive equipment, usually up to $1,000, provided you purchase a vehicle less than one-year-old. Your local automobile dealer can supply information on these programs and assist you with the application process.

- National Mobility Equipment Dealers Association (NMEDA) members are also familiar with vehicle manufacturer rebates, can help you apply for these rebates—and can provide prepurchase advice about the type of vehicle that will accommodate your adaptive equipment needs.

- Some states waive the sales tax for adaptive devices if you have a doctor's prescription for their use.

- The cost of adaptive equipment may be tax deductible. Check with a qualified tax consultant to learn more.

Licensing Requirements

All states require a valid learner's permit or driver's license to receive an on-the-road driving evaluation. You cannot be denied the opportunity to apply for a permit or license because of age or disability. However, a driver's license with restrictions may be issued based on your need for adaptive equipment.

Driver rehabilitation specialists perform comprehensive evaluations to identify the adaptive equipment most suited to your needs and medical condition. As part of this process, a rehabilitation specialist will take into consideration your future equipment needs based on your medical condition and the repetitive stress an adaptive aid may place on a particular muscle group. In addition, you can expect a complete evaluation to include vision screening as well as

- muscle strength, flexibility, and range of motion;
- coordination and reaction time;
- judgment and decision-making abilities; and
- ability to drive with adaptive equipment.

After you finish the evaluation you should receive a report containing specific recommendations on driving requirements or restrictions. You should also be given a complete list of any recommended vehicle requirements or modifications. The recommendations should suggest obtaining on-the-road training to practice safe operation of the equipment and learn safe driving habits.

Evaluate Your Needs

Driver rehabilitation specialists perform comprehensive evaluations to identify the adaptive equipment most suited to your needs and medical condition. As part of this process, a rehabilitation specialist will take into consideration your future equipment needs based on your medical condition and the repetitive stress an adaptive aid may place on a particular muscle group. In addition, you can expect a complete evaluation to include vision screening as well as:

- Muscle strength, flexibility, and range of motion;
- Coordination and reaction time;

- Judgment and decision-making abilities; and
- Ability to drive with adaptive equipment.

After you finish the evaluation you should receive a report containing specific recommendations on driving requirements or restrictions. You should also be given a complete list of any recommended vehicle requirements or modifications. The recommendations should suggest obtaining on-the-road training to practice safe operation of the equipment and learn safe driving habits.

Finding a Qualified Driver Rehabilitation Specialist

Check with a rehabilitation center in your area to find a qualified driver rehabilitation specialist to perform your evaluation. You'll find rehabilitation centers for each state listed on the websites for the Association for Driver Rehabilitation Specialists (ADED) and the American Occupational Therapy Association, Inc. (AOTA). These associations maintain lists of qualified driver rehabilitation specialists in areas across the United States and Canada.

Paying for an Evaluation

- Vocational rehabilitation agencies and workers' compensation agencies may assist in the cost of a driver evaluation.
- Your health insurance company may pay for part or all of the evaluation. Find out from your insurance company if you need a doctor's prescription or other documentation to receive such benefits.
- If you're a senior citizen, ask if your driver rehabilitation specialist offers a discount to seniors.

Determining the Best Time to Seek a Driving Evaluation

Consult with your doctor to make sure you are physically and psychologically prepared to drive. Being evaluated too soon after an injury, stroke, or other trauma may be misleading because it may show the need for adaptive equipment that you will not need in the future. You want to be functioning at your best when you have a driver evaluation. For the evaluation, you will need to take any equipment you normally use, such as a walker or neck brace. If you use a wheelchair and are planning to modify the wheelchair or obtain a new one, be sure to tell your driver rehabilitation specialist prior to the evaluation.

Evaluating Passengers with Disabilities

Driver rehabilitation specialists may also provide advice on compatibility and transportation safety issues for passengers with special needs. They determine the type of seating needed and the person's ability to enter and exit the vehicle. They provide advice on the purchase of modified vehicles and recommend appropriate wheelchair lifts or other equipment that would work in your vehicle.

If you have a child who requires a special type of safety seat, evaluators make sure the seat fits your child properly. They also make sure you can properly install the seat in your vehicle. The American Academy of Pediatrics (AAP) or your pediatrician can provide information on the safe transportation of children with special needs (www.pediatrics.aappublications.org/content/104/4/988). You can also visit the AAP website (www.aap.org) to access information about car safety seats for children with special needs.

Select the Right Vehicle

Although the purchase or lease of a vehicle is your responsibility, your mobility equipment dealer and driver rehabilitation specialist are qualified to ensure the vehicle you select can be modified to meet your adaptive equipment needs. Take the time to consult with these professionals before you make your purchase decision.

To find a qualified dealer in your area, contact the National Mobility Equipment Dealers Association (NMEDA). To find a qualified driver rehabilitation specialist, contact the Association for Driver Rehabilitation Specialists (ADED).

The following questions can help with vehicle selection. They can also help determine if you can modify a vehicle you already own:

- Does the vehicle have the cargo capacity (in pounds) to accommodate the equipment you require?
- Will there be enough space and cargo capacity to accommodate your family or other passengers once the vehicle is modified?
- Is there adequate parking space at home and at work for the vehicle and for loading/unloading a wheelchair?
- Is there adequate parking space to maneuver if you use a walker?
- What additional options are necessary for the safe operation of the vehicle?

Finding Accessible Transportation

If a third party is paying for the vehicle, adaptive devices, or modification costs, find out if there are any limitations or restrictions on what is covered. Always get a written statement on what a funding agency will pay before making your purchase. Once you select and purchase a vehicle, be aware that you will need to also purchase insurance to cover your vehicle while it's being modified—even though it will be off the road during this period.

Standard Features to Look for in a New Passenger Vehicle

Before purchasing a new vehicle, always sit in it first to make sure you are comfortable. Check to see that you can enter and exit the vehicle with ease. If possible, take it out for a test drive. How well does the car fit your body? To prevent airbag-related injury, you should keep 10 inches between your breastbone and the steering wheel, which contains the driver's side airbag. At the same time, you'll need to be able to easily reach the pedals while maintaining a comfortable line of sight above the adjusted steering wheel. Also, make sure the vehicle provides you with good visibility in all directions—front, rear, and sides. Your dealer can demonstrate the use of adaptive features, such as adjustable foot pedals and driver seats, which can help ensure a good person vehicle fit.

Check to see if the model you are considering purchasing has good crash test results and is resistant to rollover. Visit (www.safercar.gov) or call National Highway Traffic Safety Administration's (NHTSA) Vehicle Safety Hotline at 888-327-4236 to obtain government crash test results and rollover ratings for specific makes and models.

When selecting a vehicle, look for and ask about available features designed to improve both the comfort and safety of drivers with disabilities. Some of these features are:

- high or extra-wide doors;
- adjustable foot pedals;
- large interior door handles;
- oversized knobs with clearly visible labels;
- support handles to assist with entry and exit;
- large or adjustable-size print for dashboard gauges;
- seat adjusters that can move the seat in all directions—particularly raising it so the driver's line of sight is 3" above the adjusted steering wheel; and

- dashboard-mounted ignition rather than steering column-mounted ignition.

Choose a Qualified Mobility Dealer to Modify Your Vehicle

Even a half-inch change in the lowering of a van floor can affect a driver's ability to use equipment or to have an unobstructed view of the road. So it's important that you take the time to find a qualified dealer to modify your vehicle. Your driver rehabilitation specialist may be able to provide referrals depending on where you live and your vehicle modification and adaptive equipment needs.

Note: Some state agencies specify the dealer you must use if you want reimbursement. For example, some states require that dealers bidding on state vocational rehabilitation jobs be members of the National Mobility Equipment Dealer's (NMEDA's) Quality Assurance (QA) Program.

To find qualified mobility equipment dealers, begin with phone inquiries to learn about credentials, experience, and references. Ask questions about how they operate. Do they work with qualified driver rehabilitation specialists? Will they look at your vehicle before you buy it? Do they require a prescription from a physician or driver evaluation specialist? How long will it take before they can start work on your vehicle?

Also, ensure that the dealer you choose to modify your vehicle is registered with the NHTSA. In order to adapt a vehicle to meet your needs, registered equipment dealers are permitted to modify existing federally mandated safety equipment. In addition, registered mobility equipment dealers must provide you with a written statement regarding the work that was performed, as well as list any Federal Motor Vehicle Safety Standards (FMVSS) affected by their modification work on a label adjacent to the original equipment manufacturer's label or the modifier's certification label. These labels are often found inside the driver's door.

Questions to consider in evaluating a mobility equipment dealer's qualifications are listed below:

- Is the dealer registered with NHTSA?
- Is the dealer a member of NMEDA—and a participant in this organization's Quality Assurance Program?
- What type of training has the staff received?

Finding Accessible Transportation

- What type of warranty is provided on work?
- Does the dealer provide ongoing service and maintenance?
- Are replacement parts stocked and readily available?

If you are satisfied with the answers you receive, check references; then arrange to visit the dealer's facility. Once you are comfortable with a dealer's qualifications, you will want to ask more specific questions, such as:

- How much will the modification cost?
- Are third-party payments accepted?
- How long will it take to modify the vehicle?
- Can the equipment be transferred to a new vehicle in the future?
- Will existing safety features need to be modified to install the adaptive equipment?

While your vehicle is being modified, you will most likely need to be available for fittings. This prevents additional waiting time for adjustments once the equipment is fully installed. Without proper fittings, you may have problems with the safe operation of the vehicle and have to go back for adjustments.

Obtain Training on the Use of New Equipment

Both new and experienced drivers need training on how to safely use newly installed adaptive equipment. Your equipment installer and driver rehabilitation specialist should provide information on the new devices and off-road instruction. But literature and off-road instruction aren't enough to equip you to drive safely with your new adaptive equipment. This equipment can be very complex. So it's extremely important to obtain on-the-road training and practice with a driver rehabilitation specialist who has advanced expertise and knowledge of adaptive technologies. If your driver rehabilitation specialist does not offer such training, ask him or her for a referral, or inquire at your local driver licensing office. State vocational rehabilitation departments and workers' compensation will pay for driver education and training under certain circumstances. At a minimum, their staffs can help you locate a qualified driver rehabilitation specialist to provide training. Finally, remember to enlist the help of a family member or friend to drive you to all of your training sessions. (It's important to have someone else who can drive your vehicle in case of an emergency.)

Ensuring Safe Operation and Warranty Compliance

Regular maintenance is important for keeping your vehicle and specially installed adaptive features safe and reliable. It may also be mandatory for compliance with the terms of your warranty. Some warranties specify a time period during which adaptive equipment must be inspected. These equipment check-up schedules may differ from those for your vehicle. Make sure you or your modifier submit all warranty cards for all equipment. This will not only ensure coverage, but will also enable manufacturers to contact you in case of a recall.

Vehicle Safety Checklist

Your vehicle warranty and owner's manual will describe regularly required vehicle maintenance. Keep in mind that your adaptive equipment may need special attention or more frequent checkups than your vehicle alone. However, the following checklist represents basic maintenance that applies to all vehicles:

- Check tire pressure at least once a month and always before a long road trip.
- Change oil as recommended by your owner's manual, using the grade recommended.
- Check all fluids when you change the oil, including power steering fluid, brake fluid, and engine coolant.
- Routinely check headlights, brake and parking lights, reverse lights, and turn signals.
- Remember to keep your windows and headlights clean. You need to clearly see where you are going. Keeping the headlights clean will help other cars see you too.
- Check for damage from road hazards by having your vehicle put on a service lift at least once a year.

Proper maintenance can keep your vehicle running smoothly, leaving you free to concentrate on the road and enjoy the freedom of driving. However, if you think you have a problem with your modified vehicle or adaptive equipment, file a vehicle safety complaint at Safercar.

gov (www.odi.nhtsa.dot.gov/VehicleComplaint). Your information is important and could help determine if a safety issue exists.

Section 36.2

Assistance and Accommodation for Air Travel

This section includes text excerpted from "Passengers with Disabilities," U.S. Department of Transportation (DOT), January 27, 2015.

The Air Carrier Access Act (ACAA) prohibits discrimination on the basis of disability in air travel. The U.S. Department of Transportation (DOT) has a rule defining the rights of passengers and the obligations of airlines under this law. This rule applies to all flights of U.S. airlines, and to flights to or from the United States by foreign airlines. The following is a summary of the main points of the DOT rule (Title 14 CFR Part 382).

Prohibition of Discriminatory Practices

- Airlines may not refuse transportation to people on the basis of disability. Airlines may exclude anyone from a flight if carrying the person would be inimical to the safety of the flight. If a carrier excludes a person with a disability on safety grounds, the carrier must provide a written explanation of the decision.

- Airlines may not require advance notice that a person with a disability is traveling. Air carriers may require up to 48 hours' advance notice for certain accommodations that require preparation time (e.g., respirator hook-up, transportation of an electric wheelchair on an aircraft with less than 60 seats).

- Airlines may not limit the number of persons with disabilities on a flight.

- Airlines may not require a person with a disability to travel with another person, except in certain limited circumstances where the rule permits the airline to require a safety assistant. If a passenger with a disability and the airline disagree about the need for a safety assistant, the airline can require the assistant, but cannot charge for the transportation of the assistant.

- Airlines may not keep anyone out of a specific seat on the basis of disability, or require anyone to sit in a particular seat on the basis of disability, except to comply with Federal Aviation Administration (FAA) or foreign-government safety requirements. FAA's rule on exit row seating says that airlines may place in exit rows only persons who can perform a series of functions necessary in an emergency evacuation.

Accessibility of Facilities

- New aircraft with 30 or more seats must have movable aisle armrests on half the aisle seats in the aircraft.
- New twin-aisle aircraft must have accessible lavatories.
- New aircraft with 100 or more seats must have priority space for storing a passenger's folding wheelchair in the cabin.
- Aircraft with more than 60 seats and an accessible lavatory must have an on-board wheelchair, regardless of when the aircraft was ordered or delivered. For flights on aircraft with more than 60 seats that do not have an accessible lavatory, airlines must place an on-board wheelchair on the flight if a passenger with a disability gives the airline 48 hours' notice that he or she can use an inaccessible lavatory but needs an on-board wheelchair to reach the lavatory.
- Airlines must ensure that airport facilities and services that they own, lease or control are accessible in the manner prescribed in the rule.

Other Services and Accommodations

- Airlines are required to provide assistance with boarding, deplaning, and making connections. Assistance within the cabin is also required, but not extensive personal services. Where level-entry boarding is not available, there must be ramps or mechanical lifts to service most aircraft with 19 or more seats at U.S. airports with over 10,000 annual enplanements.

Finding Accessible Transportation

- Disabled passengers' items stored in the cabin must conform to FAA rules on the stowage of carry-on baggage. Assistive devices do not count against any limit on the number of pieces of carry-on baggage. Collapsible wheelchairs and other assistive devices have priority for in-cabin storage space (including in closets) over other passengers' items brought on board at the same airport, if the passenger with a disability chooses to preboard.

- Wheelchairs and other assistive devices have priority over other items for storage in the baggage compartment.

- Airlines must accept battery-powered wheelchairs, including the batteries, packaging the batteries in hazardous materials packages when necessary. The airline provides the packaging.

- Airlines must permit a passenger to use his/her portable oxygen concentrator during the flight if it is labeled as FAA-approved.

- Airlines may not charge for providing accommodations required by the rule, such as hazardous materials packaging for batteries. However, they may charge for optional services such as providing oxygen.

- Other provisions concerning services and accommodations address treatment of mobility aids and assistive devices, passenger information, accommodations for persons with vision and hearing impairments, security screening, communicable diseases and medical certificates, and service animals.

Administrative Provisions

- Training is required for airline and contractor personnel who deal with the traveling public.

- Airlines must make available specially-trained "complaints resolution officials" to respond to complaints from passengers and must also respond to written complaints. A DOT enforcement mechanism is also available.

- Airlines must obtain an assurance of compliance from contractors who provide services to passengers.

You may obtain an accessible electronic copy of 14 CFR Part 382 or call DOT at 202-366-2220 to request a copy.

Chapter 37

Family Support Services

Chapter Contents

Section 37.1—Understanding Respite and Hospice Care 410

Section 37.2—Adult Day Care 415

Section 37.1

Understanding Respite and Hospice Care

This section contains text excerpted from the following sources: Text beginning with the heading "What Is Respite Care?" is excerpted from "Respite Care," Eldercare Locator, U.S. Administration on Aging (AOA), August 2, 2004. Reviewed July 2018; Text under the heading "Where Can I Get Respite Care?" is excerpted from "Geriatrics and Extended Care—Respite Care," U.S. Department of Veterans Affairs (VA), February 18, 2017; Text beginning with the heading "How Often Is Hospice Care Covered?" is excerpted from "Your Medicare Coverage," Centers for Medicare and Medicaid Services (CMS), March 28, 2017.

What Is Respite Care?

Millions of Americans provide unpaid assistance each year to elderly family, friends, and neighbors to help them remain in their own homes and communities for as long as possible. Sometimes these caregivers need time off to relax or take care of other responsibilities. This is where respite care can be helpful. It provides the family caregivers with the break they need, and also ensures that their elderly loved one is still receiving the attention that he or she needs.

Respite care is not all the same. Respite can vary in time from part of a day to several weeks. Respite encompasses a wide variety of services including traditional home-based care, as well as adult day care, skilled nursing, home health, and short term institutional care. More specifically respite care may take any one of the following forms:

- **Adult day care:** These programs are designed to provide care and companionship for frail and disabled persons who need assistance or supervision during the day. The program offers relief to family members or caregivers and allows them the freedom to go to work, handle personal business or just relax while knowing their relative is well cared for and safe.

- **Informal and volunteer respite care:** This is as simple as it sounds. It is accepting help from other family members, friends, neighbors, or church volunteers who offer to stay with the elderly individual while you go to the store or run other errands. Sometimes your local church group or area agency on aging (AAA) will even run a formal "Friendly Visitor Program" in which volunteers may be able to provide basic respite care, as

Family Support Services

well. Many communities have formed either Interfaith Caregiver or Faith in Action Programs where volunteers from faith-based communities are matched with caregivers to provide them with some relief.

- **In-home respite care:** Generally speaking, in-home respite care involves the following four types of services for the more impaired older person:

  1. Companion services to help the family caregiver supervise, entertain, or just visit with the senior when he or she is lonely and wants company.

  2. Homemaker services to assist with housekeeping chores, preparing meals, or shopping.

  3. Personal care services to help the aged individual bathe, get dressed, go to the bathroom, and/or exercise.

  4. Skilled care services to assist the family caregiver in tending to the senior's medical needs, such as when administering medications.

How Do You Pay for Respite?

The cost of respite care varies with the type of agency and the services needed, but federal and/or state programs may help to pay for it. Long term care insurance policies may cover some of the cost of respite care. Your local area Agency on Aging (AAA) will have more information on whether financial assistance is available, depending on your situation and where you live.

Where Can I Get Respite Care?

You may be able to get respite care in a number of ways:

- A paid Home Health Aide could come to your home
- You could attend an Adult Day Health Care center
- You could go to a Community Living Center (VA Nursing Home) or a VA medical center for a short inpatient stay

Depending on the respite care services in your area, you can choose which options are best for you and your family caregiver. For example: If your caregiver has lots of errands to run or appointments, you could have a Home Health Aide come to your home while your caregiver is out of the house. If your caregiver needs time at your home alone, you could attend an Adult Day Health Care center for the day. Or, if your caregiver is out of town for a few days, you could stay at a Community Living Center (VA Nursing Home) during the time they are away.

No matter which option you use, trained staff will help you with your care needs.

Respite care services may be available up to 30 days each calendar year. These 30 days may be used in different ways. For example:

- You might stay in a Community Living Center (VA Nursing Home) for 1 visit of 30 days, or have 10 short stays of 3 days each during the year.

- You might have a Home Health Aide come to your home to stay with you for up to 6 hours in a row, day or night. Each visit (even if it is less than the 6-hour maximum) counts as 1 day of Respite Care.

You may also be able to divide your 30 days among the 3 different types of respite care.

How Often Is Hospice Care Covered?

Hospice care is usually given in your home, but it also may be covered in a hospice inpatient facility. Depending on your terminal illness and related conditions, the plan of care your hospice team creates can include any or all of these services:

- Doctor services
- Nursing care
- Medical equipment (like wheelchairs or walkers)
- Medical supplies (like bandages and catheters)
- Prescription drugs for symptom control or pain relief
- Hospice aide and homemaker services
- Physical therapy services
- Occupational therapy services
- Speech-language pathology (SLP) services
- Social work services
- Dietary counseling

Family Support Services

- Grief and loss counseling for you and your family
- Short-term inpatient care (for pain and symptom management)
- Short-term respite care
- Any other Medicare-covered services needed to manage your pain and other symptoms related to your terminal illness and related conditions, as recommended by your hospice team

When you choose hospice care, you decide you no longer want care to cure your terminal illness and/or your doctor determines that efforts to cure your illness aren't working.

Medicare won't cover any of these once your hospice benefit starts:

- Treatment intended to cure your terminal illness and/or related conditions. Talk with your doctor if you're thinking about getting treatment to cure your illness. As a hospice patient, you always have the right to stop hospice care at any time.
- Prescription drugs to cure your illness (rather than for symptom control or pain relief).
- Care from any hospice provider that wasn't set up by the hospice medical team. You must get hospice care from the hospice provider you chose. All care that you get for your terminal illness must be given by or arranged by the hospice team. You can't get the same type of hospice care from a different hospice, unless you change your hospice provider. However, you can still see your regular doctor or nurse practitioner if you've chosen him or her to be the attending medical professional who helps supervise your hospice care.
- Room and board. Medicare doesn't cover room and board if you get hospice care in your home or if you live in a nursing home or a hospice inpatient facility. If the hospice team determines that you need short-term inpatient or respite care services that they arrange, Medicare will cover your stay in the facility. You may have to pay a small copayment for the respite stay.
- Care you get as a hospital outpatient (like in an emergency room), care you get as a hospital inpatient, or ambulance transportation, unless it's either arranged by your hospice team or is unrelated to your terminal illness and related conditions.

Contact your hospice team before you get any of these services or you might have to pay the entire cost.

Who's Eligible for Hospice Care?

You can get hospice care if you have Medicare Part A (Hospital Insurance) and meet all of these conditions:

- Your hospice doctor and your regular doctor (if you have one) certify that you're terminally ill (you're expected to live 6 months or less).

- You accept palliative care (for comfort) instead of care to cure your illness.

- You sign a statement choosing hospice care instead of other Medicare-covered treatments for your terminal illness and related conditions.

Only your hospice doctor and your regular doctor (if you have one) can certify that you're terminally ill and have a life expectancy of 6 months or less.

Your Costs in Original Medicare

- $0 for hospice care.

- You may need to pay a copayment of no more than $5 for each prescription drug and other similar products for pain relief and symptom control while you're at home. In the rare case, your drug isn't covered by the hospice benefit, your hospice provider should contact your Medicare drug plan to see if it's covered under Part D.

- You may need to pay 5 percent of the Medicare-approved amount for inpatient respite care.

- Medicare doesn't cover room and board when you get hospice care in your home or another facility where you live (like a nursing home).

Section 37.2

Adult Day Care

This section includes text excerpted from "Adult Day Care," Eldercare Locator, U.S. Administration on Aging (AOA), October 16, 2015.

Adult day care centers are designed to provide care and companionship for older adults who need assistance or supervision during the day. Programs offer relief to family members and caregivers, allowing them to go to work, handle personal business, or just relax while knowing their relative is well cared for and safe.

The goals of the programs are to delay or prevent institutionalization by providing alternative care, to enhance self-esteem, and to encourage socialization. There are two types of adult day care: adult social day care and adult day healthcare. Adult social day care provides social activities, meals, recreation, and some health-related services. Adult day healthcare offers intensive health, therapeutic, and social services for individuals with serious medical conditions and those at risk of requiring nursing home care.

Older adults generally participate on a scheduled basis. Services may include the following:

- Counseling
- Education
- Evening care
- Exercise
- Health screening
- Meals
- Medical care
- Physical therapy
- Recreation
- Respite care
- Socialization
- Supervision
- Transportation
- Medication management

Center Operations

Centers are usually open during normal business hours and may stand alone or be located in senior centers, nursing facilities, places of faith, hospitals, or schools. The staff may monitor medication, serve hot meals and snacks, perform physical or occupational therapy, and arrange social activities. They may also help to arrange transportation to and from the center.

Case Study

The following is an example of someone who needs adult day care services, both for his well-being and that of his family caregivers. Paul is 69 years old and recently experienced a stroke. He needs some care and supervision, so he lives with his son, David, and daughter-in-law, Kira. Because they both work, David and Kira, need help to care for Paul during the day. They found a solution by having Kira take Paul to the local adult day care center in the morning, and having David pick him up after work. The center monitors Paul's medication and offers him lunch, some physical therapy, and a chance to socialize with other seniors.

Finding a Center

Not all states license and regulate adult day care centers. There may be a great deal of difference between individual centers; therefore, it is important to learn more about each center near you. If possible, visit the centers closest to you, and talk with the staff and other families that use the centers to determine whether the facilities meet your needs. You may also want to find out if your state has an adult day care association.

Paying for Services

Costs vary and can range from $25 to over $100 per day, depending on the services offered, type of reimbursement, and geographic region. While an adult day care center is not usually covered by Medicare insurance, some financial assistance may be available through a federal or state program (e.g., Medicaid, Older Americans Act (OAA), Veterans Health Administration (VHA)).

Local Programs

To find out more about centers where you live, contact your local aging information and assistance provider or Area Agency on Aging (AAA). For help connecting to these agencies, contact the Eldercare Locator at 800-677-1116 or www.eldercare.acl.gov. The National Adult Day Services Association (NADSA) is a good source for general information about adult day care centers, programs, and associations. Call 877-745-1440 or visit www.nadsa.org.

Part Four

Staying Healthy with a Disability

Chapter 38

Nutrition and Weight Management Issues for People with Disabilities

Chapter Contents

Section 38.1—Nutrition and Disability 420

Section 38.2—Nutrition for Swallowing Difficulties 422

Section 38.3—Overweight and Obesity among
People with Disabilities 427

Section 38.1

Nutrition and Disability

This section contains text excerpted from the following sources: Text under the heading "Does Nutrition Play a Part in Disability?" is excerpted from "The State of the World's Children 2013—Children with Disabilities," U.S. Agency for International Development (USAID), May 2013. Reviewed July 2018; Text under the heading "Accommodations for Children with Special Dietary Needs" is excerpted from "School Meals," Food and Nutrition Service (FNS), U.S. Department of Agriculture (USDA), March 9, 2017.

Does Nutrition Play a Part in Disability?

About 870 million people worldwide are thought to be undernourished. Among them, some 165 million under-fives are believed to be stunted or chronically malnourished, and more than 100 million are considered underweight. Insufficient food or a poorly balanced diet short of certain vitamins and minerals (iodine, vitamin A, iron, and zinc, for example) can leave infants and children vulnerable to specific conditions or a host of infections that can lead to physical, sensory or intellectual disabilities.

Between 250,000 and 500,000 children are considered to be at risk of becoming blind each year from vitamin A deficiency, a syndrome easily prevented by oral supplementation costing just a few cents per child. For a similarly minute amount—five cents per person per year—salt iodization remains the most cost-effective way of delivering iodine and preventing cognition damage in children in iodine-deficient areas. These low-cost measures help not only children with disabilities but also their mothers as they labor to raise infants and children in strained circumstances.

Early childhood stunting, which is measured a slow height for age, is caused by poor nutrition and diarrhea. A multi-country study showed that each episode of diarrhea in the first two years of life contributes to stunting, which is estimated to affect some 28 percent of children younger than 5 in low- and middle-income countries. The consequences of stunting, such as poor cognitive and educational performance, begin when children are very young but affect them through the rest of their lives. However, community-based efforts to improve basic health practices have been shown to reduce stunting among young children.

Nutrition and Weight Management Issues

Malnutrition in mothers can lead to a number of preventable childhood disabilities. Approximately 42 percent of pregnant women in low- and middle-income countries are anemic, and more than one in two pregnant women in these countries suffer from iron deficiency anemia. Anemia also affects more than half of preschool-aged children in developing countries. It is one of the most prevalent causes of disability in the world—and therefore, a serious global public health problem. Malnutrition in lactating mothers can also contribute to poorer infant health, increasing the risk of diseases that can cause disability. Healthy mothers can help reduce the incidence of some disabilities and are better prepared to minister to their children's needs.

While malnutrition can be a cause of disability, it can also be a consequence. Indeed, children with disabilities are at heightened risk of malnutrition. For example, an infant with cleft palate may not be able to breastfeed or consume food effectively. Children with cerebral palsy (CP) may have difficulty chewing or swallowing. Certain conditions, such as cystic fibrosis (CF), may impede nutrient absorption. Some infants and children with disabilities may need specific diets or increased calorie intake in order to maintain a healthy weight. Yet they may be hidden away from community screening and feeding initiatives. Children with disabilities who do not attend school miss out on school feeding programmes.

A combination of physical factors and attitudes may adversely affect child nutrition. In some societies, mothers may not be encouraged to breastfeed a disabled child. Stigma and discrimination may also result in a child with a disability being fed less, denied food or provided with less nutritious food than siblings without disabilities. Children with some types of physical or intellectual disabilities may also have difficulty in feeding themselves, or need additional time or assistance to eat. It is probable that in some cases what is assumed to be disability-associated ill-health and wasting may, in fact, be connected with feeding problems.

Accommodations for Children with Special Dietary Needs

Federal law and the regulations for the National School Lunch Program (NSLP) and the School Breakfast Program require schools to make accommodations for children who are unable to eat the school meal as prepared because of a disability. Accommodation generally involves substituting food items, but in some cases, schools may need to make more far-reaching accommodations to meet the needs of children. For example, some children may need to have the texture modified.

In order to make substitutions for items in reimbursable meals, the school must have on file a written statement signed by a licensed physician indicating what the child's disability is, what foods must be omitted from the child's diet, and what foods must be substituted.

Schools may, at their option, make substitutions for persons who have special needs that do not meet the definition of disability under federal law. In these instances, the school must have a written statement signed by a recognized medical authority (e.g., nurse or physician's assistant) indicating what foods should be substituted. The purpose of requiring a written statement is two-fold. First, it ensures that the nutrition integrity of the school meal will not be compromised by the substitution. More importantly, it ensures that decisions about specific food substitutes are made by persons who are highly qualified to prescribe them. Therefore, this requirement helps to protect both the child and the food service personnel who are working to meet the child's needs.

Section 38.2

Nutrition for Swallowing Difficulties

This section contains text excerpted from the following sources: Text beginning with the heading "What Is Dysphagia?" is excerpted from "Dysphagia," National Institute on Deafness and Other Communication Disorders (NIDCD), March 6, 2017; Text beginning with the heading "Tips for Safe Swallowing" is excerpted from "Safe Swallowing," U.S. Department of Veterans Affairs (VA), May 2013. Reviewed July 2018.

What Is Dysphagia?

People with dysphagia have difficulty swallowing and may even experience pain while swallowing (odynophagia). Some people may be completely unable to swallow or may have trouble safely swallowing liquids, foods, or saliva. When that happens, eating becomes a challenge. Often, dysphagia makes it difficult to take in enough calories

Nutrition and Weight Management Issues

and fluids to nourish the body and can lead to additional serious medical problems.

How Do We Swallow?

Swallowing is a complex process. Some 50 pairs of muscles and many nerves work to receive food into the mouth, prepare it, and move it from the mouth to the stomach. This happens in three stages. During the first stage, called the oral phase, the tongue collects the food or liquid, making it ready for swallowing. The tongue and jaw move solid food around in the mouth so it can be chewed. Chewing makes solid food the right size and texture to swallow by mixing the food with saliva. Saliva softens and moistens the food to make swallowing easier. Normally, the only solid we swallow without chewing is in the form of a pill or caplet. Everything else that we swallow is in the form of a liquid, a puree, or a chewed solid.

The second stage begins when the tongue pushes the food or liquid to the back of the mouth. This triggers a swallowing response that passes the food through the pharynx, or throat. During this phase,

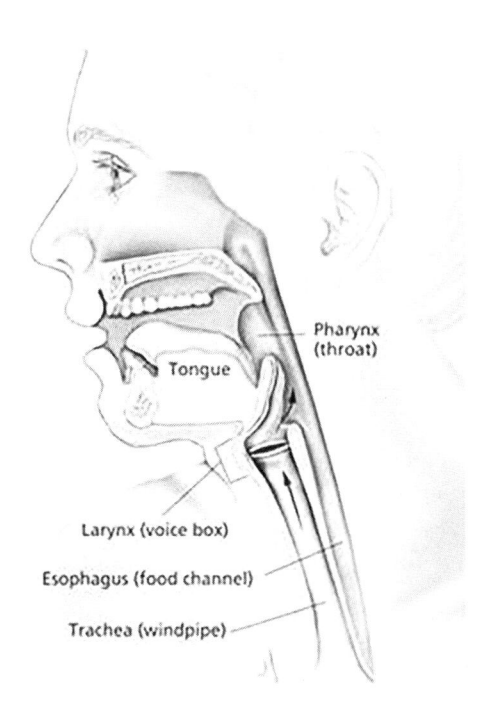

Figure 38.1. *Parts of the Mouth and Neck Involved in Swallowing*

called the pharyngeal phase, the larynx (voice box) closes tightly and breathing stops to prevent food or liquid from entering the airway and lungs.

The third stage begins when food or liquid enters the esophagus, the tube that carries food and liquid to the stomach. The passage through the esophagus, called the esophageal phase, usually occurs in about three seconds, depending on the texture or consistency of the food, but can take slightly longer in some cases, such as when swallowing a pill.

How Does Dysphagia Occur?

Dysphagia occurs when there is a problem with the neural control or the structures involved in any part of the swallowing process. Weak tongue or cheek muscles may make it hard to move food around in the mouth for chewing. A stroke or other nervous system disorder may make it difficult to start the swallowing response, a stimulus that allows food and liquids to move safely through the throat. Another difficulty can occur when weak throat muscles, such as after cancer surgery, cannot move all of the food toward the stomach. Dysphagia may also result from disorders of the esophagus.

What Are Some Problems Caused by Dysphagia?

Dysphagia can be serious. Someone who cannot swallow safely may not be able to eat enough of the right foods to stay healthy or maintain an ideal weight. Food pieces that are too large for swallowing may enter the throat and block the passage of air. In addition, when foods or liquids enter the airway of someone who has dysphagia, coughing or throat clearing sometimes cannot remove it. Food or liquid that stays in the airway may enter the lungs and allow harmful bacteria to grow, resulting in a lung infection called aspiration pneumonia. Swallowing disorders may also include the development of a pocket outside the esophagus caused by weakness in the esophageal wall. This abnormal pocket traps some food being swallowed. While lying down or sleeping, someone with this problem may draw undigested food into the throat. The esophagus may also be too narrow, causing food to stick. This food may prevent other food or even liquids from entering the stomach.

What Causes Dysphagia?

Dysphagia has many possible causes and happens most frequently in older adults. Any condition that weakens or damages the muscles

Nutrition and Weight Management Issues

and nerves used for swallowing may cause dysphagia. For example, people with diseases of the nervous system, such as cerebral palsy or Parkinson disease (PD), often have problems swallowing. Additionally, stroke or head injury may weaken or affect the coordination of the swallowing muscles or limit sensation in the mouth and throat. People born with abnormalities of the swallowing mechanism may not be able to swallow normally. Infants who are born with an opening in the roof of the mouth (cleft palate) are unable to suck properly, which complicates nursing and drinking from a regular baby bottle.

In addition, cancer of the head, neck, or esophagus may cause swallowing problems. Sometimes the treatment for these types of cancers can cause dysphagia. Injuries of the head, neck, and chest may also create swallowing problems. An infection or irritation can cause narrowing of the esophagus. Finally, for people with dementia, memory loss, and cognitive decline may make it difficult to chew and swallow.

How Is Dysphagia Treated?

There are different treatments for various types of dysphagia. Medical doctors and speech-language pathologists (SLPs) who evaluate and treat swallowing disorders use a variety of tests that allow them to look at the stages of the swallowing process. One test, the Flexible Endoscopic Evaluation of Swallowing with Sensory Testing (FEESST), uses a lighted fiber optic tube, or endoscope, to view the mouth and throat while examining how the swallowing mechanism responds to such stimuli as a puff of air, food, or liquids. A videofluoroscopic swallow study (VFSS) is a test in which a clinician takes a videotaped X-ray of the entire swallowing process by having you consume several foods or liquids along with the mineral barium to improve the visibility of the digestive tract. Such images help identify where in the swallowing process you are experiencing problems. Speech-language pathologists use this method to explore what changes can be made to offer a safe strategy when swallowing. The changes may be in food texture, size, head and neck posture, or behavioral maneuvers, such as "chin tuck," a strategy in which you tuck your chin so that food and other substances do not enter the trachea when swallowing. If you are unable to swallow safely despite rehabilitation strategies, then medical or surgical intervention may be necessary for the short term as you recover. In progressive conditions such as amyotrophic lateral sclerosis (ALS, or Lou Gehrig disease), a feeding tube in the stomach may be necessary for the long term. For some people, treatment may involve muscle exercises to strengthen weak facial muscles or to improve coordination. For others, treatment may involve learning to eat in a special way. For example, some people may have to eat with their head turned to one side or looking straight ahead. Preparing food in a certain way or avoiding certain foods may help in some situations. For instance, people who cannot swallow thin liquids may need to add special thickeners to their drinks. Other people may have to avoid hot or cold foods or drinks. For some, however, consuming enough foods and liquids by mouth may no longer be possible. These individuals must use other methods to nourish their bodies. Usually, this involves a feeding system, such as a feeding tube, that bypasses or supplements the part of the swallowing mechanism that is not working normally.

Tips for Safe Swallowing

Here are few safety tips for swallowing:

- Eat while sitting in an upright position
- Avoid distractions—focus on eating!
- Eat and drink slowly; take small bites
- Chew thoroughly and swallow completely
- Sit upright for 30 minutes after eating

Diet Level and Food Consistency

Your healthcare provider, dietitian, or speech-language pathologist will recommend the right diet level and liquid consistency for you.

- **Dysphagia Pureed**—Foods on this diet are pureed to a pudding-like consistency

- **Dysphagia Mechanically-Altered**—Foods on this diet are soft textured, moist and easy to chew. Meats must be ground or minced into pieces no larger than 1/4-inch. Vegetables must smaller than 1/2-inch pieces, thoroughly cooked and mashed with a fork. Foods from the Dysphagia Pureed diet can also be eaten on this diet.

- **Dysphagia Advanced**—Foods must be moist and cut into bite-sized pieces. No sticky, chewy, hard, or stringy foods are allowed. Foods from the dysphagia pureed and mechanically-altered diets can also be eaten on this diet.

Liquid Consistency

- **Nectar Thick**—Nectar thick liquids are thickened to the consistency of peach or pear nectar. Liquids must stay this thickness at room and body temperature. Nectar thick liquids will coat a spoon lightly.

- **Honey Thick**—Honey thick liquids are thicker than nectar thick liquids but not as thick as pudding. Liquids should pour slowly off a spoon and coat the spoon like honey. The liquid should not run off like a thin liquid or plop like pudding. Liquids must remain at this consistency at room or body temperature.

Thickeners are available to thicken thin liquids to the desired consistency; they come in powder or gel form. Follow the manufacturer's instructions for mixing. Prethickened beverages are also available.

Section 38.3

Overweight and Obesity among People with Disabilities

This section includes text excerpted from "Disability and Obesity," Centers for Disease Control and Prevention (CDC), August 1, 2017.

Overweight and obesity are both labels for ranges of weight that are greater than what is generally considered healthy for a given height. The terms also identify ranges of weight that have been shown to increase the likelihood of certain diseases and other health problems. Behavior, environment, and genetic factors can affect whether a person is overweight or obese.

Adults

For adults, overweight and obesity ranges are determined by using weight and height to calculate a number called the "body mass index" (BMI). BMI is used because, for most people, it correlates with their amount of body fat.

- An adult who has a BMI between 25 and 29.9 is considered overweight.
- An adult who has a BMI of 30 or higher is considered obese.

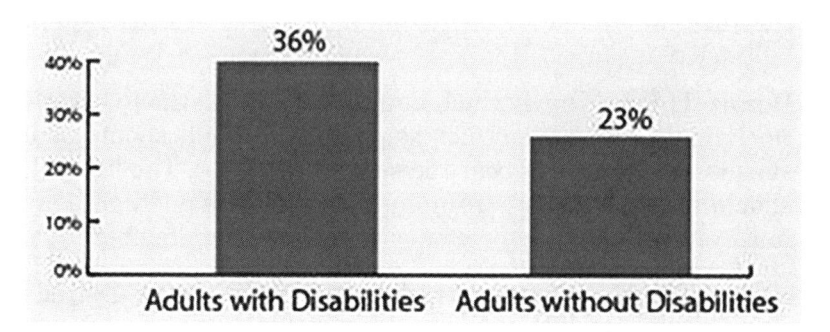

Figure 38.2. *Percentage of Obesity among Adults by Disability Status*

Children

Among children of the same age and sex, overweight is defined on Centers for Disease Control and Prevention (CDC) growth charts as a BMI at or above the 85th percentile and lower than the 95th percentile. Obesity is defined as having a BMI at or above the 95th percentile.

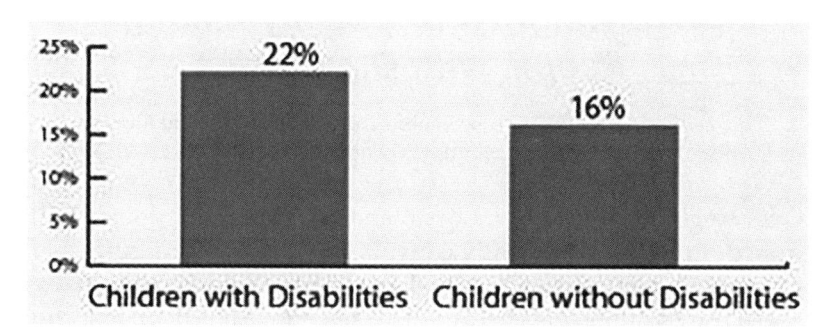

Figure 38.3. *Percentage of Obesity among Children, Ages 2–17, by Disability Status*

Challenges Facing People with Disabilities

People with disabilities can find it more difficult to always eat healthy, control their weight, and be physically active. This might be due to:

Nutrition and Weight Management Issues

- A lack of healthy food choices
- Difficulty with chewing or swallowing food, or with the taste or texture of foods
- Medications that can contribute to weight gain, weight loss, and changes in appetite
- Physical limitations that can reduce a person's ability to exercise
- Pain
- A lack of energy
- A lack of accessible environments (for example, sidewalks, parks, and exercise equipment) that can enable exercise
- A lack of resources (for example, money; transportation; and social support from family, friends, neighbors, and community members)

What Can Be Done?

Obesity is a complex problem that requires a strong call for action, at many levels, for both adults as well as children. More efforts are needed, and new federal initiatives are helping to change our communities into places that strongly support healthy eating and active living.

All people can:

- Eat more fruits and vegetables and fewer foods high in fat and sugar
- Drink more water instead of sugary drinks
- Watch less television
- Support breastfeeding
- Promote policies and programs at school, at work, and in the community that makes the healthy choice the easy choice
- Be more physically active

The Obesity Epidemic

Obesity affects different people in different ways and may increase the risk for other health conditions among people with and without disabilities.

For People with Disabilities

- Children and adults with mobility limitations and intellectual or learning disabilities are at greatest risk for obesity.
- 20 percent of children 10 through 17 years of age who have special healthcare needs are obese compared with 15 percent of children of the same ages without special healthcare needs.
- Annual healthcare costs of obesity that are related to disability are estimated at approximately $44 billion.

In the United States

- More than one-third of adults—more than 72 million people—in the United States are obese.
- Obesity rates are significantly higher among racial and ethnic groups. Non-Hispanic Blacks or African Americans have a 51 percent higher obesity prevalence and Hispanics have a 21 percent higher obesity prevalence than non-Hispanic Whites.
- Annual healthcare costs of obesity for all adults in the United States were estimated to be as high as $147 billion dollars for 2008.

Health Consequences of Overweight and Obesity

Overweight and obesity increases the risk of a number of other conditions, including:

- Coronary heart disease (CHD)
- Type 2 diabetes
- Cancers (endometrial, breast, and colon)
- High blood pressure
- Lipid disorders (for example, high total cholesterol or high levels of triglycerides)
- Stroke
- Liver and gallbladder disease
- Sleep apnea and respiratory problems
- Osteoarthritis (OA) (a degeneration of cartilage and its underlying bone within a joint)
- Gynecological problems (abnormal periods, infertility)

Chapter 39

Physical Activity for People with Disabilities

Chapter Contents

Section 39.1—Exercise Guidelines... 432
Section 39.2—Yoga for People with Disabilities 437

Section 39.1

Exercise Guidelines

This section contains text excerpted from the following sources: Text in this section begins with excerpts from "Physical Activity Is for Everybody," Centers for Disease Control and Prevention (CDC), October 18, 2017; Text beginning with the heading "Adults with Disabilities" is excerpted from "Adults with Disabilities," Centers for Disease Control and Prevention (CDC), May 6, 2014. Reviewed July 2018; Text under the heading "Key Guidelines for Adults with Disabilities" is excerpted from "2008 Physical Activity Guidelines for Americans Summary," Centers for Disease Control and Prevention (CDC), July 27, 2018.

Everybody, including people with disabilities, needs physical activity for good health. However, nearly half of adults with disabilities who are able to be physically active don't get any aerobic physical activity. Physical activity plays an important role in maintaining health, well-being, and quality of life. According to the *Physical Activity Guidelines for Americans*, physical activity can help control weight, improve mental health, and lower the risk of early death, heart disease, type 2 diabetes, and some cancers. For people with disabilities, it can help improve the ability to do activities of daily living and be self-sufficient.

In the United States, about 1 in 5 people have a disability. A disability is any condition of the body or mind that makes it more difficult for the person with the condition to do certain activities and interact with the world around them. Disability does not equal poor health, and most adults with disabilities are able to participate in regular physical activity and avoid being inactive. However, nearly half of all adults with disabilities don't get any aerobic physical activity. Aerobic physical activity is when the body's large muscles move in a rhythmic manner for a sustained period of time, thus improving heart and lung fitness. Examples of aerobic activities that might be available to adults with disabilities include walking, water aerobics, swimming, hand-crank bicycling, and various wheelchair athletics.

Healthcare Providers Play a Role

Healthcare providers are in a key position to influence physical activity participation among their adult patients with disabilities. First, adults with disabilities are more likely than those without disabilities

Physical Activity for People with Disabilities

to visit a healthcare provider on a regular basis. In addition, they are more likely to be physically active if their provider recommends it.

Adults with Disabilities

More than 21 million U.S. adults 18–64 years of age have a disability. These are adults with serious difficulty walking or climbing stairs; hearing; seeing; or concentrating, remembering, or making decisions. Most adults with disabilities are able to participate in physical activity, yet nearly half of them get no aerobic physical activity. Physical activity benefits all adults, whether or not they have a disability, by reducing their risk of serious chronic diseases, such as heart disease, stroke, diabetes, and some cancers. Only 44 percent of adults with disabilities who visited a doctor in the past year were told by a doctor to get physical activity. Yet adults with disabilities were 82 percent more likely to be physically active if their doctor recommended it.

- Adults with disabilities are 3 times more likely to have heart disease, stroke, diabetes, or cancer than adults without disabilities.
- Nearly half of all adults with disabilities get no aerobic physical activity, an important health behavior to help avoid these chronic diseases.
- Adults with disabilities were 82 percent more likely to be physically active if their doctor recommended it.

The Problem

More adults with disabilities need to get physical activity. Adults with disabilities who get no physical activity are 50 percent more likely to have certain chronic diseases than those who get the recommended amount of physical activity.

- Aerobic physical activity can help all adults avoid costly and deadly chronic diseases such as heart disease, stroke, diabetes, and some cancers.
- 1 in 2 adults with disabilities get no aerobic physical activity compared with 1 in 4 adults without disabilities.
- Adults with mobility limitations (serious difficulty walking or climbing stairs) are the least likely to get any aerobic physical

activity. Nearly 6 in 10 of them do not get any aerobic physical activity.

- Adults with disabilities face physical and emotional barriers to getting aerobic physical activity, including:

  - Knowing about and getting to programs, places, and spaces where they can be physically active;

  - Having social support for physical activity;

  - Finding fitness and health professionals who can provide physical activity options that match their specific abilities.

Inactive

54% No chronic disease
46% 1 or more chronic diseases

Active

69% No chronic disease
31% 1 or more chronic diseases

SOURCE: CDC National Center for Health Statistics, National Health Interview Survey, 2009-2012.

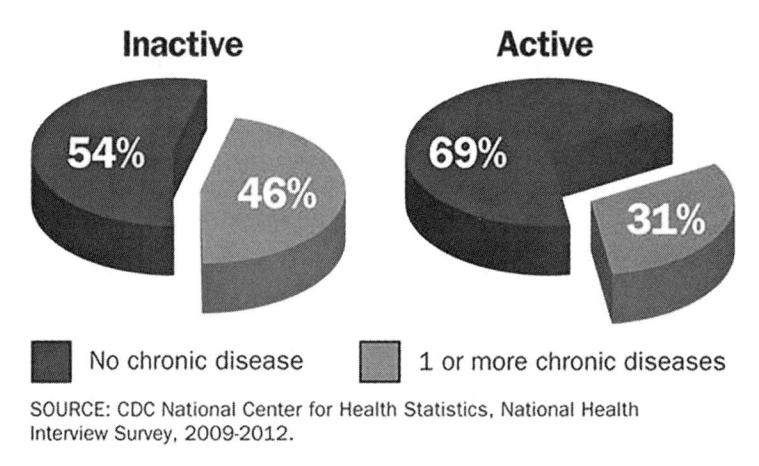

Figure 39.1. *Percentage of Adults Ages 18–64 with Disabilities Who Have One or More Chronic Diseases, by Aerobic Physical Activity Level*

Adults with disabilities are more likely to get physical activity if doctors recommend it.

- Only 44 percent of adults with disabilities who visited a doctor in the past year got a physical activity recommendation from their doctor.

- Adults with disabilities who got a physical activity recommendation from their doctor were 82 percent more likely to be physically active than those who did not get one.

- It is critical for doctors to know the *Physical Activity Guidelines* and help their patients with disabilities overcome barriers to reach their physical activity goals.

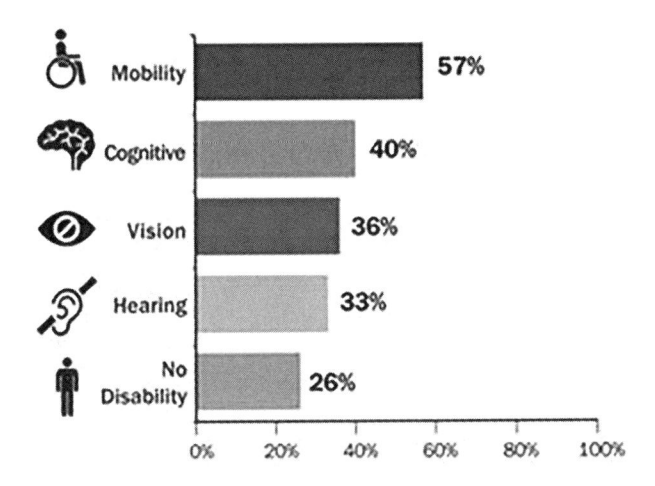

Physical Activity for People with Disabilities

Disability Type	Percentage
Mobility	57%
Cognitive	40%
Vision	36%
Hearing	33%
No Disability	26%

Mobility: Serious difficulty walking or climbing stairs

Cognitive: Serious difficulty concentrating, remembering or making decisions

Vision: Serious difficulty seeing, even wearing glasses

Hearing: Serious difficulty hearing

No Disability: Does not have any of the above disability types

SOURCE: CDC National Center for Health Statistics, National Health Interview Survey, 2009-2012.

Figure 39.2. *Percentage of Adults Ages 18–64 Who Get No Aerobic Physical Activity, by Disability Type*

What Can Be Done?

Adults with disabilities can:

- Talk to your doctor about how much and what kind of physical activity is right for you.
- Find opportunities to increase physical activity regularly in ways that meet your needs and abilities.
  - Regular aerobic physical activity increases heart and lung function; improves daily living activities and independence; decreases chances of developing chronic diseases, and; improves mental health.
- Start slowly based on your abilities and fitness level (e.g., be active for at least 10 minutes at a time, slowly increase activity over several weeks, if necessary).

Doctors and other health professionals can:

- Ask adults with disabilities about how much physical activity they get each week.

- Remind adults with disabilities to get regular physical activity. They should try to get at least 2 hours and 30 minutes a week of moderate-intensity physical activity. If this is not possible, patients with disabilities should avoid inactivity; some activity is better than none.

- Recommend physical activity options that match each person's specific abilities and connect him or her to resources that can help each person be physically active.

- Use Centers for Disease Control and Prevention's (CDC) website to find resources that can help you talk to patients with disabilities about physical activity.

States and communities can:

- Bring together adults with disabilities, health professionals, and community leaders to address resource needs to increase physical activity.

- Make sure physical activity, recreation, and sport-based program opportunities are accessible to adults with disabilities.

- Incorporate community features such as proper curb cuts on sidewalks, ramps for wheelchair access, and well-maintained trails to improve safe access to public places for physical activity.

- Encourage fitness and recreation facilities to have low-counter front desks for wheelchair users, family changing areas in locker rooms, push-button operated doors, and elevators.

Federal government is:

- Funding national and state programs to develop physical activity programs for adults with disabilities.

- Measuring state and national progress towards getting all U.S. adults physically active through the Disability and Health Data System (DHDS) and other systems.

- Providing accessible and high-quality healthcare to adults with disabilities by improving training and cultural competency for doctors and other health professionals.

Key Guidelines for Adults with Disabilities

- Adults with disabilities, who are able to, should get at least 150 minutes a week of moderate-intensity, or 75 minutes a week of vigorous-intensity aerobic activity, or an equivalent combination of moderate- and vigorous-intensity aerobic activity. Aerobic activity should be performed in episodes of at least 10 minutes, and preferably, it should be spread throughout the week.

- Adults with disabilities, who are able to, should also do muscle-strengthening activities of moderate or high intensity that involve all major muscle groups on 2 or more days a week, as these activities provide additional health benefits.

- When adults with disabilities are not able to meet the *Physical Activity Guidelines*, they should engage in regular physical activity according to their abilities and should avoid inactivity.

- Adults with disabilities should consult their healthcare provider about the amounts and types of physical activity that are appropriate for their abilities.

Section 39.2

Yoga for People with Disabilities

"Yoga for People with Disabilities,"
© 2018 Omnigraphics. Reviewed July 2018.

Yoga is an ancient spiritual practice that emerged in India from six philosophical schools of thought, or Shastras. The traditional purpose of yoga has been the attainment of self-knowledge by transcendence of the ego, characterized by inward transformation. Research confirms that yoga can offer people who are disabled overall health benefits and help to prevent disease when it is practiced alongside other regular medical treatment and therapies. Yoga should also be practiced in combination with a healthy diet and exercise.

Yoga is practiced as a spiritual discipline in Hinduism, Buddhism, and Jainism, each of which focus on self-enlightenment, or self-actualization, as the ultimate goal in life. There are many different styles of yoga—Anusara, Ashtanga, Bikram, Hatha, Iyengar, Jivamukti, Kripalu, Kundalini, Sivananda, and Vinyasa; however, Hatha yoga is one of the most popular forms practiced in the West.

Hatha Yoga

Hatha yoga is known as a discipline of force. The style is primarily known for its therapeutic value of bringing healing to the mind and the body. The practice emphasizes mastery over the body by achieving a spiritual state in which the mind is withdrawn from external factors. Hatha yoga helps practitioners develop strength, flexibility, relaxation, and mental concentration.

Hatha yoga involves postures and asanas that stem from ancient beliefs. The asanas are ideal for meditation and help the body rise above bodily consciousness. It is important to maintain a straight spine while practicing postures and asanas, as this allows the energy to flow freely upward and a state of immobility causes one to become aware of the inner energies of the body.

Health Benefits of Yoga

Research has confirmed the benefits of yoga for the disabled, including the following:

- Yoga is considered safe for people with high blood pressure, heart disease, and body aches and pains—including lower back pain.
- Yoga significantly decreases the secretion of cortisol—the hormone responsible for stress—and improves overall mental health.
- Research has shown that, among those practicing yoga, feelings of anxiety have been drastically reduced.
- Yoga improves heart health by lowering cholesterol levels. When complemented by changes in diet and life style, yoga can also lower blood pressure and reduce the risk of heart disease.
- Findings also show that yoga can reduce chronic inflammation.
- Yoga helps to improve quality of sleep, reduces pain and fatigue, and enhances your spiritual well-being.

- Studies have shown that yoga improves the physical function of people affected by arthritis and joint-related pain.
- Yoga improves flexibility and balance and when incorporated with breathing exercises and improves lung function.
- There is increasing evidence that yoga can help to relieve migraines when the vagus nerve is stimulated.
- Some studies have shown that yoga can be an effective method for practicing mindfulness and helping to control one's eating habits.
- Yoga increases strength in the upper body, builds endurance, and helps in weight loss.

Yoga Instruction for Children with Disabilities

Yoga is also proven to be therapeutic for disabled children, especially those with Down syndrome, cerebral palsy (CP), autism, attention deficiency disorder (ADD), attention deficiency hyperactivity disorder (ADHD), and learning difficulties.

References

1. "13 Benefits of Yoga That Are Supported by Science," Healthline Media, n.d.
2. "Teaching Yoga to Children with Special Needs," Yoga U, n.d.
3. "Hatha Yoga," Anandha Sangha Worldwide, n.d.
4. "Yoga for Children and Young People's Mental Health and Well-Being: Research Review and Reflections on the Mental Health Potentials of Yoga," April 2, 2014.
5. "The Origin of Yoga in Daily Life," Yoga in Daily Life, n.d.
6. "Yoga—A Guide," Focus on Disability, n.d.
7. Pizer, Ann. "Most Popular Types of Yoga Explained," May 25, 2018.

Chapter 40

Personal Hygiene for People with Disabilities

Chapter Contents

Section 40.1—Dental Care 442
Section 40.2—How to Bathe Someone with a
  Disability 447

Section 40.1

Dental Care

This section includes text excerpted from "Dental Care Everyday—A Caregiver's Guide," National Institute of Dental and Craniofacial Research (NIDCR), February 2012. Reviewed July 2018.

Taking care of someone with a developmental disability requires patience and skill. As a caregiver, you know this as well as anyone does. You also know how challenging it is to help that person with dental care. It takes planning, time, and the ability to manage physical, mental, and behavioral problems. Dental care isn't always easy, but you can make it work for you and the person you help. This booklet will show you how to help someone brush, floss, and have a healthy mouth. Everyone needs dental care every day. Brushing and flossing are crucial activities that affect our health. In fact, dental care is just as important to your client's health and daily routine as taking medications and getting physical exercise. A healthy mouth helps people eat well, avoid pain and tooth loss, and feel good about themselves.

Getting Started

Location. The bathroom isn't the only place to brush someone's teeth. For example, the kitchen or dining room may be more comfortable. Instead of standing next to a bathroom sink, allow the person to sit at a table. Place the toothbrush, toothpaste, floss, and a bowl and glass of water on the table within easy reach. No matter what location you choose, make sure you have good light. You can't help someone brush unless you can see inside that person's mouth.

Behavior. Problem behavior can make dental care difficult. Try these ideas and see what works for you.

- At first, dental care can be frightening to some people. Try the "tell-show-do" approach to deal with this natural reaction. Tell your client about each step before you do it. For example, explain how you'll help him or her brush and what it feels like. Show how you're going to do each step before you do it. Also, it might help to let your client hold and feel the toothbrush and floss. Do the steps in the same way that you've explained them.

Personal Hygiene for People with Disabilities

- Give your client time to adjust to dental care. Be patient as that person learns to trust you working in and around his or her mouth.
- Use your voice and body to communicate that you care. Give positive feedback often to reinforce good behavior.
- Have a routine for dental care. Use the same technique at the same time and place every day. Many people with developmental disabilities accept dental care when it's familiar. A routine might soothe fears or help eliminate problem behavior.
- Be creative. Some caregivers allow their client to hold a favorite toy or special item for comfort. Others make dental care a game or play a person's favorite music. If none of these ideas helps, ask your client's dentist or dental hygienist for advice.

Three Steps to a Healthy Mouth

Like everyone else, people with developmental disabilities can have a healthy mouth if these three steps are followed:

1. Brush every day
2. Floss every day
3. Visit a dentist regularly

Step 1. Brush Every Day

If the person you care for is unable to brush, these suggestions might be helpful.

- First, wash your hands and put on disposable gloves. Sit or stand where you can see all of the surfaces of the teeth.
- Be sure to use a regular or power toothbrush with soft bristles.
- Use a pea-size amount of toothpaste with fluoride, or none at all. Toothpaste bothers people who have swallowing problems. If this is the case for the person you care for, brush with water instead.
- Brush the front, back, and top of each tooth. Gently brush back and forth in short strokes.
- Gently brush the tongue after you brush the teeth.
- Help the person rinse with plain water. Give people who can't rinse a drink of water or consider sweeping the mouth with a finger wrapped in gauze.

Get a new toothbrush with soft bristles every 3 months, after a contagious illness, or when the bristles are worn.

If the person you care for can brush but needs some help, the ideas listed on the next page might work for you. You may think of other creative ways to solve brushing problems based on your client's special needs.

Make the toothbrush easier to hold.

The same kind of Velcro® strap used to hold food utensils is helpful for some people.

Others attach the brush to the hand with a wide elastic or rubber band. Make sure the band isn't too tight.

Make the toothbrush handle bigger.

You can also cut a small slit in the side of a tennis ball and slide it onto the handle of the toothbrush.

You can buy a toothbrush with a large handle, or you can slide a bicycle grip onto the handle. Attaching foam tubing, available from home healthcare catalogs, is also helpful.

Try other toothbrush options.

A power toothbrush might make brushing easier. Take the time to help your client get used to one.

Guide the toothbrush.

Help brush by placing your hand very gently over your client's hand and guiding the toothbrush. If that doesn't work, you may need to brush the teeth yourself.

Step 2. Floss Every Day

Flossing cleans between the teeth where a toothbrush can't reach. Many people with disabilities need a caregiver to help them floss. Flossing is a tough job that takes a lot of practice. Waxed, unwaxed, flavored, or plain floss all do the same thing. The person you care for might like one more than another, or a certain type might be easier to use.

- Use a string of floss 18 inches long. Wrap that piece around the middle finger of each hand.

- Grip the floss between the thumb and index finger of each hand.

- Start with the lower front teeth, then floss the upper front teeth. Next, work your way around to all the other teeth.

Personal Hygiene for People with Disabilities

- Work the floss gently between the teeth until it reaches the gumline. Curve the floss around each tooth and slip it under the gum. Slide the floss up and down. Do this for both sides of every tooth, one side at a time.

- Adjust the floss a little as you move from tooth to tooth so the floss is clean for each one.

Try a floss holder.

If you have trouble flossing, try using a floss holder instead of holding the floss with your fingers.

The dentist may prescribe a special rinse for your client. Fluoride rinses can help prevent cavities. Chlorhexidine rinses fight germs that cause gum disease. Follow the dentist's instructions and tell your client not to swallow any of the rinse. Ask the dentist for creative ways to use rinses for a client with swallowing problems.

Positioning Your Body: Where to Sit or Stand

Keeping people safe when you clean their mouth is important. Experts in providing dental care for people with developmental disabilities recommend the following positions for caregivers. If you work in a group home or related facility, get permission from your supervisor before trying any of these positions.

Step 3. Visit a Dentist Regularly

Your client should have regular dental appointments. Professional cleanings are just as important as brushing and flossing every day.

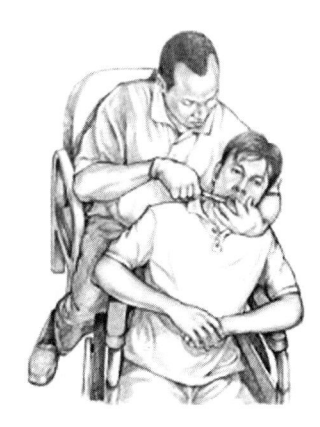

Figure 40.1. *Helping a Disabled Person Brush While Sitting*

Regular examinations can identify problems before they cause unnecessary pain. As is the case with dental care at home, it may take time for the person you care for to become comfortable at the dental office. A "get acquainted" visit with no treatment provided might help: The person can meet the dental team, sit in the dental chair if he or she wishes, and receive instructions on how to brush and floss. Such a visit can go a long way toward making dental appointments easier.

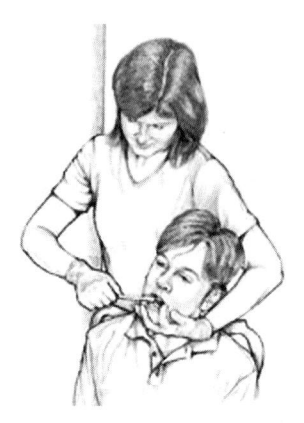

Figure 40.2. *Helping a Disabled Person Brush While Standing*

Prepare for Every Dental Visit: Your Role

- Be prepared for every appointment. You're an important source of information for the dentist. If you have questions about what the dentist will need to know, call the office before the appointment.

- Know the person's dental history. Keep a record of what happens at each visit. Talk to the dentist about what occurred at the last appointment. Remind the dental team of what worked and what didn't.

- Bring a complete medical history. The dentist needs each patient's medical history before treatment can begin.

- Bring a list of all the medications the person you care for is taking and all known allergies. Bring all insurance, billing, and legal information. Know who is responsible for payment. The dentist may need permission, or legal consent, before treatment can begin. Know who can legally give consent.

- Be on time.

Section 40.2

How to Bathe Someone with a Disability

"How to Bathe Someone with a Disability,"
© 2018 Omnigraphics. Reviewed July 2018.

Bathing someone with a disability takes time and patience, but caring for them is easier when you are prepared. Being prepared requires gathering as much information as possible about the person who is disabled. It is important to consider the following factors when bathing someone with a disability.

Bathing a Disabled Person

It is important to prepare the bath area properly before bathing a disabled person. Do not undress the person until you have organized the bathing area and arranged the clothes the disabled person will worn after the bath. Assist the person on slippery surfaces and hold him or her carefully when moving them for their bath. Make sure to follow these instructions:

- Keep bath water or water in the washing basin at room temperature. A temperature of less than 115° F prevents scalding and is considered safe for a bath.

- Keep the disabled person warm. Cover her or him with a blanket to provide privacy and warmth.

- Use a washcloth to clean the eyes. Gently wipe the eyes from the inner corners to the outward area. Rinse the cloth and leave it in the warm water.

- Use the warm washcloth to wipe the face, neck and ears. Keep rinsing the washcloth in the warm water each time you clean a portion of the body.

- Apply soap to the washcloth and clean the arms, hands, and the underarm area. Dry sensitive areas with a towel to prevent chafing.

- Add more soap as required, and wipe gently with a towel after cleaning the legs and feet with the soapy washcloth.

- If you are using a basin of water, empty the basin and refill it with warm water. Pour body lotions into the basin and use them to complete the bath.

- Lay the disabled person on his or her side and place a towel on the person's back. Check the temperature of the water before cleaning the genital area. Use separate washcloths to clean the genital area and the anus.
- Rinse the washcloth in the basin of clean water and wipe the genitals with a towel. Return the cloth to its basin and dry the area with the towel. Make sure to clean the genitals daily to prevent any form of infections.
- Use a separate washcloth to wash the anus and surrounding area, being careful to avoid contact with genitals.
- After removing the blanket, help the person dress into a set of clean clothes.

It is important to determine if the disabled person is comfortable with the way that you are assisting her or him. Communicate regularly as you bathe the person and ask if there are ways to offer improved assistance.

Bathing Aids for Disabled People

A number of reasonably priced bathing aids can make bathing a disabled person easier or allow disabled people to bathe safely without assistance. A list of a few temporary solutions follows:

- Attach a suction handrail to the bathtub to allow a disabled person to remain steady while getting into and out of the bathtub or shower.
- Attach a shower chair with a backrest or a freestanding shower stool with suction cups to the bottom of the bathtub or shower to ensure a safe bath or help a disabled person to access and use a shower safely and easily.
- Contact local disability resource groups or charities to find out how to make your home accessible for disabled people.

For people with disabilities, finding a way to care for yourself safely is one of the best ways to recover your independence and freedom without having to always rely on others.

References

1. "Be Prepared! Sport and Active Recreation Programs for People with a Disability. A Resource for Volunteers and Staff," La Trobe University. 2014.

2. "Bathing Aids for Disabled People; The Whys and Wherefores of What Can Help When Washing Becomes a Bit of a Chore," Invacare Corporation. 2018.

3. "How to Bathe the Handicapped," Our Everyday Life. September 28, 2017.

Chapter 41

Bowel and Bladder Problems Associated with Disability

What Is a Bowel Control Problem?

You have a bowel control problem if you accidentally pass solid or liquid stool or mucus from your rectum. Bowel control problems include being unable to hold a bowel movement until you reach a toilet and passing stool into your underwear without being aware of it happening. Stool, also called feces, is solid waste that is passed as a bowel movement and includes undigested food, bacteria, mucus, and dead cells. Mucus is a clear liquid that coats and protects tissues in your digestive system.

A bowel control problem—also called fecal incontinence—can be upsetting and embarrassing. Most people with a bowel control problem feel ashamed and try to hide the problem. They may not want to leave the house for fear of losing bowel control in public. They may withdraw from friends and family. Bowel control problems are often caused by a medical issue and can be treated. If you have a bowel control problem,

---

This chapter contains text excerpted from the following sources: Text beginning with the heading "What Is a Bowel Control Problem?" is excerpted from "What I Need to Know about Bowel Control," National Institute of Diabetes and Digestive and Kidney Diseases (NIDDK), December 2012. Reviewed July 2018; Text beginning with the heading "Bladder Problems" is excerpted from "Bladder Control Problems and Nerve Disease," National Institute of Diabetes and Digestive and Kidney Diseases (NIDDK), June 2012. Reviewed July 2018.

451

don't be afraid to talk about it with your doctor. Your doctor may be able to help.

How Does Bowel Control Work?

Bowel control relies on the muscles and nerves of your anus and rectum working together to:

- Hold stool in your rectum
- Let you know when your rectum is full
- Release stool when you're ready

Ringlike muscles called sphincters close tightly around your anus to hold stool in your rectum until you're ready to release the stool. Pelvic floor muscles support your rectum and a woman's vagina and also help with bowel control.

How Are Bowel Control Problems Treated?

Treatment for bowel control problems may include one or more of the following:

- Eating, diet, and nutrition
- Medicines
- Bowel training
- Pelvic floor exercises and biofeedback
- Surgery
- Electrical stimulation

Eating, Diet, and Nutrition

Changes in your diet that may improve your bowel control problem include:

- Eating the right amount of fiber. Fiber can help with diarrhea and constipation. Fiber is found in fruits, vegetables, whole grains, and beans. Fiber supplements sold in a pharmacy or health food store are another common source of fiber to treat bowel control problems. The Academy of Nutrition and Dietetics recommends getting 20–35 grams of fiber a day for adults and "age plus five" grams for children. A 7-year-old child, for

Bowel and Bladder Problems Associated with Disability

example, should get "7 plus five," or 12, grams of fiber a day. Fiber should be added to your diet slowly to avoid bloating.

- Getting plenty to drink. Drinking eight 8-ounce glasses of liquid a day may help prevent constipation. Water is a good choice. You should avoid drinks with caffeine, alcohol, milk, or carbonation if they give you diarrhea.

Medicines

If diarrhea is causing your bowel control problem, medicine may help. Your doctor may suggest using bulk laxatives to help you make more solid stools that are easier to control. Your doctor may also suggest antidiarrheal medicines that slow down your bowels and help control the problem.

Bowel Training

Training yourself to have bowel movements at certain times during the day—such as after meals—may help. Developing a regular pattern may take a while, so don't give up if it doesn't work right away.

Pelvic Floor Exercises and Biofeedback

Exercises that strengthen your pelvic floor muscles can help with bowel control. To do pelvic floor exercises, you squeeze and relax these muscles 50–100 times a day. The trick is finding the right muscles to squeeze. Your doctor can help make sure you're doing the exercises the right way. Biofeedback therapy may also help you learn to do the exercises correctly. Biofeedback therapy is painless and uses a machine to let you know when you are squeezing the right muscles. You practice what you learn at home. Success with pelvic floor exercises depends on what is causing your bowel control problem, how severe the problem is, and your motivation and ability to follow your doctor's recommendations.

Bladder Problems

For the urinary system to do its job, muscles and nerves must work together to hold urine in the bladder and then release it at the right time. Nerves carry messages from the bladder to the brain to let it know when the bladder is full. They also carry messages from the brain to the bladder, telling muscles either to tighten or release. A nerve problem might affect your bladder control if the nerves that are supposed to carry messages between the brain and the bladder do not work properly.

What Bladder Control Problems Does Nerve Damage Cause?

Nerves that work poorly can lead to three different kinds of bladder control problems.

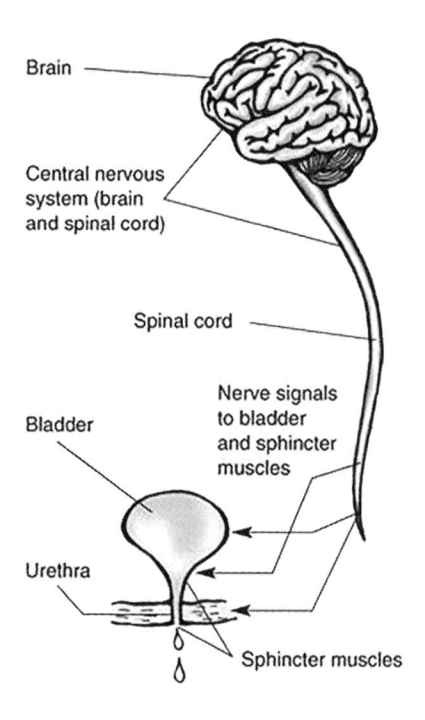

Figure 41.1. *Nerve Signals to Bladder and Sphincter Muscles*

Overactive bladder. Damaged nerves may send signals to the bladder at the wrong time, causing its muscles to squeeze without warning. The symptoms of overactive bladder include:

- Urinary frequency—defined as urination eight or more times a day or two or more times at night

- Urinary urgency—the sudden, strong need to urinate immediately

- Urge incontinence—leakage of urine that follows a sudden, strong urge to urinate

Bowel and Bladder Problems Associated with Disability

Poor control of sphincter muscles. Sphincter muscles surround the urethra and keep it closed to hold urine in the bladder. If the nerves to the sphincter muscles are damaged, the muscles may become loose and allow leakage or stay tight when you are trying to release urine.

Urine retention. For some people, nerve damage means their bladder muscles do not get the message that it is time to release urine or are too weak to completely empty the bladder. If the bladder becomes too full, urine may back up and the increasing pressure may damage the kidneys. Or urine that stays too long may lead to an infection in the kidneys or bladder. Urine retention may also lead to overflow incontinence.

How Will the Doctor Test for Nerve Damage and Bladder Control Problems?

Any evaluation for a health problem begins with a medical history and a general physical examination. Your doctor can use this information to narrow down the possible causes for your bladder problem.

If nerve damage is suspected, the doctor may need to test both the bladder itself and the nervous system, including the brain. Three different kinds of tests might be used:

- **Urodynamics.** These tests involve measuring pressure in the bladder while it is being filled to see how much it can hold and then checking to see whether the bladder empties completely and efficiently.

- **Imaging.** The doctor may use different types of equipment— X-rays, magnetic resonance imaging (MRI), and computerized tomography (CT) scans to take pictures of the urinary tract and nervous system, including the brain.

- **EEG and EMG.** An electroencephalograph (EEG) is a test in which wires with pads are placed on the forehead to sense any dysfunction in the brain. The doctor may also use an electromyograph (EMG), which uses wires with pads placed on the lower abdomen to test the nerves and muscles of the bladder.

What Are the Treatments for Overactive Bladder?

The treatment for a bladder control problem depends on the cause of the nerve damage and the type of voiding dysfunction that results.

In the case of overactive bladder, your doctor may suggest a number of strategies, including bladder training, electrical stimulation, drug therapy, and, in severe cases where all other treatments have failed, surgery.

Bladder training. Your doctor may ask you to keep a bladder diary—a record of your fluid intake, trips to the bathroom, and episodes of urine leakage. This record may indicate a pattern and suggest ways to avoid accidents by making a point of using the bathroom at certain times of the day—a practice called timed voiding. As you gain control, you can extend the time between trips to the bathroom. Bladder training also includes Kegel exercises to strengthen the muscles that hold in urine.

Electrical stimulation. Mild electrical pulses can be used to stimulate the nerves that control the bladder and sphincter muscles. Depending on which nerves the doctor plans to treat, these pulses can be given through the vagina or anus, or by using patches on the skin. Another method is a minor surgical procedure to place the electric wire near the tailbone. This procedure involves two steps. First, the wire is placed under the skin and connected to a temporary stimulator, which you carry with you for several days. If your condition improves during this trial period, then the wire is placed next to the tailbone and attached to a permanent stimulator under your skin. The U.S. Food

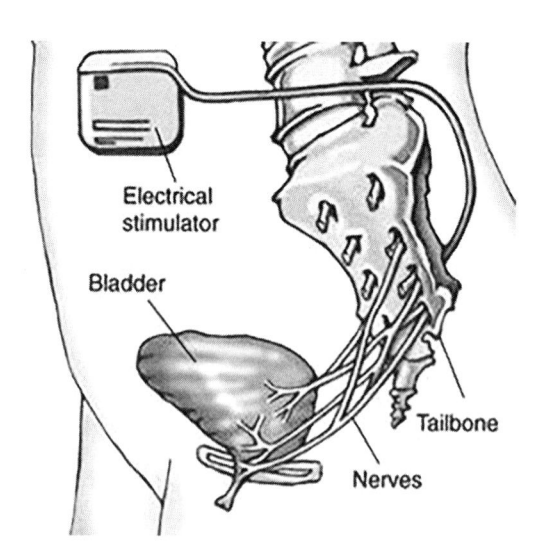

Figure 41.2. *Electrical Stimulation*

and Drug Administration (FDA) has approved this device, marketed as the InterStim system, to treat urge incontinence, urgency-frequency syndrome, and urinary retention in patients for whom other treatments have not worked.

Drug therapy. Different drugs can affect the nerves and muscles of the urinary tract in different ways.

- Drugs that relax bladder muscles and prevent bladder spasms include oxybutynin chloride (Ditropan), tolterodine (Detrol), hyoscyamine (Levsin), and propantheline bromide (Pro-Banthine), which belong to the class of drugs called anticholinergics. Their most common side effect is dry mouth, although large doses may cause blurred vision, constipation, a faster heartbeat, and flushing. A new patch delivery system for oxybutynin (Oxytrol) may decrease side effects. Ditropan XL and Detrol LA are timed-release formulations that deliver a low level of the drug continuously in the body. These drugs have the advantage of once-a-day administration. In 2004, the FDA approved trospium chloride (Sanctura), darifenacin (Enablex), and solifenacin succinate (VESIcare) for the treatment of overactive bladder.

- Drugs for depression that also relax bladder muscles include imipramine hydrochloride (Tofranil), a tricyclic antidepressant. Side effects may include fatigue, dry mouth, dizziness, blurred vision, nausea, and insomnia.

Additional drugs are being evaluated for the treatment of overactive bladder and may soon receive FDA approval.

Surgery. In extreme cases, when incontinence is severe and other treatments have failed, surgery may be considered. The bladder may be made larger through an operation known as augmentation cystoplasty, in which a part of the diseased bladder is replaced with a section taken from the patient's bowel. This operation may improve the ability to store urine but may make the bladder more difficult to empty, making regular catheterization necessary. Additional risks of surgery include the bladder breaking open and leaking urine into the body, bladder stones, mucus in the bladder, and infection.

How Do You Do Kegel Exercises?

Kegel exercises strengthen the muscles that hold up the bladder and keep it closed. The first step in doing Kegel exercises is to find the right muscles. Imagine you are trying to stop yourself from passing gas. Squeeze the muscles you would use. If you sense a "pulling" feeling, those are the right muscles for pelvic exercises.

Try not to squeeze other muscles at the same time. Be careful not to tighten your stomach, legs, or buttocks. Squeezing the wrong muscles can put more pressure on your bladder control muscles. Just squeeze the pelvic muscles. Don't hold your breath.

At first, find a quiet spot to practice—your bathroom or bedroom—so you can concentrate. Pull in the pelvic muscles and hold for a count of 3. Then relax for a count of 3. Repeat, but don't overdo it. Work up to 3 sets of 10 repeats. Start doing your pelvic muscle exercises lying down. This position is the easiest because the muscles do not need to work against gravity. When your muscles get stronger, do your exercises sitting or standing. Working against gravity is like adding more weight.

Be patient. Don't give up. It takes just 5 minutes a day. You may not feel your bladder control improve for 3–6 weeks. Still, most people do notice an improvement after a few weeks.

Some people with nerve damage cannot tell whether they are doing Kegel exercises correctly. If you are not sure, ask your doctor or nurse to examine you while you try to do them. If you are not squeezing the right muscles, you can still learn proper Kegel exercises by doing special training with biofeedback, electrical stimulation, or both.

What Are the Treatments for Lack of Coordination between the Bladder and Urethra?

The job of the sphincter muscles is to hold urine in the bladder by squeezing the urethra shut. If the urethral sphincter fails to stay closed, urine may leak out of the bladder. When nerve signals are coordinated properly, the sphincter muscles relax to allow urine to pass through the urethra as the bladder contracts to push out urine. If the signals are not coordinated, the bladder and the sphincter may contract at the same time, so urine cannot pass easily.

Drug therapy for an uncoordinated bladder and urethra. Scientists have not yet found a drug that works selectively on the urethral sphincter muscles, but drugs used to reduce muscle spasms or tremors are sometimes used to help the sphincter relax. Baclofen (Lioresal) is prescribed for muscle spasms or cramping in patients with multiple sclerosis and spinal injuries. Diazepam (Valium) can be taken as a muscle relaxant or to reduce anxiety. Drugs called alpha-adrenergic blockers (AAB) can also be used to relax the sphincter. Examples of these drugs are alfuzosin (Uroxatral), tamsulosin (Flomax), terazosin (Hytrin), and doxazosin (Cardura). The main side effects are low blood pressure, dizziness, fainting, and nasal congestion. All of these drugs have been used to relax the urethral sphincter in people whose sphincter does not relax well on its own.

Botox injection. Botulinum toxin type A (Botox) is best known as a cosmetic treatment for facial wrinkles. Doctors have also found that botulinum toxin is useful in blocking spasms like eye ticks or relaxing muscles in patients with multiple sclerosis. Urologists have found that injecting botulinum toxin into the tissue surrounding the sphincter can help it to relax. Although the FDA has approved botulinum toxin only for facial cosmetic purposes, researchers are studying the safety and effectiveness of botulinum toxin injection into the sphincter for possible FDA approval in the future.

What Are the Treatments for Urine Retention?

Urine retention may occur either because the bladder wall muscles cannot contract or because the sphincter muscles cannot relax.

Catheter. A catheter is a thin tube that can be inserted through the urethra into the bladder to allow urine to flow into a collection bag. If you are able to place the catheter yourself, you can learn to carry out the procedure at regular intervals, a practice called clean intermittent catheterization. Some patients cannot place their own catheters because nerve damage affects their hand coordination as well as their voiding function. These patients need to have a caregiver place the catheter for them at regular intervals. If regular catheter placement is not feasible, the patients may need to have an indwelling catheter that can be changed less often. Indwelling catheters have several risks, including infection, bladder stones, and bladder tumors. However, if the bladder cannot be emptied any other way, then the catheter is the only way to stop the buildup of urine in the bladder that can damage the kidneys.

Urethral stent. Stents are small tube-like devices inserted into the urethra and allowed to expand, like a spring, widening the opening for urine to flow out. Stents can help prevent urine backup when the bladder wall and sphincter contract at the same time because of improper nerve signals. However, stents can cause problems if they move or lead to infection.

Surgery. Men may consider a surgery that removes the external sphincter—a sphincterotomy—or a piece of it—a sphincter resection-to prevent urinary retention. The surgeon will pass a thin instrument through the urethra to deliver electrical or laser energy that burns away sphincter tissue. Possible complications include bleeding that requires a transfusion and, rarely, problems with erections. This procedure causes loss of urine control and requires the patient to collect urine by wearing an external catheter that fits over the penis like a condom. No external collection device is available for women.

Urinary diversion. If other treatments fail and urine regularly backs up and damages the kidneys, the doctor may recommend a urinary diversion, a procedure that may require an outside collection bag attached to a stoma, a surgically created opening where urine passes out of the body. Another form of urinary diversion replaces the bladder with a continent urinary reservoir, an internal pouch made from sections of the bowel or other tissue. This method allows the person to store urine inside the body until a catheter is used to empty it through a stoma.

Chapter 42

Pressure Sores: What They Are and How to Prevent Them

Pressure sores are areas of damaged skin caused by staying in one position for too long. They commonly form where your bones are close to your skin, such as your ankles, back, elbows, heels, and hips. You are at risk if you are bedridden, use a wheelchair, or are unable to change your position. Pressure sores can cause serious infections, some of which are life threatening. They can be a problem for people in nursing homes.

You can prevent the sores by:

- Keeping skin clean and dry
- Changing position every two hours
- Using pillows and products that relieve pressure

Pressure sores have a variety of treatments. Advanced sores are slow to heal, so early treatment is best.

This chapter contains text excerpted from the following sources: Text in this chapter begins with excerpts from "Pressure Sores," MedlinePlus, National Institutes of Health (NIH), May 2, 2016; Text beginning with the heading "Risk Factors" is excerpted from "Prevention and Management of Acute and Chronic Wounds," Federal Bureau of Prisons (BOP), March 2014. Reviewed July 2018.

Risk Factors

Patients at increased risk include those with altered sensation or limited mobility (e.g., in the case of spinal cord injury, stroke, or severe altered mental status). Any person hospitalized is at greater risk, especially inmates who are secured to the bed, limiting their mobility. Additional risk factors include those who are severely deconditioned, had a recent weight loss related to an illness, are advanced in age, have poor nutritional intake, have incontinence of either bowel or bladder, or have a medical reason to have the head of their bed elevated at or above 30 degrees for extended periods of time. In inpatient settings, a validated risk assessment tool such as the Braden Scale is commonly used to stratify risk and select appropriate interventions to decrease the possibility of ulcerations.

Mechanism of Injury

Pressure ulcerations are caused by pressure that is of sufficient force to occlude blood flow, causing tissue necrosis (tissue death). Shearing and friction are two additional mechanisms that contribute to pressure ulcers. Shearing is a deeper force where tissue is pulled away from deeper attachments. This also decreases blood flow through vessels around the area of injury. This causes undermining around wounds. Friction is the force of two surfaces moving across each other causing blistering or the removal of the top layers of the skin. This opens the tissue to invasion by microorganisms. The amount of pressure or shear needed to cause damage depends on the patient. In general, high pressure over relatively short times to moderate amounts of direct pressure over longer time periods can cause tissue damage. High-risk areas include any place where the bone is very close to the skin or the bone protrudes from the underlying weight bearing structures. The most common places include the lying surfaces of the pelvis (hips/greater trochanters and the coccyx-sacral area), the sitting surfaces of the pelvis (ischial tuberosities), and the posterior surface of the heels.

Characteristics

Pressure ulcers predominantly develop over bony surfaces. Location is often the primary sign that a wound is due to pressure injury. As described below, pressure ulcers present in multiple stages of ulceration, ranging from nonblanchable, discolored skin to deep craters extending to the bone.

- **Pressure Ulcer Stages:** In 2007, the National Pressure Ulcer Advisory Panel (NPUAP) provided updated guidance on the stages of pressure ulcers. Detailed descriptions and illustrations are available at the NPUAP website. The NPUAP scale, which is for pressure ulcers only, includes these categories: Stage I, Stage II, Stage III, Stage IV, Unstageable, and Suspected Deep Tissue Injury.

Appropriate staging should occur as soon as possible. Identifying that an ulcer is present upon admission decreases the potential for litigation in the future. Staging should be accomplished by the team only one time, unless the initial stage increases, or the ulcer is initially staged as either suspected deep tissue injury or unstageable. In the case of suspected deep tissue injury and unstageable ulcers, resolution of the necrotic tissue is necessary before definitive staging can be accomplished.

If there is no certainty regarding the stage—or whether this is, in fact, a pressure ulcer—it should just be described.

- **Reverse Staging/Healing Pressure Ulcers:** Healing pressure ulcers are not progressively staged in reverse as they heal. For example, a healing Stage III ulcer does not become a Stage II as it gets shallower; it remains a healing Stage III ulcer until closed. Once closed, it is a healed Stage III ulcer.

- **Blanchable Erythema:** Erythema over bony prominences that blanches is not considered a pressure ulcer, but may be an early indication of increased risk. It should be considered as a warning that pressure ulcer development is likely.

- **Development of Cellulitis:** If the pressure ulcer develops cellulitis, consider referral if appropriate treatment cannot be established. The development of cellulitis can expose the underlying bony structure to microorganisms, increasing the likelihood of developing osteomyelitis. If referral is not initiated, closely monitor the patient.

- **Possibility of Osteomyelitis:** If the ulceration extends close to the bone, if the bone is palpable, if the patient develops cellulitis, or if the wound is not healing in a timely manner, osteomyelitis should be ruled out. The presentation of osteomyelitis may not be obvious. Wounds with an underlying chronic osteomyelitis often appear as a small opening that tracks toward the bone, and may even repeatedly close and re-open in the absence of ongoing pressure injury.

Diagnostic Tests

Basic Testing

- **Patient history** of the ulceration, along with observation of location and characteristics, is the initial diagnostic tool for pressure ulcers.

- **Examining the patient in his/her environment,** including the bed and wheelchair, if applicable, may assist in providing clues. Looking for the location of drainage on clothing or medical equipment is also helpful.

Advanced Testing

- **Laboratory screening:** Laboratory screening for osteomyelitis can be accomplished through the use of serum sedimentation rate and/or C-reactive protein. Elevation of these serum markers indicates an ongoing acute or chronic inflammatory process, and imaging is recommended.

- **Culture:** Cultures are recommended if cellulitis develops or when the wound fails to meet healing goals after the empirical use of topical antiseptics for 2–4 weeks. Results of the culture are used to guide antibiotic therapy in treating cellulitis, as well as by wound care consultants when selecting therapy for wounds that fail to heal. Routine swab cultures are usually discouraged, as they often reflect contaminants and only poorly reflect the organisms that are responsible for inhibiting healing. If a culture is needed, a biopsy is recommended. Routine wound cultures and antibiotic use (whether topical, oral, or intravenous) is discouraged in the absence of acute cellulitis. They will rarely provide for an effective treatment of osteomyelitis without surgical removal of the bone, and their use prior to surgical debridement can create significant resistance issues.

- **Imaging:** Plain radiographs can be taken in-house to assess for bony changes, but cannot definitively rule out early osteomyelitis. A magnetic resonance imaging (MRI) is the gold standard. If the patient has retained metal, then a computed tomography (CT) or Indium Bone Scan is recommended, but are not as sensitive. Involvement of a surgeon is also strongly recommended; even intravenous (IV) antibiotics alone will most likely suppress, but not clear, the infection. Unless an acute cellulitis or sepsis is confirmed, antibiotic therapy is of little value and can be harmful for the patient, often creating resistance issues. If osteomyelitis is confirmed, the patient must be referred for surgical debridement and management, which usually includes a lengthy course of IV antibiotics. Until this can be accomplished, healing is unlikely and stabilization is the goal. Consider using Dakin's 0.125 percent solution, once or twice a day, to decrease the number of microorganisms living on the surface of the wound.

Interventions to Alleviate Mechanism of Injury

Stopping the injury process should be the initial focus of treatment efforts and are more important than the type of dressing changes. For redistribution of pressure, the affected area can functionally be divided into the parts of the body affected when sitting and lying. Those parts of the body that make contact while in bed require offloading in bed. Those on the sitting surface of the body require offloading when seated, often in a wheelchair. Ulcers on the heels can occur in bed and in the wheelchair.

The following interventions should be considered—based on the stage, location, and number of pressure ulcers present:

- A pressure redistribution mattress or overlay for the bed if the ulcer is on the lying surface of the body (e.g., the sacrum to the mid buttocks, the hips, or the posterior heel). At a minimum, this would be a Group 1 support surface specialty overlay or mattress for treatment. The Centers for Medicaid and Medicaid Services (CMS) has recommendations for multiple levels of surfaces depending on stage, location, and number of ulcers.

- A pressure-redistributing cushion for patients with a sitting ulcer who use a wheelchair. CMS defines three levels of cushions. At a minimum, a CMS-defined "skin protection wheelchair seat cushion" that offers at least 4 centimeters of immersion should be issued.

- A specialty boot if a pressure ulcer is located on the heel or foot. There are a variety of specialty boots on the market for heel-offloading. Examples of specialty boots include Heelift® Suspension Boots, HEELMEDIX™ Heel Protectors, Waffle® Heel Protectors, or Rooke® Heel Float System™ Boots.

- Equipment to elevate heels off of the bed such as pillows, blankets, or specialty boots if there is an ulcer on the heel.

- A waterproof shower cushion to offload sitting ulcers during personal hygiene.

- Pressure mapping: If the patient has an ulcer on the sitting surface of the buttocks (especially over the ischial tuberosity) that is not meeting healing goals, then consideration of pressure mapping is appropriate. It is the gold standard to ensure appropriate pressure redistribution in a wheelchair. Pressure mapping is available at many hospitals and wound care clinics. Ultimately, the effectiveness of offloading is determined by healing. If the wound is meeting healing goals, then the strategies are deemed generally appropriate. If the wound is not meeting healing goals, pressure redistribution equipment and the patient's time spent in a wheelchair must be reevaluated.

Prevention Strategies for the Spinal Cord Injury Population

In the correctional environment, any patient with a spinal cord injury should be considered at high risk for pressure ulcerations, and prevention strategies should be taken, even in the absence of a current pressure ulcer. Patient education and specialty equipment should be considered for all of these patients.

At a minimum, considerations should be made for the following durable medical equipment:

- A pressure redistribution mattress or overlay for the bed: This would be a Group 1 support surface specialty overlay or mattress. CMS has recommendations for multiple levels of surfaces depending on stage, location, and number of ulcers.

- A pressure redistributing cushion for wheelchair use: CMS defines three levels of cushions. At a minimum, a CMS-defined "skin protection wheelchair seat cushion" that offers at least 4 centimeters of immersion should be issued.

- Equipment to elevate heels off of the bed (pillows, blankets, or specialty boots) if there is an ulcer on the heel. There are a variety of specialty boots on the market for heel offloading. Examples of specialty offloading boots include Heelift® Suspension Boots, HEELMEDIX™ Heel Protectors, Waffle® Heel Protectors, or Rooke® Heel Float System™ Boots.

Pressure Sores: What They Are and How to Prevent Them

- Firm-soled shoes for use in the wheelchair if the patient does not have an existing pressure ulcer on the foot that requires special equipment to offload foot ulcers.

- A waterproof shower cushion to prevent sitting ulcers during personal hygiene.

Specific Topical Treatment Recommendations

Topical therapy should, in general, follow the recommendations discussed under the Basic Supportive Wound Care Algorithm. Avoid over-packing pressure ulcers as this can increase the amount of pressure on the wound bed over weight-bearing surfaces. In addition, if osteomyelitis is confirmed, the goal of therapy changes from healing to stabilization until surgical intervention is completed. Antibiotics are not warranted unless cellulitis develops. Antiseptics with a higher cytotoxic profile, such as Dakin's 0.125 percent solution, delivered on gauze once or twice a day, are recommended. This will decrease the number of microorganisms living on the surface of the wound and help prevent the development of an acute cellulitis until surgical intervention can be arranged.

Chapter 43

Managing Pain

Pain in its most benign form warns us that something isn't quite right, that we should take medicine or see a doctor. At its worst, however, pain robs us of our productivity, our well-being, and, for many of us suffering from extended illness, our very lives. Pain is a complex perception that differs enormously among individual patients, even those who appear to have identical injuries or illnesses.

The burden of pain in the United States is astounding. More than 100 million Americans have pain that persists for weeks to years. The financial toll of this epidemic cost $560 billion to $635 billion per year according to *Relieving Pain in America: A Blueprint for Transforming Prevention, Care, Education, and Research*, a report from an Institute of Medicine (IOM). Pain is ultimately a challenge for family, friends, and healthcare providers who must give support to the individual suffering from the physical as well as the emotional consequences of pain.

Acute Pain and Chronic Pain

There are two kinds of pain. Acute pain begins suddenly, lasts for a short time, and goes away as your body heals. You might feel acute

---

This chapter contains text excerpted from the following sources: Text in this chapter begins with excerpts from "Pain: Hope through Research," National Institute of Neurological Disorders and Stroke (NINDS), January 2014. Reviewed July 2018; Text beginning with the heading "Acute Pain and Chronic Pain" is excerpted from "Pain: You Can Get Help," National Institute on Aging (NIA), National Institutes of Health (NIH), February 28, 2018.

pain after surgery or if you have a broken bone, infected tooth, or kidney stone.

Pain that lasts for 3 months or longer is called chronic pain. This pain often affects older people. For some people, chronic pain is caused by a health condition such as arthritis. It may also follow acute pain from an injury, surgery, or other health issue that has been treated, like postherpetic neuralgia after shingles.

Living with any type of pain can be hard. It can cause many other problems. For instance, pain can:

- Get in the way of your daily activities
- Disturb your sleep and eating habits
- Make it difficult to continue working
- Be related to depression or anxiety
- Keep you from spending time with friends and family

Describing Pain

Many people have a hard time describing pain. Think about these questions when you explain how the pain feels:

- Where does it hurt?
- When did the pain start? Does it come and go?
- What does it feel like? Is the pain sharp, dull, or burning? Would you use some other word to describe it?
- Do you have other symptoms?
- When do you feel the pain? In the morning? In the evening? After eating?
- Is there anything you do that makes the pain feel better or worse? For example, does using a heating pad or ice pack help? Does changing your position from lying down to sitting up make it better?
- What medicines, including over-the-counter (OTC) medications and nonmedicine therapies have you tried, and what was their effect?

Your doctor or nurse may ask you to rate your pain on a scale of 0–10, with 0 being no pain and 10 being the worst pain you can imagine. Or, your doctor may ask if the pain is mild, moderate, or severe.

Managing Pain

Some doctors or nurses have pictures of faces that show different expressions of pain and ask you to point to the face that shows how you feel. Your doctor may ask you to keep a diary of when and what kind of pain you feel every day.

Attitudes about Pain

Everyone reacts to pain differently. Some people feel they should be brave and not complain when they hurt. Other people are quick to report pain and ask for help.

Worrying about pain is common. This worry can make you afraid to stay active, and it can separate you from your friends and family. Working with your doctor, you can find ways to continue to take part in physical and social activities despite having pain. Some people put off going to the doctor because they think pain is part of aging and nothing can help. This is not true! It is important to see a doctor if you have a new pain. Finding a way to manage pain is often easier if it is addressed early.

Treating Pain

Treating, or managing, chronic pain is important. Some treatments involve medications, and some do not. Your treatment plan should be specific to your needs. Most treatment plans focus on both reducing pain and increasing ways to support daily function while living with pain. Talk with your doctor about how long it may take before you feel better. Often, you have to stick with a treatment plan before you get relief. It's important to stay on a schedule. Sometimes this is called "staying ahead" or "keeping on top" of your pain. Be sure to tell your doctor about any side effects. You might have to try different treatments until you find a plan that works for you. As your pain lessens, you can likely become more active and will see your mood lift and sleep improve.

Medicines to Treat Pain

Your doctor may prescribe one or more of the following pain medications. Talk with your doctor about their safety and the right dose to take.

- **Acetaminophen** may help all types of pain, especially mild to moderate pain. Acetaminophen is found in over-the-counter and prescription medicines. People who have more than three drinks per day or who have liver disease should not take acetaminophen.

- **Nonsteroidal anti-inflammatory drugs (NSAIDs)** include aspirin, naproxen, and ibuprofen. Long-term use of some NSAIDs can cause side effects, like internal bleeding or kidney problems, which make them unsafe for many older adults. You may not be able to take ibuprofen if you have high blood pressure.

- **Narcotics** (also called opioids) are used for moderate to severe pain and require a doctor's prescription. They may be habit-forming. They can also be dangerous when taken with alcohol or certain other drugs. Examples of narcotics are codeine, morphine, and oxycodone.

- **Other medications** are sometimes used to treat pain. These include antidepressants, anticonvulsive medicines, local painkillers like nerve blocks or patches, and ointments and creams.

As people age, they are at risk for developing more side effects from medications. It's important to take exactly the amount of pain medicine your doctor prescribes. Don't chew or crush your pills if they are supposed to be swallowed whole. Talk with your doctor or pharmacist if you're having trouble swallowing your pills.

Mixing any pain medication with alcohol or other drugs can be dangerous. Make sure your doctor knows all the medicines you take, including over-the-counter drugs and dietary supplements, as well as the amount of alcohol you drink.

What Other Treatments Help with Pain?

In addition to drugs, there are a variety of complementary and alternative approaches that may provide relief. Talk to your doctor about these treatments. It may take both medicine and other treatments to feel better.

- **Acupuncture** uses hair-thin needles to stimulate specific points on the body to relieve pain.

- **Biofeedback** helps you learn to control your heart rate, blood pressure, muscle tension, and other body functions. This may help reduce your pain and stress level.

- **Cognitive behavioral therapy (CBT)** is a form of short-term counseling that may help reduce your reaction to pain.

Managing Pain

- **Distraction** can help you cope with acute pain, taking your mind off your discomfort.
- **Electrical nerve stimulation** uses electrical impulses to relieve pain.
- **Guided imagery** uses directed thoughts to create mental pictures that may help you relax, manage anxiety, sleep better, and have less pain.
- **Hypnosis** uses focused attention to help manage pain.
- **Massage therapy** can release tension in tight muscles.
- **Mind-body stress reduction** combines mindfulness meditation, body awareness, and yoga to increase relaxation and reduce pain.
- **Physical therapy** uses a variety of techniques to help manage everyday activities with less pain and teaches you ways to improve flexibility and strength.

Helping Yourself

There are things you can do yourself that might help you feel better. Try to:

- Keep a healthy weight. Putting on extra pounds can slow healing and make some pain worse. A healthy weight might help with pain in the knees, back, hips, or feet.
- Be physically active. Pain might make you inactive, which can lead to more pain and loss of function. Activity can help.
- Get enough sleep. It can reduce pain sensitivity, help healing, and improve your mood.
- Avoid tobacco, caffeine, and alcohol. They can get in the way of treatment and increase pain.
- Join a pain support group. Sometimes, it can help to talk to other people about how they deal with pain. You can share your thoughts while learning from others.

Chapter 44

Coping with Anxiety Disorders and Depression

Anxiety and fear are basic emotions that are experienced by everyone and are necessary for survival. Anxiety is important because it helps people prepare for a threat. Fear is important because it helps people fight or escape. The experiences of anxiety and fear are normal responses to threat or danger and are usually helpful. Anxiety and fear may be unhelpful if they interfere with a person's daily routine or prevent a person from doing things that he/she normally does. If the anxiety or fear is long-lasting and without relief, it may be a sign that a person has developed a more significant problem with anxiety, often called an "anxiety disorder." Anxiety disorders are common. Almost one-third of adults will have experienced an anxiety disorder at some point in their lifetime.

Generalized Anxiety Disorder

People with generalized anxiety disorder display excessive anxiety or worry for months and face several anxiety-related symptoms.

This chapter contains text excerpted from the following sources: Text in this chapter begins with excerpts from "Anxiety," U.S. Department of Veterans Affairs (VA), December 4, 2015; Text beginning with the heading "Generalized Anxiety Disorder" is excerpted from "Anxiety Disorders," National Institute of Mental Health (NIMH), March 2016; Text beginning with the heading "What Is Depression?" is excerpted from "Mental Health Conditions: Depression and Anxiety," Centers for Disease Control and Prevention (CDC), March 22, 2018.

Generalized anxiety disorder symptoms include:

- Restlessness or feeling wound-up or on edge
- Being easily fatigued
- Difficulty concentrating or having their minds go blank
- Irritability
- Muscle tension
- Difficulty controlling the worry
- Sleep problems (difficulty falling or staying asleep or restless, unsatisfying sleep)

Panic Disorder

People with panic disorder have recurrent unexpected panic attacks, which are sudden periods of intense fear that may include palpitations, pounding heart, or accelerated heart rate; sweating; trembling or shaking; sensations of shortness of breath, smothering, or choking; and feeling of impending doom.

Panic disorder symptoms include:

- Sudden and repeated attacks of intense fear
- Feelings of being out of control during a panic attack
- Intense worries about when the next attack will happen
- Fear or avoidance of places where panic attacks have occurred in the past

Social Anxiety Disorder

People with social anxiety disorder (sometimes called "social phobia") have a marked fear of social or performance situations in which they expect to feel embarrassed, judged, rejected, or fearful of offending others.

Social anxiety disorder symptoms include:

- Feeling highly anxious about being with other people and having a hard time talking to them
- Feeling very self-conscious in front of other people and worried about feeling humiliated, embarrassed, or rejected, or fearful of offending others

Coping with Anxiety Disorders and Depression

- Being very afraid that other people will judge them
- Worrying for days or weeks before an event where other people will be
- Staying away from places where there are other people
- Having a hard time making friends and keeping friends
- Blushing, sweating, or trembling around other people
- Feeling nauseous or sick to your stomach when other people are around

Evaluation for an anxiety disorder often begins with a visit to a primary care provider. Some physical health conditions, such as an overactive thyroid or low blood sugar, as well as taking certain medications, can imitate or worsen an anxiety disorder. A thorough mental health evaluation is also helpful, because anxiety disorders often coexist with other related conditions, such as depression or obsessive-compulsive disorder (OCD).

Risk Factors for Anxiety Disorders

Researchers are finding that genetic and environmental factors, frequently in interaction with one another, are risk factors for anxiety disorders. Specific factors include:

- Shyness, or behavioral inhibition, in childhood
- Being female
- Having few economic resources
- Being divorced or widowed
- Exposure to stressful life events in childhood and adulthood
- Anxiety disorders in close biological relatives
- Parental history of mental disorders
- Elevated afternoon cortisol levels in the saliva (specifically for social anxiety disorder)

Treatments and Therapies for Anxiety Disorders

Anxiety disorders are generally treated with psychotherapy, medication, or both.

Psychotherapy

Psychotherapy or "talk therapy" can help people with anxiety disorders. To be effective, psychotherapy must be directed at the person's specific anxieties and tailored to his or her needs. A typical "side effect" of psychotherapy is temporary discomfort involved with thinking about confronting feared situations.

Cognitive Behavioral Therapy (CBT)

CBT is a type of psychotherapy that can help people with anxiety disorders. It teaches a person different ways of thinking, behaving, and reacting to anxiety-producing and fearful situations. CBT can also help people learn and practice social skills, which is vital for treating social anxiety disorder.

Two specific stand-alone components of CBT used to treat social anxiety disorder are cognitive therapy and exposure therapy. Cognitive therapy focuses on identifying, challenging, and then neutralizing unhelpful thoughts underlying anxiety disorders.

Exposure therapy focuses on confronting the fears underlying an anxiety disorder in order to help people engage in activities they have been avoiding. Exposure therapy is used along with relaxation exercises and/or imagery. One study, called a meta-analysis because it pulls together all of the previous studies and calculates the statistical magnitude of the combined effects, found that cognitive therapy was superior to exposure therapy for treating social anxiety disorder.

CBT may be conducted individually or with a group of people who have similar problems. Group therapy is particularly effective for social anxiety disorder. Often "homework" is assigned for participants to complete between sessions.

Self-Help or Support Groups

Some people with anxiety disorders might benefit from joining a self-help or support group and sharing their problems and achievements with others. Internet chat rooms might also be useful, but any advice received over the Internet should be used with caution, as Internet acquaintances have usually never seen each other and false identities are common. Talking with a trusted friend or member of the clergy can also provide support, but it is not necessarily a sufficient alternative to care from an expert clinician.

Coping with Anxiety Disorders and Depression

Stress-Management Techniques

Stress management techniques and meditation can help people with anxiety disorders calm themselves and may enhance the effects of therapy. While there is evidence that aerobic exercise has a calming effect, the quality of the studies is not strong enough to support its use as treatment. Since caffeine, certain illicit drugs, and even some over-the-counter cold medications can aggravate the symptoms of anxiety disorders, avoiding them should be considered. Check with your physician or pharmacist before taking any additional medications.

The family can be important in the recovery of a person with an anxiety disorder. Ideally, the family should be supportive but not help perpetuate their loved one's symptoms.

Medication

Medication does not cure anxiety disorders but often relieves symptoms. Medication can only be prescribed by a medical doctor (such as a psychiatrist or a primary care provider), but a few states allow psychologists to prescribe psychiatric medications.

Medications are sometimes used as the initial treatment of an anxiety disorder, or are used only if there is insufficient response to a course of psychotherapy. In research studies, it is common for patients treated with a combination of psychotherapy and medication to have better outcomes than those treated with only one or the other.

The most common classes of medications used to combat anxiety disorders are antidepressants, antianxiety drugs, and beta-blockers. Be aware that some medications are effective only if they are taken regularly and that symptoms may recur if the medication is stopped.

Antidepressants

Antidepressants are used to treat depression, but they also are helpful for treating anxiety disorders. They take several weeks to start working and may cause side effects such as headache, nausea, or difficulty sleeping. The side effects are usually not a problem for most people, especially if the dose starts off low and is increased slowly over time.

Antianxiety Medications

Antianxiety medications help reduce the symptoms of anxiety, panic attacks, or extreme fear and worry. The most common antianxiety medications are called benzodiazepines. Benzodiazepines are first-line treatments for generalized anxiety disorder. With panic disorder or social phobia (social anxiety disorder), benzodiazepines are usually second-line treatments, behind antidepressants.

Beta-Blockers

Beta-blockers, such as propranolol and atenolol, are also helpful in the treatment of the physical symptoms of anxiety, especially social anxiety. Physicians prescribe them to control rapid heartbeat, shaking, trembling, and blushing in anxious situations.

Choosing the right medication, medication dose, and treatment plan should be based on a person's needs and medical situation, and done under an expert's care. Only an expert clinician can help you decide whether the medication's ability to help is worth the risk of a side effect. Your doctor may try several medicines before finding the right one.

You and your doctor should discuss:

- How well medications are working or might work to improve your symptoms
- Benefits and side effects of each medication
- Risk for serious side effects based on your medical history
- The likelihood of the medications requiring lifestyle changes
- Costs of each medication
- Other alternative therapies, medications, vitamins, and supplements you are taking and how these may affect your treatment
- How the medication should be stopped. Some drugs can't be stopped abruptly but must be tapered off slowly under a doctor's supervision.

What Is Depression?

Depression is more than just feeling down or having a bad day. When a sad mood lasts for a long time and interferes with normal, everyday functioning, you may be depressed. Symptoms of depression include:

- Feeling sad or anxious often or all the time
- Not wanting to do activities that used to be fun

Coping with Anxiety Disorders and Depression

- Feeling irritable, easily frustrated, or restless
- Having trouble falling asleep or staying asleep
- Waking up too early or sleeping too much
- Eating more or less than usual or having no appetite
- Experiencing aches, pains, headaches, or stomach problems that do not improve with treatment
- Having trouble concentrating, remembering details, or making decisions
- Feeling tired, even after sleeping well
- Feeling guilty, worthless, or helpless
- Thinking about suicide or hurting yourself

What Causes Depression

The exact cause of depression is unknown. It may be caused by a combination of genetic, biological, environmental, and psychological factors. Everyone is different' but the following factors may increase a person's chances of becoming depressed:

- Having blood relatives who have had depression
- Experiencing traumatic or stressful events, such as physical or sexual abuse, the death of a loved one, or financial problems
- Going through a major life change' even if it was planned
- Having a medical problem, such as cancer, stroke, or chronic pain
- Taking certain medications. Talk to your doctor if you have questions about whether your medications might be making you feel depressed.
- Using alcohol or drugs

What Are the Treatments for Depression?

Many helpful treatments for depression are available. Treatment for depression can help reduce symptoms and shorten how long the depression lasts. Treatment can include getting therapy and/or taking medications. Your doctor or a qualified mental health professional can help you determine what treatment is best for you.

- **Therapy.** Many people benefit from psychotherapy—also called therapy or counseling. Most therapy lasts for a short time and focuses on thoughts' feelings' and issues that are happening in your life now. In some cases' understanding your past can help' but finding ways to address what is happening in your life now can help you cope and prepare you for challenges in the future. With therapy, you'll work with your therapist to learn skills to help you cope with life, change behaviors that are causing problems' and find solutions. Do not feel shy or embarrassed about talking openly and honestly about your feelings and concerns. This is an important part of getting better. Some common goals of therapy include:
  - Getting healthier
  - Quitting smoking and stopping drug and alcohol use
  - Overcoming fears or insecurities
  - Coping with stress
  - Making sense of past painful events
  - Identifying things that worsen your depression
  - Having better relationships with family and friends
  - Understanding why something bothers you and creating a plan to deal with it
- **Medication.** Many people with depression find that taking prescribed medications called antidepressants can help improve their mood and coping skills. Talk to your doctor about whether they are right for you. If your doctor writes you a prescription for an antidepressant' ask exactly how you should take the medication. If you are already using nicotine replacement therapy or another medication to help you quit smoking, be sure to let your doctor know. Several antidepressant medications are available' so you and your doctor have options to choose from. Sometimes it takes several tries to find the best medication and the right dose for you, so be patient. Also be aware of the following important information:
- When taking these medications, it is important to follow the instructions on how much to take. Some people start to feel better a few days after starting the medication' but it can take up to 4 weeks to feel the most benefit. Antidepressants work

Coping with Anxiety Disorders and Depression

well and are safe for most people' but it is still important to talk with your doctor if you have side effects. Side effects usually do not get in the way of daily life' and they often go away as your body adjusts to the medication.

- Don't stop taking an antidepressant without first talking to your doctor. Stopping your medicine suddenly can cause symptoms or worsen depression. Work with your doctor to safely adjust how much you take.
- Some antidepressants may cause risks during pregnancy. Talk with your doctor if you are pregnant or might be pregnant, or if you are planning to become pregnant.
- Antidepressants cannot solve all of your problems. If you notice that your mood is getting worse or if you have thoughts about hurting yourself' it is important to call your doctor right away.

Chapter 45

Health Insurance Concerns

Chapter Contents

Section 45.1—Health Insurance for People with
            Disabilities... 486
Section 45.2—Medicaid and Children's Health
            Insurance Program 492
Section 45.3—Medicaid and Adults with Disabilities................ 496

Section 45.1

Health Insurance for People with Disabilities

This section includes text excerpted from "Coverage Options for People with Disabilities," Centers for Medicare and Medicaid Services (CMS), October 11, 2014. Reviewed July 2018.

If you have a disability, you have a number of options for health coverage. If you currently have Medicaid or Medicare, you're considered covered under the healthcare law and don't need a Marketplace plan. If you don't have health coverage, you can fill out a Marketplace application to find out if you qualify for savings on a private health plan or for coverage through Medicaid.

Social Security Disability Insurance (SSDI) and Medicare Coverage

If you get Social Security Disability Income (SSDI), you probably have Medicare or are in a 24-month waiting period before it starts. You have options in either case.

If You Get Social Security Disability Income (SSDI) and Have Medicare

- You're considered covered under the healthcare law and don't have to pay the penalty that people without coverage must pay.

- You can't enroll in a Marketplace plan to replace or supplement your Medicare coverage.

  - One exception: If you enrolled in a Marketplace plan before getting Medicare, you can keep your Marketplace plan as supplemental insurance when you enroll in Medicare. But if you do this, you'll lose any premium tax credits and other savings for your Marketplace plan.

If You Get SSDI Benefits and Are in a 24-Month Waiting Period before Getting Medicare

- You may be able to get Medicaid coverage while you wait. You can apply two ways:

Health Insurance Concerns

- Create an account or log in to complete an application. Answer "yes" when asked if you have a disability. We'll forward your application to your state Medicaid agency.
- Apply directly to your state Medicaid agency. Select your state from the menu on this Medicaid page for contact information.
- If you're eligible for Medicaid, your Medicaid eligibility may continue even after you enroll in Medicare.
- If you're turned down for Medicaid, you may be able to enroll in a private health plan through the Marketplace while waiting for your Medicare coverage to start. You may qualify for lower costs on Marketplace coverage based on your income and household size.

Supplemental Security Income (SSI) Disability and Medicaid Coverage

If you have Supplemental Security Income (SSI) Disability, you may get Medicaid coverage automatically or you may have to apply.

If You Get SSI Disability and Have Medicaid

You're considered covered under the healthcare law. You don't need to get a Marketplace plan. You won't have to pay the penalty that people without coverage must pay.

If You Get SSI Disability and Don't Have Medicaid

You can apply for Medicaid coverage. But whether you need to apply depends on your state.

- In many states, SSI recipients automatically qualify for Medicaid and don't have to fill out a Medicaid application.
- In other states, your SSI guarantees your Medicaid eligibility, but you have to sign up for it.
- In a few states, SSI doesn't guarantee Medicaid eligibility. But most people who get SSI are still eligible.

If you have SSI Disability and don't have Medicaid, you can apply for Medicaid coverage two ways:

- Select your state from the menu on this Medicaid page for contact information.

- Create an account or log in to complete an application.
  - Answer "yes" when asked if you have a disability, and we'll send your application to your state Medicaid office.
  - **Note:** When filling out your Marketplace application, don't include SSI Disability payments when estimating your income.

Waiting for a Decision on Disability Status

If you're waiting for a decision on your disability status, you have coverage options.

Apply for Medicaid or a Private Health Plan through the Marketplace

Create an account or log in to complete an application. You'll find out if you qualify for premium tax credits and lower costs on a private health plan based on your household size and income. You'll also find out if you qualify for Medicaid coverage.

- When you fill out your Marketplace application, answer "yes" when asked if you have a disability. The Centers for Medicare & Medicaid Services (CMS) will forward your application to your state Medicaid agency. If you qualify, they'll help you enroll.
- If you don't qualify for Medicaid, you may qualify for premium tax credits and other savings on a Marketplace health plan.
- You can also apply for Medicaid coverage directly through your state agency.

If You Get a Positive SSDI Disability Decision

If you get a positive disability decision, you may have to wait 24 months before Medicare coverage starts.

If You Get a Negative Disability Decision

If you get a negative disability decision, you can fill out a Marketplace application to apply for coverage. You'll find out if you qualify for a private health plan with premium tax credits and lower costs based on your household size and income. When you apply, you'll also find out if you qualify for Medicaid coverage.

Health Insurance Concerns

- When you fill out your Marketplace application, answer "yes" when asked if you have a disability. The Centers for Medicare and Medicaid Services (CMS) will forward your application to your state Medicaid agency. If you qualify, they'll help you enroll.
- If you don't qualify for Medicaid, you may qualify for savings on a Marketplace health plan.
- You can also apply for Medicaid coverage directly through your state agency.

No Disability Benefits or Health Coverage

If you have a disability, don't qualify for disability benefits, and need health coverage, you have options in the health insurance Marketplace.

Applying for Coverage through the Marketplace

Create an account or log in and fill out a Marketplace health coverage application to find out if you qualify for a private health plan with premium tax credits and other savings based on your income. You'll also find out if you qualify for Medicaid coverage.

When you fill out your application, you may be asked if you:

- Have a physical disability or mental health condition that limits your ability to work, attend school, or take care of your daily needs
- Get help with daily living activities through personal assistance, a medical facility, or nursing home

If you answer "yes" to any of these questions, a Marketplace application will be sent to your state Medicaid office to see if you qualify for Medicaid based on a disability. The state Medicaid office may contact you for more information about your disability.

You can also apply for Medicaid coverage directly to your state agency.

If You Don't Qualify for Medicaid Based on Your Disability

If you don't qualify for Medicaid based on your disability, you have two more options for health coverage through the Marketplace:

- You may qualify for Medicaid based only on your income. Some states have expanded their Medicaid programs to cover all adults who make less than a certain income level. Find out if your state is expanding Medicaid and what this means for you.

- You may qualify to enroll in a health plan through the Health Insurance Marketplace with premium tax credits and other savings that make coverage more affordable. This will depend on your household size and income.

The Fee for Not Having Coverage

Under the healthcare law, most people must have health coverage, pay a fee, or get an exemption from the fee. This applies regardless of disability status. If you don't have coverage through Medicare, Medicaid, another public program, a job, the Marketplace, or another source, you may have to pay the fee. Some people can get an exemption from the fee based on low income, hardship, or other factors.

The Marketplace Application and Disabilities

When you fill out an application for Marketplace coverage, you'll be asked several questions about disabilities. Information to help you answer the questions is below.

If you have a disability, mental health condition, or personal assistance needs, you may be eligible for Medicaid or for help paying for coverage.

Conditions That Are Considered Disabilities

If you have one or more of these conditions, you're considered disabled:

- You're blind, deaf, or hard of hearing
- You get Social Security Disability Insurance (SSDI) or Supplemental Security Insurance (SSI)
- You have a physical, cognitive, intellectual, or mental health condition, which causes one or more of these:
  - Difficulty doing errands like visiting a doctor's office or shopping
  - Serious difficulty concentrating, remembering, or making decisions
  - Difficulty walking or climbing stairs

Health Insurance Concerns

Disabilities and Children

For a child, these conditions are considered disabilities:

- They have limited ability to do the things most children of the same age can do.
- They need or use more healthcare than is usual for most children of the same age.
- They get special education services or services under a Section 504 plan.

What Happens If You Indicate You're Disabled

If you indicate you have a disability on your Marketplace application, the Centers for Medicare & Medicaid Services (CMS) will send it to your state Medical Assistance (Medicaid) office to see if you qualify for Medicaid based on your disability. If your application is sent to your state Medicaid office, they may contact you for more information on your disability. If you don't qualify for Medicaid based on your disability, you may still be eligible based on your income or you may qualify for a tax credit.

You should still indicate that you're disabled even if you're not sure if your state will consider you eligible for Medicaid based on your disability. This will help make sure you get the most help available. Your state will determine if you qualify for Medicaid.

If you say you're disabled, but your state determines you either don't qualify for Medicaid based on your income or determines that you don't have a qualifying disability, you can still buy health coverage through the Marketplace. Plans can't deny you coverage or charge you more because of your disability.

If You Need Help with Activities of Daily Living

Activities of daily living include seeing, hearing, walking, eating, sleeping, standing, lifting, bending, breathing, learning, reading, communicating, thinking, and working. If you have a cognitive or mental health condition, you may need help with these activities of daily living through coaching or instruction. If a person only needs help because he or she is too young to be able to do these activities without help, don't indicate that they need help with daily activities on your application.

Section 45.2

Medicaid and Children's Health Insurance Program

This section includes text excerpted from "Children's Health Insurance Program (CHIP)," Centers for Medicare and Medicaid Services (CMS), February 6, 2015.

The Children's Health Insurance Program (CHIP) provides health coverage to eligible children, through both Medicaid and separate CHIP programs. CHIP is administered by states, according to federal requirements. The program is funded jointly by states and the federal government.

Benefits

The CHIP provides comprehensive benefits to children. Since states have flexibility to design their own program within federal guidelines, benefits vary by state and by the type of CHIP program.

Medicaid Expansion Benefits

Medicaid expansion CHIP programs provide the standard Medicaid benefit package, including Early and Periodic Screening, Diagnostic, and Treatment (EPSDT) services, which includes all medically necessary services like mental health and dental services.

Separate CHIP Benefits Options

States can choose to provide benchmark coverage, benchmark-equivalent coverage, or Secretary-approved coverage:

- Benchmark coverage based on one of the following:
  - The standard Blue Cross/Blue Shield preferred provider option service benefit plan offered to federal employees
  - State employee's coverage plan
  - Health Maintenance Organization (HMO) plan that has the largest commercial, non-Medicaid enrollment within the state
- Benchmark-equivalent coverage must be actuarially equivalent and include:
  - Inpatient and outpatient hospital services

- Physician's services
- Surgical and medical services
- Laboratory and X-ray services
- Well-baby and well-child care, including immunizations
- Secretary-approved coverage: Any other health coverage deemed appropriate and acceptable by the Secretary of the U.S. Department of Health and Human Services (HHS).

Separate CHIP Dental Benefits

States that provide CHIP coverage to children through a Medicaid expansion program are required to provide the EPSDT benefit. Dental coverage in separate CHIP programs is required to include coverage for dental services "necessary to prevent disease and promote oral health, restore oral structures to health and function, and treat emergency conditions."

States with a separate CHIP program may choose from two options for providing dental coverage: a package of dental benefits that meets the CHIP requirements, or a benchmark dental benefit package. The benchmark dental package must be substantially equal to the:

1. the most popular federal employee dental plan for dependents,
2. the most popular plan selected for dependants in the state's employee dental plan, or
3. dental coverage offered through the most popular commercial insurer in the state.

States are also required to post a listing of all participating Medicaid and CHIP dental providers and benefit packages on InsureKidsNow.gov.

Vaccines

Coverage for age-appropriate immunizations is required in CHIP. States with a separate CHIP program (including the separate portion of a combination program) must purchase vaccines to be administered to enrolled children using only CHIP federal and state matching funds. Vaccines for federally vaccine-eligible children (through the Vaccines For Children program) should not be used by children enrolled in separate CHIP programs, and funds available under section 317 of the Public Health Service Act are designated for the purchase of vaccines for the uninsured and may not be used to purchase vaccines for children who have separate CHIP coverage.

States have two options for purchasing vaccines for children enrolled in separate CHIP programs:

1. purchase vaccines using the Centers for Disease Control and Prevention (CDC) contract and distribution mechanism, or
2. purchase vaccines through the private sector.

The Centers for Medicare and Medicaid Services (CMS) has worked with the CDC on issuing joint guidance for all states with a separate CHIP program on purchasing and claiming for vaccines administered to separate CHIP children. The guidance letter explains that, for states that purchase vaccines through the CDC, states are required to pay for vaccines at the time they are ordered. States claim federal financial participation against the CHIP allotment based on the purchase invoices rather than individual provider claims. The letter further explains that states will use a reconciliation process to ensure that future vaccine orders are adjusted based on the outstanding credit for unused vaccines from the previous order.

Eligibility

The Children's Health Insurance Program (CHIP) serves uninsured children up to age 19 in families with incomes too high to qualify them for Medicaid. States have broad discretion in setting their income eligibility standards, and eligibility varies across states.

Income Eligibility

46 states and the District of Columbia cover children up to or above 200 percent of the Federal Poverty Level (FPL), and 24 of these states offer coverage to children in families with income at 250 percent of the FPL or higher. States may get the CHIP enhanced match for coverage up to 300 percent of the FPL, which is higher than the Medicaid federal funding matching rate. States that expand coverage above 300 percent of the FPL get the Medicaid matching rate. States have the option to provide continuous eligibility to children who remain eligible for CHIP.

Waiting Periods in CHIP

A number of states have eliminated or shortened their waiting periods.

Health Insurance Concerns

New Medicaid and CHIP Coverage Options

Lawfully Residing Children and Pregnant Women

Many states have elected the option under CHIPRA to restore Medicaid and/or CHIP coverage to children and pregnant women who are lawfully residing in the United States.

Pregnant Women

CHIPRA created an explicit eligibility category for pregnant women to receive coverage through CHIP in certain circumstances. Some states have also chosen to provide prenatal care for pregnant women through the CHIP program through other available vehicles.

Children of Public Employees

The Affordable Care Act of 2010 provides states the option to extend CHIP eligibility to state employees' children. Before enactment of the Affordable Care Act children of public employees were not eligible for CHIP, regardless of their income.

Cost Sharing

States can choose to impose limited enrollment fees, premiums, deductibles, coinsurance, and copayments for children and pregnant women enrolled in CHIP, generally limited to 5 percent of a family's annual income. Cost sharing is prohibited for some services, like well-baby and well-child visits.

Medicaid Expansion Cost Sharing

States with Medicaid expansion programs must follow the Medicaid cost sharing rules.

Separate CHIP Program Cost Sharing

For families with incomes at or below 150 percent of the Federal Poverty Level (FPL), premiums cannot exceed the amount permitted in Medicaid. For families with incomes above 150 percent of the FPL, state cost-sharing requirements can't exceed 5 percent of family income.

Section 45.3

Medicaid and Adults with Disabilities

This section includes text excerpted from "Health Care Experiences of Adults with Disabilities Enrolled in Medicaid Only: Findings from a 2014–2015 Nationwide Survey of Medicaid Beneficiaries," Centers for Medicare & Medicaid Services (CMS), November 2017.

Persons who qualify for Medicaid on the basis of a disability are a diverse population group, consisting of individuals with a wide range of physical impairments, functional limitations, and intellectual and mental health disabilities. In 2015, Medicaid provided coverage for 10.2 million nonelderly individuals on the basis of a disability. Most of those individuals were adults ages 18 and older residing in a community setting. Medicaid beneficiaries with a disability may be enrolled in Medicaid alone or be dually enrolled in Medicaid and Medicare. This brief focuses on adult Medicaid beneficiaries who are not dually enrolled and qualified for Medicaid on the basis of a disability.

According to the Medicaid and CHIP Payment and Access Commission (MACPAC), research is limited on the healthcare experiences of adults with disabilities enrolled only in Medicaid (i.e., not dually enrolled in Medicare and Medicaid); however, population-based surveys indicate that they have access to care that is comparable to that of other insured persons with disabilities. A recent analysis found that nonelderly adults with disabilities enrolled in Medicaid in 2015 were more than 2.5 times as likely to have three or more functional limitations, and more than 1.5 times as likely to have 10 or more healthcare visits in a year compared to people with disabilities who were privately insured—a finding likely indicative of their greater healthcare needs.

Persons with disabilities account for a sizable share of Medicaid spending. For example, while about 15 percent of Medicaid beneficiaries were eligible for coverage on the basis of a disability, they represented 40 percent of Medicaid expenditures in federal fiscal year 2015. Understanding the healthcare experiences of persons with disabilities will support performance improvement efforts to maximize the independence, well-being, and health of people with disabilities and their families and caregivers.

The 2014–2015 Nationwide Adult Medicaid Consumer Assessment of Healthcare Providers and Systems (NAM CAHPS) survey, conducted by the Center for Medicaid and CHIP Services (CMCS), is well suited to examine access and experiences of care of adults with disabilities. The

Health Insurance Concerns

survey provides comparative information on experiences of care across states and socio-demographic subgroups. This brief focuses on adult beneficiaries (ages 18–64) who qualified for Medicaid on the basis of a disability, were living in the community, and were not dually enrolled in Medicare and Medicaid (henceforth called adults with disabilities). Indicators of access and experiences of care for this group are compared with those of all adult Medicaid beneficiaries. The intent is to provide states, the federal government, and stakeholders with information that can be used to guide continuous quality improvement efforts.

Key Findings

- Approximately 8 in 10 adults with disabilities covered by Medicaid alone (i.e., not dually enrolled in Medicare) reported they could always or usually get needed care (78%), and reported they always or usually received care quickly (82%).
- Roughly 2 in 10 adults with disabilities reported they were unable to get needed care. Coverage related barriers (e.g., beneficiary said Medicaid would not approve, cover or pay for care) were the most commonly reported reason for being unable to get care.
- Despite greater healthcare needs and more functional limitations, adults with disabilities when compared with beneficiaries overall reported similar or slightly better patient care experiences on most indicators in this brief, including:
  - How well doctors communicate (always or usually good: 89% versus 90%);
  - Customer service interactions (always or usually positive: 76% versus 76%);
  - Getting special medical equipment (always or usually easy: 55% versus 51%).
- Adults with disabilities reporting a doctor or health maintenance organization (HMO) as their usual source of care gave the highest ratings for their overall care (81% gave a score of 7–10). Adults reporting no usual source of care gave the lowest ratings (62% gave a score of 7–10).

Healthcare Experiences of Adults with Disabilities

Helping individuals with disabilities manage their needs requires access to care and coordination of care across a wide range of services.

Disabilities Sourcebook, Fourth Edition

Although a larger percentage of adults who qualified for Medicaid coverage on the basis of a disability than all adult beneficiaries reported fair/poor health, adults with disabilities reported similar or slightly better access to healthcare than adult beneficiaries overall (Table 45.1). Among adults with disabilities, 78 percent reported they could usually or always get needed care, as compared to 75 percent of all beneficiaries. Adults with disabilities also reported usually or always getting timely care more frequently than all beneficiaries (82% versus 79%).

Table 45.1. Getting Needed Care and Getting Care Quickly

Medicaid Beneficiaries		
Composite Measure	Adults with Disabilities	All Adults
Getting needed care	Percent	Percent
Never + Sometimes	22.2	24.9
Usually	26.3	26.5
Always	51.5	48.6
Getting care quickly		
Never + Sometimes	18	20.7
Usually	23	24.1
Always	59	55.2

Note: *"All Adults" includes individuals in the four NAM CAHPS sample stratum: persons with disabilities; full-benefit dual enrollees; managed care; and fee-for-service.*

Two factors that can affect getting needed care are how well doctors communicate with patients and customer service, both of which can impact patient help-seeking behaviors as well as compliance with advice from providers. Adults with disabilities reported usually or always having good doctor-patient communication (89%) as did adult beneficiaries overall (90%; see table 45.2). They also reported slightly more frequent positive customer service interactions than beneficiaries overall (78% versus 76% responded usually or always).

Table 45.2. Communication with Doctors and Customer Service

Medicaid Beneficiaries		
Composite Measure	Adults with Disabilities	All Adults
How well doctors communicate	Percent	Percent
Never + Sometimes	11.3	10.4

Health Insurance Concerns

Table 45.2. Continued

Medicaid Beneficiaries		
Composite Measure	**Adults with Disabilities**	**All Adults**
Usually	17.7	18.2
Always	71.1	71.4
Health plan information and customer service		
Never + Sometimes	22.5	23.6
Usually	21.2	21.8
Always	56.3	54.6

Note: *"All Adults" includes individuals in the four NAM CAHPS sample stratum: persons with disabilities; full-benefit dual enrollees; managed care; and fee-for-service.*

For individuals with functional limitations or medical needs, coverage for medical supplies and equipment is essential. In the NAM CAHPS survey, beneficiaries were asked if they had a need for medical equipment such as a cane, wheelchair, diabetic testing suppliers, or a nebulizer. As expected, a larger share of adults with disabilities than adults overall reported a need for special medical equipment (49% versus 39%). However, the percentage of adults with disabilities, as compared with adults overall, who reported it usually or always was easy to obtain the needed equipment did not differ greatly (55% versus 51%).

Table 45.3. Access to Special Medical Equipment

Medicaid Beneficiaries		
Survey Item	**Adults with Disabilities**	**All Adults**
Getting special medical equipment	**Percent (SE)**	**Percent (SE)**
Never + Sometimes	45.2 (0.4)	49.1 (0.3)
Usually	16.8 (0.3)	15.4 (0.2)
Always	38.1 (0.4)	35.5 (0.3)

Note: *The denominator for this indicator is the subset of respondents who reported needing medical equipment in the last 6 months. "All Adults" includes individuals in the four NAM CAHPS sample stratum: persons with disabilities; full-benefit dual enrollees; managed care; and fee-for-service. SE = standard error.*

Chapter 46

Is It a Medical Emergency?

When to Go to the Emergency Room

In some instances, such as with injuries that result in copious bleeding, it's fairly obvious when emergency treatment is necessary. But when people deal with disabilities, it can be more difficult to determine the point at which home care is no longer an option. The best way for the patient and caregivers to gain this knowledge is to have a conversation with the doctor and ask for a detailed description of the types of signs associated with the particular condition that could indicate an emergency. By becoming intimately familiar with the day-to-day symptoms and management of the condition, patients and their families will be better prepared to determine steps to be taken if the illness worsens.

In general, some signs that a visit to an emergency room or a call to 911 may be necessary include:

- Stopped breathing, or extreme difficulty breathing
- Loss of consciousness
- Uncontrollable bleeding
- Pain that is significantly beyond that normally experienced as a result of the condition
- Severe pain in the chest or jaw

"Is It a Medical Emergency?" © 2017 Omnigraphics. Reviewed July 2018.

- Changes in vision
- High fever, especially with a stiff neck
- Sudden headache
- Seizures
- Uncontrollable vomiting
- Changes in mental state, such as confusion
- Sudden paralysis, weakness, or dizziness
- Unusual abdominal pain
- Severe allergic reaction, such as in response to a new medication
- Coughing or vomiting blood
- The patient's sense that something about the condition has changed

Note that when the patient is a child who is too young to describe symptoms or changes in a medical condition, it falls to the parent or guardian to be vigilant for signs that might constitute an emergency. All of the above indicators are applicable to infants and toddlers, as well, but other signs can include:

- Turning blue
- Continuing loose stools
- Hard to wake up
- Fast heartbeat for an extended period of time
- Dry mouth
- Dry diapers for more than 18 hours
- A body part that is cold or pale

What to Do in an Emergency Situation

The advice given most often about emergencies is to remain calm. And as trite as that might sound, a panic-stricken relative or caregiver won't be able to respond appropriately or describe the situation to a first-responder or medical professional in such a way as to ensure the fastest and best treatment for the patient. And if the patient is alone when the emergency occurs, his or her physical response to panic

Is It a Medical Emergency?

(rapid heartbeat, increased breathing rate, sweating, dizziness) can exacerbate the condition itself. In addition to maintaining composure, other steps to be taken include the following:

- **Call 911 if necessary.** Certain situations leave no room for doubt that an immediate trained response is required. For example, if the patient has stopped breathing, is bleeding profusely, or has lost consciousness, he or she needs qualified emergency medical technicians (EMTs) and ambulance.

- **Assess the need for first aid.** In extreme, life-threatening cases, such as when breathing has stopped or there is no pulse, cardiopulmonary resuscitation (CPR) or other first aid needs to be administered immediately. Caregivers for patients with some chronic conditions should undergo training in order to learn proper first-aid techniques.

- **Resist the urge to transport the patient.** Although it may seem faster than waiting for an ambulance, transporting a patient in extreme distress, such as lost consciousness or stopped breathing, can delay treatment and make matters worse. Better to call 911 and follow the operator's instructions.

- **Prepare for the emergency room (ER) visit.** If it's determined that the patient may be transported safely, advanced preparation can save time at the hospital. Bring a list of the patient's medications, allergies, and immunizations, as well as the name and contact information of his or her regular doctor.

- **If unsure what to do, call a professional.** If the situation is not immediately life-threatening, and you're not sure an ER visit is necessary, call the patient's doctor or other medical professionals familiar with his or her condition. In addition, many health systems and insurance companies offer 24-hour consultation lines, which can help make an assessment.

Urgent Care Facilities

Urgent care facilities are available for patients whose doctors are unavailable or when illness occurs outside of the physician's normal office hours, and they can serve as a viable alternative to the emergency room in certain cases. Although many of their services are designed to treat such medical situations as flu, sprains and fractures, fever, and minor lacerations, they are quite well-equipped to handle many of the problems associated with chronic illnesses. For example, if the condition results in dehydration, an urgent care center can provide IV fluids while monitoring the patient's vital signs, or if pain intensifies beyond the control of the patient's normal medication, the clinic can respond with appropriate treatment.

Being Prepared

Obviously, it's not possible to prevent all medical emergencies, especially in the case of patients with chronic conditions. But advanced preparation can lessen the severity and allay some anxiety if an emergency does occur. Some ways to prepare for an emergency include:

- Keep contact information handy for doctors, hospitals, urgent care clinics, professional caregivers, and emergency advice lines.
- Have a list of medications (including dosages), allergies, and immunizations ready in advance.
- Ask the doctor for a written medical history for the patient to keep ready for EMTs or emergency-room personnel.
- Keep an appropriately equipped first-aid kit on hand.
- Be sure the patient is seeing his or her doctor for regularly scheduled appointments and is following the doctor's instructions carefully.
- Learn first-aid basics, including CPR.

Depending on the particular condition, there may be other, more specific ways to prepare for a crisis situation. The best thing to do is to discuss this with the physician supervising the case and ask about additional steps you can take to be prepared.

References

1. Kaneshiro, Neil K., MD, MHA. "When to Use the Emergency Room—Child," MedlinePlus, National Institutes of Health (NIH), November 20, 2014.

2. Martin, Laura J., MD, MPH, ABIM. "When to Use the Emergency Room—Adult," MedlinePlus, National Institutes of Health (NIH), October 27, 2014.

3. "Medical Emergency," Tufts University Office of Emergency Management, n.d.

Is It a Medical Emergency?

4. English, Taunya. "Chronic Conditions: When Do You Call the Doctor?" Center for Advancing Health (CFAH), n.d.

5. "What to Do in an Emergency," American College of Emergency Physicians (ACEP), n.d.

6. "When Should I Go to the Emergency Department?" Progressive Emergency Physicians, n.d.

Chapter 47

Rehabilitation: Options for People with Disabilities

What Is Rehabilitation Medicine?

Rehabilitation medicine describes efforts to improve function and minimize impairment related to activities that have been hampered by disease, injuries, or developmental disorders.

Injuries, illnesses, or conditions that may cause or contribute to disability can include stroke, traumatic brain injury, spinal cord injury, musculoskeletal injuries, pain, a number of intellectual and developmental disorders such as cerebral palsy (CP), fragile X syndrome, and autism spectrum disorders (ASDs), and other conditions and injuries.

The primary effects of many such conditions are physical—perhaps mobility or sensory problems. But individuals facing them can also experience intellectual, behavioral, and communication difficulties. They might have problems with making decisions, paying attention, or speaking. These can also require rehabilitation medical care.

This chapter contains text excerpted from the following sources: Text beginning with the heading "What Is Rehabilitation Medicine?" is excerpted from "Rehabilitation Medicine: Topic Information," *Eunice Kennedy Shriver* National Institute of Child Health and Human Development (NICHD), December 1, 2016; Text beginning with the heading "Model of Rehabilitation Care" is excerpted from "Chapter 4—Vision Rehabilitation: Care and Benefit Plan Models: Literature Review," Agency for Healthcare Research and Quality (AHRQ), U.S. Department of Health and Human Services (HHS), September 2012. Reviewed July 2018.

Why Might Someone Need Rehabilitation Medicine?

There are many reasons why a person may need care related to rehabilitation medicine. For example:

- Injuries and trauma, such as:
  - Burns
  - Limb loss or amputation
  - Fractures, including multiple fractures to the long bones in the limbs and fractures of the hip, spine, or skull
  - Traumatic brain injury (TBI) or concussion (mild TBI)
  - Spinal cord injury
  - Loss of sight or hearing
- Diseases and conditions that can cause loss of mobility function, such as:
  - Muscular dystrophy
  - Spina bifida
  - Cerebral palsy
  - Arthritis
  - Scoliosis or curvature of the spine
  - Damage to muscles, ligaments, tendons, or cartilage
  - Knee arthroplasty/replacement
  - Hip replacement
  - Stroke
  - Multiple sclerosis (MS)
  - Parkinson disease and related degenerative disorders
- Surgery or prolonged treatment for other diseases or illnesses that can cause loss of function, such as:
  - Chronic pain/neuropathy
  - Severe infection
  - Diabetes
  - Cancers (including chemo- and radiation therapies)

- Peripheral artery disease
- Cardiac arrest

Likewise, certain intellectual and developmental disabilities, such as autism spectrum disorders, may benefit from rehabilitation medicine in the form of occupational or physical therapy or other rehabilitation services.

Secondary Conditions

Many people who experience the disorders listed above also face their secondary effects—problems that are not necessarily part of the main diagnosis, but that can also have an impact on patients' health, independence, and quality of life.

Rehabilitation medicine may include treatments for these and other secondary symptoms:

- Muscle atrophy (wasting), blood clots or circulation issues, obesity, or other problems resulting from disuse
- Problems caused by overuse of prosthetics or medical devices
- Ulcers, bedsores, or other problems with skin integrity
- Local or widespread infections or sepsis
- Injuries resulting from falls
- Problems with balance or vision
- High blood pressure, diabetes, and other conditions
- Bladder and bowel problems
- Breathing problems, including those related to mechanical ventilation
- Emotional or cognitive difficulties, such as anger, depression, or difficulty controlling emotions or behavior

If not addressed in a timely manner, many of these secondary conditions can become serious, some of them fatal.

What Types of Activities Are Involved with Rehabilitation Medicine?

Rehabilitation medicine uses many kinds of assistance, therapies, and devices to improve function. The type of rehabilitation a person receives depends on the condition causing impairment, the bodily function that is affected, and the severity of the impairment.

The following are some common types of rehabilitation:

- **Cognitive rehabilitation therapy (CRT)** involves relearning or improving skills, such as thinking, learning, memory, planning, and decision making that may have been lost or affected by brain injury.

- **Occupational therapy** helps a person carry out daily life tasks and activities in the home, workplace, and community.

- **Pharmaco rehabilitation** involves the use of drugs to improve or restore physical or mental function.

- **Physical therapy** involves activities and exercises to improve the body's movements, sensations, strength, and balance.

- **Rehabilitative/assistive technology** refers to tools, equipment, and products that help people with disabilities move and function. This technology includes (but is not limited to):

  - Orthotics, which are devices that aim to improve movement and prevent contracture in the upper and lower limbs. For instance, pads inserted into a shoe, specially fitted shoes, or ankle or leg braces can improve a person's ability to walk. Hand splints and arm braces can help the upper limbs remain supple and unclenched after a spinal cord injury.

  - Prosthetics, which are devices designed to replace a missing body part, such as an artificial limb

  - Wheelchairs, walkers, crutches, and other mobility aids

  - Augmentative/Alternative Communication (AAC) devices, which aim to either make a person's communication more understandable or take the place of a communication method. They can include electronic devices, speech-generating devices, and picture boards.

  - Hearing aids and cochlear implants

  - Retinal prostheses, which can restore useful vision in cases in which it has been lost due to certain degenerative eye conditions

  - Telemedicine and telerehab technologies, which are devices or software to deliver care or monitor conditions in the home or community

Rehabilitation: Options for People with Disabilities

- Rehabilitation robotics
- Mobile apps to assist with speech/communication, anxiety/stress, memory, and other functions or symptoms
- **Recreational therapy** helps improve symptoms and social and emotional well-being through arts and crafts, games, relaxation training, and animal-assisted therapy.
- **Speech and language therapy** aims to improve impaired swallowing and movement of the mouth and tongue, as well as difficulties with the voice, language, and talking.
- **Surgery** includes procedures to correct a misaligned limb or to release a constricted muscle, skin grafts for burns, insertion of chips into the brain to assist with limb or prosthetic movement, and placement of skull plates or bone pins.
- **Vocational rehabilitation (VR)** aids in building skills for going to school or working at a job.
- **Music or art therapy** can specifically aid in helping people express emotion, in cognitive development, or in helping to develop social connectedness.

These services are provided by a number of different healthcare providers and specialists, including (but not limited to):

- Physiatrists (also called rehabilitation physicians)
- Occupational therapists
- Physical therapists
- Cognitive rehabilitation therapists
- Gait and clinical movement specialist
- Rehabilitation technologists
- Speech therapists
- Audiologists
- Orthopedists/surgeons
- Neurologists
- Psychiatrists/psychologists
- Biomedical engineers
- Rehabilitation engineers

Model of Rehabilitation Care

The impairments that lead to a limitation in life activities may stem from one or more of genetic conditions, acquired diseases, traumas, and aging. More recently, the "new paradigm" set forth by NIDRR (National Institute on Disability and Rehabilitation Research) characterizes disability as a product of an interaction between characteristics of the individual and characteristics of the natural, built, cultural, and social environments. The new paradigm defines a disabled person as an individual with an impairment who requires an accommodation to perform functions required to carry out life activities. This paradigm is indicative of trends towards viewing the disabled individual in his or her larger social context.

The World Health Organization developed the International Classification of Impairment, Disability, and Handicap (ICIDH) in 1980 to provide a framework and definition of illness and rehabilitation for the organization of information about the consequences of disease. Disability and handicap stem from underlying impairments and disease states, and rehabilitation interventions may be targeted at any of these different levels of patient need.

Defining a single model of rehabilitation care is challenging because of the variety of medical specialties and range of patient needs involved. The World Health Organization (WHO) classification system provides a starting point for most models. Wade and de Jong have proposed the following classification:

- **Level of impairment:** Impairment is an abnormality in structure or function at the organ system resulting from an underlying disease process, i.e., changes in a person. Interventions targeted to the level of impairment include equipment to increase functioning, patient or caregiver behavior to increase functioning, or surgery to improve structure.

- **Level of disability:** Disability is a restriction or lack of ability to perform an activity in a normal manner resulting from an impairment, i.e., changes in a person's behavior or interaction with the environment. Interventions targeted to the level of disability include retraining to achieve a goal using new methods (including equipment), or altering the personal or physical environment. The presence of multiple diseases or impairments in an individual can have a greater than additive effect on the risk for disability.

Rehabilitation: Options for People with Disabilities

- **Level of handicap:** Handicap is a disadvantage resulting from impairment or disability that limits or prevents acting in a normal role in society, i.e., changes in the person's social role functioning. Interventions address the quality and quantity of social role functioning by increasing the patient's behavioral repertoire, and through increasing opportunities for social interaction, e.g., through transport.

According to Hoenig et al., the assessment of disabilities should:

- Characterize the disability
- Identify causal impairments
- Determine underlying diseases
- Discover contributing factors

This is a holistic approach that considers social support, attitude, finances, environment, and education. The rehabilitation plan is then based on the nature of the disability and the underlying conditions. In addition, Kramer proposes assessing rehabilitation services in a way that is more inclusive of the patient's perspective. This includes specifying the system of care, services, and staff, which overlap with the structure and processes of care discussed above in the WHO classification. However, Kramer incorporates the individual's and family's decision processes. This approach is applied primarily to rehabilitation subsequent to acute care episodes while incorporating assessment across a variety of sites including inpatient, outpatient, and home care.

Because of the wide range of disability and types of intervention, there is little focus on, or consensus about, the definition and goals of rehabilitation across fields. For example, rehabilitation services can include medical or surgical therapy, environmental measures, or social and financial support services. The goals of individual programs and interventions vary with type of disability as well as with individual patient plans. While short-term goals of rehabilitation for specific conditions may differ, the field of rehabilitation encompasses common long-term goals. These include maximizing the full social integration and inclusion of the individual in the community, employment or other productive activity, and independent living of individuals of all ages with disabilities, as well as life satisfaction. Goals may also include minimizing the patient's pain and distress, as well as the distress and stress on the patient's family and caregivers. In addition, a longstanding goal of rehabilitation has been and continues to be self-sufficiency through employment.

Populations Affected

An estimated 54 million Americans are disabled. The prevalence of disability is increasing with the aging of the Nation's population. Disabilities are disproportionately concentrated in populations that are low-income, that lack access to state-of-the-art prevention tactics or interventions, and that are exposed to additional external or lifestyle risk factors. Racial, linguistic, and cultural minorities are more likely to live in poverty and lack access to healthcare and health information, and have more exposure to interpersonal violence and intentional injury that may result in disability.

Physical, social, and environmental factors create barriers to routine care for people with disabilities. These include, among other things, inadequate training and evaluation resources, insufficient referrals, lack of transportation options, remoteness of secondary and tertiary facilities, lack of financial resources, and absence of current information on disabilities. Providers often are poorly equipped to accommodate people with disabilities (i.e., they lack adaptive technologies for examination equipment) and primary care providers are often uneducated about the needs of the disabled and fail to make appropriate referrals. In addition, providers may tend to focus on the disability and overlook preventive and health maintenance care for their patients. Primary care providers need special training to better prepare them to identify, treat, and refer people with disabilities. Finally, in rural or other low-density areas where rates of disability are higher, there is frequently only one or a limited range of rehabilitation providers, restricting consumer choice.

Types of Interventions

The selection of rehabilitation services depends on the nature and conditions of the disability. Technical innovations have enormous potential for enhancing the lives of individuals with disabilities. Examples of personal functions that could benefit significantly from new technology include resting, toileting and grooming, dressing, sitting and mobility, preparing food, controlling the home environment, communicating, ensuring mobility in the community, taking long journeys, working, and recreation. However, most advances in rehabilitation have occurred in service delivery as opposed to new technology or single treatments. For example, there is an increasing focus on multidisciplinary service delivery and services that are more inclusive of the individual's particular needs in care planning. This includes assessment and consideration of economic and cultural social context, family and social relationships, and access to services. Improving access to care for people with disabilities and incorporating services that address psychosocial issues of disability remain at the forefront of changes in the field of rehabilitation.

There is an increasing recognition of the need to evaluate service delivery and outcomes from the perspectives of payers, providers, and clients. The delivery of rehabilitation services has been affected by the general shift in healthcare payment from retrospective fee-for-service (FFS) payment to prospective capitated payment. There is greater demand for demonstrating the effectiveness and cost-effectiveness of rehabilitative technologies. In particular, there is an increasing emphasis on assessing the costs and outcomes of rehabilitation from the perspective of rehabilitation service providers and third-party payers. Outcomes would include not just an improvement in ADL skill levels, but also some measure of how improved ADL skills will translate into social and economic benefits.

Models of Rehabilitation Delivery

Models of delivery refer to the settings, providers, and methods of reimbursement that enable services to be delivered to the patient. Today, there is a growing demand for rehabilitation services, due primarily to the aging of the population, increased emphasis on chronic disease and disability, and increased options for intervention. To satisfy this demand, there likewise has been an increase in the number of some types of providers of rehabilitation services and an increase in the provision of services in skilled nursing facilities, the home, and other ambulatory settings. As discussed above, there is also a trend from fee-for-service to capitated, or risk, payment.

Most rehabilitation programs employ a multidisciplinary approach to address cognitive, emotional, and family issues in addition to mobility and self-care. A meta-analysis comparing inpatient multidisciplinary rehabilitation services with usual medical care indicated the following:

- Rehabilitation services were significantly associated with better rates of survival and improved function during hospitalization, although these differences were not significant at followup.

- Rehabilitation services were significantly associated with increased rates of patients' return to and stay at home.

- There were no significant differences between rehabilitation services and usual medical care in long-term survival or functioning outcomes.

Multimodal interventions have been shown to be more effective for some conditions, for example, for prevention of falls among geriatric patients. Rehabilitation must consider social and environmental influences; further, they should account for the inevitable interaction of multiple diseases and impairments, particularly among older adults.

Types of Rehabilitation Settings of Care

Inpatient Setting

- **General acute hospital**: Compared to other settings, general acute hospitals tend to have a greater emphasis on medical care and less emphasis on custodial care. Rehabilitation efforts in this setting usually occur subsequent to an acute event (e.g., stroke), not as a response to a chronic condition (e.g., vision impairment). Because of the high costs and prevalence of prospective payment systems for inpatient care, rehabilitation services provided in this setting are likely to be subject to cost-effectiveness scrutiny.

- **Subacute rehabilitation hospital or residential nursing home:** Rehabilitation services may be provided in residential nursing homes, particularly when rehabilitation involves medical and custodial care that is not easily delivered in a home setting, or when the patient does not have a caregiver able to provide rehabilitation in a home setting. Given the prevalence of multiple interactive disabilities among the elderly, residential nursing homes are important avenues recognizing disabilities that may be secondary to the primary reason for admission.

There is little evidence regarding the relative effectiveness of inpatient versus outpatient rehabilitation. One study found that general hospital inpatients received more treatment than patients in skilled nursing facilities. In some cases, functional outcomes have been shown to be worse when care is provided in skilled nursing facilities.

Rehabilitation: Options for People with Disabilities

Outpatient Setting

- **Provider office:** Rehabilitation services may be provided in the office of a provider who may or may not specialize in the area of the patient's disability.

- **Community-based:** Community-based services have the advantage of providing social group support. Community-based rehabilitation would include activities to promote normal development, training of clients in self-care and mobility, and language and speech training.

- **Home care:** Rehabilitation services provided in the home emphasize environmental and behavioral modifications to increase independent functioning. Home care facilitates the consideration of individual psychosocial and familial factors in service provision. Rehabilitation services often include physical environmental changes made to the home. Emerging technologies such as the "Smart Houses" have the potential to support rehabilitation at home.

Payment and Access

Access to rehabilitation services and other care for people with disabilities is of increasing concern given ongoing cost-containment pressures and the traditional emphasis in healthcare delivery on acute care services.

- **Managed Care:** Several main aspects of rehabilitation services present fiscal risks to capitated healthcare plans, and thereby provide disincentives for improving access to these services. Among these are that disabled persons tend to be higher users of healthcare services, encounters with disabled patients tend to be more time consuming than most other types of visits, and it is difficult to determine accurate risk-adjustments for disabled populations. The greater financial risk posed by offering rehabilitation services to disabled populations raises the stakes for demonstrating improved functional and health outcomes and cost-effectiveness in rehabilitation.

The Healthcare Effectiveness Data and Information Set (HEDIS), the health plan "report card" intended to assist employers in selecting managed care includes measures of functioning. While capitated plans would appear to have greater disincentives to provide rehabilitation services than fee-for-service plans, actual differences are not well documented. For example, a survey of 258 people with a variety of disabilities in Massachusetts found no significant differences between their ratings of fee-for-service and managed care plans and providers. Important to patients were appointment availability, accessibility of physician offices, and physician understanding of their disabilities.

- **Industry Consolidation:** Corporate consolidation of inpatient rehabilitation services poses opportunities and threats to access. It is an opportunity in that it may offer economies of scale in products and services, standardization, and quality control. It is a threat in that it could ultimately result in diminished services in areas, such as rural areas, that are less profitable.

- **Payer Status:** Publicly paid rehabilitation services have eligibility specifications based upon clinical diagnoses. It is unclear whether eligibility standards result in over- or under-inclusiveness. In addition, the literature indicates that eligibility for Social Security Administration (SSA) and Social Security Disability Insurance (SSDI) programs may present work disincentives by discouraging individuals from seeking employment for fear of losing income-based benefits.

States rely heavily on Rehabilitation Act funds for rehabilitation services.

Private health insurance generally offers better benefits for assistive technologies. However, private-pay services may have limited financial and geographical access.

Chapter 48

Choosing a Long-Term Care Setting

What Is Long-Term Care?

Long-term care involves a variety of services designed to meet a person's health or personal care needs during a short or long period of time. These services help people live as independently and safely as possible when they can no longer perform everyday activities on their own.

Long-term care is provided in different places by different caregivers, depending on a person's needs. Most long-term care is provided at home by unpaid family members and friends. It can also be given in a facility such as a nursing home or in the community, for example, in an adult day care center.

This chapter contains text excerpted from the following sources: Text under the heading "What Is Long-Term Care?" is excerpted from "What Is Long-Term Care?" National Institute on Aging (NIA), National Institutes of Health (NIH), May 1, 2017; Text under the heading "Choosing a Nursing Home" is excerpted from "Choosing a Nursing Home," National Institute on Aging (NIA), National Institutes of Health (NIH), May 1, 2017; Text under the heading "Residential Facilities, Assisted Living, and Nursing Homes" is excerpted from "Residential Facilities, Assisted Living, and Nursing Homes," National Institute on Aging (NIA), National Institutes of Health (NIH), May 1, 2017; Text under the heading "Planning for Long-Term Care" is excerpted from "Planning for Long-Term Care," National Institute on Aging (NIA), National Institutes of Health (NIH), May 1, 2017.

The most common type of long-term care is personal care—help with everyday activities, also called "activities of daily living." These activities include bathing, dressing, grooming, using the toilet, eating, and moving around—for example, getting out of bed and into a chair.

Long-term care also includes community services such as meals, adult day care, and transportation services. These services may be provided free or for a fee.

People often need long-term care when they have a serious, ongoing health condition or disability. The need for long-term care can arise suddenly, such as after a heart attack or stroke. Most often, however, it develops gradually, as people get older and frailer or as an illness or disability gets worse.

Home-Based Long-Term Care Services

Home-based long-term care includes health, personal, and support services to help people stay at home and live as independently as possible. Most long-term care is provided either in the home of the person receiving services or at a family member's home. In-home services may be short-term—for someone who is recovering from an operation, for example—or long-term, for people who need ongoing help.

Most home-based services involve personal care, such as help with bathing, dressing, and taking medications, and supervision to make sure a person is safe. Unpaid family members, partners, friends, and neighbors provide most of this type of care.

Home Healthcare

Home healthcare involves part-time medical services ordered by a physician for a specific condition. These services may include nursing care to help a person recover from surgery, an accident, or illness. Home healthcare may also include physical, occupational, or speech therapy and temporary home health aide services. These services are provided by home healthcare agencies approved by Medicare, a government insurance program for people over age 65.

Homemaker Services

Home health agencies offer personal care and homemaker services that can be purchased without a physician's order. Personal care includes help with bathing and dressing. Homemaker services include help with meal preparation and household chores. Agencies do not have to be approved by Medicare to provide these kinds of services.

Choosing a Long-Term Care Setting

Friendly Visitor/Companion Services

Friendly visitor/companion services are usually staffed by volunteers who regularly pay short visits (less than 2 hours) to someone who is frail or living alone. You can also purchase these services from home health agencies.

Transportation Services

Transportation services help people get to and from medical appointments, shopping centers, and other places in the community. Some senior housing complexes and community groups offer transportation services. Many public transit agencies have services for people with disabilities. Some services are free. Others charge a fee.

Emergency Response Systems

Emergency response systems automatically respond to medical and other emergencies via electronic monitors. The user wears a necklace or bracelet with a button to push in an emergency. Pushing the button summons emergency help to the home. This type of service is especially useful for people who live alone or are at risk of falling. A monthly fee is charged.

Choosing a Nursing Home

A nursing home, also known as a skilled nursing facility, provides a wide range of health and personal care services. These services typically include nursing care, 24-hour supervision, three meals a day, and assistance with everyday activities. Rehabilitation services, such as physical, occupational, and speech therapy, are also available.

Some people stay at a nursing home for a short time after being in the hospital. After they recover, they go home. However, most nursing home residents live there permanently because they have ongoing physical or mental conditions that require constant care and supervision.

If you need to go to a nursing home after a hospital stay, the hospital staff can help you find one that will provide the kind of care that's best for you. If you are looking for a nursing home, ask your doctor's office for recommendations. Once you know what choices you have, it's a good idea to:

- **Consider.** What is important to you—nursing care, meals, physical therapy, a religious connection, hospice care, or special care units for dementia patients? Do you want a place close to family and friends so they can easily visit?

- **Ask.** Talk with friends, relatives, social workers, and religious groups to find out what places they suggest. Check with healthcare providers about which nursing homes they feel provide good care.

- **Call.** Get in touch with each place on your list. Ask questions about how many people live there and what it costs. Find out about waiting lists.

- **Visit.** Make plans to meet with the director and the nursing director. For example, look for:
  - Medicare and Medicaid certification
  - Handicap access
  - Residents who look well cared for
  - Warm interaction between staff and residents

- **Talk.** Don't be afraid to ask questions. For example, ask the staff to explain any strong odors. Bad smells might indicate a problem; good ones might hide a problem. You might want to find out how long the director and heads of nursing, food, and social services departments have worked at the nursing home. If key members of the staff change often, that could mean there's something wrong.

- **Visit again.** Make a second visit without calling ahead. Try another day of the week or time of day so you will meet other staff members and see different activities. Stop by at mealtime. Is the dining room attractive and clean? Does the food look tempting?

- **Understand.** Once you select a nursing home, carefully read the contract. Question the director or assistant director about anything you don't understand. Ask a good friend or family member to read over the contract before you sign it.

The Centers for Medicare and Medicaid Services (CMS) requires each State to inspect any nursing home that gets money from the government. Homes that don't pass inspection are not certified. Ask to see the current inspection report and certification of any nursing home you are considering.

Choosing a Long-Term Care Setting

Residential Facilities, Assisted Living, and Nursing Homes

At some point, support from family, friends, and local programs may not be enough. People who require help full-time might move to a residential facility that provides many or all of the long-term care services they need.

Facility-based long-term care services include: board and care homes, assisted living facilities, nursing homes, and continuing care retirement communities. Some facilities have only housing and housekeeping, but many also provide personal care and medical services. Many facilities offer special programs for people with Alzheimer disease and other types of dementia.

Board and Care Homes

Board and care homes, also called residential care facilities or group homes, are small private facilities, usually with 20 or fewer residents. Rooms may be private or shared. Residents receive personal care and meals and have staff available around the clock. Nursing and medical care usually are not provided on site.

Assisted Living

Assisted living is for people who need help with daily care, but not as much help as a nursing home provides. Assisted living facilities range in size from as few as 25 residents to 120 or more. Typically, a few "levels of care" are offered, with residents paying more for higher levels of care.

Assisted living residents usually live in their own apartments or rooms and share common areas. They have access to many services, including up to three meals a day; assistance with personal care; help with medications, housekeeping, and laundry; 24-hour supervision, security, and on-site staff; and social and recreational activities. Exact arrangements vary from state to state.

Nursing Homes

Nursing homes, also called skilled nursing facilities, provide a wide range of health and personal care services. Their services focus on medical care more than most assisted living facilities. These services typically include nursing care, 24-hour supervision, three meals a day, and assistance with everyday activities. Rehabilitation services, such as physical, occupational, and speech therapy, are also available.

Some people stay at a nursing home for a short time after being in the hospital. After they recover, they go home. However, most nursing home residents live there permanently because they have ongoing physical or mental conditions that require constant care and supervision.

Continuing Care Retirement Communities (CCRCs)

Continuing care retirement communities also called life care communities, offer different levels of service in one location. Many of them offer independent housing (houses or apartments), assisted living, and skilled nursing care all on one campus. Healthcare services and recreation programs are also provided.

In a CCRC, where you live depends on the level of service you need. People who can no longer live independently move to the assisted living facility or sometimes receive home care in their independent living unit. If necessary, they can enter the CCRC's nursing home.

Planning for Long-Term Care

You can never know for sure if you will need long-term care. Maybe you will never need it. But an unexpected accident, illness, or injury can change your needs, sometimes suddenly. The best time to think about long-term care is before you need it.

Planning for the possibility of long-term care gives you time to learn about services in your community and what they cost. It also allows you to make important decisions while you are still able.

Housing Decisions: Staying in Your Home

In thinking about long-term care, it is important to consider where you will live as you age and how your place of residence can best support your needs if you can no longer fully care for yourself.

Most people prefer to stay in their own home for as long as possible. Learn about services, products, and resources that can help older adults stay in their homes.

Decisions about Your Health

Begin by thinking about what would happen if you became seriously ill or disabled. Talk with your family, friends, and lawyer about who would provide care if you needed help for a long time.

Choosing a Long-Term Care Setting

You might delay or prevent the need for long-term care by staying healthy and independent. Talk to your doctor about your medical and family history and lifestyle. He or she may suggest actions you can take to improve your health. Healthy eating, regular physical activity, not smoking, and limited drinking of alcohol can help you stay healthy. So can an active social life, a safe home, and regular healthcare.

Talking with Relatives about Long-Term Care

It can be difficult to make the decision about whether you or a loved one needs to leave home. Sometimes, decisions about where to care for a family member need to be made quickly, for example, when a sudden injury requires a new care plan. Other times, a family has a while to look for the best place to care for an elderly relative.

You may have had a conversation with a loved one where they asked you not to "put them" in a nursing home. Many of us want to stay in our own homes. Agreeing that you will not put someone in a nursing home may close the door to the right care option for your family. The fact is that for some illnesses and for some people, professional healthcare in a long-term care facility is the only reasonable choice.

Decisions about Finances

Long-term care can be expensive. Americans spend billions of dollars a year on various services. How people pay for long-term care depends on their financial situation and the kinds of services they use. Often, they rely on a variety of payment sources, including:

- Personal funds, including pensions, savings, and income from stocks
- Government health insurance programs, such as Medicare and Medicaid
- Private financing options, such as long-term care insurance
- Veterans' benefits
- Services through the Older Americans Act (OAA)

Part Five

Special Education for Children with Disabilities

Chapter 49

Laws about Educating Children with Disabilities

Chapter Contents

Section 49.1—Individuals with Disabilities
 Education Act 530
Section 49.2—Every Student Succeeds Act 532
Section 49.3—Section 504 of the Rehabilitation Act 535

Section 49.1

Individuals with Disabilities Education Act

This section includes text excerpted from "About IDEA," U.S. Department of Education (ED), December 15, 2015.

The Individuals with Disabilities Education Act (IDEA) is a law that makes available a free appropriate public education to eligible children with disabilities throughout the nation and ensures special education and related services to those children.

The IDEA governs how states and public agencies provide early intervention, special education, and related services to more than 6.5 million eligible infants, toddlers, children, and youth with disabilities.

Infants and toddlers, birth through age two, with disabilities and their families receive early intervention services under IDEA Part C. Children and youth ages three through 21 receive special education and related services under IDEA Part B.

Additionally, the IDEA authorizes:

- Formula grants to states to support special education and related services and early intervention services.

- Discretionary grants to state educational agencies, institutions of higher education, and other nonprofit organizations to support research, demonstrations, technical assistance and dissemination, technology development, personnel preparation and development, and parent-training and information centers.

Congress reauthorized the IDEA in 2004 and most recently amended the IDEA through Public Law 114-95, the Every Student Succeeds Act (ESSA), in December 2015.

In the law, Congress states:

Disability is a natural part of the human experience and in no way diminishes the right of individuals to participate in or contribute to society. Improving educational results for children with disabilities is an essential element of our national policy of ensuring equality of opportunity, full participation, independent living, and economic self-sufficiency for individuals with disabilities.

IDEA Purpose

The stated purpose of the IDEA is:

- to ensure that all children with disabilities have available to them a free appropriate public education that emphasizes special education and related services designed to meet their unique needs and prepare them for further education, employment, and independent living;

- to ensure that the rights of children with disabilities and parents of such children are protected;

- to assist states, localities, educational service agencies, and federal agencies to provide for the education of all children with disabilities;

- to assist states in the implementation of a statewide, comprehensive, coordinated, multidisciplinary, interagency system of early intervention services for infants and toddlers with disabilities and their families;

- to ensure that educators and parents have the necessary tools to improve educational results for children with disabilities by supporting system improvement activities; coordinated research and personnel preparation; coordinated technical assistance, dissemination, and support; and technology development and media services;

- to assess, and ensure the effectiveness of, efforts to educate children with disabilities.

History of the IDEA

On November 29, 1975, President Gerald Ford signed into law the Education for All Handicapped Children Act (EAHCA) (Public Law 94-142), now known as the Individuals with Disabilities Education Act (IDEA). In adopting this landmark civil rights measure, Congress opened public school doors for millions of children with disabilities and laid the foundation of the country's commitment to ensuring that children with disabilities have opportunities to develop their talents, share their gifts, and contribute to their communities.

The law guaranteed access to a free appropriate public education (FAPE) in the least restrictive environment (LRE) to every child with a disability. Subsequent amendments, as reflected in the IDEA, have led to an increased emphasis on access to the general education curriculum, the provision of services for young children from birth through five, transition planning, and accountability for the achievement of students with disabilities. The IDEA upholds and protects the rights of infants, toddlers, children, and youth with disabilities and their families.

In the last 40+ years, we have advanced our expectations for all children, including children with disabilities. Classrooms have become more inclusive and the future of children with disabilities is brighter. Significant progress has been made toward protecting the rights of, meeting the individual needs of, and improving educational results and outcomes for infants, toddlers, children, and youths with disabilities.

Since 1975, we have progressed from excluding nearly 1.8 million children with disabilities from public schools to providing more than 6.9 million children with disabilities special education and related services designed to meet their individual needs.

Nowadays, more than 62 percent of children with disabilities are in general education classrooms 80 percent or more of their school day, and early intervention services are being provided to more than 340,000 infants and toddlers with disabilities and their families.

Section 49.2

Every Student Succeeds Act

This section includes text excerpted from "Every Student Succeeds Act (ESSA)," U.S. Department of Education (ED), December 10, 2015.

A New Education Law

The Every Student Succeeds Act (ESSA) was signed by President Obama on December 10, 2015, and represents good news for our nation's schools. This bipartisan measure reauthorizes the 50-year-old Elementary and Secondary Education Act (ESEA), the nation's national education law and longstanding commitment to equal opportunity for all students.

Laws about Educating Children with Disabilities

The new law builds on key areas of progress in recent years, made possible by the efforts of educators, communities, parents, and students across the country.

For example, today, high school graduation rates are at all-time highs. Dropout rates are at historic lows. And more students are going to college than ever before. These achievements provide a firm foundation for further work to expand educational opportunity and improve student outcomes under ESSA.

The previous version of the law, the No Child Left Behind (NCLB) Act, was enacted in 2002. NCLB represented a significant step forward for our nation's children in many respects, particularly as it shined a light on where students were making progress and where they needed additional support, regardless of race, income, zip code, disability, home language, or background. The law was scheduled for revision in 2007, and, over time, NCLB's prescriptive requirements became increasingly unworkable for schools and educators. Recognizing this fact, in 2010, the Obama administration joined a call from educators and families to create a better law that focused on the clear goal of fully preparing all students for success in college and careers.

Congress has now responded to that call.

The ESSA reflects many of the priorities of this administration.

Every Student Succeeds Act Highlights

President Obama signed the ESSA into law on December 10, 2015.

ESSA includes provisions that will help to ensure success for students and schools. Below are just a few. The law:

- Advances equity by upholding critical protections for America's disadvantaged and high-need students.

- Requires—for the first time—that all students in America be taught to high academic standards that will prepare them to succeed in college and careers.

- Ensures that vital information is provided to educators, families, students, and communities through annual statewide assessments that measure students' progress toward those high standards.

- Helps to support and grow local innovations—including evidence-based and place-based interventions developed by local leaders and educators—consistent with our Investing in Innovation and Promise Neighborhoods

- Sustains and expands this administration's historic investments in increasing access to high-quality preschool.
- Maintains an expectation that there will be accountability and action to effect positive change in our lowest-performing schools, where groups of students are not making progress, and where graduation rates are low over extended periods of time.

History of Elementary and Secondary Education Act

The Elementary and Secondary Education Act (ESEA) was signed into law in 1965 by President Lyndon Baines Johnson, who believed that "full educational opportunity" should be "our first national goal." From its inception, ESEA was a civil rights law.

ESEA offered new grants to districts serving low-income students, federal grants for textbooks and library books, funding for special education centers, and scholarships for low-income college students. Additionally, the law provided federal grants to state educational agencies to improve the quality of elementary and secondary education.

No Child Left Behind and Accountability

No Child Left Behind (NCLB) put in place measures that exposed achievement gaps among traditionally underserved students and their peers and spurred an important national dialogue on education improvement. This focus on accountability has been critical in ensuring a quality education for all children, yet also revealed challenges in the effective implementation of this goal.

Parents, educators, and elected officials across the country recognized that a strong, updated law was necessary to expand opportunity to all students; support schools, teachers, and principals; and to strengthen our education system and economy.

In 2012, the Obama administration began granting flexibility to states regarding specific requirements of NCLB in exchange for rigorous and comprehensive state-developed plans designed to close achievement gaps, increase equity, improve the quality of instruction, and increase outcomes for all students.

Laws about Educating Children with Disabilities

Section 49.3

Section 504 of the Rehabilitation Act

This section includes text excerpted from "Your Rights under Section 504 of the Rehabilitation Act," U.S. Department of Health and Human Services (HHS), June 1, 2006. Reviewed July 2018.

What Is Section 504?

Section 504 of the Rehabilitation Act of 1973 is a national law that protects qualified individuals from discrimination based on their disability. The nondiscrimination requirements of the law apply to employers and organizations that receive financial assistance from any federal department or agency, including the U.S. Department of Health and Human Services (HHS). These organizations and employers include many hospitals, nursing homes, mental health centers, and human service programs.

Section 504 forbids organizations and employers from excluding or denying individuals with disabilities an equal opportunity to receive program benefits and services. It defines the rights of individuals with disabilities to participate in, and have access to, program benefits and services.

Who Is Protected from Discrimination?

Section 504 protects qualified individuals with disabilities. Under this law, individuals with disabilities are defined as persons with a physical or mental impairment which substantially limits one or more major life activities. People who have a history of, or who are regarded as having a physical or mental impairment that substantially limits one or more major life activities, are also covered. Major life activities include caring for one's self, walking, seeing, hearing, speaking, breathing, working, performing manual tasks, and learning. Some examples of impairments which may substantially limit major life activities, even with the help of medication or aids/devices, are acquired immunodeficiency syndrome (AIDS), alcoholism, blindness or visual impairment, cancer, deafness or hearing impairment, diabetes, drug addiction, heart disease, and mental illness.

In addition to meeting the above definition, for purposes of receiving services, education or training, qualified individuals with disabilities are persons who meet normal and essential eligibility requirements.

For purposes of employment, qualified individuals with disabilities are persons who, with reasonable accommodation, can perform the essential functions of the job for which they have applied or have been hired to perform. (Complaints alleging employment discrimination on the basis of disability against a single individual will be referred to the U. S. Equal Employment Opportunity Commission (EEOC) for processing.). Reasonable accommodation means an employer is required to take reasonable steps to accommodate your disability unless it would cause the employer undue hardship.

Prohibited Discriminatory Acts in Healthcare and Human Services Settings

Section 504 prohibitions against discrimination apply to service availability, accessibility, delivery, employment, and the administrative activities and responsibilities of organizations receiving federal financial assistance. A recipient of federal financial assistance may not, on the basis of disability:

- Deny qualified individuals the opportunity to participate in or benefit from federally funded programs, services, or other benefits

- Deny access to programs, services, benefits, or opportunities to participate as a result of physical barriers

- Deny employment opportunities, including hiring, promotion, training, and fringe benefits, for which they are otherwise entitled or qualified

These and other prohibitions against discrimination based on disability can be found in the Department of Health and Human Services (DHHS) Section 504 regulation at 45 CFR Part 84.

Chapter 50

Evaluating Children for Disability

Evaluation is an essential beginning step in the special education process for a child with a disability. Before a child can receive special education and related services for the first time, a full and individual initial evaluation of the child must be conducted to see if the child has a disability and is eligible for special education. Informed parent consent must be obtained before this evaluation may be conducted. The evaluation process is guided by requirements in our nation's special education law, the Individuals with Disabilities Education Act (IDEA).

Purposes of Evaluation

The initial evaluation of a child is required by IDEA before any special education and related services can be provided to that child. The purposes of conducting this evaluation are straightforward:

- To see if the child is a "child with a disability," as defined by IDEA
- To gather information that will help determine the child's educational needs
- To guide decision making about appropriate educational programming for the child

---

This chapter includes text excerpted from "Evaluating Children for Disability," Center for Parent Information and Resources (CPIR), September 9, 2017.

IDEA's Definition of a "Child with a Disability"

IDEA lists different disability categories under which a child may be found eligible for special education and related services. These categories are:

- Autism
- Deafness
- Deaf-blindness
- Developmental delay
- Emotional disturbance
- Hearing impairment
- Intellectual disability (ID)
- Multiple disabilities
- Orthopedic impairment
- Other health impairment
- Specific learning disability
- Speech or language impairment
- Traumatic brain injury (TBI)
- Visual impairment, including blindness

Having a disability, though, does not necessarily make a child eligible for special education. Consider this language from the IDEA regulations:

> Child with a disability means a child evaluated in accordance with §§300.304 through 300.311 as having [one of the disabilities listed above] and who, by reason thereof, needs special education and related services. [emphasis added]

This provision includes the very important phrase "... *and who, by reason thereof...*" This means that, *because of the disability*, the child needs special education and related services. Many children have disabilities that do not bring with them the need for extra educational assistance or individualized educational programming. If a child has a disability but is not eligible under IDEA, he or she may be eligible for the protections afforded by other laws—such as Section 504 of the Rehabilitation Act of 1973, as amended. It's not uncommon for a child to have a 504 plan at school to address disability-related

Evaluating Children for Disability

educational needs. Such a child will receive needed assistance but not under IDEA.

Identifying Children for Evaluation

Before a child's eligibility under IDEA can be determined, however, a full and individual evaluation of the child must be conducted. There are at least two ways in which a child may be identified to receive an evaluation under IDEA:

1. Parents may request that their child be evaluated. Parents are often the first to notice that their child's learning, behavior, or development may be a cause for concern. If they're worried about their child's progress in school and think he or she might need extra help from special education services, they may call, email, or write to their child's teacher, the school's principal, or the Director of Special Education in the school district. If the school agrees that an evaluation is needed, it must evaluate the child at no cost to parents.

2. The school system may ask to evaluate the child. Based on a teacher's recommendation, observations, or results from tests given to all children in a particular grade, a school may recommend that a child receive further screening or assessment to determine if he or she has a disability and needs special education and related services. The school system must ask parents for permission to evaluate the child, and parents must give their informed written permission before the evaluation may be conducted.

Giving Parents Notice

It is important to know that IDEA requires the school system to notify parents in writing that it would like to evaluate their child (or that it is refusing to evaluate the child). This is called giving prior written notice. It is not enough for the agency to tell parents that it would like to evaluate their child or that it refuses to evaluate their child. The school must also:

- explain why it wants to conduct the evaluation (or why it refuses);
- describe each evaluation procedure, assessment, record, or report used as a basis for proposing the evaluation (or refusing to conduct the evaluation);
- where parents can go to obtain help in understanding IDEA's provisions;

- what other options the school considered and why those were rejected; and

- a description of any other factors that are relevant to the school's proposal (or refusal) to evaluate the child.

The purpose behind this thorough explanation is to make sure that parents are fully informed, understand what is being proposed (or refused), understand what evaluation of their child will involve (or why the school system is refusing to conduct an evaluation of the child), and understand their right to refuse consent for evaluation, or to otherwise exercise their rights under IDEA's procedural safeguards if the school refuses to evaluate.

All written communication from the school must be in a form the general public can understand. It must be provided in parents' native language if they do not read English, or in the mode of communication, they normally use (such as Braille or large print) unless it is clearly not feasible to do so. If parents' native language or other mode of communication is not a written language, the school must take steps to ensure:

- that the notice is translated orally (or by other means) to parents in their native language or other mode of communication,

- that parents understand the content of the notice, and

- that there is written evidence that the above two requirements have been met.

Parental Consent

Before the school may proceed with the evaluation, parents must give their informed written consent. This consent is for the evaluation only. It does not mean that the school has the parents' permission to provide special education services to the child. That requires a separate consent.

If parents refuse consent for an initial evaluation (or simply don't respond to the school's request), the school must carefully document all its attempts to obtain parent consent. It may also continue to pursue conducting the evaluation by using the law's due process procedures or its mediation procedures unless doing so would be inconsistent with state law relating to parental consent.

However, if the child is home-schooled or has been placed in a private school by parents (meaning, the parents are paying for the cost of the private school), the school may not override parents' lack of consent for initial evaluation of the child. As the U.S. Department of Education (ED) (2006) notes:

...once parents opt out of the public school system, states and school districts do not have the same interest in requiring parents to agree to the evaluation of their children. In such cases, it would be overly intrusive for the school district to insist on an evaluation over a parent's objection.

Timeframe for Initial Evaluation

In its reauthorization of IDEA in 2004, Congress added a specific timeframe: The initial evaluation must be conducted within 60 days of receiving parental consent for the evaluation—or if the state establishes its own timeframe for conducting an initial evaluation, within that timeframe. (In other words: Any timeframe established by the state takes precedence over the 60-day timeline required by IDEA.)

The Scope of Evaluation

A child's initial evaluation must be full and individual, focused on that child and only that child. This is a longstanding provision of IDEA. An evaluation of a child under IDEA means much more than the child sitting in a room with the rest of his or her class taking an exam for that class, that school, that district, or that state. How the child performs on such exams will contribute useful information to an IDEA-related evaluation, but large-scale tests or group-administered instruments are not enough to diagnose a disability or determine what, if any, special education or related services the child might need, let alone plan an appropriate educational program for the child.

The evaluation must use a variety of assessment tools and strategies to gather relevant functional, developmental, and academic information about the child, including information provided by the parent. When conducting an initial evaluation, it's important to examine all areas of a child's functioning to determine not only if the child is a child with a disability, but also determine the child's educational needs. This full and individual evaluation includes evaluating the child's:

- Health
- Vision and hearing
- Social and emotional status
- General intelligence

- Academic performance
- Communicative status
- Motor abilities

As IDEA states, the school system must ensure that—
...the evaluation is sufficiently comprehensive to identify all of the child's special education and related services needs, whether or not commonly linked to the disability category in which the child has been classified.

Review of Existing Data

Evaluation (and particularly re-evaluation) typically begins with a review of existing evaluation data on the child, which may come from the child's classroom work, his or her performance on state or district assessments, information provided by the parents, and so on.

The purpose of this review is to decide if the existing data is sufficient to establish the child's eligibility and determine educational needs, or if additional information is needed. If the group determines there is sufficient information available to make the necessary determinations, the public agency must notify parents:

- of that determination and the reason for it; and
- that parents have the right to request an assessment to determine the child's eligibility and educational needs.

Unless the parents request an assessment, the public agency is not required to conduct one.

If it is decided that additional data is needed, the group then identifies what is needed to determine:

- whether your son or daughter has a particular category of disability (e.g., "other health impairment," "specific learning disability");
- your child's present levels of performance (that is, how he or she is currently doing in school) and his or her academic and developmental needs;
- whether your child needs special education and related services; and
- if so, whether any additions or modifications are needed in the special education and related services to enable your child to

meet the goals set out in the individualized education program (IEP) to be developed and to participate, as appropriate, in the general curriculum.

An example may help crystallize the comprehensive scope of evaluations: Consider a first-grader with suspected hearing and vision impairments who's been referred for an initial evaluation. In order to fully gather relevant functional, developmental, and academic information and identify all of the child's special education and related services needs, evaluation of this child will obviously need to focus on hearing and vision, as well as, cognitive, speech/language, motor, and social/behavioral skills, to determine:

- the degree of impairment in vision and hearing and the impact of these impairments on the child;
- if there are additional impairments in other areas of functioning (including those not commonly linked to hearing and/or vision) that impact the child's aptitude, performance, and achievement; and
- what the child's educational needs are that must be addressed.

With this example, any of the following individuals might be part of this child's evaluation team: audiologist, psychologist, speech-language pathologist, social worker, occupational or physical therapist, vision specialist, regular classroom teacher, educational diagnosticians, or others.

Variety, Variety!

The evaluation must use a variety of assessment tools and strategies. This has been one of the cornerstones of IDEA's evaluation requirements from its earliest days. Under IDEA, it is inappropriate and unacceptable to base any eligibility decision upon the results of only one procedure. Tests alone will not give a comprehensive picture of how a child performs or what he or she knows or does not know. Only by collecting data through a variety of approaches (e.g., observations, interviews, tests, curriculum-based assessment, and so on) and from a variety of sources (parents, teachers, specialists, child) can an adequate picture be obtained of the child's strengths and weaknesses.

IDEA also requires schools to use technically sound instruments and processes in evaluation. Technically sound instruments generally refers to assessments that have been shown through research to be valid and reliable. Technically sound processes require that assessments and other evaluation materials be:

- administered by trained and knowledgeable personnel;
- administered in accordance with any instructions provided by the producer of the assessments; and
- used for the purposes for which the assessments or measures are valid and reliable.

In conjunction with using a variety of sound tools and processes, assessments must include those that are tailored to assess specific areas of educational need (for example, reading or math) and not merely those that are designed to provide a single general intelligence quotient or IQ.

Taken together, all of this information can be used to determine whether the child has a disability under IDEA, the specific nature of the child's special needs, whether the child needs special education and related services and, if so, to design an appropriate program.

Consider Language, Communication Mode, and Culture

Another important component in evaluation is to ensure that assessment tools are not discriminatory on a racial or cultural basis. Evaluation must also be conducted in the child's typical, accustomed mode of communication (unless it is clearly not feasible to do so) and in a form that will yield accurate information about what the child knows and can do academically, developmentally, and functionally. For many, English is not the native language; others use sign to communicate, or assistive or alternative augmentative communication devices. To assess such a child using a means of communication or response not highly familiar to the child raises the probability that the evaluation results will yield minimal, if any, information about what the child knows and can do.

Specifically, consideration of language, culture, and communication mode means the following:

- If your child has limited English proficiency, materials and procedures used to assess your child must be selected and administered to ensure that they measure the extent to which your child has a disability and needs special education, rather than measuring your child's English language skills.

Evaluating Children for Disability

This provision in the law is meant to protect children of different racial, cultural, or language backgrounds from misdiagnosis. For example, children's cultural backgrounds may affect their behavior or test responses in ways that teachers or other personnel do not understand. Similarly, if a child speaks a language other than English or has limited English proficiency, he or she may not understand directions or words on tests and may be unable to answer correctly. As a result, a child may mistakenly appear to be a slow learner or to have a hearing or communication problem.

- If an assessment is not conducted under standard conditions—meaning that some condition of the test has been changed (such as the qualifications of the person giving the test or the method of giving the test)—a description of the extent to which it varied from standard conditions must be included in the evaluation report.

- If your child has impaired sensory, manual, or speaking skills, the law requires that tests are selected and administered so as best to ensure that test results accurately reflect his or her aptitude or achievement level (or whatever other factors the test claims to measure), and not merely reflect your child's impaired sensory, manual, or speaking skills (unless the test being used is intended to measure those skills).

What about Evaluation for Specific Learning Disabilities?

IDEA's regulations specify additional procedures required to be used for determining the existence of a specific learning disability. Sections 300.307 through 300.311 spell out what these procedures are.

It's important to note, though, that IDEA 2004 made dramatic changes in how children who are suspected of having a learning disability are to be evaluated.

- States must not require the use of a severe discrepancy between intellectual ability and achievement.

- States must permit the use of a process based on the child's response to scientific, research-based intervention.

- States may permit the use of other alternative research-based procedures for determining whether a child has a specific learning disability.

- The team that makes the eligibility determination must include a regular education teacher and at least one person qualified to conduct individual diagnostic examinations of children, such as a school psychologist, speech-language pathologist, or remedial reading teacher.

Determining Eligibility

Parents were not always included in the group that determined their child's eligibility and, in fact, were often excluded. Since the IDEA Amendments of 1997, parents are to be part of the group that determines their child's eligibility and are also to be provided a copy of the evaluation report, as well as documentation of the determination of the child's eligibility.

Some school systems will hold a meeting where they consider only the eligibility of the child for special education and related services. At this meeting, your child's assessment results should be explained. The specialists who assessed your child will explain what they did, why they used the tests they did, your child's results on those tests or other evaluation procedures, and what your child's scores mean when compared to other children of the same age and grade.

It is important to know that the group may not determine that a child is eligible if the determinant factor for making that judgment is the child's lack of instruction in reading or math or the child's limited English proficiency. The child must otherwise meet the law's definition of a "child with a disability"—meaning that he or she has one of the disabilities listed in the law and, because of that disability, needs special education and related services.

If the evaluation results indicate that your child meets the definition of one or more of the disabilities listed under IDEA and needs special education and related services, the results will form the basis for developing your child's IEP.

What Happens If You Don't Agree with the Evaluation Results?

If you, as parents of a child with a disability, disagree with the results of your child's evaluation as obtained by the public agency, you have the right to obtain what is known as an Independent Educational Evaluation, or IEE. An IEE means an evaluation conducted by a qualified examiner who is not employed by the public agency responsible for the education of your child. If you ask for an IEE, the public agency

Evaluating Children for Disability

must provide you with, among other things, information about where an IEE may be obtained.

Who pays for the independent evaluation? The answer is that some IEEs are at public expense and others are paid for by the parents. For example, if you are the parent of a child with a disability and you disagree with the public agency's evaluation, you may request an IEE at public expense. "At public expense" means that the public agency either pays for the full cost of the evaluation or ensures that the evaluation is otherwise provided at no cost to you as parents. The public agency may grant your request and pay for the IEE, or it may initiate a hearing to show that its own evaluation was appropriate. The public agency may ask why you object to the public evaluation. However, the agency may not require you to explain, and it may not unreasonably delay either providing the IEE at public expense or initiating a due process hearing to defend the public evaluation.

If the public agency initiates a hearing and the final decision of the hearing officer is that the agency's evaluation was appropriate, then you still have the right to an IEE but not at public expense. As part of a due process hearing, a hearing officer may also request an IEE; if so, that IEE must be at public expense. Whenever an IEE is publicly funded, that IEE must meet the same criteria that the public agency uses when it initiates an evaluation. The public agency must tell you what these criteria are—such as location of the evaluation and the qualifications of the examiner—and they must be the same criteria the public agency uses when it initiates an evaluation, to the extent they are consistent with your right to an IEE. However, the public agency may not impose other conditions or timelines related to your obtaining an IEE at public expense.

Of course, you have the right to have your child independently evaluated at any time at your own expense. (When the same tests are repeated within a short time period, the validity of the results can be seriously weakened.) The results of this evaluation must be considered by the public agency, if it meets agency criteria, in any decision made with respect to providing your child with free appropriate public education (FAPE). The results may also be presented as evidence at a hearing regarding your child.

What Happens down the Road?

After the initial evaluation, evaluations must be conducted at least every three years (generally called a triennial evaluation) after your child has been placed in special education. Reevaluations can also occur more frequently if conditions warrant, or if you or your child's teacher request a reevaluation. Informed parental consent is also necessary for reevaluations.

As with initial evaluations, reevaluations begin with the review of existing evaluation data, including evaluations and information provided by you, the child's parents. Your consent is not required for the review of existing data on your child. As with initial evaluation, this review is to identify what additional data, if any, are needed to determine whether your child continues to be a "child with a disability" and continues to need special education and related services. If the group determines that additional data are needed, then the public agency must administer tests and other evaluation materials as needed to produce the data. Prior to collecting this additional information, the agency must obtain your informed written consent.

Or, if the group determines that no additional data are needed to determine whether your child continues to be a "child with a disability," the public agency must notify you:

- of this determination and the reasons for it; and

- of your right, as parents, to request an assessment to determine whether, for the purposes of services under IDEA, your child continues to be a "child with a disability."

A final note with respect to reevaluations: Before determining that your child is no longer a "child with a disability" and, thus, no longer eligible for special education services under IDEA, the public agency must evaluate your child in accordance with all of the provisions described above. This evaluation, however, is not required before terminating your child's eligibility due to graduation with a regular high school diploma or due to exceeding the age eligibility for FAPE under state law.

Chapter 51

Early Intervention Services

If you're concerned about the development of an infant or toddler, or you suspect that a little one has a disability, this chapter will summarize one terrific source of help—the early intervention system in your state. Early intervention services can help infants and toddlers with disabilities or delays to learn many key skills and catch up in their development. There's a lot to know about early intervention.

What Is Early Intervention?

Early intervention is a system of services that helps babies and toddlers with developmental delays or disabilities. Early intervention focuses on helping eligible babies and toddlers learn the basic and brand-new skills that typically develop during the first three years of life, such as:

- Physical (reaching, rolling, crawling, and walking)
- Cognitive (thinking, learning, solving problems)
- Communication (talking, listening, understanding)
- Social/emotional (playing, feeling secure and happy)
- Self-help (eating, dressing).

This chapter includes text excerpted from "Overview of Early Intervention," Center for Parent Information and Resources (CPIR), September 1, 2017.

Examples of Early Intervention Services

If an infant or toddler has a disability or a developmental delay in one or more of these developmental areas, that child will likely be eligible for early intervention services. Those services will be tailored to meet the child's individual needs and may include:

- Assistive technology (devices a child might need)
- Audiology or hearing services
- Speech and language services
- Counseling and training for a family
- Medical services
- Nursing services
- Nutrition services
- Occupational therapy
- Physical therapy
- Psychological services

Services may also be provided to address the needs and priorities of the child's family. Family-directed services are meant to help family members understand the special needs of their child and how to enhance his or her development.

Authorized by Law

Early intervention is available in every state and territory of the United States. The Individuals with Disabilities Education Act (IDEA) requires it—Part C of IDEA, to be precise. That's why you'll sometimes hear early intervention referred to as Part C.

Who's Eligible for Early Intervention?

Early intervention is intended for infants and toddlers who have a developmental delay or disability. Eligibility is determined by evaluating the child (with parents' consent) to see if the little one does, in fact, have a delay in development or a disability. Eligible children can receive early intervention services from birth through the third birthday (and sometimes beyond).

Early Intervention Services

For Some Children, from Birth

Sometimes it is known from the moment a child is born that early intervention services will be essential in helping the child grow and develop. Often this is so for children who are diagnosed at birth with a specific condition or who experience significant prematurity, very low birth weight, illness, or surgery soon after being born. Even before heading home from the hospital, this child's parents may be given a referral to their local early intervention office.

For Others, Because of Delays in Development

Some children have a relatively routine entry into the world, but may develop more slowly than others, experience setbacks, or develop in ways that seem very different from other children. For these children, a visit with a developmental pediatrician and a thorough evaluation may lead to an early intervention referral.

Parents don't have to wait for a referral to early intervention, however. If you're concerned about your child's development, you may contact your local program directly and ask to have your child evaluated. That evaluation is provided free of charge.

However, a child comes to be referred, evaluated, and determined eligible, early intervention services provide vital support so that children with developmental needs can thrive and grow.

What Is a Developmental Delay?

The term "developmental delay" is an important one in early intervention. Broadly speaking, it means that a child is delayed in some area of development. There are five areas in which development may be affected:

- Cognitive development
- Physical development, including vision and hearing
- Communication development
- Social or emotional development
- Adaptive development

Developmental Milestones

Think of all the baby skills that can fall under any one of those developmental areas! Babies and toddlers have a lot of new skills to learn, so it's always of concern when a child's development seems slow or more difficult than would normally be expected. Developmental milestones page (www.parentcenterhub.org/milestones-videos-in-english-and-spanish) outlines some of the typical skills that babies and toddlers learn by certain ages. It's a good resource to consult if you're concerned that a child may have a developmental delay.

Definition of "Developmental Delay"

Part C of IDEA broadly defines the term "developmental delay." But the exact meaning of the term varies from state to state, because each state defines the term for itself, including:

- Describing the evaluation and assessment procedures that will be used to measure a child's development in each of the five developmental areas.

- Specifying the level of delay in functioning (or other comparable criteria) that constitutes a developmental delay in each of the five developmental areas.

If You're Concerned about a Baby or Toddler's Development

It's not uncommon for parents and family members to become concerned when their beautiful baby or growing toddler doesn't seem to be developing according to the normal schedule of "baby" milestones.

"He hasn't rolled over yet."

"The little girl next door is already sitting up on her own!"

"She should be saying a few words by now."

Sound familiar? While it's true that children develop differently, at their own pace, and that the range of what's "normal" development is quite broad, it's hard not to worry and wonder.

What to Do

If you think that your child is not developing at the same pace or in the same way as most children his or her age, it is often a good idea to talk first to your child's pediatrician. Explain your concerns. Tell the doctor what you have observed with your child. Your child may have a disability or a developmental delay, or he or she may be at risk of having a disability or delay.

Early Intervention Services

You can also get in touch with your community's early intervention program, and ask to have your little one evaluated to see if he or she has a developmental delay or disability. This evaluation is free of charge, won't hurt your child, and looks at his or her basic skills. Based on that evaluation, your child may be eligible for early intervention services, which will be designed to address your child's special needs or delays.

How to Get in Touch with Your Community's Early Intervention Program

There are several ways to connect with the Early Intervention (EI) program in your community. Try any of these suggestions:

- Contact the Pediatrics branch in a local hospital and ask where you should call to find out about early intervention services in your area.

- Ask your pediatrician for a referral to the local early intervention system.

- Visit the Early Childhood Technical Assistance Center (ECTA) Center's early intervention "contacts" page, at: ectacenter.org/contact/ptccoord.asp

What to say to the early intervention contact person—Explain that you are concerned about your child's development. Say that you think your child may need early intervention services. Explain that you would like to have your child evaluated under Part C of IDEA.

Referral

Write down any information the contact person gives you. You will probably be referred to either your community's early intervention program or to what is known as Child Find. Child Find operates in every state to identify babies and toddlers who need early intervention services because of developmental delays or disability. You can use the Parent's Record-Keeping Worksheet (www.parentcenterhub.org/wp-content/uploads/repo_items/record-keeping.pdf) to keep track of this important information. In fact, in general, it's a good idea to write down the names and phone numbers of everyone you talk to as you move through the early intervention process.

The Evaluation and Assessment Process

Service Coordinator

Once connected with either Child Find or your community's early intervention program, you'll be assigned a service coordinator who will explain the early intervention process and help you through the next steps in that process. The service coordinator will serve as your single point of contact with the early intervention system.

Screening and/or Evaluation

One of the first things that will happen is that your child will be evaluated to see if, indeed, he or she has a developmental delay or disability. (In some states, there may be a preliminary step called screening to see if there's cause to suspect that a baby or toddler has a disability or developmental delay.) The family's service coordinator will explain what's involved in the screening and/or evaluation and ask for your permission to proceed. You must provide your written consent before screening and/or evaluation may take place.

The evaluation group will be made up of qualified people who have different areas of training and experience. Together, they know about children's speech and language skills, physical abilities, hearing and vision, and other important areas of development. They know how to work with children, even very young ones, to discover if a child has a problem or is developing within normal ranges. Group members may evaluate your child together or individually. As part of the evaluation, the team will observe your child, ask your child to do things, talk to you and your child, and use other methods to gather information. These procedures will help the team find out how your child functions in the five areas of development.

Exceptions for Diagnosed Physical or Mental Conditions

It's important to note that an evaluation of your child won't be necessary if he or she is automatically eligible due to a diagnosed physical or mental condition that has a high probability of resulting in a developmental delay. Such conditions include but aren't limited to chromosomal abnormalities; genetic or congenital disorders; sensory impairments; inborn errors of metabolism; disorders reflecting disturbance of the development of the nervous system; congenital infections; severe attachment disorders; and disorders secondary to exposure to toxic substances, including fetal alcohol syndrome. Many states have

Early Intervention Services

policies that further specify what conditions automatically qualify an infant or toddler for early intervention (e.g., Down syndrome, fragile X syndrome).

Determining Eligibility

The results of the evaluation will be used to determine your child's eligibility for early intervention services. You and a team of professionals will meet and review all of the data, results, and reports. The people on the team will talk with you about whether your child meets the criteria under IDEA and state policy for having a developmental delay, a diagnosed physical or mental condition, or being at risk for having a substantial delay. If so, your child is generally found to be eligible for services.

Initial Assessment of the Child

With parental consent, an in-depth assessment must now be conducted to determine your child's unique needs and the early intervention services appropriate to address those needs. Initial assessment will include reviewing the results of the evaluation, personal observation of your child, and identifying his or her needs in each developmental area.

Initial Assessment of the Family

With approval of the family members involved, assessments of family members are also conducted to identify the resources, concerns, and priorities of the family related to enhancing the development of your child. The family-directed assessment is voluntary on the part of each family member participating in the assessment and is based on information gathered through an assessment tool and also through an interview with those family members who elect to participate.

Who Pays for All This?

Under IDEA, evaluations and assessments are provided at no cost to parents. They are funded by state and federal monies.

Writing the Individualized Family Service Plan

Having collected a great deal of information about your child and family, it's now possible for the team (including you as parents) to sit down and write an individualized plan of action for your child and family. This plan is called the Individualized Family Service Plan, or IFSP. It is a very important document, and you, as parents, are important members of the team that develops it. Each state has specific guidelines for the IFSP. Your service coordinator can explain what the IFSP guidelines are in your state.

Guiding Principles

The IFSP is a written document that, among other things, outlines the early intervention services that your child and family will receive. One guiding principle of the IFSP is that the family is a child's greatest resource, that a young child's needs are closely tied to the needs of his or her family. The best way to support children and meet their needs is to support and build upon the individual strengths of their family. So, the IFSP is a whole family plan with the parents as major contributors in its development. Involvement of other team members will depend on what the child needs. These other team members could come from several agencies and may include medical people, therapists, child development specialists, social workers, and others.

What Information Is Included in an Individualized Family Service Plan?

Your child's IFSP must include the following:

- Your child's present physical, cognitive, communication, social/emotional, and adaptive development levels and needs
- Family information (with your agreement), including the resources, priorities, and concerns of you, as parents, and other family members closely involved with the child
- The major results or outcomes expected to be achieved for your child and family
- The specific services your child will be receiving
- Where in the natural environment (e.g., home, community) the services will be provided (if the services will not be provided in the natural environment, the IFSP must include a statement justifying why not)
- When and where your son or daughter will receive services
- The number of days or sessions he or she will receive each service and how long each session will last

Early Intervention Services

- Who will pay for the services
- The name of the service coordinator overseeing the implementation of the IFSP
- The steps to be taken to support your child's transition out of early intervention and into another program when the time comes.

The IFSP may also identify services your family may be interested in, such as financial information or information about raising a child with a disability.

Informed Parental Consent

The IFSP must be fully explained to you, the parents, and your suggestions must be considered. You must give written consent for each service to be provided. If you do not give your consent in writing, your child will not receive that service.

Reviewing and Updating the Individualized Family Service Plan

The IFSP is reviewed every six months and is updated at least once a year. This takes into account that children can learn, grow, and change quickly in just a short period of time.

Timeframes for All This

When the early intervention system receives a referral about a child with a suspected disability or developmental delay, a time clock starts running. Within 45 days, the early intervention system must complete the critical steps discussed thus far:

- screening (if used in the state),
- initial evaluation of the child,
- initial assessments of the child and family, and
- writing the IFSP (if the child has been found eligible).

That's a tall order, but important, given how quickly children grow and change. When a baby or toddler has developmental issues, they need to be addressed as soon as possible. So—45 days, that's the timeframe from referral to completion of the IFSP for an eligible child.

Who Pays for the Services?

Whether or not you, as parents, will have to pay for any services for your child depends on the policies of your state. Check with your service coordinator. Your state's system of payments must be available in writing and given to you, so there are no surprises or unexpected bills later.

What's Free to Families

Under Part C of IDEA, the following services must be provided at no cost to families:

- Child Find services;
- evaluations and assessments;
- the development and review of the IFSP; and
- service coordination.

When Services Are Not Free

Depending on your state's policies, you may have to pay for certain other services. You may be charged a "sliding-scale" fee, meaning the fees are based on what you earn. Some services may be covered by your health insurance, by Medicaid, or by Indian Health Services (IHS). The Part C system may ask for your permission to access your public or private insurance in order to pay for the early intervention services your child receives. In most cases, the early intervention system may not use your healthcare insurance (private or public) without your express, written consent. If you do not give such consent, the system may not limit or deny you or your child services.

Every effort is made to provide services to all infants and toddlers who need help, regardless of family income. Services cannot be denied to a child just because his or her family is not able to pay for them.

Chapter 52

Individualized Education Programs

An Individualized Education Program (IEP) is a written statement of the educational program designed to meet a child's individual needs. Every child who receives special education services must have an IEP. That's why the process of developing this vital document is of great interest and importance to educators, administrators, and families alike. Here's a crash course on the IEP.

What Is the Individualized Education Program's Purpose?

The IEP has two general purposes:

1. To set reasonable learning goals for a child
2. To state the services that the school district will provide for the child

---

This chapter contains text excerpted from the following sources: Text in this chapter begins with excerpts from "The Short-and-Sweet IEP Overview," Center for Parent Information and Resources (CPIR), August 1, 2017; Text beginning with the heading "What Is in the IEP?" is excerpted from "Developing Your Child's IEP," Center for Parent Information and Resources (CPIR), March 3, 2017.

Who Develops the Individualized Education Program?

The IEP is developed by a team of individuals that includes key school staff and the child's parents. The team meets, reviews the assessment information available about the child, and designs an educational program to address the child's educational needs that result from his or her disability. Want the specifics of who you'll find on an IEP team?

When Is the Individualized Education Program Developed?

An IEP meeting must be held within 30 calendar days after it is determined, through a full and individual evaluation, that a child has one of the disabilities listed in IDEA and needs special education and related services. A child's IEP must also be reviewed at least annually thereafter to determine whether the annual goals are being achieved and must be revised as appropriate.

What Is in an Individualized Education Program?

Each child's IEP must contain specific information, as listed within IDEA, our nation's special education law. This includes (but is not limited to):

- The child's present levels of academic achievement and functional performance, describing how the child is currently doing in school and how the child's disability affects his or her involvement and progress in the general curriculum.

- Annual goals for the child, meaning what parents and the school team think he or she can reasonably accomplish in a year.

- The special education and related services to be provided to the child, including supplementary aids and services (such as a communication device) and changes to the program or supports for school personnel.

- How much of the school day the child will be educated separately from nondisabled children or not participate in extracurricular or other nonacademic activities such as lunch or clubs.

- How (and if) the child is to participate in state and district-wide assessments, including what modifications to tests the child needs.

- When services and modifications will begin, how often they will be provided, where they will be provided, and how long they will last.
- How school personnel will measure the child's progress toward the annual goals.

Can Students Be Involved in Developing Their Own Individualized Education Programs?

Yes, they certainly can be! IDEA actually requires that the student be invited to any IEP meeting where transition services will be discussed. These are services designed to help the student plan for his or her transition to adulthood and life after high school.

What Is in the Individualized Education Program?

In each state or school district, the IEP form can look different. Under IDEA, the items below must be in every IEP.

- Your child's present levels of academic achievement and functional performance;
- Annual goals for your child;
- How your child's progress will be measured;
- The special education, related services, and supplementary aids and services that will be provided to (or on behalf of) your child, including program modifications or supports for school staff;
- An explanation of the extent (if any) to which your child will not participate with children without disabilities in the regular class and in school activities;
- Any modifications your child will need when taking state or district-wide assessments;
- The dates when services will begin and end, the number of services, as well as how often and where they will take place;
- How and when you will be informed of your child's progress;
- By age 16 (or younger, if the IEP team so decides), postsecondary goals and the transition services (including courses of study) that your child will need to reach those goals;

- Beginning at least one year before your child reaches the age of adulthood (usually 18–21, depending on your state law), the IEP must include a statement that your child has been informed of any rights that will transfer to him or her upon reaching this age. Reaching the age of adulthood is called the "age of majority" in IDEA.
- Not all states transfer rights upon reaching adulthood. Refer to your state's special education regulations to find out how this issue is handled.

What Is Involved in Developing My Child's Individualized Education Program?

Developing your child's IEP involves two main things:

1. The IEP meeting(s), where you, your child (at times), and school staff members together decide on an educational program for your son or daughter
2. The IEP document, which puts the decisions from that meeting in writing

Among other things, this document lists the services and supports your child will receive. The entire IEP process is a way for you and the school to talk about your child's needs and to create a plan to meet those needs. Let's look at the process, starting with the IEP meeting. The IEP meeting is somewhat formal. By law, certain people must attend. People sign in to show who is there. Lots of papers are looked at and passed around. People will talk about your child, his or her needs and strengths, and what type of educational program would be appropriate. You should feel free to ask questions and offer suggestions. You will also want to feel comfortable that the team has spent enough time talking and planning before filling out the various sections of the IEP.

Where and When Do Individualized Education Program Meetings Take Place?

You and the school agree on where and when to have the IEP meeting. Usually, meetings are held at school during regular staff time. This means the meeting can happen before, during, or after the regular school day. By law, the school must tell you in writing:

- The purpose of the meeting

Individualized Education Programs

- The time and place for the meeting
- Who will be there
- That you may invite other people who have knowledge or special expertise about your child to the meeting

Also

- The school must hold the meeting to develop your child's IEP within 30 calendar days of when your child is found eligible for special education services.
- You must agree to the program, in writing, before the school may carry out your child's first IEP.
- The IEP must be reviewed at least once every 12 months and revised as necessary.

It may take more than one meeting to write a complete IEP. If you find more time is needed, ask the team to schedule another meeting.

You may ask for an IEP meeting at any time, if you feel that changes need to be made to your child's educational program. Some teams like to meet near the end of a grading period to talk about the student's progress and to make changes to the IEP, as needed.

Measuring Your Child's Progress

Effective goals are critical parts of your child's IEP. Keeping track of your child's progress is just as important. How will you and the school know if your child is making enough progress to reach a goal by the end of the year? This information must be included in the IEP. The IEP team must decide:

- how your child's progress will be measured; and
- when periodic reports on your child's progress will be provided to you.

Often, information on how well your child must perform in order to achieve the goal is spelled out. The goal specifically mentions being able to read at the 5th-grade level or above. This type of information is called evaluation criteria.

Sound evaluation criteria are written in objective, measurable terms. These will be set by the Qualitative Reading Inventory (QRI), the test the school will be using to measure the student's reading skills.

The QRI will identify a specific score (or range of scores) that indicates a child is reading at the 5th-grade level. Your child must achieve that score, or above, in order to achieve his/her annual reading goal.

Another way the IEP team could define how your child's progress will be measured is by setting target dates for specific kinds of progress. According to his/her present levels statement, your child has difficulty decoding long words. Because decoding is a critical component of reading skill, the team might set targets for his progress in this area. For example, given a list of 20 unfamiliar words that contain 8 or more letters, the student will decode them with:

- 60 percent accuracy by December 1
- 75 percent accuracy by March 1
- 90 percent accuracy by June 15

In other instances, progress is not measured in number scores:

By June 15, the student will complete the obstacle course unassisted, as documented by the adapted physical education teacher.

In this example, the teacher will observe and take notes while the student completes the obstacle course. Teacher observation/notes are one way of checking progress. Other ways of checking progress may include:

- Reviewing class work and homework assignments
- Giving quizzes, tests, or other assessments developed by teachers
- Giving informal and/or formal assessments (the QRI or Woodcock-Johnson, for example)

In addition to describing how your child's progress will be measured, the IEP must also describe when periodic reports on that progress will be given to you as parents. As examples, IDEA mentions the use of quarterly reports that come out at the same time as report cards. But the periodic reports may take another form or schedule, depending on the policies or practices in your area.

Chapter 53

Supports, Modifications, and Accommodations for Students

For many students with disabilities—and for many without—the key to success in the classroom lies in having appropriate adaptations, accommodations, and modifications made to the instruction and other classroom activities. Some adaptations are as simple as moving a distractible student to the front of the class or away from the pencil sharpener or the window. Other modifications may involve changing the way that material is presented or the way that students respond to show their learning.

Adaptations, accommodations, and modifications need to be individualized for students, based upon their needs and their personal learning styles and interests. It is not always obvious what adaptations, accommodations, or modifications would be beneficial for a particular student, or how changes to the curriculum, its presentation, the classroom setting, or student evaluation might be made. This chapter is intended to help teachers and others find information that can guide

---

This chapter includes text excerpted from "Supports, Modifications, and Accommodations for Students," Center for Parent Information and Resources (CPIR), February 8, 2017.

them in making appropriate changes in the classroom based on what their students need.

A Quick Look at Terminology

You might wonder if the terms supports, modifications, and adaptations all mean the same thing. The simple answer is: No, not completely, but yes, for the most part. (Don't you love a clear answer?) People tend to use the terms interchangeably, to be sure, and we will do so here, for ease of reading, but distinctions can be made between the terms.

Sometimes people get confused about what it means to have a modification and what it means to have an accommodation. Usually, a modification means a change in what is being taught to or expected from the student. Making an assignment easier so the student is not doing the same level of work as other students is an example of a modification.

An accommodation is a change that helps a student overcome or work around the disability. Allowing a student who has trouble writing to give his answers orally is an example of an accommodation. This student is still expected to know the same material and answer the same questions as fully as the other students, but he doesn't have to write his answers to show that he knows the information.

What is most important to know about modifications and accommodations is that both are meant to help a child to learn.

Different Types of Supports

Special Education

By definition, special education is "specially designed instruction" (§300.39). And Individuals with Disabilities Education Act (IDEA) defines that term as follows:

> (3) Specially designed instruction means adapting, as appropriate to the needs of an eligible child under this part, the content, methodology, or delivery of instruction—(i) To address the unique needs of the child that result from the child's disability; and(ii) To ensure access of the child to the general curriculum, so that the child can meet the educational standards within the jurisdiction of the public agency that apply to all children. [§300.39(b)(3)]

Thus, special education involves adapting the "content, methodology, or delivery of instruction." In fact, the special education field can

Supports, Modifications, and Accommodations for Students

take pride in the knowledge base and expertise it's developed in the past 30-plus years of individualizing instruction to meet the needs of students with disabilities. It's a pleasure to share some of that knowledge with you now.

Adapting Instruction

Sometimes a student may need to have changes made in class work or routines because of his or her disability. Modifications can be made to:

- What a child is taught?
- How a child works at school?

For example:
Jack is an 8th-grade student who has learning disabilities in reading and writing. He is in a regular 8th-grade class that is team-taught by a general education teacher and a special education teacher. Modifications and accommodations provided for Jack's daily school routine (and when he takes state or district-wide tests) include the following:

- Jack will have shorter reading and writing assignments.
- Jack's textbooks will be based upon the 8th-grade curriculum but at his independent reading level (4th grade).
- Jack will have test questions read/explained to him, when he asks.
- Jack will give his answers to essay-type questions by speaking, rather than writing them down.

Modifications or accommodations are most often made in the following areas:

Scheduling

For example:

- Giving the student extra time to complete assignments or tests
- Breaking up testing over several days

Setting

For example:

- Working in a small group

- Working one-on-one with the teacher

Materials

For example:

- Providing audiotaped lectures or books
- Giving copies of teacher's lecture notes
- Using large print books, Braille, or books on CD (digital text)

Instruction

For example:

- Reducing the difficulty of assignments
- Reducing the reading level
- Using a student/peer tutor

Student Response

For example:

- Allowing answers to be given orally or dictated
- Using a word processor for written work
- Using sign language, a communication device, Braille, or native language if it is not English.

Because adapting the content, methodology, and/or delivery of instruction is an essential element in special education and an extremely valuable support for students, it's equally essential to know as much as possible about how instruction can be adapted to address the needs of an individual student with a disability. The special education teacher who serves on the Individualized Education Program (IEP) team can contribute his or her expertise in this area, which is the essence of special education.

Related Services

One look at IDEA's definition of related services at §300.34 and it's clear that these services are supportive in nature, although not in the same way that adapting the curriculum is. Related services support children's special education and are provided when necessary to help

Supports, Modifications, and Accommodations for Students

students benefit from special education. Thus, related services must be included in the treasure chest of accommodations and supports we're exploring. That definition begins:

§300.34 Related services.

a. General. Related services means transportation and such developmental, corrective, and other supportive services as are required to assist a child with a disability to benefit from special education, and includes:

Here's the list of related services in the law.

- Speech-language pathology and audiology services
- Interpreting services
- Psychological services
- Physical and occupational therapy
- Recreation, including therapeutic recreation
- Early identification and assessment of disabilities in children
- Counseling services, including rehabilitation counseling
- Orientation and mobility services
- Medical services for diagnostic or evaluation purposes
- School health services and school nurse services
- Social work services in schools

This is not an exhaustive list of possible related services. There are others (not named here or in the law) that states and schools routinely make available under the umbrella of related services. The IEP team decides which related services a child needs and specifies them in the child's IEP.

Supplementary Aids and Services

One of the most powerful types of supports available to children with disabilities are the other kinds of supports or services (other than special education and related services) that a child needs to be educated with nondisabled children to the maximum extent appropriate. Some examples of these additional services and supports, called supplementary aids and services in IDEA, are:

- Adapted equipment—such as a special seat or a cut-out cup for drinking

- Assistive technology—such as a word processor, special software, or a communication system
- Training for staff, student, and/or parents
- Peer tutors
- A one-on-one aide
- Adapted materials—such as books on tape, large print, or highlighted notes
- Collaboration/consultation among staff, parents, and/or other professionals

The IEP team, which includes the parents, is the group that decides which supplementary aids and services a child needs to support his or her access to and participation in the school environment. The IEP team must really work together to make sure that a child gets the supplementary aids and services that he or she needs to be successful. Team members talk about the child's needs, the curriculum, and school routine, and openly explore all options to make sure the right supports for the specific child are included.

Program Modifications or Supports for School Staff

If the IEP team decides that a child needs a particular modification or accommodation, this information must be included in the IEP. Supports are also available for those who work with the child, to help them help that child be successful. Supports for school staff must also be written into the IEP. Some of these supports might include:

- Attending a conference or training related to the child's needs
- Getting help from another staff member or administrative person
- Having an aide in the classroom
- Getting special equipment or teaching materials

Accommodations in Large Assessments

IDEA requires that students with disabilities take part in state or district-wide assessments. These are tests that are periodically given to all students to measure achievement. It is one way that schools determine how well and how much students are learning. IDEA now states

Supports, Modifications, and Accommodations for Students

that students with disabilities should have as much involvement in the general curriculum as possible. This means that, if a child is receiving instruction in the general curriculum, he or she could take the same standardized test that the school district or state gives to nondisabled children. Accordingly, a child's IEP must include all modifications or accommodations that the child needs so that he or she can participate in state or district-wide assessments.

The IEP team can decide that a particular test is not appropriate for a child. In this case, the IEP must include:

- An explanation of why that test is not suitable for the child, and
- How the child will be assessed instead (often called alternate assessment).

Ask your state and/or local school district for a copy of their guidelines on the types of accommodations, modifications, and alternate assessments available to students.

Even a child with many needs is to be involved with nondisabled peers to the maximum extent appropriate. Just because a child has severe disabilities or needs modifications to the general curriculum does not mean that he or she may be removed from the general education class. If a child is removed from the general education class for any part of the school day, the IEP team must include in the IEP an explanation for the child's nonparticipation.

Because accommodations can be so vital to helping children with disabilities access the general curriculum, participate in school (including extracurricular and nonacademic activities), and be educated alongside their peers without disabilities, IDEA reinforces their use again and again, in its requirements, in its definitions, and in its principles. The wealth of experience that the special education field has gained over the years since IDEA was first passed by Congress is the very resource you'll want to tap for more information on what accommodations are appropriate for students, given their disability, and how to make those adaptations to support their learning.

Chapter 54

Students with Disabilities Preparing for Postsecondary Education

Postsecondary education is one of the most important postschool goals; and research has demonstrated that it is the primary goal for most students with disabilities. As students with disabilities transition from secondary school to postsecondary education, training, and employment, it is critical that they are prepared academically and financially. Postsecondary options, with the help of the Vocational Rehabilitation (VR) program, include two- and four-year colleges and universities, trade and vocational schools, adult education programs, and employment outcomes in competitive integrated employment or supported employment. This chapter will describe specific actions to be taken and available services and supports for students and youth with disabilities. The services described in this section are provided at the secondary and postsecondary levels to help students and youth with disabilities succeed in their postschool goals.

This chapter includes text excerpted from "A Transition Guide to Postsecondary Education and Employment for Students and Youth with Disabilities," U.S. Department of Education (ED), May 2017.

Postsecondary Education and Training Options

Preparing for College

Secondary School

Whether in middle or high school, if an Individuals with Disabilities Education Act (IDEA)-eligible student is planning to attend college, there are a number of critical steps to be taken to become college-ready. Early in the transition process, a student is encouraged to:

- Take interesting and challenging courses that prepare him or her for college;
- Be involved in school or community-based activities that allow him or her to explore career interests, including work-based learning or internship opportunities;
- Meet with school guidance counselors to discuss career goals, such as vocational and educational goals, programs of study, college requirements, including the admissions process and any standardized tests required for admission; and
- Be an active participant during the Individualized Education Program (IEP) meetings.

As noted earlier, the IEP Team is responsible for ensuring that the student's IEP includes the specialized instruction, supports, and services needed to assist the student in preparing for college and/or other postsecondary schools. Students with disabilities and their families interested in higher education are encouraged to consider the college environment that provides the best educational program and support services to assist students with meeting their needs and career goals.

IDEA-eligible students with disabilities will benefit from discussions with their parents, school guidance counselor, vocational rehabilitation (VR) counselor (if applicable), and other professional support staff about the services and supports needed to be successful in postsecondary education or training. For IDEA-eligible students whose eligibility terminates because the student has graduated from secondary school with a regular high school diploma or the student has exceeded the age of eligibility for free appropriate public education (FAPE) under State law, the school district must provide the student with an standard operating procedure (SOP) that documents the student's academic achievement, functional performance and recommendations on how to assist the student in meeting his or her postsecondary goals.

Postsecondary Education

Paying for College

The Office of Federal Student Aid (FSA) in the U.S. Department of Education (ED) plays a central role in the nation's postsecondary education community. Through the FSA, the department awards about $150billion a year in grants, work-study funds, and low-interest loans to approximately 13 million students. There are three types of Federal student aid:

- **Grants and Scholarships:** Financial aid that does not have to be repaid, including the Federal Pell grant that can award as much as $5,815 to each low-income student per year;
- **Work-Study:** A program that allows students to earn money for their education; and
- **Low Interest Loans:** Aid that allows students to borrow money for their education; loans must be repaid with interest.

The following website provides information about the three types of student aid: studentaid.ed.gov. Completing the Free Application for Federal Student Aid (FAFSA®) is the first step toward getting financial aid for college. The FAFSA® not only provides access to the $150 billion in grants, loans, and work-study funds that the federal government has available, but many states, schools, and private scholarships require students to submit the FAFSA® before they will consider offering any financial aid. That is why it is important that every college-bound student complete the FAFSA®. FAFSA® is free, and there is help provided throughout the application at fafsa.ed.gov/help.htm. It is also easier than ever to complete, taking only an average time of less than thirty minutes.

Choosing the Right College

College is a big investment in time, money, and effort; and, therefore, it is important to research and understand the types of schools, tuition and costs, programs available, student enrollment, and a variety of other important factors when choosing the right school. When researching potential college programs, students and their families are advised to work closely with the disability support services (DSS) office on campus to discuss disability-related concerns and needs, and the disability support services available to students at that postsecondary school. Many DSS offices empower, support, and advocate for students with disabilities to achieve their goals by providing access to education and other programs through the coordination of appropriate accommodations and academic adjustments, assistive technology, alternative formats, and other support. Disability support services, including academic adjustments and auxiliary aids, are provided in compliance with Section 504 and Title II of the Americans with Disabilities Act (ADA) (Title II). Information about the DSS office may be found at the postsecondary school's website. The U.S. Department of Education (ED) publication" College Scorecard" (collegescorecard.ed.gov) also provides data on outcomes and affordability to help select the right college.

Rights and Responsibilities in Postsecondary Education and Training

Students with disabilities are encouraged to be well informed about their rights and responsibilities, as well as the responsibilities of postsecondary schools. Being informed about their rights and responsibilities will help ensure that students have full opportunity to enjoy the benefits of the postsecondary education experience without disruption or delay. A postsecondary student with a disability is not entitled to the same services and supports that the student received in high school. While students with disabilities are entitled to comprehensive supports under the FAPE requirements of IDEA or Section 504, if applicable, while in high school, they are no longer entitled to FAPE under IDEA or Section 504 if they graduate with a regular high school diploma. At the postsecondary level, Section 504 prohibits discrimination on the basis of disability by recipients of federal financial assistance, and Title II prohibits discrimination on the basis of disability by public entities, regardless of receipt of federal funds. Note that if the postsecondary institution is a private college or university that is not a religious entity, it would be covered by Title III of the ADA (Title III). The U.S. Department of Education (ED) does not enforce the Title III rights of postsecondary students with disabilities. The U.S. Department of Justice (DOJ) enforces Title III.

Section 504 and Title II require that the postsecondary educational institution provide students with disabilities with accommodations, including appropriate academic adjustments and auxiliary aids and services, that are necessary to afford an individual with a disability an equal opportunity to participate in a school's program.

Postsecondary educational institutions are not required to make adjustments or provide aids or services that would result in a fundamental alteration of their academic program or impose an undue financial or administrative burden on the postsecondary institution's programs.

To receive these supports, a student with a disability must inform the college that he or she has a disability and needs one or more accommodations. The college is not required to identify the student as having a disability or assess the student's needs prior to receiving a request for an accommodation. Colleges may set reasonable requirements for documentation that students must provide. While an IEP or Section 504 plan from high school may be helpful in identifying services that have been effective for the student, such a plan will generally not be sufficient documentation by itself.

The IEP Team, VR counselor, or support professionals can provide specific guidance to prepare the student for postsecondary education and training. For example, they may provide an overview of how to self-disclose individual needs or functional limitations in the postsecondary educational setting.

An overview of the rights and responsibilities of students with disabilities who are preparing to attend postsecondary schools, as well as the obligations of a postsecondary school to provide academic adjustments, including auxiliary aids and services, is available on the department's website.

Structural Supports and Physical Accessibility

Section 504 and the ADA contain requirements related to the physical accessibility of facilities, including those used for higher education purposes. In the last few decades, the removal of architectural barriers, such as providing curb cuts, ramps, and elevators, helped make higher education more inclusive for students with disabilities. Structural accommodations involve making buildings accessible to individuals with disabilities. Typical structural accommodations include ramp availability, elevators, convenient parking, doorway, and restroom facilities modifications, and architectural barriers removal or modifications. In situations where architectural barriers cannot be removed, some institutions have changed the location of classes or other activities to a site that is accessible.

Vocational Rehabilitation Supports for Postsecondary Education

The VR program assists individuals with disabilities, including students and youth with disabilities, to acquire the knowledge and skills needed to achieve employment that can sustain economic independence. If it is determined to be necessary and is included on the individual's IPE, the VR agencies can provide financial support to eligible individuals to pay for or offset higher education-related expenses, including college expenses not covered by student financial aid, or disability-related expenses, such as personal assistants, interpreters, readers, and education support services.

The student's IPE lists the services that the VR agency and other responsible parties will provide. VR financial support commonly listed in an IPE could include the following postsecondary expenses:

- Vocational and other training services;

- Personal and vocational adjustment training; and

- Advanced training in the fields of science, technology, engineering, or mathematics, computer science, medicine, law, or business in an institution of higher education (universities, colleges, vocational schools, technical institutes, hospital schools of nursing, or any other postsecondary education institution) books, tools; and other training materials.

Before the VR agency can provide financial support for most VR services, the VR agency, and the student must identify other sources of funding. This requirement is frequently referred to as a search for comparable benefits under the VR program. With respect to the provision of training, including postsecondary education at an institution of higher education (IHE), both the VR counselor and student or representative, as appropriate, must make every effort to secure grant assistance from other sources to pay for that training prior to the VR agency providing financial support. Pell grants are identified as grant assistance through the FAFSA® and would be included in a search for comparable benefits. However, scholarships or awards based on merit or student loans do not count as grant assistance, for purposes of searching for comparable benefits, under the VR program. The VR program does not require a student to apply for merit-based scholarships or awards or apply for student loans. If a student accepts a merit-based scholarship that is restricted to specific costs, such as tuition, fees, room, and board, the VR program will take that reduction in expenses into consideration when calculating the amount it could pay to assist the student in order to avoid duplication in funding.

Postsecondary Education and Training Programs and Opportunities

The following are examples of such programs that are funded through the U.S. Department of Education (ED):

Gallaudet University

Gallaudet University, federally charted in 1864, is a bilingual, diverse, multicultural institution of higher education that ensures the intellectual and professional advancement of deaf and hard of hearing individuals through American Sign Language and English. Deaf and hard-of-hearing undergraduate students can choose from more than 40 majors leading to a Bachelor of Arts or a Bachelor of Science degree.

National Technical Institute for the Deaf (NTID)

National Technical Institute for the Deaf (NTID) is a special institution that is funded by Office of Special Education and Rehabilitative Services (OSERS). It is one of the nine colleges within Rochester Institute of Technology (RIT), a leading career-oriented, technological university. Approximately 1, 200 students who are deaf or hard-of-hearing attend NTID. NTID offers students two-year, career-focused degree programs, opportunities to participate in the university's cooperative education program, a faculty who specialize in educating deaf and hard-of-hearing students, and the opportunity to enroll in RIT's four-year degree programs.

Model Transition Programs for Students with Intellectual Disabilities (TPSID) into Higher Education

The Higher Education Opportunity Act (HEOA) includes provisions to increase access and opportunities for youth and adults with intellectual disabilities who are interested in participating in higher education programs. The Department's Office of Postsecondary Education (OPE) funded 25 TPSID projects in 2015 to serve students with intellectual disabilities by providing access to academically inclusive college courses, enhancing participation in internships and competitive integrated employment, and encouraging engagement in social and personal development activities. OPE also funds a national coordinating center to provide support, coordination, training, and evaluation services for TPSID grantees and other programs for students with intellectual disabilities nationwide. The national coordinating center is administered by Think College, a project team at the Institute for Community Inclusion at the University of Massachusetts Boston.

Examples of State and Local Collaboration to Support Postsecondary Options for Individuals with Disabilities

Autism Services

A VR agency, secondary school, and a local community college collaborated in a grant-funded project, which provided comprehensive supports to individuals with autism enrolled at a local community college. At the conclusion of the grant, the VR agency identified a staff person to continue providing supports to 20 students enrolled at three community colleges in the community college system, with some participants transitioning to four-year universities. Supports included faculty trainings, career guidance, self-advocacy instruction, and increased communication with VR counselors, faculty, and family members.

Supported Education

A VR agency collaborated with a community college to develop a supported education program. This initiative provides additional tutoring, study skills training, college life, and other training for transition students who enroll in the community college, and seek remedial courses before matriculating into a degree or certificate program. The goal is to make community college education and training an option for more transition-age students with disabilities, and increase their success rate in college. A student suffered a stroke at a very young age, and afterward, was unable to walk, talk, or breathe on his own. However, he did not have any cognitive damage that impacted his intellectual functioning during the stroke. Despite his challenges, he graduated from high school and entered a rigorous four-year college. This student received a bachelor's degree in fine arts. His postsecondary educational success can be largely attributed to his own personal drive, supportive parents, and knowledgeable service providers.

Chapter 55

Transitioning Students with Disabilities to Higher Education and Adulthood

Are Students with Disabilities Entitled to Changes in Standardized Testing Conditions on Entrance Exams for Institutions of Postsecondary Education?

It depends. In general, tests may not be selected or administered in a way that tests the disability rather than the achievement or aptitude of the individual. In addition, federal law requires changes to the testing conditions that are necessary to allow a student with a disability to participate as long as the changes do not fundamentally alter the examination or create undue financial or administrative burdens. Although some institutions of postsecondary education may have their own entrance exams, many use a student's score on commercially available tests. In general, in order to request one or more changes in standardized testing conditions, which test administrators may also refer to as "testing accommodations," the student will need to contact the institution of postsecondary education or the entity that administers the exam and provide documentation of a disability and

---

This chapter includes text excerpted from "Transition of Students with Disabilities to Postsecondary Education: A Guide for High School Educators," U.S. Department of Education (ED), March 2011. Reviewed July 2018.

the need for a change in testing conditions. The issue of documentation is discussed below. Examples of changes in testing conditions that may be available include, but are not limited to:

- Braille
- Large print
- Fewer items on each page
- Tape recorded responses
- Responses on the test booklet
- Frequent breaks
- Extended testing time
- Testing over several sessions
- Small group setting
- Private room
- Preferential seating
- The use of a sign language interpreter for spoken directions

Are Students Obligated to Inform Institutions That They Have a Disability?

No. A student has no obligation to inform an institution of postsecondary education that he or she has a disability; however, if the student wants an institution to provide an academic adjustment or assign the student to accessible housing or other facilities, or if a student wants other disability-related services, the student must identify himself or herself as having a disability. The disclosure of a disability is always voluntary. For example, a student who has a disability that does not require services may choose not to disclose his or her disability.

What Are Academic Adjustments and Auxiliary Aids and Services?

Academic adjustments are defined in the Section 504 regulations at 34 C.F.R. § 104.44(a) as:

> [S]uch modifications to [the] academic requirements as are necessary to ensure that such requirements do not discriminate or

have the effect of discriminating, on the basis of [disability] against a qualified ... applicant or student [with a disability]. Academic requirements that the recipient can demonstrate are essential to the instruction being pursued by such student or to any directly related licensing requirement will not be regarded as discriminatory within the meaning of this section. Modifications may include changes in the length of time permitted for the completion of degree requirements, substitution of specific courses required for the completion of degree requirements, and adaptation of the manner in which specific courses are conducted.

Academic adjustments also may include a reduced course load, extended time on tests and the provision of auxiliary aids and services. Auxiliary aids and services are defined in the Section 504 regulations at 34 C.F.R. § 104.44(d), and in the Title II regulations at 28 C.F.R. § 35.104. They include note-takers, readers, recording devices, sign language interpreters, screen-readers, voice recognition and other adaptive software or hardware for computers, and other devices designed to ensure the participation of students with impaired sensory, manual or speaking skills in an institution's programs and activities. Institutions are not required to provide personal devices and services such as attendants, individually prescribed devices, such as eyeglasses, readers for personal use or study, or other services of a personal nature, such as tutoring. If institutions offer tutoring to the general student population, however, they must ensure that tutoring services also are available to students with disabilities. In some instances, a state Vocational Rehabilitation (VR) agency may provide auxiliary aids and services to support an individual's postsecondary education and training once that individual has been determined eligible to receive services under the VR program.

In General, What Kind of Documentation Is Necessary for Students with Disabilities to Receive Academic Adjustments from Institutions of Postsecondary Education?

Institutions may set their own requirements for documentation so long as they are reasonable and comply with Section 504 and Title II. It is not uncommon for documentation standards to vary from institution to institution; thus, students with disabilities should research documentation standards at those institutions that interest them. A student must provide documentation, upon request, that he or she has a disability, that is, an impairment that substantially limits a major life activity and that supports the need for an academic adjustment. The documentation should identify how a student's ability to function is limited as a result of her or his disability. The primary purpose of the documentation is to establish a disability in order to help the institution work interactively with the student to identify appropriate services. The focus should be on whether the information adequately documents the existence of a current disability and need for an academic adjustment.

Who Is Responsible for Obtaining Necessary Testing to Document the Existence of a Disability?

The student. Institutions of postsecondary education are not required to conduct or pay for an evaluation to document a student's disability and need for an academic adjustment, although some institutions do so. If a student with a disability is eligible for services through the state VR Services program, he or she may qualify for an evaluation at no cost. High school educators can assist students with disabilities in locating their state VR agency at rsa.ed.gov. If students with disabilities are unable to find other funding sources to pay for necessary evaluation or testing for postsecondary education, they are responsible for paying for it themselves.

At the elementary and secondary school levels, a school district's duty to provide a free appropriate public education (FAPE) encompasses the responsibility to provide, at no cost to the parents, an evaluation of suspected areas of disability for any of the district's students who is believed to be in need of special education or related aids and services. School districts are not required under Section 504 or Title II to conduct evaluations that are for the purpose of obtaining academic adjustments once a student graduates and goes on to postsecondary education.

If It Is Clear That a Student Has a Disability, Why Does an Institution Need Documentation?

Students who have the same disability may not necessarily require the same academic adjustment. Section 504 and Title II require that institutions of postsecondary education make individualized determinations regarding appropriate academic adjustments for each individual student. If the student's disability and need for an academic adjustment are obvious, less documentation may be necessary.

Must Institutions Provide Every Academic Adjustment a Student with a Disability Wants?

It depends. Institutions are not required to provide an academic adjustment that would alter or waive essential academic requirements. They also do not have to provide an academic adjustment that would fundamentally alter the nature of a service, program, or activity or result in undue financial or administrative burdens considering the institution's resources as a whole. For example, an appropriate academic adjustment may be to extend the time a student with a disability is allotted to take tests, but an institution is not required to change the substantive content of the tests.

In addition, an institution is not required to make modifications that would result in undue financial or administrative burdens. Public institutions are required to give primary consideration to the auxiliary aid or service that the student requests, but can opt to provide alternative aids or services if they are effective. They can also opt to provide an effective alternative if the requested auxiliary aid or service would fundamentally alter the nature of a service, program, or activity or result in undue financial or administrative burdens. For example, if it would be a fundamental alteration or undue burden to provide a student with a disability with a note-taker for oral classroom presentations and discussions and a tape recorder would be an effective alternative, a postsecondary institution may provide the student with a tape recorder instead of a note-taker.

If Students Want to Request Academic Adjustments, What Must They Do?

Institutions may establish reasonable procedures for requesting academic adjustments; students are responsible for knowing these procedures and following them. Institutions usually include information on the procedures and contacts for requesting an academic adjustment in their general information publications and websites. If students are unable to locate the procedures, they should contact an institution official, such as an admissions officer or counselor.

How Do Institutions Determine What Academic Adjustments Are Appropriate?

Once a student has identified him- or herself as an individual with a disability, requested an academic adjustment and provided appropriate documentation upon request, institution staff should discuss with the student what academic adjustments are appropriate in light of the student's individual needs and the nature of the institution's program. Students with disabilities possess unique knowledge of their individual disabilities and should be prepared to discuss the functional challenges they face and, if applicable, what has or has not worked for them in the past. Institution staff should be prepared to describe the barriers students may face in individual classes that may affect their full participation, as well as to discuss academic adjustments that might enable students to overcome those barriers.

Who Pays for Auxiliary Aids and Services?

Once the needed auxiliary aids and services have been identified, institutions may not require students with disabilities to pay part or all of the costs of such aids and services, nor may institutions charge students with disabilities more for participating in programs or activities than they charge students who do not have disabilities. Institutions generally may not condition their provision of academic adjustments on the availability of funds, refuse to spend more than a certain amount to provide academic adjustments, or refuse to provide academic adjustments because they believe other providers of such services exist.

In many cases, institutions may meet their obligation to provide auxiliary aids and services by assisting students in either obtaining them or obtaining reimbursement for their cost from an outside agency or organization, such as a state VR agency. Such assistance notwithstanding, institutions retain ultimate responsibility for providing necessary auxiliary aids and services and for any costs associated with providing such aids and services or utilizing outside sources.

However, as noted above, if the institution can demonstrate that providing a specific auxiliary aid or service would result in undue financial or administrative burdens, considering the institution's resources as a whole, it can opt to provide another effective one.

Keys to Success: Attitude, Self-Advocacy, and Preparation

The attitude and self-advocacy skills of students with disabilities may be two of the most important factors in determining their success or failure in postsecondary education. Students with disabilities need to be prepared to work collaboratively with the institution's disability coordinator to enable them to have an equal opportunity to participate in an institution's programs and activities. To ensure that students with disabilities possess the desired levels of self-advocacy to succeed in postsecondary education, high school educators may want to encourage the students to:

- **Understand their disabilities.** Students with disabilities need to know the functional limitations that result from their disabilities and understand their strengths and weaknesses. They should be able to explain their disabilities to an institution's disability coordinators or other appropriate staff. As part of this process, students should be able to explain where they have had difficulty in the past, as well as what has helped them overcome such problems and what specific adjustments might work in specific situations. To assist students in this area, high school educators can encourage high school students to be active participants in their individualized education program (IEP) or Section 504 meetings. High school personnel also can suggest that students practice explaining their disabilities, as well as why they need certain services, to appropriate secondary staff or through role-playing exercises to prepare them to engage in such conversations with confidence in a postsecondary setting.

- **Accept responsibility for their own success.** All students, including those with disabilities, must take primary responsibility for their success or failure in postsecondary education. Students with disabilities, in particular, are moving from a system where parents and school staff usually advocated on their behalf to a system where they will be expected to advocate for themselves. An institution's staff will likely communicate directly with students when issues arise and are generally not required to interact with students' parents.

In general, students with disabilities should expect to complete all course requirements, such as assignments and examinations. Students with disabilities need to identify the essential academic and technical standards that they will be required to meet for admission and continued participation in an institution's program. Students also need to identify any academic adjustments they may need as a result of their disabilities to meet those standards and how to request those adjustments. Students with disabilities need to understand that, while federal disability laws guarantee them an equal opportunity to participate in these laws do not guarantee that students will achieve a particular outcome, for example, good grades.

- **Take an appropriate preparatory curriculum.** Because all students will be expected to meet an institution's essential standards, students with disabilities need to take a high school curriculum that will prepare them to meet those standards. If students with disabilities plan to attend a rigorous postsecondary institution, they, like their peers without disabilities, need to make high school curriculum choices that support that goal. High school guidance counselors and state Vocational Rehabilitation (VR) agency counselors, in particular, can play an important role in students' curriculum planning.

For all students, good study skills and the ability to write well are critical factors of success in postsecondary education. High school educators can help students in these areas by offering or identifying opportunities, such as workshops, courses, or tutoring programs, that emphasize the importance of reading, writing, and good study skills. In addition, staff should encourage students to enroll in classes that will focus on writing and study skills in their freshman year of postsecondary education.

- **Learn time management skills.** Although a primary role of high school educators is to provide monitoring, direction and guidance to students as they approach the end of their high school career, staff also need to prepare students to act independently and to manage their own time with little to no supervision. High school educators can assist students by identifying resources that will help them learn time management and scheduling skills.

- **Acquire computer skills.** Because postsecondary students use computers to complete a multitude of tasks, from registering for classes to accessing course material and obtaining grades, it is essential that students learn to use computers if they are to be prepared for postsecondary education. Ideally, students with disabilities need to start using computers as early as possible in school to increase their familiarity with, and their comfort level in using computers. Students with visual impairments, hearing impairments, learning disabilities, or mobility impairments may have problems with inputting data or reading a computer monitor. Assistive technology can help certain students with disabilities use computers and access information.

- **Consider supplemental postsecondary education preparatory programs.** A variety of institutions of postsecondary education have summer programs in which students can participate while they are still in high school, or after graduation, to ease their transition to postsecondary education. These programs often expose students to experiences that they are likely to encounter in postsecondary education, such as living in dorms, relating to other students and eating in dining halls. The programs may also focus on instruction in certain subject areas, such as math or English, or in certain skills, such as computer, writing or study skills, that can prepare a student to be successful in postsecondary education. High school educators can assist students with disabilities by identifying such program opportunities in their area of residence.

- **Research postsecondary education programs.** Students with disabilities may select any program for which they are qualified but should be advised to review carefully documentation standards and program requirements for their program or institution of interest. For example, students should pay close attention to an institution's program requirements, such as language or math, to avoid making a large financial and time commitment only to realize several years into a program that they cannot, even with academic adjustments, meet an essential requirement for program completion. Campus visits, which include visits to the disability services office, can be helpful in locating an environment that best meets a student's interests and needs. In addition, while all institutions have a legal obligation to provide appropriate services, certain colleges may be able to provide better services than others due to their size or location.

- **Get involved on campus.** To help students avoid the isolation that can occur away from home during the first year of postsecondary education, high school educators should encourage students to live on campus and to become involved in campus activities. Attendance at orientation programs for freshmen is a good first step in discovering ways to get involved in the postsecondary education environment.

Part Six

Legal, Employment, and Financial Concerns for People with Disabilities

Chapter 56

A Guide to Disability Rights Laws

Americans with Disabilities Act

The Americans with Disabilities Act (ADA) prohibits discrimination on the basis of disability in employment, state and local government, public accommodations, commercial facilities, transportation, and telecommunications. It also applies to the United States Congress.

To be protected by the ADA, one must have a disability or have a relationship or association with an individual with a disability. An individual with a disability is defined by the ADA as a person who has a physical or mental impairment that substantially limits one or more major life activities, a person who has a history or record of such an impairment, or a person who is perceived by others as having such an impairment. The ADA does not specifically name all of the impairments that are covered.

ADA Title I: Employment

Title I requires employers with 15 or more employees to provide qualified individuals with disabilities an equal opportunity to benefit from the full range of employment-related opportunities available to others. For example, it prohibits discrimination in recruitment,

---

This chapter includes text excerpted from "A Guide to Disability Rights Laws," ADA.gov, U.S. Department of Justice (DOJ), July 2009. Reviewed July 2018.

hiring, promotions, training, pay, social activities, and other privileges of employment. It restricts questions that can be asked about an applicant's disability before a job offer is made, and it requires that employers make reasonable accommodation to the known physical or mental limitations of otherwise qualified individuals with disabilities, unless it results in undue hardship. Religious entities with 15 or more employees are covered under title I.

Title I complaints must be filed with the U. S. Equal Employment Opportunity Commission (EEOC) within 180 days of the date of discrimination, or 300 days if the charge is filed with a designated state or local fair employment practice agency. Individuals may file a lawsuit in federal court only after they receive a "right-to-sue" letter from the EEOC.

Charges of employment discrimination on the basis of disability may be filed at any EEOC field office. Field offices are located in 50 cities throughout the U.S. and are listed in most telephone directories under "U.S. government."

ADA Title II: State and Local Government Activities

Title II covers all activities of state and local governments regardless of the government entity's size or receipt of federal funding. Title II requires that state and local governments give people with disabilities an equal opportunity to benefit from all of their programs, services, and activities (e.g., public education, employment, transportation, recreation, healthcare, social services, courts, voting, and town meetings).

State and local governments are required to follow specific architectural standards in the new construction and alteration of their buildings. They also must relocate programs or otherwise provide access in inaccessible older buildings, and communicate effectively with people who have hearing, vision, or speech disabilities. Public entities are not required to take actions that would result in undue financial and administrative burdens. They are required to make reasonable modifications to policies, practices, and procedures where necessary to avoid discrimination, unless they can demonstrate that doing so would fundamentally alter the nature of the service, program, or activity being provided.

Complaints of title II violations may be filed with the U.S. Department of Justice (DOJ) within 180 days of the date of discrimination. In certain situations, cases may be referred to a mediation program sponsored by the Department. The Department may bring a lawsuit where it has investigated a matter and has been unable to resolve violations.

Title II may also be enforced through private lawsuits in federal court. It is not necessary to file a complaint with the DOJ or any other federal agency, or to receive a "right-to-sue" letter, before going to court.

ADA Title II: Public Transportation

The transportation provisions of title II cover public transportation services, such as city buses and public rail transit (e.g., subways, commuter rails, Amtrak). Public transportation authorities may not discriminate against people with disabilities in the provision of their services. They must comply with requirements for accessibility in newly purchased vehicles, make good faith efforts to purchase or lease accessible used buses, remanufacture buses in an accessible manner, and, unless it would result in an undue burden, provide paratransit where they operate fixed-route bus or rail systems. Paratransit is a service where individuals who are unable to use the regular transit system independently (because of a physical or mental impairment) are picked up and dropped off at their destinations.

ADA Title III: Public Accommodations

Title III covers businesses and nonprofit service providers that are public accommodations, privately operated entities offering certain types of courses and examinations, privately operated transportation, and commercial facilities. Public accommodations are private entities who own, lease, lease to, or operate facilities such as restaurants, retail stores, hotels, movie theaters, private schools, convention centers, doctors' offices, homeless shelters, transportation depots, zoos, funeral homes, day care centers, and recreation facilities including sports stadiums and fitness clubs. Transportation services provided by private entities are also covered by title III.

Public accommodations must comply with basic nondiscrimination requirements that prohibit exclusion, segregation, and unequal treatment. They also must comply with specific requirements related to architectural standards for new and altered buildings; reasonable modifications to policies, practices, and procedures; effective communication with people with hearing, vision, or speech disabilities; and other access requirements. Additionally, public accommodations must remove barriers in existing buildings where it is easy to do so without much difficulty or expense, given the public accommodation's resources.

Courses and examinations related to professional, educational, or trade-related applications, licensing, certifications, or credentialing must be provided in a place and manner accessible to people with disabilities, or alternative accessible arrangements must be offered.

Commercial facilities, such as factories and warehouses, must comply with the ADA's architectural standards for new construction and alterations.

Complaints of title III violations may be filed with the U.S. Department of Justice. In certain situations, cases may be referred to a mediation program sponsored by the Department. The Department is authorized to bring a lawsuit where there is a pattern or practice of discrimination in violation of title III, or where an act of discrimination raises an issue of general public importance. Title III may also be enforced through private lawsuits.

ADA Title IV: Telecommunications Relay Services

Title IV addresses telephone and television access for people with hearing and speech disabilities. It requires common carriers (telephone companies) to establish interstate and intrastate telecommunications relay services (TRS) 24 hours a day, 7 days a week. TRS enables callers with hearing and speech disabilities who use TTYs (also known as TDDs), and callers who use voice telephones to communicate with each other through a third party communications assistant. The Federal Communications Commission (FCC) has set minimum standards for TRS services. Title IV also requires closed captioning of federally funded public service announcements.

Telecommunications Act

Section 255 and Section 251(a)(2) of the Communications Act of 1934, as amended by the Telecommunications Act of 1996, require manufacturers of telecommunications equipment and providers of telecommunications services to ensure that such equipment and services are accessible to and usable by persons with disabilities, if readily achievable. These amendments ensure that people with disabilities will have access to a broad range of products and services such as telephones, cell phones, pagers, call-waiting, and operator services, that were often inaccessible to many users with disabilities.

Fair Housing Act

The Fair Housing Act, as amended in 1988, prohibits housing discrimination on the basis of race, color, religion, sex, disability, familial status, and national origin. Its coverage includes private housing, housing that receives federal financial assistance, and state and local government housing. It is unlawful to discriminate in any aspect of selling or renting housing or to deny a dwelling to a buyer or renter because of the disability of that individual, an individual associated with the buyer or renter, or an individual who intends to live in the residence. Other covered activities include, for example, financing, zoning practices, new construction design, and advertising.

The Fair Housing Act requires owners of housing facilities to make reasonable exceptions in their policies and operations to afford people with disabilities equal housing opportunities. For example, a landlord with a "no pets" policy may be required to grant an exception to this rule and allow an individual who is blind to keep a guide dog in the residence. The Fair Housing Act also requires landlords to allow tenants with disabilities to make reasonable access-related modifications to their private living space, as well as to common use spaces. (The landlord is not required to pay for the changes.) The Act further requires that new multifamily housing with four or more units be designed and built to allow access for persons with disabilities. This includes accessible common use areas, doors that are wide enough for wheelchairs, kitchens, and bathrooms that allow a person using a wheelchair to maneuver, and other adaptable features within the units.

Additionally, the DOJ can file cases involving a pattern or practice of discrimination. The Fair Housing Act may also be enforced through private lawsuits.

Air Carrier Access Act

The Air Carrier Access Act (ACAA) prohibits discrimination in air transportation by domestic and foreign air carriers against qualified individuals with physical or mental impairments. It applies only to air carriers that provide regularly scheduled services for hire to the public. Requirements address a wide range of issues including boarding assistance and certain accessibility features in newly built aircraft and new or altered airport facilities. People may enforce rights under the Air Carrier Access Act by filing a complaint with the U.S. Department of Transportation (DOT), or by bringing a lawsuit in federal court.

Voting Accessibility for the Elderly and Handicapped Act

The Voting Accessibility for the Elderly and Handicapped Act (VAEHA) of 1984 generally requires polling places across the United States to be physically accessible to people with disabilities for federal elections. Where no accessible location is available to serve as a polling place, a political subdivision must provide an alternate means of casting a ballot on the day of the election. This law also requires states to make available registration and voting aids for disabled and elderly voters, including information by TTYs (also known as TDDs) or similar devices.

National Voter Registration Act

The National Voter Registration Act (NVRA) of 1993, also known as the "Motor Voter Act," makes it easier for all Americans to exercise their fundamental right to vote. One of the basic purposes of the Act is to increase the historically low registration rates of minorities and persons with disabilities that have resulted from discrimination. The Motor Voter Act requires all offices of state-funded programs that are primarily engaged in providing services to persons with disabilities to provide all program applicants with voter registration forms, to assist them in completing the forms, and to transmit completed forms to the appropriate state official.

Civil Rights of Institutionalized Persons Act

The Civil Rights of Institutionalized Persons Act (CRIPA) authorizes the U.S. Attorney General to investigate conditions of confinement at state and local government institutions such as prisons, jails, pretrial detention centers, juvenile correctional facilities, publicly operated nursing homes, and institutions for people with psychiatric or developmental disabilities. Its purpose is to allow the Attorney General to uncover and correct widespread deficiencies that seriously jeopardize the health and safety of residents of institutions. The Attorney General does not have authority under CRIPA to investigate isolated incidents or to represent individual institutionalized persons.

The Attorney General may initiate civil lawsuits where there is reasonable cause to believe that conditions are "egregious or flagrant," that they are subjecting residents to "grievous harm," and that they are part of a "pattern or practice" of resistance to residents' full enjoyment

A Guide to Disability Rights Laws

of constitutional or federal rights, including title II of the ADA and section 504 of the Rehabilitation Act.

Individuals with Disabilities Education Act

The Individuals with Disabilities Education Act (IDEA) (formerly called P.L. 94-142 or the Education for all Handicapped Children Act of 1975) requires public schools to make available to all eligible children with disabilities a free appropriate public education in the least restrictive environment appropriate to their individual needs.

IDEA requires public school systems to develop appropriate Individualized Education Programs (IEP's) for each child. The specific special education and related services outlined in each IEP reflect the individualized needs of each student.

IDEA also mandates that particular procedures be followed in the development of the IEP. Each student's IEP must be developed by a team of knowledgeable persons and must be at least reviewed annually. The team includes the child's teacher; the parents, subject to certain limited exceptions; the child, if determined appropriate; an agency representative who is qualified to provide or supervise the provision of special education; and other individuals at the parents' or agency's discretion.

If parents disagree with the proposed IEP, they can request a due process hearing and a review from the state educational agency if applicable in that state. They also can appeal the state agency's decision to state or federal court.

Rehabilitation Act

The Rehabilitation Act prohibits discrimination on the basis of disability in programs conducted by federal agencies, in programs receiving federal financial assistance, in federal employment, and in the employment practices of federal contractors. The standards for determining employment discrimination under the Rehabilitation Act are the same as those used in title I of the ADA.

Section 501

Section 501 requires affirmative action and nondiscrimination in employment by federal agencies of the executive branch. To obtain more information or to file a complaint, employees should contact their agency's U.S. Equal Employment Opportunity Office (EEOC).

Section 503

Section 503 requires affirmative action and prohibits employment discrimination by federal government contractors and subcontractors with contracts of more than $10,000.

Section 504

Section 504 states that "no qualified individual with a disability in the United States shall be excluded from, denied the benefits of, or be subjected to discrimination under" any program or activity that either receives federal financial assistance or is conducted by any Executive agency or the United States Postal Service (USPS).

Each federal agency has its own set of section 504 regulations that apply to its own programs. Agencies that provide federal financial assistance also have section 504 regulations covering entities that receive federal aid. Requirements common to these regulations include reasonable accommodation for employees with disabilities; program accessibility; effective communication with people who have hearing or vision disabilities; and accessible new construction and alterations. Each agency is responsible for enforcing its own regulations. Section 504 may also be enforced through private lawsuits. It is not necessary to file a complaint with a federal agency or to receive a "right-to-sue" letter before going to court.

Section 508

Section 508 establishes requirements for electronic and information technology developed, maintained, procured, or used by the federal government. Section 508 requires federal electronic and information technology to be accessible to people with disabilities, including employees and members of the public.

An accessible information technology system is one that can be operated in a variety of ways and does not rely on a single sense or ability of the user. For example, a system that provides output only in visual format may not be accessible to people with visual impairments and a system that provides output only in audio format may not be accessible to people who are deaf or hard of hearing. Some individuals with disabilities may need accessibility-related software or peripheral devices in order to use systems that comply with Section 508.

A Guide to Disability Rights Laws

Architectural Barriers Act

The Architectural Barriers Act (ABA) requires that buildings and facilities that are designed, constructed, or altered with federal funds, or leased by a federal agency, comply with federal standards for physical accessibility. ABA requirements are limited to architectural standards in new and altered buildings and in newly leased facilities. They do not address the activities conducted in those buildings and facilities. Facilities of the USPS are covered by the ABA.

Chapter 57

Questions and Answers about the Americans with Disabilities Act

Title I of the Americans with Disabilities Act (ADA) of 1990 prohibits private employers, state and local governments, employment agencies and labor unions from discriminating against qualified individuals with disabilities in job application procedures, hiring, firing, advancement, compensation, job training, and other terms, conditions, and privileges of employment. The ADA covers employers with 15 or more employees, including state and local governments. It also applies to employment agencies and to labor organizations. The ADA's nondiscrimination standards also apply to federal sector employees under section 501 of the Rehabilitation Act, as amended, and its implementing rules.

This chapter contains text excerpted from the following sources: Text in this chapter begins with excerpts from "Facts about the Americans with Disabilities Act," U.S. Equal Employment Opportunity Commission (EEOC), April 9, 2016; Text beginning with the heading "What Employers Are Covered by the ADA, and When Is the Coverage Effective?" is excerpted from "The ADA: Questions and Answers," U.S. Equal Employment Opportunity Commission (EEOC), February 1, 2001. Reviewed July 2018.

What Employers Are Covered by the Americans with Disabilities Act, and When Is the Coverage Effective?

The employment provisions of title I of the ADA apply to private employers, state and local governments, employment agencies, and labor unions. Employers with 25 or more employees were covered starting July 26, 1992, when title I went into effect. Employers with 15 or more employees were covered two years later, beginning July 26, 1994.

In addition, the employment practices of state and local governments of any size are covered by title II of the ADA, which goes into effect on January 26, 1992. The standards to be used under title II for determining whether employment discrimination has occurred depends on whether the public entity at issue is also covered by title I. Beginning July 26, 1992, if the public entity is covered by title I, then title I standards will apply. If not, the standards of section 504 of the Rehabilitation Act will apply. From January 26, 1992, when title II went into effect, until July 26, 1992, when title I went into effect, public entities were subject to the section 504 standards.

What Practices and Activities Are Covered by the Employment Nondiscrimination Requirements?

The ADA prohibits discrimination in all employment practices, including job application procedures, hiring, firing, advancement, compensation, training, and other terms, conditions, and privileges of employment. It applies to recruitment, advertising, tenure, layoff, leave, fringe benefits, and all other employment-related activities.

Who Is Protected against Employment Discrimination?

Employment discrimination is prohibited against "qualified individuals with disabilities." Persons discriminated against because they have a known association or relationship with a disabled individual also are protected. The ADA defines an "individual with a disability" as a person who has a physical or mental impairment that substantially limits one or more major life activities, has a record of such an impairment, or is regarded as having such an impairment.

The first part of the definition makes clear that the ADA applies to persons who have substantial, as distinct from minor, impairments, and that these must be impairments that limit major life activities such as seeing, hearing, speaking, walking, breathing, performing

Questions and Answers about the ADA

manual tasks, learning, caring for oneself, and working. An individual with epilepsy, paralysis, a substantial hearing or visual impairment, mental retardation, or a learning disability would be covered, but an individual with a minor, nonchronic condition of short duration, such as a sprain, infection, or broken limb, generally would not be covered.

The second part of the definition would include, for example, a person with a history of cancer that is currently in remission or a person with a history of mental illness.

The third part of the definition protects individuals who are regarded and treated as though they have a substantially limiting disability, even though they may not have such an impairment. For example, this provision would protect a severely disfigured qualified individual from being denied employment because an employer feared the "negative reactions" of others.

Who Is a "Qualified Individual with a Disability"?

A qualified individual with a disability is a person who meets legitimate skill, experience, education, or other requirements of an employment position that he or she holds or seeks, and who can perform the "essential functions" of the position with or without reasonable accommodation. Requiring the ability to perform "essential" functions assures that an individual will not be considered unqualified simply because of inability to perform marginal or incidental job functions. If the individual is qualified to perform essential job functions except for limitations caused by a disability, the employer must consider whether the individual could perform these functions with a reasonable accommodation. If a written job description has been prepared in advance of advertising or interviewing applicants for a job, this will be considered as evidence, although not necessarily conclusive evidence, of the essential functions of the job.

Does an Employer Have to Give Preference to a Qualified Applicant with a Disability over Other Applicants?

No. An employer is free to select the most qualified applicant available and to make decisions based on reasons unrelated to the existence or consequence of a disability. For example, if two persons apply for a job opening as a typist, one a person with a disability who accurately types 50 words per minute, the other a person without a disability who accurately types 75 words per minute, the employer may hire the applicant with the higher typing speed, if typing speed is needed for successful performance of the job.

What Is "Reasonable Accommodation"?

Reasonable accommodation is a modification or an adjustment to a job or the work environment that will enable a qualified applicant or employee with a disability to participate in the application process or to perform essential job functions. Reasonable accommodation also includes adjustments to assure that a qualified individual with a disability has rights and privileges in employment equal to those of nondisabled employees.

What Kinds of Actions Are Required to Reasonably Accommodate Applicants and Employees?

Examples of reasonable accommodation include making existing facilities used by employees readily accessible to and usable by an individual with a disability; restructuring a job; modifying work schedules; acquiring or modifying equipment; providing qualified readers or interpreters; or appropriately modifying examinations, training, or other programs. Reasonable accommodation also may include reassigning a current employee to a vacant position for which the individual is qualified, if the person becomes disabled and is unable to do the original job. However, there is no obligation to find a position for an applicant who is not qualified for the position sought. Employers are not required to lower quality or quantity standards in order to make an accommodation, nor are they obligated to provide personal use items such as glasses or hearing aids.

The decision as to the appropriate accommodation must be based on the particular facts of each case. In selecting the particular type of reasonable accommodation to provide, the principal test is that of effectiveness, i.e., whether the accommodation will enable the person with a disability to do the job in question.

Must Employers Be Familiar with the Many Diverse Types of Disabilities to Know Whether or How to Make a Reasonable Accommodation?

No. An employer is required to accommodate only a "known" disability of a qualified applicant or employee. The requirement generally will be triggered by a request from an individual with a disability, who frequently can suggest an appropriate accommodation. Accommodations must be made on an individual basis, because the nature and extent of a disabling condition and the requirements of the job will vary in each case. If the individual does not request an accommodation, the employer is not obligated to provide one. If a disabled person requests, but cannot suggest, an appropriate accommodation, the employer and the individual should work together to identify one. There are also many public and private resources that can provide assistance without cost.

What Are the Limitations on the Obligation to Make a Reasonable Accommodation?

The disabled individual requiring the accommodation must be otherwise qualified, and the disability must be known to the employer. In addition, an employer is not required to make an accommodation if it would impose an "undue hardship" on the operation of the employer's business. "Undue hardship" is defined as "an action requiring significant difficulty or expense" when considered in light of a number of factors. These factors include the nature and cost of the accommodation in relation to the size, resources, nature, and structure of the employer's operation. Where the facility making the accommodation is part of a larger entity, the structure and overall resources of the larger organization would be considered, as well as the financial and administrative relationship of the facility to the larger organization. In general, a larger employer would be expected to make accommodations requiring greater effort or expense than would be required of a smaller employer.

Must an Employer Modify Existing Facilities to Make Them Accessible?

An employer may be required to modify facilities to enable an individual to perform essential job functions and to have equal opportunity to participate in other employment-related activities. For example, if an employee lounge is located in a place inaccessible to a person using a wheelchair, the lounge might be modified or relocated, or comparable facilities might be provided in a location that would enable the individual to take a break with coworkers.

May an Employer Inquire as to Whether a Prospective Employee Is Disabled?

An employer may not make a preemployment inquiry on an application form or in an interview as to whether, or to what extent, an individual is disabled. The employer may ask a job applicant whether he or she can perform particular job functions. If the applicant has a disability known to the employer, the employer may ask how he or she can perform job functions that the employer considers difficult or impossible to perform because of the disability, and whether an accommodation would be needed. A job offer may be conditioned on the results of a medical examination, provided that the examination is required for all entering employees in the same job category regardless of disability, and that information obtained is handled according to confidentiality requirements specified in the Act. After an employee enters on duty, all medical examinations and inquiries must be job related and necessary for the conduct of the employer's business. These provisions of the law are intended to prevent the employer from basing hiring and employment decisions on unfounded assumptions about the effects of a disability.

Does the Americans with Disabilities Act Take Safety Issues into Account?

Yes. The ADA expressly permits employers to establish qualification standards that will exclude individuals who pose a direct threat—i.e., a significant risk of substantial harm—to the health or safety of the individual or of others, if that risk cannot be lowered to an acceptable level by reasonable accommodation. However, an employer may not simply assume that a threat exists; the employer must establish through objective, medically supportable methods that there is genuine risk that substantial harm could occur in the workplace. By requiring employers to make individualized judgments based on reliable medical or other objective evidence rather than on generalizations, ignorance, fear, patronizing attitudes, or stereotypes, the ADA recognizes the need to balance the interests of people with disabilities against the legitimate interests of employers in maintaining a safe workplace.

Can an Employer Refuse to Hire an Applicant or Fire a Current Employee Who Is Illegally Using Drugs?

Yes. Individuals who currently engage in the illegal use of drugs are specifically excluded from the definition of a "qualified individual with a disability" protected by the ADA when an action is taken on the basis of their drug use.

Is Testing for Illegal Drugs Permissible under the Americans with Disabilities Act?

Yes. A test for illegal drugs is not considered a medical examination under the ADA; therefore, employers may conduct such testing of applicants or employees and make employment decisions based on the results. The ADA does not encourage, prohibit, or authorize drug tests.

Are People with Acquired Immunodeficiency Syndrome (AIDS) Covered by the Americans with Disabilities Act?

Yes. The legislative history indicates that Congress intended the ADA to protect persons with acquired immunodeficiency syndrome (AIDS) and human immunodeficiency virus (HIV) disease from discrimination.

How Does the Americans with Disabilities Act Recognize Public Health Concerns?

No provision in the ADA is intended to supplant the role of public health authorities in protecting the community from legitimate health threats. The ADA recognizes the need to strike a balance between the right of a disabled person to be free from discrimination based on unfounded fear and the right of the public to be protected.

What Is Discrimination Based on "Relationship or Association"?

The ADA prohibits discrimination based on relationship or association in order to protect individuals from actions based on unfounded assumptions that their relationship to a person with a disability would affect their job performance, and from actions caused by bias or misinformation concerning certain disabilities. For example, this provision would protect a person with a disabled spouse from being denied employment because of an employer's unfounded assumption that the applicant would use excessive leave to care for the spouse. It also would protect an individual who does volunteer work for people with AIDS from a discriminatory employment action motivated by that relationship or association.

Will the Americans with Disabilities Act Increase Litigation Burdens on Employers?

Some litigation is inevitable. However, employers who use the period prior to the effective date of employment coverage to adjust their policies and practices to conform to ADA requirements will be much less likely to have serious litigation concerns. In drafting the ADA, Congress relied heavily on the language of the Rehabilitation Act of 1973 and its implementing regulations. There is already an extensive body of law interpreting the requirements of that Act to which employers can turn for guidance on their ADA obligations. The U.S. Equal Employment Opportunity Commission (EEOC), which has issued regulations implementing the ADA's title I employment provisions, published a technical assistance manual with guidance on how to comply and will provide other assistance to help employers meet ADA requirements. Equal employment opportunity for people with disabilities will be achieved most quickly and effectively through widespread voluntary compliance with the law, rather than through reliance on litigation to enforce compliance.

How Are the Employment Provisions Enforced?

The employment provisions of title I of the ADA are enforced under the same procedures applicable to race, sex, national origin, and religious discrimination under Title VII of the Civil Rights Act of 1964. Complaints regarding actions that occur on or after July 26, 1992, may be filed with the EEOC or designated state human rights agencies. Remedies may include hiring, reinstatement, back pay, court orders to stop discrimination, and reasonable accommodation. Compensatory damages may be awarded for actual monetary losses and for future monetary losses, mental anguish, and inconvenience. Punitive damages may be available as well, if an employer acts with malice or reckless indifference. Attorney's fees may also be awarded.

Chapter 58

Housing and Safety Issues for People with Disabilities

Chapter Contents

Section 58.1—Centers for Independent Living for
Disabled People 612
Section 58.2—Disability Rights in Housing 614
Section 58.3—Understanding the Fair Housing
Amendments Act 631
Section 58.4—Housing Rights for People with
Disabilities.. 637
Section 58.5—Fire Safety for People with
Disabilities and Their Caregivers 640
Section 58.6—Disaster Preparedness for People
with Disabilities and Special Needs................... 642

Section 58.1

Centers for Independent Living for Disabled People

This section includes text excerpted from "Centers for Independent Living," Administration for Community Living (ACL), July 16, 2018.

Administration for Community Living's (ACL) independent living programs work to support community living and independence for people with disabilities across the nation based on the belief that all people can live with dignity, make their own choices, and participate fully in society. These programs provide tools, resources, and supports for integrating people with disabilities fully into their communities to promote equal opportunities, self-determination, and respect.

What Is Independent Living?

Independent living can be considered a movement, a philosophy, or specific programs. In the context of ACL, independent living programs are supported through funding authorized by the Rehabilitation Act of 1973, as amended (The Act). Title VII, chapter 1 of the Act states the current purpose of the program is to "promote a philosophy of independent living including a philosophy of consumer control, peer support, self-help, self-determination, equal access, and individual and system advocacy, in order to maximize the leadership, empowerment, independence, and productivity of individuals with disabilities, and the integration and full inclusion of individuals with disabilities into the mainstream of American society."

Key provisions of the Act include responsibilities of the Designated State Entity (DSE), provisions for the Statewide Independent Living Councils (SILCs), requirements for the State Plan for Independent Living (SPIL), and Centers for Independent Living (CILs) standards and assurances.

To receive funding, states must jointly develop and submit a State Plan for Independent Living (SPIL), which is a three-year plan for providing independent living services in the state. The Designated State Entity (DSE) is the agency that, on behalf of the state, receives, accounts for and disburses funds received under Subpart B of the Act. The Statewide Independent Living Council (SILC) is an independent entity responsible to monitor, review, and evaluate the implementation of the SPIL. Centers for Independent Living are consumer-controlled, community-based, cross-disability, nonresidential private nonprofit agency that is designed and operated within a local community by individuals with disabilities, and provides an array of independent living services.

Workforce Innovation and Opportunity Act

In July 2014, the Workforce Innovation and Opportunity Act (WIOA) was signed into law, transferring the Independent Living programs, the National Institute on Disability, Independent Living, and Rehabilitation Research (NIDILRR), and the Assistive Technology programs to ACL. WIOA also included statutory changes that affect independent living programs, including the addition of new core services, shifts in the process of developing and adopting state plans and changes in the functions of the SILC. ACL developed a final rule to implement the relevant provisions of the Workforce Innovation and Opportunity Act of 2014, and will continue to issue guidance as needed.

Independent Living Services Programs

The Independent Living Services (ILS) program provides financial assistance, through formula grants, to states and territories for providing, expanding, and improving the provision of independent living services. To be eligible to receive financial assistance, states must:

1. develop, submit and receive approval on a State Plan for Independent Living (SPIL), and
2. establish and maintain a Statewide Independent Living Council (SILC).

The SILC and the Centers for Independent Living (CILs) within the state develop a State Plan for Independent Living (SPIL), a document required by law that indicates how the state IL Network is going to execute and improve independent living services over the next three years.

Funds are also made available for the provisions of training and technical assistance to SILCs. The ILS program funding provides resources to the state to support the work of the SILC and the Designated State Entity (DSE), the state entity responsible to receive, account for, and disburse the ILS funds. The remainder of funds may be used for the following activities as reflected in an approved SPIL:

1. Providing independent living (IL) services to individuals with significant disabilities, particularly those in unserved areas of the state;

2. Demonstrating ways to expand and improve IL services;

3. Supporting the operation of CILs;

4. Increasing the capacity of public or nonprofit organizations and other entities to develop comprehensive approaches or systems for providing IL services;

5. Conducting studies and analyses, developing model policies and procedures, and presenting information, approaches, strategies, findings, conclusions, and recommendations to federal, state, and local policymakers;

6. Training individuals with disabilities and individuals providing services to individuals with disabilities and other persons regarding the IL philosophy; and

7. Providing outreach to populations that are unserved or underserved by programs under this title, including minority groups and urban and rural populations.

Section 58.2

Disability Rights in Housing

This section includes text excerpted from "U.S. Department of Housing and Urban Development," U.S. Department of Justice (DOJ), August 6, 2015.

The U.S. Department of Justice (DOJ) and the U.S. Department of Housing and Urban Development (HUD) are jointly responsible for enforcing the federal Fair Housing Act, which prohibits discrimination in housing on the basis of race, color, religion, sex, national origin, familial status, and disability. One type of disability discrimination prohibited by the Act is the refusal to make reasonable accommodations in rules, policies, practices, or services when such accommodations may be necessary to afford a person with a disability the equal opportunity to use and enjoy a dwelling. HUD and DOJ frequently respond to complaints alleging that housing providers have violated the Act by refusing reasonable accommodations to persons with disabilities. This statement provides technical assistance regarding the rights and obligations of persons with disabilities and housing providers under the Act relating to reasonable accommodations.

What Types of Discrimination against Persons with Disabilities Does the Act Prohibit?

The Act prohibits housing providers from discriminating against applicants or residents because of their disability or the disability of anyone associated with them and from treating persons with disabilities less favorably than others because of their disability. The Act also makes it unlawful for any person to refuse "to make reasonable accommodations in rules, policies, practices, or services, when such accommodations may be necessary to afford person(s) (with disabilities) equal opportunity to use and enjoy a dwelling." The Act also prohibits housing providers from refusing residency to persons with disabilities, or placing conditions on their residency, because those persons may require reasonable accommodations. In addition, in certain circumstances, the Act requires that housing providers allow residents to make reasonable structural modifications to units and public/common areas in a dwelling when those modifications may be necessary for a person with a disability to have full enjoyment of a dwelling. With certain limited exceptions, the Act applies to privately and publicly owned housing, including housing subsidized by the federal government or rented through the use of Section 8 voucher assistance.

Who Must Comply with the Fair Housing Act's Reasonable Accommodation Requirements?

Any person or entity engaging in prohibited conduct—i.e., refusing to make reasonable accommodations in rules, policies, practices, or services, when such accommodations may be necessary to afford a person with a disability an equal opportunity to use and enjoy a dwelling—may be held liable unless they fall within an exception to the Act's coverage. Courts have applied the Act to individuals, corporations, associations, and others involved in the provision of housing and residential lending, including property owners, housing managers, homeowners and condominium associations, lenders, real estate agents, and brokerage services. Courts have also applied the Act to state and local governments, most often in the context of exclusionary zoning or other land-use decisions. Under specific exceptions to the Fair Housing Act, the reasonable accommodation requirements of the Act do not apply to a private individual owner who sells his own home so long as he

1. does not own more than three single-family homes;
2. does not use a real estate agent and does not employ any discriminatory advertising or notices;
3. has not engaged in a similar sale of a home within a 24-month period; and
4. is not in the business of selling or renting dwellings. The reasonable accommodation requirements of the Fair Housing Act also do not apply to owner-occupied buildings that have four or fewer dwelling units.

Who Qualifies as a Person with a Disability under the Act?

The Act defines a person with a disability to include

1. individuals with a physical or mental impairment that substantially limits one or more major life activities;
2. individuals who are regarded as having such an impairment; and
3. individuals with a record of such an impairment.

The term "physical or mental impairment" includes, but is not limited to, such diseases and conditions as orthopedic, visual, speech and hearing impairments, cerebral palsy, autism, epilepsy, muscular dystrophy, multiple sclerosis, cancer, heart disease, diabetes, Human Immunodeficiency Virus infection, mental retardation, emotional illness, drug addiction (other than addiction caused by current, illegal use of a controlled substance) and alcoholism.

The term "substantially limits" suggests that the limitation is "significant" or "to a large degree."

The term "major life activity" means those activities that are of central importance to daily life, such as seeing, hearing, walking, breathing, performing manual tasks, caring for one's self, learning, and speaking. This list of major life activities is not exhaustive.

Housing and Safety Issues for People with Disabilities

Does the Act Protect Juvenile Offenders, Sex Offenders, Persons Who Illegally Use Controlled Substances, and Persons with Disabilities Who Pose a Significant Danger to Others?

No, juvenile offenders and sex offenders, by virtue of that status, are not persons with disabilities protected by the Act. Similarly, while the Act does protect persons who are recovering from substance abuse, it does not protect persons who are currently engaging in the current illegal use of controlled substances.

Additionally, the Act does not protect an individual with a disability whose tenancy would constitute a "direct threat" to the health or safety of other individuals or result in substantial physical damage to the property of others unless the threat can be eliminated or significantly reduced by reasonable accommodation.

How Can a Housing Provider Determine If an Individual Poses a Direct Threat?

The Act does not allow for exclusion of individuals based upon fear, speculation, or stereotype about a particular disability or persons with disabilities in general. A determination that an individual poses a direct threat must rely on an individualized assessment that is based on reliable objective evidence (e.g., current conduct, or a recent history of overt acts). The assessment must consider:

1. the nature, duration, and severity of the risk of injury;
2. the probability that injury will actually occur; and
3. whether there are any reasonable accommodations that will eliminate the direct threat.

Consequently, in evaluating the history of overt acts, a provider must take into account whether the individual has received intervening treatment or medication that has eliminated the direct threat (i.e., a significant risk of substantial harm). In such a situation, the provider may request that the individual document how the circumstances have changed so that he no longer poses a direct threat. A provider may also obtain satisfactory assurances that the individual will not pose a direct threat during the tenancy. The housing provider must have reliable, objective evidence that a person with a disability poses a direct threat before excluding him from housing on that basis.

Example 1: A housing provider requires all persons applying to rent an apartment to complete an application that includes information on the applicant's current place of residence. On her application to rent an apartment, a woman notes that she currently resides in Cambridge House. The manager of the apartment complex knows that Cambridge House is a group home for women receiving treatment for alcoholism. Based solely on that information and his personal belief that alcoholics are likely to cause disturbances and damage property, the manager rejects the applicant. The rejection is unlawful because it is based on a generalized stereotype related to a disability rather than an individualized assessment of any threat to other persons or the property of others based on reliable, objective evidence about the applicant's recent past conduct. The housing provider may not treat this applicant differently than other applicants based on his subjective perceptions of the potential problems posed by her alcoholism by requiring additional documents, imposing different lease terms, or requiring a higher security deposit. However, the manager could have checked this applicant's references to the same extent and in the same manner as he would have checked any other applicant's references. If such a reference check revealed objective evidence showing that this applicant had posed a direct threat to persons or property in the recent past and the direct threat had not been eliminated, the manager could then have rejected the applicant based on direct threat.

Example 2: James X, a tenant at the Shady Oaks apartment complex, is arrested for threatening his neighbor while brandishing a baseball bat. The Shady Oaks' lease agreement contains a term prohibiting tenants from threatening violence against other residents. Shady Oaks' rental manager investigates the incident and learns that James X threatened the other resident with physical violence and had to be physically restrained by other neighbors to keep him from acting on his threat. Following Shady Oaks' standard practice of strictly enforcing its "no threats" policy, the Shady Oaks rental manager issues James X a 30-day notice to quit, which is the first step in the eviction process. James X's attorney contacts Shady Oaks' rental manager and explains that James X has a psychiatric disability that causes him to be physically violent when he stops taking his prescribed medication. Suggesting that his client will not pose a direct threat to others if proper safeguards are taken, the attorney requests that the rental manager grant James X an exception to the "no threats" policy as a reasonable accommodation based on James X's disability. The Shady Oaks rental manager need only grant the reasonable accommodation if James X's

Housing and Safety Issues for People with Disabilities

attorney can provide satisfactory assurance that James X will receive appropriate counseling and periodic medication monitoring so that he will no longer pose a direct threat during his tenancy. After consulting with James X, the attorney responds that James X is unwilling to receive counseling or submit to any type of periodic monitoring to ensure that he takes his prescribed medication. The rental manager may go forward with the eviction proceeding, since James X continues to pose a direct threat to the health or safety of other residents.

What Is a "Reasonable Accommodation" for Purposes of the Act?

A "reasonable accommodation" is a change, exception, or adjustment to a rule, policy, practice, or service that may be necessary for a person with a disability to have an equal opportunity to use and enjoy a dwelling, including public and common use spaces. Since rules, policies, practices, and services may have a different effect on persons with disabilities than on other persons, treating persons with disabilities exactly the same as others will sometimes deny them an equal opportunity to use and enjoy a dwelling. The Act makes it unlawful to refuse to make reasonable accommodations to rules, policies, practices, or services when such accommodations may be necessary to afford persons with disabilities an equal opportunity to use and enjoy a dwelling.

To show that a requested accommodation may be necessary, there must be an identifiable relationship, or nexus, between the requested accommodation and the individual's disability.

Example 1: A housing provider has a policy of providing unassigned parking spaces to residents. A resident with a mobility impairment, who is substantially limited in her ability to walk, requests an assigned accessible parking space close to the entrance to her unit as a reasonable accommodation. There are available parking spaces near the entrance to her unit that are accessible, but those spaces are available to all residents on a first come, first served basis. The provider must make an exception to its policy of not providing assigned parking spaces to accommodate this resident.

Example 2: A housing provider has a policy of requiring tenants to come to the rental office in person to pay their rent. A tenant has a mental disability that makes her afraid to leave her unit. Because of her disability, she requests that she be permitted to have a friend mail her rent payment to the rental office as a reasonable accommodation.

The provider must make an exception to its payment policy to accommodate this tenant.

Example 3: A housing provider has a "no pets" policy. A tenant who is deaf requests that the provider allows him to keep a dog in his unit as a reasonable accommodation. The tenant explains that the dog is an assistance animal that will alert him to several sounds, including knocks at the door, sounding of the smoke detector, the telephone ringing, and cars coming into the driveway. The housing provider must make an exception to its "no pets" policy to accommodate this tenant.

Are There Any Instances When a Provider Can Deny a Request for a Reasonable Accommodation without Violating the Act?

Yes. A housing provider can deny a request for a reasonable accommodation if the request was not made by or on behalf of a person with a disability or if there is no disability-related need for the accommodation. In addition, a request for a reasonable accommodation may be denied if providing the accommodation is not reasonable i.e., if it would impose an undue financial and administrative burden on the housing provider or it would fundamentally alter the nature of the provider's operations. The determination of undue financial and administrative burden must be made on a case-by-case basis involving various factors, such as the cost of the requested accommodation, the financial resources of the provider, the benefits that the accommodation would provide to the requester, and the availability of alternative accommodations that would effectively meet the requester's disability-related needs.

When a housing provider refuses a requested accommodation because it is not reasonable, the provider should discuss with the requester whether there is an alternative accommodation that would effectively address the requester's disability-related needs without a fundamental alteration to the provider's operations and without imposing an undue financial and administrative burden. If an alternative accommodation would effectively meet the requester's disability-related needs and is reasonable, the provider must grant it. An interactive process in which the housing provider and the requester discuss the requester's disability-related need for the requested accommodation and possible alternative accommodations is helpful to all concerned because it often results in an effective accommodation for the requester that does not pose an undue financial and administrative burden for the provider.

Example: As a result of a disability, a tenant is physically unable to open the dumpster placed in the parking lot by his housing provider for trash collection. The tenant requests that the housing provider send a maintenance staff person to his apartment on a daily basis to collect his trash and take it to the dumpster. Because the housing development is a small operation with limited financial resources and the maintenance staff are on site only twice per week, it may be an undue financial and administrative burden for the housing provider to grant the requested daily trash pick-up service. Accordingly, the requested accommodation may not be reasonable. If the housing provider denies the requested accommodation as unreasonable, the housing provider should discuss with the tenant whether reasonable accommodations could be provided to meet the tenant's disability-related needs—for instance, placing an open trash collection can in a location that is readily accessible to the tenant so the tenant can dispose of his own trash and the provider's maintenance staff can then transfer the trash to the dumpster when they are on site. Such an accommodation would not involve a fundamental alteration of the provider's operations and would involve little financial and administrative burden for the provider while accommodating the tenant's disability-related needs.

There may be instances where a provider believes that, while the accommodation requested by an individual is reasonable, there is an alternative accommodation that would be equally effective in meeting the individual's disability-related needs. In such a circumstance, the provider should discuss with the individual if she is willing to accept the alternative accommodation. However, providers should be aware that persons with disabilities typically have the most accurate knowledge about the functional limitations posed by their disability, and an individual is not obligated to accept an alternative accommodation suggested by the provider if she believes it will not meet her needs and her preferred accommodation is reasonable.

What Is a "Fundamental Alteration"?

A "fundamental alteration" is a modification that alters the essential nature of a provider's operations.

Example: A tenant has a severe mobility impairment that substantially limits his ability to walk. He asks his housing provider to transport him to the grocery store and assist him with his grocery shopping as a reasonable accommodation to his disability. The provider does not provide any transportation or shopping services for its tenants, so granting this request would require a fundamental alteration in the nature of the provider's operations. The request can be denied, but the provider should discuss with the requester whether there is any alternative accommodation that would effectively meet the requester's disability-related needs without fundamentally altering the nature of its operations, such as reducing the tenant's need to walk long distances by altering its parking policy to allow a volunteer from a local community service organization to park her car close to the tenant's unit so she can transport the tenant to the grocery store and assist him with his shopping.

What Happens If Providing a Requested Accommodation Involves Some Costs on the Part of the Housing Provider?

Courts have ruled that the Act may require a housing provider to grant a reasonable accommodation that involves costs, so long as the reasonable accommodation does not pose an undue financial and administrative burden and the requested accommodation does not constitute a fundamental alteration of the provider's operations. The financial resources of the provider, the cost of the reasonable accommodation, the benefits to the requester of the requested accommodation, and the availability of other, less expensive alternative accommodations that would effectively meet the applicant or resident's disability-related needs must be considered in determining whether a requested accommodation poses an undue financial and administrative burden.

What Happens If No Agreement Can Be Reached through the Interactive Process?

A failure to reach an agreement on an accommodation request is in effect a decision by the provider not to grant the requested accommodation. If the individual who was denied an accommodation files a Fair Housing Act complaint to challenge that decision, then the agency or court receiving the complaint will review the evidence in light of applicable law and decide if the housing provider violated that law.

May a Housing Provider Charge an Extra Fee or Require an Additional Deposit from Applicants or Residents with Disabilities as a Condition of Granting a Reasonable Accommodation?

No. Housing providers may not require persons with disabilities to pay extra fees or deposits as a condition of receiving a reasonable accommodation.

Example 1: A person who is substantially limited in his ability to walk uses a motorized scooter for mobility purposes. He applies to live in an assisted living facility that has a policy prohibiting the use of motorized vehicles in buildings and elsewhere on the premises. It would be a reasonable accommodation for the facility to make an exception to this policy to permit the person to use his motorized scooter on the premises for mobility purposes. Since allowing the person to use his scooter in the buildings and elsewhere on the premises is a reasonable accommodation, the facility may not condition his use of the scooter on payment of a fee or deposit or on a requirement that he obtain liability insurance relating to the use of the scooter. However, since the Fair Housing Act does not protect any person with a disability who poses a direct threat to the person or property of others, the person must operate his motorized scooter in a responsible manner that does not pose a significant risk to the safety of other persons and does not cause damage to other persons' property. If the individual's use of the scooter causes damage to his unit or the common areas, the housing provider may charge him for the cost of repairing the damage (or deduct it from the standard security deposit imposed on all tenants), if it is the provider's practice to assess tenants for any damage they cause to the premises.

Example 2: Because of his disability, an applicant with a hearing impairment needs to keep an assistance animal in his unit as a reasonable accommodation. The housing provider may not require the applicant to pay a fee or a security deposit as a condition of allowing the applicant to keep the assistance animal. However, if a tenant's assistance animal causes damage to the applicant's unit or the common areas of the dwelling, the housing provider may charge the tenant for the cost of repairing the damage (or deduct it from the standard security deposit imposed on all tenants), if it is the provider's practice to assess tenants for any damage they cause to the premises.

When and How Should an Individual Request an Accommodation?

Under the Act, a resident or an applicant for housing makes a reasonable accommodation request whenever she makes clear to the housing provider that she is requesting an exception, change, or adjustment to a rule, policy, practice, or service because of her disability. She should explain what type of accommodation she is requesting and, if the need for the accommodation is not readily apparent or not known to the provider, explain the relationship between the requested accommodation and her disability.

An applicant or resident is not entitled to receive a reasonable accommodation unless she requests one. However, the Fair Housing Act does not require that a request be made in a particular manner or at a particular time. A person with a disability need not personally make the reasonable accommodation request; the request can be made by a family member or someone else who is acting on her behalf. An individual making a reasonable accommodation request does not need to mention the Act or use the words "reasonable accommodation." However, the requester must make the request in a manner that a reasonable person would understand to be a request for an exception, change, or adjustment to a rule, policy, practice, or service because of a disability.

Although a reasonable accommodation request can be made orally or in writing, it is usually helpful for both the resident and the housing provider if the request is made in writing. This will help prevent misunderstandings regarding what is being requested, or whether the request was made. To facilitate the processing and consideration of the request, residents or prospective residents may wish to check with a housing provider in advance to determine if the provider has a preference regarding the manner in which the request is made. However, housing providers must give appropriate consideration to reasonable accommodation requests even if the requester makes the request orally or does not use the provider's preferred forms or procedures for making such requests.

Example: A tenant in a large apartment building makes an oral request that she be assigned a mailbox in a location that she can easily access because of a physical disability that limits her ability to reach and bend. The provider would prefer that the tenant make the accommodation request on a preprinted form, but the tenant fails to complete the form. The provider must consider the reasonable accommodation request even though the tenant would not use the provider's designated form.

Must a Housing Provider Adopt Formal Procedures for Processing Requests for a Reasonable Accommodation?

No. The Act does not require that a housing provider adopt any formal procedures for reasonable accommodation requests. However, having formal procedures may aid individuals with disabilities in making requests for reasonable accommodations and may aid housing providers in assessing those requests so that there are no misunderstandings as to the nature of the request, and, in the event of later disputes, provide records to show that the requests received proper consideration.

A provider may not refuse a request, however, because the individual making the request did not follow any formal procedures that the provider has adopted. If a provider adopts formal procedures for processing reasonable accommodation requests, the provider should ensure that the procedures, including any forms used, do not seek information that is not necessary to evaluate if a reasonable accommodation may be needed to afford a person with a disability equal opportunity to use and enjoy a dwelling.

Is a Housing Provider Obligated to Provide a Reasonable Accommodation to a Resident or Applicant If an Accommodation Has Not Been Requested?

No. A housing provider is only obligated to provide a reasonable accommodation to a resident or applicant if a request for the accommodation has been made. A provider has notice that a reasonable accommodation request has been made if a person, her family member, or someone acting on her behalf requests a change, exception, or adjustment to a rule, policy, practice, or service because of a disability, even if the words "reasonable accommodation" are not used as part of the request.

What If a Housing Provider Fails to Act Promptly on a Reasonable Accommodation Request?

A provider has an obligation to provide prompt responses to reasonable accommodation requests. An undue delay in responding to a reasonable accommodation request may be deemed to be a failure to provide a reasonable accommodation.

What Inquiries, If Any, May a Housing Provider Make of Current or Potential Residents Regarding the Existence of a Disability When They Have Not Asked for an Accommodation?

Under the Fair Housing Act, it is usually unlawful for a housing provider to

1. ask if an applicant for a dwelling has a disability or if a person intending to reside in a dwelling or anyone associated with an applicant or resident has a disability, or
2. ask about the nature or severity of such persons' disabilities. Housing providers may, however, make the following inquiries, provided these inquiries are made of all applicants, including those with and without disabilities:

- An inquiry into an applicant's ability to meet the requirements of tenancy;
- An inquiry to determine if an applicant is a current illegal abuser or addict of a controlled substance;
- An inquiry to determine if an applicant qualifies for a dwelling legally available only to persons with a disability or to persons with a particular type of disability; and
- An inquiry to determine if an applicant qualifies for housing that is legally available on a priority basis to persons with disabilities or to persons with a particular disability.

Example 1: A housing provider offers accessible units to persons with disabilities needing the features of these units on a priority basis. The provider may ask applicants if they have a disability and if, in light of their disability, they will benefit from the features of the units. However, the provider may not ask applicants if they have other types of physical or mental impairments. If the applicant's disability and the need for the accessible features are not readily apparent, the provider may request reliable information/documentation of the disability-related need for an accessible unit.

Example 2: A housing provider operates housing that is legally limited to persons with chronic mental illness. The provider may ask

Housing and Safety Issues for People with Disabilities

applicants for information needed to determine if they have a mental disability that would qualify them for the housing. However, in this circumstance, the provider may not ask applicants if they have other types of physical or mental impairments. If it is not readily apparent that an applicant has a chronic mental disability, the provider may request reliable information/documentation of the mental disability needed to qualify for the housing.

In some instances, a provider may also request certain information about an applicant's or a resident's disability if the applicant or resident requests a reasonable accommodation.

What Kinds of Information, If Any, May a Housing Provider Request from a Person with an Obvious or Known Disability Who Is Requesting a Reasonable Accommodation?

A provider is entitled to obtain information that is necessary to evaluate if a requested reasonable accommodation may be necessary because of a disability. If a person's disability is obvious, or otherwise known to the provider, and if the need for the requested accommodation is also readily apparent or known, then the provider may not request any additional information about the requester's disability or the disability-related need for the accommodation.

If the requester's disability is known or readily apparent to the provider, but the need for the accommodation is not readily apparent or known, the provider may request only information that is necessary to evaluate the disability-related need for the accommodation.

Example 1: An applicant with an obvious mobility impairment who regularly uses a walker to move around asks her housing provider to assign her a parking space near the entrance to the building instead of a space located in another part of the parking lot. Since the physical disability (i.e., difficulty walking) and the disability-related need for the requested accommodation are both readily apparent, the provider may not require the applicant to provide any additional information about her disability or the need for the requested accommodation.

Example 2: A rental applicant who uses a wheelchair advises a housing provider that he wishes to keep an assistance dog in his unit even though the provider has a "no pets" policy. The applicant's disability is readily apparent but the need for an assistance animal is not obvious to the provider. The housing provider may ask the applicant to provide information about the disability-related need for the dog.

Example 3: An applicant with an obvious vision impairment requests that the leasing agent provide assistance to her in filling out the rental application form as a reasonable accommodation because of her disability. The housing provider may not require the applicant to document the existence of her vision impairment.

If a Disability Is Not Obvious, What Kinds of Information May a Housing Provider Request from the Person with a Disability in Support of a Requested Accommodation?

A housing provider may not ordinarily inquire as to the nature and severity of an individual's disability. However, in response to a request for a reasonable accommodation, a housing provider may request reliable disability-related information that

1. is necessary to verify that the person meets the Act's definition of disability (i.e., has a physical or mental impairment that substantially limits one or more major life activities),
2. describes the needed accommodation, and
3. shows the relationship between the person's disability and the need for the requested accommodation.

Depending on the individual's circumstances, information verifying that the person meets the Act's definition of disability can usually be provided by the individual himself or herself (e.g., proof that an individual under 65 years of age receives Supplemental Security Income (SSI) or Social Security Disability Insurance (SSDI) benefits or a credible statement by the individual). A doctor or other medical professional, a peer support group, a nonmedical service agency, or a reliable third party who is in a position to know about the individual's disability may also provide verification of a disability. In most cases, an individual's medical records or detailed information about the nature of a person's disability is not necessary for this inquiry.

Once a housing provider has established that a person meets the Act's definition of disability, the provider's request for documentation should seek only the information that is necessary to evaluate if the reasonable accommodation is needed because of a disability. Such information must be kept confidential and must not be shared with other persons unless they need the information to make or assess a decision to grant or deny a reasonable accommodation request or unless disclosure is required by law (e.g., a court-issued subpoena requiring disclosure).

If a Person Believes She Has Been Unlawfully Denied a Reasonable Accommodation, What Should That Person Do If She Wishes to Challenge That Denial under the Act?

When a person with a disability believes that she has been subjected to a discriminatory housing practice, including a provider's wrongful denial of a request for reasonable accommodation, she may file a complaint with HUD within one year after the alleged denial or may file a lawsuit in federal district court within two years of the alleged denial. If a complaint is filed with HUD, HUD will investigate the complaint at no cost to the person with a disability.

There are several ways that a person may file a complaint with HUD:

- By placing a toll-free call to 800-669-9777 or toll-free TTY 800-927-9275;
- By completing the "online" complaint form available on the HUD Internet site: www.hud.gov; or
- By mailing a completed complaint form or letter to:

Office of Fair Housing and Equal Opportunity (FHEO)
U.S. Department of Housing and Urban Development (HUD)
451 Seventh St., S.W., Rm. 5204
Washington, DC 20410-2000

Upon request, HUD will provide printed materials in alternate formats (large print, audio tapes, or Braille) and provide complainants with assistance in reading and completing forms.

The Civil Rights Division of the U.S. Department of Justice (DOJ) brings lawsuits in federal courts across the country to end discriminatory practices and to seek monetary and other relief for individuals whose rights under the Fair Housing Act have been violated. The Civil Rights Division initiates lawsuits when it has reason to believe that a person or entity is involved in a "pattern or practice" of discrimination or when there has been a denial of rights to a group of persons that raises an issue of general public importance. The Division also participates as amicus curiae in federal court cases that raise important legal questions involving the application and/or interpretation of the Act. To alert the Justice Department to matters involving a pattern or practice of discrimination, matters involving the denial of rights to groups of persons, or lawsuits raising issues that may be appropriate for amicus participation, contact:

U.S. Department of Justice (DOJ)
Civil Rights Division
Housing and Civil Enforcement Section – G St.
950 Pennsylvania Ave., N.W.
Washington, DC 20530

For more information on the types of housing discrimination cases handled by the Civil Rights Division, please refer to the Housing and Civil Enforcement Section's website (www.justice.gov/crt/housing-and-civil-enforcement-section).

A HUD or DOJ decision not to proceed with a Fair Housing Act matter does not foreclose private plaintiffs from pursuing a private lawsuit. However, litigation can be an expensive, time-consuming, and uncertain process for all parties. HUD and the DOJ encourage parties to Fair Housing Act disputes to explore all reasonable alternatives to litigation, including alternative dispute resolution procedures, such as mediation. HUD attempts to conciliate all Fair Housing Act complaints. In addition, it is the DOJ's policy to offer prospective defendants the opportunity to engage in presuit settlement negotiations, except in the most unusual circumstances.

Section 58.3

Understanding the Fair Housing Amendments Act

This section includes text excerpted from "The Fair Housing Act," U.S. Department of Justice (DOJ), December 21, 2017.

Fair Housing Act

The Fair Housing Act, 42 U.S.C. 3601 et seq., prohibits discrimination by direct providers of housing, such as landlords and real estate companies as well as other entities, such as municipalities, banks or other lending institutions and homeowners insurance companies whose discriminatory practices make housing unavailable to persons because of:

- Race or color
- Religion
- Sex
- National origin
- Familial status, or
- Disability

In cases involving discrimination in mortgage loans or home improvement loans, the department may file suit under both the Fair Housing Act and the pattern or practice of discrimination or where a denial of rights to a group of persons raises an issue of general public importance. Where force or threat of force is used to deny or interfere with fair housing rights, the U.S. Department of Justice (DOJ) may institute criminal proceedings. The Fair Housing Act also provides procedures for handling individual complaints of discrimination. Individuals who believe that they have been victims of an illegal housing practice, may file a complaint with the U.S. Department of Housing and Urban Development (HUD) or file their own lawsuit in federal or state court. The DOJ brings suits on behalf of individuals based on referrals from HUD.

Discrimination in Housing Based upon Race or Color

One of the central objectives of the Fair Housing Act, when Congress enacted it in 1968, was to prohibit race discrimination in sales and rentals of housing. Nevertheless, more than 30 years later, race discrimination in housing continues to be a problem. The majority of the Justice Department's pattern or practice cases involve claims of race discrimination. Sometimes, housing providers try to disguise their discrimination by giving false information about availability of housing, either saying that nothing was available or steering homeseekers to certain areas based on race. Individuals who receive such false information or misdirection may have no knowledge that they have been victims of discrimination. The DOJ has brought many cases alleging this kind of discrimination based on race or color. In addition, the Department's Fair Housing Testing Program seeks to uncover this kind of hidden discrimination and hold those responsible accountable. Most of the mortgage lending cases brought by the department under the Fair Housing Act and Equal Credit Opportunity Act (ECOA) have alleged discrimination based on race or color. Some of the Department's cases have also alleged that municipalities and other local government entities violated the Fair Housing Act when they denied permits or zoning changes for housing developments, or relegated them to predominantly minority neighborhoods, because the prospective residents were expected to be predominantly African-Americans.

Discrimination in Housing Based upon Religion

The Fair Housing Act prohibits discrimination in housing based upon religion. This prohibition covers instances of overt discrimination against members of a particular religion as well less direct actions, such as zoning ordinances designed to limit the use of private homes as a place of worship. The number of cases filed since 1968 alleging religious discrimination is small in comparison to some of the other prohibited bases, such as race or national origin. The Act does contain a limited exception that allows noncommercial housing operated by a religious organization to reserve such housing to persons of the same religion.

Discrimination in Housing Based upon Sex, Including Sexual Harassment

The Fair Housing Act makes it unlawful to discriminate in housing on the basis of sex. The department's focus in this area has been to challenge sexual harassment in housing. Women, particularly those who are poor, and with limited housing options, often have little recourse but to tolerate the humiliation and degradation of sexual harassment or risk having their families and themselves removed from their homes. The department's enforcement program is aimed at landlords who create an untenable living environment by demanding sexual favors from tenants or by creating a sexually hostile environment for them. In this manner, the department seeks both to obtain relief for tenants who have been treated unfairly by a landlord because of sex and also deter other potential abusers by making it clear that they cannot continue their conduct without facing repercussions. In addition, pricing discrimination in mortgage lending may also adversely affect women, particularly minority women. This type of discrimination is unlawful under both the Fair Housing Act and Equal Credit Opportunity Act (ECOA).

Discrimination in Housing Based upon National Origin

The Fair Housing Act prohibits discrimination based upon national origin. Such discrimination can be based either upon the country of an individual's birth or where his or her ancestors originated. Census data indicate that the Hispanic population is the fastest growing segment of the nation's population. The U.S. Department of Justice (DOJ) has taken enforcement action against municipal governments that have tried to reduce or limit the number of Hispanic families that may live in their communities. It has sued lenders under both the Fair Housing Act and the Equal Credit Opportunity Act (ECOA) when they have imposed more stringent underwriting standards on home loans or made loans on less favorable terms for Hispanic borrowers. The department has also sued lenders for discrimination against Native Americans. Other areas of the country have experienced an increasing diversity of national origin groups within their populations. This includes immigrants from Southeastern Asia, such as the Hmong, the former Soviet Union, and other portions of Eastern Europe. The department has taken action against private landlords who have discriminated against such individuals.

Discrimination in Housing Based upon Familial Status

The Fair Housing Act, with some exceptions, prohibits discrimination in housing against families with children under 18. In addition to prohibiting an outright denial of housing to families with children, the Act also prevents housing providers from imposing any special requirements or conditions on tenants with custody of children. For example, landlords may not locate families with children in any single portion of a complex, place an unreasonable restriction on the total number of persons who may reside in a dwelling, or limit their access to recreational services provided to other tenants. In most instances, the amended Fair Housing Act prohibits a housing provider from refusing to rent or sell to families with children. However, some facilities may be designated as Housing for Older Persons (55 years of age). This type of housing, which meets the standards set forth in the Housing for Older Persons Act (HOPA) of 1995, may operate as "senior" housing. The U.S. Department of Housing and Urban Development (HUD) has published regulations and additional guidance detailing these statutory requirements.

Discrimination in Housing Based upon Disability

The Fair Housing Act prohibits discrimination on the basis of disability in all types of housing transactions. The Act defines persons with a disability to mean those individuals with mental or physical impairments that substantially limit one or more major life activities. The term mental or physical impairment may include conditions such as blindness, hearing impairment, mobility impairment, human immunodeficiency virus (HIV) infection, mental retardation, alcoholism, drug addiction, chronic fatigue, learning disability, head injury, and mental illness. The term major life activity may include seeing, hearing, walking, breathing, performing manual tasks, caring for one's self, learning, speaking, or working. The Fair Housing Act also protects persons who have a record of such an impairment, or are regarded as having such an impairment. Current users of illegal controlled substances, persons convicted for illegal manufacture or distribution of a controlled substance, sex offenders, and juvenile offenders are not considered disabled under the Fair Housing Act, by virtue of that status. The Fair Housing Act affords no protection to individuals with or without disabilities who present a direct threat to the persons or property of others. Determining whether someone poses such a direct threat must be made on an individualized basis, however, and cannot be based on general assumptions or speculation about the nature of a disability. The Division's enforcement of the Fair Housing Act's protections for persons with disabilities has concentrated on two major areas. One is insuring that zoning and other regulations concerning land use are not employed to hinder the residential choices of these individuals, including unnecessarily restricting communal, or congregate, residential arrangements, such as group homes. The second area is insuring that newly constructed multifamily housing is built in accordance with the Fair Housing Act's accessibility requirements so that it is accessible to and usable by people with disabilities, and, in particular, those who use wheelchairs. There are other federal statutes that prohibit discrimination against individuals with disabilities, including the Americans with Disabilities Act (ADA), which is enforced by the Disability Rights Section (DRS) of the Civil Rights Division.

Discrimination in Housing Based upon Disability
Group Homes

Some individuals with disabilities may live together in congregate living arrangements, often referred to as "group homes." The Fair Housing Act prohibits municipalities and other local government entities from making zoning or land use decisions or implementing land use policies that exclude or otherwise discriminate against individuals with disabilities. The Fair Housing Act makes it unlawful:

To utilize land use policies or actions that treat groups of persons with disabilities less favorably than groups of nondisabled persons. An example would be an ordinance prohibiting housing for persons with disabilities or a specific type of disability, such as mental illness, from locating in a particular area, while allowing other groups of unrelated individuals to live together in that area.

To take action against, or deny a permit, for a home because of the disability of individuals who live or would live there. An example would be denying a building permit for a home because it was intended to provide housing for persons with mental retardation.

To refuse to make reasonable accommodations in land use and zoning policies and procedures where such accommodations may be necessary to afford persons or groups of persons with disabilities an equal opportunity to use and enjoy housing. What constitutes a reasonable accommodation is a case-by-case determination. Not all requested modifications of rules or policies are reasonable. If a requested modification imposes an undue financial or administrative burden on a local government, or if a modification creates a fundamental alteration in a local government's land use and zoning scheme, it is not a "reasonable" accommodation.

Discrimination in Housing Based upon Disability—Accessibility Features for New Construction

The Fair Housing Act defines discrimination in housing against persons with disabilities to include a failure "to design and construct" certain new multi-family dwellings so that they are accessible to and usable by persons with disabilities, and particularly people who use wheelchairs. The Act requires all newly constructed multi-family dwellings of four or more units intended for first occupancy after March 13, 1991, to have certain features: an accessible entrance on an accessible route, accessible common and public use areas, doors sufficiently wide to accommodate wheelchairs, accessible routes into and through each dwelling, light switches, electrical outlets, and thermostats in accessible location, reinforcements in bathroom walls to accommodate grab bar installations, and usable kitchens and bathrooms configured so that a wheelchair can maneuver about the space.

Developers, builders, owners, and architects responsible for the design or construction of new multi-family housing may be held liable under the Fair Housing Act if their buildings fail to meet these design requirements. The U.S. Department of Justice has brought many enforcement actions against those who failed to do so. Most of the cases have been resolved by consent decrees providing a variety of types of relief, including: retrofitting to bring inaccessible features into compliance where feasible and where it is not—alternatives (monetary funds or other construction requirements) that will provide for making other housing units accessible; training on the accessibility requirements for those involved in the construction process; a mandate that all new housing projects comply with the accessibility requirements, and monetary relief for those injured by the violations. In addition, the department has sought to promote accessibility through building codes.

Section 58.4

Housing Rights for People with Disabilities

This section includes text excerpted from "Disability Rights in Housing," U.S. Department of Housing and Urban Development (HUD), August 13, 2003. Reviewed July 2018.

The State of Housing for People with Disabilities

Federal laws define a person with a disability as "Any person who has a physical or mental impairment that substantially limits one or more major life activities; has a record of such impairment; or is regarded as having such an impairment."

In general, a physical or mental impairment includes hearing, mobility and visual impairments, chronic alcoholism, chronic mental illness, acquired immunodeficiency syndrome (AIDS), AIDS-related complex, and mental retardation that substantially limits one or more major life activities. Major life activities include walking, talking, hearing, seeing, breathing, learning, performing manual tasks, and caring for oneself.

Disability Rights in Private and Public Housing

Regardless of whether you live in private or public housing, federal laws provide the following rights to persons with disabilities:

- Prohibits discrimination against persons with disabilities. It is unlawful for a housing provider to refuse to rent or sell to a person simply because of a disability. A housing provider may not impose different application or qualification criteria, rental fees or sales prices, and rental or sales terms or conditions than those required of or provided to persons who are not disabled.

Example: A housing provider may not refuse to rent to an otherwise qualified individual with a mental disability because she/he is uncomfortable with the individual's disability. Such an act would violate the Fair Housing Act because it denies a person housing solely on the basis of their disability.

- Requires housing providers to make reasonable accommodations for persons with disabilities. A reasonable accommodation is a change in rules, policies, practices, or services so that a person with a disability will have an equal opportunity to use and enjoy a dwelling unit or common space. A housing provider should do everything s/he can to assist, but she/he is not required to make changes that would fundamentally alter the program or create an undue financial and administrative burden. Reasonable accommodations may be necessary at all stages of the housing process, including application, tenancy, or to prevent eviction.

Example: A housing provider would make a reasonable accommodation for a tenant with mobility impairment by fulfilling the tenant's request for a reserved parking space in front of the entrance to their unit, even though all parking is unreserved.

- Requires housing providers to allow persons with disabilities to make reasonable modifications. A reasonable modification is a structural modification that is made to allow persons with disabilities the full enjoyment of the housing and related facilities.

  Examples of a reasonable modification would include allowing a person with a disability to: install a ramp into a building, lower the entry threshold of a unit, or install grab bars in a bathroom.

  Reasonable modifications are usually made at the resident's expense. However, there are resources available for helping fund building modifications. Additionally, if you live in federally assisted housing the housing provider may be required to pay for the modification if it does not amount to an undue financial and administrative burden.

- Requires that new covered multifamily housing be designed and constructed to be accessible. In covered multifamily housing consisting of 4 or more units with an elevator built for first occupancy after March 13, 1991, all units must comply with the following seven design and construction requirements of the Fair Housing Act:

  - Accessible entrance on an accessible route
  - Accessible public and common-use areas
  - Usable doors
  - Accessible route into and through the dwelling unit
  - Accessible light switches, electrical outlets, thermostats, and environmental controls

Housing and Safety Issues for People with Disabilities

- Reinforced walls in bathrooms
- Usable kitchens and bathrooms

In covered multifamily housing without an elevator that consists of 4 or more units built for first occupancy after March 13, 1991, all ground floor units must comply with the Fair Housing Act seven design and construction requirements.

These requirements apply to most public and private housing. However, there are limited exemptions for owner-occupied buildings with no more than four units, single-family housing sold or rented without the use of a broker, and housing operated by organizations and private clubs that limit occupancy to members.

If you live in a federally-assisted multifamily housing consisting of 5 or more units, 5 percent of these units (or at least one unit whichever is greater) must meet more stringent physical accessibility requirements. Additionally, 2 percent of units (or at least one unit whichever is greater) must be accessible for persons with visual or hearing disabilities.

People with Disabilities in Federally Assisted Housing

Federal law makes it illegal for an otherwise qualified individual with a disability to be excluded, solely because of his or her disability, from programs receiving federal financial assistance.

- **Zoning and Land Use:** It is unlawful for local governments to utilize land use and zoning policies to keep persons with disabilities from locating to their area.
- **State and Local Laws:** Many states and localities have fair housing laws that are substantially equivalent to the Federal Fair Housing Act. Some of these laws prohibit discrimination on additional bases, such as source of income or marital status. Some of these laws may impose more stringent design and construction standards for new multifamily housing.
- **The Americans with Disabilities Act (ADA):** In most cases, the ADA does not apply to residential housing. Rather, the ADA applies to places of public accommodation such as restaurants, retail stores, libraries, and hospitals as well as commercial facilities such as offices buildings, warehouses, and factories. However, Title III of the ADA covers public and common use areas at housing developments when these public areas are, by

their nature, open to the general public. For example, it covers the rental office since the rental office is open to the general public.

Title II of the ADA applies to all programs, services, and activities provided or made available by public entities. This includes housing when the housing is provided or made available by a public entity. For example, housing covered by Title II of the ADA includes public housing authorities that meet the ADA definition of "public entity," and housing operated by states or units of local government, such as housing on a state university campus.

Section 58.5

Fire Safety for People with Disabilities and Their Caregivers

This section includes text excerpted from "Fire Safety Outreach Materials for People with Disabilities," U.S. Fire Administration (FA), January 4, 2018.

The U.S. Fire Administration (USFA) reviews and collects resources that can be used in public outreach activities to help keep people with disabilities safe from home fires. The free materials are yours to use when educating these community members about the importance of practicing home fire safety.

Statistics

Each year:

- There are approximately 700 home fires involving people with physical disabilities.

- There are approximately 1,700 home fires involving people with mental disabilities.

- Kitchens and cooking areas are the primary areas where these fires start.

Housing and Safety Issues for People with Disabilities

Fire Safety Messages to Share

Millions of people live with physical and mental disabilities. It is important for them to know how to stay safe from fire.

Understand Your Fire Risk

- Having physical or mental disabilities doesn't mean you can't keep you and your family safe from fire.
- Build your home safety plan around your abilities.

Install and Maintain Smoke Alarms

- Smoke alarms with a vibrating pad or flashing light are available for people who are deaf or hard of hearing.
- Smoke alarms with a strobe light outside the home to catch the attention of neighbors, and emergency call systems for summoning help, are also available.
- Ask the manager of your building, or a friend or relative, to install at least one smoke alarm on each level of your home.
- Test smoke alarm batteries every month and change them at least once a year. If you can't reach the test button on your smoke alarm, ask someone to test it for you.

Live near an Exit

- Although you have the legal right to live where you choose, you'll be safest on the ground floor if you live in an apartment building.
- If you live in a multistory home, arrange to sleep on the first floor.
- Being on the ground floor and near an exit will make your escape easier.

Plan Your Escape

- Plan your escape around your capabilities.
- Know at least two exits from every room.
- If you use a walker or wheelchair, check all exits to be sure you can get through the doorways.

- Make any necessary changes, such as installing exit ramps and widening doorways, to make an emergency escape easier.

Don't Isolate Yourself

- Speak to your family members, building manager or neighbors about your fire safety plan and practice it with them.
- Contact your local fire department's nonemergency line and explain your needs. They can suggest escape plan ideas and may perform a home fire safety inspection if you ask.
- Ask emergency providers to keep your needs information on file.
- Keep a phone near your bed and be ready to call 911 or your local emergency number if a fire occurs.
- Fire Safety for People with disabilities flyer
- fire safety for people with disabilities

Section 58.6

Disaster Preparedness for People with Disabilities and Special Needs

This section includes text excerpted from "Disaster Preparedness for People with Disabilities," Federal Emergency Management Agency (FEMA), April 13, 2018.

The keys to effective disaster preparedness—be informed, make a plan and take action—apply to all of us, but people with access and functional needs or disabilities, should approach preparedness planning with additional considerations.

Additional considerations could include:

- Creating a support network. Check with those who can assist you, if needed. Keep a contact list in a watertight container in your emergency kit.

Housing and Safety Issues for People with Disabilities

- Planning ahead for accessible transportation for evacuation or getting to a medical clinic. Work with local services, public transportation or paratransit to identify local or private accessible transportation options.
- Informing a support network where your emergency supplies are; you may want to give one member a key to your house or apartment.
- Knowing location and availability of more than one facility for dialysis if dialysis is part of a health maintenance plan or routine or other life-sustaining treatment.
- Preparing to use medical equipment if a power outage occurs.
- Wearing medical alert tags or bracelets.
- Making note of the best way to communicate with you in an emergency if you have a communications disability.
- Planning how to evacuate with assistive devices or how to replace equipment if lost or destroyed. Keep model information and note where the equipment came from such as Medicaid, Medicare or private insurance.

Build a Kit

In addition to having basic survival supplies, an emergency kit should contain items to meet individual needs in various emergencies. Consider items used daily and those needed to add to a kit.

Tips for People Who Are Deaf or Hard of Hearing

Include:

- A weather radio with text display and a flashing alert
- Extra hearing-aid batteries
- A teletypewriter (TTY)
- Pen and paper in case you have to communicate with someone who does not know sign language

Tips for People Who Are Blind or Have Low Vision

Include:

- Mark emergency supplies with Braille labels or large print. Keep a list of your emergency supplies on a portable flash drive, or make an audio file that is kept in a safe place where you can access it.

- Keep a Braille, or deaf-blind communications device in an emergency supply kit.

Tips for People with a Mobility Disability

Include:

- If you use a power wheelchair, have a lightweight manual chair available as a backup. Show others how to operate your wheelchair.
- Know the size and weight of your wheelchair, and if it is collapsible for transportation.
- Keep an extra mobility device such as a cane or walker, if you use one.
- If you use a seat cushion to protect your skin or maintain your balance, and you must evacuate without your wheelchair, take your cushion with you.

The Florida Division of Emergency Management (FDEM), in coordination with each local emergency management agency in the state, developed a registry to allow residents with special needs to register with their local emergency management agency to receive assistance during a disaster. The statewide registry provides first responders with valuable information to prepare for disasters or other emergencies.

For more on the tips above and disaster planning for those with access and functional needs or disabilities, or for children, visit www.ready.gov. The range of needs runs wide and effective planning runs deep. Be ready for hurricanes—and for any other disaster and help those who may need neighborly assistance.

Federal Emergency Management Agency's (FEMA) Mission: Helping people before, during, and after disasters. Disaster recovery assistance is available without regard to race, color, religion, nationality, sex, age, disability, English proficiency or economic status. If you or someone you know has been discriminated against, call FEMA toll-free at 800-621-FEMA (800-621-3362). For toll-free TTY call 800-462-7585.

Chapter 59

Employees with Disabilities

Chapter Contents

Section 59.1—Why Work Matters to People with Disabilities.. 646

Section 59.2—In the Workplace: Reasonable Accommodations for Employees with Disabilities.. 648

Section 59.3—Job Accommodation Situations and Solutions 650

Section 59.4—Accommodating Mental Illness in the Workplace... 654

Section 59.1

Why Work Matters to People with Disabilities

This section includes text excerpted from "Disability Employment," U.S. Office of Personnel Management (OPM), November 14, 2010. Reviewed July 2018.

Job Seekers

The federal government is actively recruiting and hiring persons with disabilities. It offers a variety of exciting jobs, competitive salaries, excellent benefits, and opportunities for career advancement. Hiring people with disabilities into federal jobs is fast and easy. People with disabilities can be appointed to federal jobs noncompetitively through a process called Schedule A. Learn how to be considered for federal jobs under the noncompetitive process. People with disabilities may also apply for jobs through the traditional or competitive process.

Getting a Job

Learn the difference between the competitive and noncompetitive hiring processes, how to use the Schedule A Authority, and how to conduct a job search in the federal government.

Find a Selective Placement Program Coordinator

Most federal agencies have a Selective Placement Program Coordinator (SPPC), a Special Emphasis Program Manager (SEPM) for Employment of Adults with Disabilities, or equivalent, who helps to recruit, hire and accommodate people with disabilities at that agency.

Reasonable Accommodations

The federal government may provide you reasonable accommodation in appropriate cases. Requests are considered on a case-by-case basis.

Federal Agencies

As the Nation's largest employer, the federal government has a special responsibility to lead by example in including people with disabilities in the workforce. The website (www.usajobs.gov) contains important information for federal agencies to use in recruiting, hiring, and retaining individuals with disabilities and targeted disabilities.

Background

On July 26, 2010, President Obama issued Executive Order 13548, which provides that the federal government, as the Nation's largest employer, must become a model for the employment of individuals with disabilities. The order directs Executive departments and agencies (agencies) to improve their efforts to employ federal workers with disabilities and targeted disabilities through increased recruitment, hiring, and retention of these individuals. This is not only the right thing to do, but it is also good for the government, as it increases the potential pool of highly qualified people from which the federal government draws its talent. Importantly, the Executive Order adopts the goal set forth in Executive Order 13163 of hiring 100,000 people with disabilities into the federal government over 5 years, including individuals with targeted disabilities.

The Executive Order also instructed the Director of the Office of Personnel Management (OPM), in consultation with the Secretary of Labor, the Chair of the U.S. Equal Employment Opportunity Commission (EEOC), and the Director of the Office of Management and Budget (OMB), to design model recruitment and hiring strategies for agencies to facilitate their employment of people with disabilities.

In addition to the Executive Order, federal agencies are obligated under the Rehabilitation Act of 1973, as amended to affirmatively employ people with disabilities. The specific requirements of this obligation are spelled out in the Equal Employment Opportunity Commission Management Directive (MD) 715.

Recruiting

The recruiting section contains recruiting information and resources for selective placement program coordinators, human resources professionals, managers and hiring officials.

Hiring

There are two types of hiring processes. In the noncompetitive hiring process, agencies use a special authority (Schedule A) to hire persons with disabilities without requiring them to compete for the job. In the competitive process, applicants compete with each other through a structured process.

Retention

Retention is essential to making the investment of identifying and hiring people pay off. Learn helpful practices for retaining people with disabilities.

Providing Accommodation

In order to meet their accommodation obligations, agencies should think creatively about ways to make their workplace more accessible and create an environment where their employees who have disabilities can thrive. Here are some suggestions that relate specifically to reasonable accommodation issues.

Section 59.2

In the Workplace: Reasonable Accommodations for Employees with Disabilities

This section includes text excerpted from "Disability Employment—Reasonable Accommodations," U.S. Office of Personnel Management (OPM), January 20, 2013. Reviewed July 2018.

Federal agencies are required by law to provide reasonable accommodation to qualified employees with disabilities. The federal government may provide you with a reasonable accommodation based on appropriate requests (unless so doing will result in undue hardship to the agencies).

Reasonable accommodations can apply to the duties of the job and/or where and how job tasks are performed. The accommodation should make it easier for the employee to successfully perform the duties of the position. Examples of reasonable accommodations include providing interpreters, readers, or other personal assistance; modifying job duties; restructuring work sites; providing flexible work schedules or work sites (i.e., telework) and providing accessible technology or other workplace adaptive equipment. Telework provides employees additional flexibility by allowing them to work at a geographically convenient alternative worksite, such as home or a telecenter, on an average of at least one day per week.

Requests are considered on a case-by-case basis. To request reasonable accommodations,

- look at the vacancy announcement
- work directly with person arranging the interviews
- contact the agency Selective Placement Program Coordinator (SPPC)
- contact the hiring manager and engage in an interactive process to clarify what the person needs and identify reasonable accommodations
- make an oral or written request; no special language is needed

Additional Resources Relating to Reasonable Accommodations, Assistive Technology, and Accessibility

- ABLEDATA: Assistive technology (www.abledata.acl.gov)—Provides information on assistive technology and rehabilitation equipment available from domestic and international sources for use within the United States.
- Executive Order 13164 (www.gpo.gov/fdsys/pkg/FR-2000-07-28/pdf/00-19323.pdf)—Requires Federal agencies to establish procedures to facilitate the provision of reasonable accommodations.
- Job Accommodation Network (JAN) (www.askjan.org)—Provides information about job accommodations, the ADA and employment of people with disabilities.
- University of Wisconsin-Madison: Trace Research and Development Center (www.tracecenter.org)—Provides information on technology and disabilities.

- U.S. Equal Employment Opportunity Commission's (EEOC) "Enforcement Guidance: Reasonable Accommodation and Undue Hardship under the ADA" (www.eeoc.gov/policy/docs/accommodation.html)

- U. S. Department of Education (ED): Assistive Technology (www2.ed.gov/policy/gen/guid/assistivetech.html)—Uses assistive technology to assist ED employees and customers with disabilities.

- U.S. Department of Defense (DoD)/Office of Secretary of Defense (OSD): Computer/Electronic Accommodations Program (CAP) (www.cap.mil/)—Provides assistive technology to employees with disabilities at the Department of Defense and other federal agencies.

- U.S. General Services Administration (GSA): Federal Relay Service (www.gsa.gov/technology/technology-purchasing-programs/telecommunications-and-network-services/federal-relay-fedrelay)—Describes the federal relay service.

Section 59.3

Job Accommodation Situations and Solutions

This section includes text excerpted from "Investing in People: Job Accommodation Situations and Solutions," U.S. Department of Labor (DOL), August 2005. Reviewed July 2018.

All employees need the right tools and work environment to effectively perform their jobs. Similarly, individuals with disabilities may need workplace adjustments—or accommodations—to maximize the value they can add to their employer.

An accommodation can be simple, such as putting blocks under a table's legs so that a person who uses a wheelchair can roll up to it. It might involve advanced technology, such as installing a screen reader on a computer so that a person who is blind can manage documents. It may be procedural, such as altering a work schedule or job assignments.

When thinking about accommodations, the focus should not be on the person's disability but rather on essential job tasks and the physical functions necessary to complete them. Consider a receptionist who cannot answer the phone because he or she cannot grasp the receiver. A handle could be attached to the receiver to enable him or her to balance it on the hand. Or, the receptionist could use a headset, eliminating the need for grasping altogether. The reason the person can't grasp the receiver is immaterial. With a simple accommodation, the employee can answer the phone.

Because accommodations are for individuals, they are individual in nature. But by requiring employers and employees to think creatively about how tasks are accomplished, an accommodation can benefit more than a single employee—it can benefit business. Devising accommodations can uncover strategies that help others, regardless of whether they have disabilities. For instance, headsets may help other receptionists better perform their duties and reduce neck strain. Similarly, magnifying glasses at workstations help people with visual disabilities read documents and may reduce eye strain for others. When an accommodation has widespread benefit, it is referred to as universal design. Perhaps the most ubiquitous example of universal design is curb cuts. These were designed to enable people who use wheelchairs to get on and off sidewalks, but they are routinely used by people for other purposes, such as pushing strollers or carts.

Thus, an accommodation is an investment that promises an immediate return—an investment in a qualified worker who happens to have a disability and is, or could become, a valuable asset to a business. Moreover, accommodations usually are not expensive. According to the Job Accommodation Network (JAN), a free and confidential service from the U.S. Department of Labor's (DOL) Office of Disability Employment Policy (ODEP) that provides individualized accommodation solutions, two-thirds of accommodations cost less than $500, with nearly a quarter costing nothing at all. Yet, more than half of the employers surveyed said that each accommodation benefited their organization an average of $5,000.

Below are real-life examples of successful accommodations that were implemented by employers after consulting JAN.

Situation: A woman with a severe developmental disability worked in an envelope manufacturing facility operating a machine that stacked boxes. She needed to stack 20 boxes at a time, but could not keep a mental count past 10.

Solution: The employer installed a punch counter and trained the woman to include punching in her routine—tape, stack, punch; tape, stack, punch. As the woman's productivity soared, the employer realized that keeping count is difficult for many people and decided to install counters at other machines.

Cost: $10

Situation: A person who is blind was a switchboard operator for a large building. As such, she needed to know which telephone lines were on hold, in use or ringing.

Solution: The employer installed a light probe that emitted a noise signaling which console buttons were blinking and which ones were steadily lit. The console was also modified to audibly differentiate incoming calls from internal calls.

Cost of light probe: $45. Console modifications were made at no cost to the employer.

Situation: A student with cerebral palsy obtained a work-study position with the landscape crew of his university. His supervisor was concerned that he could not safely operate a push mower because of his motor impairment. The individual agreed that his gait and balance were a concern in safely operating a push mower.

Solution: His supervisor assigned him other tasks, such as mulching, weeding and picking up litter.

Cost: None.

Situation: A college chemistry teacher who used a wheelchair needed to work in a lab designed to accommodate students at a standing height.

Solution: The college provided the teacher with an elevating wheelchair.

Cost: $7,000.

Situation: A warehouse worker whose job involved maintaining and delivering supplies had difficulty with the job's physical demands due to fatigue from cancer treatment.

Employees with Disabilities

Solution: The individual was provided a three-wheeled scooter at work to reduce the amount of walking required, and the warehouse was rearranged to reduce the amount of climbing and reaching.

Cost: $1,500.

Situation: A secretary had a back impairment and experienced pain when reaching for things such as documents, files, and the phone receiver.

Solution: To reduce the need for reaching, she was provided an adjustable workstation, a telephone headset, a copy holder and a horizontal filing cabinet.

Cost: Adjustable workstation, $900; headset, $50; copy holder, $35; horizontal filing cabinet, $300.

Situation: A clerical worker who stamped paperwork for several hours each day had difficulty pinching and gripping due to carpal tunnel syndrome.

Solution: The stamp handles were wrapped in antivibration wrap and cut tennis balls were placed on the top to eliminate the need for fine motor pinching and gripping to operate them.

Cost: Antivibration wrap, $15; tennis balls, $3.

Situation: A teacher with multiple sclerosis was not able to effectively communicate with students because his speech became soft and slurred when he was fatigued.

Solution: He was provided with a personal speech amplifier so that he would not have to strain to project his voice and was allowed to schedule his classes to allow periodic rest breaks.

Cost: $210.

Situation: A saw operator with a learning disability had trouble measuring to the fraction of an inch.

Solution: His employer gave him a small pocket-sized card that listed the fractions on an enlarged picture of an inch. The employee used the card to determine correct fractions by visually comparing it with the ruler when measuring wood cuts.

Cost: None.

Situation: An office manager who had been treated for stress and depression had difficulty concentrating when trying to complete assignments.

Solution: She was allowed to schedule blocks of time each week during which she could focus on tasks without interruption and modify her hours to allow more time for counseling and exercise. Her supervisor also arranged stress-management training for all employees and informed them about the company's employee assistance program.

Cost: None.

Situation: A meter reader with hearing loss needed to be alerted to the sound of barking dogs and other sudden noises that might present dangers while working in city neighborhoods.

Solution: His employer provided him a device that vibrates in response to sudden noises.

Cost: $300.

Section 59.4

Accommodating Mental Illness in the Workplace

> This section includes text excerpted from "Accommodating Mental Illness in the Workplace," Substance Abuse and Mental Health Services Administration (SAMHSA), June 22, 2016.

Mental illness can present unique challenges to employment. Unlike physical disabilities that can be seen and recognized, employers may not realize that a person with a mental health condition is experiencing an issue and needs a workplace accommodation to remain employed and productive.

Not every person experiencing mental illness will have difficulty at work, but some will. "Hidden" disabilities such as depression, post-traumatic stress disorder (PTSD), schizophrenia, obsessive-compulsive

Employees with Disabilities

disorder (OCD), traumatic brain injury (TBI), and intellectual and learning disabilities (e.g., attention deficit disorder (ADD) and attention deficit hyperactivity disorder (ADHD)) can affect a person's ability to perform his or her job.

Also, unlike a physical disability that may be permanent, shifts in mental health can trigger and recede without warning. When someone experiences a cognitive challenge, it can be difficult to focus, process, think clearly, remember details, organize thoughts and tasks, and stop and start activities.

For these individuals, Title I of the Americans with Disabilities Act Amendments Act of 2008 (ADAAA) requires employers to make "reasonable accommodations" to help people with mental health conditions do their jobs. The ADAAA does not list medical conditions that are disabilities, but rather gives a general definition of disability. A doctor may be required to validate the need for accommodation.

"Employers have to understand that you can't always know what a person is living with," says Beth Loy, Ph.D., who is a principal consultant with the U.S. Department of Labor's (DOL) Job Accommodation Network (JAN). "There may be limitations due to medication, or a flexible schedule might be needed for a person to go to therapy appointments."

The JAN is a comprehensive resource for employees, managers and business owners, behavioral health providers, physicians, and rehabilitation counselors. People who want to understand their rights regarding disabilities and possible accommodations can access information on JAN's website or reach out to them directly. Experts at JAN respond to questions, provide training, and conduct outreach to raise awareness about disability rights and job accommodations.

What Accommodations Look Like

Because every person is unique and may have different needs, there are many options for mental health accommodations. "Sometimes small adjustments to how the work is organized, a workday schedule, or headphones that help block out distracting noise can make a big difference," explains Carlton Speight, a public health advisor with Substance Abuse and Mental Health Services Administration's (SAMHSA) Center for Mental Health Services (CMHS). "Also, for a person who may be easily triggered or anxious, a service dog can help with grounding. It just depends on the individual and what will help in their particular experience."

Melanie Whetzel, MA, CBIS, the lead consultant on the Cognitive Neurological Team at JAN, says, "Most of the mental impairment questions we receive relate to service animals, flexible schedules, flexibility to leave the workstation if someone feels panicked and needs to get grounded, comfortable and private space to take breaks, and insulation to abate noise."

She also notes that sometimes the process of exploring accommodation can lead to a job change. "When an employer learns about the accommodation needed, they may offer the opportunity to shift to a different job that will make the accommodation easier or the job task will be more manageable," she says. "And sometimes the employee will realize that there could be a better environment in which to work, where managing mental health and triggers will be easier."

Most accommodations in the workplace can be established with little or no cost. They just require some flexibility and creativity, and can often be put in place quickly, if the need arises. Such accommodations may include:

- Creating a supportive environment—It is critical for individuals with mental health conditions to work with colleagues and leadership who are positive, open, and welcoming.

- Removing or mitigating workplace stressors—Working in an office or workspace that is quiet, with less traffic, may be more comfortable and manageable. Open floor plans can be very stress-provoking for persons living with mental health conditions.

- Adjusting the approach to supervising—It could be as simple as scheduling recurring one-on-one meetings to see how things are going. Check-ins may also help people manage problems before they become stressful and overwhelming.

- Offering flexible schedules—Flexible arrival and departure times also allow individuals to perform duties when they can be most productive. Flexible or extended breaks may also help them manage stress or attend healthcare appointments.

- Providing opportunity to telework—Telework may remove the exposure to the stressors of commuting and eliminating that time on the road, making it easier to be productive when beginning the workday. Working from home may also provide a substantially more comfortable environment for the employee, which may significantly reduce stress and anxiety.

Employees with Disabilities

With the ADAAA regulations in place, requesting an accommodation is designed to be a simple and straightforward process for employees. Workers may be requested to substantiate a disability with medical information, but it is not required. The U.S. Equal Employment Opportunity Commission (EEOC) also offers some guidance on accommodation procedures.

When an accommodation is needed, it is often helpful for the employer and the employee to discuss the request together to determine what will work and how that can be achieved.

"I think it is critical for employers to understand that workplace accommodations create substantial benefits for the organization," says Matthew Aumen, a program analyst in SAMHSA's Center for Substance Abuse Prevention (CSAP). "Accommodations remove barriers, which allows employees to maximize their potential and performance. That's something every employer wants."

Chapter 60

Scholarships and Financial Aid Available to Students with Disabilities

Chapter Contents

Section 60.1—Finding and Applying for Scholarships 660

Section 60.2—Scholarships for Students with
　　　　　　　Intellectual Disabilities 662

Section 60.1

Finding and Applying for Scholarships

This section includes text excerpted from "Finding and Applying for Scholarships," Federal Student Aid, U.S. Department of Education (ED), July 15, 2012. Reviewed July 2018.

Scholarships are gifts. They don't need to be repaid. There are thousands of them, offered by schools, employers, individuals, private companies, nonprofits, communities, religious groups, and professional and social organizations.

What Kinds of Scholarships Are Available?

Some scholarships for college are merit-based. You earn them by meeting or exceeding certain standards set by the scholarship-giver. Merit scholarships might be awarded based on academic achievement or on a combination of academics and a special talent, trait, or interest. Other scholarships are based on financial need.

Many scholarships are geared toward particular groups of people; for instance, there are scholarships for women or high school seniors. And some are available because of where you or your parent work, or because you come from a certain background (for instance, there are scholarships for military families).

A scholarship might cover the entire cost of your tuition, or it might be a one-time award of a few hundred dollars. Either way, it's worth applying for, because it'll help reduce the cost of your education.

How Do I Find Scholarships?

You can learn about scholarships in several ways, including contacting the financial aid office at the school you plan to attend and checking information in a public library or online. But be careful. Make sure scholarship information and offers you receive are legitimate; and remember that you don't have to pay to find scholarships or other financial aid. Check out our information on how to avoid scams.

Try these free sources of information about scholarships:

- the financial aid office at a college or career school
- a high school or TRIO counselor
- the U.S. Department of Labor's (DOL) FREE scholarship search tool

Scholarships and Financial Aid

- federal agencies
- your state grant agency
- your library's reference section
- foundations, religious or community organizations, local businesses, or civic groups
- organizations (including professional associations) related to your field of interest
- ethnicity-based organizations
- your employer or your parents' employers

When Do I Apply for Scholarships?

That depends on each scholarship's deadline. Some deadlines are as early as a year before college starts, so if you're in high school now, you should be researching and applying for scholarships during the summer between your junior and senior years. But if you've missed that window, don't give up! Look at scholarship information to see which ones you can still apply for now.

How Do I Apply for Scholarships?

Each scholarship has its own requirements. The scholarship's website should give you an idea of who qualifies for the scholarship and how to apply. Make sure you read the application carefully, fill it out completely, and meet the application deadline.

How Do I Get My Scholarship Money?

That depends on the scholarship. The money might go directly to your college, where it will be applied to any tuition, fees, or other amounts you owe, and then any leftover funds given to you. Or it might be sent directly to you in a check. The scholarship provider should tell you what to expect when it informs you that you've been awarded the scholarship. If not, make sure to ask.

How Does a Scholarship Affect My Other Student Aid?

A scholarship will affect your other student aid because all your student aid added together can't be more than your cost of attendance at your college or career school. So, you'll need to let your school know if you've been awarded a scholarship so that the financial aid office can subtract that amount from your cost of attendance (and from certain other aid, such as loans, that you might have been offered). Then, any amount left can be covered by other financial aid for which you're eligible. Questions? Ask your financial aid office.

Section 60.2

Scholarships for Students with Intellectual Disabilities

This section includes text excerpted from "Students with Intellectual Disabilities," Federal Student Aid, U.S. Department of Education (ED), July 15, 2012. Reviewed July 2018.

If you have an intellectual disability, you may receive funding from the Federal Pell Grant, Federal Supplemental Educational Opportunity Grant (FSEOG), and Federal Work-Study (FWS) programs if you

- are enrolled or accepted for enrollment in a comprehensive transition and postsecondary (CTP) program for students with intellectual disabilities at an institution of higher education (a college or career school) that participates in the federal student aid programs;
- are maintaining satisfactory academic progress; and
- meet the basic federal student aid eligibility requirements, except that you are not required to have a high school diploma or General Educational Development (GED) and are not required to be pursuing a degree or certificate.

A CTP program for students with intellectual disabilities means a degree, certificate, or nondegree program that

- is offered by a college or career school and approved by the U.S. Department of Education (ED);

Scholarships and Financial Aid

- is designed to support students with intellectual disabilities who want to continue academic, career, and independent living instruction to prepare for gainful employment;
- offers academic advising and a structured curriculum; and
- requires students with intellectual disabilities to participate, for at least half of the program, in
  - regular enrollment in credit-bearing courses with nondisabled students,
  - auditing or participating (with nondisabled students) in courses for which the student does not receive regular academic credit,
  - enrollment in noncredit-bearing, nondegree courses with nondisabled students, or
  - internships or work-based training with nondisabled individuals.

The following states have schools that offer CTP programs:

- Arkansas
- California
- Delaware
- Florida
- Georgia
- Illinois
- Iowa
- Kansas
- Kentucky
- Louisiana
- Minnesota
- Mississippi
- Missouri
- Nevada
- New Jersey
- New York
- North Carolina
- Ohio
- Oregon
- Pennsylvania
- Rhode Island
- South Carolina
- South Dakota
- Tennessee
- Utah
- Virginia
- Washington

Disabilities Sourcebook, Fourth Edition

Table 60.1. CTP Programs Approved to Participate in the Federal Student Aid Programs*

School	Location
South Arkansas Community College	El Dorado, Arkansas
University of Arkansas	Fayetteville, Arkansas
Pulaski Technical College	North Little Rock, Arkansas
California State University	Fresno, California
University of California	Los Angeles, California
San Diego City College	San Diego, California
San Diego Mesa College	San Diego, California
San Diego Miramar College	San Diego, California
Santa Rosa Junior College	Santa Rosa, California
Taft College	Taft, California
University of Delaware	Newark, Delaware
Florida Atlantic University	Boca Raton, Florida
Florida Panhandle Technical College	Chipley, Florida
Santa Fe College	Gainesville, Florida
Florida Keys Community College	Key West, Florida
Southeastern University	Lakeland, Florida
University of Georgia	Athens, Georgia
Georgia Institute of Technology	Atlanta, Georgia
University of West Georgia	Carrollton, Georgia
Kennesaw State University	Kennesaw, Georgia
Georgia Southern University	Statesboro, Georgia
East Georgia State College	Swainsboro, Georgia
National Louis University	Chicago, Illinois
Elmhurst College	Elmhurst, Illinois
Lewis and Clark Community College	Godfrey, Illinois
Heartland Community College	Normal, Illinois
University of Iowa	Iowa City, Iowa
University of Kansas	Lawrence, Kansas
Northern Kentucky University	Highland Heights, Kentucky
Murray State University	Murray, Kentucky
Bossier Parish Community College	Bossier City, Louisiana
Southeastern Louisiana University	Hammond, Louisiana
Nicholls State University	Thibodaux, Louisiana

Scholarships and Financial Aid

Table 60.1. Continued

School	Location
Central Lakes College	Brainerd, Minnesota
Rochester Community and Technical College	Rochester, Minnesota
Bethel University	Saint Paul, Minnesota
Ridgewater College	Willmar, Minnesota
Mississippi State University	Mississippi State, Mississippi
University of Missouri—Kansas City	Kansas City, Missouri
University of Missouri—Saint Louis	Saint Louis, Missouri
Missouri State University	Springfield, Missouri
University of Central Missouri	Warrensburg, Missouri
University of Nevada, Las Vegas	Las Vegas, Nevada
University of Nevada, Reno	Reno, Nevada
Camden County College	Blackwood, New Jersey
The College of New Jersey	Ewing, New Jersey
Keuka College	Keuka, New York
Orange County Community College	Middletown, New York
New York Institute of Technology	Old Westbury, New York
Monroe Community College	Rochester, New York
Roberts Wesleyan College	Rochester, New York
Syracuse University	Syracuse, New York
Appalachian State	Boone, North Carolina
Western Carolina University	Cullowhee, North Carolina
The University of North Carolina at Greensboro	Greensboro, North Carolina
University of Cincinnati	Cincinnati, Ohio
Ohio State University	Columbus, Ohio
Kent State University	Kent, Ohio
University of Toledo	Toledo, Ohio
Portland State University	Portland, Oregon
Mercyhurst University	Erie, Pennsylvania
Arcadia University	Glenside, Pennsylvania
Millersville University	Millersville, Pennsylvania
Temple University	Philadelphia, Pennsylvania
Lehigh Carbon Community College	Schnecksville, Pennsylvania

Table 60.1. Continued

School	Location
Slippery Rock University	Slippery Rock, Pennsylvania
West Chester University of Pennsylvania	West Chester, Pennsylvania
Rhode Island College	Providence, Rhode Island
College of Charleston	Charleston, South Carolina
Clemson University	Clemson, South Carolina
University of South Carolina	Columbia, South Carolina
Coastal Carolina University	Conway, South Carolina
Winthrop University	Rock Hill, South Carolina
Augustana University	Sioux Falls, South Dakota
Union University	Jackson, Tennessee
University of Tennessee	Knoxville, Tennessee
University of Memphis	Memphis, Tennessee
Lipscomb University	Nashville, Tennessee
Vanderbilt University	Nashville, Tennessee
Utah State University	Logan, Utah
George Mason Universlty	Fairfax, Virginia
Virginia Commonwealth University	Richmond, Virginia
Highline College	Des Moines, Washington
Spokane Community College	Spokane, Washington

*As of June 29, 2018

If you have questions about your eligibility, contact the financial aid office at your college or career school.

Chapter 61

Social Security Disability Benefits

Disability is something most people don't like to think about. But the chances that you'll become disabled probably are greater than you realize. Studies show that a 20-year-old worker has a 1-in-4 chance of becoming disabled before reaching full retirement age. This chapter provides basic information on Social Security disability benefits and isn't meant to answer all questions. For specific information about your situation, you should speak with a Social Security representative. We pay disability benefits through two programs: the Social Security Disability Insurance (SSDI) program and the Supplemental Security Income (SSI) program.

Who Can Get Social Security Disability Benefits?

Social Security pays benefits to people who can't work because they have a medical condition that's expected to last at least one year or result in death. Federal law requires this very strict definition of disability. While some programs give money to people with partial disability or short-term disability, Social Security does not.

Certain family members of disabled workers can also receive money from Social Security.

This chapter includes text excerpted from "Disability Benefits," U.S. Social Security Administration (SSA), January 2017.

In general, to get disability benefits, you must meet two different earnings tests:

1. A recent work test, based on your age at the time you became disabled; and
2. A duration of work test to show that you worked long enough under Social Security.

Certain blind workers have to meet only the duration of work test.

The following table shows the rules for how much work you need for the recent work test, based on your age when your disability began. We base the rules in this table on the calendar quarter in which you turned or will turn a certain age.

The calendar quarters are:

First quarter: January 1 through March 31
Second quarter: April 1 through June 30
Third quarter: July 1 through September 30
Fourth quarter: October 1 through December 31

Table 61.1. Rules for Recent Work Test

If You Become Disabled...	Then You Generally Need:
In or before the quarter you turn age 24	1.5 years of work during the three-year period ending with the quarter your disability began.
In the quarter after you turn age 24 but before the quarter you turn age 31	Work during half the time for the period beginning with the quarter after you turned 21 and ending with the quarter you became disabled. Example: If you become disabled in the quarter you turned age 27, then you would need three years of work out of the six-year period ending with the quarter you became disabled.
In the quarter you turn age 31 or later	Work during five years out of the 10-year period ending with the quarter your disability began.

The following table shows examples of how much work you need to meet the duration of work test if you become disabled at various selected ages. For the duration of work test, your work doesn't have to fall within a certain period of time.

NOTE: This table doesn't cover all situations.

Social Security Disability Benefits

Table 61.2. Duration of Work Test

If You Become Disabled...	Then You Generally Need:
Before age 28	1.5 years of work
Age 30	2 years
Age 34	3 years
Age 38	4 years
Age 42	5 years
Age 44	5.5 years
Age 46	6 years
Age 48	6.5 years
Age 50	7 years
Age 52	7.5 years
Age 54	8 years
Age 56	8.5 years
Age 58	9 years
Age 60	9.5 years

How Do I Apply for Disability Benefits?

There are two ways that you can apply for disability benefits. You can

1. apply online at www.socialsecurity.gov; or
2. call the toll-free number, 800-772-1213, to make an appointment to file a disability claim at your local Social Security office or to set up an appointment for someone to take your claim over the telephone. The disability claims interview lasts about one hour. If you're deaf or hard of hearing, you may call the toll-free TTY number, 800-325-0778, between 7 a.m. and 7 p.m. on business days. If you schedule an appointment, we'll send you a Disability Starter Kit to help you get ready for your disability claims interview. The Disability Starter Kit also is available online at www.socialsecurity.gov/disability.

You have the right to representation by an attorney or other qualified person of your choice when you do business with Social Security.

When Should I Apply and What Information Do I Need?

You should apply for disability benefits as soon as you become disabled. Processing an application for disability benefits can take 3–5 months. To apply for disability benefits, you'll need to complete an application for Social Security benefits. You can apply online at www.socialsecurity.gov. The Social Security office may be able to process your application faster if you help them by getting any other information we need.

The information we need includes

- your Social Security Number (SSN);
- your birth or baptismal certificate;
- names, addresses, and phone numbers of the doctors, caseworkers, hospitals, and clinics that took care of you, and dates of your visits;
- names and dosage of all the medicine you take;
- medical records from your doctors, therapists, hospitals, clinics, and caseworkers that you already have in your possession;
- laboratory and test results;
- a summary of where you worked and the kind of work you did; and
- a copy of your most recent W-2 Form (Wage and Tax Statement) or, if you're self-employed, your federal tax returns for the past year.

In addition to the basic application for disability benefits, you'll also need to fill out other forms. One form collects information about your medical condition and how it affects your ability to work. Other forms give doctors, hospitals, and other healthcare professionals who have treated you, permission to send them information about your medical condition.

Don't delay applying for benefits if you can't get all of this information together quickly. We'll help you get it.

Can My Family Get Benefits?

Certain members of your family may qualify for benefits based on your work. They include:

- Your spouse, if he or she is age 62 or older;
- Your spouse at any age, if he or she is caring for a child of yours who is younger than age 16 or disabled;

Social Security Disability Benefits

- Your unmarried child, including an adopted child, or, in some cases, a stepchild or grandchild. The child must be younger than age 18 (or younger than 19 if still in high school);
- Your unmarried child, age 18 or older, if he or she has a disability that started before age 22. The child's disability must also meet the definition of disability for adults.

NOTE: In some situations, a divorced spouse may qualify for benefits based on your earnings, if he or she was married to you for at least 10 years, is not currently married, and is at least age 62. The money paid to a divorced spouse doesn't reduce your benefit or any benefits due to your current spouse or children.

When Do I Get Medicare?

You'll get Medicare coverage automatically after you've received disability benefits for two years.

What Do I Need to Know about Working?

After you start receiving Social Security disability benefits, you may want to try working again. Social Security has special rules called work incentives that allow you to test your ability to work and still receive monthly Social Security disability benefits. You can also get help with education, rehabilitation, and training you may need to work. If you do take a job or become self-employed, tell about it right away. We need to know when you start or stop work and if there are any changes in your job duties, hours of work, or rate of pay. You can call them toll-free at 800-772-1213. If you're deaf or hard of hearing, you may call the TTY number, 800-325-0778.

Chapter 62

Amputation and Social Security Benefits

Statistics from the Amputee Coalition (www.amputee-coalition.org) confirm that 300–500 amputations occur daily in the United States and that almost two million Americans have lost a limb to amputation. Researchers project that this American amputee population will increase to 3.6 million by the year 2050. The leading cause of limb loss in the United States is vascular disease, which includes diabetes and peripheral arterial disease (often caused by fatty deposits in artery walls), at 54 percent. Trauma, including vehicular accidents, is the second leading cause of limb loss, at 45 percent. A little less than two percent of Americans also lose limbs to cancer.

Amputees usually experience phantom limb pain, as the brain continues to receive pain signals from the nerve endings at the amputation site. Phantom limb pain causes amputees to feel pain and a continuing sense of loss, and often results in depression. While phantom limb pain usually decreases over time, it is important to check with a healthcare provider if the pain continues more than six months after an amputation.

Losing a limb can affect your ability to work and live life as usual. While prosthetics—typically a cane or crutch or artificial limb—are

---

"Amputation and Social Security Benefits," © 2018 Omnigraphics. Reviewed July 2018.

considered effective solutions for ambulation, phantom limb pain can reduce an amputee's ability to effectively use prosthetics. Barriers to prosthetic use can arise due to stump complications or other related problems that prevent the effective use of prosthetics. In these cases, American amputees may apply for Social Security disability benefits.

How to Qualify for Social Security Benefits If You Have an Amputation?

Despite technological advancements, many amputees are unable to use prosthetics for one reason or the other. If you fall into the category of a physically challenged person and are working or living independently, you may qualify for Social Security disability benefits based on your physical condition. You can refer to the Social Security Blue Book (www.disability-benefits-help.org/glossary/social-security-blue-book) to find out if you meet the requirements of the Social Security disability benefits.

How the Social Security Blue Book Can Help Your Case

The Social Security Blue Book lists the various disabling impairments that qualify someone for Social Security disability benefits, including the following conditions:

- A medical disorder that prevents you from performing your daily routine or chores, i.e., bathing, dressing, cooking, or eating
- An amputation that may last more than a year or result in death
- Disability in one hand or above the ankle, inability to walk normally
- Stump complications at the amputation site
- If both hands are amputated or in the case of a hip disarticulation.

A specific list of amputations is also included under the Social Security Listing 1.05 of the Social Security Blue Book.

Social Security Disability Benefits Approval Process

It is important to provide accurate and detailed information in order to increase your chances of being approved for Social Security

Amputation and Social Security Benefits

disability benefits. The detailed record of your medical history and your test results will be examined by the concerned authority. Make sure to make available to investigators copies of the following documentation:

- **X-rays.** The severity of your amputation will likely be determined by X-rays.

- **Blood tests and tissue samples.** Complications resulting from an amputation will likely be determined through an examination of the results of blood tests and tissue samples, which are the easiest way to confirm the presence of disease.

- **Computed tomography (CT) and magnetic resonance imaging (MRI) scans.** Complications that are not easily detected through the above methods can be efficiently determined by documentation from CT and MRI scans, particularly in cases of walking disabilities.

- **General medical history.** Investigators will need to review the compilation of notes made by your healthcare provider(s), which describe in detail your medical condition and other related disorders that resulted in the amputation of your limb.

- **Physical therapy notes.** Physical therapy aftercare reports can provide investigators with valuable insight into your ability to take care of yourself.

If you need further clarification on whether your amputee complication(s) will qualify you for Social Security disability benefits, ask your healthcare provider to complete a Residual Functional Capacity (RFC) test.

Residual Functional Capacity Test

A Residual Functional Capacity (RFC) test will determine whether you are capable of performing normal activities. For lower limb amputations, Social Security will monitor your ability to walk on certain surfaces that require body balancing and perform other activities such as crawling, kneeling, climbing, and bending at the knees. Fine motor movements, typing, writing, and your ability to hold and lift objects will be assessed in the case of upper-limb amputations. In some cases, specific details about your amputation may be relevant. For instance, an amputation of a dominant hand may prevent you from working, even if your amputation does not fit all specific criteria mentioned. This detail may still result in your being declared eligible for disability benefits.

Other Disability Benefits

You may qualify for welfare other disability benefits, including:

- **Medical vocational allowance.** If, under the examination of the U.S. Social Security Administration (SSA), you are deemed unfit to perform certain assigned activities, then you will be considered eligible for disability benefits through the Medical Vocational Allowance exception.

Resources

The following resources may provide more helpful advice and information:

- **Social security disability attorney.** Applying for disability benefits can be time- consuming. If you are worried about the application process, you can hire a Social Security disability attorney.
- **Disability benefits finder.** You can call a Welfare benefits advisor in case of any queries on 800-644-0815 or 01245-216669 or send an e-mail to benefits@limbless-association.org

References

1. "How to Qualify for Social Security Benefits with an Amputation," Disability Benefits Help, n.d.
2. "Limbless Association—Supporting Lives Beyond Limb Loss," The Limbless Association, n.d.
3. "Applying for Disability After an Amputation," Disability Secrets, 2018.
4. "Amputation and Social Security Disability Benefits," n.d.
5. "Social Security Blue Book," n.d.

Chapter 63

Tax Benefits and Credits for People with Disabilities

Taxpayers with disabilities and parents of children with disabilities may qualify for a number of Internal Revenue Service (IRS) tax credits and benefits. Listed below are six tax credits and other benefits which are available if you or someone else listed on your federal tax return is disabled.

Income

All income is taxable unless it is specifically excluded by law. The following discussions highlight some taxable and nontaxable income items.

Dependent Care Benefits

Dependent care benefits include the following.

- Amounts your employer paid directly to you or your care provider for the care of your qualifying person(s) while you worked.

- The fair market value of care in a daycare facility provided or sponsored by your employer.

This chapter includes text excerpted from "Tax Highlights for Persons with Disabilities," Internal Revenue Service (IRS), 2017.

- Pretax contributions you made under a dependent care flexible spending arrangement.

Exclusion or deduction. If your employer provides dependent care benefits under a qualified plan, you may be able to exclude these benefits from your income. Your employer can tell you whether your benefit plan qualifies.

If you are self-employed and receive benefits from a qualified dependent care benefit plan, you are treated as both employer and employee. Therefore, you would not get an exclusion from wages. Instead, you would get a deduction on one of the following Form 1040 schedules: Schedule C, line 14; Schedule E, line 19 or 28; or Schedule F, line 15. To claim the deduction, you must use Form 2441.

The amount you can exclude or deduct is limited to the smallest of the following.

1. The total amount of dependent care benefits you received during the year.
2. The total amount of qualified expenses you incurred during the year.
3. Your earned income.
4. Your spouse's earned income.
5. $5,000 ($2,500 if married filing separately).

Statement for employee. Your employer must give you a statement, showing the total amount of dependent care benefits provided to you during the year under a qualified plan.

Qualifying person(s). A qualifying person is any of the following.

- A qualifying child who is under age 13 whom you can claim as a dependent. If the child turned 13 during the year, the child is a qualifying person for the part of the year he or she was under age 13.

- Your disabled spouse who is not physically or mentally able to care for themselves.

- Any disabled person who was not physically or mentally able to care for themselves whom you can claim as a dependent (or could claim as a dependent except that the person had gross income of $4,050 or more or filed a joint return).

- Any disabled person who was not physically or mentally able to care for themselves whom you could claim as a dependent except

Tax Benefits and Credits for People with Disabilities

that you (or your spouse if filing jointly) could be claimed as a dependent on another taxpayer's 2017 return.

Social Security and Railroad Retirement Benefits

My Social Security account. Social security beneficiaries may quickly and easily obtain the following information from the Social Security Administration's (SSA) website with my Social Security account.

- Keep track of your earnings and verify them every year.
- Get an estimate of your future benefits if you are still working.
- Get a letter with proof
- of your benefits if you currently receive them.
- Change your address. Start or change your direct deposit.
- Get a replacement Medicare card.
- Get a replacement SSA-1099 or SSA-1042S for the tax season.

If you received social security or equivalent Tier 1 railroad retirement (RRTA) benefits during the year, part of the amount you received may be taxable.

Are any of your benefits taxable? If the only income you received during the year was your social security or equivalent Tier 1 RRTA benefits, your benefits generally are not taxable.

If you received income during the year in addition to social security or equivalent Tier 1 RRTA benefits, part of your benefits may be taxable if all of your other income, including tax-exempt interest, plus half of your benefits are more than:

- $25,000 if you are single, head of household, or qualifying widow(er);
- $25,000 if you are married filing separately and lived apart from your spouse for all of 2017;
- $32,000 if you are married filing jointly; or
- $-0- if you are married filing separately and lived with your spouse at any time during 2017.

Supplemental security income (SSI) payments. Social security benefits do not include SSI payments, which are not taxable. Do not include these payments in your income.

Disability Pensions

If you retired on disability, you must include in income any disability pension you receive under a plan that is paid for by your employer. Minimum retirement age generally is the age at which you can first receive a pension or annuity if you are not disabled. Beginning on the day after you reach minimum retirement age, payments you receive are taxable as a pension or annuity.

Retirement and profit-sharing plans. If you receive payments from a retirement or profit-sharing plan that does not provide for disability retirement, do not treat the payments as a disability pension. The payments must be reported as a pension or annuity.

Accrued leave payment. If you retire on disability, any lump-sum payment you receive for accrued annual leave is a salary payment. The payment is not a disability payment. Include it in your income in the tax year you receive it.

Military and Government Disability Pensions

Generally, you must report disability pensions as income, but do not include certain military and government disability pensions.

U.S. Department of Veterans Affairs (VA) disability benefits. Do not include disability benefits you receive from the VA in your gross income.

Do not include in your income any veterans' benefits paid under any law, regulation, or administrative practice administered by the VA. These include

- education, training, and subsistence allowances;
- disability compensation and pension payments for disabilities paid to veterans or their families;
- grants for homes designed for wheelchair living;
- grants for motor vehicles for veterans who lost their sight or the use of their limbs;
- veterans' insurance proceeds and dividends paid to veterans or their beneficiaries, including the proceeds of a veteran's endowment policy paid before death;
- interest on insurance dividends left on deposit with the VA;
- benefits under a dependent care assistance program;
- the death gratuity paid to a survivor of a member of the Armed Forces who died after September 10, 2001; or

Tax Benefits and Credits for People with Disabilities

- payments made under the VA's compensated work therapy program.

Other Payments

You may receive other payments that are related to your disability. The following payments are not taxable.

- Benefit payments from a public welfare fund, such as payments due to blindness.
- Workers' compensation for an occupational sickness or injury if paid under a workers' compensation act or similar law.
- Compensatory (but not punitive) damages for physical injury or physical sickness.
- Disability benefits under a "no-fault" car insurance policy for loss of income or earning capacity as a result of injuries.
- Compensation for permanent loss or loss of use of a part or function of your body, or for your permanent disfigurement

Long-Term Care Insurance

Long-term care insurance contracts generally are treated as accident and health insurance contracts. Amounts you receive from them (other than policyholder dividends or premium refunds) generally are excludable from income as amounts received for personal injury or sickness.

Accelerated Death Benefits

You can exclude from income accelerated death benefits you receive on the life of an insured individual if certain requirements are met. Accelerated death benefits are amounts received under a life insurance contract before the death of the insured. These benefits also include amounts received on the sale or assignment of the contract to a viatical settlement provider. This exclusion applies only if the insured was a terminally ill individual or a chronically ill individual.

Itemized Deductions

Medical Expenses

When figuring your deduction for medical expenses, you can generally include medical and dental expenses you pay for yourself, your spouse, and your dependents.

Medical expenses are the cost of diagnosis, cure, mitigation, treatment, or prevention of disease, and the costs for treatments affecting any part or function of the body. They include the costs of equipment, supplies, diagnostic devices, and transportation for needed medical care and payments for medical insurance.

You can deduct only the amount of your medical and dental expenses that is more than 7.5 percent of your adjusted gross income shown on Form 1040, line 38.

The following list highlights some of the medical expenses you can include in figuring your medical expense deduction.

- Artificial limbs, contact lenses, eyeglasses, and hearing aids.

- The part of the cost of Braille books and magazines that is more than the price of regular printed editions.

- Cost and repair of special telephone equipment for hearing-impaired persons.

- Cost of a wheelchair used mainly for the relief of sickness or disability, and not just to provide transportation to and from work. The cost of operating and maintaining the wheelchair is also a medical expense.

- Cost and care of a guide dog or other animal aiding a person with a physical disability.

- Costs for a school that furnishes special education if a principal reason for using the school is its resources for relieving a mental or physical disability. This includes the cost of teaching Braille and lip reading and the cost of remedial language training to correct a condition caused by a birth defect.

- Premiums for qualified long-term care insurance, up to certain amounts.

- Improvements to a home that do not increase its value if the main purpose is medical care. An example is constructing entrance or exit ramps.

Impairment-Related Work Expenses

If you are disabled, you can take a business deduction for expenses that are necessary for you to be able to work. If you take a business deduction for these impairment-related work expenses, they are not subject to the 7.5 percent limit that applies to medical expenses.

Tax Benefits and Credits for People with Disabilities

You are disabled if you have:

- a physical or mental disability (for example, blindness or deafness) that functionally limits your being employed; or
- a physical or mental impairment (including, but not limited to, a sight or hearing impairment) that substantially limits one or more of your major life activities, such as performing manual tasks, walking, speaking, breathing, learning, or working.

Impairment-related expenses defined. Impairment-related expenses are those ordinary and necessary business expenses that are:

- necessary for you to do your work satisfactorily;
- for goods and services not required or used, other than incidentally, in your personal activities; and
- not specifically covered under other income tax laws.

Tax Credits

This discussion highlights three tax credits which may lower your tax due and may be refundable.

Child and Dependent Care Credit

If you pay someone to care for your dependent under age 13 or your spouse or dependent who is not able to care for themselves, you may be able to get a credit of up to 35 percent of your expenses. To qualify, you must pay these expenses so you can work or look for work. The care must be provided for

1. your qualifying child who is your dependent and who was under age 13 when the care was provided;
2. your spouse who was not physically or mentally able to care for themselves and lived with you for more than half the year; or
3. A person who was not physically or mentally able to care for themselves, lived with you for more than half the year, and either
   a. was your dependent, or
   b. would have been your dependent except that
      i. he or she received gross income of $4,050 or more,
      ii. he or she filed a joint return, or
      iii. you, or your spouse if filing jointly, could be claimed as a dependent on someone else's 2017 return.

Credit for the Elderly or the Disabled

You may be able to claim this credit if you are a U.S. citizen or a resident alien and either of the following applies.

- You were 65 or older at the end of 2017.
- You were under 65 at the end of 2017, and retired on permanent or total disability.

Earned Income Credit

This credit is for people who work and have a qualifying child or who meet other qualifications. You can get the credit if your adjusted gross income for 2017 is less than

- $15,010 ($20,600 for married filing jointly) if you do not have a qualifying child,
- $39,617 ($45,207 for married filing jointly) if you have one qualifying child,
- $45,007 ($50,597 for married filing jointly) if you have two qualifying children, or
- $48,340 ($53,930 for married filing jointly) if you have three or more qualifying children.

Qualifying child. To be a qualifying child, your child must be younger than you (or your spouse if married filing jointly) and under age 19 or a full-time student under age 24 at the end of 2017, or permanently and totally disabled at any time during 2017, regardless of age.

Earned income. If you are retired on disability, benefits you receive under your employer's disability retirement plan are considered earned income until you reach minimum retirement age. However, payments you received from a disability insurance policy that you paid the premiums for are not earned income.

Household Employers

If you pay someone to work in your home, such as a babysitter or housekeeper, you may be a household employer who has to pay employment taxes. A person you hire through an agency is not your employee if the agency controls what work is done and how it is done. This control could include setting the fee, requiring regular reports, and providing rules of conduct and appearance. In this case, you do not

Tax Benefits and Credits for People with Disabilities

have to pay employment taxes on the amount you pay. But if you control what work is done and how it is done, the worker is your employee. If you possess the right to discharge a worker, that worker is generally considered to be your employee. If a worker is your employee, it does not matter that you hired the worker through an agency or from a list provided by an agency.

Business Tax Incentives

If you own or operate a business, or you are looking for work, you should be aware of the following tax incentives for businesses to help persons with disabilities.

- **Deduction for costs of removing barriers to the disabled and the elderly**—This is a deduction a business can take for making a facility or public transportation vehicle more accessible to and usable by persons who are disabled or elderly.
- **Disabled access credit**—This is a nonrefundable tax credit for an eligible small business that pays or incurs expenses to provide access to persons with disabilities. The expenses must be to enable the eligible small business to comply with the Americans With Disabilities Act of 1990.
- **Work opportunity credit**—This credit provides businesses with an incentive to hire individuals from targeted groups that have a particularly high unemployment rate or other special employment needs. One targeted group consists of vocational rehabilitation referrals. These are individuals who have a physical or mental disability that results in a substantial handicap to employment.

ABLE Account

Compare ABLE programs on the websites of state governments to see which program is best suited for you.

- An ABLE account is a tax-favored savings account that can accept contributions for an eligible blind or disabled individual who is the designated beneficiary and owner of the account. The account is used to provide for qualified disability expenses.
- An ABLE account is disregarded for purposes of determining eligibility for benefits under Supplemental Security Income (SSI)

and certain other means-tested federal programs. For further information, go to SSA.gov.

- A designated beneficiary is limited to only one ABLE account at a time.

- Earnings in an ABLE account aren't taxed unless a distribution exceeds a designated beneficiary's qualified disability expenses. A designated beneficiary doesn't include distributions for qualified disability expenses in their income. Qualified disability expenses include any expenses incurred at a time when the designated beneficiary is an eligible individual. The expenses must relate to blindness or disability, including expenses for maintaining or improving health, independence, or quality of life.

- Contributions to an ABLE account are not tax deductible and must be in cash or cash equivalents. Anyone, including the designated beneficiary, can contribute to an ABLE account. An ABLE account is subject to an annual contribution limit and a cumulative balance limit.

- Upon your death, as a designated beneficiary, any state may file a claim (either with the person with signature authority over your ABLE account or the executor of your estate) for the amount of the total medical assistance paid to you under the state's Medicaid plan after you (or a person with authority to open an ABLE account on your behalf) established an ABLE account. The amount paid in satisfaction of such a claim is not a taxable distribution from your ABLE account. Further, this amount is paid to the state only after all your qualified disability expenses have been paid from your ABLE account and the amount paid to satisfy the state's claim is reduced by the amount of all premiums you paid to a Medicaid Buy-In program under that state's Medicaid plan.

Chapter 64

Guardianship for People with Disability

According to the National Guardianship Association (NGA), Inc.: "Guardianship, also referred to as conservatorship, is a legal process, utilized when a person can no longer make or communicate safe or sound decisions about his/her person and/or property or has become susceptible to fraud or undue influence. Because establishing a guardianship may remove considerable rights from an individual, it should only be considered after alternatives to guardianship have proven ineffective or are unavailable."

Before we can begin evaluating guardianship or making recommendations for how to improve it, it is important to define and ensure a basic understanding of what guardianship is. Although the previous quote may seem like a reasonable definition from which to start, it contains value judgments—which are worthy of consideration—such as what constitutes "safe or sound decisions"; who gets to make that determination for an individual; and how an individual's safety should balance against his or her right to experience the dignity of risk.

This chapter includes text excerpted from "Beyond Guardianship: Toward Alternatives That Promote Greater Self-Determination," National Council on Disability (NCD), March 22, 2018.

Despite the oft-cited proposition that all people have certain inalienable rights, once someone is declared incapacitated and is appointed a guardian, many of their rights are taken away and their ability to make decisions in a wide variety of areas given to another person.

Therefore, although guardianship is largely a creature of state law, it nonetheless raises

fundamental questions concerning federal civil rights and constitutional due process. An adult

usually becomes subject to guardianship when the court finds that:

- the individual is incapable of making all or some of their own financial or personal decisions, and
- it is necessary to appoint a guardian to make those choices on their behalf.

Rights at Risk in Guardianships

Guardianships are typically separated into two categories, guardianships of the person and guardianships of the property (also sometimes referred to as conservatorship). When the guardian controls decisions regarding both person and property, the guardianship is called plenary. However, there are really three types of rights that are at issue in guardianships:

- Rights that can be taken from an individual but not given to another individual
- Rights that can be taken from a person and exercised by someone else on their behalf
- Rights that a guardian needs a court order to exercise on the individual's behalf

A person who is determined incapacitated generally can have the following rights removed, but these rights cannot be exercised by someone else. These include the right to:

- marry,
- vote,
- drive, or
- seek or retain employment.

Still, other rights can be removed and transferred to a guardian who can exercise these rights on behalf of the individual, such as the right to:

- contract,
- sue and defend lawsuits,
- apply for government benefits,
- manage money or property,
- decide where to live,
- consent to medical treatment, and
- decide with whom to associate or be friends.

In many states, there are also some rights that a guardian can exercise on behalf of the individual subject to guardianship, but only after the court has issued a specific order allowing the action, such as:

- committing the person to a facility or institution,
- consenting to biomedical or behavioral experiments,
- filing for divorce,
- consenting to the termination of parental rights, and
- consenting to sterilization or abortion.

A Word on Language

When a petition is filed with the court that alleges that the individual is incapacitated, the individual is often referred to as the alleged incapacitated person, or AIP for short. If the court finds that the person does lack capacity and appoints a guardian to manage some or all of their affairs, the individual is often referred to as the ward. In this report, we will use the term AIP, but because the term ward is viewed by many as stigmatizing and inappropriate, whenever possible, consistent with National Council on Disability's (NCD) longstanding commitment of avoiding stigmatizing language, we will refer to individuals for whom a guardian has been appointed as an individual subject to guardianship. This is also consistent with the Uniform Guardianship, Conservatorship and Other Protective Arrangements Act (UGCOPAA), which is the latest iteration of the uniform guardianship statute that has been approved by the Uniform Law Commission (ULC). However, it should be noted that the term ward will appear when it appears in a direct quote.

Process of Obtaining Guardianship

Guardianship petitions may be filed in a wide variety of situations: by parents when a child with an intellectual disability turns 18; by a son or daughter when a parent begins to show signs of dementia severe enough that there is concern for their safety; for a person with a severe disability due to sudden trauma; or when there is concern that a bad actor is exercising undue influence over a person with a disability in order to exploit the individual in some way. There are also times when guardianship is filed for less altruistic reasons, such as to gain access to the person's assets or public benefits or to exploit the individual. Whether the guardianship is over person, property, or both, or whether it is limited or plenary may be determined, at least in part, by the circumstances that give rise to the perceived need for guardianship. Due to our federalist system of government, guardianship is a creature of state, rather than federal law, and all 50 states and the District of Columbia have revised their statutes regarding guardianship numerous times. However, it is not clear that in statute or in practice guardianship law has been able to keep pace with the nation's changing understanding of disability, autonomy, and due process. Although the process is different in every state, making it difficult to provide a singular description of the guardianship process, there are certain generalities that are helpful to discuss before examination of whether or not guardianship is working for people with disabilities, their families, and communities. The following steps are generalities that may or may not align with the laws in a given state, so it is important for interested individuals to consult their state's laws for more accurate, detailed information.

General Steps to Guardianship

1. Filing the petitions
2. Notice that a guardianship petition has been filed
3. Appointment of an attorney to represent the alleged incapacitated person
4. Capacity evaluation
5. Hearing

6. Letters of guardianship
7. Guardianship plan and initial reports

Guardianship as a Disability Policy Issue

Guardianship is often overlooked, and, when it becomes part of the national policy conversation, it is often viewed as an issue impacting older Americans and not thought of as an important disability issue. However, guardianship must be understood as a disability policy issue worthy of examination, reflection, and reform. After all, an adult becomes subject to guardianship only if a court has determined that he or she cannot manage property or meet essential requirements for health and safety. Additionally, at least 11 states have laws that provide for alternate, and generally less rigorous, procedures when the individual who allegedly needs a guardian is an adult with intellectual and/or developmental disabilities. Regardless of whether one is a young adult with a congenital developmental disability subject to guardianship because the court determined he or she lacked the ability to make decisions him or herself, or whether one is in his or her 80s and the court believes that Alzheimer disease (AD) has advanced to the point where he or she can no longer make decisions for his or herself, the reason to impose guardianship is disability in both instances. In order to fully understand guardianship as a disability issue, we need to come from a common understanding of it within the context of the evolution of disability policy, particularly as it relates to issues of liberty, autonomy, and self-determination. This chapter provides an overview of the evolution of disability policy from the eugenics movement to the Convention on the Rights of Persons with Disabilities (CRPD) in order to provide context for our discussion of guardianship and to help ground our recommendations in National Council on Disability (NCD) long tradition of advancing policies that promote the dignity, self-determination, and maximum independence of all people with disabilities regardless of their age.

Chapter 65

Advance Directives and Advance Care Planning for People with Physical and Intellectual Disabilities

What Is Advance Care Planning?

Whether someone is facing an acute illness, a long-term chronic illness or a terminal illness, advance care planning can help alleviate unnecessary suffering, improve quality of life and provide better understanding of the decision-making challenges facing the individual and his or her caregivers. An advance care plan can be used at any stage of life and should be updated as circumstances change.

"Advance care plans can be developed at any time, whether you are sick or well," said Joanne Lynn, MD, a geriatrician and hospice

---

This chapter contains text excerpted from the following sources: Text under the heading "What Is Advance Care Planning?" is excerpted from "Advance Care Planning: Ensuring Your Wishes Are Known and Honored If You Are Unable to Speak for Yourself," Centers for Disease Control and Prevention (CDC), 2012. Reviewed July 2018; Text beginning with the heading "Advance Care Planning for People with Physical Disability" is excerpted from "Advance Directives and Advance Care Planning for People with Intellectual and Physical Disabilities," Office of the Assistant Secretary for Planning and Evaluation (ASPE), October 2007. Reviewed July 2018.

physician who heads the Center on Elder Care and Advanced Illness for the Altarum Institute. "Once you are sick and disabled with a progressive illness that will last until death, you really need a comprehensive care plan that considers your social supports, your preferences, and your likely course. Advance care planning is an essential part of such a plan."

Advance care planning is about planning for the "what ifs" that may occur across the entire lifespan, such as being maimed in a motorcycle crash at a young age, and not just for older adults approaching the end of their lives, Dr. Lynn said. Those plans can be revised and updated throughout the person's life as health status and living circumstances change, she added.

Comprehensive advance care planning involves discussion of disease trajectory and multiple conditions, said Kathleen Tschantz Unroe, MD, Assistant Research Professor of Medicine, Indiana University (IU) Center for Aging Research. "The patient and family need to understand the patient's medical and functional condition and what that might look like over the next months or a year and try to anticipate events that can happen. The goal is to try to more proactively make decisions and understand patient values rather than just reacting to changes in condition," Dr. Unroe said.

Advance care planning is especially important if a patient does not want aggressive treatment, Dr. Unroe said. "The default in our medical system is aggressive care unless there is a clearly written, in-your-face, advance directive." Otherwise, "a 95-year old who is unresponsive is getting coded (a reference to a "code blue" patient status in a hospital when a team quickly moves to revive a patient without a heartbeat). If they can get a pulse back and get them into the intensive care unit (ICU), that is what is going to happen. That is the American culture and the American medical culture," she said.

Advance Care Planning for People with Physical Disability

There are limited research studies, position papers, or materials on advance care planning about or for people with physical disabilities. In view of the extensive professional literature and discourse during the past two decades on end-of-life and palliative care, as well as on advance care planning and healthcare decisionmaking, it may appear that the attitudes and concerns of people with physical disabilities have largely been absent from the radar screen of many in the health professions, even in the literature concerning end-of-life care (EoLC) and diverse cultural communities.

While the literature on advance care planning for people with physical disabilities is limited, disability theorists, advocates, and organizations have addressed related issues of autonomy in end-of-life decisionmaking, mainly in the context of assisted suicide and surrogate decision making. First, because of a history of unequal access to health services, advocates forcefully responded to societal discussions during the 1990s and beyond on whether or not assisted suicide should be legalized and on the impact of assisted suicide on the disability community. At the same time, the legal battle over the care for Terri Schiavo encouraged discussion regarding the parameters of surrogate decisionmaking on behalf of people with disabilities who lack decisional capacity. Debate regarding these matters provides some insight on the disability community concerns that may influence advance care planning, such as the degree to which healthcare professionals (and society) value and respect the lives and perspectives of people with disabilities, as well as overall access to healthcare.

Policy and professional discussion on the legalization of assisted suicide resulted in numerous articles, primarily (although not entirely) opposed to physician aid-in-dying (PAD). Gill examines the literature on the attitudes of healthcare professionals on disability, and relates these attitudes to perspectives on assisted suicide and a lack of regard for people with disabilities. In contrast to studies finding that most people with disabilities are "glad to be alive" and rate "the quality of their lives as good to excellent," regardless of "degree of physical impairment," she describes research on the attitudes of healthcare professionals towards people with disabilities that:

- Are as negative as public attitudes, and sometimes more so. More specifically, health professionals significantly underestimate the quality of life of persons with disabilities compared with the actual assessments made by persons with disabilities themselves... Such pessimistic professional views of life with disability are implicitly conveyed to patients and their families while they are in the midst of decisionmaking about new disabilities... [and] are related to professionals' views about whether or not to offer life-sustaining treatment options to persons with disabilities.

These attitudes are found to carry over into medical care, through recurrent "distressing encounters" with physicians and other health professionals described as lacking "aware[ness] of disability issues, patronizing, and disrespectful. A common concern... is, 'Doctors need to realize that I have a real life and it's a valuable life.

Furthermore, research suggests that physician attitudes regarding disability may predict whether or not life-sustaining care is provided. In a study of ventilator use with patients with severe neuromuscular diseases, such as Duchenne muscular dystrophy (DMD) and amyotrophic lateral sclerosis (ALS) (Lou Gehrig's Disease), Bach reported that clinic directors who "most underestimated the ventilator users' life satisfaction... were least likely to encourage ventilator use... Physicians' assessment of patients' quality of life and about the relative desirability of certain types of existence determine the likelihood of individuals receiving therapeutic interventions like mechanical ventilation." Bach concludes that the "patient's attitude towards the use of ventilatory aids seems to reflect his/her physician's attitude and the nature of the treatment options being presented rather than his/her own informed rational decision.

Gill's findings are reflected in the numerous websites of disability advocacy organizations, such as Not Dead Yet and the Disability Rights Education and Defense Fund (DREDF), that post documents opposing assisted suicide. DREDF lists 12 nationally prominent disability organizations that have stated their opposition to the legalization of assisted suicide. The National Council on Disability (NCD) issued a position paper summarizing the perspective of disability groups:

- Current evidence indicates clearly that the interests of the few people who would benefit from legalizing physician-assisted suicide are heavily outweighed by the probability that any law, procedures, and standards that can be imposed to regulate physician-assisted suicide will be misapplied to unnecessarily end the lives of people with disabilities and entail an intolerable degree of intervention by legal and medical officials in such decisions.

Hwang attempts to deflect attention from national disability advocacy organizations to emphasize the views of individuals with physical disabilities regarding assisted suicide. Using websites frequented by members of the physical disability community, she conducted polls on attitudes towards assisted suicide, self-perceptions of "vulnerability," and acceptability of assisted suicide for oneself. While the sample was self-selected and relatively small, Hwang uses her "exploratory" findings to show that "people with disabilities hold a wide variety of views with regard to [physician-assisted suicide] that cannot be easily summed up by any one position... Ultimately, the question, 'What kind of life is worth living?' is a highly individual one" that transcends the positions of disability advocacy groups.

The concerns of disability advocates regarding the withholding or withdrawal of life-sustaining interventions are a logical extension of the assisted suicide debate. For example, Werth argues that many more people with disabilities will die through decisions to forgo treatments than through assisted suicide." Therefore, the fears behind the assisted suicide debate—societal (and more specifically, physician) devaluation of the lives of people with disabilities, the costs of care, and resource allocation—are equally applicable to decisions to withhold or withdraw treatments and to futility decisions.

In response to the legal debates and public attention surrounding the care of Terri Schiavo, leading disability advocacy organizations issued policy statements on life-sustaining care. A Statement of Common Principles on Life-Sustaining Care and Treatment of People with Disabilities, coordinated by the Center on Human Policy (CHP) at Syracuse University (SU), declared that the "rights to life-sustaining care and treatment and to self-determination and autonomy" are "fundamental rights." The Statement notes that "disability has been used as a justification for depriving people of their fundamental rights." Therefore,

- Absent clear and convincing evidence of the desires of people with disabilities to decline life-sustaining care or treatment, such care and treatment should not be withheld or withdrawn unless death is genuinely imminent and the care or treatment is objectively futile and would only prolong the dying process.

Although not explicitly stated, it can be presumed that advance directives are "clear and convincing evidence of desires—informed decisions [that] must be respected" and could be encouraged.

Likewise, United Cerebral Palsy (UCP), The Arc, and the American Association of People with Disabilities (AAPD) declared that "the provision of medical treatment must always be nondiscriminatory and never denied, delayed or withheld due to the existence of a disability." The organizations argued: "[t]he courts, the political system, and the general public must not allow policy to develop that will de-value any individual, no matter what the extent of that individual's disability or incapacity." This statement also notes that individuals may document their preferences through advance directives.

It is encouraging that these organizational statements explicitly support the use of advance directives by individuals with disabilities.

A handful of other disability organizations have taken a more direct approach in support of advance care planning. For example, the Multiple Sclerosis Association of America (MSAA) published a detailed article for consumers explaining the importance advance directives as part of life-planning, with instructions and resources for their completion. Clinical practice guidelines developed for the Paralyzed Veterans of America supported discussion of advance directives with patients following spinal cord injury to determine the validity of documents completed prior to traumatic injury. These guidelines might also encourage discussion of advance directives among patients with capacity following spinal cord injury when there are no earlier documents. Finally, Allen and her colleagues described a unique effort to use American Sign Language (ASL) to survey Deaf seniors on end-of-life concerns and present educational information on healthcare directives and end-of-life care (EoLC).

Advance Care Planning for People with Intellectual Disability

There is a legal presumption that all persons have the capacity to make their own healthcare decisions unless they are declared incompetent through a legal process. However, adults with intellectual disability "have historically been excluded from various spheres of decision-making about their lives, on the presumption that they are incapable of making informed decisions." Healthcare providers, administrators, and families commonly assumed a protective stance toward people with intellectual disabilities, even when decision-specific capacity may have existed. Recent trends have encouraged providers, researchers, and advocates to question this paternalistic approach for three reasons.

First, medical advances are increasing the longevity of people with intellectual disabilities. For example, life expectancy for people with Down syndrome (DS) has doubled during the 1980s and 1990s. As individuals with intellectual disabilities (ID) age, they and their caregivers face issues of aging and chronic illness as never before. Second, this time period has witnessed significant cultural changes regarding medical decisionmaking, EoLC, and advance care planning, as bioethical principles evolved from a paternalistic to an autonomy-based approach. Third, although the needs of people with intellectual disabilities were largely absent from early discussions to promote advance care planning and palliative approaches to care, providers and advocates have sought to bolster the autonomy of community members and brought their concerns to the table.

Advance Directives and Advance Care Planning

Decisional Capacity

Advance care planning by and for people with intellectual disabilities is complicated by the wide range of cognitive abilities and limitations and by differing needs for assistance among members of this community. For example, those with mild impairments may reside independently in the community, with a support system that includes social services staff, personal care attendants, family and community advocates, and vocational and residential services. These individuals "usually need information on their service options when confronting life-threatening illness, especially on hospice and palliative care services, assistance in documenting their preferences through advance directives, and support in navigating their way through complex healthcare systems." Others with more serious cognitive impairments have intermittent decisionmaking abilities or have never had the capacity to make healthcare decisions. Their "health-related decisions are made by surrogates, primarily parents, and other (public or private) guardians, who act in their child's or ward's best interest and need information and support in selecting the most appropriate healthcare."

People with intellectual disabilities should not be presumed to lack capacity for making healthcare decisions. A panel convened by the Midwest Bioethics Center (now known as the Center for Practical Bioethics) in 1996 issued guidelines to facilitate individual decisionmaking and more accurate professional assessments of decisional capacity. The guidelines provide recommendations to assess "whether patients meet a minimum level of understanding." Limitations in intellect and communication abilities are bolstered by supporting areas of individual strength and by offering assistance.

Clinical practice and legal standards have moved away from global determinations of capacity to more finely-tuned task-specific determinations of capacity. The capacity to make healthcare decisions has been defined as the ability to understand the information about a proposed care plan, appreciate the consequences of a decision, and reach and communicate an informed decision. Unlike competency, which is an "all or nothing" judicial determination, capacity is specific to the decision at hand. This more flexible methodology to assessing abilities creates a multi-tiered approach to decisionmaking. For example, individuals who lack abilities to express preferences or goals of care in a living will may be able to appoint a healthcare proxy. Similarly, those unable to make decisions about life-sustaining interventions may have the capacity to make less complex decisions, such as on low-risk medications, diet, or recreation. Beltran summarizes the challenge in accurately assessing decisionmaking capacity: "There is a need to balance protection from harm with the patient's right to self-determination. This balancing requires skilled listening, the proper level of advocacy from caregivers, and pragmatic models of shared decisionmaking."

A 2003 study assessed healthcare capacity among adults with mild, moderate, and no mental retardation to make "low-risk" medical treatment decisions. The study used standardized treatment vignettes to measure the capacity of adults to reason about treatment-related information. Cea and Fisher found that "most adults with mild (86%) and no (95%) mental retardation and almost half of adults with moderate mental retardation (45%) were able to make and justify treatment choices and fully or partially understand treatment information." These findings are used to support claims that many adults with mild mental retardation, and some adults with moderate retardation, "do indeed have the ability to provide adequate consent to standard low-risk health-related treatments." Moreover, capacity to consent "could be enhanced with supportive decisionmaking or educational techniques in preparation for treatments or procedures requiring their consent."

Policy Statements

Key intellectual disability organizations support efforts to promote rights to autonomy and self-determination. The American Association on Intellectual and Developmental Disabilities (AAIDD, formerly called the American Association on Mental Retardation (AAMR)) issued a Position Statement on Caring at the End of Life in 2005. The statement advocates:

- Discovering and honoring the treatment wishes of persons with intellectual disabilities through: observing and interacting with individuals over time to understand what is important to them; encouraging expressions of preferences regarding EoLC "before situations requiring decisionmaking occur"; and for capable individuals, documenting preferences through "living wills, personal vision statements, healthcare proxy instructions, and other indicators of one's wishes."

- "Withdrawing or withholding care may be appropriate in some situations," but not "because the person has a disability."

- "The presumption should always be in favor of treatment ... [but] may be overcome in ... clearly specified situations."

Advance Directives and Advance Care Planning

- These situations, where "continued life may not be in the person's best interest include:
  1. where "life-sustaining treatment is clearly ineffective and would only prolong the process of dying with no prospect of reversing it;
  2. the person is in an irreversible coma or permanent vegetative state; or
  3. the treatment itself would impose excessive pain and suffering."
- Hospice care and adequate pain relief should be available.
- "Permissible treatment options at the end-of-life are the same for persons with intellectual or developmental disabilities as for everyone else."

Similarly, a 2002 joint policy statement of The Arc of the United States (formerly called the Association for Retarded Citizens) and AAIDD, supported the availability, use, and "honoring" of advance directives for individuals with mental retardation "whenever informed consent is assured." In addition, the "decisions involving the refusal of medical treatments, or nutrition and hydration when such refusal will result in the death of the individual,... should be confined to those situations in which the person's condition is terminal, death is imminent, and any continuation or provision of treatment, nutrition and/or hydration would only serve to prolong dying." Unlike the 2005 policy statement of AAIDD, the earlier position does not list irreversible coma or permanent vegetative state as permissible reasons to forgo life-sustaining care.

Resources and Innovations

Materials and innovative approaches to advance care planning have been developed to promote better end-of-life decisions. Last Passages, a three-year public-private partnership funded by the U.S. Administration on Developmental Disabilities (ADD) and the Project on Death in America, provides an array of electronic materials to assist service providers, policymakers, and consumers. Resources include descriptive information, a manual about EoLC for people with developmental disabilities, sample documents for advance care planning, links to national organizations and projects, and an extensive bibliography.

NYSARC, Inc., in collaboration with Last Passages, developed a monograph and resource manual (primarily focused on New York State) to inform consumers, family members, and providers about hospice and EoLC, advance care planning, and bereavement. The Center for Practical Bioethics's Healthcare Treatment Decision-Making Guidelines for Adults with Developmental Disabilities provides model standards for policymakers considering revisions to public or institutional policies on healthcare decisionmaking or advance directives.

Kingsbury advocates "person-centered planning" to help consumers, family members, and providers identify and document preferences for EoLC. "Person-centered planning is not an event; it is a process" for advance care planning discussions with people with intellectual limitations. "Person-centered planning can help people identify their wishes, such as who they would like to have present, how they would like to be made comfortable, what kinds of treatment they wish to have or not have, [and] what religious or spiritual support they want." Planning tools involve deliberate, ongoing communication that emphasizes listening, learning, understanding, and acting on what is important to support people who are aging and dying, and their caregivers.

Is it possible to augment the decisionmaking capacity of individuals with cognitive limitations? Friedman supports the concept of "assisted capacity," through which "individuals who may be unable to make advance directives decisions completely independently, but who could participate in decisionmaking with the proper degree of assistance and support from others." Such support could come from families, friends, clergy, advocates, and formal healthcare and service providers. While this strategy may facilitate advance care planning, there is the potential for helper influence to act as a coercive force in decisions that are made.

To help elicit the preferences of people with disabilities with varying degrees of decisional capacity, the Center for Practical Bioethics and Missouri's largest public guardianship office (the Jackson County Public Administrator), established Project BRIDGE. Through an intensive process of "inviting" public wards to express their healthcare preferences, "listening" carefully when the invitation is accepted, and "reporting" relayed stories and preferences to public guardians, project staff offered individuals who were often overlooked the opportunity to express and document their preferences to inform the guardians who made decisions for them. Although this approach requires significant staff time, it offers a creative way of understanding the wishes and values of people with limited capacity, as well as those with limited communication abilities.

Advance Directives and Advance Care Planning

For individuals with limited and no decisionmaking capacity, Beltran and Martyn propose a standard of "best respect" (similar to a best interests decisionmaking standard), with healthcare choices made by a team rather than an individual surrogate. The proponents of "best respect" suggest convening those individuals most familiar with the patient's life and values for an informed dialogue that results in a consensus on treatment decisions. This "shared decisionmaking" (distinguished from the shared decisionmaking between patient and provider) should occur within the context of the patient's "community of care," which may be a developmental center, community group home, or independent living arrangement. An ethics committee could convene key parties, such as family members, friends, or other supportive caregivers, as well as the interdisciplinary team caring for the individual. In the best respect model, physicians offer "objective" information about the patient, including diagnosis, prognosis, available treatment choices, and quality of life issues. Subsequently, the:

- search for subjective information… [examines] what the person has communicated in the past about her own life and its pleasures, pains, dignities, indignities, and dependencies. Second, the group should consider what this information tells them about the subjective value of life to this patient. Finally, given what has been shared, [a determination would be made on] which decision best respects the individual expression of this unique individual.

With more effective public outreach promoting the benefits of advance care planning, some parents and guardians of individuals with limited or no capacity desire to complete advance directives on their children's or ward's behalf. These parents and guardians, motivated by the desire to plan for their own death or incapacity, are surprised to learn that they cannot do so—that directives may be completed only by individuals with capacity to do so. In response, Beltran encourages parents/guardians to "write a letter expressing their values and concerns" for placement into their child's/ward's permanent planning records. While noting that such "values" letters have no legal force, they can "provide guidance to healthcare providers seeking to provide treatments that are in keeping with the patient's values." Beltran recommends the development of a "legal mechanism for parents to document values to assure their wishes are carried out after they die." Physician orders—such as Physician Orders for Life-Sustaining Treatment (POLST), where patient and surrogate preferences are incorporated into doctors' orders, or out-of-hospital Do-Not-Resuscitate

Orders—may provide models for such long-range planning if the hurdles regarding decisionmaking can be surmounted.

Professional education has been recognized as a critical component to improving EoLC and promoting better-informed advance care plans and medical decisions. Frequently, healthcare professionals (physicians, nurses, social workers, clergy, and others), including hospice and palliative care staff, lack training on the special needs of people with intellectual disabilities and on methods to assess their decisional capacity. Furthermore, staff of public agencies and private organizations serving people with disabilities should be trained in the special needs of people with intellectual disabilities for advance care planning, options for hospice and palliative care to manage life-threatening illnesses, and special concerns in providing and consenting to care. For example, in a rare study of end-of-life decisions in a developmental center (where residents commonly have more severe intellectual disabilities than those living in community placements), Lohiya and her colleagues found that among 38 residents who had died during a 2½ year period, only ten residents (26%) had an end-of-life decision made on their behalf. Of 850 residents, only two had ever completed an advance directive. The researchers suggest that more frequent discussions of patients' best interests before death might lead to better EoLC.

Part Seven

Additional Help and Information

Chapter 66

Glossary of Terms Related to Disabilities

access: An individual's ability to obtain appropriate healthcare services. Barriers to access can be financial, geographic, organizational, and sociological. Efforts to improve access often focus on providing/improving health coverage.

activities of daily living (ADLs): Basic personal activities that include bathing, eating, dressing, mobility, transferring from bed to chair, and using the toilet. ADLs are used to measure how dependent a person may be on requiring assistance in performing any or all of these activities.

acute care: Recovery is the primary goal of acute care. Physician, nurse, or other skilled professional services are typically required and usually provided in a doctor's office or hospital. Acute care is usually short term.

adult day care: A daytime community-based program for functionally impaired adults that provides a variety of health, social, and related support services in a protective setting.

adult day services: Services provided during the day at a community-based center. Programs address the individual needs of functionally

---

This glossary contains terms excerpted from documents produced by several sources deemed reliable.

or cognitively impaired adults. These structured but not 24-hour care. Many adult day service programs include health-related services.

Alzheimer disease (AD): Progressive, degenerative form of dementia that causes severe intellectual deterioration. First symptoms are impaired memory, followed by impaired thought and speech, and finally complete helplessness.

arthritis: Disease involving inflammation of a joint or joints in the body.

assistive devices: Any device that helps a person with hearing loss or a voice, speech, or language disorder to communicate. These terms often refer to devices that help a person to hear and understand what is being said more clearly or to express thoughts more easily. With the development of digital and wireless technologies, more and more devices are becoming available to help people with hearing, voice, speech, and language disorders communicate more meaningfully and participate more fully in their daily lives.

attention deficit disorder (ADD): A severe difficulty in focusing and maintaining attention. Often leads to learning and behavior problems at home, school, and work. Also called attention deficit hyperactivity disorder (ADHD).

audiologists: Assess and treat persons with hearing and related disorders. May fit hearing aids and provide auditory training. May perform research related to hearing problems.

biopsy: A procedure in which tissue or other material is removed from the body and studied for signs of disease.

birth defects: Conditions that cause structural changes in one or more parts of the body; are present at birth; and have an adverse effect on health, development, or functional ability.

bronchiectasis: A condition in which damage to the airways causes them to widen and become flabby and scarred. The airways are tubes that carry air in and out of your lungs.

cardiomyopathy: Diseases of the heart muscle. In cardiomyopathy, the heart muscle becomes enlarged, thick, or rigid. In rare cases, the muscle tissue in the heart is replaced with scar tissue.

caregiver: Person who provides support and assistance with various activities to a family member, friend, or neighbor. May provide emotional or financial support, as well as hands-on help with different tasks. Caregiving may also be done from long distance.

Glossary of Terms Related to Disabilities

carrier: An individual who doesn't have a disease but has one normal gene and one gene for a genetic disorder and is, therefore, capable of passing this disease to her or his children.

cartilage: A tough, elastic tissue that covers the ends of the bones where they meet to form joints. In rheumatoid arthritis, the inflamed synovium invades and destroys joint cartilage.

cerebral: Relating to the two hemispheres of the human brain.

chromosomes: Genetic structures that contains DNA.

cochlear implant: A cochlear implant is an implanted electronic hearing device, designed to produce useful hearing sensations to a person with severe to profound nerve deafness by electrically stimulating nerves inside the inner ear.

cognitive impairment: Deterioration or loss of intellectual capacity that requires continual supervision to protect the person or others, as measured by clinical evidence and standardized tests that reliably measure impairment in the area of (1) short- or long-term memory, (2) orientation as to person, place and time, or (3) deductive or abstract reasoning. Such loss in intellectual capacity can result from Alzheimer disease or similar forms of dementia.

cyclothymic disorder (cyclothymia): A mild form of bipolar disorder. People with cyclothymia have episodes of hypomania as well as mild depression for at least two years. However, the symptoms do not meet the diagnostic requirements for any other type of bipolar disorder.

developmental delay: Behind schedule in reaching the milestones of early childhood development.

developmental disability: A disability that originates before age 18, can be expected to continue indefinitely, and constitutes a substantial handicap to the disabled's ability to function normally.

diabetic retinopathy: Diabetic retinopathy is a complication of diabetes and a leading cause of blindness. It occurs when diabetes damages the tiny blood vessels inside the retina in the back of the eye.

disability: The limitation of normal physical, mental, social activity of an individual. There are varying types (functional, occupational, learning), degrees (partial, total), and durations (temporary, permanent) of disability.

dyscalculia: A severe difficulty in understanding and using symbols or functions needed for success in mathematics.

dysgraphia: A severe difficulty in producing handwriting that is legible and written at an age-appropriate speed.

dyslexia: A severe difficulty in understanding or using one or more areas of language, including listening, speaking, reading, writing, and spelling.

dyspraxia: A severe difficulty in performing drawing, writing, buttoning, and other tasks requiring fine motor skill, or in sequencing the necessary movements.

electromyography (EMG): A recording and study of the electrical properties of skeletal muscle.

epilepsy: A person is diagnosed with epilepsy when they have had two or more seizures. Also called a seizure disorder.

glaucoma: Glaucoma is a group of diseases that can damage the eye's optic nerve and result in vision loss and blindness.

group home: Residence that offers housing and personal care services for 3 to 16 residents. Services (such as meals, supervision, and transportation) are usually provided by the owner or manager. May be single family home. Also called adult care home or board and care home.

hearing difficulty: Deaf or having serious difficulty hearing (DEAR).

home healthcare: A range of health-related services such as assistance with medications, wound care, intravenous (IV) therapy, and help with basic needs such as bathing, dressing, mobility, etc., which are delivered at a person's home.

impairment: Any loss or abnormality of psychological, physiological, or anatomical function.

independent living difficulty: Because of a physical, mental, or emotional problem, having difficulty doing errands alone such as visiting a doctor's office or shopping (DOUT).

individualized education program (IEP): A written statement of the educational program designed to meet a child's individual needs. Every child who receives special education services must have an IEP.

inflammation: A reaction of body tissues to injury or disease, typically marked by five signs swelling, redness, heat, pain, and loss of function.

Glossary of Terms Related to Disabilities

learned helplessness: A tendency to be a passive learner who depends on others for decisions and guidance. In individuals with learning disabilities, continued struggle and failure can heighten this lack of self-confidence.

learning disability: A disorder in one or more of the basic psychological processes involved in understanding or in using language, spoken or written, which may manifest itself in an imperfect ability to listen, think, speak, read, write, spell, or to do mathematical calculation. The term includes such conditions as perceptual handicaps, brain injury, and minimal brain dysfunction.

long-term care: A range of medical and/or social services designed to help people who have disabilities or chronic care needs. Services may be short- or long-term and may be provided in a person's home, in the community, or in residential facilities (e.g., nursing homes or assisted living facilities).

lupus: A chronic inflammatory condition in which the immune system attacks the skin, joints, heart, lungs, blood, kidneys, and brain. Also called systemic lupus erythematosus.

mental disability: Conditions that include a learning disability, an intellectual disability, developmental disability, Alzheimer disease, senility, or dementia, or some other mental or emotional condition that seriously interferes with daily activity.

neuron: The structural and functional unit of the nervous system, also known as a nerve cell. A neuron consists of a cell body and its processes an axon and one or more dendrites.

newborn screening: Identifies conditions that can affect a child's long-term health or survival. Early detection, diagnosis, and intervention can prevent death or disability and enable children to reach their full potential.

nursing home: Facility licensed by the state to offer residents personal care as well as skilled nursing care on a 24-hour-a-day basis. Provides nursing care, personal care, room and board, supervision, medication, therapies, and rehabilitation. Rooms are often shared, and communal dining is common.

occupational therapy: Help patients improve their independence with activities of daily living through rehabilitation, exercises, and the use of assistive devices. May be covered in part by Medicare.

osteoporosis: A disease in which the bones become weak and are more likely to break. People with osteoporosis most often break bones in the hip, spine, and wrist.

otolaryngologist: An otolaryngologist is a physician specializing in ear, nose, and throat disorders who can determine the cause of hearing loss as well as possible treatment options.

palsy: Paralysis or the lack of control over voluntary movement.

pancreatitis: Inflammation of the pancreas. Pancreatitis can be acute or chronic. Either form is serious and can lead to complications. In severe cases, bleeding, infection, and permanent tissue damage may occur.

paralysis: The inability to control movement of a part of the body.

paraplegia: A condition involving paralysis of the legs.

physical therapy: Designed to restore/improve movement and strength in people whose mobility has been impaired by injury and disease. May include exercise, massage, water therapy, and assistive devices. May be covered in part by Medicare.

pneumothorax: Air or gas can build up in the pleural space. When this happens, it's called a pneumothorax. A lung disease or acute lung injury can cause a pneumothorax. Some lung procedures also can cause a pneumothorax. Examples include lung surgery, drainage of fluid with a needle, bronchoscopy, and mechanical ventilation.

presbycusis: One form of hearing loss, presbycusis, comes on gradually as a person ages. Presbycusis can occur because of changes in the inner ear, auditory nerve, middle ear, or outer ear.

rehabilitation: The combined and coordinated use of medical, social, educational, and vocational measures for training or retaining individuals disabled by disease or injury to the highest possible level of functional ability. Several different types of rehabilitation are distinguished—vocational, social, psychological, medical, and educational.

related condition (RC): Severe chronic disability attributed to a condition other than mental illness but found to be closely related to intellectual disability. The condition results in impairment of general intellectual functioning or adaptive behavior similar to that of people with intellectual disabilities and requires treatment or services similar to those required for people with intellectual disabilities. It

Glossary of Terms Related to Disabilities

is manifested before the person reaches age 22, is likely to continue indefinitely, and results in substantial functional limitations in at least three of the following areas of major life activity: self-care, understanding and use of language, learning, mobility, self-direction, and capacity for independent living.

respite care: Trained professionals or volunteers come into the home to provide short-term care (from a few hours to a few days) for a disabled person to allow caregivers some time away from their caregiving role.

rubella (also known as German measles): A viral infection that can damage the nervous system of an unborn baby if a mother contracts the disease during pregnancy.

sacral: Part of the spine in the hip area.

sensory disability: Conditions that include blindness, deafness, or a severe vision or hearing impairment.

social security disability insurance (SSDI): A program that pays monthly benefits to citizens who are insured by workers' contributions to the Social Security Trust Fund, who become disabled before reaching retirement age and are unable to work.

special education: A type of education some children with disabilities receive. Special education may include specially designed instruction in classrooms, at home, or in private or public institutions, and may be accompanied by related services such as speech therapy, occupational and physical therapy, psychological counseling, and medical diagnostic services necessary to the child's education.

speech-language pathologists (SLPs) (sometimes called speech therapists): Assess, diagnose, treat, and help to prevent communication and swallowing disorders in patients. Speech, language, and swallowing disorders result from a variety of causes, such as a stroke, brain injury, hearing loss, developmental delay, a cleft palate, cerebral palsy, or emotional problems.

support groups: Group of people who share a common bond (e.g., caregivers) who come together on a regular basis to share problems and experiences. May be sponsored by social service agencies, senior centers, religious organizations, as well as organizations such as the Alzheimer's Association.

traumatic brain injury (TBI): A form of acquired brain injury, occurs when a sudden trauma causes damage to the brain. TBI can result when the head suddenly and violently hits an object or when an object pierces the skull and enters brain tissue.

vision difficulty: Blind or having serious difficulty seeing, even when wearing glasses (DEYE).

X-ray: A procedure in which low-level radiation is passed through the body to produce a picture called a radiograph. X-rays of joints affected by rheumatoid arthritis are used to determine the degree of joint destruction.

yoga: Yoga is a mind and body practice with origins in ancient Indian philosophy. The various styles of yoga typically combine physical postures, breathing techniques, and meditation or relaxation.

Chapter 67

Directory of Organizations That Help People with Disabilities

Government Agencies That Provide Information about Disabilities

Administration on Aging (AOA)
U.S. Department of Health and Human Services (HHS)
One Massachusetts Ave. N.W.
Washington, DC 20001
Website: www.acl.gov
E-mail: aoainfo@aoa.gov

Agency for Healthcare Research and Quality (AHRQ)
Office of Communications and Knowledge Transfer
5600 Fishers Ln.
Rockville, MD 20857
Phone: 301-427-1364
Website: www.ahrq.gov

Resources in this chapter were compiled from several sources deemed reliable; all contact information was verified and updated in July 2018.

Centers for Disease Control and Prevention (CDC)
1600 Clifton Rd.
Atlanta, GA 30329-4027
Toll-Free: 800-CDC-INFO
(800-232-4636)
Phone: 404-639-3311
Toll-Free TTY: 888-232-6348
Website: www.cdc.gov
E-mail: cdcinfo@cdc.gov

Disability.gov
U.S. Department of Labor (DOL)
200 Constitution Ave. N.W.
Washington, DC 20210
Toll-Free: 866-ODEP-DOL
(866-633-7365)
Website: www.dol.gov/odep/topics/disability.htm

Eldercare Locator
Administration on Aging (AOA)
Toll-Free: 800-677-1116
Website: eldercare.acl.gov/Public/Index.aspx
E-mail: eldercarelocator@n4a.org

Eunice Kennedy Shriver *National Institute of Child Health and Human Development (NICHD)*
P.O. Box 3006
Rockville, MD 20847
Toll-Free: 800-370-2943
Toll-Free TTY: 888-320-6942
Toll-Free Fax: 866-760-5947
Website: www.nichd.nih.gov
E-mail: NICHDInformationResourceCenter@mail.nih.gov

Federal Communications Commission (FCC)
445 12th St. S.W.
Washington, DC 20554
Toll-Free: 888-225-5322
Toll-Free TTY: 888-835-5322
Toll-Free Fax: 866-418-0232
Website: www.fcc.gov
E-mail: fccinfo@fcc.gov

Healthfinder®
U.S. Department of Health and Human Services (HHS)
1101 Wootton Pkwy
Rockville, MD 20852
Website: healthfinder.gov
E-mail: healthfinder@hhs.gov

Library of Congress (LOC)
101 Independence Ave. S.E.
Washington, DC 20540
Phone: 202-707-5000
Website: www.loc.gov

National Cancer Institute (NCI)
9609 Medical Center Dr.
BG 9609 MSC 9760
Bethesda, MD 20892-9760
Toll-Free: 800-4-CANCER
(800-422-6237)
Website: www.cancer.gov
E-mail: cancergovstaff@mail.nih.gov

Directory of Organizations That Help People with Disabilities

National Center for Health Statistics (NCHS)
3311 Toledo Rd.
Rm. 2217
Hyattsville, MD 20782-2064
Toll-Free: 800-CDC-INFO
(800-232-4636)
Phone: 301-458-4901
Website: www.cdc.gov/nchs/nhis/contact.htm
E-mail: nhis@cdc.gov

National Council on Disability (NCD)
1331 F St. N.W.
Ste. 850
Washington, DC 20004
Phone: 202-272-2004
TTY: 202-272-2074
Fax: 202-272-2022
Website: www.ncd.gov
E-mail: ncd@ncd.gov

National Heart, Lung, and Blood Institute (NHLBI)
NHLBI Health Information Center
31 Center Dr.
Bldg. 31
Bethesda, MD 20892
Website: www.nhlbi.nih.gov
E-mail: nhlbiinfo@nhlbi.nih.gov

National Institute of Arthritis and Musculoskeletal and Skin Diseases (NIAMS)
Information Clearinghouse,
National Institutes of Health (NIH)
1 AMS Cir.
Bethesda, MD 20892-3675
Toll-Free: 877-22-NIAMS
(877-226-4267)
Phone: 301-495-4484
TTY: 301-565-2966
Fax: 301-718-6366
Website: www.niams.nih.gov
E-mail: NIAMSInfo@mail.nih.gov

National Institute of Dental and Craniofacial Research (NIDCR)
National Institutes of Health (NIH)
31 Center Dr. MSC 2190
Bldg. 31, Rm. 5B55
Bethesda, MD 20892-2190
Toll-Free: 866-232-4528
Phone: 301-496-4261
Website: www.nidcr.nih.gov
E-mail: nidcrinfo@mail.nih.gov

National Institute of Mental Health (NIMH)
Science Writing, Press, and Dissemination Branch
6001 Executive Blvd.
Bethesda, MD 20892-9663
Toll-Free: 866-615-6464
Phone: 301-443-4513
Toll-Free TTY: 866-415-8051
Fax: 301-443-4279
Website: www.nimh.nih.gov
E-mail: nimhinfo@nih.gov

*National Institute of
Neurological Disorders and
Stroke (NINDS)*
NIH Neurological Institute
P.O. Box 5801
Bethesda, MD 20824
Toll-Free: 800-352-9424
Phone: 301-496-5751
Fax: 301-402-2186
Website: www.ninds.nih.gov
E-mail: braininfo@ninds.nih.gov

*National Institute on Aging
(NIA)*
Bldg. 31, Rm. 5C27
31 Center Dr. MSC 2292
Bethesda, MD 20892
Toll-Free: 800-222-2225
Phone: 301-496-1752
Toll-Free TTY: 800-222-4225
Website: www.nia.nih.gov

*National Institute on
Deafness and Other
Communication Disorders
(NIDCD)*
National Institutes of Health
(NIH)
31 Center Dr.
MSC 2320
Bethesda, MD 20892-2320
Toll-Free: 800-241-1044
Phone: 301-827-8183
Toll-Free TTY: 800-241-1055
Fax: 301-402-0018
Website: www.nidcd.nih.gov
E-mail: nidcdinfo@nidcd.nih.gov

*National Institute
on Disability and
Rehabilitation Research
(NIDRR)*
Administration for Community
Living (ACL), U.S. Department
of Health and Human Services
(HHS)
330 C St. S.W.
Rm. 1304
Washington, DC 20201
Phone: 202-795-7398
Fax: 202-205-0392
Website: www.acl.gov/about-acl/about-national-institute-disability-independent-living-and-rehabilitation-research
E-mail: nidilrr-mailbox@acl.hhs.gov

*National Technical
Information Service (NTIS)*
5301 Shawnee Rd.
Alexandria, VA 22312
Toll-Free: 800-363-2068
Phone: 703-605-6060
Fax: 703-605-6880
Website: www.ntis.gov
E-mail: helpdesk@ntis.gov

*National Women's Health
Information Center (NWHIC)*
Office on Women's Health
(OWH)
200 Independence Ave. S.W.
Washington, DC 20201
Toll-Free: 800-994-9662
Phone: 202-690-7650
Fax: 202-205-2631
Website: www.womenshealth.gov

Directory of Organizations That Help People with Disabilities

Office of Disability Employment Policy (ODEP)
U.S. Department of Labor (DOL)
200 Constitution Ave. N.W.
Washington, DC 20210
Toll-Free: 866-4-USA-DOL (866-487-2365)
Toll-Free TTY: 877-889-5627
Website: www.dol.gov/odep

U.S. Department of Education (ED)
400 Maryland Ave. S.W.
Washington, DC 20202
Toll-Free: 800-USA-LEARN (800-872-5327)
Phone: 202-401-2000
Toll-Free TTY: 800-437-0833
Website: www2.ed.gov

U.S. Department of Justice (DOJ)
950 Pennsylvania Ave. N.W.
Washington, DC 20530-0001
Toll-Free: 800-514-0301
Toll-Free TTY: 800-514-0383
Fax: 202-307-1197
Website: www.justice.gov/crt/disability-rights-section

U.S. Department of Veterans Affairs (VA)
810 Vermont Ave. N.W.
Washington, DC 20420
Toll-Free: 800-827-1000
Website: www.va.gov

U.S. Equal Employment Opportunity Commission (EEOC)
131 M St. N.E. Fourth Fl.
Ste. 4NWO2F
Washington, DC 20507-0100
Toll-Free: 800-669-4000
Toll-Free TTY: 800-669-6820
Fax: 202-419-0739
Website: www.eeoc.gov/field/washington/index.cfm
E-mail: info@eeoc.gov

U.S. Food and Drug Administration (FDA)
10903 New Hampshire Ave.
Silver Spring, MD 20993
Toll-Free: 888-INFO-FDA (800-463-6332)
Website: www.fda.gov

U.S. Government Printing Office (GPO)
732 N. Capitol St. N.W.
Washington, DC 20401
Toll-Free: 866-512-1800
Phone: 202-512-1800
Website: www.gpo.gov/who-we-are/our-agency/office-locations
E-mail: contactcenter@gpo.gov

U.S. National Library of Medicine (NLM)
8600 Rockville Pike
Bethesda, MD 20894
Toll-Free: 888-FIND-NLM
(888-346-3656)
Website: www.nlm.nih.gov
E-mail: custserv@nlm.nih.gov

U.S. Social Security Administration (SSA)
Office of Public Inquiries
1100 W. High Rise
6401 Security Blvd.
Baltimore, MD 21235
Toll-Free: 800-772-1213
Toll-Free TTY: 800-325-0778
Website: www.ssa.gov

Private Agencies That Provide Information about Disabilities

AARP
601 E. St. N.W.
Washington, DC 20049
Toll-Free: 888-OUR-AARP
(888-687-2277)
Toll-Free TTY: 877-434-7598
Website: www.aarp.org

AbilityJobs
8941 Atlanta Ave.
Huntington Beach, CA 92646
Website: www.abilityjobs.com

Alzheimer's Association
225 N. Michigan Ave.
Fl. 17
Chicago, IL 60601
Toll-Free: 800-272-3900
Website: www.alz.org

Alzheimer's Foundation of America
322 Eighth Ave.
Seventh Fl.
New York, NY 10001
Toll-Free: 866-232-8484
Fax: 646-638-1546
Website: www.alzfdn.org
E-mail: info@alzfdn.org

American Academy of Family Physicians (AAFP)
11400 Tomahawk Creek Pkwy
Leawood, KS 66211-2680
Toll-Free: 800-274-2237
Phone: 913-906-6000
Fax: 913-906-6075
Website: www.aafp.org/home.html
E-mail: contactcenter@aafp.org

American Academy of Physical Medicine and Rehabilitation (AAPM&R)
9700 W. Bryn Mawr Ave., Ste. 200
Rosemont, IL 60018
Toll-Free: 877-227-6799
Phone: 847-737-6000
Fax: 847-737-6001
Website: www.aapmr.org
E-mail: info@aapmr.org

American Council of the Blind Inc
1703 N. Beauregard St., Ste. 420
Arlington, VA 22311
Toll-Free: 800-424-8666
Phone: 202-467-5081
Fax: 703-465-5085
Website: www.acb.org

Directory of Organizations That Help People with Disabilities

American Foundation for the Blind (AFB)
1401 S. Clark St.
Ste. 730
Arlington, VA 22202
Toll-Free: 800-AFB-LINE
(800-232-5463)
Phone: 212-502-7600
Website: www.afb.org
E-mail: info@afb.net

American Heart Association (AHA)
National Center
7272 Greenville Ave.
Dallas, TX 75231
Toll-Free: 800-AHA-USA-1
(800-242-8721)
Website: www.heart.org

American Medical Association (AMA)
AMA Plaza, 330 N. Wabash Ave.
Ste. 39300
Chicago, IL 60611-5885
Website: www.ama-assn.org

American Parkinson Disease Association (APDA)
135 Parkinson Ave.
Staten Island, NY 10305
Toll-Free: 800-223-2732
Phone: 718-981-8001
Fax: 718-981-4399
Website: www.apdaparkinson.org
E-mail: apda@apdaparkinson.org

American Printing House for the Blind (APH)
1839 Frankfort Ave.
Louisville, KY 40206
Toll-Free: 800-223-1839
Phone: 502-895-2405
Fax: 502-899-2284
Website: www.aph.org
E-mail: info@aph.org

American Psychological Association (APA)
750 First St. N.E.
Washington, DC 20002-4242
Toll-Free: 800-374-2721
Phone: 202-336-5500
TTY: 202-336-6123
Website: www.apa.org

American Society on Aging (ASA)
575 Market St.
Ste. 2100
San Francisco, CA 94105-2869
Toll-Free: 800-537-9728
Phone: 415-974-9600
Fax: 415-974-0300
Website: www.asaging.org
E-mail: info@asaging.org

American Speech-Language-Hearing Association (ASHA)
2200 Research Blvd.
Rockville, MD 20850-3289
Toll-Free: 800-638-8255
Phone: 301-296-5700
TTY: 301-296-5650
Fax: 301-296-8580
Website: www.asha.org
E-mail: actioncenter@asha.org

Amputee Coalition of America
900 E. Hill Ave.
Ste. 390
Knoxville, TN 37915
Toll-Free: 888-AMP-KNOW
(888-267-5669)
TTY: 865-525-4512
Fax: 865-525-7917
Website: www.amputee-coalition.org

Amyotrophic Lateral Sclerosis (ALS) Association
1275 K St. N.W.
Ste. 250
Washington, DC 20005
Toll-Free: 800-782-4747
Fax: 202-289-6801
Website: www.alsa.org
E-mail: alsinfo@als-national.org

The Arc
1825 K St. N.W., Ste. 1200
Washington, DC 20006
Toll-Free: 800-433-5255
Phone: 202-534-3700
Fax: 202-534-3731
Website: www.thearc.org
E-mail: info@thearc.org

ARCH National Respite Network and Resource Center
Website: www.archrespite.org

Arthritis Foundation
1355 Peachtree St. N.E.
Sixth Fl.
Atlanta, GA 30309
Phone: 404-872-7100
Website: www.arthritis.org

Assisted Living Federation of America (ALFA)
1650 King St., Ste. 602
Alexandria, VA 22314
Phone: 703-894-1805
Website: www.alfa.org

Associated Services for the Blind and Visually Impaired (ASB)
919 Walnut St.
Philadelphia, PA 19107
Phone: 215-627-0600
Fax: 215-922-0692
Website: www.asb.org

Association of University Centers on Disabilities (AUCD)
1010 Wayne Ave.
Ste. 1000
Silver Spring, MD 20910
Phone: 301-588-8252
Fax: 301-588-2842
Website: www.aucd.org
E-mail: aucdinfo@aucd.org

Autism Society
4340 East-West Hwy
Ste. 350
Bethesda, MD 20814
Toll-Free: 800-328-8476
Website: www.autism-society.org

Birth Defect Research for Children, Inc. (BDRC)
976 Lake Baldwin Ln.
Ste. 104
Orlando, FL 32814
Phone: 407-895-0802
Website: www.birthdefects.org
E-mail: staff@birthdefects.org

Directory of Organizations That Help People with Disabilities

Brain Injury Association of America (BIAA)
1608 Spring Hill Rd.
Ste. 110
Vienna, VA 22182
Toll-Free: 800-444-6443
Phone: 703-761-0750
Fax: 703-761-0755
Website: www.biausa.org
E-mail: braininjuryinfo@biausa.org

Brain Trauma Foundation (BTF)
Website: www.braintrauma.org

Cleveland Clinic
9500 Euclid Ave.
Cleveland, OH 44195
Toll-Free: 800-223-2273
TTY: 216-444-0261
Website: my.clevelandclinic.org

Cystic Fibrosis (CF) Foundation
4550 Montgomery Ave.
Ste. 1100 N
Bethesda, MD 20814
Toll-Free: 800-344-4823
Phone: 301-951-4422
Website: www.cff.org
E-mail: info@cff.org

Easterseals
141 W. Jackson Blvd.
Ste. 1400A
Chicago, IL 60604
Toll-Free: 800-221-6827
Phone: 312-726-6200
Fax: 312-726-1494
Website: www.easterseals.com
E-mail: info@easterseals.com

Health in Aging
40 Fulton St.
Fl. 18
New York, NY 10038
Toll-Free: 800-563-4916
Phone: 212-308-1414
Website: www.healthinaging.org

Family Caregiver Alliance (FCA)
101 Montgomery St.
Ste. 2150
San Francisco, CA 94104
Toll-Free: 800-445-8106
Phone: 415-434-3388
Website: www.caregiver.org

Goodwill Industries
15810 Indianola Dr.
Rockville, MD 20855
Toll-Free: 800-741-0186
Website: www.goodwill.org
E-mail: contactus@goodwill.org

Job Accommodation Network (JAN)
Toll-Free: 800-526-7234
Toll-Free TTY: 877-781-9403
Website: www.askjan.org
E-mail: jan@askjan.org

The John F. Kennedy Center for the Performing Arts
2700 F St. N.W.
Washington, DC 20566
Toll-Free: 800-444-1324
Phone: 202-467-4600
Website: education.kennedy-center.org

March of Dimes
1275 Mamaroneck Ave.
White Plains, NY 10605
Phone: 914-997-4488
Website: www.marchofdimes.com

National Adult Day Services Association (NADSA)
11350 Random Hills Rd.
Ste. 800
Fairfax, VA 22030
Toll-Free: 877-745-1440
Fax: 919-825-3945
Website: www.nadsa.org
E-mail: info@nadsa.org

National Alliance for Caregiving (NAC)
4720 Montgomery Ln.
Ste. 205
Bethesda, MD 20814
Phone: 301-718-8444
Fax: 301-951-9067
Website: www.caregiving.org
E-mail: info@caregiving.org

National Association of the Deaf (NAD)
8630 Fenton St.
Ste. 820
Silver Spring, MD 20910
Phone: 301-587-1788
TTY: 301-587-1789
Fax: 301-587-1791
Website: www.nad.org

National Center for Learning Disabilities (NCLD)
32 Laight St.
Second Fl.
New York, NY 10013
Phone: 212-545-7510
Fax: 212-545-9665
Website: www.ncld.org
E-mail: info@ncld.org

National Center on Health, Physical Activity and Disability (NCHPAD)
4000 Ridgeway Dr.
Birmingham, AL 35209
Toll-Free: 800-900-8086
Fax: 205-313-7475
Website: www.ncpad.org
E-mail: email@nchpad.org

National Center on Deaf-Blindness (NCDB)
345 N. Monmouth Ave.
Monmouth, OR 97361
Phone: 503-838-8754
Fax: 503-838-8150
Website: www.nationaldb.org
E-mail: info@nationaldb.org

National Down Syndrome Society (NDSS)
8 E 41st St.
Eighth Fl.
New York, NY 10017
Toll-Free: 800-221-4602
Fax: 646-870-9320
Website: www.ndss.org
E-mail: info@ndss.org

Directory of Organizations That Help People with Disabilities

National Federation of the Blind (NFB)
200 E. Wells St.
Baltimore, MD 21230
Phone: 410-659-9314
Fax: 410-685-5653
Website: www.nfb.org
E-mail: info@ndss.org

National Hospice and Palliative Care Organization (NHPCO)
1731 King St.
Ste. 100
Alexandria, VA 22314
Toll-Free: 800-658-8898
Phone: 703-837-1500
Website: www.nhpco.org
E-mail: nhpco_info@nhpco.org

National Multiple Sclerosis Society (NMSS)
733 Third Ave.
Third Fl.
New York, NY 10017
Toll-Free: 800-344-4867
Phone: 212-463-7787
Fax: 212-986-7981
Website: www.nationalmssociety.org
E-mail: info@msnyc.org

National Organization for Rare Disorders (NORD)
55 Kenosia Ave.
Danbury, CT 06810
Phone: 203-744-0100
Fax: 203-263-9938
Website: www.rarediseases.org

National Rehabilitation Information Center (NARIC)
8400 Corporate Dr.
Ste. 500
Landover, MD 20785
Toll-Free: 800-346-2742
Phone: 301-459-5900
TTY: 301-459-5984
Fax: 301-459-4263
Website: www.naric.com
E-mail: naricinfo@heitechservices.com

National Spinal Cord Injury Association
75-20 Astoria Blvd.
Ste. 120
Jackson Heights, NY 11370
Toll-Free: 800-962-9629
Phone: 718-512-0010
Toll-Free Fax: 866-387-2196
Website: www.spinalcord.org
E-mail: info@spinalcord.org

National Stroke Association
9707 E. Easter Ln.
Ste. B
Centennial, CO 80112-3747
Toll-Free: 800-787-6537
Website: www.stroke.org
E-mail: info@stroke.org

Nemours Foundation Center for Children's Health Media
1600 Rockland Rd.
Wilmington, DE 19803
Phone: 302-651-4046
Website: www.kidshealth.org
E-mail: info@kidshealth.org

*Parkinson's Disease
Foundation*
1359 Bdwy.
Ste. 1509
New York, NY 10018
Toll-Free: 800-473-4636
Website: www.pdf.org
E-mail: helpline@parkinson.org

PsychCentral
55 Pleasant St.
Ste. 207
Newburyport, MA 01950
Website: www.psychcentral.com
E-mail: talkback@psychcentral.com

Shirley Ryan AbilityLab
355 E. Erie
Chicago, IL 60611
Toll-Free: 844-355-ABLE (844-355-2253)
Phone: 312-238-1000
Website: www.sralab.org

Spina Bifida Association (SBA)
1600 Wilson Blvd.
Ste. 800
Arlington, VA 22209
Toll-Free: 800-621-3141
Phone: 202-944-3285
Fax: 202-944-3295
Website: www.spinabifidaassociation.org
E-mail: sbaa@sbaa.org

United Cerebral Palsy (UCP)
1825 K St. N.W.
Ste. 600
Washington, DC 20006
Toll-Free: 800-872-5827
Phone: 202-776-0406
Fax: 202-776-0414
Website: www.ucp.org

United Spinal Association
120-34 Queens Blvd.
Ste. 320
Kew Gardens, NY 11415
Phone: 718-803-3782
Fax: 718-803-0414
Website: www.unitedspinal.org

Visiting Nurses Associations of America (VNAA)
1800 Diagonal Rd.
Ste. 600
Alexandria, VA 22314
Phone: 571-527-1520
Fax: 202-384-1444
Website: www.vnaa.org

Web Accessibility Initiative (WAI)
MIT/CSAIL, Bldg. 32-G530, 32 Vassar St.
Cambridge, MA 02139
Phone: 617-253-2613
Website: www.w3.org/WAI

Directory of Organizations That Help People with Disabilities

Americans with Disabilities Act National Network Centers

Great Lakes ADA Center
Serves Region 5 (Illinois, Indiana, Michigan, Minnesota, Ohio, and Wisconsin), University of Illinois/Chicago Department on Disability and Human Development
1640 W. Roosevelt Rd.
Rm. 405
Chicago, IL 60608
Toll-Free: 800-949-4232
Phone: 312-413-1407
Fax: 312-413-1856
Website: www.adagreatlakes.org

Mid-Atlantic ADA Center
Serves Region 3 (Delaware, District of Columbia, Maryland, Pennsylvania, Virginia, and West Virginia), TransCen, Inc.,
12300 Twinbrook Pkwy
Ste. 350
Rockville, MD 20852
Toll-Free: 800-949-4232
Phone: 301-217-0124
Fax: 301-251-3762
Website: www.adainfo.org

New England ADA Center
Serves Region 1 (Connecticut, Maine, Massachusetts, New Hampshire, Rhode Island, and Vermont), Institute for Human Centered Design
180-200 Portland St.
Ste. 1
Boston, MA 02114
Toll-Free: 800-949-4232
Phone: 617-695-0085
Fax: 617-482-8099
Website: www.newenglandada.org
E-mail: ADAinfo@NewEnglandADA.org

Northeast ADA Center
Serves Region 2 (New Jersey, New York, Puerto Rico, and the U.S. Virgin Islands), Cornell University
201 Dolgen Hall
Ithaca, NY 14853
Toll-Free: 800-949-4232
Phone: 607-225-6686
Fax: 607-255-2763
Website: www.dbtacnortheast.org
E-mail: northeastada@cornell.edu

Pacific ADA Center

Serves Region 9 (Arizona, California, Hawaii, Nevada, and the Pacific Basin)
555 12th St.
Ste. 1030
Oakland, CA 94607-4046
Toll-Free: 800-949-4232
Phone: 510-285-5600
Fax: 510-285-5614
Website: www.adapacific.org

Rocky Mountain ADA Center

Serves Region 8 (Colorado, Montana, North Dakota, South Dakota, Utah, and Wyoming), Meeting the Challenge, Inc.
3630 Sinton Rd.
Ste. 103
Colorado Springs, CO 80907
Toll-Free: 800-949-4232
Phone: 719-444-0268
Fax: 719-444-0269
Website: www.adainformation.org
E-mail: email@rockymountainada.org

Southwest ADA Center

Serves Region 6 (Arkansas, Louisiana, New Mexico, Oklahoma, and Texas),
TIRR Memorial Hermann – ILRU
1333 Moursund
Houston, TX 77030
Toll-Free: 800-949-4232
Phone: 713-797-7171
Fax: 713-520-5785
Website: www.southwestada.org
E-mail: swdbtac@ilru.org

Chapter 68

Directory of Organizations for Athletes with Disabilities

Organizations That Provide Information on Multiple Sports

Adaptive Sports Center
10 Crested Butte Way
Treasury Center Lower Level
Mt. Crested Butte, CO 81225
Toll-Free: 866-349-2296
Phone: 970-349-5075
Website: www.adaptivesports.org
E-mail: info@adaptivesports.org

Adaptive Sports USA
P.O. Box 621023
Littleton, CO 80162
Phone: 720-412-7979
Toll-Free Fax: 866-204-8918
Website: adaptivesportsusa.org
E-mail: nationaloffice@adaptivesportsusa.org

Disabled Sports USA
451 Hungerford Dr.
Ste. 608
Rockville, MD 20850
Phone: 301-217-0960
Fax: 301-217-0968
Website: disabledsportsusa.org
E-mail: info@dsusa.org

National Sports Center for the Disabled (NSCD)
Broncos Stadium at Mile High
1801 Mile High Stadium Cir.
Ste. 1500
Denver, CO 80204
Fax: 303-293-5448
Website: www.nscd.org
E-mail: info@nscd.org

Resources in this chapter were compiled from several sources deemed reliable; all contact information was verified and updated in July 2018.

Special Olympics
1133 19th St. N.W.
Washington, DC 20036-3604
Toll-Free: 800-700-8585
Phone: 202-628-3630
Fax: 202-824-0200
Website: www.specialolympics.org
E-mail: info@specialolympics.org

SPLORE (Special Populations Learning Outdoor Recreation and Education)
774 E. 3300 S.
Ste. 105
Salt Lake City, UT 84106
Phone: 801-484-4128
Fax: 801-484-4177
Website: splore.org
E-mail: info@splore.org

United States Association of Blind Athletes (USABA)
One Olympic Plaza
Colorado Springs, CO 80909
Phone: 719-866-3224
Fax: 719-866-3400
Website: www.usaba.org

United States Paralympic Team
United States Olympic Committee (USOC)
One Olympic Plaza
Colorado Springs, CO 80909
Phone: 719-632-5551
Website: www.teamusa.org

Wilderness Inquiry
808 14th Ave. S.E.
Minneapolis, MN 55414
Phone: 612-676-9400
Fax: 612-676-9401
Website: www.wildernessinquiry.org
E-mail: info@wildernessinquiry.org

World T.E.A.M. Sports
4250 Veterans Memorial Hwy
Ste. 420 E.
Holbrook, NY 11741-4020
Toll-Free: 855-987-8326
Toll-Free Fax: 855-288-3377
Website: www.worldteamsports.org
E-mail: info@worldteamsports.org

Organizations for Blind and Deaf Athletes

American Blind Bowling Association (ABBA)
Website: www.abba1951.org

American Blind Skiing Foundation (ABSF)
609 Crandell Ln.
Schaumburg, IL 60193
Phone: 312-409-1605
Website: www.absf.org
E-mail: absf@absf.org

Directory of Organizations for Athletes with Disabilities

National Softball Association for the Deaf (NSAD)
Website: www.nsad.org
E-mail: info@nsad.org

Skating Athletes Bold at Heart (SABAH)
2607 Niagara St.
Buffalo, NY 14207
Phone: 716-362-9600
Fax: 716-362-9601
Website: www.sabahinc.org
E-mail: sabah@sabahinc.org

Ski for Light, Inc.
1455 W. Lake St.
Minneapolis, MN 55408
Phone: 612-827-3232
Website: www.sfl.org
E-mail: info@cosfl.org

United States Blind Golf Association (USBGA)
Website: usblindgolf.com
E-mail: info@usblindgolf.com

United States Deaf Cycling Association (USDCA)
Website: www.usdeafcycling.org

U.S. Deaf Ski Snowboard Association (USDSSA)
76 Kings Gate N.
Rochester, NY 14617
Website: www.usdssa.org

USA Deaf Soccer Association
Website: www.usdeafsoccer.com

USA Deaf Sports Federation (USADSF)
P. O. Box 22011
Santa Fe, NM 87502
Website: www.usdeafsports.org
E-mail: support@usdeafsports.org

USA Deaf Track and Field
Website: www.usadtf.org
E-mail: info@usadtf.org

Organizations That Provide Information on Specific Sports

Achilles International
42 W. 38th St.
Fourth Fl.
New York, NY 10018
Phone: 212-354-0300
Fax: 212-354-3978
Website: www.achillesinternational.org
E-mail: info@achillesinternational.org

American Amputee Hockey Association (AAHA)
150 York St.
Stoughton, MA 02072
Phone: 781-297-1393
Fax: 781-341-8715
Website: amputeehockey.sportsengine-prelive.com
E-mail: aaha@nesinai.org

American Amputee Soccer Association
Website: www.ampsoccer.org

American Wheelchair Bowling Association (AWBA)
16006 Congo Ln.
Houston, TX 77040
Phone: 713-849-9052
Website: www.awba.org
E-mail: info@awba.org

Dancing Wheels Company and School
3030 Euclid Ave.
Ste. 100
Cleveland, OH 44115
Phone: 216-432-0306
Fax: 216-432-0308
Website: dancingwheels.org

Fishing Has No Boundaries, Inc. (FHNB)
15453 County Hwy B
P.O. Box 175
Hayward, WI 54843
Toll-Free: 800-243-3462
Phone: 715-634-3185
Fax: 715-634-1305
Website: www.fhnbinc.org

International Wheelchair Aviators (IWA)
82 Corral Dr.
Keller, TX 76244
Phone: 817-229-4634
Website: www.wheelchairaviators.org
E-mail: wheelchairaviators@yahoo.com

International Wheelchair Basketball Federation (IWBF)
Website: www.iwbf.org

National Alliance for Accessible Golf
One World Golf Pl.
St. Augustine, FL 32092-2724
Phone: 904-940-4204
Website: www.accessgolf.org
E-mail: info@accessgolf.org

National Amputee Golf Association (NAGA)
701 Orkney Ct.
Smyrna, TN 37167-6395
Website: nagagolf.org

National Shooting Sports Foundation (NSSF)
Flintlock Ridge Office Center
11 Mile Hill Rd.
Newtown, CT 06470-2359
Phone: 203-426-1320
Fax: 203-426-1087
Website: www.nwba.org
E-mail: info@nssf.org

National Wheelchair Basketball Association (NWBA)
1130 Elkton St.
Ste. A
Colorado Springs, CO 80907
Phone: 719-266-4082
Fax: 719-266-4876
Website: www.nwba.org

Directory of Organizations for Athletes with Disabilities

National Wheelchair Poolplayers Association (NWPA)
90 Flemons Dr.
Somerville, AL 35670
Website: www.nwpainc.org

Professional Association of Therapeutic Horsemanship (PATH) International
8670 Wolff Ct., Ste. 210
Westminster, CO 80031
Toll-Free: 800-369-RIDE (800-369-7433)
Fax: 303-252-4610
Website: www.pathintl.org
E-mail: pathintl@pathintl.org

Physically Challenged Bowhunters of America, Inc. (PCBA)
Toll-Free: 855-247-7222
Website: physicallychallengedbowhuntersofamerica-inc.org

United Foundation for Disabled Archers (UFFDA)
20 N.E. Ninth Ave.
P.O. Box 251
Glenwood, MN 56334
Phone: 320-634-3660
Website: www.uffdaclub.com
E-mail: info@uffdaclub.com

United States Electric Wheelchair Hockey Association (U.S.EWHA)
c/o U.S. EWHA
7216 39th Ave. No.
Minneapolis, MN 55427
Phone: 612-568-7216
Website: www.powerhockey.com
E-mail: info@powerhockey.com

United States Sailing Center
5489 E. Ocean Blvd.
Long Beach, CA 90803
Phone: 562-433-7939
Fax: 562-433-3668
Website: www.ussclb.org

United States Tennis Wheelchair
United States Tennis Association (USTA)
70 W. Red Oak Ln.
White Plains, NY 10604
Phone: 914-696-7000
Website: www.usta.com/en/home/play/lots-of-ways-to-play/wheelchair.html

USA Swimming
1 Olympic Plaza
Colorado Springs, CO 80909
Phone: 719-866-4578
Website: www.usaswimming.org

USA Water Ski
1251 Holy Cow Rd.
Polk City, FL 33868-8200
Phone: 863-324-4341
Fax: 863-325-8259
Website: www.usawaterski.org

USRowing
2 Wall St.
Princeton, NJ 08540
Toll-Free: 800-314-4ROW (800-314-4769)
Website: www.usrowing.org

Chapter 69

How Can I Get Help Finding and Paying for Assistive Technology?

Administration for Community Living

Administration for Community Living's (ACL) Center for Integrated Programs, Office of Consumer Access and Self-Determination, oversees the State Grant for Assistive Technology Program and the Assistive Technology National Activities funded under the Assistive Technology Act of 1998, as amended (AT Act of 2004).

- The **State Grant for Assistive Technology Program** (#AG90) supports state efforts to improve the provision of assistive technology to individuals with disabilities of all ages through comprehensive, statewide programs that are consumer-responsive. The State Grant for Assistive Technology Program makes assistive technology devices and services more available and accessible to individuals with disabilities and their families.

This chapter contains text excerpted from the following sources: Text beginning with the heading "Administration for Community Living" is excerpted from "Assistive Technology," Administration for Community Living (ACL), July 17, 2018; Text beginning with the heading "Programs for Disability Assistance" is excerpted from "Disability Assistance," Benefits.gov, U.S. Department of Labor (DOL), August 11, 2016.

The program provides one grant to each state, the District of Columbia, Puerto Rico, and the outlying areas (American Samoa, the Commonwealth of the Northern Mariana Islands, Guam, and the U.S. Virgin Islands). The State Grant for Assistive Technology Program is a formula grant program; there are no grant competitions. The amount of each state's annual award is based largely on state population.

- General contact information for state assistive technology programs can be found in the State Assistive Technology Program Directory (www.at3center.net/stateprogram) on the AT3 Center website. Specific program contact information, including Lead Agency and Implementing Entity, for the State Grant for Assistive Technology (AT) programs is contained in the State Plan.

- The **Assistive Technology National Activities Program** (#AN90) provides information and technical assistance through grants, contracts, or cooperative agreements, on a competitive basis, to individuals, service providers, states, protection and advocacy entities, and others to support and improve the implementation of the AT Act of 2004. Grants awarded under this program are competitive and open to public or private entities, including for-profit organizations and institutions of higher education with relevant expertise.

- Mandatory funding allocation information is available.

In FY 2005, Congress amended the AT Act to eliminate the separate Alternative Financing Program authorization and instead authorized an AT State grant program that is inclusive of financing activities, including alternative financing loan programs. Each State Grant for Assistive Technology program includes financing activities. In FY 2015, FY 2016, and FY 2017 Congress appropriated funding separate and apart from the Assistive Technology Act for the purposes of making Alternative Financing program grants.

Assistive Technology State Plans

The AT Act of 2004 requires states to submit an application in order to receive funds under the State Grant for AT Program. The application must be in the form of a three-year State Plan for Assistive Technology (AT). The State AT Plans describe how states will implement their program. During the three-year period covered by the plan, a state may be required to submit amendments and updates. Individual state plans can be accessed along with a summary of State AT Program information.

Programs for Disability Assistance

Architectural Barriers Act Enforcement

This program assists individuals subject to discrimination on the basis of disability within the domain of Federally assisted programs.

Assistance for Indian Children with Severe Disabilities

The purpose of the program is to provide special education and related services to Native American children with severe disabilities, in accordance with the Individuals with Disabilities Education Act (IDEA).

Job Accommodation Network (JAN)

The Job Accommodation Network (JAN) provides free, expert and confidential technical assistance to both employees and employers regarding workplace accommodations and disability employment issues.

Nondiscrimination in Federally Assisted and Conducted Programs (On the Basis of Disability)

The program is designed to prohibit discrimination on the basis of disability in programs or activities receiving Federal financial assistance.

Services and Aid for Blind Veterans

U.S. Department of Veterans Affairs (VA) provides personal and social adjustment programs and medical or health-related services for eligible blinded Veterans at selected VA Medical Centers maintaining blind rehabilitation centers. Assistance comes in many forms. Services include assessment skill training, counseling, peer support, family education, and the provision of and training with assistive technology such as magnification devices, and adapted computers.

VA—Birth Defects Assistance—Payments for Children with Spina Bifida Whose Parents Served in Vietnam or Korea

Spina bifida patients who are natural children of Vietnam and Korea Veterans may be eligible for a monthly monetary allowance.

If you want to apply for either of the other spina bifida benefits (healthcare assistance or vocational training), you must start by applying for the monthly allowance.

Nondiscrimination in Federally Assisted and Conducted Programs (On the Basis of Disability)

The program is designed to prohibit discrimination on the basis of disability in programs or activities receiving Federal financial assistance.

Supplemental Security Income (SSI)

Supplemental Security Income is a federally funded program administered by the U.S. Social Security Administration (SSA). SSI provides financial help to disabled adults and children who have limited income and assets.

Index

Index

Page numbers followed by 'n' indicate a footnote. Page numbers in *italics* indicate a table or illustration.

A

AAFP *see* American Academy of Family Physicians
AAP *see* American Academy of Pediatrics
AAPMR *see* American Academy of Physical Medicine and Rehabilitation
AARP, contact 720
AbilityJobs, contact 720
"About IDEA" (ED) 530n
ACAA *see* Air Carrier Access Act
accelerated death benefits, tax benefits and credits 681
access, defined 707
accessibility
　assistive devices 312
　communicating with and about people with disabilities 49
　deaf-blind 168
　home modifications 327
　housing and safety issues 636
　transportation 406
"Accommodating Mental Illness in the Workplace" (SAMHSA) 654n
accommodations
　air travel 405
　Americans with Disabilities Act (ADA) 606
　disability rights 595
　disabled students 565
　employees with disabilities 648
　housing and safety issues 619
　nutrition and weight management issues 421
　rehabilitation 512
　see also reasonable accommodations
Acetaminophen, managing pain 471
Achilles International, contact 731
acquired immunodeficiency syndrome (AIDS)
　Americans with Disabilities Act (ADA) 609
　deaf-blindness 167
　Section 504 435
activities of daily living (ADL)
　assistive technology (AT) 307
　autism spectrum disorder (ASD) 211
　cerebral palsy (CP) 92
　defined 707
　exercise guidelines 432
　health insurance concerns 491
　long-term care 520
　occupational therapists (OTs) 378

741

Disabilities Sourcebook, Fourth Edition

activities of daily living (ADL), *continued*
    Parkinson disease (PD) 263
    spinal cord injuries (SCIs) 299
activity limitation
    disabilities statistics 17
    disability 3
    recreational therapy 388
acupuncture
    Parkinson disease (PD) 274
    spinal cord injuries (SCIs) 297
acute care
    defined 707
    rehabilitation care 513
AD *see* Alzheimer disease
ADA *see* Americans with Disabilities Act
"The ADA: Questions and Answers" (EEOC) 603n
"Adapting Motor Vehicles for People with Disabilities" (NHTSA) 396n
adaptive development, development delay 551
Adaptive Sports Center, contact 729
Adaptive Sports USA, contact 729
ADHD *see* attention deficit hyperactivity disorder
ADL *see* activities of daily living
Administration for Community Living (ACL)
    publications
        amputation and limb loss 276n
        assistive technology (AT) 735n
        home modifications 327n
        independent living 612n
Administration on Aging (AOA), contact 715
adult day care
    defined 707
    long-term care 519
    overview 415–6
    respite care 410
"Adult Day Care" (AOA) 415n
adult day services, defined 707
"Adults with Disabilities" (CDC) 432n
advance care planning, overview 693–704

"Advance Care Planning: Ensuring Your Wishes Are Known and Honored If You Are Unable to Speak for Yourself" (CDC) 693n
"Advance Directives and Advance Care Planning for People with Intellectual and Physical Disabilities" (ASPE) 693n
"Advancing Women and Girls with Disabilities" (USAID) 69n
aerobic exercise, chest physical therapy 108
aerobic physical activity, exercise guidelines 432
Affordable Care Act, insurance coverage 495
age-related macular degeneration (AMD)
    low vision 358
    sensory disabilities 151
Agency for Healthcare Research and Quality (AHRQ)
    contact 715
    publication
        vision rehabilitation 507n
aggression *see* aggressive behavior
aggressive behavior
    childhood bullying 60
    children with developmental disabilities 63
"Aggressive Behavior and Violence" (CDC) 63n
AHT *see* abusive head trauma
AIDS *see* acquired immunodeficiency syndrome
Air Carrier Access Act (ACAA)
    described 597
    service animal 392
air travel, assistance 405
alcohol-related birth defects (ARBD), fetal alcohol spectrum disorders (FASDs) 192
alcohol-related neurodevelopmental disorder (ARND), fetal alcohol spectrum disorders (FASDs) 192
alcohol use
    attention deficit hyperactivity disorder (ADHD) 222
    depression 482

742

Index

ALDs *see* assistive listening devices
ALS *see* amyotrophic lateral sclerosis
Alzheimer disease
 aging 38
 aphasia 176
 cognitive changes 257
 defined 708
 guardianship 691
 overview 232–7
 Parkinsonism 266
Alzheimer's Association, contact 720
"Alzheimer's Disease Fact Sheet" (NIA) 232n
Alzheimer's Foundation of America, contact 720
AMD *see* age-related macular degeneration
American Academy of Family Physicians (AAFP), contact 720
American Academy of Physical Medicine and Rehabilitation (AAPM&R), contact 720
American Amputee Hockey Association (AAHA), contact 731
American Amputee Soccer Association, contact 732
American Blind Bowling Association (ABBA), contact 730
American Blind Skiing Foundation (ABSF), contact 730
American Council of the Blind Inc, contact 720
American Foundation for the Blind (AFB), contact 721
American Heart Association (AHA), contact 721
American Medical Association (AMA), contact 721
American Parkinson Disease Association (APDA), contact 721
American Printing House for the Blind (APH), contact 721
American Psychological Association (APA), contact 721
American Sign Language (ASL), hearing loss 349
American Society on Aging (ASA), contact 721
American Speech-Language-Hearing Association (ASHA), contact 721

American Wheelchair Bowling Association (AWBA), contact 732
Americans with Disabilities Act (ADA)
 communication 48
 described 593
 disability myths 25
 housing 635
 mobility aids 319
 telecommunication relay services 355
amniocentesis
 birth defects 79
 Down syndrome 188
 prenatal screening 106
"Amputation and Social Security Benefits" (Omnigraphics) 673n
amputations
 overview 276–83
 physical therapists 383
 rehabilitation 382
 Social Security benefits 673
Amputee Coalition of America, contact 722
amyotrophic lateral sclerosis (ALS), overview 238–9
Amyotrophic Lateral Sclerosis (ALS) Association, contact 722
"Amyotrophic Lateral Sclerosis (ALS) Information Page" (NINDS) 238n
antidepressant medication
 depression 256
 pain management 482
 see also selective serotonin reuptake inhibitor
"Anxiety" (VA) 475n
anxiety disorders
 coping 475
 described 221
"Anxiety Disorders" (NIMH) 475n
AOA *see* Administration on Aging
AOTA *see* American Occupational Therapy Association
Apgar score, cerebral palsy (CP) 88
aphasia, overview 176–80
"Aphasia" (NIDCD) 176n
apraxia, overview 180–3
"Apraxia of Speech" (NIDCD) 180n
ARBD *see* alcohol-related birth defects

The Arc, contact 722
ARCH National Respite Network and Resource Center, contact 722
architectural barriers, physical accessibility 577
Architectural Barriers Act (ABA), described 601
ARND *see* alcohol-related neurodevelopmental disorder
arthritis
 defined 708
 overview 239–42
"Arthritis" (NIAMS) 239n
Arthritis Foundation, contact 722
art therapy, overview 385–9
"Artificial Retina Receives FDA Approval" (NSF) 360n
ASD *see* autism spectrum disorder
ASHA *see* American Speech-Language-Hearing Association
assisted living
 home modifications 330
 housing and safety 623
 long-term care 523
Assisted Living Federation of America (ALFA), contact 722
assistive listening devices (ALDs), hearing loss 143
assistive devices
 arthritis 242
 birth defects 80
 defined 708
 described 92
 hearing 346
 Medicaid 308
 transportation 407
 wheelchairs 320
 see also mobility aids
"Assistive Devices for People with Hearing, Voice, Speech, or Language Disorders" (NIDCD) 346n
assistive technology (AT), overview 307–9
"Assistive Technology" (ACL) 735n
"Assistive Technology" (AOA) 307n
Associated Services for the Blind and Visually Impaired (ASB), contact 722
Association for Driver Rehabilitation Specialists (ADED), transportation 400

Association of University Centers on Disabilities (AUCD), contact 722
AT *see* Assistive technologies; *see also* mobility aid
ataxia
 cerebral palsy (CP) 83
 multiple sclerosis (MS) 154
attention deficit disorder (ADD)
 autism 216
 defined 708
attention deficit hyperactivity disorder (ADHD)
 bullying 60
 described 222
 overview 217–20
"Attention-Deficit/Hyperactivity Disorder (ADHD)—Basic Information" (CDC) 217n
attitudinal barriers, defined 20
audiologists
 cochlear implant 339
 defined 708
 hearing loss 142
auditory nerve, cochlear implant 338
Autism Society, contact 722
"Autism Spectrum Disorder Fact Sheet" (NINDS) 211n
autism spectrum disorders (ASD)
 overview 211–6
 rehabilitation medicine 507
autoimmune disease, multiple sclerosis (MS) 249
auxiliary aids
 hearing loss 334
 postsecondary education 576
axons, multiple sclerosis (MS)

B

back pain, overview 284–9
Baclofen (Lioresal), uncoordinated bladder and urethra 458
balance
 benefits of exercise 39
 caregiving tips 56
 cerebral palsy (CP) 90
 cystic fibrosis (CF) 105
 multiple sclerosis (MS) 246
 pallidotomy and thalamotomy 272

Index

balance, *continued*
   rehabilitation medicine 510
   telecommunication relay
      services 356
"Basics about FASDs" (CDC) 190n
"Basics about Hearing Loss in
   Children" (CDC) 146n
bathing
   abuse against women with
      disabilities 72
   assistive technology (AT) 307
   disability 447
   occupational therapists 378
bed sores *see* pressure sores
behavior disorder, sleep problems 263
behind-the-ear (BTE), hearing
   aids 341
beta-blockers, anxiety disorders
   medications 480
"Beyond Guardianship: Toward
   Alternatives That Promote Greater
   Self-Determination" (NCD) 687n
biofeedback
   bowel control problems 452
   pain treatments 472
biofeedback therapy, bowel control
   problems 453
biopsy
   defined 708
   muscle biopsies 127
   pressure sores 464
bipolar disorder
   autism 215
   bipolar and related disorders 223
   multiple sclerosis (MS) 246
Birth Defect Research for Children,
   Inc. (BDRC), contact 722
birth defects
   cleft lip and palate 95
   defined 708
   Down syndrome 189
   low vision 358
   overview 75–81
   prenatal diagnosis 136
"Birth Defects" (NICHD) 75n
bladder, depicted *456*
bladder control problems
   Kegel exercises 458
   multiple sclerosis (MS) 245

bladder control problems, *continued*
   nerve damage 454
   overactive bladder 455
"Bladder Control Problems and Nerve
   Disease" (NIDDK) 451n
bladder training, overactive bladder 456
blindness
   ABLE account 686
   child with a disability 538
   co-robotic cane 373
   developmental birth defects 76
   diabetic retinopathy 162
   discrimination in housing based
      upon disability 634
   glaucoma 155
   high blood pressure 41
   robotic glove 374
   shaken baby syndrome 195
   see also vision impairment
blood clots
   bleeding in the brain 86
   cardiovascular problem 41
   circulatory problems 296
   rehabilitation medicine 509
blood pressure
   atrial fibrillation 41
   autonomic dysreflexia 296
   cerebral palsy (CP) 91
   circulatory problems 296
   levodopa/carbidopa 269
   nonsteroidal anti-inflammatory
      drugs 472
   optic nerve damage 156
   Parkinson disease (PD) 258
   spinal cord injury (SCI) 291
   yoga 438
Blue Cross/Blue Shield, Children's
   Health Insurance Program 492
BMI *see* body mass index
body mass index (BMI), overweight
   and obesity 427
Botulinum toxin type A (Botox),
   uncoordinated bladder and urethra 459
bowel control problem, changes in
   diet 452
bradykinesia
   drug-induced Parkinsonism 267
   pallidotomy and thalamotomy 272
   Parkinson disease (PD) 261

braille
  communication systems 170
  low vision 643
  overview 366–70
  Web-Braille 370
braille alphabet, described 368
braille books
  braille transcribers and
    proofreaders 370
  history of braille 367
  medical expenses 682
  Web-Braille 371
braille transcribers, described 369
Brain Injury Association of America
  (BIAA), contact 723
Brain Trauma Foundation (BTF),
  contact 723
brain tumor, aphasia 176
breathing problems
  arthritis 241
  pulmonary rehabilitation 109
  rehabilitation medicine 509
breech position, cerebral palsy (CP) 88
bronchiectasis
  cystic fibrosis (CF) 104
  defined 708
bronchodilators, cystic fibrosis
  (CF) 108
BTF *see* Brain Trauma Foundation
bullying
  conduct disorder 226
  overview 60–3
"Bullying and Children and Youth
  with Disabilities and Special Health
  Needs" (HHS) 60n
"The Burden of Vision Loss" (CDC) 150n

C

C-reactive protein, pressure
  sores 464
caffeine, bowel control problems 453
canes
  assistive technologies 309
  physical therapy 383
captions, overview 332–7
"Captions for Deaf and Hard-of-
  Hearing Viewers" (NIDCD) 332n

cardiomyopathy
  defined 708
  muscular dystrophy
    (MD) 124
cardiopulmonary resuscitation (CPR),
  medical emergency 503
cardiovascular
  aging 44
  aphasia 180
caregivers
  autism 216
  children 67
  defined 708
  dental care 443
  fire safety 640
  medical emergency 503
  respite care 410
  sensory disabilities 168
  shaken baby syndrome 195
  speech disorders 352
"Caregiving Index—Alzheimer's
  Disease and Healthy Aging"
  (CDC) 55n
caregiving tips, described 55
carrier, defined 709
cartilage
  defined 709
  obesity 430
  rehabilitation 508
cataracts
  described 158
  myotonic dystrophy 131
catheters
  hospice care 412
  urine retention 459
cauda equina syndrome,
  defined 286
CDC *see* Centers for Disease Control
  and Prevention
Center for Parent Information and
  Resources (CPIR)
  publications
    accommodations for
      students 565n
    disability evaluation 537n
    early intervention 549n
    Individualized Education
      Program (IEP) 559n

746

Index

Centers for Disease Control and
  Prevention (CDC)
  contact 716
  publications
    adults with disabilities 432n
    advance care planning 693n
    aggressive behavior and
      violence 63n
    Alzheimer disease 55n
    attention deficit hyperactivity
      disorder (ADHD) 217n
    birth defects 75n
    child abuse 63n
    children speech-language
      pathology 352n
    cleft lip and cleft palate 95n
    common barriers 19n
    communicating with people
      with disabilities 47n
    depression and anxiety 475n
    disabilities 3n
    disability and functioning 11n
    disability and health 3n
    disability and obesity 427n
    disability statistics 11n
    Down syndrome 186n
    family caregivers 55n
    fetal alcohol spectrum
      disorders (FASDs) 190n
    hearing loss in children 146n
    language and speech
      disorders 352n
    physical activity guidelines 432n
    shaken baby syndrome 194n
    traumatic brain injury 300n
    vision loss 150n
    women with disabilities 33n
Centers for Independent Living
  (CILs), independent living
  programs 613
"Centers for Independent Living"
  (ACL) 612n
Centers for Medicare and Medicaid
  Services (CMS)
  health insurance concerns 494
  publications
    Children's Health Insurance
      Program (CHIP) 492n

Centers for Medicare and Medicaid
  Services (CMS)
  publications, *continued*
    insurance for people with
      disabilities 486n
    Medicaid beneficiaries 496n
    Medicare coverage 410n
central nervous system (CNS)
  fetal alcohol spectrum disorders
    (FASDs) 191
  multiple sclerosis (MS) 247
central pain, multiple sclerosis
  (MS) 255
cerebral, defined 709
cerebral palsy (CP)
  dysphagia 425
  housing 616
  occupational therapist 383
  overview 83–93
  rehabilitation medicine 508
  shaken baby syndrome 196
"Cerebral Palsy: Hope through
  Research" (NINDS) 83n
cerebrospinal fluid (CSF), neurological
  disorders 265
cervical cancer, disabilities 34
CF *see* cystic fibrosis
"Chapter 4—Vision Rehabilitation:
  Care and Benefit Plan Models:
  Literature Review" (AHRQ) 507n
chest physical therapy (CPT), cystic
  fibrosis (CF) 107
Chiari II malformation, spina
  bifida 135
child abuse
  cerebral palsy (CP) 85
  posttraumatic stress disorder
    (PTSD) 228
  shaken baby syndrome 195
Child Find
  early intervention services 554
  fetal alcohol spectrum disorders
    (FASDs) 194
childhood stunting, nutrition 420
children
  apraxia of speech (AOS) 182
  attention deficit hyperactivity
    disorder (ADHD) 219

747

children, *continued*
  autism spectrum disorder (ASD) 212
  bowel control problems 452
  caregivers 55
  cerebral palsy (CP) 90
  childhood bullying 60
  cochlear implant 338
  cystic fibrosis (CF) 101
  deaf-blindness 165
  dyspraxia 209
  early intervention 551
  hearing loss 146
  housing 633
  juvenile arthritis (JA) 240
  language therapy 353
  limb loss 276
  Medicaid 492
  muscular dystrophy (MD) 122
  nutrition 420
  social barriers 23
  Social Security 671
  special education 527
  spina bifida 136
  transportation 400
Children's Health Insurance Program (CHIP), Medicaid 492
"Children's Health Insurance Program (CHIP)" (CMS) 492n
CHIP *see* Children's Health Insurance Program
"Choosing a Nursing Home" (NIA) 519n
chorionic villus sampling (CVS)
  described 79
  Down syndrome 188
  genetic counseling 126
chromosomal disorder, noninvasive prenatal testing (NIPT) 79
chromosomes
  defined 709
  Down syndrome 189
  muscular dystrophy (MD) 122
CILs *see* Centers for Independent Living
CJD *see* Creutzfeldt-Jakob disease
cleft lip
  birth defects 76
  defined 709
  depicted *95*
  overview 95–9

cleft palate
  depicted *96*
  described 96
clefts, birth defects 97
Cleveland Clinic, contact 723
"Closed Captioning on Television" (FCC) 332n
clubbing, cystic fibrosis (CF) 105
CNS *see* central nervous system
cochlear implants
  birth defects 80
  overview 337–40
"Cochlear Implants" (NIDCD) 337n
cognitive assistance, assistive technologies 309
cognitive behavioral therapy (CBT), pain management 472
cognitive development, development delay 551
cognitive disability, rehabilitative technologies 313
cognitive impairment
  defined 709
  see cognitive disability
cognitive rehabilitation therapy (CRT), defined 510
"Common Barriers to Participation Experienced by People with Disabilities" (CDC) 19n
"Communicating with and about People with Disabilities" (CDC) 47n
"Communicating with and about People with Disabilities" (DOL) 47n
communication
  abuse 69
  alcohol spectrum disorders 191
  assistive devices 92
  autism spectrum disorder (ASD) 212
  barriers 21
  braille 366
  deaf-blind 168
  disabled children 544
  disaster preparedness 643
  early intervention 556
  hearing aids 341
  hearing loss 148
  language therapy 354
  real-time captioning 333
  rehabilitative technologies 510

Index

communication, *continued*
  speech disorders 178
  telecommunication 355
  workplace 53
communication barrier, described 21
communication development,
  development delay 551
communities
  disability myths 26
  Every Student Succeeds Act
    (ESSA) 533
  housing discrimination 633
  physical activities 436
  respite care 410
  sensory disabilities 173
  statistics 14
complementary and alternative
  therapy, cerebral palsy (CP) 93
completely-in-canal (CIC), canal
  aids 145
computed tomography (CT)
  Alzheimer disease 236
  aphasia 178
  cerebral palsy (CP) 89
  shaken baby syndrome 196
  spina bifida 137
  traumatic brain injury 303
"Computer Models Could Help
  Design Physical Therapy Regimens"
  (NIBIB) 381n
computers
  assistive technology (AT) 92, 315
  attention deficit hyperactivity
    disorder (ADHD) 220
  dysgraphia 208
  students 583
  visual impairment 373
congenital myasthenic syndrome,
  muscular dystrophy (MD) 124
congenital myopathy, muscular
  dystrophy (MD) 124
constipation
  autonomic dysreflexia 297
  bowel and bladder problems 256
  muscular dystrophy (MD) 131
  nutrition 452
contact lenses, low vision 358
cornea, depicted *155*
corticosteroid, muscular dystrophy
  (MD) 129

"Coverage Options for People with
  Disabilities" (CMS) 486n
CP *see* cerebral palsy
CPT *see* chest physical therapy
cranial ultrasound, defined 89
"Creative Arts Therapies Fact Sheet"
  (VA) 385n
"Creative Arts Therapy a Useful Tool
  for Military Patients" (NEA) 385n
CPR *see* cardiopulmonary
  resuscitation
crutches
  assistive devices 309
  physical therapist 383
  rehabilitation 510
  spina bifida 138
CT *see* computed tomography
CVD *see* cardiovascular disease
CVS *see* chorionic villus sampling
cyclothymia, bipolar disorder 223
cyclothymic disorder (cyclothymia),
  defined 709
cystic fibrosis (CF), overview 101–13
"Cystic Fibrosis" (NHLBI) 101n
Cystic Fibrosis (CF) Foundation,
  contact 723

D

dalfampridine, multiple sclerosis
  (MS) 254
Dancing Wheels Company and School,
  contact 732
DBS *see* deep brain stimulation
deaf
  captions 332
  cochlear implants 337
  communication tips 53
  disability benefits 671
  education 579
  hearing loss 143
  safety 641
  Section 508 600
  speech language therapy 354
  see also hearing impairment
deaf-blindness, overview 165–74
"Debunking the Three Biggest Myths
  about Disability Benefits and Work"
  (SSA) 25n

deep brain stimulation (DBS)
  described 272
  tremor 254
degenerative disorder
  birth defects 76
  Parkinson disease (PD) 257
dementia
  aging 41
  Alzheimer disease 236
  deep brain stimulation 273
  dyslexia 206
  dysphagia 425
  long-term care 523
  Parkinson disease (PD) 263
dental care, overview 442–6
"Dental Care Everyday—A
  Caregiver's Guide" (NIDCR) 442n
Department of Education (ED) *see*
  U.S. Department of Education
Department of Health and Human
  Services (DHHS; HHS) *see* U.S.
  Department of Health and Human
  Services
Department of Housing and Urban
  Development (HUD) *see* U.S.
  Department of Housing and Urban
  Development
Department of Justice *see* U.S.
  Department of Justice
dependent care benefits, described 677
depression
  amyotrophic lateral sclerosis 239
  autism 216
  bullying 61
  conduct disorder 226
  coping 475
  described 256
  emotional issues 112
  Parkinson disease (PD) 262
  spina bifida 136
deoxyribonucleic acid (DNA)
  Alzheimer disease (AD) 235
  autism spectrum disorder (ASD) 215
  multiple sclerosis (MS) 248
"Developing Your Child's IEP"
  (CPIR) 559n
developmental delay
  autism spectrum disorders
    (ASDs) 213

developmental delay, *continued*
  defined 709
  described 551
  inherited disorders 117
  speech disorders 353
developmental disabilities
  advanced care planning 701
  children 63
  Civil Rights of Institutionalized
    Persons Act (CRIPA) 598
  muscular dystrophy (MD) 123
developmental disability, defined 709
developmental milestones
  cerebral palsy (CP) 84
  developmental delay 551
"Developmental Dyspraxia
  Information Page" (NINDS) 209n
diabetes
  aging 38
  Alzheimer disease 235
  bullying 61
  cataracts 159
  cystic fibrosis (CF) 104
  described 42
  multiple sclerosis (MS) 248
  orofacial clefts 97
  spina bifida 137
diabetic retinopathy (DR)
  defined 709
  described 162
  low vision 358
*Diagnostic and Statistical Manual
  of Mental Disorders* DSM-IV,
  fetal alcohol spectrum disorders
  (FASDs) 192
diarrhea
  bowel and bladder problems 452
  catechol-O-methyltransferase
    (COMT) inhibitors 270
  cystic fibrosis (CF) 111
Diazepam (Valium), bladder
  problems 458
dietary supplement
  cerebral palsy (CP) 93
  complementary and supportive
    therapies 273
  inborn errors 120
dieticians, swallowing 263
dilated eye exam, defined 153

Index

diplopia, multiple sclerosis (MS) 253
disability
  abuse 70
  aging 35
  air travel 405
  Americans with Disabilities Act (ADA) 593
  apraxia 181
  bowel and bladder problems 451
  bullying 60
  children 537
  communication 50
  deaf-blindness 166
  defined 709
  degenerative diseases 231
  dental care 442
  early intervention 549
  employment discrimination 605
  evaluation 538
  guardianship 687
  health insurance 487
  home use devices 324
  housing 614
  Individuals with Disabilities Education Act (IDEA) 538
  living space 327
  mental disorders 221
  multiple sclerosis (MS) 243
  myths 25
  nutrition 420
  overview 3–9
  personal hygiene 447
  postsecondary education 576
  rehabilitation medicine 507
  service animals 393
  shaken baby syndrome 196
  Social Security benefits 667
  spina bifida 134
  statistics 11
  students 586
  traumatic and injury 275
  women 33
"Disability and Functioning (Noninstitutionalized Adults Aged 18 and Over)" (CDC) 11n
"Disability and Health—Disability Overview" (CDC) 3n
"Disability and Obesity" (CDC) 427n
"Disability Assistance" (DOL) 735n

"Disability Benefits" (SSA) 667n
"Disability Employment" (OPM) 646n
"Disability Employment—Reasonable Accommodations" (OPM) 648n
Disability.gov, contact 716
disability harassment, described 61
"Disability in Older Adults" (NIH) 35n
disability pensions, described 680
"Disability Rights in Housing" (HUD) 637n
disability support services (DSS), college 575
Disabled Sports USA, contact 729
disaster preparedness, overview 642–4
"Disaster Preparedness for People with Disabilities" (FEMA) 642n
distraction, pain treatment 472
DMD *see* Duchenne muscular dystrophy
DNA *see* deoxyribonucleic acid
DOJ *see* U.S. Department of Justice
domestic violence, women 71
donepezil, Alzheimer disease 237
dopamine, Parkinson disease (PD) 258
Down syndrome
  birth defects 76
  overview 186–9
drooling, cerebral palsy (CP) 91
driver's license, disabled 398
drug abuse, occupational therapy 380
drug therapy
  muscular dystrophy (MD) 129
  Parkinson disease (PD) 267
DSM-IV *see* Diagnostic and Statistical Manual of Mental Disorders
Duchenne muscular dystrophy (DMD), advance care planning 696
dysarthria, aphasia 176
dyscalculia
  defined 709
  overview 201–6
dysesthesias, multiple sclerosis (MS) 255
dysgraphia
  defined 710
  described 200
"Dysgraphia Information Page" (NINDS) 208n

751

dyslexia
  defined 710
  overview 206–7
"Dyslexia Information Page"
  (NINDS) 206n
dysphagia, described 422
"Dysphagia" (NIDCD) 422n
dyspraxia
  defined 710
  described 209
dystonia, Parkinson disease (PD) 261

E

early and periodic screening,
  diagnostic, and treatment (EPSDT),
  Medicaid 492
Early Childhood Technical Assistance
  Center (ECTA), early intervention
  services 553
early intervention
  birth defects 81
  Down syndrome 189
  fetal alcohol spectrum disorders
    (FASDs) 193
  Individuals with Disabilities
    Education Act (IDEA) 530
  services overview 549
Easterseals, contact 723
ED *see* U.S. Department of Education
education
  individualized education program
    (IEP) 560
  military and government disability
    pensions 680
  postsecondary 573
  scholarships 660
educational program
  child's initial evaluation 541
  individualized education 172
EEOC *see* Equal Employment
  Opportunity Commission
"Effective Interaction: Communicating
  with and about People with
  Disabilities in the Workplace"
  (DOL) 47n
Eldercare Locator, contact 716
electrical stimulation
  bowel control problems treatment 452

electrical stimulation, *continued*
  complementary and alternative
    therapies 93
  overactive bladder treatment 456
  physical therapy 130
  spinal cord injury (SCI) 297
electrical stimulator for bladder
  control, depicted *456*
electroencephalogram, cerebral palsy
  (CP) 89
electroencephalograph (EEG),
  nerve damage and bladder control
  problems 455
electromyography (EMG)
  defined 710
  neurophysiology studies 128
Elementary and Secondary Education
  Act (ESEA), Every Student Succeeds
  Act 532
EMG *see* electromyography
emotional support, service
  animal 392
employment
  Americans with Disabilities Act
    (ADA) 593, 603
  discrimination 536
  household employers 684
  IDEA purpose 531
  model transition programs 579
  postsecondary education 573
  rehabilitation 299
  rehabilitation act 599
  scholarships for students with
    intellectual disabilities 663
  testing for illegal drugs 609
employment discrimination
  Americans with Disabilities Act
    (ADA) 604
  discrimination of qualified
    individuals with disabilities 536
  rehabilitation act 599
end-of-life care, advance care
  planning 695
environmental factors
  activity limitation and participation
    restriction 5
  age-related macular
    degeneration 152
  aging and disabilities 37
  anxiety disorders 222

752

Index

environmental factors, *continued*
  attention deficit hyperactivity disorder (ADHD) 219
  autism spectrum disorder (ASD) 215
  depressive disorders 224
  schizophrenia 227
  spina bifida 134
epilepsy
  autism spectrum disorder (ASD) 213
  childhood bullying 60
  defined 710
  employment discrimination 605
  neuroimaging techniques 89
Equal Credit Opportunity Act (ECOA)
  discrimination in housing based upon national origin 633
  discrimination in housing based upon race or color 632
  discrimination in housing based upon sex, including sexual harassment 633
Equal Employment Opportunity Commission (EEOC)
  litigation burdens on employers 610
  section 504 of the rehabilitation act 536
ESEA *see* Elementary and Secondary Education Act
ethnic group
  autism spectrum disorder (ASD) 211
  cystic fibrosis (CF) 102
  vision loss 150
Eunice Kennedy Shriver National Institute of Child Health and Human Development
  contact 716
  publications
    assistive devices 307n
    birth defects 75n
    dyscalculia 201n
    learning disabilities 198n
    rehabilitation medicine 507n
    rehabilitative and assistive technology (AT) 311n
"Evaluating Children for Disability" (CPIR) 537n
Every Student Succeeds Act (ESSA), overview 532–4
"Every Student Succeeds Act (ESSA)" (ED) 532n
evoked potential (EP), multiple sclerosis (MS) 249
exercise
  bowel control problems 452
  cognitive behavioral therapy 478
  complementary and supportive therapies 274
  guidelines overview 432–7
  Kegel exercises 457
  postsurgical period 280
  yoga 437
eye diseases
  Down syndrome 189
  low vision 358
eye exam
  age-related macular degeneration 153
  cataract 161
  diabetes 164
  diabetic retinopathy 163
  glaucoma 156

F

"Facts about Age-Related Macular Degeneration" (NEI) 150n
"Facts about Birth Defects" (CDC) 75n
"Facts about Cataract" (NEI) 150n
"Facts about Cleft Lip and Cleft Palate" (CDC) 95n
"Facts about Diabetic Eye Disease" (NEI) 150n
"Facts about Down Syndrome" (CDC) 186n
"Facts about Glaucoma" (NEI) 150n
"Facts about the Americans with Disabilities Act" (EEOC) 603n
failure
  dyslexia 199
  interactive process 622
  learning disabilities 28
  reasonable accommodation request 626
  self-advocacy skills 586
Fair Housing Act
  amendments 631
  described 597

Fair Housing Act, *continued*
   disability rights in housing 614
   disability rights in private and public housing 637
   discrimination in housing based upon disability 634
   discrimination in housing based upon national origin 633
   discrimination in housing based upon race or color 631
   discrimination in housing based upon religion 632
   service animal 392
"The Fair Housing Act" (DOJ) 631n
Family Caregiver Alliance (FCA), contact 723
"Family Caregivers" (CDC) 55n
family history
   bipolar and related disorders 223
   cystic fibrosis carrier testing 106
   decisions about your health 525
   genetic counseling 126
   muscular dystrophy (MD) 123
   newborn screening 78
   open-angle glaucoma 156
   prenatal screening 79
   schizophrenia 227
FAPE *see* free appropriate public education
FASDs *see* fetal alcohol spectrum disorders
fatigue
   bipolar and related disorders 223
   cystic fibrosis (CF) 105
   generalized anxiety disorder 476
   multiple sclerosis (MS) 244
   sexual issues 256
   vision problems 253
   yoga 438
FDA *see* U.S. Food and Drug Administration
"FDA Approves Implantable Device That Changes the Shape of the Cornea to Correct near Vision" (FDA) 364n
fecal incontinence, bowel control problem 451
Federal Bureau of Prisons (BOP) publication
      pressure sores 461n

Federal Communications Commission (FCC)
   contact 716
   publication
      closed captioning 332n
Federal Emergency Management Agency (FEMA)
   publication
      disaster preparedness 642n
Federal Poverty Level (FPL), health insurance 494
Federal Student Aid
   publications
      scholarships 660n
      students with intellectual disabilities 662n
feeding tube
   cystic fibrosis (CF) 110
   dysphagia 425
   muscular dystrophies treatment 129
festination, Parkinson disease (PD) 262
fetal alcohol spectrum disorders (FASDs), overview 190–4
fetal alcohol syndrome (FAS)
   birth defects 77
   deaf-blindness 167
   fetal alcohol spectrum disorders (FASDs) 191
fetal surgery, spina bifida 137
fibromyalgia, low back pain 287
financial assistance
   Fair Housing Act 597
   family support services 411
   federally assisted housing 639
   independent living services programs 613
   postsecondary education and training 576
   Rehabilitation Act 599
   Section 504 of the Rehabilitation Act 535
"Finding and Applying for Scholarships" (Federal Student Aid) 660n
fire safety, overview 640–2
"Fire Safety Outreach Materials for People with Disabilities" (FA) 640n
firm-soled shoes, pressure sores 467

Index

Fishing Has No Boundaries, Inc. (FHNB), contact 732
"Five Innovations Harness New Technologies for People with Visual Impairment, Blindness" (NEI) 373n
flare-ups, multiple sclerosis (MS) 250
folic acid
  birth defects 81
  spina bifida 134, 138
Food and Drug Administration (FDA) see U.S. Food and Drug Administration
Food and Nutrition Service (FNS)
  publication
    nutrition and disability 420n
fragile X syndrome
  autism spectrum disorder (ASD) 213
  functional or developmental birth defects 76
  rehabilitation medicine 507
free appropriate public education (FAPE)
  Individuals with Disabilities Education Act (IDEA) 530
  postsecondary education and training options 574
"Frequently Asked Questions about Home Use Devices" (FDA) 324n
functional impairment, spina bifida complications 135

G

GAD see generalized anxiety disorder
gait
  below-knee amputations 277
  cerebral palsy (CP) 84
  complementary and supportive therapies 273
  exercise 274
  orthopedic surgery 92
  Parkinson disease (PD) 262
  Parkinsonism 265
  physical therapy regimens 383
  rehabilitation 511
galantamine (Razadyne®), mental function 237
GCS see Glasgow coma scale
gene therapy, birth defects 80
genes
  autism spectrum disorder (ASD) 214
  birth defects 77
  cerebral dysgenesis 86
  cleft lip and palate 97
  cystic fibrosis (CF) 101
  dyslexia 206
  inborn errors of metabolism 116
  multiple sclerosis (MS) 248
  muscular dystrophy (MD) 124
  Parkinson disease (PD) 259
genetic factors
  apraxia of speech 181
  autism 215
  overweight and obesity 427
general anesthesia
  muscle biopsies 127
  muscular dystrophy (MD) 131
generalized anxiety disorder (GAD)
  antianxiety medications 480
  anxiety disorders 475
genetic abnormalities, cerebral palsy (CP) 85
genetic counselor, birth defects 77
genetic disorder
  amniocentesis 79
  autism spectrum disorder (ASD) 213
  birth defects 81
genetic test
  age-related macular degeneration 152
  cystic fibrosis (CF) 105
"Geriatrics and Extended Care— Respite Care" (VA) 410n
glaucoma
  cataract 160
  defined 710
  low vision 358
  overview 155–8
  visual impairment 373
global aphasia, speech disorders 178
Goodwill Industries, contact 723
gout
  arthritis 240
  inborn errors of metabolism 116
Great Lakes ADA Center, contact 727
grief
  creative art therapy 386
  hospice care 413

group home
  defined 710
  discrimination in housing 635
"A Guide to Disability Rights Laws" (DOJ) 593n
"A Guide to Interacting with People Who Have Disabilities" (DHS) 25n

H

hallucinations
  amantadine 271
  dementia or other cognitive problems 264
  levodopa 269
  moderate Alzheimer disease 234
  schizophrenia 227
head injury
  aphasia 176
  apraxia of speech 181
  cerebral palsy (CP) 85
  deaf-blindness 167
  discrimination in housing 634
  dysphagia 425
  posttraumatic Parkinsonism 265
"Health Care Experiences of Adults with Disabilities Enrolled in Medicaid Only: Findings from a 2014–2015 Nationwide Survey of Medicaid Beneficiaries" (CMS) 496n
Health in Aging, contact 723
health insurance *see* insurance coverage
health maintenance organization (HMO), children's health insurance program 492
health screening
  adult day care 415
  women with disabilities 33
healthcare professionals
  advance care planning 695
  autism 216
  cerebral palsy (CP) 90
Healthfinder®, contact 716
hearing aids
  assistive listening devices 347
  hearing loss 142
  overview 340–5
  see also in-the-canal (ITC)

"Hearing Aids" (NIDCD) 340n
hearing difficulty, defined 710
hearing disability, assistive devices 314
hearing impairment
  assistive devices 312
  child with a disability 538
  communication barriers 21
  discrimination in housing 634
  impairment-related work expenses 683
  telecommunication relay services 355
hearing loop, assistive listening devices 347
hearing loss
  birth defects 76
  Down syndrome 189
  hearing aids 341
  overview 142–6
  speech-language pathologists (SLPs) 353
  tabulated *48*
  see also presbycusis
"Hearing Loss and Older Adults" (NIDCD) 142n
heart rate
  cystic fibrosis (CF) 105
  low apgar score 88
  orthostatic hypotension 264
  pain treatment 472
  panic disorder 476
HHS *see* U.S. Department of Health and Human Services
high-fiber diet, bladder control and constipation 256
hip disarticulation, amputation 278
HIV *see* human immunodeficiency virus
home care
  adult day care 415
  continuing care retirement communities 524
  medical emergency 501
  outpatient setting 517
home healthcare
  assistive technology (AT) 307
  defined 710
  described 520
  healthy mouth 444

Index

home modifications, adapt living spaces 327
"Home Modifications" (ACL) 327n
"How to Bathe Someone with a Disability" (Omnigraphics) 447n
home use devices, home use medical devices 324
"Home Use Devices" (FDA) 324n
home use medical devices, overview 324–6
homelessness, schizophrenia 228
homemaker services
 described 520
 family support services 411
hospice care
 nursing home 521
 overview 412–4
hospitalizations, traumatic brain injury 300
housing, overview 614–40
HUD see U.S. Department of Housing and Urban Development
human immunodeficiency virus (HIV)
 Americans with Disabilities Act (ADA) 609
 assistive devices 314
Huntington disease, Parkinsonism 266
hydrocephalus, spina bifida 135
hypertonia, cerebral palsy (CP) 84
hypomanic episode, bipolar and related disorders 223
hypotonia, cerebral palsy (CP) 84

I

IDEA see Individuals with Disabilities Education Act
IEP see individualized education program
impairment, defined 710
in-the-canal (ITC), hearing aids 145, 342
in-the-ear (ITE), hearing aids 145, 342
income level, Medicaid 490
incontinence
 bladder control problems 454
 Parkinson disease (PD) 266
 pressure sores 462

independent living difficulty, defined 710
Individualized Education Program (IEP)
 defined 710
 overview 559–64
Individuals with Disabilities Education Act (IDEA)
 described 599
 early intervention services 550
 overview 530–2
induction loop systems, hearing aids 145, 342
infants
 autism spectrum disorder (ASD) 212
 birth defects 78
 cerebral palsy (CP) 84
 cleft lip 97
 dysphagia 425
 early intervention services 549
 Individuals with Disabilities Education Act (IDEA) 530
 occupational therapists (OTs) 380
 shaken baby syndrome (SBS) 196
inflammation
 Alzheimer disease (AD) 234
 arthritis 239
 back pain 285
 cerebral palsy (CP) 87
 defined 710
 multiple sclerosis (MS) 245
 muscular dystrophy (MD) 127
 Parkinson disease (PD) 259
 spinal cord injury (SCI) 292
 yoga 438
"Infographic: Does Your Child Struggle with Math?" (NICHD) 201n
"Inherited Disorders of Metabolism" (Omnigraphics) 115n
insurance coverage
 aging and disabilities 37
 see also Social Security Disability Insurance (SSDI)
insurance plan, assistive technology (AT) 308
intellectual and developmental disabilities (IDD)
 advance care planning 700
 birth defects 76
 rehabilitation medicine 509

757

Internal Revenue Service (IRS)
publication
tax benefits 677n
International Classification of Functioning, Disability and Health (ICF), mental impairment 5
International Wheelchair Aviators (IWA), contact 732
International Wheelchair Basketball Federation (IWBF), contact 732
"Interveners and Children Who Are Deaf-Blind" (ED) 165n
Intimate Partner Violence (IPV), women with disabilities 34
intracranial hemorrhage, cerebral palsy (CP) 86
intravenous (IV), medicines 108
"Investing in People: Job Accommodation Situations and Solutions" (DOL) 650n
IPV *see* Intimate Partner Violence
IRS *see* Internal Revenue Service
"Is It a Medical Emergency?" (Omnigraphics) 501n

J

Job Accommodation Network (JAN)
contact 723
disability assistance program 737
employees with disabilities 649
The John F. Kennedy Center for the Performing Arts, contact 723
Justice Department *see* U.S. Department of Justice
juvenile arthritis (JA), defined 240
juvenile offenders, controlled substances 617

K

"Keeping Children with Disabilities Safe" (CDC) 63n
Kegel exercises, described 457
"Key Findings: Prevalence of Disability in the US" (CDC) 11n

L

"Language and Speech Disorders" (CDC) 352n
laser surgery
age-related macular degeneration (AMD) 154
proliferative diabetic retinopathy (PDR) 165
laughing, involuntary expressions 256
laxative
bladder control problems 256
bowel control problems 453
LD *see* learning disabilities
learned helplessness, defined 711
learning disabilities (LD)
attention deficit hyperactivity disorder (ADHD) 219
childhood bullying 61
mental illness 655
overview 198–209
spina bifida 136
see also dyscalculia; dysgraphia; dyslexia; dyspraxia
learning disability, defined 711
lens, depicted *155*
Library of Congress (LOC), contact 716
life expectancy
aging and disabilities 35
hospice care 414
multiple sclerosis (MS) 243
muscular dystrophy (MD) 128
people with intellectual disability 698
life-sustaining treatment, advance care 695
limb loss
amputation 276
disability 4
rehabilitation medicine 508
"Limb Prosthetics Services and Devices" (NIST) 276n
living will, advance care 699
long-term care
defined 711
overview 519–25
Lou Gehrig's Disease *see* amyotrophic lateral sclerosis (ALS)

Index

low back pain, overview 284–9
"Low Back Pain Fact Sheet" (NINDS) 284n
Low birthweight, cerebral palsy (CP) 87
low blood pressure
  cerebral palsy (CP) 86
  Parkinson disease (PD) 269
  spinal cord injury (SCI) 296
lung disease
  cerebral palsy (CP) 91
  cystic fibrosis (CF) 109
lupus
  arthritis 241
  defined 711
  multiple sclerosis (MS) 244

M

macula, depicted *155*
macular degeneration
  described 151
  low vision 358
magnetic resonance imaging (MRI)
  Alzheimer disease (AD) 236
  aphasia 178
  bladder control problems 455
  cerebral palsy (CP) 89
  multiple sclerosis (MS) 243
  Parkinson disease (PD) 267
  pressure sores 464
  shaken baby syndrome (SBS) 196
  spina bifida 137
  spinal cord injury (SCI) 294
magnifiers
  assistive technology (AT) 315
  cerebral palsy (CP) 93
major depressive disorder (MDD), mental health 224
malnutrition, cerebral palsy (CP) 91
manic episode, bipolar disorder 223
manual wheelchair, mobility aids 319
March of Dimes, contact 724
masked face, Parkinson disease (PD) 262
massage therapy
  managing pain 473
  Parkinson disease (PD) 274
maternal infections, cerebral palsy (CP) 86

math learning disabilities *see* dyscalculia
MCI *see* mild cognitive impairment
MDD *see* major depressive disorder
medical emergency, overview 501–5
medical equipment
  assistive technology (AT) 308
  hospice care 412
  pressure sores 464
  tabulated *499*
memantine (Namenda®)
  Alzheimer disease (AD) 237
  Parkinson disease (PD) 264
meningitis
  cerebral palsy (CP) 85
  deaf-blindness 167
  hearing loss 149
  spina bifida 135
meningocele, spina bifida 134
mental disability, defined 711
mental disorders
  psychiatric disability, overview 221–9
  rehabilitation medicine 507
"Mental Disorders" (SAMHSA) 221n
"Mental Health Conditions: Depression and Anxiety" (CDC) 475n
mental retardation
  advance care 700
  shaken baby syndrome (SBS) 195
metabolic disorder
  birth defects 76
  cerebral palsy (CP) 90
Mid-Atlantic ADA Center, contact 727
middle ear implant, hearing aids 146
mild cognitive impairment (MCI)
  aging and disabilities 38
  Alzheimer disease (AD) 233
mobility aids
  assistive technology (AT) 309
  overview 318–21
  rehabilitation medicine 510
mobility impairment
  fundamental alteration 621
  people with disabilities 53
  physical barriers 21
mortgage loans, Fair Housing Act 631

motor vehicles, people with
   disabilities 396
MRI *see* magnetic resonance imaging
multiple sclerosis
   disability 4
   overview 243–57
   tabulated *48*
"Multiple Sclerosis: Hope Through
   Research" (NINDS) 243n
muscle biopsy, described 127
muscle spasm
   bladder control problem 458
   multiple sclerosis (MS) 245
   muscular dystrophy (MD) 129
muscular dystrophy
   assistive technology (AT) 314
   birth defects 76
   childhood bullying 60
   overview 121–32
   rehabilitation medicine 508
   tabulated *49*
"Muscular Dystrophy: Hope through
   Research" (NINDS) 121n
myelomeningocele, spina bifida 134
myopathy *see also* cardiomyopathy

N

narcotics (opioids), pain 472
National Adult Day Services
   Association (NADSA), contact 724
National Alliance for Accessible Golf,
   contact 732
National Alliance for Caregiving
   (NAC), contact 724
National Amputee Golf Association
   (NAGA), contact 732
National Association of the Deaf
   (NAD), contact 724
National Cancer Institute (NCI),
   contact 716
National Center for Health Statistics
   (NCHS), contact 717
National Center for Learning
   Disabilities (NCLD), contact 724
National Center on Deaf-Blindness
   (NCDB), contact 724
National Center on Health, Physical
   Activity and Disability (NCHPAD),
   contact 724

National Council on Disability (NCD)
   contact 717
   publication
      guardianship 687n
National Down Syndrome Society
   (NDSS), contact 724
National Endowment For The Arts
   (NEA)
   publications
      arts and health 385n
      creative arts therapy 385n
"The National Endowment for the
   Arts Guide to Community-Engaged
   Research in the Arts and Health"
   (NEA) 385n
National Eye Institute (NEI)
   publications
      age-related macular
         degeneration 150n
      cataract 150n
      diabetic eye disease 150n
      glaucoma 150n
      low vision 358n
      low vision devices 373n
National Federation of the Blind
   (NFB), contact 725
National Heart, Lung, and Blood
   Institute (NHLBI)
   contact 717
   publication
      cystic fibrosis (CF) 101n
National Highway Traffic Safety
   Administration (NHTSA)
   publication
      adaptive technologies 396n
National Hospice and Palliative Care
   Organization (NHPCO), contact 725
National Institute of Arthritis and
   Musculoskeletal and Skin Diseases
   (NIAMS)
   contact 717
   publication
      arthritis 239n
National Institute of Biomedical
   Imaging and Bioengineering
   (NIBIB)
   publications
      physical therapy 381n
      tongue-driven wheelchairs 320n

760

Index

National Institute of Dental and
Craniofacial Research (NIDCR)
contact 717
publication
dental care 442n
National Institute of Diabetes and
Digestive and Kidney Diseases
(NIDDK)
publication
bowel and bladder control
problems 451n
National Institute of Mental Health
(NIMH)
contact 717
publication
anxiety disorders 475n
National Institute of Neurological
Disorders and Stroke (NINDS)
contact 718
publications
amyotrophic lateral sclerosis
(ALS) 238n
autism spectrum disorder
(ASD) 211n
cerebral palsy (CP) 83n
developmental dyspraxia 209n
dysgraphia 208n
dyslexia 206n
low back pain 284n
multiple sclerosis (MS) 243n
muscular dystrophy (MD) 121n
pain management 469n
Parkinson disease (PD) 257n
shaken baby syndrome 194n
spina bifida 133n
spinal cord injury (SCI) 289n
traumatic brain injury 300n
National Institute of Standards and
Technology (NIST)
publication
limb prosthetics 276n
National Institute on Aging (NIA)
contact 718
publications
aging and chronic diseases 35n
Alzheimer disease 232n
assisted living 519n
long-term care 519n
manage pain 469n

National Institute on Deafness and
Other Communication Disorders
(NIDCD)
contact 718
publications
aphasia 176n
apraxia of speech 180n
assistive hearing devices 346n
closed captions 332n
cochlear implants 337n
dysphagia 422n
hearing aids 340n
hearing loss and older
adults 142n
telecommunications relay
services 355n
National Institute on Disability and
Rehabilitation Research (NIDRR),
contact 718
National Institutes of Health (NIH)
publications
aphasia 176n
disability in older adults 35n
dyslexia 206n
pressure sores 461n
"National Limb Loss Resource Center"
(ACL) 276n
National Mobility Equipment Dealers
Association (NMEDA), accessible
transportation 397
National Multiple Sclerosis Society
(NMSS), contact 725
National Organization for Rare
Disorders (NORD), contact 725
National Organization on Fetal
Alcohol Syndrome (NOFAS),
treatment 193
National Rehabilitation
Information Center (NARIC),
contact 725
National Science Foundation (NSF)
publication
artificial retina 360n
National Shooting Sports Foundation
(NSSF), contact 732
National Softball Association for the
Deaf (NSAD), contact 731
National Spinal Cord Injury
Association, contact 725

National Sports Center for the Disabled (NSCD), contact 729
National Stroke Association, contact 725
National Technical Information Service (NTIS), contact 718
National Wheelchair Basketball Association (NWBA), contact 732
National Wheelchair Poolplayers Association (NWPA), contact 733
National Women's Health Information Center (NWHIC), contact 718
NCI *see* National Cancer Institute
NCLD *see* National Center for Learning Disabilities
Nemours Foundation Center for Children's Health Media, contact 725
nerve damage
 bladder control problem 454
 diabetes 4
 neurophysiology study 128
 overactive bladder 455
 spina bifida 135
 structural impairments 5
 urine retention 455
neural tube defects
 birth defects 76
 noninvasive prenatal testing (NIPT) 79
 prenatal screening 78
neurogenic pain, spinal cord injury (SCI) 297
neuron
 Alzheimer disease (AD) 232
 amyotrophic lateral sclerosis (ALS) 238
 defined 711
 multiple sclerosis (MS) 246
 Parkinson disease (PD) 257
 spinal cord injury (SCI) 289
neurotransmitter
 Parkinson disease (PD) 258
 spinal cord injury (SCI) 292
New England ADA Center, contact 727
newborn screening
 cystic fibrosis (CF) 105
 defined 711

newborn screening, *continued*
 described 78
 inherited metabolic disorders 119
NHLBI *see* National Heart, Lung, and Blood Institute
NHTSA *see* National Highway Traffic Safety Administration
NIA *see* National Institute on Aging
NIAMS *see* National Institute of Arthritis and Musculoskeletal and Skin Diseases
NIDCD *see* National Institute on Deafness and Other Communication Disorders
NIDCR *see* National Institute of Dental and Craniofacial Research
NIMH *see* National Institute of Mental Health
NINDS *see* National Institute of Neurological Disorders and Stroke
"NLS Factsheet: About Braille" (LOC) 366n
No Child Left Behind (NCLB) Act, described 534
NOFAS *see* National Organization on Fetal Alcohol Syndrome
noise-induced hearing loss, defined 143
nonsteroidal anti-inflammatory drugs (NSAIDs), pain 427
Northeast ADA Center, contact 727
nursing facilities
 adult day care center 415
 inpatient setting 516
 nursing home 523
nursing home
 defined 711
 described 521
 long-term care 519
 Medicare 413
 pressure sores 461
 Section 504 535
nutrition, disability 420
nutritional counseling, pulmonary rehabilitation (PR) 109
nutritional therapy, cystic fibrosis (CF) 110
nystagmus, multiple sclerosis (MS) 253

Index

O

obesity
　Alzheimer disease 235
　chronic disease in older age 39
　disability 427
　health consequences 430
　muscular dystrophy (MD) 131
　older adults 37
　rehabilitation medicine 509
　statistics 428
obsessive-compulsive disorder (OCD)
　described 226
　social anxiety disorder 477
occulta, described 134
occupational therapists
　deaf-blindness 171
　overview 378–81
　Parkinson disease (PD) 263
　rehabilitative or assistive technology (AT) 314
　spinal cord injury (SCI) 298
"Occupational Therapists" (BLS) 378n
occupational therapy
　adult day care 415
　amyotrophic lateral sclerosis (ALS) 239
　cerebral palsy (CP) 90
　defined 711
　described 378
　early intervention service 550
　fatigue 255
　hospice care 421
　muscular dystrophy (MD) 130
　rehabilitation
　spinal cord injury (SCI) 299
"Occupational Therapy—VA Boston Healthcare System" (VA) 378n
"Occupational Therapy—VA Palo Alto Healthcare System" (VA) 378n
OCD see obsessive-compulsive disorder
ODEP see Office of Disability Employment Policy Employment Policy
odynophagia, dysphagia 422
Office of Disability Employment Policy (ODEP), contact 719
Office of the Assistant Secretary for Planning and Evaluation (ASPE)
　publication
　　　advance care planning 693n
Office on Women's Health (OWH)
　publication
　　　women with disabilities 69n
OI see osteogenesis imperfecta
older adults
　adult day care 415
　Alzheimer disease 234
　assistive technology (AT) 307
　disability 35
　dysphagia 424
　exercise 39
　hearing loss 142
　nonsteroidal anti-inflammatory drug (NSAID) 472
Older Americans Act (OAA)
Omnigraphics
　publications
　　　amputation and social security benefits 673n
　　　dyscalculia 201n
　　　inherited disorders of metabolism 115n
　　　medical emergency 501n
　　　personal hygiene 447n
　　　Web-Braille 370n
　　　yoga 437n
oppositional defiant disorder (ODD)
　child abuse 63
　described 225
opsoclonus, multiple sclerosis (MS) 253
optic nerve
　age-related macular degeneration (AMD) 152
　argus retinal prosthesis 360
　cataract 161
　depicted *155*
　diabetic retinopathy 162
　glaucoma 155
　multiple sclerosis (MS) 243
oral medication, cerebral palsy (CP) 91
orientation
　creative arts therapists 387
　deaf-blindness 171

orofacial clefts
 defined 95
 occurrence 97
orthostatic hypotension
 described 264
 Parkinson disease (PD) 270
orthotic devices, cerebral palsy (CP) 90
osteoarthritis
 aging 46
 back pain 287
 defined 240
 overweight and obesity 430
osteogenesis imperfecta (OI)
 aging 46
 assistive devices 314
osteoporosis
 cystic fibrosis (CF) 105
 defined 712
 diuretic 41
 exercise 39
 quit smoking 289
OTC *see* over-the-counter
otolaryngologist
 defined 712
 hearing loss 142
over-the-counter (OTC)
 aging 40
 birth defects 81
 home use devices 325
 pain 470
overactive bladder
 cerebral palsy (CP) 92
 nerve damage 454
 treatment 455
"Overview of Early Intervention" (CPIR) 549n
"Overview on Deaf-Blindness" (ED) 165n
overweight
 disability 427
 muscular dystrophy (MD) 129
OWH *see* Office on Women's Health
oxygen therapy
 cerebral palsy (CP) 93
 cystic fibrosis (CF) 109

P

Pacific ADA Center, contact 728

"Pain: Hope through Research" (NINDS) 469n
"Pain: You Can Get Help" (NIA) 469n
palliative care
 decisional capacity 699
 hospice care 414
 physical disability 694
pallidotomy, defined 272
palsy, defined 712
pancreatitis, defined 712
panic disorder, described 476
paralysis, defined 712
paraplegia, defined 712
parental consent
 child evaluation 540
 initial assessment 555
Parkinson disease (PD)
 dysphagia 425
 mobility function 508
 overview 257–74
 speech-language pathologist (SLP) 353
Parkinson's Disease Foundation, contact 726
"Parkinson's Disease: Hope Through Research" (NINDS) 257n
"Passengers with Disabilities" (DOT) 405n
patient support group, cystic fibrosis (CF) 113
"People with Disabilities" (CDC) 3n
pensions
 disability 680
 military and government 680
percutaneous umbilical blood sampling (PUBS), Down syndrome 189
periventricular leukomalacia (PVL), cerebral palsy (CP) 86
personal hygiene, overview 442–9
pervasive developmental disorder not otherwise specified (PDD-NOS), autism spectrum disorder (ASD) 211
PET *see* positron emission tomography
phantom limb pain, amputation 673
pharynx (throat), depicted *423*
physiatrists, overview 381–4
"Physical Activity Is for Everybody" (CDC) 432n

Index

physical barriers
  disability 21
  Section 504 536
physical development, developmental delay 551
physical disability
  advance care planning 694
  assistive devices 314
  Marketplace health coverage 489
  medical expenses 682
"Physical Medicine and Rehabilitation—PM&R" (VA) 381n
physical therapists
  cystic fibrosis (CF) 107
  overview 381–4
"Physical Therapists" (BLS) 381n
physical therapy
  adult day care 415
  cerebral palsy (CP) 90
  defined 712
  Down syndrome 189
  early intervention services 550
  fatigue 255
  muscular dystrophy (MD) 128
  Parkinson disease (PD) 262
  walking and balance 254
Physically Challenged Bowhunters of America, Inc. (PCBA), contact 733
"Planning for Long-Term Care" (NIA) 519n
pneumonia
  cystic fibrosis (CF) 104
  spinal cord injury (SCI) 295
pneumothorax, defined 712
policy barriers, described 21
polyps, cystic fibrosis (CF) 104
positron emission tomography (PET), Alzheimer disease 236
postsecondary education, students with disabilities 573
posttraumatic Parkinsonism, described 265
posttraumatic stress disorder (PTSD)
  art therapy 386
  described 228
  employment 654
postural instability, Parkinson disease (PD) 262

posture
  cerebral palsy (CP) 83
  dyspraxia 209
  multiple sclerosis (MS) 255
  occupational therapy 90
  scoliosis 131
power wheelchair
  Medicaid 308
  mobility devices 318
  mobility disability 644
PR *see* pulmonary rehabilitation
pregnancy
  antidepressants 483
  birth defect 77
  cerebral palsy (CP) 87
  chorionic villus sampling (CVS) 80
  cleft lip and cleft palate 95
  diabetic retinopathy 163
  Down syndrome 186
  fetal alcohol spectrum disorders (FASDs) 190
  hearing loss 148
  prenatal screening 78
  schizophrenia 227
  spina bifida 133
premature birth, cerebral palsy (CP) 87
prenatal screening
  cystic fibrosis (CF) 106
  described 78
  muscular dystrophies 128
presbycusis
  defined 712
  hearing loss 142
prescription
  birth defects 81
  cataract 160
  home use devices 325
  hospice care 412
  insurance company 399
  original medicare 414
  pain treatment 471
pressure redistribution mattress
  interventions to alleviate mechanism of injury 465
  prevention strategies for the spinal cord injury (SCI) 466
pressure sores
  overview 461–7

pressure sores, *continued*
  spinal cord injury (SCI) 297
"Pressure Sores" (NIH) 461n
"Prevention and Management
  of Acute and Chronic Wounds"
  (BOP) 461n
Professional Association of
  Therapeutic Horsemanship (PATH)
  International, contact 733
programmatic barriers, described 22
progressive muscular atrophy (PMA),
  complex rehabilitative technology 314
progressive neurological disease,
  aphasia 176
prosthetics
  amputation and social security
    benefits 673
  rehabilitation medicine 509
PsychCentral, contact 726
psychotherapy
  anxiety disorders treatment 477
  treatments for depression 482
psychotic disorders
  defining characteristic 227
  Parkinson disease (PD) 265
PTSD *see* posttraumatic stress
  disorder
public accommodations, Americans
  with Disabilities Act 334, 595
public transportation
  business tax incentives 685
  independent living 8
  occupational therapist 380
  transportation barriers 23
pulmonary rehabilitation (PR)
  described 109
  lung problems 107
PVL *see* periventricular leukomalacia
  (PVL)

Q

QDWI *see* Qualified Disabled and
  Working Individuals Program
quadriplegia, spinal cord injury
  (SCI) 289
"Questions You May Want to Ask
  Your Child's Speech-Language
  Pathologist" (CDC) 352n

R

radiculopathy, low back pain 285
recreational therapy
  art therapy, overview 385–9
  rehabilitation medicine 511
"Recreation Therapy Service Fact
  Sheet" (VA) 385n
"Recreational Therapy: Restoring
  Function, Recreating Lives"
  (VA) 385n
rectal prolapse, cystic fibrosis
  (CF) 104
"Reducing Chronic Disease in Older
  Age" (NIA) 35n
regulations
  medical device 325
  policy barriers 21
rehabilitation, defined 712
Rehabilitation Act
  bullying 61
  described 599
  overview 535–6
Rehabilitation Engineering and
  Assistive Technology Society of
  North America (RESNA), home
  modifications 327
rehabilitation medicine, overview
  507–18
"Rehabilitation Medicine: Topic
  Information" (NICHD) 507n
rehabilitation physicians
  Physical Medicine and
    Rehabilitation (PM&R) 381
  rehabilitation medicine 511
rehabilitative and assistive
  technology, overview 311–5
"Rehabilitative and Assistive
  Technology: Condition Information"
  (NICHD) 311n
related condition (RC)
  defined 712
  hospice care 412
  social anxiety disorder 477
relaxation
  drug therapy 129
  fatigue 255
  managing pain 473
  occupational therapists (OTs) 379

Index

relaxation, *continued*
  rehabilitation medicine 511
  yoga 438
relaxation therapy, arthritis 242
religious discrimination, Fair Housing Act 632
"Residential Facilities, Assisted Living, and Nursing Homes" (NIA) 519n
RESNA *see* Rehabilitation Engineering and Assistive Technology Society of North America
respiratory muscle, muscular dystrophy (MD) 126
respite care
  adult day care 415
  defined 713
  overview 410–2
"Respite Care" (AOA) 410n
retina
  age-related macular degeneration (AMD) 151
  depicted *155*
  diabetic retinopathy 163
  shaken baby syndrome (SBS) 196
Rh incompatibility, cerebral palsy (CP) 87
rheumatoid arthritis
  low back pain 287
  multiple sclerosis (MS) 244
rigidity, Parkinson disease (PD) 261
rivastigmine (Exelon®)
  Alzheimer disease (AD) 237
  Parkinson disease (PD) 264
Rocky Mountain ADA Center, contact 728
rubella (also known as German measles)
  cerebral palsy (CP) 87
  deaf-blindness 167
  defined 713
  disability 4

S

sacral
  defined 713
  low back pain 286
"Safe Swallowing" (VA) 422n
SAMHSA *see* Substance Abuse and Mental Health Services Administration
SBA *see* Spina Bifida Association
schizophrenia, described 227
"School Meals" (FNS) 420n
SCI *see* spinal cord injury
sciatica, low back pain 285
scoliosis
  medical conditions 508
  muscular dystrophy (MD) 130
  skeletal irregularities 286
SCIs *see* spinal cord injuries
seizures
  autism spectrum disorder (ASD) 216
  birth defects 76
  cerebral palsy (CP) 84
  shaken baby syndrome (SBS) 195
"Service Animals" (DOJ) 391n
self-care task, disability 6
self-esteem
  adult day care 415
  cerebral palsy (CP) 91
  multiple sclerosis (MS) 256
  speech disorders 179
sensory disability, defined 713
sensory-motor therapy, birth defects 80
sensory problem
  birth defects 76
  rehabilitation medicine 507
sensory processing, Alzheimer disease (AD) 233
service animals, overview 391–4
sexual abuse
  depression 481
  women with disabilities 70
sexual function, spinal cord injury (SCI) 298
sexual harassment, housing and safety issues 632
sexual issues, multiple sclerosis (MS) 256
sexual problems, multiple sclerosis (MS) 246
shaken baby syndrome, overview 194–6
"Shaken Baby Syndrome" (CDC) 194n

"Shaken Baby Syndrome Information Page" (NINDS) 194n
Shirley Ryan AbilityLab, contact 726
"The Short-and-Sweet IEP Overview" (CPIR) 559n
sinuses, cystic fibrosis (CF) 101
Skating Athletes Bold at Heart (SABAH), contact 731
skeletal irregularities, low back pain 286
Ski for Light, Inc., contact 731
skin problem
  Parkinson disease (PD) 263
  spina bifida 136
SLP *see* speech-language pathologist
social activities
  adult day care 415
  Americans with Disabilities Act (ADA) 594
  managing pain 471
social anxiety disorder, described 476
social barriers, described 22
social impairment, autism spectrum disorder (ASD) 212
Social Security Disability (SSD)
  amputation 674
  benefits overview 667–71
Social Security Disability Insurance (SSDI)
  defined 713
  health insurance 486
Social Security Number (SSN), disability benefits 670
Southwest ADA Center, contact 728
spasm
  drug therapy 129
  lower back pain 285
  multiple sclerosis (MS) 245
  spinal cord injury (SCI) 296
spasticity
  amyotrophic lateral sclerosis 239
  bladder control and constipation 255
  cerebral palsy (CP) 83
  oral medications 91
  orthopedic surgery 92
  shaken baby syndrome 195
  spinal cord injury (SCI) 295

special education
  Braille 370
  children with disability 537
  deaf-blindness 165
  disability 7
  dyspraxia 209
  fetal alcohol spectrum disorders (FASDs) 193
  higher education and adulthood 584
  Individualized Education Program (IEP) 560
  Individuals with Disabilities Education Act (IDEA) 530, 599
  itemized deductions 682
  rehabilitative and assistive technology (AT) 314
  speech disorders 352
Special Olympics, contact 730
special teaching technique, dyslexia 207
speech disorders
  child speech-language therapy 352
  overview 175–83
  see also aphasia; apraxia
speech-language pathologists
  defined 713
  described 353
  dysphagia 425
"Speech-Language Pathologists" (BLS) 352n
speech-language therapy
  aphasia 178
  apraxia of speech 183
speech pathologist, aphasia 179
speech therapy
  child's speech language pathologist 354
  complementary and supportive therapies 273
  dyspraxia 209
  muscular dystrophy (MD) 131
  nursing home 521
spina bifida
  assistive devices 314
  bullying 60
  overview 133–9
  rehabilitation medicine 508
  structural birth defects 76
Spina Bifida Association (SBA), contact 726

768

Index

"Spina Bifida Fact Sheet" (NINDS) 133n
spinal cord injuries (SCIs)
  advance care planning 698
  assistive devices 314
  overview 294–9
  pressure sores 462
  rehabilitation 507
"Spinal Cord Injury: Hope through Research" (NINDS) 289n
spinal decompression, spinal cord injuries (SCIs) 294
spinal column
  cerebral palsy (CP) 92
  spinal cord injuries (SCIs) 293
  spondylolisthesis 286
spinal stenosis, defined 286
SPLORE (Special Populations Learning Outdoor Recreation and Education), contact 730
spondylitis
  arthritis 240
  lower back pain 287
spondyloarthropathy, lower back pain 287
sports
  Americans with Disabilities Act (ADA) 595
  assistive technology (AT) 309
  children with intellectual disabilities 68
  disabilities 9
  electronic newsroom captions (ENR) 333
  occupational therapist (OT) 381
  recreation therapy 90, 388
  rehabilitation 299
  traumatic brain injury (TBI) 301
SSA *see* U.S. Social Security Administration
SSDI *see* Social Security Disability Insurance
SSI *see* Supplemental Security Income
"The State of the World's Children 2013 — Children with Disabilities" (USAID) 420n
statistics
  amputation 673
  overview 11–7

stem cell therapy, complementary and alternative therapies 93
steroids
  multiple sclerosis (MS) 250
  Parkinson disease (PD) 260
strength exercise, aging 39
strength training, cerebral palsy (CP) 90
stress management
  anxiety disorder 479
  multiple sclerosis (MS) 255
stroke
  adult day care 416
  aging 37
  Alzheimer disease (AD) 235
  aphasia 176
  apraxia 181
  deaf-blindness 167
  depression 481
  dysphagia 424
  hearing loss 143
  hypertension and atrial fibrillation (AF) 41
  intracranial hemorrhage 86
  magnetic resonance imaging (MRI) 90
  occupational therapist (OT) 379
  overweight and obesity 430
  Parkinson disease (PD) 265
  physical therapist (PT) 383
  pressure sores 462
  rehabilitation medicine 507
  rehabilitative technologies 313
  shaken baby syndrome (SBS) 194
  speech-language pathologists (SLPs) 353
supported education 580
"Students with Intellectual Disabilities" (Federal Student Aid) 662n
substance abuse
  anxiety disorders 221
  disability rights in housing 617
  mental illness 654
Substance Abuse and Mental Health Services Administration (SAMHSA)
  publications
    mental disorders 221n
    mental illness in the workplace 654n

769

sunlight
  cataract 160
  multiple sclerosis (MS) 248
Supplemental Security Income (SSI)
  ABLE account 685
  defined 738
  described 487
  myths about disability benefits 30
  tax benefits and credits 679
supplementary aids and services
  described 569
  Individualized Education Program (IEP) 560
support groups
  anxiety disorders 478
  caregiving tips 56
  cleft lip and palate 99
  cystic fibrosis (CF) 113
  defined 713
  disability 9
  low vision 359
  National Limb Loss Resource Center 283
  speech disorders 179
supported education, supported education 580
"Supporting Students with Learning Disabilities—Myths and Misconceptions" (DOL) 25n
"Supports, Modifications, and Accommodations for Students" (CPIR) 565n
surgical procedures
  birth defects 80
  cerebral palsy (CP) 92
  cochlear implant 339
  overactive bladder 456
swallowing difficulties
  nutrition 422
  see also dysphagia
swallowing disorder
  dysphagia 425
  speech-language pathologists (SLPs) 353, 713
  see also dysphagia
sweat test
  described 105
  see also cystic fibrosis
"Symptoms" (Omnigraphics) 201n

T

tax credits
  health insurance 486
  overview 683–4
  tax benefits 677
"Tax Highlights for Persons with Disabilities" (IRS) 677n
tax incentives, described 685
TBI see traumatic brain injury
"TBI: Get the Facts" (CDC) 300n
telecommunications
  augmentative and alternative communication 349
  communicating with disabled people 51
  deaf and hard-of-hearing viewers 334
  disability rights laws 596
  telecommunications relay service 355
telecommunications relay services
  augmentative and alternative communication 349
  disability rights laws 596
  overview 355–6
"Telecommunications Relay Services" (NIDCD) 355n
teletypewriter (TTY)
  augmentative and alternative communication 349
  hearing kit 643
  telecommunications relay service (TRS) 355
tendon
  muscular dystrophy (MD) 124
  occupational therapists 381
  orthopedic surgery 92
  rehabilitation medicine 508
  sprains and strains 285
tests
  aging and disabilities 39
  Alzheimer disease (AD) 236
  Americans with Disabilities Act (ADA) 606
  arthritis 241
  attention deficit hyperactivity disorder (ADHD) 217
  autism spectrum disorder (ASD) 213

Index

tests, *continued*
  birth defects 78
  bullying 61
  cerebral palsy (CP) 89
  cervical cancer screening 34
  cystic fibrosis (CF) 101
  diagnostic tests 464
  Down syndrome 188
  dyscalculia 203
  dyslexia 207
  dysphagia 425
  evaluating children for
    disability 541
  Fair Housing Amendments Act 632
  fetal alcohol spectrum disorders
    (FASDs) 192
  health insurance 499
  hearing aid 341
  hearing loss 142
  Individualized Education Program
    (IEP) 560
  inherited disorders of
    metabolism 119
  misconceptions about disabilities 28
  multiple sclerosis (MS) 249
  muscular dystrophy (MD) 121
  nerve damage 455
  Parkinson disease (PD) 260
  percutaneous umbilical blood
    sampling (PUBS) 189
  physical therapist 384
  sensory disabilities 148
  social security disability benefits 668
  speech disorders 178
  spina bifida 136
  spinal cord injuries (SCIs) 294
  support of students 570
  tongue-driven wheelchairs 320
  traumatic brain injury (TBI) 302
tobacco
  attention deficit hyperactivity
    disorder (ADHD) 219
  cystic fibrosis (CF) 112
  managing pain 473
  near vision correction 365
toddlers
  aggressive behavior 64
  cerebral palsy (CP) 89
  early intervention services 549

toddlers, *continued*
  Individuals with Disabilities
    Education Act (IDEA) 530
  medical emergency 502
  occupational therapist 380
tongue drive system (TDS), tongue-
  driven wheelchairs 320
"Tongue-Driven Wheelchair Out-
  Maneuvers the Competition"
  (NIBIB) 320n
toxoplasmosis
  cerebral palsy (CP) 87
  deaf-blindness 167
"A Transition Guide to Postsecondary
  Education and Employment
  for Students and Youth with
  Disabilities" (ED) 573n
"Transition of Students with
  Disabilities to Postsecondary
  Education: A Guide for High School
  Educators" (ED) 581n
transition planning, Individuals
  with Disabilities Education Act
  (IDEA) 532
transition services, Individualized
  Education Program (IEP) 561
transportation
  air travel 405
  disability rights laws 593
  disaster preparedness 643
  family support services 413
  fundamental alteration 622
  itemized deductions 682
  long-term care 520
  nutrition and weight
    management 429
  occupational therapist (OT) 379
  passengers with disabilities 400
  rehabilitation 514
  transportation barriers 23
transportation barrier, described 23
transportation services
  Americans with Disabilities Act
    (ADA) 595
  long-term care 520
traumatic brain injury (TBI)
  assistive devices 314
  children with disability 538
  defined 713

771

traumatic brain injury (TBI), *continued*
  disability 4
  mental illness 655
  overview 300–3
  rehabilitation 507
  shaken baby syndrome (SBS) 196
"Traumatic Brain Injury Information Page" (NINDS) 300n
travel
  air travel 405
  assistive technology (AT) 7, 307
  behind-the-ear (BTE) 144
  caregiving tips 57
  hearing aids 341
  hearing loop 347
  neurophysiology studies 128
  photodynamic therapy (PDT) 154
  plaques 243
  radiculopathy 285
  rehabilitative and assistive technology (AT) 314
  transcranial direct current stimulation (tDCS) 313
tremor
  cerebral palsy (CP) 84
  defined 254
  Parkinson disease (PD) 257
  uncoordinated bladder and urethra 458
trisomy 21 *see* Down syndrome
tuberous sclerosis, autism spectrum disorder (ASD) 213
"2008 *Physical Activity Guidelines for Americans* Summary" (CDC) 432n

U

ultrasound
  birth defects 78
  cleft lip diagnosis 98
  diagnostic imaging 127
  Down syndrome diagnosis 188
  multiple sclerosis (MS) 255
  optical coherence tomography (OCT) 153, 163
  pallidotomy and thalamotomy 272
  spina bifida diagnosis 136

United Cerebral Palsy (UCP), contact 726
United Foundation for Disabled Archers (UFFDA), contact 733
United Spinal Association, contact 726
United States Association of Blind Athletes (USABA), contact 730
United States Blind Golf Association (USBGA), contact 731
United States Deaf Cycling Association (USDCA), contact 731
United States Electric Wheelchair Hockey Association (U.S.EWHA), contact 733
United States Paralympic Team, contact 730
United States Sailing Center, contact 733
United States Tennis Wheelchair, contact 733
upper-limb amputations, Residual Functional Capacity (RFC) 675
urinary catheters *see* catheters
urinary frequency
  defined 454
  multiple sclerosis (MS) 255
urinary tract infections, bladder and bowel problems 298
urinary urgency, defined 454
urine retention
  defined 455
  treatment 459
USA Deaf Soccer Association, contact 731
USA Deaf Sports Federation (USADSF), contact 731
USA Deaf Track and Field, contact 731
USA Swimming, contact 733
USA Water Ski, contact 733
USABA *see* United States Association of Blind Athletes
USRowing, contact 733
U.S. Administration on Aging (AOA)
  publications
    adult day care 415n
    respite care 410n

Index

U.S. Agency for International
Development (USAID)
    publications
        children with disabilities 420n
        women with disabilities 69n
U.S. Bureau of Labor Statistics (BLS)
    publications
        occupational therapists 378n
        physical therapists 381n
        speech-language pathologists 352n
U.S. Deaf Ski Snowboard Association (USDSSA), contact 731
U.S. Department of Education (ED)
    contact 719
    publications
        deaf-blindness 165n
        Every Student Succeeds Act (ESSA) 532n
        Individuals with Disabilities Education Act (IDEA) 530n
        postsecondary education and employment 573n
        respite care 410n
        transition to postsecondary education 581n
U.S. Department of Health and Human Services (HHS)
    publications
        bullying 60n
        Section 504 535n
U.S. Department of Homeland Security (DHS)
    publication
        communication tips 25n
"U.S. Department of Housing and Urban Development" (DOJ) 614n
U.S. Department of Housing and Urban Development (HUD)
    publication
        housing rights 637n
U.S. Department of Justice (DOJ)
    contact 719
    publications
        assistive devices 318n
        disability rights laws 593n
        Fair Housing Act 631n
        right to housing 614n
        service animals 391n

U.S. Department of Labor (DOL)
    publications
        communicating with and about people with disabilities 47n
        disability assistance 735n
        job accommodation situations and solutions 650n
        myths and misconceptions about people with disabilities 25n
U.S. Department of Transportation (DOT)
    publication
        air travel assistance 405n
U.S. Department of Veterans Affairs (VA)
    contact 719
    publications
        anxiety 475n
        art therapy 385n
        creative arts therapies 385n
        occupational therapy 378n
        physical medicine and rehabilitation 381n
        recreation therapy 385n
        respite care 410n
        safe swallowing 422n
U.S. Equal Employment Opportunity Commission (EEOC)
    contact 719
    publication
        Americans with Disabilities Act (ADA) 603n
U.S. Fire Administration (FA)
    publication
        fire safety 640n
U.S. Food and Drug Administration (FDA)
    contact 719
    publications
        home use devices 324n
        low vision devices 364n
U.S. Government Printing Office (GPO), contact 719
U.S. Library of Congress (LOC)
    publication
        braille 366n
U.S. National Library of Medicine (NLM), contact 720

U.S. Office of Personnel Management
    (OPM)
  publications
    disability employment 646n
    employee accommodation 648n
U.S. Social Security Administration
    (SSA)
  contact 720
  publications
    disability benefits 667n
    disability myths 25n

V

vehicle safety checklist,
    described 404
verbal aggression, aggressive
    behavior 64
Veterans Health Administration
    (VHA)
  adult day care 416
  therapeutic recreation 387
VHA *see* Veterans Health
    Administration
violence
  abuse of children 63
  conduct disorder 226
  fetal alcohol spectrum disorders
      (FASDs) 193
  housing and safety 618
  posttraumatic stress disorder
      (PTSD) 229
  rehabilitation 514
  social barriers 23
  spinal cord injuries (SCIs) 291
  women with disabilities 69–72
"Violence against Women with
    Disabilities" (OWH) 69n
viruses
  Americans with Disabilities Act
      (ADA) 609
  assistive devices 314
  housing and safety 616, 634
  multiple sclerosis (MS) 247
  plaques 243
vision aids
  assistive devices 92
  see also magnifiers

vision difficulty, defined 714
vision impairment
  communication barriers 21
  housing and safety 628
  vision loss 150
  see also blindness
Visiting Nurses Associations of
    America (VNAA), contact 726
visual acuity test
  cataract 161
  diabetic retinopathy 163
  glaucoma 157
  macular degeneration 153
visual art therapy, art and
    recreational therapy 386
visual field test, defined 157
visual impairment
  Americans with Disabilities Act
      (ADA) 605
  assistive devices 314
  children with disability 538
  computer skills 588
  discrimination 535
  housing rights 637
  new technologies 373
vitamin D
  back health 289
  sunlight 248
vocational rehabilitation
  defined 511
  disability myths 31
  higher education for students 583
  motor vehicles 397
  postsecondary education 577
  spinal cord injuries (SCIs) 299

W

walkers
  accessible transportation 399
  assistive technology (AT) 7, 309
  cerebral palsy (CP) 93
  disaster preparedness 644
  fire safety 641
  hospice care 412
  housing and safety 627
  mobility aids 318
  multiple sclerosis (MS) 254

Index

walkers, *continued*
  muscular dystrophy (MD) 130
  physical therapist (PT) 383
  rehabilitation medicine 510
  spina bifida 138
  spinal cord injuries (SCIs) 299
walking problems, multiple sclerosis (MS) 254
Web Accessibility Initiative (WAI), contact 726
Web-Braille, overview 370–2
"Web-Braille" (Omnigraphics) 370n
"What Are Some Types of Assistive Devices and How Are They Used?" (NICHD) 307n
"What Are the Indicators of Learning Disabilities?" (NICHD) 198n
"What I Need to Know about Bowel Control" (NIDDK) 451n
"What Is Aphasia" (NIH) 176n
"What Is Art Therapy?" (VA) 385n
"What Is Dyslexia?" (NIH) 206n
"What Is Long-Term Care?" (NIA) 519n
"What You Should Know" (NEI) 358n
wheelchairs
  air travel 407
  assistive technologies (AT) 7, 309
  cerebral palsy (CP) 93
  communicating with disabled people 51
  defined 318
  Fair Housing Act 597
  housing 635
  job accommodation 651
  physical barriers 21
  physical therapy 130
  postsurgical period 281
  rehabilitation medicine 510
  spina bifida 138
  tongue-driven wheelchairs 320
"Wheelchairs, Mobility Aids, and Other Power-Driven Mobility Devices" (DOJ) 318n
Wilderness Inquiry, contact 730

women with disabilities
  overview 33–4
  violence 69–72
"Women with Disabilities" (CDC) 33n
World T.E.A.M. Sports, contact 730
workplace
  Americans with Disabilities Act (ADA) 608
  assistive devices 92, 312
  communicating with disabled people 52
  federal agencies 648
  Job Accommodation Network (JAN) 737
  mental illness 654
  occupational therapist (OT) 379
  occupational therapy 130
  spinal cord injuries (SCIs) 299
  tongue-driven wheelchairs 321
work test, Social Security Disability Benefits 668

X

X chromosome
  inborn errors 116
  muscular dystrophy (MD) 122
X-linked disorder, muscular dystrophy (MD) 122
X-ray
  arthritis test 241
  birth defects 78
  Children's Health Insurance Program (CHIP) 493
  computed tomography (CT) 89
  cystic fibrosis (CF) diagnosis 106
  defined 714
  dysphagia 425
  Social Security benefits 675
  spina bifida diagnosis 137, 294
  traumatic brain injury (TBI) 303

Y

Y chromosome, muscular dystrophy (MD) 122

yoga
  complementary and supportive
    therapies 274
  defined 714
  overview 437–9
  stress reduction 473
"Yoga for People with Disabilities"
  (Omnigraphics) 437n

young adults, multiple sclerosis
  (MS) 243
"Your Medicare Coverage"
  (CMS) 410n
"Your Rights under Section 504
  of the Rehabilitation Act"
  (HHS) 535n